The Rise of Commercial Empires

*England and the Netherlands in the Age of
Mercantilism, 1650–1770*

In early modern Europe, and particularly in the Netherlands, commercial empires were held together as much by cities as by unified nation
states. David Ormrod here takes a regional economy as his preferred unit
of analysis: the North Sea economy, an interlocking network of trades
shaped by public and private interests, and the matrix within which
Anglo-Dutch competition, borrowing and collaboration took shape. He
shows how England's increasingly coherent mercantilist objectives undermined Dutch commercial hegemony, in ways which contributed to
the restructuring of the North Sea staplemarket system. The commercial revolution has rightly been identified with product diversification
and the expansion of long-distance trading, but the reorganisation of
England's nearby European trades was equally important, providing the
foundation for eighteenth-century commercial growth and facilitating
the expansion of the Atlantic economy. With the Anglo-Scottish union
of 1707, the last piece of a *national* British entrepôt system was put into
place.

DAVID ORMROD is Reader in Economic and Cultural History at the
University of Kent, and a leading authority on British and Dutch commercial history in the early modern period.

Cambridge Studies in Modern Economic History

Cambridge Studies in Modern Economic History is a major new initiative in economic history publishing, and a flagship series for Cambridge University Press in an area of scholarly activity in which it has long been active. Books in this series will primarily be concerned with the history of economic performance, output and productivity, assessing the characteristics, causes and consequences of economic growth (and stagnation) in the western world. This range of enquiry, rather than one methodological or analytic approach, will be the defining characteristic of volumes in the series.

For a complete list of titles in the series, please see end of volume

The Rise of Commercial Empires

England and the Netherlands in the Age of Mercantilism, 1650–1770

David Ormrod

University of Kent

CAMBRIDGE UNIVERSITY PRESS
Cambridge, New York, Melbourne, Madrid, Cape Town, Singapore, São Paulo

Cambridge University Press
The Edinburgh Building, Cambridge CB2 8RU, UK

Published in the United States of America by Cambridge University Press, New York

www.cambridge.org
Information on this title: www.cambridge.org/9780521819268

First published 2003
Third printing 2005
This digitally printed version (with corrections) 2008

A catalogue record for this publication is available from the British Library

ISBN 978-0-521-81926-8 hardback
ISBN 978-0-521-04864-4 paperback

For Patrick and Kate

Contents

Maps and illustrations

Figures

Tables

Preface and acknowledgements

The British industrial revolution can no longer be regarded as the critical moment of transition in European economic history. Its transformative aspects are not in doubt, but to paraphrase de Vries and van der Woude, the industrial revolution contributed to a larger process of modernisation within a European zone larger than England. That zone is best described as the North Sea economy, within which the Dutch republic established a short-lived but striking position of dominance between the truce of 1609 and the outbreak of the first Anglo-Dutch War of 1652: a *pax Neerlandica*. But in what sense did the Dutch golden age mark the starting point of European modernity, and how does the subsequent history of Dutch decline and British growth fit into revisionist perspectives of this sort? De Vries and van der Woude have described European modernisation in terms of two cycles of growth, crisis and stagnation: the first pioneered by the Netherlands from some point in the sixteenth century to 1850, and a second beginning between 1780 and 1850 which 'affected the whole of the western world'.

In some respects, this is a useful way of scaling down and recontextual-ising the British commercial and industrial revolutions, but it rests on an assumption more appropriate to the nineteenth than to the sixteenth or seventeenth centuries: that of the 'national cycle' of growth and de-cline set out most clearly by Kindleberger. In early modern Europe, and particularly in the Netherlands, commercial empires were held together as much by cities as by unified nation states. The prior existence of in-tegrated national economies cannot be assumed, and their emergence surely deserves an important place in narratives of growth. This study takes a regional economy as its preferred unit of analysis: the North Sea economy, an interlocking network of trades shaped by public and private interests, and the matrix within which Anglo-Dutch competition, bor-rowing and collaboration took shape. It attempts to show how England's increasingly coherent mercantilist objectives succeeded in undermining Dutch commercial hegemony, in ways which contributed to the restruc-turing of the North Sea staplemarket system. The commercial revolution has rightly been identified with product diversification and the expansion of long-distance trading, but the reorganisation of England's nearby European trades was equally important, providing the foundation for eighteenth-century commercial growth and facilitating the expansion of the Atlantic economy. With the Anglo-Scottish union of 1707, the last piece of a *national* British entrepôt system was put into place.

It was the late Jack Fisher who initially suggested this topic as a focus for postgraduate research. From LSE, I went off to Cambridge to pursue it under the kindly supervision of Charles Wilson and, for a brief period, David Joslin, in the congenial surroundings of Christ's College. The encouragement and unfailing generosity of all three compounded a debt which I can never repay. My doctoral dissertation was presented in 1973, the year of Britain's entry into the European Community, and these circumstances meant that I was soon combining university teaching with museum work, gathering together objects and writing the scenario for a major exhibition at the Museum of London on 'The Dutch in London, 1550–1800', as part of the government's 'Fanfare for Europe'. In the following year, I first encountered Immanuel Wallerstein at a memorable symposium in Montreal, along with a small group of younger American scholars which included Jan de Vries, Robert Brenner and Franklin Mendels. The issues raised in Montreal and the possibility of developing an interest in histories of material culture persuaded me to shelve the dissertation, and to undertake further research on the international grain trade and the neglected history of re-exports. The former was central to both Wallerstein's world systems analysis and to the so-called 'Brenner debate' about the origins of agrarian capitalism which were unfolding during the 1970s. My involvement with museums and cultural history had to wait until the 1990s, but, in 1985, I published a monograph on English grain exports and agrarian capitalism which engaged with questions raised by Wallerstein and Brenner, parts of which appear in modified form in chapter 7 of the present volume. The results of work on the re-export trade appeared in the *festschrift* presented to Charles Wilson in 1984, *Enterprise and History*, and likewise form the core of one of the following chapters. The present study, however, is a substantially revised and extended treatment of my previously published and unpublished work, and attempts to trace a path, at times eccentric, through the proliferating literature on British and Dutch commercial history of the past thirty years.

I have benefited enormously from the stimulus and criticism of many friends, mediated particularly through seminars at the Institute of Historical Research. Patrick O'Brien's advice and constant support have been invaluable, and I owe special debts of gratitude to Jan de Vries and Derek

Keene. Members of the Preindustrial England seminar have contributed in a variety of ways to improving the book, especially Negley Harte, Nuala Zahedieh, Larry Epstein, Vanessa Harding, Peter Earle and David Mitchell. I am grateful to several scholars for giving me the opportunity to benefit from their unpublished work, including Norris Nash, Margaret Spufford, Michael Berlin, Regina Grafe, Karen Newman, Jake Knoppers and Hugh Dunthorne. Various friends in the Netherlands have helped me over the years, none more than the late Simon Hart, who placed his intimate knowledge of the Amsterdam city archives at my disposal. Alice Carter was as helpful with Dutch sources as she was in procuring supplies of *Bokma* for the LSE bar. Joop Faber, Johan de Vries, Leo Noordegraaf, Marjolein 't Hart, Clé Lesger, Pieter Jansen and Jan Willem Veluwenkamp have all supplied me with essential information, for which I am most grateful.

I am much indebted to the several librarians and archivists in Britain and the Netherlands, whose institutions are listed in the bibliography. Special thanks are due to those who provided illustrations, together with permission to reproduce them: James Hellings and Martin Royalton-Kisch of the Department of Prints and Drawings at the British Museum; the staff of the Map Room at the British Library; Chris Rich at the National Maritime Museum; Jaap Oosterhoff at the Centraal Museum, Utrecht; Mariette Halkema at the Mauritshuis, the Hague; Joyce Edwards at the Amsterdam Historical Museum; and Spencer Scott of the University of Kent's photographic department. Last, but certainly not least, I must thank Richard Fisher and Michael Watson of Cambridge University Press for their encouragement and forbearance.

Aucher House   D. J. O.
Canterbury
Easter 2002

Abbreviations

AAG Bijdragen	*Bijdragen*, Afdeling Agrarische Geschiedenis, Wageningen Universiteit
Add Mss	Additional manuscripts, British Library
AHN	*Acta Historiae Neerlandicae*
BIHR	*Bulletin of the Institute of Historical Research*
BL	British Library
BMGN	*Bijdragen en mededelingen betreffende de geschiedenis der Nederlanden*
BMHG	*Bijdragen en mededelingen van het historisch genootschap gevestigd te Utrecht*
BPP	British Parliamentary Papers
Brants	Archief Brants, Gemeente Archief, Amsterdam
C	Chancery records, Public Record Office
CO	Colonial Office records, Public Record Office
CSPC	*Calendar of State Papers, Colonial Series*
CTBP	*Calendar of Treasury Books and Papers*
Cust. 3	Ledgers of the Inspector General, Public Record Office
Cust. 50–101	Outport records, Public Record Office
DNB	*Dictionary of National Biography*
EcHR	*Economic History Review*
EHJ	*Economisch-Historisch Jaarboek*
EIC	(English) East India Company
ESHJ	*Economisch- en Sociaal-Historisch Jaarboek*
ESHN	*Economic and Social History in the Netherlands*
GAA	Gemeente Archief, Amsterdam
GAR	Gemeente Archief, Rotterdam
Hanson	L. W. Hanson, *Contemporary Printed Sources for British Irish and Economic History, 1701–1750*, Cambridge, 1963
HMC	Historical Manuscripts Commission
JCTP	*Journal of the Commissioners for Trade and Plantations*

JEEH	*Journal of European Economic History*
JEH	*Journal of Economic History*
JHC	*Journals of the House of Commons*
JMH	*Journal of Modern History*
MADBR	Maatschappij van Assurantie, Discontering en Beleening, Rotterdam
NEHA	Nederlandsch Economisch-Historisch Archief
NA	Notarial Archives
NRO	Northumberland Record Office, Melton Park
NRON	Norfolk Record Office, Norwich
PP	*Past and Present*
PRO	Public Record Office, London
RHC	*Reports from Committees of the House of Commons*
SP84	State Papers, Holland, Public Record Office
T	Treasury Papers, Public Record Office
TRHS	*Transactions of the Royal Historical Society*
TvG	*Tijdschrift voor Geschiedenis*
VOC	Dutch East India Company (Verenigde Oost-Indische Compagnie)
WIC	West India Company (West-Indische Compagnie)

1 National economies and the history of the market

Unsurprisingly perhaps, the most comprehensive history of the earlier centuries of British overseas trade, Adam Anderson's *Origin of Commerce*, was first published in the 1760s as the mercantile age was at its height. It was 'To the instrumentality of Commerce *alone*', the author suggested, that 'the Britannic Empire is most peculiarly indebted for its Opulence and Grandeur, its Improvements in Arts and Knowledge; and, in general, for the great Bulk of its solid Comforts and Conveniences'.[1] During the preceding century, trade and navigation came to occupy an unprecedented place in the national esteem. Their progress was reported in numerous tracts and journals as an indicator of national well-being and prosperity, and naval power was equated with national security. It is undeniable that a sense of British national identity was strengthened during the course of the Anglo-French wars of the eighteenth century.[2] But the making of national *character* and a sense of Englishness involved earlier and more subtle processes in which similarity and difference were constantly negotiated and renegotiated.[3] Although far less costly and wasteful of human life, the Anglo-Dutch wars of the 1650s, '60s and '70s involved an equally momentous struggle for maritime supremacy, between people whose religious and social lives were marked by similarity rather than difference. That struggle produced some of the most potent images of a maritime nation, which laid the basis for the English school of eighteenth-century marine painting. Yet the images produced by the van de Veldes, as Dutch immigrants, contain no hint of propaganda, serving to emphasise the importance of admiration, emulation and subtle rivalry in the

---

[1] A. Anderson, *An Historical and Chronological Deduction of the Origin of Commerce*, 4 vols., 1764, vol. I, p. v. For a discussion of the value of Anderson's treatise, see J. Dorfman, 'An Eighteenth Century Guide Book for Economic Policy', prefaced to the 1967 reprint of the four-volume 1801 edition, A. M. Kelley, New York.

[2] L. Colley, *Britons. Forging the Nation, 1707–1837*, 1992, Introduction.

[3] On the distinction between national character and national identity, see P. Anderson, 'Fernand Braudel and National Indentity', *London Review of Books*, 9 May 1991, pp. 4–8, reprinted in Anderson, *A Zone of Engagement*, 1992.

Wisdom and Youth .   *Published according to the Act of Parl.t Jan.y 30,1753.*

Illustration 1.1 Unknown artist and engraver, 'Wisdom and Youth', engraved for J. Hanway, *Travels*, 1754.

making of national identity. The period also saw the multiplication of images of the British merchant and his calling. Jonas Hanway's publisher, for example, depicted the merchant and his cargoes at the heart of a prosperous and godly community, for the instruction of Youth, attended by the muse of Wisdom. The gentleman merely dispenses charity, and the husbandman sows, as he has since time immemorial.[4]

For many contemporaries, foreign trade was seen as the prime-mover in the economy, and controlled commercial expansion was closely linked with a growing sense of national identity and assertiveness. The home market, on the other hand, was seriously neglected, although Gregory King estimated its size at four times the volume of imports and exports.[5] Such an outlook, in broad terms, has been described as *mercantilist*. Although modern economic historians have expressed a diversity of views on the subject, the pre-war generations found the concept indispensable and relatively unproblematic. R. H. Tawney, for example, opened his LSE lectures on early modern English history with the statement that 'Trade is the dynamic which sets everything in motion.' Tawney, in fact, explained British economic development in the sixteenth and seventeenth centuries through the maturing of a specifically commercial form of capitalism, and expressed his distaste for it by quoting the early eighteenth-century clergyman economist, Dean Tucker, who believed that 'to fight for trade is a species of madness reserved only for Britons'.[6] The post-war generation, however, was inclined to downgrade or dismiss the significance and coherence of mercantilist thought, preferring instead to measure and delineate the commodity structures of overseas trade. Relatively little attention was given to either the political context or the global structures within which commercial patterns evolved, and the main preoccupation was to estimate the contribution of overseas trade to the growth of the British economy in the eighteenth and nineteenth centuries.

The growth perspectives of the 1960s viewed commercial expansion as an economic act performed within an essentially Ricardian framework, in which overseas trade was assumed to be inter-*national*.[7] The reality described by Dean Tucker, however, was a more variegated world of nation states in the making, of city states and maritime provinces, and of colonies, plantations and 'remote and marginal worlds' untouched by

---

[4] J. Hanway, *An Historical Account of the British Trade over the Caspian Sea: with a Journal of Travels from London through Russia into Persia; and back again through Russia, Germany and Holland . . . added, The Revolutions of Persia during the present century*, London, second edn 1754, vol. II, frontispiece.

[5] L. Gomes, *Foreign Trade and the National Economy. Mercantilist and Classical Perspectives*, 1987, pp. 76 7.

[6] British Library of Political and Economic Science: Tawney Papers, Box 5/1, Lectures on Economic History, 1485 1800; D. J. Ormrod, 'R. H. Tawney and the Origins of Capitalism', *History Workshop*, 18 (1984), p. 147.

[7] Kenneth Berrill was one of the few economist historians to draw attention to the regional basis underlying supposedly 'national' commercial networks in earlier periods: 'International Trade and the Rate of Economic Growth', *EcHR*, 12 (1960), pp. 351 9.

European influence.[8] It was the city states, indeed, which played the leading role in European commercial life before the territorial states rose to prominence in the eighteenth century. Inequality, both political and economic, was thus the starting point of exchange in the early modern world.

Since the mid-1970s, the proponents of a new history of development have attempted to overcome the limited assumptions of orthodox commercial history to take account of disparities of resource endowment and degrees of economic backwardness. Originally set out by Immanuel Wallerstein, and re-interpreted by Fernand Braudel, a new descriptive framework has now emerged by which the expansion of European commerce may be understood in terms of a hierarchy of zones and markets, in which unequal exchange and coercion are acknowledged realities. The three centuries between 1450 and 1750 are seen as the critical period during which the integration of European trade networks incorporated increasing areas of the world into a European world-economy or world system. A world-economy (*economie-monde* or *weltwirtschaft*) should not be confused with *the* world economy as a whole. It refers rather to a fragment of the world, 'an economically autonomous section of the planet able to provide for most of its own needs [with]...a certain organic unity'.[9] As Wallerstein explains, the framework is one within which the development of sovereign states or nations can be described merely as one kind of organisational structure among others. It presupposes a single division of labour within an area larger than any one political unit.[10]

It would be misleading to represent the proponents of the new history of development as constituting a unified 'school'. Significant variations in emphasis are apparent between Wallerstein, Braudel and other writers who adopt a world-systems framework.[11] For both Wallerstein and Braudel, the world-economy is conceived in terms of a strong central (or core) zone, a developed middle zone and a vast underdeveloped periphery. In the long run, the core shifts from one part of the system to another, and the system as a whole experiences periods of expansion and contraction. Both share a similar conceptualisation of time, in which historical change occurs within cyclical rather than linear patterns. Here, Wallerstein relies on the Braudellian logistic, derived from Simiand: the

---

[8] F. Braudel, *Civilisation and Capitalism, 15th–18th Century*, vol. III, *The Perspective of the World* (1979) 1984, p. 441.

[9] Ibid., p. 22.

[10] I. Wallerstein, *The Modern World-System*, vol. I, *Capitalist Agriculture and the Origins of the European World-Economy in the Sixteenth Century*, 1974, p. 7; I. Wallerstein, 'Failed Transitions or Inevitable Decline of the Leader?' in F. Krantz & P. Hohenberg (eds.), *Failed Transitions to Modern Industrial Society: Renaissance Italy and Seventeenth Century Holland*, Montreal, 1975, p. 76.

[11] P. K. O'Brien, 'European Economic Development: the Contribution of the Periphery', *EcHR*, 35 (1982), p. 2.

long cycle of three centuries, consisting of two phases, one of growth (A) and one of stagnation (B). It is especially during phase B movements that repositioning occurs within the system, and capital is concentrated in the core, as in the period *c*.1620–1750. It is within the spatial dimension, in fact, that the most notable differences arise within the world systems approach.

For Wallerstein, the hierarchy of zones represents a series of analytical categories rather than a number of specific sites and locations, defined by the logic of unequal exchange. He assumes a single, dynamic core area which may, however, be occupied by one or more states or regions.[12] Braudel, on the other hand, stresses the pivotal role of specific leading cities, of 'high-voltage' urban economies which dominated their hinterlands, taking advantage of the backwardness of others. From the early thirteenth century until the rise of Antwerp around 1500, the European world-economy, according to Braudel, was dominated by Bruges and Venice, acting as its northern and southern poles. During Antwerp's brief golden age, the northern zone began to establish its leading position. After the closure of the Scheldt in 1585, however, the system lapsed into a further bi-polar phase as Genoa took up the position of southern pole, while the Low Countries retained something of their former dominance. The role of the leading city essentially involves an uncertain struggle for economic and political control, in which long periods of stability are followed by crisis, and an ensuing process of 'de-centring' and 're-centring'. His *economie-monde* is less monolithic than Wallerstein's, liable to fragment into its constituent elements, the two great circuits of trade or regional economies centring on the Mediterranean and the North Sea.

Around 1600, the balance shifted decisively northwards, as Amsterdam assumed Antwerp's former hegemonic position. This did not merely involve a transfer of activity from Antwerp to Amsterdam, but represented a permanent and massive shift of gravity from southern to north-western Europe, at a time when the European economy as a whole was expanding. Following the provocative suggestion of Violet Barbour, Braudel described Amsterdam as the last of a series of economically dominant cities, which prolonged the old pattern of European history. Like those of Venice and Antwerp, Amsterdam's golden age was one in which 'a veritable empire of trade and credit could be held by a city in her own right, unsustained by the forces of a modern state'.[13] In the succeeding phase, marked by the shift of power to London, the territorial state

---

[12] I. Wallerstein, *The Modern World System*, II, *Mercantilism and the Consolidation of the European World-Economy, 1600–1750*, 1980, p. 37.
[13] V. Barbour, *Capitalism in Amsterdam in the Seventeenth Century* (1950), Ann Arbor, 1963, p. 13.

and the national economy took on a new significance. Pushing Braudel's logic one stage further, we can characterise the contrast between Amsterdam and London in terms of the emergence of a new kind of entrepôt system: the one a modification of the old city-centred staple system, a central staplemarket; the other, a modern commercial metropolis with an integrated national economy as its hinterland. In this sense, the rise of the British nation state provided the basis and the starting point for a new pattern of economic development.

In Braudel's view then, one or more leading cities dominate the entire network of commercial relations. Development springs partly from the drive to monopolise commercial profits, and partly from the agglomeration of economies, skills and precocious technologies of an urban environment. Wallerstein, in contrast, places much more emphasis on relations between core and periphery as the dynamic of development. The exploitation of the periphery, secured especially through unequal exchange and labour control, is constituted in the 'development of underdevelopment'. In his account of the sixteenth-century *origins* of the modern world system, Wallerstein attaches no special significance to the territory of the nation state, and the core exists as a single zone which may comprise several cities, states and regions. By 1600, that zone is identified as 'firmly located in northwest Europe, that is in Holland and Zeeland; in London, the Home Counties, and East Anglia; and in northern and western France'.[14] In the following decades however, and especially after 1650, economic crisis and demographic stagnation produced more intense forms of economic nationalism, and a major struggle was played out in the core, as Britain and France challenged Dutch hegemony over the world-economy. In the second of Wallerstein's volumes, dealing with the contraction of the European world-economy during the long seventeenth century, much greater emphasis is placed on the nation state and commercial rivalry, the Colbertian *combat perpetuel*. England and the Dutch Republic are seen as two equally-matched nation states, equally capable of devising and implementing effective mercantilist strategies, although, in practice, Dutch strength and productive efficiency were such that only limited forms of state intervention were necessary. This, as we shall see, is a misleading assumption, which neglects important differences in the pattern of state formation, especially those arising from the entanglements of cities and states.[15] It underestimates the extent of intercity rivalries in Holland and greatly exaggerates the strength and effectiveness of the Dutch state.

[14] Wallerstein, *Modern World System*, vol. II, p. 37.
[15] C. Tilly, 'Entanglements of European Cities and States', in C. Tilly & W. P. Blockmans (eds.), *Cities and the Rise of States in Europe, AD 1000–1800*, Boulder, 1994, pp. 1–27.

An even more serious anachronism in Wallerstein's 'world-system' is the supposition that, by 1640, the economies of Europe and its overseas possessions were sufficiently integrated to constitute a 'new European division of labour' based on the flow of resources between core and periphery. The movement of international wheat prices indeed shows a slow but steady integration of northern and southern cereal markets between 1300 and 1650, but trade-flows between Asia, the Americas and Europe were insignificant before the mid seventeenth century.[16] Although intercontinental trade accelerated thereafter, O'Brien, following Bairoch, suggests that commerce with the peripheral areas probably accounted for no more than 4% of Western Europe's GNP by 1800. In terms of capital formation, this is unlikely to have exceeded 1% of GNP. For the Netherlands and Britain, of course, long-distance trade played a more important role, but O'Brien calculates that, even in Britain's case, trade with the periphery generated surpluses which can hardly have financed more than 7% of gross annual investment during the 1780s.[17] This figure represents a slight underestimate, based as it is on the three years immediately following the American War of Independence when transatlantic trade and re-exports remained at abnormally low levels (1784–6). Re-exports at that time amounted to only one-sixth the value of total exports, whereas from 1771 to 1775 for example, the proportion was over one-third.[18] The logic of world-systems theory, however, posits that the primary products of the periphery were indeed purchased cheap, hence the argument is one which cannot be resolved by a national accounts approach, however refined the statistical evidence. As both proponents and critics of world-systems theory have admitted, their differences are of a paradigmatic kind.[19]

Whatever the contribution of mercantile profits to capital accumulation and investment, it is clear that the most palpable benefits of trade with the periphery accrued to the consumer, particularly during the first half of the eighteenth century. From c. 1710 to 1735, prices for colonial and Asian goods either stagnated or collapsed. Demand for semi-luxuries such as tea, coffee, sugar, tobacco and Indian textiles was both income- and

---

[16] S. R. Epstein, *Freedom and Growth. The Rise of States and Markets in Europe, 1300–1750*, 2000, ch. 7.
[17] O'Brien, 'Contribution of the Periphery', p. 17.
[18] Ibid., Table 1, p. 6, excludes the Baltic and Northern European periphery, and selects the years 1784–6, immediately following the end of the American War of Independence when re-exports were abnormally reduced at £3.6mill.; for 1771–5, for example, re-exports averaged £5.75mill. In 1784–6, re-exports amounted to 17% of the value of total exports, whereas from 1772 to 1774, the figure was 34.7%.
[19] A. G. Frank, *Re-Orient: Global Economy in the Asian Age*, Berkeley, Los Angeles, London, 1998, p. 42.

price-elastic, and a wider spectrum of the population was now able to enjoy them. In developmental terms, long-distance trade released Europeans from their own resource endowments, but colonial raw materials and primary products made only a modest contribution to industrial growth, until the rapid expansion of West Indian cotton-wool imports from the mid-1780s.[20] More important than colonial sources of supply were the peripheral and 'semi-peripheral' regions of the Baltic, Eastern Europe, Ireland and Scotland. The contribution of these local peripheries to English economic development is excluded from O'Brien's calculations, but their significance was felt at two levels, as sources of essential 'strategic' imports and, through the pursuit of import substitution policies, as low-cost alternative producers. Baltic flax, hemp, timber and naval stores were paid for by re-exports of plantation goods and Asian textiles to Europe, and the Irish and Scottish linen industries supplied England's growing home market with replacements for more expensive European fabrics.

The world systems perspective is a useful corrective to neo-classical theory, but the measurable economic gains from Europe's colonial and transoceanic trades were smaller than Wallerstein suggests, and the size and weight of the European system in 1750 was only modest in real global terms. Gundar Frank has recently drawn attention to the eurocentricity of Wallerstein and Braudel's models. In a grand polemic which revises his own earlier views, Frank reduces its proportions to an appendage of a much larger Afro-Eurasian world economy, itself the magnet which led to the 'discovery' of the New World and the incorporation of the Americas into the European economy. In spite of appearances, Frank is close to agreeing with O'Brien that Wallerstein's great European division of labour straddling core and periphery needs scaling down. In the chapters which follow, some elements of a Braudellian world systems framework will be retained, including the role of leading cities and a hierarchy of zones in which regional economies were drawn into closer forms of integration within the larger (real) global economy. The assumption that the wealth of the European 'core' countries depended on the resources of a global periphery, however, is rejected, and, with it, Wallerstein's sketch of Anglo-Dutch rivalry as a struggle between two equally strong core states attempting to control those resources. Access to colonial markets was, of course, an important issue for English and Dutch statesmen, but Anglo-Dutch competition was played out primarily in the North Sea – Baltic zone, a region large enough to contain its own periphery. That contest involved industrial competition, a struggle for the carrying trades

---

[20] O'Brien, 'Contribution of the Periphery', pp. 10–12.

of the region, access to the primary products of the Baltic and Eastern Europe and, for the English, a drive to reduce dependence on the Dutch staplemarket. National rivalries obviously played a critical role in this, but so too did conflict and co-operation between mercantile cities.

Braudel and Wallerstein's European 'world-system' is most properly seen as an intermediate zone within the larger global economy. The North Sea – Baltic economy formed its northern pole, and existed as a distinct regional economy comparable in scale to the trading world of the Mediterranean. Like its southern European counterpart, the North Sea zone contained a highly urbanised core in the Low Countries and southern England, but state formation and city-state relations followed a different course in each case. Whereas in northern and central Italy, territorial states dominated by a single city persisted into the nineteenth century, the Dutch succeeded in creating a durable federation of city-states. In England, a high degree of political centralisation together with weak urban jurisdictions permitted the emergence of a national urban hierarchy at an early stage. As the potential for urban expansion moved steadily northwards during the seventeenth century, a new pattern of large city growth emerged in which London and Amsterdam expanded far beyond the size and weight achieved by the mercantile cities of northern Italy. The relative dynamism of north-western Europe during the B-phase of the growth cycle, it seems, was closely bound up with the concentration of skills, capital, commercial intelligence and external economies in a handful of large mercantile cities, supported by the resources of the state. A number of questions remain, however, about the configuration of urban growth and the role of the state in England and the northern Netherlands. What were the relative positions of London and Amsterdam within their respective urban hierarchies, port systems and hinterlands? How effective was the state in opposing the vested interests of urban oligarchies and in promoting market growth in England and the Republic? How far and in what ways were 'strong core states' able to use taxation as a means of promoting commercial and industrial growth?

Leading cities and their hinterlands

Recent work by Dutch demographic historians has confirmed Braudel's suggestion that, in relation to the towns of the United Provinces, 'Amsterdam stood in the same position as did Venice to those of the *Terraferma*'.[21] Like London, Amsterdam was indeed unique in the

---

[21] Braudel, *Perspective of the World*, p. 182. In 1600, the population of Venice was 139,000; that of Verona lay within the range 50–60,000, Brescia 40–50,000, Padua 30–40,000,

national urban hierarchy, but was surrounded by several populous towns and small cities in a way that London was not. By 1622, just over half the total population of Holland was urbanised, and during the seventeenth century as a whole, between a quarter and one-third of the Dutch population lived in towns and cities with populations in excess of 10,000 (Table 1.1).[22] By far the greater proportion of these urban dwellers lived in places other than Amsterdam. At the height of the Dutch golden age, the English provinces had nothing to compare with Leiden's population of 67,000, or Haarlem's 38,000, and Rotterdam, Middleburg and Utrecht were all 50% larger than Norwich or Bristol, with populations of around 30,000.[23] Even during the first half of the eighteenth century when the United Provinces experienced urban decline, the proportion of town dwellers remained close to 20% of the total.[24]

In England and Wales during the seventeenth century, a relatively small proportion of the national population lived in urban areas outside London, and not until the first half of the eighteenth century was a significant rise registered in the population of sizeable provincial towns. The tendency in both countries was for the capital city to grow at a disproportionately rapid rate before 1700, as the European economy became increasingly integrated and leading cities extended their functions over a wider hinterland. By the turn of the century, Amsterdam, like London, contained more than 10% of the national population, but Amsterdam's dominance was much less pronounced than London's. Following de Vries, Diederiks emphasises the singularity of Dutch urban history in terms of the absence of a single multi-functional urban centre, noting that, while Amsterdam indeed developed into by far the largest of the Dutch commercial cities, a single metropolis failed to emerge in the northern Netherlands. Instead, the whole western area of the province of post-medieval Holland may be considered as a 'decentralised metropolis'.[25] In Diederiks's view, Amsterdam never functioned as a primate city, or

and Bergamo, 20–30,000 (C. Wilson and G. Parker (eds.), *An Introduction to the Sources of European Economic History, 1500–1800*, 1977, p. 5).

[22] J. A. Faber, H. K. Roessingh, *et al.*, 'Population Changes and Economic Developments in the Netherlands: An Historical Survey', *AAG Bijdragen*, 12 (1965), p. 53; J. de Vries, *European Urbanisation, 1500–1800*, 1984, Appendix 1, pp. 270–87.

[23] Population figures for 1650, assembled by de Vries, *European Urbanisation*.

[24] E. A. Wrigley, 'Urban Growth and Agricultural Change: England and the Continent in the Early Modern Period', *Journal of Interdisciplinary History*, 15 (1985), and reprinted in Wrigley, *People, Cities and Wealth. The Transformation of a Traditional Society*, Oxford, 1987, p. 180.

[25] H. Diederiks, 'The Netherlands, the Case of a Decentralised Metropolis', in E. Aerts and P. Clark (eds.), *Metropolitan Cities and their Hinterlands in Early Modern Europe*, Leuven, 1990, pp. 86–97.

Table 1.1 *English and Dutch urbanisation, 1600–1750*

	1600	1650	1700	1750
Number of towns of 10,000 +				
England & Wales	6	8	11	21
United Provinces	19	19	20	18
Total population (millions)				
England & Wales	4.11	5.23	5.06	5.77
United Provinces	1.50	1.87	1.90	1.90

	1600		1650		1700		1750	
	'000	%	'000	%	'000	%	'000	%
Population living in towns								
of 10,000 +								
England & Wales,								
excluding London	55	1.3	95	1.8	143	2.8	346	6.0
London	200	4.9	400	7.6	575	11.5	675	11.7
Total	255	6.2	495	9.5	718	14.2	1,021	17.7
United Provinces,								
excluding Amsterdam	299	19.9	428	22.9	439	23.1	370	19.5
Amsterdam	65	4.3	175	9.4	200	10.5	210	11.1
Total	364	24.3	603	32.3	639	33.6	580	30.5

Sources: de Vries, *European Urbanisation*, pp. 270–1; J. A. Faber, 'De achttiende eeuw', in J. H. van Stuijvenberg (ed.), *De economische geschiedenis van Nederland*, p. 120; Groningen, 1977, ch. 4, esp. E. A. Wrigley & R. S. Schofield, *The Population History of England, 1541–1871. A reconstruction*, Cambridge, 1981, pp. 208–9.

the hub in a central place system, as Dutch towns always tended to exercise complementary functions.[26] Others have likewise drawn attention to Amsterdam's dependence on other towns within its own region, particularly in the earlier phase of growth before 1585.[27]

In comparative terms then, the positions of London and Amsterdam in relation to their immediate hinterlands around 1700 suggest a contrast between, on the one hand, a national metropolis which exercised key political, administrative, manufacturing and commercial roles, and, on the other, a mercantile city-state occupying the territory of the western part of the province of Holland. The city of Amsterdam functioned simply

[26] Ibid. p. 96; a different view is expressed by P. M. Hohenberg and L. H. Lees, *The Making of Urban Europe, 1000–1950*, Cambridge, Mass., and London, 1985, p. 66.
[27] C. Lesger, 'Clusters of Achievement. The Economy of Amsterdam in its Golden Age', in P. K. O'Brien *et al.* (eds.), *Urban Achievement in Early Modern Europe*, Cambridge, 2001, p. 78.

Table 1.2 *The English and Dutch port systems, 1600–1800: population size of major ports, '000*

	1600	1650	1700	1750	1800
LONDON	200	400	575	675	865
Bristol	11	20	25	45	65
Newcastle/Sunderland	10	13	19	39	52
Exeter	10	10	14	16	17
Ipswich	0	?	8	12	11
King's Lynn	0	5	5	9	10
Yarmouth	0	10	10	10	15
Hull	0	0	6	6	28
Liverpool	0	0	6	22	78
London as a percentage of total 9	86.6	87.3	86.1	80.9	75.9
AMSTERDAM	65	175	200	210	217
Rotterdam	13	30	48	44	57
Middleburg	20	30	25	24	20
Dordrecht	15	20	22	16	18
Enkhuizen	17	22	14	7	7
Hoorn	12	16	13	10	10
Amsterdam as a percentage of total 6	45.8	59.7	62.1	67.5	66.0

Source: J. de Vries, *European Urbanisation*, Appendix 1.

as *primus inter pares*. This contrast is also reflected in the structures of the English and Dutch port systems, that is, the distribution and degree of concentration of overseas and inland trade within a range of ports of different sizes, given the prevailing situation in which not all had equal means of access to their respective hinterlands (Table 1.2).[28] As is well known, London's dominance of English overseas trade represented the continuation of a centuries-old pattern, one which was heightened during the course of the seventeenth century before declining, albeit only in relative terms, during the eighteenth. It is of course true that, for most purposes, the volume or value of trade constitutes a better measure of the relative importance of different ports than their population size. In the absence of comparable international measures, however, the latter provides a rough means of comparison which only slightly exaggerates the commercial importance of the great entrepôt cities. In 1687, for example,

[28] C. Lesger, 'Intraregional Trade and the Port System in Holland, 1400–1700', in K. Davids & L. Noordegraaf, *The Dutch Economy in the Golden Age*, NEHA, Amsterdam, 1995, pp. 186–217.

London contributed rather less than 82% of the national customs revenue, while Amsterdam in 1698 contributed around 51% of the Dutch total.[29] Table 1.2 can therefore be taken to indicate the bare outlines of the English and Dutch port systems.

Although Amsterdam's lead over the other Dutch ports was substantial, and the city continued to grow at a modest rate throughout the eighteenth century, its dominance was far from complete. Rivalry with other neighbouring ports was an ever-present reality, particularly with Rotterdam, which handled the trade with England, Scotland and France.[30] Furthermore, Amsterdam had emerged as the premier port of Holland at a comparatively late stage in the history of the Netherlands, taking second place to Dordrecht in the mid fourteenth century. By the 1540s, Amsterdam was handling a much wider range of goods than its rivals and the value of its exports was three times that of all the other Dutch ports. Its 'meteoric' rise to prominence, however, occurred after 1585. As one of the Zuider Zee ports, Amsterdam acted as an intermediary between north and south, acting principally as Holland's main gateway to the north German ports and the Baltic. Less important was the east–west trade of the Rhine–Meuse delta, which linked the North Sea trade with the Republic's eastern hinterland. Until the early years of the seventeenth century, the delta ports were dominated by Dordrecht, when Rotterdam began its slow rise to prominence.[31]

The excellence and accessibility of inland water transport throughout the Dutch Republic, together with the early establishment of the *beurtvaart*, a network of regular inland shipping services, go a long way towards explaining why the Dutch port system was less concentrated than England's.[32] On the other hand, the dependence of Dutch cities on imported Baltic grain before 1700 ensured that Amsterdam would maintain an important central role as an intermediary port linking international with inland trade. In ways such as these, it is possible to note important differences between the circumstances shaping the roles of Amsterdam and London as major entrepôts and as leading cities at the apex of their

[29] W. E. Minchinton (ed.), *The Growth of English Overseas Trade in the Seventeenth and Eighteenth Centuries*, 1969, p. 33; J. Hovy, *Het voorstel van 1751 tot instelling van een beperkt vrijhavenstelsel in de republiek*, Groningen, 1966, Tables I–V, pp. 7–18 (the Convoy and Licence yield for the Zeeland Admiralty is unavailable for 1698, and the nearest available figure, that of 1689, is inserted to complete the total).

[30] Joh. de Vries, *Amsterdam–Rotterdam. Rivaliteit in economisch-historisch perspectief*, Bussum, 1965, pp. 43–69.

[31] Lesger, 'The Economy of Amsterdam', pp. 64–5.

[32] On the *beurtvaart*, see Lesger, 'Intraregional Trade', pp. 195–9; J. de Vries, 'Barges and Capitalism. Passenger Transportation in the Dutch Economy, 1632–1839', *AAG Bijdragen*, 21, 1978.

respective urban hierarchies. From the late sixteenth through to the later seventeenth century, however, before Dutch economic decline and demographic stagnation set in, it is clear that the overall pattern of urban growth and change came to exhibit more points of similarity than difference. Between 1550 and 1680, as Wrigley has shown, England and Wales and the northern Netherlands experienced comparable rates of population growth (64% and 58% respectively), and the pace of urbanisation in the former began to quicken.[33] Most significantly, London and Amsterdam attained positions of comparable size within their own urban hierarchies. The reasons for this convergence become apparent as one shifts one's focus to trends within Europe as a whole.

In his general account of the process of European urbanisation in the period 1500–1800, de Vries suggests that the northern Netherlands approached a ceiling in terms of urban potential by the mid-seventeenth century. During the preceding century, the stock of urban centres from which the expanding Dutch cities were drawn remained stable, whereas England possessed a much larger endowment of potential cities, with hundreds of small market towns and industrial villages. By the early nineteenth century, British levels of urbanisation reached those attained by the Dutch a century earlier: from 1680 to 1820, the population of England and Wales grew by 133%, while that of the Dutch Republic increased by only 8%. In both countries, however, a single dominating commercial centre had emerged during what de Vries describes as the 'middle phase' of European urbanisation extending from roughly 1600 to 1750, characterised by large-city growth. The first phase coincides with the 'long' sixteenth century (1500–1600/50) and is marked by general urban growth at all levels: the emerging hierarchy of cities at this stage may be described as polycentric. The second (or middle) phase characterised by large-city growth precedes a final phase, running from c. 1750 to the early nineteenth century, in which the expansion of smaller cities reduced large-city growth to a level proportionate to that of total population growth. The emerging pattern, described as 'new urbanisation', was an urban growth from below.

Above all, de Vries has emphasised that, during the period 1500–1800, the cities of Europe came to form a single urban system which 'deployed and developed the resources of the entire European zone'. The disproportionate growth of London in the seventeenth century and, to a lesser extent, that of Amsterdam occurred at a critical juncture in this process, and represented the intensification of urban civilisation across the

[33] E. A. Wrigley, 'The Growth of Population in Eighteenth-century England: A Conundrum Resolved', *PP*, 98 (1983), reprinted in Wrigley, *People, Cities and Wealth*, p. 216.

core zone of north-western Europe. For a brief period, from roughly 1670 to 1720, south-eastern England and the Dutch Republic seemed to have reached a point of convergence within the urbanisation process, with around 40% of the population living in cities, in both regions.[34] In the English case, of course, the urban population was mainly concentrated in a single city, London. Significantly, it was during these years that London's rise to pre-eminence was underpinned by Amsterdam's financial and commercial resources, especially after 1689. The diffusion of the entrepôt function thus occurred at a definite point of continuity in the development of the urban system. The sustained growth of London's population thereafter, together with that of the English outports and manufacturing centres, carried the process of urban growth beyond the ceiling reached by the Low Countries. In both demographic and economic terms, Europe's centre of gravity was moving further north, as the culmination of a long-run reorientation of commodity markets and capital flows, and improved access to commercial and manufacturing skills. It was during the 1720s and '30s that London's dependence on Amsterdam receded most conspicuously, the moment when Dutch primacy in world trade finally collapsed.[35]

Cities, states and mercantilist policy

The independence and political weight of the Dutch cities in relation to the state were rooted in economic realities, and the Dutch urban economy represented a precocious development of the traditional staplemarket structure, transformed by large flows of skilled immigrant craftsmen and traders. The central staplemarket function developed out of an agglomeration of local and regional mart towns, at the apex of a hierarchy of exchanges. As an active entrepôt, Amsterdam exercised price leadership, stablised commodity flows and provided a range of financial and shipping services.[36] As J. A. Faber has emphasised, the Republic relied on overseas producers for much of its food and raw material supplies, while its principal exports consisted of commercial and shipping services, colonial

---

[34] J. de Vries, 'Problems in the Measurement, Description, and Analysis of Historical Urbanisation', in A. M. van der Woude, J. de Vries and A. Hayami (eds.), *Urbanisation in History. A Process of Dynamic Interactions*, Oxford, 1990, p. 48.
[35] J. I. Israel, *The Dutch Republic. Its Rise, Greatness, and Fall, 1477–1806*, Oxford, 1995, pp. 998–9.
[36] Joh. de Vries, *De Economische Achteruitgang de Republiek in de Achttiende Eeuw*, Amsterdam, 1959, p. 16; T. P. van der Kooy, *Hollands Stapelmarket en haar Verval*, Amsterdam 1931, ch. 1; K. Glamann, 'The Changing Patterns of Trade', in E. E. Rich & C. H. Wilson (eds.), *The Cambridge Economic History of Europe*, vol. V, *The Economic Organization of Early Modern Europe*, Cambridge, 1977, ch. IV, esp. p. 286.

products, and manufactured goods with a high import content.[37] Most of the linen bleached at Haarlem was imported from Germany and the fine cloths of Leiden were made from imported Spanish wool. English malt and barley sustained the brewing and distilling industries of the Maas towns during the eighteenth century, as did English and Scottish coal, which additionally supplied the needs of sugar refiners, saltmakers and smiths. Textile finishing was merely one of a large group of processing and finishing industries which dominated the industrial sector. Their dependence on imports is reflected in a language which has no exact equivalent in English: *trafiekbedrijf, verkeersnijverheid, verkeersindustrieën.*[38] Fundamentally, this was an economy which depended on the staple-market. In the eighteenth century, over half the labour force was employed in shipping, trade and commercial services, and the processing industries.[39]

The British entrepôt system, on the other hand, developed during the course of the seventeenth century on a much broader economic base. London, like Amsterdam, possessed 'the whole panoply of economic power' including shipping, finance, commercial and industrial strength but drew on its own, home-produced supplies of food, fuel and raw materials to a degree that the Dutch cities did not. A nation-wide network of agents provided the capital city with inland supplies of food, fuel and semi-finished goods.[40] London merchants, unlike their Amsterdam counterparts, invested in provincial manufacturing on a large scale, frequently with a controlling interest arising from their involvement in finishing and marketing.[41] Nor should the extent of manufacturing in early modern London be underestimated.[42] Seventeenth-century occupational patterns in the metropolis reflect a strong bias towards production rather than exchange, in a proportion of roughly 3:1. In addition, London functioned as the locus of central government and political decision-making,

[37] J. A. Faber, 'The Economic Decline of the Dutch Republic in the Second Half of the Eighteenth Century and the International Terms of Trade', in W. G. Heeres *et al.* (eds.), *From Dunkirk to Danzig. Shipping and Trade in the North Sea and the Baltic, 1350–1850*, Hilversum, 1988, p. 107; Joh. de Vries, *Economische Achteruitgang*, p. 13.

[38] Z. W. Sneller, *Geschiedenis van den Steenkolenhandel van Rotterdam*, Groningen, 1946, pp. 60–1.

[39] J. A. Faber, 'Structural Changes in the European Economy during the Eighteenth Century as Reflected in the Baltic Trade', in Heeres *et al.* (eds.), *Dunkirk to Danzig*, p. 87.

[40] J. A. Chartres, 'Food Consumption and Internal Trade', in A. L. Beier & R. Finlay (eds.), *London, 1500–1700. The Making of a Metropolis*, 1986, pp. 184–8; J. A. Chartres, 'The Marketing of Agricultural Produce', in J. Thirsk (ed.), *The Agrarian History of England and Wales, 1640–1750*, vol. V (II), *Agrarian Change*, Cambridge, 1985, pp. 491–3.

[41] Ibid., p. 161.

[42] A. L. Beier, 'Engine of Manufacture: the Trades of London', in Beier & Finlay (eds.), *London, 1500–1700*, p. 150.

and important social and cultural differences between London and Amsterdam affected their commercial life. The former seems to have developed at least a reputation for conspicuous consumption and luxury, so that, by 1715, London was fast becoming the equal of Paris in terms of fashionable taste. Amsterdam, on the other hand, retained a 'glorious simplicity'. Although 'the better sort' had made 'a great alteration... in their equipages, entertainments, and whole manner of living' since the days when Temple complained of Dutch frugality, it seemed to Mandeville that the majority still harboured a strong aversion to luxury.[43] London's population, in addition, was more than twice that of Amsterdam, and represented the largest single concentration of consumers in Britain and Europe.

In several key respects, then, London's position in the European economy was entirely different from that of Amsterdam or Venice, and, from the late seventeenth century, we move into a new context: as Braudel noted, 'this great city had at its command the English national market and later that of the entire British Isles'.[44] A major threshold existed for Braudel between the city-centred economies of the European past and the rise of national economies. Wallerstein, on the other hand, registers no major discontinuity in the shift of power from Holland to Britain. Instead, the starting point of European modernisation lies in the political events which separated the failure of Charles V's drive towards world-empire and the rise of the Dutch Republic as 'the first hegemonic power of the capitalist world-economy'. For Wallerstein, economic leadership at the core of the world-economy requires, a fortiori, productive efficiency backed by the power of the nation state; and the Dutch state, in this view, was just as strong and effective as the political order which emerged in England after 1688. De Vries and van der Woude also emphasise the same elements of modernity underlying the success of the Dutch economy, including early industrial growth, high productivity and an integrated national economy, but are less optimistic about the part played by government.[45]

In emphasising these differences, we inevitably encounter a major historiographical divide which originates in the arguments of the German Historical School and its critics, about the role of the state in economic affairs and the significance of the change from municipal to 'national' policy. Following Schmoller's lead, it was Heckscher especially who

[43] D. Regin, *Traders, Artists and Burghers. A Cultural History of Amsterdam in the 17th Century*, Assen, 1976, pp. 211–13; B. Mandeville, *The Fable of the Bees, or Private Vices, Public Benefits*, 6th edn, 1723, pp. 206–8.
[44] Braudel, *Perspective of the World*, p. 35.
[45] J. de Vries & A. van der Woude, *The First Modern Economy. Success, Failure, and Perseverance of the Dutch Economy, 1500–1815*, Cambridge, 1997, p. 695.

defined the notion of a consistent medieval town policy and described the ways in which mercantilism challenged municipal autonomy and attempted to 'nationalise the economic features of town life'. Heckscher distinguished five basic economic principles of medieval town policy: to secure abundant supplies of food and raw materials; to reserve trade, commerce and manufactures for the town; to discriminate against strangers; to support the staplemarket function, by 'driving as much traffic as possible into the city'; and to apply the general social ethic of the Middle Ages, which required that every person with a calling was to be assured of the means of subsistence. The last-mentioned principle required that competition be circumscribed, following the ideal represented by the handicraft gilds.[46] The challenge to medieval municipal policy, according to Heckscher, was most successful in England, the country in which it had been least constructive.[47]

Few of Heckscher's criteria apply without modification to the towns of the Dutch Republic, yet the contrast between London and Amsterdam, and particularly between London and the smaller Dutch cities which comprised the 'decentralised metropolis' of Holland, is plain. Before the collapse of their trade to the Low Countries in the 1660s, the Merchant Adventurers in Middleburg, Dordrecht and Rotterdam enjoyed the protection of the *stapelrecht*, based on law merchant, in return for the payment of tolls and their adherence to the discipline of the staplemarket.[48] German merchants likewise established the staple for Westphalian linens at Rotterdam, before its demise in 1672. Groningen exerted its market monopoly over a wide area, and several smaller towns claimed staple privileges and the right to levy tolls.[49] Conflict of interest between the Dutch cities was endemic, especially between Amsterdam, with its relatively open markets, and the staple towns. Differences in economic orientation towards either trade or manufacture provided the main source of longrunning tension, while disputes about inland navigation were common.[50]

---

[46] E. F. Heckscher, *Mercantilism* (1931), revised edn, ed. E. F. Soderlund, 1955, pp. 128–36.

[47] E. F. Heckscher, 'Mercantilism', in D. C. Coleman, *Revisions in Mercantilism*, 1969, pp. 22–3.

[48] P. Huvelin, *Essai historique sur le droit des marchés et des foires*, Paris, 1897, p. 209; B. van Rijswick, *Geschiedenis van het Dordtsche Stapelrecht*, 's-Gravenhage, 1900, ch. 8; R. H. I. Palgrave, *Dictionary of Political Economy*, vol. I, 1894, pp. 460–3.

[49] De Vries & van der Woude, *First Modern Economy*, p. 173.

[50] J. L. Price, *Holland and the Dutch Republic in the Seventeenth Century. The Politics of Particularism*, Oxford, 1994, ch. 5. In addition to inter-city rivalries, L. Noordegraaf emphasises the domination of the countryside by town authorities through the purchase of manorial rights; serious urban–rural conflict continued into the eighteenth century ('Domestic Trade and Domestic Trade Conflicts in the Low Countries; Autonomy, Centralisation and State-formation in the Pre-industrial Era' in S. Groenveld & M.

Municipal self-interest also expressed itself through gild organisation, which remained intact in most Dutch cities, especially Leiden, long after it collapsed in mid-seventeenth-century London.[51] In the promotion of new ventures in industry, the provincial and central authorities played no part whatsoever; it was at the level of municipal government that public support was given.[52]

Although disagreement about staple rights often produced local conflict, staplemarket trading was in principle subject to a transnational code of practice derived from the law merchant, a body of customary rules applied on the high seas and in the conduct of fairs and marts across Europe. With the consolidation of state power and the development of mercantilist ideas and practices, the law merchant was incorporated into national jurisdictions.[53] In England, King's Bench and the Courts of Common Pleas replaced merchants' courts from 1606 to 1640, and, under Lord Mansfield, law merchant was absorbed into the common law in the 1750s. In the northern Netherlands, the most coherent expression of law merchant was found in the *Dordtsche stapelrecht*, the staple law of Dordrecht, the oldest of the Dutch ports standing at the head of the Waal and Maas navigation. The weakness of central authority in the United Provinces ensured at least the formal survival of the *stapelrecht*.

After 1588, the newly established States of Holland increasingly arrogated to themselves the sovereign laws over the *graafschap* or county, and took the lead in interpreting the *Dortsche stapelrecht* through the exercise of a casting vote. They could also issue pronouncements in the event of disputes, which were frequent.[54] The most serious conflicts were with Rotterdam, especially those of 1618–20 when Dordrecht attempted to extend the staple to include the former's growing wine trade with France. This particular dispute began with the seizure of Rotterdam wine ships and an attempt to impose fines for attempted evasion of the *stapelrecht*. Rotterdam reacted by convoying her ships through Dordrecht, which in turn produced armed reprisals, with several dead and wounded. The affair was settled by provincial authority, but no attempt was made to

---

Wintle (eds.), *State and Trade: Government and Economy in Britain and the Netherlands since the Middle Ages*, Zutphen, 1992, pp. 22–3).

[51] G. Unwin, 'De Leidsche Textielnijverheid', in R. H. Tawney (ed.), *Studies in Economic History. The Collected Papers of George Unwin*, 1927, pp. 399–403.

[52] K. Davids, 'Beginning Entrepreneurs and Municipal Governments in Holland at the Time of the Dutch Republic', in C. Lesger & L. Noordegraaf (eds.), *Entrepreneurs and Entrepreneurship in Early Modern Times. Merchants and Industrialists within the Orbit of the Dutch Staple Market*, Hollandse Historische Reeks, 24, The Hague, 1985, p. 167.

[53] C. M. Schmitthoff, 'International Business Law: A New Law Merchant', in C.-J. Cheng (ed.), *Clive M. Schmitthoff's Select Essays on International Trade Law*, Dordrecht, Boston and London 1988, pp. 21–7.

[54] Van Rijswick, *Dordtsche Stapelrecht*, p. 97.

limit or circumscribe the *stapelrecht*. Throughout the seventeenth century, shipmasters who complained of seizures and the arbitrary actions of the Dordrecht authorities met with the pronouncement that, 'beyond all question the stapelrecht [is] not at fault'. In 1630, for example, difficulties arose over the export of timber along the Ijssel and Lek for the account of the Admiralty of the Maas, and in 1649 over the free transport of Scottish and English coal. Efforts to tighten up searches continued, notably in 1657, the 1660s (three), 1707 and the 1740s (three).[55] Gradually, however, Dordrecht gave way on issues of principle, and in the long run was powerless against the continued evasion of the law and the united opposition of the neighbouring towns.[56]

In practical terms, these disagreements probably did little to disrupt the mainstream of commercial life, but they indicate the 'pre-national' origins and the mercantile rationale of the staplemarket economy. In common with intermittent disputes about gild regulations and the protection of industrial interests against foreign competition, they underline the weakness and limitations of the Dutch state as an economic agent. Historians are uncertain as to whether the congeries of municipal and regional economies which formed the Dutch Republic actually functioned as a coherent national economy, a fact which many contemporaries questioned. De Vries and van der Woude conclude that, despite decentralised economic policy formation and an absence of political unity, market forces produced a degree of economic coherence.[57] In good times, provincial collaboration was the norm and local interests were respected. But the pursuit of mercantilist policies by neighbouring states left the Republic in a vulnerable and passive position. Adopting criteria suggested by Tilly, Blockmans and others, it is difficult to describe the Dutch model as anything other than a decentralised federation of cities, supported by a somewhat fragmented state apparatus. The coercive power at its disposal, for both internal and external use, was weak, but capital-intensive. It was, however, a state system that was both transnational and city-based. Its economy far exceeded the boundaries of the state to form a commercial empire, yet the state lacked the trappings of empire.[58]

Given these ambiguities, it is not surprising that debates about the nature of the Dutch state, in terms of its strength, effectiveness and

---

[55] Ibid., pp. 104–5.

[56] H. C. Hazewinkel, *Geschiedenis van Rotterdam*, vol. II, Amsterdam, 1940, pp. 120–1.

[57] De Vries & van der Woude, *First Modern Economy*, pp. 172–9.

[58] The possibilities for describing such a hybrid are no doubt endless. Within Blockmans' threefold classification of city states, territorial states and composite states, the Dutch Republic is a composite, centralised to some degree under the authority of the States General (M. 't Hart, *The Making of a Bourgeois State. War, Politics and Finance during the Dutch Revolt*, Manchester, 1993, p. 11).

modernity, remain inconclusive. Wallerstein, as we have noticed, takes an exaggeratedly optimistic view of all three, while Israel credits the state with a crucial role in the advancement of the country's commerce.[59] Dutch historians, however, are becoming increasingly critical of the weak federalism that came into being between 1579 and 1588. In practice, key resolutions in the States General were taken by majority vote rather than unanimously, as theory demanded, but policy-making was undoubtedly slowed down by the need to form coalitions of interest. Even Israel describes the state mechanism as a hybrid, 'a cross between federal state and confederacy, with more of the confederacy in form and theory, and more of the federal state in substance and practice'.[60] Contemporary political theorists in the Netherlands mostly abhorred the notion of strong government, and provincial autonomy was jealously guarded.[61] The result of this weak form of federalism was the absence of a unified tax and tariff structure, which left limited scope for a coherent economic policy. The most recent study of Dutch public finance, following Tilly, concludes that the absence of a central bureaucracy was no obstacle to efficient fiscal organisation, but accepts that advantages of decentralisation were balanced by the fact that no powerful state body existed to express and represent vital commercial interests.[62]

The disadvantages of weak federal government became increasingly apparent as the golden age drew to a close, and have been invoked by historians as a major factor in the economic decline of the eighteenth century.[63] In any explanation of the Republic's loss of hegemony over the world-economy, and its transfer to England, the limitations of state power must be acknowledged. Like the question of economic decline, the issue of state power is a relative one, and the Republic's vulnerability became increasingly evident as economic nationalism became more strident from the later seventeenth century. After eighty years of struggle against the power of Spain, further participation in expensive and protracted warfare, commercial or otherwise, would seriously strain the Republic's political and financial resources as it approached its natural 'tax ceiling' by the

[59] Wallerstein, *Modern World-System*, vol. I, pp. 211–13; vol. II, pp. 60–1; J. I. Israel, *Dutch Primacy in World Trade, 1585–1740*, Oxford, 1989, pp. 410–13.

[60] Israel, *Dutch Republic*, pp. 276–7.

[61] E. H. Kossman, 'The Development of Dutch Political Theory in the Seventeenth Century', in J. S. Bromley & E. H. Kossman (eds.), *Britain and the Netherlands*, vol. I, 1960, pp. 91–110.

[62] 't Hart, *Making of a Bourgeois State*, pp. 5–7, 216–26.

[63] Joh. de Vries, *Economische Achteruitgang*, p. 177; K. W. Swart, 'Holland's Bourgeoisie and the Retarded Industrialization of the Netherlands', in F. Krantz & P. Hohenberg (eds.), *Failed Transitions to Modern Industrial Society: Renaissance Italy and Seventeenth Century Holland*, Montreal, 1975, pp. 44–8; Hovy, *Voorstel van 1751*, p. 617.

Table 1.3 *British and Dutch taxation compared, 1670–1794*

	% of national income appropriated by taxation		tax revenue per capita (gl)		% direct taxes		% indirect taxes	
	Britain	Holland	Britain	Holland	Britain	Holland	Britain	Holland
	a	*b*	*c*	*d*	*e*	*f*	*g*	*h*	*i*
1670s	–	3.4	11.0	2.9	26.0	–	–	–	–
1720	8.0	10.8	10.5	11.5	23.0	26	50	69	44
1750	8.0	10.5	13.5	13.2	28.0	28	55	71	40
1788–94	–	–	12.0	–	34.0	–	50	–	41
1790	10.0	12.3	–	24.1	–	17	–	75	–

Sources: Columns *a*, *c*, *e*: Fritschy, 'Taxation in Britain, France and the Netherlands', Table 4. Figures in column *c* represent the mid-point of a narrow range. Columns *b*, *d*: derived from P. K. O'Brien, 'The Political Economy of British Taxation, 1660–1815', *EcHR*, 2nd ser., 41 (1988); E. A. Wrigley & R. S. Schofield, *Population History*; exchange rates taken from J. J. McCusker, *Money and Exchange in Europe and America*, 2nd edn, London and Basingstoke, 1992. Current prices utilised in columns *d* and *e*. Columns *f–i*: Fritschy, Table 5 (other minor sources of revenue excluded). Note that Holland contributed between 60 and 70% of the Republic's revenue.

early decades of the eighteenth century.[64] Yet it was primarily through taxation that early modern governments were able to influence the course of economic change, albeit within narrow limits.[65]

Recent work in the field of public finance enables us to provide a fairly clear picture of the comparative history of fiscal arrangements in Britain and the United Provinces. As we have already noticed, autonomous fiscal regimes produced different levels of taxation in the Dutch provinces. Holland contributed the lion's share, varying from 60 to 70% of the total. In the Republic as a whole, the tax burden (tax revenue per capita) was much higher than in Britain, being almost twice as high in 1716–20. As per capita incomes were also higher, though, the percentage of the national income appropriated by taxation was only slightly larger than in Britain (Table 1.3). The Dutch, in the early eighteenth century, were prosperous enough to bear a heavy tax burden, but slow economic decline produced no capacity for further expansion. Indeed, tax revenues declined in real terms, as prices rose in the later eighteenth century.[66] In Britain, the reverse was the case: economic growth and prudent taxation policies provided the basis for a real increase in the tax burden

[64] W. Fritschy, 'Taxation in Britain, France and the Netherlands in the Eighteenth Century', *ESHN*, 2 (1990–1), pp. 62, 65.

[65] P. K. O'Brien, 'Political Preconditions for the Industrial Revolution', in P. K. O'Brien & R. Quinault (eds.), *The Industrial Revolution and British Society*, 1993, p. 125.

[66] Fritschy, 'Taxation in Britain, France and the Netherlands', pp. 59–66.

to levels comparable with those prevailing in Holland, by 1790. The emphasis throughout was on indirect taxation, especially excises, whereas the Dutch relied more heavily on direct taxes such as those levied on government investments, houses, land and farm stock. The success of the Hanoverian state in raising these sums without provoking social discontent is remarkable, but even more striking was the speed with which enormous tax increases were implemented in late seventeenth-century England. By 1720, the percentage of the national income appropriated by taxation had risen to three times the corresponding figure for the 1670s.[67]

For much of the early modern period, the capacity of the English state to regulate the economy and to protect and extend the nation's commerce remained limited. Yet by 1713, after a twenty-year struggle waged against Louis XIV, newly united Britain rose to great-power status. Its enhanced military capability no longer served merely defensive purposes, but would be used to support strategic foreign and imperial policies designed to weaken rival commercial empires.[68] Historians have rightly attached enormous significance to the fiscal and financial revolutions, which, by creating a securely funded national debt, provided the resources needed for Britain's new role in Europe and beyond. Certainly, the size of the Dutch Republic's tax burden made its further participation in major European wars almost impossible after 1713. The drift towards a policy of neutrality, which had the added bonus of stimulating the carrying trade, was in part dictated by financial constraints.[69] In Britain, an efficient and centralised fiscal apparatus undoubtedly enhanced the state's capacity and determination to act, and centralised decision-making facilitated the resolution of competing mercantile interests. Historians, however, have not fully taken the measure of the British 'fiscal-military' state that emerged in the decades following the Glorious Revolution. Some, indeed, have outlined a slow shift towards parliamentary taxation as a consequence of recurring bouts of royal financial mismanagement, involving the creation of a 'tax state' on the ruins of the 'demesne state' during the years c. 1590–1670.[70] However, consideration of long-run changes in national income and revenue from 1485 to 1815 clearly marks

---

[67] P. K. O'Brien, 'British Taxation, 1660–1815', *EcHR*, 41 (1988), pp. 1–32; P. Mathias & P. K. O'Brien, 'Taxation in England and France, 1715–1810: A Comparison of the Social and Economic Incidence of Taxes Collected for the Central Governments', *JEEH*, 5 (1976), pp. 601–50.

[68] O'Brien, 'Political Preconditions', pp. 135–44.

[69] Fritschy, 'Taxation in Britain, France and the Netherlands', pp. 62–3; A. M. C. Carter, *The Dutch Republic in Europe in the Seven Years' War*, 1971, p. xiii.

[70] M. J. Braddick, *Parliamentary Taxation in Seventeenth-Century England*, Woodbridge, 1994, Introduction.

out the Glorious Revolution and the Anglo-French wars of 1689–1713 as the decisive moment in which the state learned how to tax its citizens.[71] In a parallel movement, the reorganisation of public credit after 1688 mobilised the resources of the 'monied interest', and this distinct but related phenomenon has been appropriately described as a financial revolution.[72]

Unfortunately, these familiar processes of fiscal and financial restructuring have rarely been integrated with the complex of changes involved in the redirection and reorganisation of English overseas trade, also labelled in terms borrowed from politics (and invented by Bolingbroke in the 1730s) as a 'commercial revolution'.[73] For mercantilist writers, the connections were relatively clear if somewhat circular, whereby the expansion of commerce was both a means and an end in itself: 'foreign trade produces riches, riches power, power preserves our trade and religion', as Child pronounced.[74] By increasing the supply of colonial products carried in English shipping, and by generating favourable trade balances, the commercial revolution potentially enlarged the state's traditional taxable resource, the King's customs, and, therefore, the capacities of the fiscal-military state. The scale of operations during the wars of the Grand Alliance, however, required huge resources. As D. W. Jones has emphasised, England's strategy of a 'double-forward commitment' on land and sea endangered the protection of English trade, the availability of shipping, naval stores and seamen, and therefore the ability to continue to earn trade surpluses out of which remittances for the supply of English and allied troops would be paid. The strain of the war effort was intense during the 1690s, and commercial growth failed to deliver the war economy from a serious monetary crisis, in the wake of bullion export. Survival, it seems, depended on the activities of the coinage clippers. By the 1700s, however, export growth was sufficiently buoyant to enlarge the surplus out of which remittances were paid, serving to remind us that the redirection of trade flows provided Britain with a means of meeting its overseas obligations and facilitating the conduct of war.[75]

---

[71] P. K. O'Brien & P. H. Hunt, 'The Rise of a Fiscal State in England, 1485–1815', *Historical Research*, 66 (160), 1993, pp. 129–76; H. V. Bowen, *War and British Society, 1688–1815*, Cambridge, 1998, p. 29.

[72] P. G. M. Dickson, *The Financial Revolution in England. A Study in the Development of the Public Credit, 1688–1756*, 1967, ch. 1.

[73] J. H. Plumb, *The Growth of Political Stability in England, 1675–1725*, 1967, p. 3.

[74] J. Child, 'A Treatise concerning the East India Trade', 1681, cited J. Viner, 'Power versus Plenty as Objectives of Foreign Policy in the Seventeenth and Eighteenth Centuries', in D. C. Coleman (ed.), *Revisions in Mercantilism*, 1969, p. 76.

[75] D. W. Jones, *War and Economy in the Age of William and Marlborough*, Oxford, 1988, ch. 2; D. W. Jones, 'Sequel to Revolution: The Economics of England's Emergence as a Great Power, 1688–1712', in J. I. Israel, *The Anglo-Dutch Moment. Essays on the*

A remittance-induced export boom, however, was only one of several benefits which a strong commercial economy could contribute to the success of the fiscal-military state. In particular, it was the selective taxation of overseas trade and its correlate, the application of subsidies, which gave parliament a degree of control which has been persistently underestimated. For most purposes, including the allocation of government expenditure, historians have been content to utilise the concept of 'tax receipts at the exchequer', ignoring the gross sums collected from taxpayers. In the case of most direct taxes and certain excises, the gap between the two was relatively small. Customs revenue, however, presents a different picture. The payment of drawbacks on re-exports,[76] together with bounties and subsidies, all of which were usually met from the proceeds of duties already collected, produced a sizeable and a growing margin, which increased during the first half of the eighteenth century, as the subsidised grain export trade expanded. From a margin of £1.1 million in 1720, the margin between the gross and net yield of customs revenue increased to £2.3 million in 1750. Gross customs revenue, as Table 1.4 shows, was comparable in magnitude with the yield from excise and stamp duties, generally considered to be the most important branch of the revenue throughout the eighteenth century.

For the mercantilist state, variation of the tariff structure together with the redistribution of a large and growing customs revenue, via bounties, drawbacks and tax exemptions, provided the means to promote industrial interests, to encourage import saving, to stimulate the growth of re-exports vis-à-vis domestic consumption, and to modify the terms of trade between British exports and imports of foreign goods and raw materials. Some of these marginal adjustments and their consequences will be examined below. Here, we will simply draw a broad comparison with the Dutch fiscal system, which relied heavily on direct taxation. Net customs revenue in Holland rarely rose above 5% of total revenue, compared to between 20 and 28% in Britain during the years 1700–90. For the Republic as a whole, the sums involved were tiny, fluctuating around the equivalent of £0.1 to £0.25 millions in the same period. The means at its disposal for the promotion of mercantilist policies were comparatively limited, therefore.

Debates about the efficiency of the decentralised Dutch state remain unsettled, but there can be little doubt that Dutch mercantilism was weak

---

Glorious Revolution and its World Impact, Cambridge 1991, pp. 389–406; J. Brewer, *The Sinews of Power. War, Money and the English State, 1688–1783*, New York 1988, ch. 7.
[76] 'Drawback' involved the repayment of import duties or excise, in whole or in part, after goods were re-exported.

Table 1.4 *Distribution of British tax revenues compared with the level of Dutch customs receipts, 1670–1770 (£m)*

	1 tax receipts (net)	2 direct taxes	3 gross excises & stamps	4 net excises & stamps	5 gross customs	6 net customs	7 United Provinces, customs
1670	1.39	1.0		0.2		0.2	0.1
1680	1.51	0.5		0.4		0.5	0.2
1690	2.05	1.4		0.9		0.7	0.2
1700	4.40	1.9		1.7		1.2	0.3
1710	5.13	2.1		1.9		1.3	0.1
1712			2.0	1.7	2.2	1.3	
1720	5.81	1.6	2.7	2.4	2.8	1.7	0.1
1730	6.04	1.5	3.1	2.8	3.0	1.6	0.2
1740	5.62	1.5	3.0	2.7	2.9	1.4	0.2
1750	7.33	2.0	3.6	3.3	3.7	1.7	0.2
1760	8.51	2.3				1.9	0.2
1770	9.70	1.9	4.7	4.2	3.9	2.6	0.2

Sources: Columns 1, 2, and 4 (1670–1710) and 6 (1670–1710), P. K. O'Brien, 'Political Economy of British Taxation', Tables 2 and 4, pp. 3, 9. Columns 3 and 4 (1712–60), 5 and 6 (1712–70). J. Sinclair, *History of the Public Revenue of the British Empire*, 1804, vol. III, pp. 165–74. All figures in columns 1–6 are five-year averages centring on the year indicated, with the exception of those for 1712. Column 7, H. E. Becht, *Statistische gegevens betreffende den handelsomzet van de Republiek der Vereenigde Nederlanden gederende de 17e eeuw (1579–1715)*, 's-Gravenhage, 1908, Table 1; Hovy, *Voorstel van 1751*, Tables I–V, pp. 7–18.

and vulnerable in the face of English and European competition. The striving for national unity and power, which Schmoller considered to be the hallmark of mercantilism, hardly existed in the Republic. Insofar as they constituted an integrated national economy, the United Provinces have been described as 'deviant to the point of being puzzling'.[77] Amsterdam, as we have already emphasised, functioned as an advanced type of world entrepôt, a central staplemarket whose continuous markets were focused on the Bourse, but it nonetheless represented a development of the much older city-centred stapling function.[78] To the extent that the English challenge to Dutch hegemony in world trade was based on the modernisation of older forms of commercial organisation, the emergence of a new type of entrepôt system centred on London depended, in part, on the dismantling of privileged corporate access to the mart towns of Holland and the creation of new frameworks for conducting trade with nearby Europe. It is to these processes that we now turn.

[77] J. De Vries and van der Woude, *First Modern Economy*, p. 172.
[78] Ibid., p. 692.

Part I

England, Holland and the commercial revolution

2   Dutch trade hegemony and English competition, 1650–1700

Throughout Holland's golden age, it seemed clear to many English observers that Dutch foreign policy was driven primarily by commercial interests, and that this was a society in which merchants directed their own affairs, both individually and in corporate terms. Thurloe, for example, writing in 1656, considered that earlier efforts to forge a defensive Anglo-Dutch alliance had failed because 'the United Provinces always found it necessary for them to mingle therewith the consideration of trade... The Hollanders had rather His Highness [Cromwell] be alone in it than that they should lose a tun of sack or a frail of raisins.'[1] Although conflict between Orangists and republicans shifted the balance of emphasis between, on the one hand, Calvinist orthodoxy and warfare and, on the other, toleration and pacifism (or neutrality), an agreed *handelspolitiek* based on the priority of staplemarket trading and low duties hardly changed in its essentials. The ordinary tariff, in fact, rarely exceeded 5%, while domestic taxes remained high.[2]

In mid-seventeenth-century England, on the other hand, a major cause of political conflict lay in the existence of two distinct models of commercial and fiscal practice, based on either formal corporate monopoly or open trade. Both assumed a degree of external protection, and contemporary usage of the phrase 'free trade' to describe the latter option accommodated a range of assumptions far removed from those of the mid-Victorians. The first involved the organisation of overseas trade within privileged, corporate bodies with a restricted membership whose livelihood depended upon the royal prerogative rather than parliamentary sanction. Amongst other things, the system depended on

---

[1] Cited in Viner, 'Power versus Plenty', reprinted in Coleman (ed.), *Revisions in Mercantilism*, p. 84; K. W. Swart, *The Miracle of the Dutch Republic as seen in the Seventeenth Century*, Inaugural Lecture, University College, London, 1969.

[2] M. 't Hart, 'Freedom and Restrictions. State and Economy in the Dutch Republic, 1570–1670', in K. Davids & L. Noordegraaf (eds.), *The Dutch Economy in the Golden Age, Nine Studies*, Amsterdam (NEHA), 1993, p. 109; P. Klein, 'A New Look at an Old Subject: Dutch Trade Policies in the Age of Mercantilism', in Groenveld & Wintle (eds.), *State and Trade*, pp. 39–40.

the willingness of the companies to provide fees, gifts and loans to the Crown, while the membership paid customs duties in return for their privileges. The 'regulated' model was especially suited to a monarchical system in a commercial world dominated by bilateral trading relations, including privileged access to staple rights in the mart towns of north-western Europe. The second model approximated more closely to the Dutch fiscal–commercial system. It combined low customs duties with formally open trading, the latter moderated in reality by a range of informal restrictive practices. Some proponents of the Dutch model proposed that the shortfall in customs revenue might be made up through alternative forms of taxation, such as the excise. In the event, an effective compromise was reached after 1689 in which urgent fiscal needs were balanced against the interests of landowners and merchants, the latter operating within a web of multilateral trading relationships. The dynamics of change, which broke down the older system, arose from the growing complexity of English commerce in the seventeenth century, especially the development of the import trades which involved re-exports and triangular trading (or 'internal multilaterality'), combined with the force of Dutch competition.[3]

The piecemeal reorganisation of English commerce, as distinct from its redirection, occupied the years from 1651 to 1689, prior to the establishment of a new institutional framework during the 1690s. In essence, this involved two related bodies of legislation: the passage of the Navigation Act of 1651 and its successors of 1660 and 1663 – which codified and extended a number of earlier experimental measures – and the phasing-out of company trading on the regulated pattern.[4] Cromwell's Navigation Act, it has been said, represented the climax of a process of 'conscious economic re-orientation', dating from the 1620s, which aimed to develop an entrepôt system similar to that which had grown up spontaneously at Amsterdam.[5] The method was staggeringly ambitious: to create an overarching *national* monopoly within which English shipping and long-distance trade could develop – especially the re-export trades in colonial and Asian staples.[6] By prohibiting the import of Asian, African or American goods in foreign ships, and by insisting that commodities imported into England should come directly from the country

[3] R. Brenner, *Merchants and Revolution. Commercial Change, Political Conflict, and London's Overseas Traders, 1550–1653*, Cambridge, 1993, pp. 598–9.
[4] E. Lipson, *The Economic History of England* (1931) 1948, vol. III, pp. 116 ff.; Harper, *The English Navigation Laws*, New York, 1939, chs. 2–6.
[5] C. H. Wilson, *England's Apprenticeship, 1603–1763*, 1965, p. 61 ff.
[6] J. E. Farnell, 'The Navigation Act of 1651, the First Dutch War and the London Merchant Community', *EcHR*, 16 (1964), pp. 439–54; Brenner, *Merchants and Revolution*, pp. 625–8.

which produced them, the Act dealt a deadly blow to the Dutch carrying trade. The second measure, the permanent withdrawal of the Merchant Adventurers' corporate monopoly in 1689, followed a period in which the company's trade to Holland slowly disintegrated during the Anglo-Dutch wars. It was succeeded by a series of parliamentary attacks on regulated trading in general during the 1690s. Much has been written about the impact of the Navigation Acts, but the demise of regulated trading has received much less attention. In fact the latter followed naturally in the wake of the former, as an indirect consequence of fifteen years of intense Anglo-Dutch rivalry, warfare and hostility generated by the new navigation code. At the same time, the proponents of the original Navigation Act, the so-called new-merchants of London, were in the forefront of the attack on the corporate privileges of the Merchant Adventurers, as Robert Brenner has shown.

Anglo-Dutch rivalry, national monopoly and deregulation

The Dutch Republic, commonly regarded as a commercial rival, was also admired as the prototype for a new kind of mercantile state.[7] Formally recognised by Spain in 1648, a matter of months before the English republic or Commonwealth came into being, it emerged as something of a hybrid and an 'odd variant', markedly different from the centralised absolutist monarchies which had arisen elsewhere. It was, in fact, a federation of city states, albeit one with an urban population which exceeded that of Britain and Scandinavia combined.[8] Compared with the Mediterranean and Hanseatic city states, its population of 2 million people was substantial, while the economy of its compact provinces was integrated to a degree unknown in pre-revolutionary France.[9] One of the bestsellers of the seventeenth century was Sir William Temple's *Observations upon the United Provinces of the Netherlands*, first published in 1673, the year following the French invasion of Holland. Temple, who had served as British Ambassador at the Hague during the 1660s, observed that the new

---

[7] C. H. Wilson, *England's Apprenticeship*, pp. 168–9, 210; H. Roseveare, *The Treasury. The Evolution of a British Institution*, 1969, p. 65; J. Appleby, *Economic Thought and Ideology in Seventeenth Century England*, Princeton, 1980, pp. 73–98; B. E. Supple, 'The Nature of Enterprise' in Rich & Wilson (eds.), *Cambridge Economic History of Europe*, vol. V, p. 452; C. C. Barfoot, ' "Envy, Fear and Wonder"; English Views of Holland and the Dutch, 1673–1764', in C. C. Barfoot & R. Todd (eds.), *The Great Emporium. The Low Countries as a Cultural Crossroads in the Renaissance and the Eighteenth Century*, Amsterdam, 1992, pp. 207–47.
[8] De Vries and van der Woude, *First Modern Economy*, p. 671.
[9] Ibid., pp. 172–3.

Republic had not 'grown rich by any native commodities, but by force of Industry; by Improvement and Manufacture of all Foreign Growths; by being the general magazine of all Europe, and furnishing all parts with whatever the Market wants or invites; and by their Sea-men, being, as they have properly been called, the common Carriers of the World'.[10]

The great surge of overseas trade from 1648 to 1651, following the lifting of the Spanish embargoes, represented the peak of Dutch commercial expansion. Although historians cannot decide exactly where to place the turning-point between growth and stagnation, it seems clear that the Dutch golden age had passed its zenith by the time Temple had completed his *Observations*.[11] In the late 1640s, however, English merchants and statesmen were totally dazzled by the Dutch economic miracle, as Dutch traders began to recapture Baltic and Mediterranean markets previously lost to the English. From 1649 to 1651, the number of English ships sailing to the Baltic fell by half, while, in the Mediterranean, they were suddenly outnumbered by Dutch vessels at Leghorn, the chief centre for English shipping in the region.[12] Yet astonishingly, it seemed for a brief moment that a policy of co-operation might emerge in place of rivalry and intermittent conflict. While the Commonwealth government was considering a possible alliance with the Dutch in 1650, the newly created Council of Trade discussed proposals for the establishment of a free-port system to help reduce the burden of customs on the re-export trade, and, in so doing, to place the English entrepôt on a more competitive level with the Dutch ports. Above all, it was the group which Brenner describes as 'new merchants' – Atlantic traders, colonists and interloping East India merchants, whose interests lay in the import and re-export trades – who dominated the Council of Trade and made the

---

[10] Sir William Temple, *Observations upon the United Provinces of the Netherlands*, (1673) 1705, Preface, A3 and pp. 210–11.

[11] The majority of specialists would accept the view of de Vries and van der Woude that the Dutch golden age ended in the 1660s and '70s (*First Modern Economy*, pp. 673 ff.). On the commercial aspects of the issue, which reasserts the primacy of trade with the Baltic region, see Lindblad, 'The Foreign Trade of the Dutch Republic in the Seventeenth Century', in Davids & Noordegraaf (eds.), *Dutch Economy in the Golden Age*, pp. 219–49. See also I. Schöffer, 'Did Holland's Golden Age Co-incide with a Period of Crisis?' *AHN*, 1 (1966), pp. 82–107; P. W. Klein, 'De zeventiende eeuw, 1585–1700', in J. H. van Stuijvenberg (ed.), *De economische geschiedenis van Nederland*, Groningen, 1977, p. 79; J. C. Riley, 'The Dutch Economy after 1650: Decline or Growth?' *JEEH*, 13 (1984), pp. 521–69; Israel, *Dutch Primacy*, pp. 259–69, 377–98; and J. de Vries, 'The Decline and Rise of the Dutch Economy, 1675–1900', in G. Saxonhouse and G. Wright (eds.), *Technique, Spirit and Form in the Making of Modern Economies: Essays in Honour of William N. Parker*, Greenwich, 1984, p. 149.

[12] R. Davis, *The Rise of the English Shipping Industry in the Seventeenth and Eighteenth Centuries*, 1962, p. 12.

running.[13] Indeed, by the early 1650s, mercantile opinion had become much more influential in shaping the course of government policy than was the case before the Civil War.

It would be out of place here to describe the failure of the mid-century Anglo-Dutch rapprochement, and its rapid descent into war and acute commercial rivalry embodied in the Navigation Acts.[14] Suffice it to say that if union with the Dutch was politically impracticable at mid-century, it seemed to many that protracted commercial rivalry and war were unavoidable. English mercantile opinion was substantially united in its desire to reduce the impact of Dutch competition, and the accretion of naval power achieved during the commonwealth period seemed to make this a practical possibility. There was, however, one influential merchant group whose interests ran counter to those of national monopoly: the Merchant Adventurers trading to the Low Countries.[15] It was, above all, the London import merchants who were most anxious to restrict the flow of imports carried by the Dutch, especially merchants of the Levant, Eastland, Greenland and Russia Companies, as well as the new-merchant leadership, the Atlantic traders and interlopers. The Merchant Adventurers, on the other hand, still the richest and most powerful of the London merchant groups, depended heavily on Dutch co-operation in the mart towns and beyond. With a primary business interest in the export of English woollens to the Dutch staplemarket, their chief concern was to protect their own privileges at both ends of the chain: either from attack by jealous rivals in London, or from possible reprisals which the Dutch authorities might take during a trade war.[16] In an important sense, the Adventurers placed the interests of a localised Anglo-Dutch-German consortium above those of the national entrepôt. In the long run, an effective national monopoly would render local monopolies and cartels, driving an artificially restricted volume of trade at high prices, redundant.

In the meantime, the company attempted to resist attacks by government, merchant-clothiers and interlopers, and in doing so delayed the reorganisation of the main branch of England's export trade to Europe. The slow demise of the Merchant Adventurers serves as a reminder of the extent to which the period was marked by the resilience of traditional notions as to how merchants might best maintain a stable level of

[13] Brenner, *Merchants and Revolution*, pp. 608–25.
[14] The predominant English view was that negotiations broke down primarily because the Dutch had insisted on concentrating their efforts to expand their share of Anglo-Dutch trade. See C. H. Wilson, *England's Apprenticeship*, p. 62.
[15] The Hamburg Merchant Adventurers, on the other hand, regarded aggression and war against the Dutch as very much in their interest: see Farnell, 'Navigation Act', p. 450.
[16] C. H. Wilson, *Profit and Power. A Study of England and the Dutch Wars*, 1957, p. 56.

trade, while maintaining prices, profits and employment. Examination of the day-to-day business of company members suggests that dynamics of change arose as much from their struggle with competitors and suppliers, that is, interloping merchants and clothiers, as from the observations of disinterested theorists (pursued in chapter 4).

To a large extent, the parliamentary movement against commercial monopoly and for increased freedom of participation in trade centred on the East India Company's affairs in the 1680s and '90s. It is true that the Adventurers' case failed to generate a comparable pamphleteering war, but their activities gave rise to a more protracted political struggle, stretching back to the early seventeenth century.[17] In 1604, provincial resentment of London's commercial dominance and the Merchant Adventurers' monopoly exploded in the so-called 'free-trade' debate in parliament. At this stage, the company's critics were concerned less with the existence of monopoly as such than with the financial exactions and supervision exercised by the Crown.[18] More serious was the parliamentary onslaught of the early 1620s, which marked a major turning point in the company's fortunes. In 1624, parliament persuaded the Privy Council to confine its privileges to the export of undressed cloth. This opened up the trade in new draperies and the cheaper varieties of cloth until the year 1634, when Charles I renewed the company's original monopoly in return for a payment of 60,000gl. from the city of Rotterdam.[19] It was here that the staple was re-established for the next twenty years, after periods at Middleburg (1611–21) and Delft (1621–35), while the German staple remained fixed at Hamburg from 1611.[20] All manner of concessions were provided by the company's Dutch

---

[17] B. E. Supple, *Commercial Crisis and Change in England, 1600–1642*, Cambridge, 1959, ch. 3.

[18] W. R. Scott, *The Constitution and Finance of English, Scottish and Irish Joint-Stock Companies to 1720*, vol. I, Cambridge, 1912, p. 126; R. Ashton, 'The Parliamentary Agitation for Free Trade in the Opening Years of the Reign of James I', *PP*, 38 (1967), pp. 40–4; R. Ashton, *The Court and the City, 1603–1643*, Cambridge, 1979, ch. 3; Brenner, *Merchants and Revolution*, pp. 205–18.

[19] Supple, *Commercial Crisis*, pp. 52–72; R. Bijlsma, *Rotterdams Welvaren, 1550–1650*, 's-Gravenhage, 1918, p. 146.

[20] There is no comprehensive history of the company, but see W. E. Lingelbach, 'The Internal Organisation of the Merchant Adventurers of England', *TRHS*, new ser., XVI (1902), pp. 19–67; E. Lipson, *Economic History of England*, vol. II, 1948, pp. 196–269; G. Unwin, 'The Merchant Adventurers' Company in the Reign of Elizabeth', in R. H. Tawney (ed.), *Studies in Economic History: The Collected Papers of George Unwin*, 1927, pp. 133–220; G. D. Ramsay, *The Queen's Merchants and the Revolt of the Netherlands*, Manchester, 1986. On the German staple, see W.-R. Baumann, *The Merchants Adventurers and the Continental Cloth Trade, 1560s–1620s*, Berlin, 1990, and E. K. Newman, 'Anglo-Hamburg Trade in the Late Seventeenth and Early Eighteenth Centuries', unpublished University of London Ph.D. thesis, 1979; on the Dutch staple, see C. Te Lintum, *De Merchant Adventurers in de Nederlanden*, 's-Gravenhage, 1905.

hosts, including provision of an Episcopalian church, a new bourse, and the laying out of an entire English quarter. Within a matter of months, around sixty English merchants, apprentices and factors established themselves under the company's jurisdiction, and trade flourished for the next seven years.[21] The outbreak of the English Civil War, however, seriously divided the Rotterdam community, although the majority of the fellowship at home and abroad opted for Parliament.[22]

The introduction of the first Navigation Act had only a limited impact on Rotterdam's trade with England – which was mostly carried on in English ships – but the First Anglo-Dutch War brought commercial relations to a complete standstill.[23] The company moved temporarily to Flanders and Brabant, but decided to resettle at Dordrecht shortly before Cromwell ratified its privileges in 1656.[24] For the next few years, the company struggled on in Holland, in the face of heavy competition from interloping merchants and a deteriorating political climate which culminated in the Second Anglo-Dutch War. In 1663, the States-General levied additional impositions against English woollens in retaliation against the new Navigation Acts, and from this point the Adventurers directed the bulk of their woollen exports through Germany. To make matters worse, interloping merchants succeeded in winning formal approval for intermittent periods of free trade, from 1662 to 1663 and 1666 to 1667. In 1672, the few remaining company factors in Holland left Dordrecht for Hamburg.[25]

The efforts of the Merchant Adventurers to maintain their privileges in an increasingly competitive world, in which rivalry between different trading centres was endemic, seem to have created more uncertainty than might otherwise have obtained in an open market. During the first Anglo-Dutch war, the Rotterdam court lost its tax exemptions and other privileges, and the future of the Dutch staple looked increasingly vulnerable. The company's move to Dordrecht in 1655 proved to be unsettling and unpopular. The city authorities there were delighted to steal a march over their younger rival on the Maas, Rotterdam, and incurred more expense in establishing the court than any of the earlier mart towns.[26]

[21] Te Lintum, *De Merchant Adventurers*, pp. 103–25; Bijlsma, *Rotterdams Welvaren*, pp. 143–50; H. C. Hazewinkel, *Geschiedenis van Rotterdam*, vol. II, pp. 127–37. By 1648–9, the community numbered at least sixty-five.

[22] M. Ashley, *Financial and Commercial Policy under the Cromwellian Protectorate*, Oxford, 1934, p. 122; P. W. Klein, ' "Little London": British Merchants in Rotterdam during the Seventeenth and Eighteenth Centuries', in D. C. Coleman and P. Mathias (eds.), *Enterprise and History. Essays in Honour of Charles Wilson*, Cambridge, 1984, pp. 120–1; Bijlsma, *Rotterdams Welvaren*, pp. 150–1.

[23] Bijlsma, *Rotterdams Welvaren*, p. 158.

[24] Ashley, *Financial and Commercial Policy*, p. 123.

[25] Te Lintum, *De Merchant Adventurers*, pp. 208–24.   [26] Ibid., p. 208.

The English factors, however, were unimpressed: 'we wonder', wrote one of them, 'that our compa[ny in London] regard us no more, to bring us here & leane us'. Tax exemptions were less advantageous than those originally provided by Rotterdam, and the Adventurers' cloths were excised at between 10 and 16 gilders per piece – whilst country cloths were sold free of tax.[27] The re-establishment of court and staple at Dordrecht seems to have brought no improvement in the company's position, and, if anything, probably facilitated the interlopers' trade at Rotterdam. In March 1657, company members complained that they were obliged to 'take the market after the interlopers. What our merchants cannot find at Amsterdam & Rottd. & Middelburgs they are forced to buy of us.'[28]

The economy of Rotterdam, in fact, suffered little from the departure of the Adventurers, and it is possible that some returned to continue as unregulated traders. By mid-century, the bulk of Anglo-Dutch trade, as well as Dutch-French trade, was concentrated there, both regulated and unregulated, and trade with Scotland and Ireland also developed during the later seventeenth century. Indeed, Klein suggests that, in the decades which followed the passage of the Navigation Acts, Rotterdam was uniquely placed to gain what other Dutch towns had lost. The continuing English presence there ensured that the city was relatively immune to the restrictive import policies aimed against the Dutch, as the bulk of its trade with England passed into the hands of the English community.[29] Rotterdam's trade with its German and southern Netherlands hinterland, it seems, remained wholly in the hands of indigenous Dutch merchants, but resident English overseas traders provided the vital commercial link with the protected British entrepôt before 1667, when the Treaty of Breda modified the provisions of the Navigation Acts in relation to the transit trade.[30] Henceforth, it was agreed that all merchandise brought from the Republic's 'natural hinterland' of Germany and the Spanish Netherlands should be regarded as Dutch goods, and consequently could be exported to England in Dutch vessels. The staple for Westphalian linens was established at Rotterdam, and a certain stability was restored to Anglo-Dutch commercial relations.[31]

The English community in Rotterdam became increasingly well established as time went on, and foreign visitors came to describe it as 'little London'. By the mid eighteenth century, one-third of the depositors of

---

[27] PRO C109/19, R. Gay & T. Bale, Dordrecht, to W. Attwood, London, 22 Dec. 1656.
[28] C109/19, R. Gay & T. Bale, Dordrecht, to W. Attwood, London, 9 March 1657.
[29] Klein, 'Little London', p. 122.   [30] Ibid.
[31] Z. W. Sneller, *Rotterdams bedrijfsleven in het verleden*, Amsterdam, 1940, p. 78; C. H. Wilson, *Profit and Power*, pp. 141 2; Anderson, *Origin of Commerce*, vol. II, p. 493.

the Bank of Rotterdam were English, Scots or Irish, some of whom had taken out Dutch nationality.[32] In 1721, the Tory propagandist Charles King estimated 'by the best information' he could gather in Holland, that more than 100,000 of the Dutch population 'were either Deserters from this Nation, or Descendents of such Deserters', which, he calculated, represented an annual diminution of the national income of £600,000.[33] By the 1760s, however, the English community in Rotterdam was well assimilated.[34]

As we have already indicated, the 1660s constituted a watershed for the Merchant Adventurers when, for a variety of reasons, the company's trade through the Dutch staplemarket came to a virtual standstill. The majority of members were now trading via Hamburg, and some were shifting the balance of their trade towards linen imports.[35] It is, of course, well known that English commerce during the period 1660–89 was characterised by an upsurge of import-led growth, associated with the development of the re-export trades. Domestic production and exports of woollen goods, on the other hand, experienced stagnation and possibly decline, and the tendency towards defensive government action which had most obviously manifested itself during the 1620s again found expression in a series of officially sanctioned periods of open trade, in 1662–3 and 1666–7. As in 1624, free-trading merchants laid their case against the company's monopoly before parliament and the Privy Council, demanding intervention in order to promote trade and employment. Demoralised by the interlopers' political successes at home and the progress of foreign rivals, the Adventurers were prepared by 1674 to surrender their charter if their corporate debt might be waived.[36]

The position of the Merchant Adventurers was thus weakening until, in 1689, the woollen trade was thrown open by statute (rather than proclamation), on a basis which proved to be permanent. The introduction and extension of the Navigation Acts clearly played a major part in hastening the demise of regulated trade to the Low Countries. Although the provisions of the Acts were relaxed by the Treaty of Breda, this came too late to prevent the transfer of regulated trade to Hamburg

---

[32] A. M. C. Carter, 'Britain as a European Power, from her Glorious Revolution to the French Revolutionary War', in J. S. Bromley & E. H. Kossman, *Britain and the Netherlands*, vol. III, *Britain and the Netherlands in Europe and Asia*, 1968, p. 118.

[33] C. King, *The British Merchant*, 1721, vol. I, p. 121.

[34] See below, chapter 3, pp. 90–1.

[35] This was the strategy adopted by Thomas Attwood, whose business is discussed below, chapter 4.

[36] H. Roseveare, *Markets and Merchants of the Late Seventeenth Century. The Marescoe–David Letters, 1668–1680* (British Academy, Records of Social and Economic History, new ser., 12) 1987, p. 178; Lipson, *Economic History of England*, vol. II, pp. 256–6.

alongside an increasing volume of 'free' Anglo-Hamburg trade. Between 1633 and 1740, the number of English ships arriving in Hamburg more than doubled, from 61 to 138 per year.[37] In 1688, the English consul in Amsterdam observed that the trade of Hamburg was 'accounted the third in Europe, and comes next to London and Amsterdam, she being now become the magazine of Germany, and of the Baltic and Northern Seas'.[38]

The conclusion of the Second Anglo-Dutch War is rightly seen as a turning point in Anglo-Dutch relations. Economic and colonial rivalry receded, and, in Sir George Clark's words, 'the ensuing period laid the foundations for a community of interest which ultimately found expression in alliance'.[39] The Dutch had secured major concessions over the European transit trade which were balanced by the cession of New Amsterdam to the English, as New York. Thus, a major loophole was closed in the operation of the navigation laws relating to the colonial carrying trade. Although Dutch merchants continued to involve themselves in the North American and Caribbean coasting trade, the revised navigation code proved effective in substantially excluding them from the colonial carrying trade with Europe.[40] By 1750, almost half the British merchant fleet was engaged in transatlantic traffic.[41] It is clear, however, that not all colonial merchandise destined for European consumers passed through the British entrepôt according to the formula required by law. In the 1690s, the government found it necessary to embark on a concerted programme of action to tighten up the operation of the navigation code, including extension of the network of enforcement abroad. In 1693, the customs authorities attempted to install an English consul at Rotterdam, Abraham Kick, whose principal duty would be to enforce the provisions of the navigation code relating to the trade in plantation goods. The English community successfully resisted, claiming that 'the justice of this Government towards us and the easiness of accesse wch we have always had upon any occasion to the Magistracy here, hath made [consular representation] ... altogether as unnecessary & superfluous as it would be in the Citty of London'. The petitioners included several influential Anglo-Huguenot merchants: Sir Theodore Janssen, Sir Peter Delmé, Samuel Lethieullier, William DesBouverie and Abraham Houblon. Five years later, Kick reported that large-scale frauds were continuing, involving English, Irish and colonial ships sailing directly from

---

[37] J. A. Faber, 'De achttiende eeuw', in J. H. van Stuijvenberg, *De economische geschiedenis van Nederland*, Groningen, 1977, p. 137.
[38] Anderson, *Origin of Commerce*, vol. II (1801 edn), p. 580.
[39] G. N. Clark, *The Later Stuarts, 1660–1714*, Oxford, 1934, p. 68.
[40] Around 1650, 'dozens' of Dutch ships laded colonial tobacco cargoes for Europe (Davis, *Shipping Industry*, p. 12). See also below, chapter 10, pp. 310–13.
[41] Ibid., p. 42.

the plantations, with tobacco and other goods, to Holland, Hamburg and Bremen, without entering in English ports; foreign merchandise was laden in the same ports and carried directly back to the plantations, without touching in England.[42] The Commissioners for Trade and Plantations reported similar breaches of the navigation code during the 1690s.[43]

It is impossible to estimate exactly how much progress was made in halting these abuses. In 1730, for example, the Privy Council expressed concern to the Commissioners that 'great cargoes of goods [were] carried from Holland to the West Indies by English ships that touch in Holland under pretence of buying a cargo of goods for the coast of Africa'. The greater part of these goods, it was claimed, were in fact exported to the plantations. After making enquiries of their own, the Commissioners produced the unconvincing reply that 'we do not find sufficient reason to believe that any such trade is carried on'.[44] As the historian of the navigation code reminds us, the legislation was intended to achieve two major objectives: to prevent Dutch shipping from dominating England's carrying trade, and to break English merchants from the habit of depending on the Dutch staplemarket.[45] Amongst other evidence, comparison of entries in the port books after 1660 with the Sound Toll records suggests that the first was readily achieved: the Acts seem to have had a powerful influence in undermining the role of the Dutch as third-party carriers in England's trade with other countries. In the direct trade between England and Holland too, the proportion of English shipping increased markedly in the second half of the seventeenth century: from 57% prior to 1651 to 92% after 1660, in the case of the incoming trade of the outports.[46]

In relation to the second objective, however, the Dutch entrepôt continued to function as a market for commodity exports for a much longer period, and, to a lesser extent, as an indirect source of imports. The Navigation Acts clearly played some part in reducing the latter during the first half of the eighteenth century. Nevertheless, as a redistributive centre for English raw materials, manufactured goods, and re-exports of colonial and Asian goods, the Dutch entrepôt retained a position of major importance until the 1720s and '30s. In 1717, an official calculated that 'near half as much shipping' was engaged in carrying plantation goods from England to their final destinations in Germany, Holland and

---

[42] PRO CO388/6 A5, A6, Petitions of Diverse Merchants . . . tradeing to Rotterdam, 1695, July 1696; CO388/7, fols. 68–70, Proposals for preventing frauds, 29 December 1698; Harper, *English Navigation Laws*, p. 93.

[43] 'State of the Trade of the Kingdom in 1697', representation from the Commissioners laid before the House of Lords, *Calendar of House of Lords Mss*, new ser., vol. X, p. 162 (23 December 1697).

[44] CO389/28, fo. 435, 'Report to the Lords of Commerce in Council', 19 June 1730.

[45] Harper, *English Navigation Laws*, pp. 299–300.   [46] Ibid., pp. 301–2.

other foreign countries as was employed in carrying them directly from the colonies.[47] Although the volume of English trade chanelled through Holland, however, was maintained in the early years of the eighteenth century, the financial involvement of English merchants declined markedly. Roles were reversed as Dutch and other continental merchants came to London either as buyers or commission agents acting for principals in Amsterdam and Rotterdam, or to settle permanently and trade on their own accounts. As the central staplemarket took on an increasingly passive character, Dutch merchants had little choice but to play a more active part in the commercial life of London, Hamburg and other European centres.

This process was facilitated by the de-regulation of English trade with nearby Europe, from 1689, a development which coincided with the growth of commercial and financial opportunities in general in late seventeenth-century London. The East India Company's quarterly sales in London were attracting growing numbers of Dutch, German and eastern European dealers, encouraged by the boom of the mid-1680s.[48] At the same time, the size of the Huguenot mercantile community was swollen by the influx of Huguenot refugees in general. At least 7,000 arrived in London during the 1680s, several of whom were merchants specialising in the wine, silk and paper trades.[49] It was during the following decade, as D. W. Jones has shown, that immigrant German, Dutch and Baltic merchants gained a significant hold over London's overseas trade, alongside the established Huguenot firms. The forerunners of the Anglicised Dutch financial community of eighteenth-century London – van Necks, van Hemerts, Muilmans and van Nottens – were the less conspicuous commodity traders such as Vanheythuson, Cornelisen, Vanderstegen, Vanhatten and Viroot.[50] Some, such as the linen merchant Matthew Decker, who arrived in London in 1700, or the Huguenot wine importer Dennis Dutry, moved from commodity trade to merchant banking within a few years, providing a kind of link between the two groups.[51]

---

[47] Ibid., p. 272.
[48] K. N. Chaudhuri, *The Trading World of Asia and the English East India Company, 1660–1760*, Cambridge, 1978, pp. 132–3, 508.
[49] G. C. Gibbs, 'The Reception of the Huguenots in England and the Dutch Republic, 1680–1690', in O. Grell, J. Israel & N. Tyacke (eds.), *From Persecution to Toleration. The Glorious Revolution and Religion in England*, Oxford, 1991, p. 278; D. W. Jones, 'London Merchants and the Crisis of the 1690s', in P. Clark and P. Slack (eds.), *Crisis and Order in English Towns, 1500–1700*, 1972, p. 329.
[50] D. W. Jones, *War and Economy*, Table 8.3, pp. 254–5.
[51] Both picked up knighthoods in the process. C. H. Wilson, 'The Anglo-Dutch Establishment in Eighteenth Century England', in A. G. Dickens (ed.), *The Anglo-Dutch Contribution to the Civilization of Early Modern Society*, British Academy, 1976, pp. 11–32; C. H. Wilson, *Anglo-Dutch Commerce and Finance in the Eighteenth Century*, Cambridge, 1941, pp. 88–136.

Immigrant Dutch merchants, as Charles Wilson pointed out, were not part of the inner court entourage of William III, but many arrived in his wake, along with army contractors, bankers and others.[52]

The 1690s: internal 'free trade' and external protection

The primary consequence of the Glorious Revolution on economic and commercial life has generally been identified as the war against French trade, which William needed so badly, and the emergence of a 'fiscal-military state', underpinned by new financial techniques and institutions. Alongside the newly created national debt, the financial demands of war called for a massive increase in the public revenue, achieved mainly by an increase in the land tax and customs revenue. Ralph Davis considered that a substantial rise in import duties was inevitable in these circumstances.[53] In fact, this is by no means clear, since a general excise had been proposed in 1666, but failed to win parliamentary approval. By 1686–8, customs and excise duties each contributed one quarter of the total public revenue, and a convincing case could be made for substantially increasing the latter.[54] The customs revenue, it could plausibly be argued, had already reaped the gains of the commercial revolution, and the discouragement of particular imports by high duties might actually damage the revenue in the long term.[55] With rather less than the force of inevitability, the 1690s nevertheless stand out as the decade which above all others witnessed the rise of protection in England.

Equally, if not more, significant than the emergence of the fiscal-military state was a series of changes in the commercial sphere whose rationale was more apparent to nineteenth-century liberal writers than to modern economic historians: the impact of constitutional monarchy and parliamentary government on commercial life and institutions. In place of the Crown and Privy Council's controlling interest, parliamentary regulation became the order of the day. As Macaulay pointed out, the Bill of Rights and the Convention were silent on the extent of the Crown's powers for the regulation of trade, involving the prescription of weights and measures, coinage, the authorisation of fairs and markets, of legal quays for the loading and unloading of ships, and the grant of

---

[52] C. H. Wilson, 'Anglo-Dutch Establishment', p. 12.

[53] R. Davis, 'The Rise of Protection in England, 1689–1786', *EcHR*, 19 (1966), pp. 306–7.

[54] The annual average public revenue for Michaelmas 1686 – Michaelmas 1688 stood at £2.13m., of which customs contributed £0.538m. (25.2%), excise £0.548m. (25.7%) and hearth tax receipts £0.232m. (10.9%) (C. K. Chandaman, *The English Public Revenue, 1660–1688*, Oxford, 1975, pp. 360–1).

[55] Ibid., pp. 10–11.

commercial privileges to individuals and corporate bodies.[56] The subject was too sensitive to be put into a clear formula, but parliament acted nonetheless. A concerted effort to abolish monopolies established by royal authority was made in the Statute of Monopolies of 1624, but numerous exceptions existed, including the overseas trading companies. Following its close association with the court of James II, and the earlier offensive against prominent Whig members such as Papillon and Barnardistone, it was hardly surprising that the case of the East India Company would rise in the political agenda, and, with it, the wider issue of commercial monopolies. The abolition of the Merchant Adventurers' privileges, like the opening up of participation in the East India trade, took shape as the natural resolution of the political tensions of the 1680s within the London merchant community, when both companies had gone out of their way to secure concessions from the Crown and its Tory supporters.

As we have seen, the position of the Merchant Adventurers was weakening until, in 1689, the woollen trade was thrown open by statute (rather than proclamation), on a basis which proved to be permanent.[57] Long-distance trade to Asia, Africa and Hudson's Bay was supported by joint-stock organisation and quasi-sovereign powers, but the nearby trades were substantially de-regulated and freed from the constraints of corporate privilege. Non-merchants, retailers and foreign buyers were now permitted to compete with free-trading English merchants in the nation's premier export business. Thus, the new situation protected the English entrepôt rather than the nationality and status of the exporter. In practical terms, the continuation of local, corporate monopoly proved incompatible with that of a national monopoly created by the Navigation Acts, particularly in relation to the maintenance of the Adventurers' court and staple in Holland during the third quarter of the seventeenth century. The resources of private traders and the accumulation of expertise and credit by established communities of free merchants in Rotterdam, Amsterdam and the German ports were sufficient to sustain a moderate level of cloth exports during these years, so that special privileges were no longer necessary. By 1711 it was said that the company's residence at Dordrecht was ruined 'and not an English merchant left there'.[58]

In both a practical and a symbolic sense, the manner in which change was effected reflected a decisive shift in the shaping of commercial policy,

---

[56] C. H. Firth (ed.), The History of England, from the Accession of James II, by Lord Macaulay, 1914, vol. V, pp. 2091–2.

[57] By 1 Will. & M. c. 32. The Act is dated 1688 in the statute book but the correct date is 1689; see Lipson, Economic History of England, vol. II, p. 266, n. 4. The monopoly of the Levant, Eastland, Russian and African companies remained.

[58] CO388/14, letter received from the Hamburg Company, 22 April 1711.

of the kind which had produced the first Navigation Act of 1651: the basis was parliamentary initiative in place of the exercise of royal prerogative and court patronage. As Horwitz has pointed out, the greater recourse to parliamentary legislation after 1689 reflected the enhanced authority of statute, which was most apparent in the case of the chartered trading companies. Those companies that did manage to preserve their privileged status now required firm parliamentary support. After the Hudson's Bay Company had secured a parliamentary charter by private act in May 1690, the directors 'promptly wrote to their agents in the Bay in triumphant tones that "whatever was eluded to as prerogative before" by interlopers "is now the law of our land and as such to be enforced" '.[59] The reformed companies, as Gauci reminds us, preserved some element of continuity within London's mercantile politics, but, on balance, the 1690s witnessed a decisive shift towards a much more liberal commercial environment. The Lockean emphasis on natural liberty and individual freedom was paralleled by a more inclusive approach to economic matters, in both thought and practice, a development which has sometimes been obscured by a one-sided emphasis on the rise of protection after 1689. The task of promoting employment, it can be shown, 'gained priority over the accumulation of a national stock of money' and consumption gained an importance in its own right.[60] Apprenticeship regulations were enforced in a more liberal manner, increasingly determined by local custom rather than public compulsion. In 1701, after rejecting the petitions of several groups of woolcombers protesting against illegal apprenticeships in London and the provinces, parliament pronounced the maxim 'Trade ought to be free and not restrained.'[61]

The establishment of internal free trade, however, was linked indissolubly with external protection, at two distinct levels: the tightening-up of the navigation code, and the raising of protective duties on a range of manufactured imports. In relation to the former, a Commons Committee was established in 1694 to investigate the operation of the Navigation Acts in response to the complaints of the merchants of Bristol and Liverpool, and of customs officials. The committee drew on the specialist knowledge of those members who were merchants, and included William Culliford, soon to become the first Inspector-General of Imports and Exports. Their extensive deliberations resulted in the passage of the

---

[59] H. Horwitz, *Parliament, Policy and Politics in the Reign of William III*, Manchester, 1977, p. 315.

[60] P. Gauci, *The Politics of Trade. The Overseas Merchant in State and Society, 1660–1720*, Oxford, 2001, pp. 112–26; J. A. W. Gunn, *Politics and the Public Interest in the Seventeenth Century*, 1969, p. 245; C. H. Wilson, 'The Other Face of Mercantilism', *TRHS*, 5th ser., 9 (1959).

[61] E. Lipson, *The History of the English Woollen and Worsted Industries*, 1921, pp. 116–17.

1696 Act which confined colonial trade in its entirety to English-built shipping. Registration of ownership was now required, and, although the registers were not made public, the Act required authentication of British build and ownership for customs officials.[62] Renewed efforts were made to tighten up administration of the code at the waterside, especially in the Dutch ports. The Dutch government, unsurprisingly, had high hopes that William's accession might provide an opening for the repeal of the Navigation Acts, and the Dutch envoys in 1689 pressed the matter, together with an appeal for the reduction of various other duties. The Dutch, however, were prepared to offer no concessions in return, and the British commissioners took up the position that they were unable to reverse arrangements enacted by parliament.[63]

The reaffirmation and strengthening of the Navigation Acts in the new political context of the 1690s was one of a number of measures which served to consolidate a closer relationship between the merchant and the state. Since the early 1650s, merchants had been able to play a more active part in the formulation of commercial policy, in which the notion of the national economy took on an increasingly tangible form. Tawney suggested something of this sort when he wrote, 'Before the Civil War, "mercantilism", if that word is to be employed, is a policy imposed by the executive on the business world; after, it is a policy imposed by the business world on the executive.'[64] The navigation code was nationalist in a double sense. Its immediate objective was to reduce the commercial hegemony and competition of a rival nation, the Dutch, and the advantages which it offered could be exploited by the merchant community as a whole, rather than specific groups, companies or sectional interests claiming special privileges. Although the interests of individual merchants frequently diverged, economic thought and administrative practice were shifting towards the establishment of public institutions which might reflect the national interest in commercial matters. As Benjamin Worsley put it, trade was an affair of policy, the ends of which were distinct from the intrigues and private designs of merchants, and should proceed 'upon unvariable reason to the general good and concern of the nation'.[65]

---

[62] 7 & 8 Will. III c. 22; Harper, *English Navigation Laws*, p. 390. The Act was extended to introduce a public register of shipping in 1786, by 26 Geo. III c. 60 (Davis, *Shipping Industry*, p. 109).

[63] G. N. Clark, *The Dutch Alliance and the War Against French Trade, 1688–1697*, Manchester, 1923, pp. 25–6.

[64] British Library of Political and Economic Science: Tawney Papers, Box 1/8, Lectures on Economic History, 1485–1800. Lecture 10, 'The Restoration (i) The Political Situation', p. 27.

[65] P. Laslett, 'John Locke, the Great Recoinage, and the Origins of the Board of Trade: 1695–1698', *William and Mary Quarterly*, 14 (1957), pp. 377–8.

It was this kind of thinking which lay behind the permanent establishment of the Board of Trade in 1696, properly known as the Commission for Trade and Plantations. Committees of the Privy Council and special commissions had sat intermittently since the early 1620s to deal with issues arising from particular trades and colonies, and Charles II had revived these in 1660, prior to establishing a single Council for Trade and Plantations in 1672. This body, however, was disestablished in 1675. By the early 1690s, anxiety about the scale of French captures and the conduct of the war produced mounting demands for a Council of Trade with executive powers, appointed by parliament. Sir William Petty had already devised two schemes for an 'economic parliament', a representative assembly of members drawn from all parts of Britain and the colonies, while James Whiston published a similar proposal in 1693.[66] Anxious to avoid an unwelcome invasion of his prerogative, William III moved rapidly towards the establishment of a permanent Commission. The early Board of Trade, however, represented more than a short-term response to a minor political crisis. It embodied a comparatively new principle in administration, namely, that the prerequisite for effective regulation is enquiry into and knowledge about what is to be regulated.[67] While its functions included the formulation of proposals for the improvement of commerce and 'redressing of all grievances and burdens upon trade', the Commission also exercised an important information-gathering role.[68]

British consuls residing abroad received their instructions from the Commissioners, as did the governors of the American plantations, and each in turn supplied a flow of commercial intelligence. The effectiveness of the new body stemmed in no small part from the improved accuracy and availability of commercial statistics from the late 1690s, which statesmen had been requesting since the 1670s and '80s. It was largely the establishment of Treasury control in the late 1660s and the reform of the customs service after 1671 which produced the need and the capacity for more accurate estimates of the revenue and of the balance of trade.[69] The commercial expansion of the post-Restoration decades also raised new questions in the minds of statesmen about the impact of the Navigation Acts, the rate of growth of colonial trade, the growing problem of

[66] Ibid., p. 375, n. 10.   [67] D. Ogg, *William III*, 1956, p. 107.
[68] The phrase is Anderson's (*Origin of Commerce*, vol. II (1801 edn), p. 623). For the debates leading to the creation of a new Board of Trade, see Gauci, *Politics of Trade*, pp. 180–94.
[69] The 'farming' of customs was ended in September 1671, when Commissioners were appointed to manage the customs revenue under the control, shortly afterwards, of a Receiver-General (H. Atton & H. H. Holland, *The King's Customs. An Account of Maritime Revenue and Contraband Traffic in England, Scotland and Ireland, from the Earliest Times to the Year 1800*, 1908, ch. 5); R. C. Jarvis, Introduction to E. E. Hoon, *The Organisation of the English Customs System, 1696–1786* (1938) Newton Abbott, 1968, pp. vii–xxvii.

luxury imports from France and, by the mid-1690s, the currency crisis. Unsurprisingly, therefore, one of the duties of the new Commission was to 'enquire, examine into, and take an account of the state and condition of the general trade of England, ... and to ... examine what trades are or may prove hurtful, or are or may be made beneficial to our Kingdom of England'.[70] The Commissioners of Customs, however, were unable to meet the increased demand for more exact commercial statistics, and, in 1696, the Treasury agreed to support a new office within the customs establishment with the specific task of compiling comprehensive annual accounts of the volume and value of English overseas trade. This department, the office of the Inspector General of Imports and Exports, owed nothing of substance to Dutch or French example, and was the first in the world to collect such comprehensive statistical material.[71]

Although it is difficult to trace a direct connection, it seems likely that the creation of the Inspector General's office owed much to the growing interest in the 'political arithmetic' of Petty, Graunt, Davenant and others, which fostered a quantitative approach to economic issues.[72] The calculations of the political arithmeticians, it may be suggested, were remarkable not so much for their accuracy as for their use of a new unit of analysis, the national economy.[73] Although systematic national income statistics were not compiled by contemporaries, the Inspector General's ledgers at the very least attempted to provide a rough indication of the nation's economic progress as reflected in the annual balance of trade. Their layout, which distinguished London's trade from that of the aggregated trade of the outports, indicates something of significance about the dominating role of the English commercial metropolis at the end of the seventeenth century. National or metropolitan aggregates were, of course, totally absent from the port books, which simply documented the commercial life of their localities. The Inspector General's ledgers and the work of the political arithmeticians, on the other hand, represented a new effort to imagine and delineate the national economy in ways which were consistent with rudimentary attempts at economic management.

These administrative improvements, which accompanied the financial revolution and fiscal reforms of the 1690s, facilitated the movement to

[70] Quoted in G. N. Clark, *Guide to English Commercial Statistics, 1696–1782*, Royal Historical Society, 1938, p. 1.

[71] Ibid., pp. 3–8.

[72] Ibid., p. xiii. Gregory King was employed by the Treasury when the office was established.

[73] A classic example is Gregory King's attempt to measure the relative sizes of the population, wealth and rate of capital accumulation for England, France and Holland in 1688 and 1695.

link a more competitive internal market with a higher level of external protection. Until at least the 1730s, the Commissioners for Trade maintained an active and useful existence, helping to balance and resolve the interests of merchants, manufacturers, planters and mariners, while keeping a close watch on the progress of foreign manufactures.[74] The character of English protectionism, which was 'endlessly and minutely modified' after the major duty increases of William's reign, owed a good deal to the Commission's advisory role.[75] Its effectiveness stemmed especially from its dual function of reporting on the state of overseas trade in European and colonial markets, while considering 'by what means profitable manufactures, already settled, may be further improved; and how other new and profitable manufactures may be introduced'.[76]

It was during the fifteen-year period from 1690 to 1704, in Ralph Davis's words, that 'the English tariff structure was transformed from a generally low level fiscal system into a moderately high level system which, though still fiscal in its purposes, had become in practice protective'.[77] From almost negligible proportions, the general level of import duties roughly quadrupled in the same period. The adjustment of duties on imports and exports, however, formed only part of the story. The enforcement of old-fashioned prohibitions and navigation laws and the application of bounties and subsidies completed the panoply of protectionist mechanisms available to the mercantilist state. Compared to their Dutch counterparts, English statesmen were, in the long term, driven to give equal attention to the protection of manufacturing, agricultural and commercial interests. For the Dutch of course, the last-mentioned remained of paramount importance. Yet, prior to the Glorious Revolution, the English tariff system provided little direct protection for home industry.[78] The temporary prohibition of trade with France in 1678 gave some encouragement to the luxury trades, and a strong measure of agricultural protection was provided in the Bounty Acts of 1672, made permanent in 1689. The Navigation Acts, of course, protected the English entrepôt from 1651, so that import merchants engaged in the colonial trades and re-export business received special consideration throughout.

It is possible to interpret in a variety of ways the state's protectionist motives during the wars against Louis XIV. By concentrating merely

---

[74] See especially the earlier volumes of the *Journal of the Commissioners for Trade and Plantations, 1704–1782*, 14 vols., 1920. Proceedings prior to 1704 are summarised in the *Calendar of State Papers, Colonial Series, America and West Indies*.

[75] Davis, 'Rise of Protection', p. 307.

[76] *JHC*, 13, p. 298 (from W. Blathwayt's report on the work of the Commission during the first four years of its existence, 23 March 1701).

[77] Davis, 'Rise of Protection', p. 307.   [78] Ibid., p. 308.

on tariffs and the flow of legislation, Davis took the view that parliament moved reluctantly, even accidentally, towards industrial protection before 1704, holding that the process only gathered momentum with Walpole's great customs reform of 1722.[79] Thus, parliament was slow to protect the woollen industry from the great influx of Asian textiles in the later seventeenth century; the duty increases of the 1690s were applied indiscriminately to all imported manufactured imports, whether or not they competed with home industries; and raw materials, including dyestuffs, were taxed. Urgent fiscal needs predominated, and, according to Davis, examination of the legislation suggests neither the influence of economic theories nor ministers' long-term commercial policies. It would be wrong, however, to view these various objectives and desiderata as alternatives, and the preambles to the statutes of the period often reveal less of the ideologies and assumptions of those who framed them than was the case, for example, in the later sixteenth century. For these, one must look elsewhere. Moreover, the details of specific protectionist policies often hinged on the political resolution of differences between varied competing industrial and commercial interests. Unsurprisingly, earlier historians influenced by the German school of historical economists took a more robust view of the state's protectionist intentions. Cunningham invented the label 'Parliamentary Colbertism' to describe the drift of economic policy in England after 1689, while Lipson directed attention towards those widely held 'general maxims of trade' which shaped the pattern of industrial protectionism.[80] Recent work on the role of protectionism in the rise of the English cotton industry has shifted the emphasis back to the interplay of mercantilist regulation with political forces representing the relevant industrial interests. The form and content of the legislation which fostered the cotton textile industry, it has been suggested, can best be explained 'as the product of bargaining among interest groups, constrained by Parliament's perception of strategic and political necessities and conditioned by the ideological preconceptions of a mercantilist age'.[81]

The ideal of national self-sufficiency was an old one, but took on a new momentum from the 1540s, and was promoted with special vigour under

[79] North and Thomas conclude, even more brusquely, that the rise of protection 'was the accidental consequence of taxation for revenue' (R. Floud & D. McCloskey, *The Economic History of Britain*, vol. I, *1700–1860*, Cambridge, 1981, p. 93).

[80] W. Cunningham, *The Growth of English Industry and Commerce*, Cambridge, 1882 (1912 edn), p. 406; Lipson, *Economic History of England*, vol. III, pp. 13–15.

[81] P. K. O'Brien, T. Griffiths & P. Hunt, 'Political Components of the Industrial Revolution: Parliament and the English Cotton Textile Industry, 1660–1774', *EcHR*, 44 (3) (1991), pp. 396–7; C. H. Wilson, 'Government Policy and Private Interest in Modern English History', in C. H. Wilson, *Economic History and the Historian: Collected Essays*, 1969, p. 153.

Burleigh from the 1570s when licences and patents were used to promote the introduction of new industries from abroad. By the later seventeenth century, however, industrial monopolies were discredited, and the emphasis in mercantilist thinking shifted from an obsession with bullion and the balance of trade towards home production and the protection of manufacturing industry.[82] As the English economy became increasingly import-led, economic writers and statesmen judged the significance of imports less in terms of their value to the consumer than their impact on the home producer.[83] During the first half of the eighteenth century, a rising level of import duties was linked with a series of measures designed to promote import substitution, in an effort to reduce the nation's dependence on foreign manufactured goods: bounties, premiums and drawbacks of duty were now combined with the older policy of encouraging skilled immigrant craftsmen from abroad. Industrial protectionism did not, of course, spring into life, fully formed, during the 1690s when the issue was crystallised by a lengthy and complicated struggle between the East India Company and its opponents, including the woollen, silk, linen and calico-printing interests. Fine adjustments to the tariff system were in any case unnecessary during the war period. Prohibitions against trade with France were in force from 1689 and 1702, which, together with the general disruption of trade, generated major import savings and brought about an immediate expansion in the output of a number of home industries, including the production of canvas, silk, salt and distilling.[84] The policy of import substitution matured over a much longer period, but the substantial raising of the general tariff level during the 1690s was an integral part of that policy, and was governed by more than fiscal necessity.

The raising of tariffs and import substitution policies obviously discriminated in favour of English manufacturers while affecting mercantile interests in a variety of ways. Those engaged in the import trades from nearby Europe probably suffered most in the long term, although wartime prohibitions produced a more serious impact on the import trades from southern Europe, chiefly in wine and salt.[85] Colonial import merchants were unaffected and those re-exporting European manufactures to the plantations, especially linen goods, were actually better placed than exporters of British-made products through the

[82] J. Thirsk, *Economic Policy and Projects. The Development of a Consumer Society in Early Modern England*, Oxford, 1978, p. 8; P. J. Thomas, *Mercantilism and the East India Trade*, 1926, pp. 21 4.

[83] P. J. Thomas, *East India Trade*, ch. 4. This, indeed, was the essence of Cunningham's notion of 'Parliamentary Colbertism'.

[84] Jones, *War and Economy*, pp. 175 80.   [85] Ibid., p. 175.

operation of the 'drawback' system, whereby the bulk of duties paid
were refunded, provided re-export took place within a given period.
Exporting merchants gained a good deal when the 5% duty on woollen
cloth exports was removed in 1700, and, in broad terms, the overall
policy can be seen as one which aimed to shift the structure of English
overseas trade towards the mercantilist ideal of an export-led system.
The payment of drawbacks, which emerged during the reign of James I,
was specifically designed to encourage the re-export trade, and largely
succeeded in its dual aim of fostering the growth both of an entrepôt
system, and of a domestic manufacturing base. By 1700, the method
of claiming drawbacks had become so complicated that an alternative
was devised: the warehousing system, whereby imports were stored in
bonded warehouses under the joint locks of the customs service and the
merchant. Duty was paid only when goods were delivered out for home
consumption.[86] By the early years of the eighteenth century, therefore,
the drive to undercut Dutch and French competition had shaped an
entrepôt system distinguished by high external tariffs, and a unified,
restrictive and highly formalised customs mechanism. At the same time,
the organisation of London's wholesale markets and overseas trade was,
by Dutch standards, relatively free from restrictive practice.

In Holland, the institutional basis of staplemarket trade and finance
was more or less in place in Amsterdam by the 1620s, and the system of
low import duties remained in force with only minor modifications until
the Batavian period, and the subsequent imposition of the protective
tariff of 1816. It has been argued that free trade as such was not a
principle in the Republic. Rather, the policy was 'staplemarket-minded',
assuming a more defensive character at the end of the seventeenth
century.[87] The tariff reform of 1725 brought only marginal changes and
attempted, unsuccessfully, to reduce evasion by introducing a simplified
ad valorem duty of 3% as the basis of the new system.[88] Following more
than two decades of commercial stagnation, the proposals of 1751 for a
limited free-port system failed to get off the ground.[89] In general, it could

[86] See below, chapter 6, pp. 184–5.
[87] Joh. de Vries, *Economische Achteruitgang*, pp. 45–6; H. R. C. Wright, *Free Trade and
      Protection in the Netherlands, 1816–1830*, Cambridge, 1955, ch. 3.
[88] W. Heeres, 'Annual Values of Amsterdam's Imports and Exports, 1697–1798', in Heeres,
      Dunkirk to Danzig, pp. 263–80; Joh. de Vries, 'De ontduiking der convooien en licenten
      in de Republiek tijdens de achttiende eeuw', *TvG*, 71 (1958), pp. 349–61; J. L. F.
      Engelhard, *Het generaalplakkaat van 31 juli 1725 op de convooien en licenten en het lastgeld
      op de schepen*, Assen, 1970.
[89] *Groot Placaatboek*, vol. VI, Amsterdam, 1795, pp. 1371–2; Anon. [T. B.], *The Holland
      Merchant's Companion*, Rotterdam, 1715, p. 72, and 1748, pp. 75–6; H. R. C. Wright,
      Free Trade and Protection, p. 60; Hovy, *Voorstel van 1751*, pp. 653–9.

be said that the Republic's external tariff was of less significance to her trading partners than occasional temporary prohibitions and informal restrictive practices pursued by indigenous staplemarket traders.

Several writers, including van der Kooy, Barbour and Posthumus, have emphasised the pervasiveness and range of monopolistic practices pursued by Dutch merchants. Price data suggests that monopolistic tendencies prevailed in the wholesale trade for at least 169 out of a total of 223 commodities, during the seventeenth and eighteenth centuries.[90] P. W. Klein, following Schumpeter, has argued that the attempt to control prices through monopolisation of supply helped to reduce risk, which, in turn, promoted growth and reinvestment in stocks.[91] Even Klein's critics would accept that strategies designed to avoid competition were not incompatible with innovations of a kind which may have actually strengthened the staplemarket.[92] The cost, it seems, was measured in a loss of long-term competitiveness. In time, a defensive strategy based on the storage and stockpiling of goods was likely to give way to speculative tendencies and short-range investment decisions. In any case, total monopolisation of supply could only be realised in very special circumstances where staple products came from a single production area, such as copper and tar purchased through the Swedish crown monopoly. More usual, according to Veluwenkamp, were 'monopolistically competitive' practices. Through product differentiation, specialisation and the development of customer loyalty, merchants evaded conditions of perfect competition as each attempted to control his own market. Thus, the Dutch staplemarket was 'not one big integrated market but was composed rather of a large number of "partial markets", the "private markets" of the separate merchants'.[93] Veluwenkamp's view was based on his analysis of the major Amsterdam firm of de Neufville, whose principal business was the export of linen to England. As we shall see, de Neufville's strategy was undermined especially by the availability of new sources of supply from Ireland, Scotland and home producers, as the

[90] P. W. Klein, 'Entrepreneurial Behaviour and the Economic Rise and Decline of the Netherlands in the Seventeenth and Eighteenth Centuries', *Annales Cisalpines d'Histoire Sociale*, 1 (1970), pp. 14–15.

[91] P. W. Klein, *De Trippen in de 17e eeuw. Een studie over het ondernemersgedrag op de Hollandse stapelmarkt*, Assen, 1965; Klein, 'De zeventiende eeuw, 1585–1700', p. 102; Klein, 'Handel, geld- en bankwezen', *Algemene Geschiedenis der Nederlanden*, 8 (1979, Haarlem), pp. 177–81.

[92] P. W. Klein & J. W. Veluwenkamp, 'The Role of the Entrepreneur in the Economic Expansion of the Dutch Republic', in Davids & Noordegraaf (eds.), *Dutch Economy in the Golden Age* (sections 1 & 4 by Klein, sections 2 and 3 by Veluwenkamp), p. 39; J. de Vries & van der Woude, *First Modern Economy*, pp. 670–1.

[93] J. W. Veluwenkamp, *Ondernemersgedrag op de Hollandse Stapelmarkt in de tijd van de Republiek*, Leiden, 1981, pp. 5–30.

English government's policy of import substitution developed.[94] In parallel to monopolistic or quasi-monopolistic practice, merchants also strove to reduce uncertainty by increasing the quantity and quality of commercial information available. Indeed one of the distinguishing characteristics of the Amsterdam staplemarket was its unique capacity to analyse, process and transfer commercial and financial intelligence through specialised information brokers and publications.[95] Information gathering, however, generated restrictive practice in its wake, through the linking of insurance provision with credit and shipping services on the Amsterdam Bourse.[96]

Aside from informal restrictive practices, institutionalised corporate monopoly played an enduring and significant role in Dutch commercial life. The establishment of the Dutch East India Company (VOC) in 1602 was followed by the Northern Company of 1614, the West India Company (WIC) of 1621, the directorate of Mediterranean Trade of 1625, and the Society of Surinam of 1682.[97] Although much has been claimed for the VOC as a well-managed bureaucracy, it is far from clear that the commercial companies were well placed to respond to changes in demand patterns as the seventeenth century progressed.[98] In the industrial sphere, municipal sponsorship supported new initiatives through bounties, patents, monopolies, loans, tax exemptions and other arrangements, especially in the period 1575–1620. If spectacular failures were not wholly balanced by modest successes, at least costs were low and many schemes helped to reduce the cost of poor relief.[99] A National Organisation of Cloth Buyers first emerged in 1616 in the wake of the Cockayne crisis, and the Commissioners of the Great Fishery required producers to function as a consortium from the third quarter of the sixteenth century.[100]

---

[94] See below, chapter 5.

[95] W. D. Smith, 'The Function of Commercial Centers in the Modernization of European Capitalism: Amsterdam as an Information Exchange in the Seventeenth Century', *JEH*, 44 (1984), pp. 985–1005.

[96] By the eighteenth century, it was common for brokers to offer combined packages of insurance, credit, freight and warehousing facilities. See F. C. Spooner, *Risks at Sea. Amsterdam Insurance and Maritime Europe, 1766–1780*, Cambridge, 1983, p. 19.

[97] Israel, *Dutch Primacy*, pp. 16–17.

[98] See below, chapter 6; L. Blussé & F. Gaastra (eds.), *Companies and Trade. Essay on Overseas Trading Companies during the Ancien Régime*, Leiden, 1981, especially the editors' introduction, and the essays by Klein, Gaastra, Emmer and Steensgaard.

[99] C. A. Davids, 'Beginning Entrepreneurs and Municipal Governments in Holland at the Time of the Dutch Republic', in C. Lesger & L. Noordegraaf (eds.), *Entrepreneurs and Entrepreneurship in Early Modern Times*, Hollandse Historische Reeks, 24, Den Haag, 1995, pp. 167–83.

[100] N. M. Posthumus, *De Nationale Organisatie der Lakenkoopers tijdens de Republiek*, Utrecht, 1927, p. viii; de Vries & van der Woude, *First Modern Economy*, p. 246.

In spite of their free ports, the Dutch were 'still very remote' from Adam Smith's ideal of a liberal commercial society, as he was forced to acknowledge.[101] By the 1690s, their commercial policies and practices came to represent a mirror image of those which the English were adopting. Yet, in different ways, both monopolistic practices and mercantilist policies involved attempts to manipulate commodity flows and exercise price control. Whereas the former relied on private and informal initiatives which were prone to speculative fever, the latter rested on a strong centralised state and the stabilising hand of bureaucracy. The situation contained a certain irony, given that the period of 'high protectionism' in England had been called into being by William's war against French trade, and the need to raise large tax revenues at record speed.

The adoption of protectionist policies by Britain and other neighbouring states was clearly a major factor in the Republic's economic decline. In 1751, a century after the passage of the original Navigation Act, and at a time when the Dutch economy was passing through a severe depression, the merchants of Amsterdam were unanimous in attributing a major part of their difficulties to the long-term effects of English protectionist legislation.[102] Historians, however, are less certain, and cannot agree on the relative weight to be attached to internal structural problems, external influences, and the declining secular trend of European population and demand after 1650, the Braudellian *renversement de la tendance séculaire*. Certainly, a much lower proportion of the Dutch national income was internally generated than was the case in England, and prosperity depended heavily on external economic relations. Thus, many would accept the argument that Dutch trade expanded precisely because of a lack of expansion in that of other countries.[103] It is difficult, however, to estimate precisely how important the commercial sector was to the economy as a whole. As far as the raising of English tariffs is concerned, it is true that the English market was not crucial for Dutch exporters.[104] The central point at issue, however, was England's competitive role on several fronts: as a supplier of manufactured goods to Europe and North America; as a major source of raw and processed colonial and Asian goods, including sugar, tobacco, groceries and Indian textiles; as a bulk

---

[101] A. Smith, *Inquiry into the Nature and Causes of the Wealth of Nations*, ed. J. R. McCulloch, 1838, p. 220.

[102] Argued in the 'Propositions' presented to the States General, reprinted and translated in J. R. McCulloch, *A Select Collection of Scarce and Valuable Tracts on Commerce*, 1859, pp. 441–8.

[103] Lindblad, 'Foreign Trade', p. 221.

[104] As J. I. Israel points out in 'England's Mercantilist Response to Dutch World Trade Primacy, 1647–74', in Israel, *Conflicts of Empires. Spain, the Low Countries and the Struggle for World Supremacy, 1585–1713*, 1997, p. 315.

Table 2.1 *Estimated values of English and Dutch foreign trade, 1622–1790 (£'000)*

Constant prices as follows: England from 1690 to 1715(official values); United Provinces, constant prices based on 1753 = 100

	English imports	English re-exports	English domestic exports	combined total ENGLISH	combined total DUTCH	Dutch VOC & WIC
1622	2,619	–	2,320	4,939	–	–
1624–5	–	–	–	–	12,163	557
1640s	–	–	–	–	17,110	1,106
1660s	4,395	900	3,239	8,534	12,200	1,626
1690s	–	–	–	–	17,529	2,224
1699–1701	5,849	1,986	4,433	12,268	–	–
1716–20	6,054	2,291	4,739	13,084	–	–
1733–5	7,757	3,104	5,717	16,578	–	–
1749–55	8,144	3,438	8,645	20,227	–	–
1753	8,625	3,511	8,732	20,868	16,392	4,067
1764–76	–		–	–	–	–
1772–4	12,735	5,818	9,853	28,406	–	–
1779	10,660	5,580	7,013	23,253	15,784	3,308
1784–8	15,303	4,286	11,050	30,639	–	–
1790	17,443	4,828	14,057	36,328	14,350	2,759

Sources: *England*: BL Add Mss 36785 and PRO Cust. 3 (official values); based on totals given by Davis, 'English Foreign Trade, 1660–1700', *EcHR*, 6 (1954) (including Davis's estimated figure for outport woollen exports of £700,000 for 1663–9, incorporated into Table 2.1); 'English Foreign Trade, 1700–1774', *EcHR*, 15 (1962); Schumpeter, *English Overseas Trade Statistics*, Tables XII and XIII.

United Provinces: Convoy and Licence returns, from estimates given by Joh. de Vries, *Economische Achteruitgang*, pp. 26–8. Turnover for the Dutch East India Company based on totals for domestic selling prices and carriage and handling costs, given in J. P. de Korte, *De Jaarlijkse Financiele Verantwoording in de VOC*, Leiden, 1984, Appendix 13; *Algemene Geschiedenis der Nederlanden*, vol. IX, Haarlem, 1980, p. 463. Turnover for the Dutch West India Company, 1779 and 1790, based on van der Oudermeulen's estimate for 1779 (Joh. de Vries, *Economische Achteruitgang*, p. 27); 1753 and 1690s, projected back from 1779, on the basis of figures for coffee and sugar sales, 1753–90, given in J. P. van der Voort, *De Westindische Plantages van 1720 tot 1795*, *Financien en Handel*, Eindhoven, 1973, p. 150. Estimates for the West India Company's turnover are not included in the figures for 1624–5, 1640s and 1660s, being less than £0.3m. De Vries's estimates have been adjusted as follows: 1753 = 100; 1779 = 167 (van der Oudermeulen); 1790 = 200. Dutch currency was converted to sterling at rates given in McCusker, *Money and Exchange*, and W. Beawes, *Lex Mercatoria Rediviva*, 1783, within the range £1: gl. 10.2–11.0.

It is worth noting that the estimates for the value of Dutch trade with Asia and the Americas, given here are slightly more generous than those produced by N. Steensgaard for the year 1753. Steensgaard arrives at a figure equivalent to 17.3% of the value of the Republic's trade with Europe, while Table 2.1 suggests a figure of 24.8% (N. Steensgaard, 'The Growth and Composition of the Long-distance Trade of England and the Dutch Republic before 1750', in J. D. Tracy (ed.), *The Rise of Merchant Empires: Long-Distance Trade in the Early Modern World, 1350–1750*, Cambridge, 1990, pp. 147–51).

supplier of foodstuffs and raw materials to European markets and to the staplemarket itself, especially grain and coal; and as a leading provider of shipping and commercial services.

Some indication of the chronology involved in the build-up of English competition may be found in a comparison of the available Dutch and English commercial statistics. The English materials, although requiring much care in their interpretation, were at least designed to be read by well-informed contemporaries as a record of the state and progress of English, and later British, overseas trade. Very few of the Dutch official commercial statistics have survived, however, and, in their absence, we must rely on extrapolated figures derived from provincial tax materials. Evasions, exemptions, changes in tax rates, and a degree of ambiguity about the use of fixed and ad valorem rates combine to make this an extremely hazardous enterprise, although an extensive literature highlights the problems involved.[105] Although the figures in Table 2.1 are far from exact estimates, they perhaps indicate the broad trends.

It seems reasonably clear that the Republic's overseas trade still compared favourably with that of England and Wales during the 1690s. Although the war years saw a decline from the buoyant years of the 1680s, the late 1690s witnessed a recovery following the Peace of Rijswick of 1697, with customs yields (*convooien en licenten*) reaching a seventeenth-century peak in 1688 and 1698.[106] The likelihood is that Dutch and English foreign trade were roughly equivalent in value during the second quarter of the eighteenth century, and the Inspector General's estimates indicate that English trade surged ahead during the 1740s, prior to a second and much more substantial burst of growth in the 1770s and

---

[105] On the use of the English materials, see: Clark, *Guide*, pp. 33–42; T. S. Ashton's introduction to E. B. Schumpeter, *English Overseas Trade Statistics, 1697–1808*, Oxford, 1960, pp. 1–14; R. Davis, *The Industrial Revolution and British Overseas Trade*, Leicester, 1979, pp. 11–12, and Appendix, pp. 77–86; J. J. McCusker, 'The Current Value of English Exports, 1697–1800', in McCusker, *Essays in the Economic History of the Atlantic World*, 1997, pp. 222–44; S. D. Smith, 'Prices and the Value of English Exports in the Eighteenth Century: Evidence from the North American Colonial Trade', *EcHR*, 48 (1995), pp. 575–90. On the Dutch materials, see above, p. 52, n. 88, and J. C. Westerman, 'Statistische gegevens over den handel van Amsterdam in de zeventiende eeuw', *TvG*, 61 (1948), pp. 3–30; Israel, *Dutch Primacy*, pp. 280–3; J. L. van Zanden, L. Noordegraaf and J. I. Israel, 'Discussie over J. I. Israel, *Dutch Primacy in World Trade*', in *BMGN*, 106 (1991), pp. 451–79; Lindblad, 'Foreign Trade', pp. 223–31.

[106] Lindblad, 'Foreign Trade', p. 228 and Appendix I, p. 241; Joh. de Vries, *Economische Achteruitgang*, pp. 185–93; H. E. Becht, *Statistische gegevens*, Appendix, Tables 1–3. Johan de Vries's suggestion that England's exports amounted to less than one-third of Holland's at the end of the seventeenth century, taken from Sombart's *Moderne Kapitalismus*, seriously overstates the strength of the Dutch position, based as it was on temporary post-war boom conditions; at the same time, English re-exports are excluded from the picture (*Economische Achteruitgang*, p. 30).

'80s. Dutch overseas trade may have emerged from several decades of stagnation by the later eighteenth century, but its rate of growth lagged far behind that of England and Wales. Although the expansion of the post-Restoration period petered out in the 1690s, the value of English commerce by this time must have exceeded the level of that attained by the United Provinces during the depressed years of the 1670s.

3 English commercial expansion and the Dutch staplemarket, 1700–1770

England's challenge to Dutch competition in world markets depended on the ability to exercise domination over several great circuits of trade, which, taken together, formed the market structure of the European world-economy. These circuits or zones within the world-economy have been variously described as compartments, regional economies or maritime economies, and their overall character has been convincingly described in terms of the impact of topography on the pattern of communications. Lucien Febvre, for example, suggested that 'the Mediterranean is the sum of its routes, land routes and sea routes, routes along the rivers and routes along the coasts, an uneven network of regular and casual connections'.[1] For convenience, we will refer to them as regional economies. In a sense, they form the building blocks from which the emerging European world-economy was constructed, as in Braudel's notion of 'a juxtaposition of zones interconnected at different levels'. Around 1700, we can distinguish four of them: the Mediterranean, the North Sea / Baltic economy (described by Braudel as a 'double-sea space'), the Atlantic economy, and the trading world of Asia.

The great regional economies overlapped and intersected with the core and peripheral zones of the world-economy in different ways, but each contained *within itself* a local hierarchy of zones. Even within the Atlantic economy, often seen as a vast undifferentiated periphery stretching from Maryland to Brazil, a core zone began to emerge in the seventeenth century, centred on the northern and middle American mainland colonies.[2] In the first instance, leading cities rose to a position of dominance over their respective regional economies before achieving hegemony within the core of the larger world-economy. Amsterdam's leadership was initially

[1] In *Annales d'Histoire Sociale* (1940), cited by F. Braudel, *The Mediterranean and the Mediterranean World in the Age of Philip II*, vol. I, London, 1972, p. 276.
[2] Wallerstein, *Modern World-System*, vol. II, p. 179. Gundar Frank implies that the periphery was synonymous with the colonial world in the eighteenth century (*World Accumulation, 1492–1789*, 1978, p. 216).

Table 3.1 *Distribution of English shipping between the major circuits of world trade, 1663 to 1771–3 ('000 tons; percentages shown in italics)*

	1663		1686		1771–3	
1 North Sea economy						
i. nearby Europe	39	*40.0*	41	*21.6*	92	*24.5*
ii. Scandinavia & Baltic	13	*10.3*	28	*14.7*	74	*19.7*
2 Mediterranean	30	*23.8*	39	*20.5*	27	*7.2*
3 Atlantic	36	*28.6*	70	*36.8*	153	*40.8*
4 Asia	8	*6.3*	12	*6.3*	29	*7.7*

Source: Davis, *Shipping Industry*, p. 17.

secured through the extension of trade with the northern European periphery: by monopolising the bulk trades of the North Sea / Baltic region, drawing grain, timber and naval stores from Poland and Livonia, via the eastern Baltic cities, in exchange for fish and salt. To these trades, Norwegian timber and Swedish iron were added, paid for in some measure by Dutch woollens, tiles and earthenwares. By 1650, Dutch *fluytschips* were carrying perhaps ten times as much as any of their competitors out of the Baltic.[3] Seventeenth-century Dutch hegemony within the European world-economy, in fact, was achieved principally by linking the bulk trades of the North Sea and the Baltic with the rich trades of the Mediterranean, to form an integrated world trade network. The rise of the English entrepôt in some degree involved recapitulating Dutch success in integrating the circuits of north–south European trade, and the century after 1570 was marked by intense Anglo-Dutch rivalry in the Baltic and the Mediterranean.

English traders first moved into the Baltic during the 1570s and '80s, while the Dutch were distracted during the early stages of their struggle for independence, but made little headway before the mid seventeenth century. Dutch competition progressively undermined the Eastland Company's bilateral trade in which English woollens were exchanged for Baltic grain, flax and naval stores, until a measure of state protection was provided under the umbrella of the Navigation Acts. In 1673, the company's monopoly was curtailed, leaving English merchants free to trade to Sweden and Denmark–Norway. Within two years however, war broke out between the Scandinavian countries, and the Dutch soon joined a coalition against Sweden and France. For a brief period, only the

[3] R. Davis, *The Rise of the Atlantic Economies*, 1973, p. 181.

English were neutral, and these adventitious circumstances gave them a firm foothold in the Baltic which they never lost.[4] English dependence on Swedish iron grew steadily thereafter, but the Dutch soon re-established their position in all spheres of Baltic trade, facilitated, not least, by their ability to make payment in bullion and specie.

The rich trades of the Mediterranean proved initially more susceptible to English penetration, where shipping costs were a less significant factor than new market opportunities for English textiles, in the decades following the collapse of the Antwerp entrepôt.[5] From the 1620s, the decline of the Italian woollen industry opened up new possibilities for Dutch and English producers, but the ending of the Twelve Years' Truce with Spain, in 1621, created major obstacles for the former. During the 1620s and '30s, Dutch–Mediterranean trade experienced a 'disastrous slump and contraction', and Dutch merchants lost their leading position to their English competitors.[6] In 1615 and 1622, Orders in Council were approved, limiting the carriage of imports from the Mediterranean and the Baltic, respectively, to English ships alone – in effect, precursors of the Navigation Act of 1651.[7] Lacking comparative cost advantages over the Dutch in handling and shipping charges, the English were prepared to utilise whatever natural and artificial means lay at their disposal to neutralise Dutch competition. The abundance and variety of English wool facilitated the diversification of textile production to meet the different demands of western and eastern Mediterranean markets, with the new draperies dominating the trade to the Iberian peninsula and broadcloths finding ready markets in the Levant. The restriction of the export of raw wool in 1614, together with the Orders in Council, foreshadowed the lengths to which the English nation state was prepared to go in pursuit of a clearly defined commercial policy. The Dutch continued to provide serious competition in the Levant trade, but English merchants were able to hold their own. During the years 1647–88, England's seaborne trade with Turkey exceeded that of the Dutch by a ratio of about 5 to 4.[8] Not until the war years of the 1690s, and especially during the War of

[4] R. W. K. Hinton, *The Eastland Trade and the Common Weal in the Seventeenth Century*, Cambridge, 1959, ch. 9.

[5] R. Davis, 'England and the Mediterranean, 1570–1670', in F. J. Fisher (ed.), *Essays in the Economic and Social History of Tudor and Stuart England*, Cambridge, 1961, pp. 117–37.

[6] J. I. Israel, 'The Phases of the Dutch *Straatvaart*, 1590–1713: A Chapter in the Economic History of the Mediterranean', in Israel, *Empires and Entrepots. The Dutch, the Spanish Monarchy and the Jews, 1585–1713*, 1990, pp. 144–5.

[7] R. Davis, *English Overseas Trade, 1500–1700*, 1973, ch. 3.

[8] R. Grassby, *The English Gentleman in Trade. The Life and Works of Sir Dudley North, 1641–1691*, Oxford, 1994, p. 31; Israel, 'Phases of the Dutch *Straatvaart*', p. 152.

the Spanish Succession, did Dutch–Mediterranean trade lapse into prolonged decline.

The success of English commercial expansion in the Mediterranean played some part in hastening the economic decline of Italy, and signalled the first stage of England's domination of world markets.[9] Business which had previously been channelled through the Italian cities passed directly into English hands, and Venetian and Florentine merchant houses withdrew from London. English merchants established a dominant position in the Levant trade on the eve of the Civil War, a commerce which was to expand rapidly during the 1650s, '60s and early '70s. During these years, English cloth exports to Turkey rose from an average of 13,600 pieces per year from 1666 to 1671 to a peak figure of 30,000 in 1672. The Dutch were exporting roughly half this quantity.[10] The Mediterranean carrying trade between foreign countries was gradually taken over by English shipowners and merchants at the expense of the Italians and, to a lesser extent, of the Dutch. In short, there was a 'complete reversal of the economic roles of England and Italy'.[11] By the late seventeenth century, the former core of the world-economy had sunk back into the position of eastern Europe and the Baltic countries, to form part of the European 'old periphery'.[12] A new disposition of economic power emerged in which the dominant players were the maritime powers of the North Sea and Atlantic seaboards.

The growth of trade with both northern and southern Europe, however, was overshadowed by the spectacular expansion of the Atlantic economy. The West Indies and the American mainland colonies, particularly the southern plantations, formed what was, in effect, a 'new periphery', which absorbed increasing quantities of English merchant capital and credit, and, of course, slave labour. In the late 1680s, the tonnage of English shipping accounted for by transatlantic trade had already grown to equal that employed in the nearby European trades together with northern Europe and the Baltic. By the early 1770s, the volume of shipping in both circuits of trade had more than doubled. At the same time, trade with the Far East expanded to occupy a volume of shipping comparable to that trading to the Mediterranean (Table 3.1).

The British Atlantic colonies are conventionally divided into two groups: on the one hand are the West Indies and the southern and middle

[9] Grassby, *English Gentleman*, p. 23; Cipolla, 'The Economic Decline of Italy', in B. Pullan (ed.), *Crisis and Change in the Venetian Economy in the Sixteenth and Seventeenth Centuries*, 1968, p. 144.
[10] Grassby, *English Gentleman*, p. 61; Israel, 'Phases of the Dutch *Straatvaart*', p. 151.
[11] Davis, 'England and the Mediterranean', p. 133.
[12] Wallerstein, *Modern World-System*, vol. II, p. 167.

plantation colonies, and, on the other, the northern colonies from Pennsylvania to New England and Canada. As Davis emphasised, of all the areas which called on the services of English shipping during the eighteenth century, it was the plantation colonies, the 'new periphery', which grew most rapidly, generating a fourfold increase in import values between 1700 and the early 1770s.[13] The Navigation Acts proved effective in substantially excluding the Dutch from the colonial carrying trade, and helped to secure a seemingly unlimited supply of tobacco, sugar, indigo and other primary products for British importers at prices which provided assured markets in Britain and Europe. During the third quarter of the eighteenth century, however, American population growth provided important new markets for British manufactured goods so as to secure a much more balanced pattern of trade, at even higher levels. As early as 1715, the Commissioners for Trade and Plantations noted how the mainland colonies 'are of late years very much increased in their Numbers of people, particularly the Northerly Ones'. A population of roughly a quarter of a million in 1700 reached 1.2 millions in 1750–1, and 2.28 millions in 1770–1.[14]

Transatlantic trade thus took on a special significance for Britain in its rise to a position of commercial hegemony. More than two centuries earlier, the merchants of Antwerp and, later, Amsterdam had begun to integrate the southern and northern poles of the European world-economy, centred on the Mediterranean and the North Sea / Baltic. In a comparable way, merchants in London and the western ports succeeded in integrating the trading world of the Atlantic with Europe, while enlarging their trade with the Far East. An important preliminary, however, was the establishment of competitiveness with the Dutch in the traditional trading areas of Europe, expanding trade across the North Sea and the Baltic, and commanding the trade routes of the eastern and western Mediterranean.

The expansion of long-distance trade, however, and the development of re-export business in colonial and Asian goods involved a more thorough redirection of shipping, commercial services and merchant capital than had been necessary simply to break into the old-established European trades. During the last four decades of the seventeenth century, the rate of new investment in commerce, as contrasted with industry,

---

[13] Davis, *Shipping Industry*, p. 267. Import values from the W. Indies, Virginia, Maryland and the Carolinas rose from £1.008m. in 1699–1701 to £4.054m. in 1771–3 (pp. 298–9).

[14] PRO CO390/12, 'Representation to the Commissioners for Trade and Plantations in relation to the Decrease of the Exportation of the Woollen Manufacture', 1715, fo. 37; S. D. Smith, 'The Market for Manufactures in the Thirteen Continental Colonies, 1698–1776', *EcHR* (1998), pp. 676–708; J. M. Price, 'The Imperial Economy, 1700–1776', in P. J. Marshall (ed.), *The Oxford History of the British Empire*, vol. II, *The Eighteenth Century*, Oxford, 1998, p. 100.

was, as Ralph Davis put it, 'abnormally high', and the amount of capital needed for carrying on trade grew much faster than the value of trade itself.[15] The so-called 'commercial revolution' required new sources of capital and enterprise, and, to a certain extent, some of this originated in the process of colonial development itself. The slow accumulation of profits on plantation goods, as new natural resources were exploited, provided a modest stock of colonial and metropolitan capital.[16] In the early eighteenth century, however, especially from 1713 to 1730, the price of colonial staples in European markets was low and falling, putting pressure on the capital of merchants and planters. In the absence of buoyant commercial profits, the continuing capital requirements of long-distance trade could only be met from improvements in commercial organisation, such as the lowering of transaction costs, increased turnover of merchant capital, and the transfer of risk to trading partners.

The last-mentioned was particularly important. As the following chapters will show, it is clear that Dutch merchant capital flowed into the old-established channels of Anglo-European trade during the late seventeenth and early eighteenth centuries, in ways which enabled British merchants to redirect their energies and limited capital resources towards the Atlantic frontier. During a period of slow demographic and economic growth, marked by recurrent commercial crises and expensive European wars, the restructuring of the North Sea economy played a significant part in facilitating the expansion of the British Atlantic system.[17] The chapters which follow will examine this process in detail, analysing the dual mechanism by which changes in commercial organisation and the movement of Dutch capital into the more important branches of British North Sea trade transformed the relationship of the maritime economies. In an indirect sense, Dutch merchant capital helped to facilitate the British 'Atlantic thrust' suggesting that, in certain circumstances, development on the periphery depended upon readjustments within the core of the world-economy during the eighteenth century, rather than vice versa. At the same time, the intensification of urban civilisation across the north-western core of Europe provided a dense local market for imported colonial and Asian goods, whose growth was sustained by new cultures of

[15] Davis, 'English Foreign Trade, 1700–1774', p. 93; R. Davis, *A Commercial Revolution*, Historical Association, 1967, p. 12.
[16] R. Pares, *Merchants and Planters*, *EcHR*, Supplement 4 (1960), pp. 49–50.
[17] See ch. 10 below. During the first half of the seventeenth century, European population as a whole declined by 4.3%, and recovered only slowly during the next half-century, when the population of England and Wales actually declined, from 5.6 to 5.4m., and that of the Netherlands remained stable at 1.9m. (J. de Vries, *European Urbanization*, 1984, Table 3.6, p. 36).

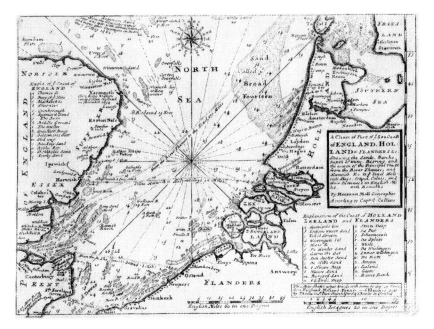

Illustration 3.1 H. Moll, early eighteenth-century chart of the North
Sea, *c.* 1710.

consumption, which relied on product innovation and increasingly sophisticated marketing.[18]

The North Sea / Baltic economy: stability and growth

If we focus on trade values rather than shipping tonnage, and on the
sale and marketing of trade goods rather than their acquisition and import, it is clear that the starting point of English commercial hegemony
lay in the old-established trade networks which were concentrated in
the southern core of the North Sea area, rather than in the new long-
distance trades. Triangular as well as bilateral voyages across the North
Sea linked the mainstream of Anglo-Dutch trades with others originating in Scotland, the Baltic, Russia and the Scandinavian countries as
well as northern France, the southern Netherlands and north Germany.
The trans-shipment of goods along the great river systems of northern

---

[18] M. Berg, 'Manufacturing the Orient. Asian Commodities and European Industry,
1500–1800', in S. Cavaciocchi (ed.), *Prodotti e Tecniche d'Oltremare nelle Economie Europee. Secc. XIII–XVIII*, Prato, 1998, pp. 385 420.

Europe, especially the Rhine and the Elbe, drew large parts of the German hinterland into this extensive circuit of commerce. With some justification therefore, the North Sea economy may be compared in its scale and complexity with the Mediterranean economy of the sixteenth century, or the Atlantic economy of the late colonial period.

Although the English economy grew only slowly during the first half of the eighteenth century, overseas trade continued to expand steadily, if at a less rapid rate than that achieved between the Restoration and the revolution of 1688.[19] Exports, including re-exports, rose much more rapidly than the national income, and, by the 1740s, it is likely that the total value of English overseas trade overtook that of the Dutch Republic, as we have seen.[20] With the exception of a brief revival in the 1720s, and a period of respite during the Seven Years' War when Dutch traders benefited from their status as neutral carriers, the Republic's commercial sector experienced stagnation and serious *relative* decline.[21] It is difficult, because of the revaluation of the French currency in 1726, to arrive at comparable values for French overseas trade, expressed in constant prices. It undoubtedly grew more rapidly than that of England, however, showing a three-fold increase in volume between 1716–20 and the 1780s, which in part represented a recovery from very low levels of trade at the close of the War of the Spanish Succession. Nevertheless, French trade with Spain and its American empire, along with West Indian sugar and coffee cultivation, represented real elements of buoyancy.[22]

Dutch commercial decline was indeed a relative process, and also one which was causally related to the progress of the Republic's neighbours and competitors. In part it was a result of England's growing domination of the North Sea trades, and the exclusion of the Dutch from a major role in the Atlantic trades by the Navigation Acts. Steensgaard estimates the contribution of Dutch extra-European trade at 20–25%

---

[19] Coleman estimates an average annual compound growth rate for overseas trade of 0.5% for the years from 1699–1701 to 1722–4, compared with 0.9% for the years 1663/9 to 1699–1701 (D. C. Coleman, *The Economy of England, 1450–1750*, Oxford, 1977, p. 133).

[20] N. Crafts, 'The Industrial Revolution', in R. Floud & D. McCloskey (eds.), *The Economic History of Britain since 1700*, vol. I, *1700–1860*, 1981, p. 48; C. H. Wilson, *England's Apprenticeship*, p. 264.

[21] See above, ch. 2, p. 55, n. 102; J. de Vries & van der Woude, *First Modern Economy*, pp. 490–503; and Joh. de Vries, *Economische Achteruitgang*, pp. 26–9.

[22] E. Levasseur, *Histoire du Commerce de la France*, Paris, 1911, vol. I, p. 512; F. Crouzet, 'England and France in the Eighteenth Century: A Comparative Analysis of two Economic Growths', in F. Crouzet, *Britain Ascendant: Comparative Studies in Franco-British Economic History*, Cambridge, 1990 (first published in *Annales*, 21 (1966)), pp. 18–21; G. Daudin, 'French International Trade 1716–1792: What do we know, and why do we care?', *Papers presented to the Annual Conference of the Economic History Society*, Oxford, 1999, pp. 113–17.

of the Republic's total trade for the years 1752–4, including re-exports, which compares with a figure of roughly 50% for England, and 33% for France.[23] The Republic continued to rely on its Baltic trade, which revived during the second half of the eighteenth century. By this time, however, the Dutch had lost their comparative advantage both in the shipping of bulk goods, especially timber, and in the distribution and sale of colonial goods. Again, the Navigation Acts played a decisive role in excluding them from the carrying of Baltic cargoes to English markets after 1660. Before the Danish–Swedish War of 1675–9, over half the ships sailing through the Sound were Dutch. By the second half of the eighteenth century, Scandinavian and British shippers had reached positions of equality with their Dutch counterparts.[24]

Attempts to arrive at exact measures of the visible trade of maritime economies such as those of the Netherlands and Britain are frustrated by, amongst other things, the existence of a sizeable *voorbijlandvaart*, or a traffic in goods which, for a variety of reasons, by-passed the metropolitan entrepôt.[25] The growth of commission business, linked with the provision of financial and shipping services, together with the development of increasingly complex patterns of multilateral trade, tended to undermine centralised warehousing. Dutch commerce especially was affected by these changes as the eighteenth century wore on.[26] In the case of England, the Navigation Acts succeeded in channelling the bulk of the nation's overseas trade through London and the outports, although conspicuous exceptions were occasionally reported, as we have seen, involving voyages by English, Irish and colonial vessels sailing directly from the plantations to continental Europe.[27] Ship's masters also conducted a small port-to-port trade on their own accounts along the North Sea coast. 'Leakages' such as these were probably small, but three important 'triangular' Atlantic trades generated a turnover of at least £1.3m. per year in the eighteenth century: the African slave trade, sales of Newfoundland fish to southern Europe, and the provisioning of the north American

---

[23] N. Steensgaard, 'Growth and Composition', pp. 102–52. The figure for England, which includes relatively small quantities of re-exports from Europe, such as German linens shipped to the plantations, is 49.8%, based on the Inspector General's official values (annual average for 1751–5, calculated from Schumpeter, *English Overseas Trade Statistics*, Tables I–IV, pp. 15–18).

[24] J. A. Faber, 'Structural Changes', pp. 83–94; see below, ch. 9.

[25] The proportion of vessels by-passing the staplemarket – the *voorbijlandvaart* – increased substantially as foreign competition in the carrying trade mounted. Estimates for the growth of this traffic suggest minimum levels of 40 vessels per year during the 1710s, rising to 170 by the 1750s – an increase from 9% to 16% of Dutch vessels passing the Sound – though the true level was probably much higher. See below, ch. 9, p. 282.

[26] Joh. de Vries, *Economische Achteruitgang*, p. 32.   [27] See above, ch. 2, pp. 40–1.

colonies from Ireland.[28] At the same time, England's high tariff structure gave rise to a sizeable smuggling trade, which came principally from France and the Low Countries. Around 1717, the Inspector General estimated its value at about £100,000 or one-third of the legitimate trade from those countries.[29] By 1746, a Commons Committee noted that specie worth over £1m. per year may have been exported to pay for smuggled goods, to say nothing of illegal shipments of raw wool exported for the same purpose.[30]

Aside from these omissions, the defects of the Inspector General's 'official values' have often been rehearsed. It is well known that entries are expressed in formalised, unit values which closely match the level of wholesale prices prevailing during the years 1696–1709, when the official list became fossilised. The figures are therefore best suited to measuring changes in the volume rather than the value of trade, although their use as a guide to values is only seriously invalidated by the sharp price increases of the 1790s. Exports and imports were valued f.o.b. (free on board), that is, exclusive of freight, insurance and merchant's profit, while re-export goods included an element to cover these items only prior to their actual re-export – in other words, no c.i.f. (cost, insurance, freight) supplement was made in respect of their sale overseas. In the case of East Indian goods, the Inspector General produced a uniform valuation mid-way between the cost price in Asia and the selling price in London, resulting in their overvaluation as imports and their undervaluation as traded re-exports.[31] These particular figures therefore underestimate the surpluses generated in an important branch of the re-export trade, while several other categories of imports may also have been valued above their cost clear on board in foreign ports.[32] In view of these difficulties and omissions, it is clear that the customs ledgers cannot be used as a basis for reconstructing the balance of payments without a much more sophisticated series of adjustments on the invisible and capital accounts than anything so far attempted.[33]

[28] R. C. Nash, 'The Balance of Payments and Foreign Capital Flows in Eighteenth-Century England: A Comment', *EcHR*, 50 (1997), p. 112.

[29] Ashton, introduction to Schumpeter, *English Overseas Trade Statistics*, p. 3; Clark, *Guide*, pp, 34, 105–14; W. A. Cole. 'Trends in Eighteenth Century Smuggling', *EcHR*, 10 (1958), pp. 395–410; H.-C. & L. H. Mui, 'Trends in Eighteenth Century Smuggling Reconsidered', *EcHR*, 28 (1975), pp. 28–42; W. A. Cole, 'The Arithmetic of Eighteenth Century Smuggling; A Rejoinder', *EcHR*, 28 (1975), pp. 44–9.

[30] Cole, 'Trends', p. 409.

[31] K. Chaudhuri, *The Trading World of Asia and the English East India Company, 1660–1760*, Cambridge, 1978, pp. 13–14.

[32] Clark, *Guide*, p. 71.

[33] For a demonstration of the range of adjustments required and the pitfalls involved in such an exercise, see E. S. Brezis, 'Foreign Capital Flows in the Century of Britain's

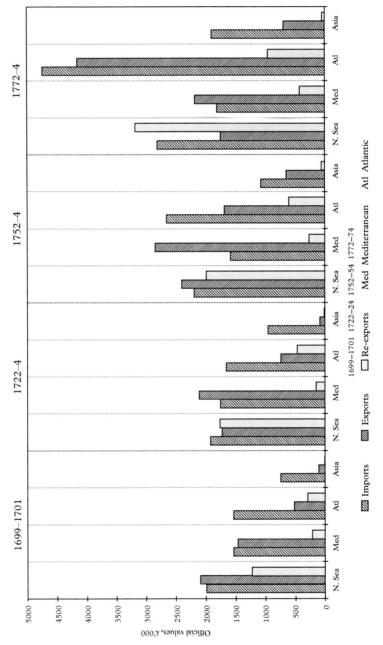

Figure 3.1 English overseas trade flows, 1699–1774

The 'official values' nevertheless shed some light on developments underlying the steady expansion of trade which occurred during the first half of the eighteenth century. In essence, they arose from the impact of the commercial revolution on traditional trading patterns and in the first instance involved the sustained growth of re-exports across the North Sea. The value of England's total North Sea / Baltic trade still exceeded that with the Mediterranean, with Asia and the Americas. From the 1720s, however, exports of home-produced manufactures to southern Europe and the Mediterranean, mainly to Spain and Portugal, overtook those to the North Sea area. Much of this trade was destined for the Spanish and Portuguese possessions in the Americas, so that England was vicariously participating in the expansion of the Iberian Atlantic empire several decades before North America emerged as a major consumer of manufactured goods.[34] In the long term, however, it was the massive growth of exports to the British Atlantic zone that transformed the composition and significance of English overseas trade, with important consequences for the industrial sector. Almost all of the *increase* in exports of home-produced goods during the first three-quarters of the eighteenth century arose from the combined sources of colonial demand.[35] By the eve of the American Revolution, English merchants and shipowners dominated intercontinental trade as a result, in Brinley Thomas's words, of monopolistic mercantilism rather than competitive capitalism.[36]

It was during the early stages of the War of the Spanish Succession that the primary objective of English commercial policy was clearly expressed as the domination of the Atlantic periphery in the face of French and Spanish competition. In 1705, Queen Anne warned parliament, 'if the French king continues master of the Spanish monarchy, the balance of power in Europe is utterly destroyed, and he will be able in a short time to engross the trade and wealth of the world'.[37] The Board of Trade, whose permanent establishment in 1696 had been brought about by the scale of French privateering and the conduct of the war, soon took on the character of a Board of Anglo-American trade, and an instrument of colonial administration and control.[38] Although they were not central to the peace negotiations, the Spanish succession question pushed colonies

---

Industrial Revolution: New Estimates, Controlled Conjectures', *EcHR*, 48 (1995), pp. 46–67; R. C. Nash, 'Balance of Payments', pp. 110–28.

[34] H. E. S. Fisher, *The Portugal Trade*, 1971, Introduction; Jones, *War and Economy*, p. 317.

[35] *Viz.*, those of the American mainland colonies, the West Indies and the Spanish and Portuguese empires.

[36] B. Thomas, *The Industrial Revolution and the Atlantic Economy*, 1993, p. 34.

[37] Cited J. Black, *The Rise of the European Powers, 1679–1793*, 1990, p. 8.

[38] I. K. Steele, *Politics of Colonial Policy. The Board of Trade in Colonial Administration, 1696–1720*, Oxford, 1968, p. xiii.

and commerce to the forefront of politics. More than one historian has emphasised the apparent contradiction between the expressed aims of a self-consciously imperial commercial policy and the day-to-day realities of a commercial world in which the bulk of English overseas trade was still conducted with nearby Europe.[39] But the growth of the Atlantic economy and long-distance trade depended to a large degree on a strong European trading position, and on Britain's ability to exercise leverage at the core of the European world-economy, the North Sea / Baltic zone, as power shifted from Amsterdam to London.

At a formal level, we can distinguish four strategic aspects of this process. First, it was necessary to enforce the navigation code at both ends of the chain, in the Americas and the ports of nearby Europe, especially those of Holland. Second, an entrepôt system was required to dispose of colonial re-exports close to the growing urban markets of nearby Europe, at favourable prices. Third, since the navigation code ruled out a free-port system, the taxation of overseas trade would need to be effected in such a way as to encourage the re-export trade, as well as exports, while at the same time encompassing measures to promote import saving. Finally, direct and unimpeded access to essential supplies of Scandinavian timber, naval stores and other raw materials from the Baltic countries were essential to maintain a powerful navy and the shipping requirements of long-distance trade. Efforts to encourage North American timber, pitch and iron exports produced no significant results, and Anglo-Baltic trade thus took on a highly strategic character in the eighteenth century.[40] Competition for northern primary products constituted an axis of potential conflict amongst the core powers, and one which was fully exploited by Sweden by imposing punitive import duties on manufactured goods from 1726, and by creating various monopoly arrangements, notably the *produktplakat* of 1724.[41] Defoe, among others, bemoaned the failure of colonial supplies, so that trade was 'running in a wrong Channel, to the infinite Advantage of the Danes, Swedes, Poles, Prussians and Muscovites, and the enriching the (otherwise) poorest and most worthless, and I had almost said the beggarly Nations in the World'.[42]

[39] Colley, *Britons*, pp. 68–9; Plumb, *Political Stability*, p. 4; P. J. Cain & A. G. Hopkins, *British Imperialism, Innovation and Expansion, 1688–1914*, 1993, pp. 87–8.

[40] H. S. Kent, *War and Trade in Northern Seas*, Cambridge, 1973, ch. 1; J. J. Murray, 'Baltic Commerce and Power Politics in the Early Eighteenth Century', *Huntington Library Quarterly*, 6 (1942–3), pp. 293–312.

[41] Kent, *War and Trade*, p. 5; J. J. Murray, *George I, The Baltic and the Whig Split*, 1969, ch. 2; H. C. Johansen, 'How to Pay for Baltic Products?' in W. Fischer, R. McInnis & J. Schneider (eds.), *The Emergence of a World Economy, 1500–1914*, Part I, *1500–1850*, Wiesbaden, 1986, pp. 123–42.

[42] D. Defoe, *A Plan of the English Commerce*, 1728, p. 222.

Although departing from modern standards of political correctness, Defoe's comments highlight both the inability of the northern countries to purchase English goods and the resulting payments problem. With all their imperfections and omissions, the Inspector General's returns indicate something of the scale of the visible trading deficit with the Baltic countries, which so aggravated mercantilist consciences: a deficit of £248,000 around 1700 had risen to £1.081m. by the early 1770s (Appendix 1).[43] Substantial exports of coin and bullion were indeed recorded in the customs ledgers. Between 1699 and 1719, nearly £13 million worth was exported, but over 70% of this was destined for Asia, supplemented by purchases made by the East India Company's agents on the Dutch bullion market.[44] Less than 5% was sent to northern Europe, and virtually all of this went to Russia. The remainder consisted largely of coin and bullion shipments to Holland, moving in response to exchange rate fluctuations, alongside the transit trade in Portuguese-Brazilian gold.[45] All the evidence suggests that, by the 1690s, multilateral exchange operations centred on Amsterdam had become the dominant means by which England's heavy import requirements from northern Europe were financed.[46]

It was the large visible trade surplus with Holland and nearby Europe which enabled English merchants to utilise Dutch credits and precious metals to settle the large and growing trading deficit with the north, particularly with Russia. During the first half of the eighteenth century, the surplus arising from commodity trade with Holland averaged £1.35m.

---

[43] The omissions include smuggling, freight charges, the cost of foreign wars, interest payments on foreign loans, travel, tourism and the cost of maintaining foreign embassies. See C. H. Wilson, 'Treasure and Trade Balances: The Mercantilist Problem', *EcHR*, 2 (1949), and reprinted in C. H. Wilson, *Economic History and the Historian*, p. 58.

[44] Henry Martin's 'Account', printed in Clark, *Guide*, pp. 77–9. A. Attman, *Dutch Enterprise in the World Bullion Trade*, Gothenburg, 1983, p. 54. During the 1690s, the East India Company's agents in Amsterdam purchased 7–8 million gilders-worth of Dutch silver ducatoons per year (K. N. Chaudhuri, *Trading World*, ch. 8).

[45] The organised Anglo-Portuguese bullion trade arose from the large surplus on the English and colonial trade account with Portugal, which was settled mainly with gold coin, carried by English men-of-war. Dutch and German trading surpluses with Portugal were also carried from Lisbon to Holland, via London (Fisher, *Portugal Trade*, pp. 105–6; N. Magens, *The Universal Merchant, containing the rational of commerce*, 1753, p. 67; J. Sperling, 'The International Payments Mechanism in the Seventeenth and Eighteenth Centuries', *EcHR*, 14 (1962), p. 453, n. 2.

[46] Sperling, 'International Payments', pp. 446–68; J. L. Price, 'Multilateralism and/or Bilateralism: The Settlement of British Trade Balances with "the North", ca. 1700', *EcHR*, 14 (1961), pp. 254–74; C. H. Wilson, 'Treasure and Trade Balances', pp. 152–61; E. F. Heckscher, 'Multilateralism, Baltic Trade, and the Mercantilists', *EcHR*, 3 (1950), pp. 219–28; C. H. Wilson, 'Treasure and Trade Balances: Further Evidence', *EcHR*, 4 (1951), pp. 231–42; S. E. Aström, *From Cloth to Iron. The Anglo-Baltic Trade in the late Seventeenth Century*, Helsingfors, 1963, Part I, pp. 77–121.

per annum, and with nearby Europe as a whole, £2.14m. (according to the official values). Before Isaac Gervaise produced his *System or Theory of the Trade of the World* in 1720, mercantilist writers consistently failed to provide an adequate description of the existing multilateral payments system, and invariably misconstrued the significance of bullion movements and the consequences of an adverse balance of trade in particular cases.[47] Commercial relations were continually described in terms of bilateral 'trades', either in favourable or pejorative terms which indicated, as Donald Coleman put it, 'a concept of commerce as a series of separate, self-financing, national, quasi-political acts'.[48] Nevertheless, the experience of the 1690s, when the recoinage crisis and an acute shortage of bills came close to endangering the war effort, shows that their emphasis on measures designed to maximise the trading surplus with Europe was not entirely chimerical.[49]

With the break-up of Sweden's Baltic empire at the close of the Great Northern War in 1721, Anglo-Russian trade grew steadily via the newly opened port of St Petersburg. While the volume of Swedish iron and timber imports altered little during the course of the eighteenth century, England drew increasing quantities of pitch and tar, masts, hemp, flax, linen, hides and iron from Russia and the eastern provinces, now under Russian control. Between the 1740s and '70s, the volume of Anglo-Russian trade increased three-fold, in spite of the continuing structural imbalance (Appendix 2). It was at this point that the British were able to exercise a degree of leverage by relaxing the restraints of the navigation code in favour of their Dutch-Baltic associates, who in return made good their chronic shortage of funds in northern Europe. As Jennifer Newman has shown, Dutch merchants used the proceeds of their own Baltic trade, along with those accruing from their intermediary role in organising the French wine and salt trades in the region, to provide loans to the British merchant community in St Petersburg and elsewhere, in return for bills payable in Amsterdam and Rotterdam.[50] In several instances, British merchants gave their Dutch colleagues access to protected colonial markets, by including goods shipped from Holland in mixed cargoes, in return for preferential funding arrangements.[51] Although the logic of English

[47] Sperling, 'International Payments', pp. 449 50.
[48] D. C. Coleman, 'Politics and Economics in the Age of Anne: The Case of the Anglo-French Trade Treaty of 1713', in D. C. Coleman & A. H. John (eds.), *Trade, Government, and Economy in Pre-Industrial England*, 1976, p. 202.
[49] Jones, *War and Economy*, ch. 2.
[50] J. Newman, 'Anglo-Dutch Commercial Co-operation and the Russia Trade in the Eighteenth Century', in J. M. van Winter (ed.), *The Interactions of Amsterdam and Antwerp with the Baltic Region, 1400–1800*, Leiden, 1983, p. 102.
[51] Ibid., p. 99.

commercial policy was directed against Dutch interests, a degree of informal co-operation provided Dutch merchants with ample opportunities for profit.

The Inspector General's figures reflect the dominance and continuing importance of Anglo-Dutch trade and the English visible trade surplus with Holland. This, of course, included the proceeds of the river trade along the Rhine and Main to the markets of south Germany and beyond. It was the expansion of trade to Hamburg, however, which provided a real element of growth within the North Sea zone as a whole. If we exclude the transit trade through Holland, the figures suggest a doubling in the volume of English exports to Germany during the first sixty years of the eighteenth century, while imports from nearby Europe stagnated (Appendix 2).[52] It was the corresponding increase in the visible trade surplus that helped to finance the rapid growth of Russian and other Baltic imports, from the 1730s onwards.

After the demise of the Merchant Adventurers in the Low Countries during the 1660s, several company members transferred their business to Hamburg. The English merchant community rapidly assumed a leading role, although, by 1675, its monopoly of English cloth there also began to slip away, as interlopers and their German associates took an increasing share.[53] By 1678, English imports of all kinds exceeded those from Spain and Holland, and, a century later, it was said that the English in Hamburg still 'make a great figure here, different from those of all other nations'.[54] With a channel to Lubeck and the Baltic, the city became a major rival of Amsterdam during the eighteenth century, as a great entrepôt in the exchange of Baltic goods for Mediterranean groceries. It also functioned as a staple for Swedish copper and iron, and the colonial products of Holland, Britain and France, as well as the latter's wine.

J. A. Faber has convincingly explained the rise of Hamburg in terms of a dispersal of the North Sea staple function resulting from structural changes in Baltic trade and the growth of population in the countries bordering the North Sea – with the exception, significantly, of the United Provinces.[55] During the first half of the eighteenth century, the number of Dutch vessels passing the Sound fell by 12%, compared with the period 1650–1700, while those belonging to the Republic's competitors rose by 25%. From admittedly low levels, English and Scottish

---

[52] Imports of linen from Hamburg grew steadily up to 1740, while those from Holland contracted throughout the period (see below, ch. 5).

[53] Roseveare, *Markets and Merchants*, p. 178.

[54] M. Postlethwayt, *Universal Dictionary of Trade and Commerce*, vol. I, 1774 ('Hamburg' entry); Roseveare, *Markets and Merchants*, p. 51.

[55] Faber, 'Structural Changes', p. 91. The city's new constitution of 1712 and ensuing political stability also deserve emphasis.

vessels increased by over 70%. At the same time, the average size of Dutch vessels was falling, whereas the tonnage of British ships sharply increased around the mid eighteenth century.[56] As the Dutch share of Baltic trade declined, and, with it, the emphasis on cereal shipments, the range of commodities shipped westwards through the Sound was extended. In the reverse direction, colonial re-exports from northern Europe found increasing sales in the Baltic area, channelled principally through Amsterdam and Hamburg.[57] The markets of the North Sea / Baltic zone as a whole experienced 'enlargement, dispersal and stabilisation'.[58]

English trade with the Dutch staplemarket

It is clear, therefore, that profound structural changes were at work during the later seventeenth century to reduce English dependence on the Dutch staplemarket. At the same time, new consumption patterns were transforming commercial relations. Since the early sixteenth century, cycles of growth and crisis in the English economy had been closely bound up with the stability of England's premier export industry, woollen textiles, and their disposal in nearby Europe, via the Low Countries and Germany. During the 1550s, and again in the 1620s, disruption of the Merchant Adventurers' trade with the northern European entrepôt brought commerce to a standstill, and drove the textile industry into depression.

By the 1690s, however, the establishment of a more competitive and flexible framework for the disposal of woollen exports had reduced the impact of commercial crises, while the growth of the home market for imported goods provided merchants with a broader range of investment opportunities.[59] Amongst other things, the emergence of a consumer society was reflected in the diversity of goods now imported from the Low Countries: maps and engravings, paintings, lacquered ware, clocks, perspective glasses, wainscotting, harpsichords, 'Rhenish' wines and Dutch

---

[56] Snapper points outs that Dutch-Baltic tonnage declined especially from 1709 to 1744, with the exception of ships sailing to Russian ports ('The Influence of British and Dutch Convoys on the Development of British Baltic Trade', in W. E. Minchinton (ed.), *Britain and the Northern Seas*, 1988, p. 94).

[57] The total shipment of colonial products through the Sound increased tenfold between 1700–9 and 1780–3, but the trade was dominated by the Dutch, who shipped three times the English volume before 1740, while the French began to catch up in the 1760s (H. C. Johansen, 'How to Pay for Baltic Products?' p. 129).

[58] Faber, 'Structural Changes', p. 94.

[59] On the seventeenth-century shift from export-led to import-led commercial expansion, see F. J. Fisher, 'London as an "Engine of Growth" ', in J. S. Bromley & E. H. Kossman (eds.), *Britain and the Netherlands*, vol. IV, *Metropolis, Dominion and Province*, The Hague, 1971, p. 8.

jenever, fine spices, and thrown silk – the list is endless.[60] The Customs Ledger for 1697–8 lists more than 270 separate species of goods exported to Holland, well over 500 categories of imports, and a proliferating range of re-exports. Especially significant were those items which represented the flow of technology across national boundaries. Even in the mid eighteenth century, English manufacturers sometimes relied on Dutch industrial techniques and equipment. Nottinghamshire manufacturers imported large numbers of Dutch 'frames or engines for the making and knitting stockings, gloves &c.', and chalk moulds were shipped to Hull from Amsterdam, 'intended as patterns for manufacturers of Earthenware in Staffordshire'.[61]

In spite of this growing diversification, Anglo-Dutch trade was still dominated by the exchange of English woollens for Dutch or Dutch-bleached linens, and contemporaries sometimes used this as a shorthand basis for discussing trade with the United Provinces as a whole.[62] Alongside the linen trade was a quantity of associated imports: sailcloths and canvas, thread, tapes, paper and flax.[63] On the export account, the dominance of a single commodity, woollens, was more marked than was the case with the import account. Because of their shipping requirements, the bulk export trades in coal and grain occupied places of commanding importance: the value of the latter often exceeded £100,000 per annum. Other valuable exports were metal wares and ores, mainly lead and tin, and fish.[64] Comparable in value with home-produced exports was the re-export trade to Holland, consisting of groceries – chiefly sugar, tea, coffee, and tobacco – and East Indian textiles, calicoes and silks.[65] Finally, there existed a sharply fluctuating export of bullion.

The movement away from dependence on a central European staple-market gathered pace during the seventeenth century, as the commodity composition of English trade broadened out. From 1689, however, it was reversed, as several countervailing influences made themselves felt,

---

[60] O. Burrish, *Batavia Illustrata*, 1728, p. 576. French wines and brandies were imported from Holland under the denomination 'Rhenish Wines' (p. 378).

[61] PRO Cust. 92/4 (Hull Collector-Board), 27 May and 16 July, 25 October 1755.

[62] E.g. Huet, *Memoirs*, p. 68; T. Mortimer, *A New and Complete Dictionary of Trade & Commerce*, 1766–7 ('linens' entry).

[63] Other valuable imports included raw silk and madder; bulky low-value goods were imported as ballast cargoes, mainly tiles, bricks and stones (J. Houghton, *A Collection for the Improvement of Husbandry and Trade*, 1727, vol. II, pp. 26, 29, 30, 40).

[64] Contrary to the impression often given by contemporaries, exports of herrings to Holland exceeded imports. The Dutch had engrossed the trade in pickled (white) herrings, but the trade in red herrings remained in English hands; see *JHC*, 12, p. 151 (10 March 1698).

[65] Burrish estimated that one-third of British tobacco imports were sent annually to Holland (*Batavia Illustrata*, p. 378).

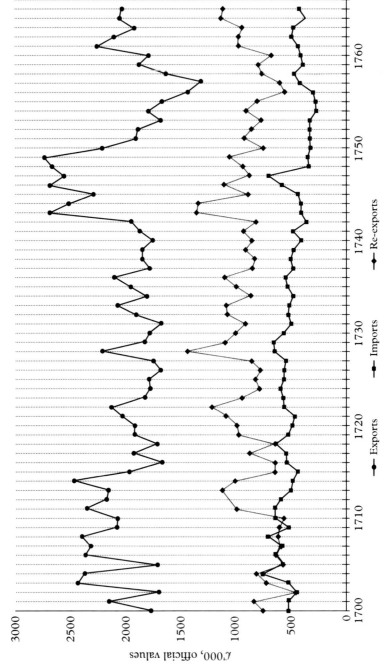

Figure 3.2 Anglo-Dutch trade, 1700–1765

arising from the outbreak of prolonged warfare. First, Amsterdam's role as a provider of financial and commercial services, combined with the exigencies of war finance, produced an intermittent downward pressure on the exchanges, which in effect cheapened British exports in the Low Countries. Second, the multiplication of risks at sea resulting from privateering and enemy depredation encouraged merchants to make maximum use of the nearby Dutch staplemarket, a situation which recurred during the War of the Austrian Succession and the Seven Years' War. Third, the prohibition of trade with France, first implemented during the years 1678–85, was reimposed for the duration of the wars of the Grand Alliance, while duties were raised to prohibitive levels against the few remaining goods falling outside the embargo. During the five-year peace, from 1697 to 1702, most French goods were paying *ad valorem* duties of at least 50%. Anglo-French trade was now diverted through Holland on a larger scale than ever before, 'the Dutch having made themselves masters of the inland trade of France, by the help of Refugees'.[66] The failure of the proposed commercial treaty with France in 1713 effectively perpetuated the situation.[67]

As far as the first of these groups of influences is concerned, it is true that several contemporaries, invariably Tory propagandists, exaggerated the use made by Britain of Dutch commercial and financial services together with the negative consequences for the balance of trade.[68] In fact it was only during wartime that English merchants made much use of Dutch shipping and insurers, and, to an increasing extent, these payments were counterbalanced by a reciprocal use of English shipping by Dutch merchants in peacetime. Rotterdam merchants, especially, regularly chartered English vessels for triangular voyages between the North Sea ports after the peace of 1713. It was during the 1720s that the London marine insurance market took off, effectively displacing the services of Amsterdam and Rotterdam. The fact that the bulk of England's European payments were cleared in Amsterdam, however, continued to exert a depressive effect on the London–Amsterdam exchange.[69]

The heaviest pressures on sterling, however, arose from transfer payments, of which the largest and most concentrated were remittances sent abroad during wartime for the payment and supply of troops, and for

---

[66] Macpherson, *Origin of Commerce*, 1805, vol. III, p. 8. Linen imports from France declined thus (million ells): 1669, 3.70; 1686, 2.13; 1699–1700 (annual average), 0.18 (E. K. Newman, 'Anglo-Hamburg Trade in the Late Seventeenth and Early Eighteenth Centuries', unpublished University of London Ph.D. thesis, 1979, p. 195).

[67] D. C. Coleman, 'Politics and Economics', p. 202.

[68] J. A. de Serionne, *Le Commerce de la Hollande*, Amsterdam, 1765–8, vol. III, p. 79.

[69] See Sperling, 'International Payments', pp. 451–5.

subsidies to allied governments, which were made chiefly via Holland.[70] During the War of the Spanish Succession, these payments averaged £1.8m. annually and reached similar levels during the War of the Austrian Succession. In the course of the Seven Years' War, however, it seems that more than £3m. per year was sent to the continent for these purposes, and, in addition, large sums were now directed to North America.[71] In 1759, for example, subsidies to allies amounted to almost £2m. while most of the £1.5m. in the army estimates was remitted to Europe for the expeditionary forces. A further £1m. was earmarked for the North American forces, including the direct supply of provisions worth almost £0.25 mill.[72]

A second transfer item, smaller in scale than remittances but which nevertheless acquired an exaggerated significance for many contemporaries, consisted of interest charges on Dutch holdings in the English national debt.[73] In spite of periodic temporary movements of Dutch funds out of Britain,[74] these holdings grew in size during the first three-quarters of the eighteenth century, rising from an estimated maximum figure of £10m. in 1739 to about £20m. in 1762.[75] A contemporary French estimate, quoted in 1771, placed annual interest payments to Dutch investors

[70] T. S. Ashton, *An Economic History of England: The Eighteenth Century*, 1955, p. 195.
[71] Figures extracted from the *CTBP* by D. W. Jones suggest that total military payments to Europe amounted to £7.9m. during the Nine Years' War and £19.9m. during the War of the Spanish Succession (*War and Economy*, p. 38). For subsequent conflicts, sums voted by parliament together with extraordinary expenses are given in the *JHC*, but on an inconsistent basis which involves double-counting. The estimates quoted above are based on known subsidies to foreign troops, to which is added a sum equivalent to 50% of the known total army expenditure during these years, excluding ordnance, given in BPP 1868–9, 25 (2), pp. 697–700. The allied subsidies are as follows, with total military expenditure, excluding ordnance and subsidies, shown in brackets (£m.): 1689–1697, £0.32 (£19.69); 1702–12, £7.12 (£23.37); 1740–8, £6.81 (£17.17); 1756–63, £9.55 (£32.43). For the War of the Austrian Succession, see *CTBP*, 1742–5, pp. 461–2; P. G. M. Dickson, *Finance and Government under Maria Theresa*, Oxford, 1987, vol. II, pp. 157–84.
[72] BPP 1868–9, 25(2), p. 699; *JHC*, 28, pp. 328–30, 342–3, 361, 369. Of the £983,300 in the North American estimates, 56% was intended for pay items, 24% covered provisions supplied directly, while 9% was remitted in specie and 8% in bills for the purchase of supply items.
[73] C. Davenant, 'A Second Report to the Honourable Commissioners for Stating the Public Accounts', 1711, in Davenant's *Political and Commercial Works*, ed. C. Whitworth, vol. IV, 1771, pp. 434–8; Magens, *Universal Merchant*, p. 67; de Serionne, *Commerce de la Hollande*, vol. III, p. 79; Macpherson, *Origin of Commerce*, vol. III, pp. 230–1.
[74] T. S. Ashton, *Eighteenth Century*, p. 193.
[75] C. H. Wilson, 'Dutch Investment in Eighteenth Century England: A Note on Yardsticks', *EcHR*, 12 (1960), p. 434, drawing on Mrs A. M. C. Carter's published work. The process of transfer of dividends is described in C. H. Wilson, *Anglo-Dutch Commerce*, pp. 142–3; J. F. Wright, 'The Contribution of Overseas Savings to the Funded National Debt of Great Britain, 1750–1815', *EcHR*, 50 (1997), pp. 657–74.

at a figure of £1.4m., which in the light of modern research may be corrected to about £1.05m.[76] Finally, it is likely that spending by English travellers visiting Holland produced a net loss of income owing to the English habit of the Grand Tour – though on nothing like the scale sometimes claimed for this, 'the most expensive of our national follies'. 'We expend more on travels than all Europe does besides', claimed a newspaper correspondent in 1727, and 'since Queen Anne's Peace, the Nation has thrown away near a Million of Species in foreign chaise-hire for our young quality'.[77] Of these various deficit items, there is no doubt that the first, the financial impact of military expenditure abroad, was the primary influence shaping the course of the London–Amsterdam exchange rate.[78]

To some extent, these payments were absorbed by the inward flow of capital from Holland, but the fact remains that for 47 out of the 61 years from 1700 to 1760, the exchange fell below par. As we would expect, sterling reached its lowest levels during wartime, particularly during the years 1703–12, 1718, 1743–4, 1758–9 and 1761, as remittances poured into Amsterdam. Interest payments to Dutch investors put little strain on the exchanges as long as the flow of capital was towards England.[79] When that flow was reversed, however, sterling came under pressure and interest payments assumed a greater burden. Movement of the exchange against Britain during years of peace is probably explained by withdrawals of Dutch capital from England, particularly during the financial crisis of 1721 and during the late 1720s and early '30s.[80]

A number of factors, therefore, caused the exchange on Amsterdam to fall below specie export point from time to time, giving rise to a fluctuating trade in bullion and specie. Its extent, indeed, troubled many contemporaries and caused much misunderstanding of the balance of trade with Holland in the early eighteenth century.[81] Arbitrage operations between bills and bullion, however, were already well organised by London goldsmith bankers during the 1680s, such as Evance, Child and others. As Stephen Quinn has shown, arbitrage opportunities increased

---

[76] Quoted by de Pinto, *Traité de la Circulation et du Credit*, 1771, in turn quoted by C. H. Wilson, *Anglo-Dutch Commerce*, p. 71. The estimate was based on the assumption that one-third of the English national debt was in Dutch hands. The correct figure is close to one quarter, and the whole amount can be scaled down proportionally (C. H. Wilson, 'Note on Yardsticks').

[77] Quoted in J. Black, *The Grand Tour in the Eighteenth Century*, 1992, p. 86; A. M. C. Carter, 'Britain as a European Power', p. 117.

[78] P. Einzig, *The History of Foreign Exchange*, 1962, p. 134.

[79] T. S. Ashton, *Eighteenth Century*, p. 193.

[80] Einzig, *History of Foreign Exchange*, p. 134; Wilson, *Anglo-Dutch Commerce*, pp. 107–8.

[81] See above, p. 73.

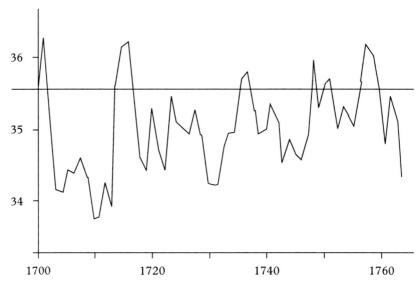

Figure 3.3 The Course of the Exchange. London on Amsterdam, 1700–1765. Schellingen per £1 Sterling (par of exchange at 35.625 sch.)

as a result of the demands of war finance after 1689, when remittance operations were handled mainly by private syndicates. Even during the crisis years of the 1690s, remittances were made in bills rather than bullion, although Evance and his partners covered their costs and no doubt made sizeable profits by exchanging bills for silver.[82] As English trade with Portugal developed after the Methuen treaty of 1703, and English trade surpluses there were translated into gold imports, the Anglo-Dutch bullion trade expanded significantly. From the early 1720s to the close of the War of the Austrian Succession, bullion and specie exports to Holland usually exceeded £1 million per year.[83] Because imports of precious metals went unrecorded, declared coin and bullion exports do not represent net outflows, nor do they include exports of specie which financed the smuggling trade. Nevertheless, the figures do indicate a close correlation

[82] S. Quinn, 'Gold, Silver and the Glorious Revolution: Arbitrage between Bills of Exchange and Bullion', *EcHR*, 41 (1996), p. 434.
[83] Cust. 3; figures for the years 1698–1719 are given in Add Ms 10,453, fo. 175, reprinted in Clark, *Guide*, p. 78. Although precious metals entered for export appear under the denomination 'foreign coin and bullion', a good deal of this consisted of British coin and bullion (the export of which was prohibited) moving in response to exchange rate fluctuations, in addition to quantities of foreign bullion which passed through London and other English ports *en route* for Holland.

between exchange rate movements and bullion exports to Holland.[84] From the 1720s onwards, it seems that enlarged supplies of precious metals (especially gold) and conditions of relative safety in transporting them contributed towards the stabilisation of exchange rates.[85]

In several respects, it was the innovative solutions to the problems of war finance devised during the crisis years of the 1690s that provided a firm basis for the relative financial stability of the eighteenth century, involving parliamentary guarantees for loans on supply, the establishment of the Bank of England, the reorganisation of public credit and the restoration of the coinage. Reorganisation of the remittance system under Lord Treasurer Godolphin enabled the government to transfer a much larger volume of funds to the continent during the War of the Spanish Succession than during the previous conflict, in ways which neither disrupted the exchanges nor involved the direct export of specie from London. Two leading city financiers, Sir Henry Furnese and Sir Theodore Janssen, established a network of agents in northern Europe, Portugal and Italy to purchase bullion, specie and bills representing English trade credits. Payments to the Spanish theatre were mostly consigned in coin and bullion, while remittances to Holland were transferred by bills of exchange.[86] Long-term borrowing was now sufficient to cover deficit spending, but the state was still dependent on the size of export surpluses to accommodate the transfer of funds abroad. It was, in a real sense, intercepting the foreign earnings of English exporters which otherwise would have been returned as imports.[87] This, of course, was a doubly difficult strategy, bearing in mind that even larger export surpluses were needed to cover the cost of increasing quantities of timber and naval stores imported from the Baltic to satisfy wartime demands.

Although 'direct supply' was not attempted, the government was keenly aware of the need to balance military requirements against the flow of exports to the Low Countries. During the Nine Years' War, Furnese had handled clothing contracts for several regiments, and during the War of the Spanish Succession continued to supply clothing while facilitating the

[84] Notable falls in the exchange were accompanied by substantially increased bullion exports in 1709–12, 1717–19, 1723, 1727–31, 1742–5, 1750, 1758 and 1761. For a close examination of the position during the War of the Spanish Succession, see Sperling, 'International Payments', pp. 465–6.
[85] Sperling, 'International Payments', p. 456; see also L. M. Cullen, *Anglo-Irish Trade, 1660–1800*, Manchester, 1968, p. 177, for a similar situation in eighteenth-century Anglo-Irish trade.
[86] J. G. Sperling, 'Godolphin and the Organisation of Public Credit, 1702–1710', unpublished Cambridge Ph.D. thesis, 1955, pp. 298–9; Sperling, 'International Payments', p. 464.
[87] Jones, 'London Merchants', pp. 321–2.

shipment of grain for the army bread contractors in Flanders and Spain, at Godolphin's request.[88] In 1707, Secretary-at-War St John assured the Paymaster-General of the army, James Brydges, 'I shall improve here as much as I can the impression that it is the universal inclination to have as much English manufacture as possible sent abroad for the service of the Queen's troops and of the allys', after making arrangements to secure shipping for a consignment of woollen goods from Kent.[89] Dutch purchasers of English goods, of course, were stimulated by the falling value of sterling, while English exporters were encouraged by 'easy money' conditions: ready money was available with minimum delay as remitters purchased their bills drawn on foreign customers.[90] Brydges himself made full use of his inside knowledge and his position at the centre of Anglo-Dutch financial networks to encourage his friends to make the most of the situation, who in turn provided him with commercial and political intelligence.[91] His circle included Matthew Decker and Denis Dutry in London, and John Drummond, Andrew Pels and Walter Senserf in Amsterdam.

The Inspector General's statistics indicate the extent to which merchants trading to the Low Countries took advantage of boom conditions generated by large-scale government remittances. Exports of home-produced goods to Holland, especially serges, perpetuanas and other woollen goods, grew rapidly between 1703 and 1710, only to collapse in the post-war period.[92] A modest revival during the 1740s replicated the boom conditions of the 1700s on a smaller scale. Re-exports responded less positively, but nevertheless grew steadily up to the mid-1730s. At the same time, the flow of imports from Holland contracted, discouraged by the falling exchange rate and high wartime taxation which reduced consumer spending – though here, the trend was clearly one of slow, long-term decline. The logic of the situation was one which encouraged import saving, and this was intensified by the state's policy of selective increases in the level of import duties after 1689, coupled with measures to promote import substitution. Thus, the course of trade altered in such a way as to produce the real transfer involved in overseas remittance

[88] Sperling, 'Organisation of Public Credit', p. 207.
[89] Huntington Library, Brydges Papers, ST58/1, St John to Brydges, Margate, 24 March 1706/7.
[90] Jones, 'London Merchants', p. 322.
[91] G. Davies, 'The Seamy Side of Marlborough's Wars', *Huntington Library Quarterly*, 15 (1951), pp. 21–44; R. Hatton, 'John Drummond in the War of the Spanish Succession', in R. Hatton & M. S. Anderson, *Studies in Diplomatic History*, London, 1970, pp. 75–7.
[92] The 1709 downward revision of values makes the high exports of these years appear even higher than they in fact are, especially in the case of cloths, which were 'devalued' by 45%.

payments, and, to a large extent, the export surplus was enlarged out of which a part of the remittances were financed.[93] When this was insufficient, it was supplemented by foreign borrowing. The volume of Dutch investment in England before 1720 cannot be exactly quantified, but contemporaries assumed that it was substantial. Davenant noted 'the large effects they have in our annuities and stocks, and all other funds', while Erasmus Philips, writing in 1726, estimated long-term foreign lending at about £1m. between 1690 and 1702, and £6½m. between 1702 and 1714. Although several prominent London Dutch and Huguenot investors played a major role, however, foreign investment in Bank and East India stock was actually very limited before 1713.[94]

The remittance effect clearly exerted a powerful influence in creating wartime boom conditions in the main branches of England's export trade to the Low Countries, but several real, non-monetary factors also played an important role.[95] The relative safety of the nearby Dutch market, the possibility of trading with the enemy via Holland, and the necessity of military supply through the Low Countries all tended to enlarge the entrepôt functions of Holland, as Davenant explained in 1711:

late exports thither [to Holland] seem rather forced... While navigation to other parts was insecure, while we had no trade with France and Spain, and while the business of the war took our thoughts from trade, and while, at the same time, such vast sums were to be drawn from England for the subsistence of troops abroad, and payment of the subsidies, such as were concerned in the remittances thought Holland the best market for our native produced and re-exported goods, and found it their interest to drive thither the whole stream of trade.[96]

The disruption of foreign markets and the abundance of English textiles in Holland naturally depressed prices. An Exeter merchant, Thomas Townshend, wrote in 1705 that 'Mixt goods of all sorts were never so cheap here as now', while, three years later, an English commission agent in Rotterdam complained that mixed kerseys were 'mighty hard' to sell: sometimes, they lay on hand for a year.[97] Stockpiling of goods in the expectation of peace contributed to what Davenant described as 'forced export'. The prices of serges would undoubtedly rise, Townshend predicted, after the allied invasion of Catalonia, 'if good news come from Spain'.[98]

---

[93] Jones, 'London Merchants', pp. 320–3, for a detailed explanation of the remittance-induced export boom of the 1690s.
[94] Davenant, 'Second Report', p. 450; Dickson, *Financial Revolution*, pp. 304–6.
[95] See below, ch. 5, pp. 104, 136.   [96] Davenant, 'Second Report', p. 436.
[97] Brants 924, T. Townshend Jr, Exeter, to D. Leeuw, Amsterdam, 1 Dec. 1705; NRO ZBL 192 (Blackett Letter Book) p. 9, John Blackett, Rotterdam, to Henry Witton, Wakefield, 28 Dec. 1708.
[98] Brants 924, T. Townshend Jr, Exeter, to D. Leeuw, Amsterdam, 24 April 1706.

Wartime disruption of trade with France and Spain was more serious for English than for Dutch merchants. It was with great reluctance that the States General yielded to English pressure to accept a prohibition of commerce and correspondence with France and Spain early in 1703.[99] Rotterdam and Amsterdam were hopelessly divided over the issue, since the former, 'in case it can open a free trade [with France] hopes to draw the greater part of it to its self, by the convenience and nearness of its haven'.[100] In fact the embargoes lasted only a year on the Dutch side, while England maintained a total prohibition of trade with the enemy. Dutch shipping, however, still required passes to enter French ports, privateering was a constant danger, and the Dutch hold on trade with Spain was weakened when Dutch factors left the Spanish ports in large numbers, leaving business in the hands of local commission agents.[101] The Leiden textile industry went into sharp decline, particularly the manufacture of *greinen* or camlets – lightweight fabrics which normally found ready markets in Spain and the Mediterranean. In 1710, an English diplomat visiting Leiden noted how, 'since the war with France, their trade is dead and the town much impoverished'.[102] The situation was exacerbated by the fact that English serges were to some extent used to clothe Dutch troops, in place of native manufactures.[103] Indeed, sixty years later, Boswell noted that English textiles were still used to supply Dutch regiments.[104]

Holland's trade with Spain was much reduced during the War of the Spanish Succession, as well as its hold on the Spanish American market.[105] Some compensation was provided, however, by the diversion of Anglo-French trade via Holland. The Treaty of Ryswick had strengthened the basis of Dutch commercial relations with France, by establishing

[99] PRO CO388/8 Part II, fo. 340, 'Some observation relating to trade with France and Spain, 25 Sept, 1701'; SP84/224, Part II, fo. 274, 'Extract of Mr Secretary Hedges' Letter to Mr Stanhope', 12 Jan. 1703.

[100] PRO SP84/224 Part I, fo. 50, 'The information of an English merchant in Amsterdam given to Richard Warre Esqre. and reported to the Earl of Nottingham', Amsterdam, 23 May 1702.

[101] Israel, *Dutch Primacy*, pp. 367 8.

[102] Production of camlets (*greinen*) fell from 36.9 thousand pieces in 1700 to 4.7 thousand pieces in 1703, while cloths (*lakens*) declined from 85 to 45.6 thousand pieces in the same period (N. W. Posthumus, *Geschiedenis van de Leidsche Lakenindustrie*, 's-Gravenhage, 1939, vol. III, Table 151, pp. 1098 9; Add Mss 15,570, John Farrington's Account of a Journey through Holland, Friesland, Westphalia &c, in several letters to a friend: to Mr N. H., p. 16 (Leiden, 16 Sept. 1710)).

[103] CO388/8, Part III, fo. 493 4, 'Letter from Haarlem', 13 Feb. 1703.

[104] F. A. Pottle (ed.), *Boswell in Holland, 1763–4*, 1952, p. 281, J. Boswell, Utrecht, to W. J. Temple, 17 June 1764.

[105] Israel, *Dutch Primacy*, p. 369.

a scale of preferential import duties.[106] In the late autumn of 1705, Davenant had visited Holland in order to collect information on this subject for the Godolphin ministry, and the result was his 'Memorial concerning the free trade now tolerated between France and Holland'.[107] The purpose of this document was to serve a distinct political objective, a fact made doubly plain when, five years later, the same information was used by the author to justify precisely the opposite ends under a new ministry.[108] The details of these policies need not detain us here;[109] the essential point to note is that the same material was used in both cases, that is, information gained from the 'most knowing and disinterested persons I could meet with'.[110] It clearly shows that a vigorous trade was being carried on between the two countries in which the re-export of English commodities to France played an important part. In addition to the great quantities of East Indian goods which were said to reach France by way of the Spanish Netherlands, Davenant claimed that by 'the same way', the Dutch

steal into that kingdom much of our lead, tin, and no inconsiderable quantities of our woollen manufactures; and 'tis known that of late one person from Gaunt had a permission to bring thither to the value of 50,000 crowns in English kersies and bays which he bought at Amsterdam, such permission being to be obtained by bribes to the Spanish Intendents.[111]

---

[106] As an English observer commented a few years later, 'The Dutch made an advantageous treaty of commerce with France ... they may import woollen manufactery, herrings and other goods: that is not permitted the English nation. Whereby it happens that the Dutch ships have all the French trade, whilst the English stand spectators' (CO388/8 Part II, fo. 340, 'Some observation relating to trade with France and Spain', 25 Sept. 1701).

[107] The copy used here is the ms version, CO 389/18, fols. 501–33 (printed copies also exist in the Bodleian Library, British Museum and the Goldsmiths Library).

[108] Published as *New Dialogues upon the Present Posture of Affairs . . . and the Trade now carried on between France and Holland, by the Author of the 'Ways and Means'*, London, 1710.

[109] D. Coombs, 'Dr Davenant and the Debate on Franco-Dutch trade', *EcHR*, 10 (1957), pp. 94–103. In 1705 the memorial was used to prove that the French were profiting from their 'free trade' at the expense of Holland. In order to preserve the Dutch alliance, the Godolphin ministry realised it must allow Franco-Dutch trade to continue, so that Davenant's arguments were used to silence those critics of the government who claimed that the Dutch were drawing out the war in order to prolong their supposed profitable trade with France. With the change of ministry in 1710, Davenant used this same information to show that, in fact, the Dutch were profiting from this trade, a situation which the conclusion of peace would rectify.

[110] CO 389/18, 'Memorial', fo. 504. In fact, Davenant conferred at length with two merchants in Amsterdam, M. Denelle, a French refugee, and John Drummond, later Harley's personal agent (Coombs, 'Debate on Franco-Dutch Trade', p. 99).

[111] Entry from Limburg into the Spanish Netherlands was free; see CO 388/16, fo. 17, Letter from Bolingbroke to the Commissioners for Trade, 25 July 1713: 'The Deputies of Brabant were positively refused the liberty of establishing any custom house officers in the Comptoirs of Vento, Buremonde, or other places of the Spanish Guelder' ('Memorial', fols. 509, 10).

He went on to say that 'good quantities of English stockings and stuffs' were conveyed into France by way of Nancy, from where they were also conveyed to other frontier places.[112] The size of this trade in English goods Davenant found 'impossible to compute', but considered it to be of such a size as made it 'doubtful whether or no it is so very much our interest that this free trade should be quite determined [terminated] since it certainly occasions a vent of many of our commodities, which could no other ways be conveyed thither in time of war'.[113] This judgement was doubtless influenced by the interests of Davenant's political masters, who were anxious to prevent renewal of the prohibition in order to preserve the Dutch alliance. Yet in 1710 when he was arguing the opposite case, he still repeated his earlier evidence and this same opinion, although the latter was styled as the viewpoint of 'the Hollanders', which implied a greater degree of doubt.[114]

Through a combination of 'real' and monetary factors therefore, the wartime situation tended to increase English dependence on the Dutch staplemarket, particularly in the case of woollen textiles. By 1715, however, the wartime boom had evaporated, and the Commissioners for Trade concluded that 'the clothing trade of this Kingdom is manifestly exposed by the increase of the Woollen Manufactures in other countries'.[115] Certainly, contemporary opinion was agreed that the woollen industries of Silesia, the Lausitz and western Poland were now able to compete effectively with English woollens in the markets of north Germany, and, in relation to the Dutch market itself, it seems clear that English exports were exposed to the short-term recovery of the Dutch woollen industry.[116] From a low point of 45,000 pieces in 1703, production at Leiden reached 82,000 pieces by 1718.[117] In 1714, a Leiden clothier explained to his London correspondent 'seeing the peace [between] the King of Spain and the States General is concluded, by which, the fabric of camlets begins to increase'.[118]

The overall impact of the Wars of the Grand Alliance thus reestablished, for a brief period, the traditional bilateral pattern of North

---

[112] In the *New Dialogues* (1710), this appears as 'considerable parcels', and instead of 'Nancy', 'Nantz' is printed. This can hardly be a reference to Nantes and must be a misprint.

[113] 'Memorial', fols. 510–11.   [114] *New Dialogues*, pp. 227–8.

[115] CO390/12, Representation, fo. 48.

[116] J. de L. Mann, 'Clothiers and Weavers in Wiltshire during the Eighteenth Century', in L. S. Pressnell (ed.), *Studies in the Industrial Revolution presented to T. S. Ashton*, 1960, p. 86.

[117] Posthumus, *Leidsche Lakenindustrie*, vol. III, p. 1098.

[118] Guildhall Library, Radcliffe Papers, Ms 6645/2, Jan van Eems, Leiden, to Ralph Radcliffe, London, 11 Sept. 1714.

Sea trade in which England relied on the redistributive functions of the Dutch staplemarket. In spite of deteriorating political relations with The Hague during the 1710s, joint English and Dutch naval operations in the Baltic kept vital trade routes with northern Europe open during the Great Northern War of 1700–21. Not until the peace of Nystad, however, did British trade with the Baltic and Russia surge forward, following a similar pattern to the expansion of trade with Hamburg. During the two decades following the Glorious Revolution, the intensity of the Anglo-Dutch commercial and financial relationship was mirrored by a unity of purpose and mutual trust in international politics; but the latter began to break down in 1711 when England started to negotiate separate peace terms with France under the new Tory ministry. Defoe, a loyal friend of the Dutch, wrote at the time, 'We will fight hand to hand, and back to back, against France, against tyranny, against popery; but we fight hand to hand, and face to face in our trade, in all parts of the world, where our trading interests clash; nor is it any breach of our alliance in other things.'[119] English dependence on the Dutch staplemarket in wartime was relatively short-lived, but the security and accessibility of London's commodity and money markets, after 1689, proved irresistible to Dutch traders for several decades to come. Questions about the timing and the extent of Dutch investment in the English national debt continue to attract the attention of historians; but in fact the export of capital was preceded by extensive Dutch investment in English commodity trade, encouraged by the special conditions of the wartime alliance.

The merchant community

In the long term, capital export and investment in commodity trade depended on confidence and mutual trust between merchants, rather than an identity of political outlook and purpose on the part of statesmen. As we have seen, the later seventeenth century saw a transformation of the structure of the Anglo-Dutch merchant community when the old framework of regulated trading collapsed, along with the obligations entailed in Crown patronage. The Merchant Adventurers' monopoly of the Dutch market was finally dissolved in 1689 and, in its place, an informal network of firms, partnerships and individual traders provided a more liberal commercial environment.[120]

---

[119] *A Weekly Review*, 7 (1710–11), p. 210, quoted in P. Earle, *The World of Defoe*, 1976, p. 98.
[120] G. L. Cherry, 'The Development of the English Free Trade Movement in Parliament, 1689–1702', *JMH*, 25 (1953), pp. 103–19.

Outside Huguenot circles, however, the unifying force of religious belief and affiliation ceased to play a significant role in business, as toleration replaced persecution. The English churches in the Netherlands never functioned as 'refugee churches' in quite the same way or on the same scale as the Dutch, Walloon and French churches in London and the provinces. During the early years of the Dutch revolt, membership of the Dutch reformed church at Austin Friars increased dramatically, reaching 2,300 in 1577, and contemporary estimates suggest that an even larger number of 'strangers' in London were 'not yet joined to any particular church'.[121] In the early seventeenth century, the flow was reversed and the number of English emigrants to Holland peaked during the late 1620s and '30s, when the Caroline church introduced more aggressive policies towards puritan nonconformists. Even then, the two principal English churches in Amsterdam claimed no more than 750 members. Of these, about 450 attended the English reformed church in the Begijnhof, established in 1607, while the remaining 300 gathered at the Separatist (Brownist) church on the Lange Houtstraat, dating from 1596.[122] In Rotterdam, the English reformed church of 1619 was transformed into a model Congregational community during the 1630s by the radical puritan, Hugh Peter. From 1635, however, this was counterbalanced by the Laudian arrangements put into place at the Merchant Adventurers' church, following the company's move from Dordrecht. One of the conditions of the reinstatement of the Adventurers' trading monopoly in the previous year was that the company 'exercise the Christian reformed religion according to the discipline and order of the Church of England', a great victory for Laud. Indeed, the company was given a monopoly of English religion in Rotterdam, but this proved impossible to enforce, to the dismay of Anglican members.[123]

During the 1650s, impecunious royalists, expelled Anglican clergymen and growing numbers of Quakers began to arrive in Holland. At the Restoration, the tide turned once more, and schismatics, rebels and

---

[121] I. Scouloudi, 'Alien Immigration into and Communities in London, 1558–1640', University of London M.Sc. thesis, 1936, Appendix 1; A. Pettegree, *Foreign Protestant Communities in Sixteenth Century London*, Oxford, 1986, ch. 9; J. Lindeboom, *Austin Friars. History of the Dutch Reformed Church in London, 1550–1950*, The Hague, 1950, chs. 1 and 2; O. P. Grell, *Dutch Calvinists in Early Stuart London. The Dutch Church in Austin Friars, 1603–42*, Leiden, 1989, pp. 249–53.

[122] A. M. C. Carter, *The English Reformed Church in Amsterdam in the Seventeenth Century*, Amsterdam, 1964, p. 116; A. M. C. Carter, 'The Ministry to the English Churches in the Netherlands in the Seventeenth Century', *BIHR*, 33 (1960), pp. 166–79; K. L. Sprunger, *Dutch Puritanism. A History of English and Scottish Churches of the Netherlands in the Sixteenth and Seventeenth Centuries*, Leiden, 1982, chs. 3 and 4.

[123] Sprunger, *Dutch Puritanism*, pp. 162–75, 248–51.

prominent republicans sought refuge there, but these were political exiles rather than religious radicals.[124] The theological disputes of earlier
decades died down and all the English churches in the Netherlands were
gradually brought within the control of the Dutch reformed church. Only
the Scots in Rotterdam maintained the godly discipline and enthusiasm
of the 1640s. From its foundation in 1643 until the Glorious Revolution,
the Scottish church in Rotterdam served as 'the unofficial headquarters of
militant Presbyterians'.[125] By 1700, membership of the English reformed
church in the Begijnhof numbered only 150. Significantly, the final
initiative in establishing an English ministry in the Netherlands, made in
1699, involved raising the salary for an Episcopal clergyman who would
divide his time between Amsterdam and Rotterdam.[126]

By the time of the Glorious Revolution then, assimilation and intermarriage between successive waves of religious refugees had left a residue
of strong family and personal connections in the trading centres of
Britain and the Netherlands. Several prominent merchant families in
Holland were of English and Scottish descent, such as the Hopes, Furlys
and Crawfurds in Rotterdam and the Cliffords, Chittys and Kirbys in
Amsterdam, who 'remain here in Splendour and Plenty'.[127] Amongst
the Dutch business community in London, names such as Cornelissen
and Corsellis suggest some continuity with the earlier history of Austin
Friars, but the great majority were recent arrivals, accepting denization or
naturalisation after 1660.[128] The transformative years for the London
merchant community in fact came in the 1680s and '90s, with the massive influx of Huguenot refugees – between 40,000 and 50,000 – and the
creation of a new Anglo-Dutch and Huguenot establishment at the core
of the city's financial and commercial life. Many Huguenots arrived in
England via the Netherlands, and the events of 1689 prompted the return from Holland of many of the ultra-protestant exiles, together with a
large outer circle of merchants, army contractors and bankers who came

[124] J. Walker, 'The English Exiles in Holland during the reigns of Charles II and James II',
  TRHS, 4th ser. 30 (1948), pp. 111–25.
[125] Sprunger, *Dutch Puritanism*, p. 432; Carter, 'English Churches in the Netherlands',
  p. 167.
[126] J. Loosjes, *History of Christ Church, Amsterdam 1698–1932*, Amsterdam, 1932,
  pp. 13–19.
[127] C. H. Wilson, *Anglo-Dutch Commerce*, pp. xiii, 28–9, 67; C. Forman, *Letter to the
  Merchants of Great Britain*, 1732, p. xvi.
[128] Grell, *Dutch Calvinists*, Appendixes I and II; D. M. Mitchell, ' "It will be easy to make
  money." Merchant Strangers in London, 1580–1689', in Lesger & Noordegraaf (eds.),
  Entrepreneurs and Entrepreneurship, pp. 119–45; Gauci, *Politics of Trade*, pp. 38–43.
  Gauci's sample of 850 London merchants in the 1690s shows that first-generation
  immigrant Dutch merchants outnumbered those of the second generation by 3:1.

in William's wake, distinct from his inner court entourage.[129] The invading Dutch armies in Britain and Ireland contained more than 2,000 Huguenot officers and men and, as Jonathan Israel emphasises, the revolution which they helped to create reshaped political discourse within the larger Huguenot diaspora. A new political outlook emerged which espoused 'the revolution of armed resistance to illegal royal authority proclaimed by William III and the Whigs', and it was one which large numbers of Huguenots were prepared to underwrite financially in their support of a protestant war against Louis XIV.[130]

For more than half a century after 1689, a large cluster of Dutch and Huguenot firms played a disproportionately large role in London's financial and commercial life. The Dutch were represented by the van Necks, Deckers, Muilmans, de Neufvilles, van Lenneps, Crayesteyns and van Nottens, together with a smaller number of Dutch Portuguese Jews, the Sephardim.[131] Both were easily outnumbered by Huguenot firms, too numerous to list, whose members continued to maintain their allegiance to the immigrant churches across the generations, unlike the Dutch. Nevertheless, Dutch and Huguenot families frequently intermarried and pursued joint business ventures. Many acted as attorneys for Dutch and other foreign investors in English government stocks, while a small elite stood at the heart of government finance, as bankers and military contractors. Around 10% of the national debt was held by Huguenot investors during the 1690s, and several dealers combined a financial role with mercantile and entrepreneurial activity, such as Sir Theodore Janssen, Thomas Papillon, the Reneus, Seignorets and Pettits. At least twenty-five directors of the Bank of England came from these circles from 1719 to 1785, as well as several directors of the East India Company.[132] In 1744, at the time of the city's declaration of loyalty to George II, 542

---

[129] P. Joutard, 'The Revocation of the Edict of Nantes: End or Renewal of French Calvinism?' in Prestwich, *International Calvinism, 1541–1715*, Oxford, 1985, pp. 346–54; R. D. Gwynn, *Huguenot Heritage. The History and Contribution of the Huguenots in Britain*, 1985, pp. 23–4; G. Gibbs, 'The Reception of the Huguenots in England and the Dutch Republic, 1680–1690', in O. Grell, J. I. Israel & N. Tyacke (eds.), *From Persecution to Toleration. The Glorious Revolution and Religion in England*, Oxford, 1991, pp. 295–8; C. H. Wilson, 'Anglo-Dutch Establishment', pp. 11–20.

[130] Israel, *Anglo-Dutch Moment*, p. 34.

[131] C. H. Wilson, *Anglo-Dutch Commerce*, ch. 4.

[132] A. M. C. Carter, 'The Huguenot Contribution to the Early Years of the Funded Debt, 1694–1714', in Carter (ed.), *Getting, Spending and Investing in Early Modern Times*, Assen, 1975, p. 87; C. H. Wilson, 'Anglo-Dutch Establishment', p. 20. On the wealth and political influence of Huguenot silk importers and merchants trading with nearby Europe, see G. S. de Krey, *A Fractured Society. The Politics of London in the First Age of Party, 1688–1715*, Oxford, 1985, pp. 137, 141–7. The deregulation of the woollen export trade plays a large part in explaining why the latter, as independent merchants, 'slipped farther from their former position of civic leadership' (p. 144).

merchants added their signatures to a document which has often, and rightly, been quoted as evidence of the strong foreign presence in London's mercantile affairs. At least one-third of the signatories were of non-British descent. The Dutch numbered 37, another 40 were Jewish, almost all Sephardim, while over 100 were Huguenot. On the occasion of another similar declaration, the accession of George III in 1760, the proportions were remarkably similar.[133]

The events of 1685 and 1689 had helped to prise open London's commercial culture. In Amsterdam, on the other hand, trade and finance remained 'under the very active control of Dutch merchants and capitalists, excluding foreign interests almost completely'.[134] In its golden age, Amsterdam was a highly cosmopolitan city and its worldwide commercial orientation owed much to the enterprise of Antwerp immigrants. Its municipal government, however, remained under the tight control of an inner circle of the *regentenpatriciaat*, animated by local pride and patriotism.[135] It was through their historic links with Rotterdam that the English and Scots were able to play a prominent and decisive role in the commercial life of Holland and the conduct of North Sea trade in general. Soon after the transfer of the English staple from Delft to Rotterdam in 1635, the latter established its enduring position as the central conduit for Anglo-Dutch trade. The departure of the Merchant Adventurers in 1656 caused little concern, as the fortunes of the company moved into rapid decline. By the 1720s, Rotterdam's prosperity depended on the trades with Britain and Ireland, which it possessed almost to the exclusion of the other towns of Holland. At mid-century, a reliable observer claimed that, apart from these trades, the city 'has nothing to support her but the sugar and wine trades'.[136] The closeness and excellence of Rotterdam's harbour, esteemed the best in Holland, attracted English merchants. Vessels could normally load and unload there and make returns to England in the time it would take a similar ship to clear Amsterdam and the Texel. 'Ships of very large burthen', it was noted, 'can not only come up to the town,

[133] S. D. Chapman, *Merchant Enterprise in Britain, from the Industrial Revolution to World War I*, Cambridge, 1992, p. 30. Gauci's sampling suggests that roughly a quarter of London's overseas traders were of identifiable foreign ancestry during the 1690s (Gauci, *Politics of Trade*, Table 1.5, p. 39).

[134] Klein, 'Little London', in D. C. Coleman & P. Mathias (eds.), *Enterprise and History*, Cambridge, 1984, p. 117.

[135] J. G. van Dillen, 'Amsterdam's Role in Seventeenth-Century Dutch Politics and its Economic Background', in Bromley & Kossman (eds.), *Britain and the Netherlands*, vol. II, p. 141. On the English in Amsterdam, see Carter, *English Reformed Church*, part II, and Carter, 'English Churches in the Netherlands', pp. 166–79.

[136] SP84/451, R. Wolters to the Duke of Newcastle, fo. 354, 31 October 1749; Bijlsma, *Rotterdams Welvaren*, pp. 142–60; Hazewinkel, *Geschiedenis van Rotterdam*, vol. II, pp. 127–38.

Illustration 3.2 J. Quack, The Rotterdam Bourse, 1665, engraving.

but likewise by means of several deep canals, come even into the middle of the town, & land their goods at the very doors of their merchants.'[137]

In the 1690s, Englishmen spoke of Rotterdam as 'Little London', with its two English churches and a high proportion of citizens who could speak good English. The Scottish community continued to thrive, and, in spite of the formal settlement of their staple at Veere from 1675, the greater part of an expanding volume of Dutch trade with Scotland was channelled through Rotterdam. The influx of British settlers reached a peak in the 1720s when one in five of those admitted as burghers was English or Scots, and, in 1743, the size of the English colony was estimated at between 3,000 and 4,000, or about 8% of the total population.[138] The British community in Rotterdam was thus much larger than its Dutch equivalent in London, which by 1700 had shrunk to a few hundred souls. But the respective impact of each of these communities on the wider worlds of business and politics is not easily represented in terms of mere size. The Dutch in London and their Huguenot relatives and partners clearly exercised an influence over the city's financial and commercial affairs which was out of all proportion to their numbers. In a different

[137] Add Mss 15,764, Diary of Jeremiah Milles, 1736, fo. 106; W. Carr, *An Accurate Description of the United Netherlands*, 1691, p. 7.
[138] Anon., *A Description of Holland, or the Present State of the United Provinces*, 1743, p. 33; Klein, 'Little London', pp. 121, 126–7.

way, the economic significance of the numerically larger community of British in Rotterdam, although localised, extended beyond a provincial role, in both a literal and a figurative sense. Clearly, they handled the lion's share of Anglo-Dutch trade, including the bulk trades in coal and grain, as well as medium- and high-value trades in lead, tin, woollens and tobacco, all imported from Britain. In addition, they performed a decisive strategic function arising from the constraints of the Navigation Acts. The Acts had little immediate effect on imports from England but, before the 1667 amendments to the Treaty of Breda, exports from Holland and its German hinterland were seriously curtailed. Much of this trade was henceforth channelled through the hands of English residents, a position which changed little after the liberalisation of trade of 1667, which allowed German goods into England via Holland. There is some evidence too that British merchants in Rotterdam facilitated direct trade between the American colonies and Holland, in defiance of the navigation code. More significant than either of these loopholes, however, was the enormous expansion of British shipping tonnage in the nearby European trades which the navigation code set out to achieve, and which the British in Rotterdam willingly exploited, as merchants, shipmasters and chartering agents.[139]

The growing domination of British shipping in the North Sea was given a powerful stimulus by an emerging division of labour in the wholesale trade of Rotterdam between two separate groups of merchants. The first group, the *zeehandelaars*, specialised in overseas trade, while a second group organised the inland trade, including dealings with an extensive foreign hinterland. The latter became the exclusive preserve of indigenous Dutch traders, to which outsiders 'had no access whatsoever'.[140] The British, on the other hand, established a firm foothold in south Holland's overseas trade with the encouragement of the navigation code. In time, as we shall see in chapter 9, the Hollando-British came to organise and finance not merely Anglo-Dutch commodity trade but also an extensive network of North Sea shipping, by chartering British vessels for triangular and multilateral voyages across the entire North Sea / Baltic zone.

By the 1760s, the English community in Rotterdam was well integrated to the extent that a large minority intermarried, and 'most of our British merchants residing here consider themselves as Dutch', according to a diplomatic source. National sentiments were easily revived on civic occasions such as the coronation of George III when 'the most public marks of zeal and loyalty, such as firing and illuminating of ships' were displayed by

[139] Klein, 'Little London', pp. 122–8; see below, pp. 288–92, 338, 341.
[140] Klein, 'Little London', p. 122.

British residents.[141] The Dutch community in London amongst whom the accession of William and Mary seems to have generated little interest, appears to have been relatively immune to such feelings. It was only the enthusiasm of the French churches in London that produced a joint deputation honouring William, in January 1689, for saving 'the British Israel from invading Popery and everlasting slavery'.[142] The Dutch church at Austin Friars was no longer the focus of a large stranger community as it had been during Elizabeth's reign, and only a minority of Dutch settlers who came in the wake of William's accession became members. The van Necks were a prominent exception.[143]

It has often been emphasised that Calvinism was marked by feelings of international solidarity, but the leading role of protestant entrepreneurs in European business life owed much more to their mobility and identity as migrants than to Calvinist piety or doctrinal orthodoxy.[144] Intermarriage and the continuing strength of kinship ties within the 'protestant capitalist international' helped to maintain bonds of trust and mutual dependability in an environment where reputation and respectability were all-important. As members of a large dispersed business community, Huguenot merchants enjoyed the benefits of mutual trust to a greater degree than most, and, for them, religious discipline still mattered, supported by voluntary educational and charitable provision. Between 1688 and 1700, the number of French refugee churches in London grew from six to twenty-six.[145]

In two important respects, Huguenot traders helped to reshape the pattern of northern European commerce: by the development of transnational commercial operations, which linked European with North American markets, and through product specialisation. More than any other single group, it was the Huguenot immigrants of the 1690s who provided the basis for the enduring cosmopolitan character of London's

---

[141] SP84/509, R. Wolters to the Earl of Sandwich, 22 January 1765; SP84/494, R. Wolters to E. Weston, 25 September 1761.

[142] O. P. Grell, 'From Persecution to Integration: The Decline of the Anglo-Dutch Communities in England, 1648–1702', in O. P. Grell, J. I. Israel & N. Tyacke (eds.), *From Persecution to Toleration*, Oxford, 1991, p. 98.

[143] Ibid., p. 99.

[144] H. Schilling, 'Innovation through Migration: The Settlements of Calvinistic Netherlanders in Sixteenth- and Seventeenth-Century Central and Western Europe', *Social History*, 16 (1983), p. 32; O. Grell, 'Merchants and Ministers: The Foundations of International Calvinism', in A. Pettegree, A. Duke & G. Lewis (eds.), *Calvinism in Europe, 1540–1620*, Cambridge, 1994, pp. 254–73.

[145] Grell *et al.*, *Persecution to Toleration*, Introduction, p. 10; N. Zahedieh, 'Credit, Risk and Reputation in late Seventeenth-Century Colonial Trade', in O. U. Janzen (ed.), *Merchant Organization and Maritime Trade in the North Atlantic, 1660–1815*, St John's, 1998, pp. 53–74; J. F. Bosher, 'Huguenot Merchants and the Protestant International in the Seventeenth Century', *William and Mary Quarterly*, 52 (1995), p. 77.

trading culture. At the same time, they played a key role in the expansion of Anglo-American commercial networks. Around 2,000 Huguenots emigrated to America before 1700, settling mainly in New York, Massachusetts and South Carolina.[146] Although numbers were small compared with the flow of British emigrants across the Atlantic, their role in international trade was disproportionately large and distinctive. By 1703, 28% of the New York mercantile community was of French origin, compared with 26% of English and 33% of Dutch nationality.[147] During the eighteenth century, however, it was from South Carolina that Huguenots made their greatest impact on the trading world of the Atlantic. While the first generation of Huguenot merchants may have lacked substantial trading capital, those who arrived after 1700 possessed larger resources based on trading connections with relatives established in London. Several of these later emigrants were the younger sons of London Huguenots acting as resident agent for family firms, and their conspicuous role in the London–Carolina trade lasted until the 1720s, by which time the dominance of English firms increased.[148]

Because of their pre-existing international commitments to the European wine, silk and paper trades, immigrant Huguenot merchants accentuated the tendency towards commodity specialisation in London's overseas commerce during the 1690s. The extent of specialisation was already considerable by this time, evident both in the nearby European trades and in colonial commerce, where the tobacco and sugar trades were conducted by two distinct merchant groups.[149] The London Port Books strongly suggest that merchants committed themselves to either exports or imports, the latter giving rise to a wider range of specialist options. Diversification, when it developed, was often related to a merchant's speciality. It occurred most frequently amongst those with strong interests in shipowning, and seems to have increased with the scale of operations. During the first three-quarters of the eighteenth century, a rising volume (and value) of trade was becoming concentrated into fewer hands, and increasing mercantile wealth was often accompanied by an extension in the geographical range of an individual's trading connections.[150] In

[146] J. Butler, *The Huguenots in America. A Refugee People in New World Society*, Cambridge, Mass., 1983, p. 49.
[147] Ibid., p. 152.
[148] R. C. Nash, 'The Huguenot Diaspora and the Development of the Atlantic Economy: Huguenots and the Growth of the South Carolina Economy, 1680–1775', in Janzen (ed.), *Merchant Organization and Maritime Trade*, pp. 85–90.
[149] D. W. Jones, 'London Merchants', pp. 326–9; R. C. Nash, 'English Transatlantic Trade, 1660–1730: A Quantitative Study', University of Cambridge Ph.D. thesis, 1982, p. 135.
[150] Chapman, *Merchant Enterprise in Britain*, p. 22; Jones, 'London Merchants', p. 328; R. G. Wilson, *Gentlemen Merchants, The Merchant Community in Leeds, 1700–1830*, Manchester, 1971, pp. 13–16.

1763, fewer than 5% of London merchants were prepared to describe themselves as 'general merchants' in a comprehensive directory of the city's traders, but well over half refused to define their interests in terms of a single trading area or geographical region. Of those that did, we find that the group describing itself as Dutch merchants, comprising forty-six individuals, was the largest of its kind, with the exception of the Italian merchants.[151]

By the middle of the eighteenth century therefore, it is clear that the movement of commodities, shipping, credit and capital across the North Sea was controlled by a looser network of firms, partnerships, brokers and chartering agents than was the case a century earlier, in the days of regulated trade. Many of the larger merchant houses had, by 1700, established branches in both Amsterdam and London, whether of Dutch origin, such as Muilman, van Neck, de Neufville or van Notten, or British, such as Hope or Clifford. The larger British firms in Rotterdam such as Hope, Wilkinson and Furly emphasised the shipping rather than the financial aspects of their business; the latter remained concentrated, for the most part, in London and Amsterdam. Those firms without established branches in both countries would devise appropriate agency arrangements, and it was common for younger sons of merchant families to attach themselves to a business house abroad, either as apprentices or informal agents, for periods ranging from a few months to several years. Ralph Radcliffe for example, heir to the Radcliffe fortune, was apprenticed in 1702 to Matthew Chitty of Amsterdam at the age of nineteen for a period of five years, to be 'taught and exercised in the art and trade of a merchant'. The Northumberland coal-owner Sir Edward Blackett established his son John as an independent commission agent in Rotterdam from 1708 to 1712, advising his father and other merchants on the state of the Dutch market for coal.[152]

The use of agents, of course, depended on the nature and circumstances of each branch of commodity trade, but the overwhelming tendency for London merchants engaged in Anglo-Dutch trade was to cease dealing on their own account. As the position of the Dutch staplemarket weakened and overseas trade became increasingly specialised, London merchants preferred to act as commission agents and brokers for Dutch and other foreign principals. Commission dealings, in addition, allowed for a greater degree of flexibility in the purchase and disposal of the increasingly broad and diverse range of Asian and colonial re-exports

---

[151] J. Mortimer, *Universal Director of London and Westminster and their Environs*, 1763.
[152] Guildhall Library Ms 6645/2, Articles of Agreement, 1702; NRO ZBL192, Blackett Letter Book.

entering into European trade. At the centre of these changes were the vicissitudes of the traditional woollen export and linen import trades, which in 1700 still remained the mainstay of England's trade with Europe. As time went on, English merchants became increasingly reluctant to trade on their own accounts in woollen goods. As was the case with Dutch merchants during the golden age, British merchants who were engaged in trade with nearby Europe preferred the low but predictable gains from commission sales, a shift which eased the transition to colonial American markets where similar tendencies were at work.

Part II

English trade with the Dutch staplemarket

4   Rivalry, crisis and reorganisation in the woollen export trade

The permanent restructuring of England's relations with the Dutch staplemarket during the first half of the eighteenth century was nowhere expressed more clearly than in the traditional area of woollen textile exports.[1] Since the collapse of the Antwerp mart in the third quarter of the sixteenth century, English merchants had shifted their operations between the Dutch and north German mart towns, from Middleburg to Hamburg, as the vicissitudes of war and commercial rivalry dictated. By 1700, half the total value of English exports was still accounted for by woollen textiles, described then as 'the greatest and most profitable commodity of this kingdom on which the value of lands and the trade of the nation do chiefly depend'.[2] By far the largest share of that trade was disposed of through Dutch ports. Yet by 1720, Holland's important role as the main recipient of English woollens was receding rapidly, and English exporters had already ceased to involve themselves. What had previously been an all-important branch of English commerce, led by English exporters, contracted and transformed itself into a Dutch import trade, driven by Dutch merchants and Dutch capital. The decline of the staplemarket function in this case (an example of what Johan de Vries termed 'external contraction') was emphatically not accompanied by the assumption of an increasingly passive role on the part of the Dutch merchant.[3] As we shall see, the reality and logic of the situation stimulated his more active involvement at an admittedly lower level of trade.

In spite of reorganisation and a sharp degree of post-war contraction, this traditional avenue of commerce was accorded an exaggerated importance by some contemporaries. Defoe in 1728 put the value of woollens

---

[1] The word 'cloth' is used throughout in the narrow sense to indicate broadcloth, corresponding to the Dutch *laken*. To avoid confusion, the generic term 'woollens' or 'woollen manufacture' is applied to the whole species, to include worsteds. This follows contemporary usage.

[2] Lipson, *Economic History of England*, vol. II, pp. 10–11.

[3] For the argument about external contraction, see Joh. de Vries, *Economische Achteruitgang*, pp. 34–45.

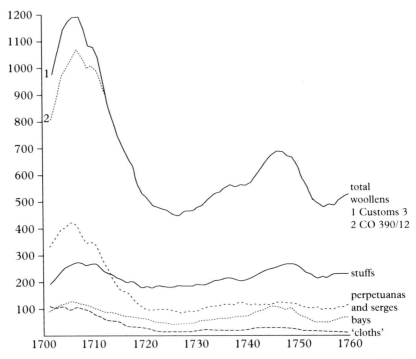

Figure 4.1 English woollens exported to Holland, 1702–1760 (Official values, £'000: nine-year moving averages)
Note: On pre-1709 values, see 'Note on statistics', in Appendixes, pp. 352–3.

exported to Holland at 'above two millions sterling'.[4] In fact the peak figure recorded for the eighteenth century was £1.4 million, reached in 1708, as shown in Figures 4.1 and 4.2. During the years from 1720 to 1760, the value of the trade fluctuated narrowly around £0.5 million annually – at a time when exports of English woollens to other markets were increasing substantially.[5]

During these middle decades therefore, the pattern is a familiar one of relative rather than absolute decline in a hitherto valuable staplemarket trade.[6] To the extent that Dutch commercial decline as a whole represents a case of relative decline, the trade in imported English woollens

---

[4] Defoe, *Plan*, p. 163. He refers to his earlier statement, p. 144, that 'it was affirmed to the Parliament in a particular debate on that subject, that they took off two millions yearly of our Woollen Manufacture'.

[5] See below, pp. 352–3, for a brief review of the problems in interpreting this material.

[6] Joh. de Vries, *Economische Achteruitgang*, ch. 2.

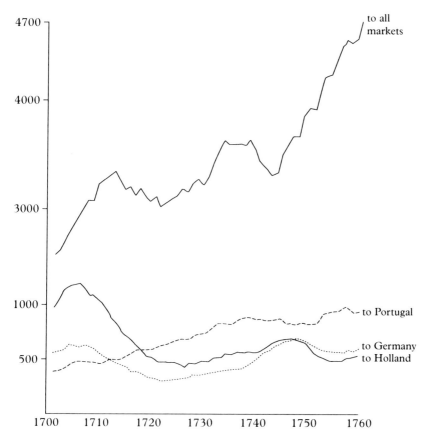

Figure 4.2 English woollen exports, 1702–1760 (Official values, £'000: nine-year moving averages)
Note: On pre-1709 values, see 'Note on statistics', in Appendixes, pp. 352–3.

conforms to the general pattern. The Dutch woollen industry itself, however, was subject to absolute decline during the eighteenth century, and the question arises as to whether the 'falling behind' of Dutch commerce was responsible in some measure for absolute decline in certain industrial sectors. For the fact is that many branches of Dutch textile activity relied on imports, whether of raw wool for domestic production, or semi-finished cloths from abroad awaiting dyeing and further dressing. In this sense, woollen textile production in the United Provinces bore some of the characteristics of a 'traffic industry'. There were of course several types of textile manufacture in which all stages of production were carried out in the United Provinces. But because the structure of the industry as a whole was integrated with the staplemarket, international commercial rivalry had a powerful impact on production itself. Anglo-Dutch rivalry in the woollen textile trade had a long history, and, in order to understand its outlines, we must disaggregate the trade into its component parts. The discontinuities between the Dutch and English industries which accounted for the varying fortunes of their products in world markets arose from differences in raw material supplies, dyeing and finishing techniques and relative costs of production.

Commercial rivalry, protectionism and their impact on production

Woollen textile manufacture was carried out in many parts of the United Provinces but, unlike in England, was concentrated in the towns, particularly those of Holland. One centre dominated the rest, with its workshops and heavy use of child labour drawn from its orphanages: the city of Leiden. It represented 'the largest single industrial concentration in Europe' and its annual output of woollens amounted to about half the value of the entire British cloth export trade, and between 85 and 90% of total Dutch production, around the middle of the seventeenth century.[7] The Leiden manufacture reached its peak output of 139,000 pieces in 1671, after which a process of slow decline set in, continuing throughout the eighteenth century. From a production figure of 85,000 pieces in 1700, output fell to 54,000 pieces in 1750 declining to 41,400 pieces by 1775.[8] A similar pattern was followed by the subsidiary woollen centres with the exception of Tilburg to which some of the activities of Leiden and, later, Hilversum, had transferred, attracted no doubt by cheaper labour.[9] This experience stands in marked contrast to that of the English industry. In spite of the absence of comparable production figures, it is fairly clear that the output of the English woollen industry grew steadily throughout the eighteenth century. For the years 1741–72, it has been

---

[7] C. H. Wilson, 'Cloth Production and International Competition in the Seventeenth Century', *EcHR*, 13 (1960), and reprinted in Wilson, *Economic History and the Historian*, p. 103; J. L. van Zanden, 'Economic Growth in the Golden Age: The Economy of Holland, 1500–1650', in Davids & Noordegraaf (eds.), *Dutch Economy in the Golden Age*, p. 9.

[8] Posthumus, *Leidsche Lakenindustrie*, vol. III, pp. 930–1, 1098–9.

[9] Joh. de Vries, *Economische Achteruitgang*, p. 84; J. Mun, *Observations on British Wool*, 1738, p. 45. The textiles industry in and around Haarlem may also constitute an exception to the general pattern, and may have experienced extensive expansion (L. Noordegraaf, 'Dutch Industry in the Golden Age', in Davids & Noordegraaf (eds.), *Dutch Economy in the Golden Age*, pp. 152–3, n. 2).

estimated that raw material input to the industry increased by an average of 14% per decade.[10]

The main problem facing Dutch manufacturers had long been a deficiency in the quality and quantity of domestic wool supplies, especially of long combing wools. In the 1730s, Dutch wool was described as coarse and short, with a high proportion of stichel – a stiff white fibre which was impossible to dye.[11] A good deal of fine-quality merino wool was supplied by Spain, mohair yarn was imported from Turkey, and coarser wools were drawn from Germany and Poland. After the mid-century peace with Spain, the manufacturers of Leiden applied themselves increasingly to the production of fine broadcloth or *lakens*, which used Spanish wool.[12] By concentrating on broadcloth manufacture, the Dutch were able to hold out against English competition when this was at its most intense, that is, during the period of the Anglo-Dutch Wars and the years immediately following. Charles Wilson suggested that these contrasting situations in the two major European textile industries were 'the result of direct competition, product by product, between them'.[13] In fact, conditions of free competition were limited by the English ban on raw wool exports, and by Dutch restrictions on the import of dyed and finished textiles from England. Both sets of measures dated from the years 1614–16, the period of Anglo-Dutch commercial disputes arising from the so-called 'Cockayne Project', the East India trade and the North Sea fisheries. The situation might therefore be described more accurately as one of rivalry bolstered by protectionism. Just as the English prohibition on wool export encouraged the Dutch to concentrate on the production of *lakens*, Dutch protectionism greatly boosted the English manufacture of worsteds and mixtures dyed in the yarn.

The long-term significance of the Dutch prohibitions of 1614 has been given much less attention than their immediate impact in exacerbating the commercial crisis of 1614–17.[14] At the same time, the character of Dutch mercantilism has sometimes been portrayed as weak and ineffective. It is true that Dutch commercial and industrial interests were frequently

[10] P. Deane, 'The Output of the British Woollen Industry in the Eighteenth Century', in *JEH*, 17 (1957), pp. 207–23.
[11] Mun, *Observations*, pp. 3, 46.
[12] The process began after the outbreak of war between France and Spain in 1636, and the consequent rerouting of Spanish wool supplies from Brabant via Calais, to Leiden via Dover: Israel, *Dutch Primacy*, p. 194; Posthumus, *Leidsche Lakenindustrie*, vol. III, pp. 754–66; C. H. Wilson, 'Cloth Production', p. 105.
[13] C. H. Wilson, 'Cloth Production', p. 105.
[14] For the former, see A. Friis, *Alderman Cockayne's Project and the Cloth Trade*, Copenhagen and London, 1927, ch. 4; Supple, *Commercial Crisis*, ch. 2; Brenner, *Merchants and Revolution*, pp. 210–11.

Illustration 4.1 Unknown Utrecht artist, cloth manufacture in sixteen stages, *c.* 1760 (oil on canvas).

divided and unable to assent to a common *handelspolitiek*, unlike their English counterparts who supported a total import ban on all foreign woollens. The character of Dutch protectionism in fact was shaped by three groups of interests: those of the manufacturer, who desired a complete prohibition of all woollen imports; those of the staplemarket trader requiring free import, particularly for the transit trade through Holland; and those of the dyeing and finishing industries which required a moderate degree of protection through the restriction of fully finished imports. The merchant clothier stood somewhere between the first two groups according to the balance of his interests as industrialist and dealer in foreign goods.[15]

The conflict of interest between Dutch woollen manufacturers and staplemarket traders was never resolved. It formed one of the principal obstacles to the realisation of the project for a limited free-entrepôt system in the early 1750s, when the decline of the Republic's trade had become glaringly obvious. But the long-established dyeing and finishing industries of Holland fared better, and since 1614 had enjoyed a fair measure of protection. In the early seventeenth century, the greater proportion of English broadcloth had been sent to Holland in an undyed and undressed state, where Dutch craftsmen carried out the finishing processes and added a new value to the cloth. It was in 1614, however, that James I acceded to the pressure of a group of Eastland merchants, led by Alderman Cockayne, to prohibit the export of undyed and unfinished cloth in order, at least on the surface of things, to give some encouragement to the domestic cloth-finishing industry. As one recent historian of this episode has put it, 'England's prosperity had become the object of a gigantic gamble, at least on the part of the government, as to whether England was capable of producing, and Holland willing to buy, a new type of product.' As the Merchant Adventurers had predicted, however, the States General retaliated by issuing a *placaat* forbidding the import of dyed and dressed cloth; and although the English lifted their ban within two years, the Dutch retained theirs and extended it at intervals, notably in 1643 and 1725. In the mid-1650s, members of the English company observed that prohibited cloths were sold in Rotterdam illegally.[16]

What, in the long term, was the impact of Dutch and English protectionist legislation on the woollen trade, and to what extent did it serve to modify the course of industrial development by encouraging product differentiation? The English ban on the export of wool, although it was

[15] H. R. C. Wright, *Free Trade and Protection*, pp. 62–3.
[16] PRO C109/19, Robert Gay and Thomas Bale, Rotterdam, to William Attwood, London, 14 May 1655; Supple, *Commercial Crisis*, p. 34.

frequently circumvented, undoubtedly hurt Dutch industry by depriving it of highly accessible raw material supplies.[17] The Dutch *placaats*, however, in trying to appease different industrial and commercial interests, inevitably contained formalised exceptions and exemptions, as well as loopholes. Thus, the placaat of 1614 related only to cloths dyed in the piece. Cloths dyed in the yarn, which commonly supplied the transit trade to Germany, were excluded from its provisions and this encouraged English clothiers to experiment with alternatives, as Adam Anderson realised when he explained the origins of 'Spanish cloths' or 'medleys'. It was to overcome the Dutch restrictions of 1614, he claimed, that 'English clothiers ingeniously discovered the art of making of mixtures dyed in the wool, rather than lose all the advantages of dyeing and dressing. This has ever since got the appellation of Medley Cloth. All woollen cloth before this time being only of one single colour dyed in the cloth, as black, blue, red, &c.'

Anderson's explanation of the origins of medley cloth is, no doubt, too simple. Their manufacture is recorded in Somerset in the early 1580s, when Benedict Webb of Taunton described them as his 'invention', a claim later upheld by John Aubrey.[18] It was indeed during the 1620s, however, that the export of medleys developed apace (known also as 'Spanish cloths' because Spanish wool was sometimes used in their production), finding their principal market in the Low Countries.[19] By 1722, 80% by value of the cloths exported to Dutch ports consisted of Spanish cloths. A category of fine-quality cloth was thus created which enabled English exporters and staplemarket traders, to whom the prosperity of the Dutch dyeing and finishing industries was of little consequence, to circumvent the Dutch prohibition. In addition, the 'new draperies' and mixed fabrics also lay outside the scope of the prohibition, and for this reason alone must have appeared increasingly attractive to those trading to the United Provinces. These mixed fabrics, of which the most

---

[17] The prohibition was initially effected by royal proclamation in 1614, repeated by Charles I and Cromwell, before being embodied in statutes of 1660 and 1662. Reports of illegal wool exports to Rotterdam from Scotland and north-east England may be found in CO388/5 Part III, fols. 218, 229, 266 (1697); CO388/7 fo. 75 (1699); for the illegal export of wool from Ireland, see CO388/22, 30 Sept. 1720. On the English tendency to exaggerate Dutch dependence on illegal wool exports, see J. Marshall, *Travels through Holland, Flanders, Germany, Denmark, Sweden, Lapland, Russia, the Ukraine and Poland; in the years 1768, 1769, and 1770*, 1772, vol. I, p. 35.

[18] E. Kerridge, *Textile Manufactures in Early Modern England*, Manchester, 1985, pp. 37–8. See also G. D. Ramsay, *The Wiltshire Woollen Industry in the Sixteenth and Seventeenth Centuries*, Oxford, 1943, ch. 8; C. H. Wilson, 'Cloth production', p. 99.

[19] Spanish cloths or medleys were not exported on any scale in the early seventeenth century; Supple found no record of their export from London in the Port Book of 1622 (*Commercial Crisis*, p. 149).

important were serges, perpetuanas, bays and shalloons, were often dyed in the wool and hence could be produced in a variety of patterns. They were especially responsive to changes in fashion.[20] The diversification of the English textile industry during the seventeenth century is of course to be explained by a variety of factors, including changes in taste and unfavourable production costs for traditional broadcloths. Dutch competition in the manufacture of *lakens* and the determination of the Dutch dyeing and finishing industries to obtain a measure of protection, however, played a key role. For much of the seventeenth century in fact, the Dutch dyeing and finishing industries succeeded in maintaining their reputation for excellence and quality.[21] The fine colours of Leiden were universally admired, and one prominent London merchant confessed to a German correspondent in 1694 that 'Dyeing in Holland far exceeds ours, or might have a good trade of it for such sort of cloth.'[22]

During the seventeenth century, the prosperity of the Leiden woollen industry became dependent on the production of *lakens*, and the excellence of its dyeing and finishing facilities; and since the latter were in some measure dependent on the staplemarket, they benefited from a limited form of protection. The situation facing the Leiden clothiers, however, was a highly vulnerable one, and, by about 1700, production of *lakens* also fell into decline. A generation earlier, Dutch fine cloth was considered much better than the English equivalent, but, by 1715, English merchants trading to Danzig claimed that, in comparison with the English product, Dutch fine cloths were 'thin and slight' and less durable in quality.[23] Unlike new drapery products, *lakens* required much labour-intensive finishing and English improvements in this sphere counterbalanced any remaining advantage which the Dutch still possessed in the dyeing processes. As was so often the case, burdensome gild regulations in the Dutch cities tended to protect long-established rights and duties at the expense of the general interest: 'Green-dyers, black-dyers and blue-dyers must not encroach on one another, nor even the dyers of different varieties of cloth. Neither dyers nor shearmen must deal in piece-goods, nor must merchants employ finishers, except within certain limits.'[24]

---

[20] D. C. Coleman, 'Textile Growth', in Harte & Ponting (eds.), *Textile History and Economic History*, p. 21; D. T. Jenkins & K. G. Ponting (eds.), *The British Wool Textile Industry, 1770–1914*, Aldershot, 1982, p. 1; J. Thirsk, 'The Fantastical Folly of Fashion; The English Stocking Knitting Industry, 1500–1700', in Harte & Ponting (eds.), *Textile History and Economic History*, pp. 50–73.

[21] Posthumus, *Leidsche Lakenindustrie*, vol. II, p. 314.

[22] PRO C111/127 Part II, Journal of Henry Phill, 1692–1700, copy of letter to B. Aylosse? Konigsberg, 26 July 1694.

[23] PRO CO388/20, fo. 63, 'A State of the British Trade in Dantzig, 1715', received 29 February 1716.

[24] Unwin, 'Leidsche Textielnijverheid', p. 401.

Illustration 4.2 J. Luiken, sketch for *De Veruwer* (the dyer), for the *Spiegel van het Menselijk Bedrijf*, Amsterdam 1718, pen and wash.

More important, as the eighteenth century progressed and Asian textiles became increasingly available, European taste continued to move in favour of the lighter fabrics to the advantage of the English industry. At Leiden the production of *lakens* fell from its seventeenth-century peak of 28,100 pieces in 1698 to 6,700 pieces in 1750, while during the same period total English exports of stuffs (the most popular of the lighter fabrics) increased sixfold in volume. During the first half of the eighteenth century, the English obsession with preventing the export of wool was especially intense, particularly in relation to long combing wool suitable for new drapery manufacture, 'that sort of wool which our rivals covet most'. At the same time, as the Leiden industry entered a permanent state of crisis, Dutch demands for protection against English competition became more intense.[25]

It was in 1725, at a time of general trade recession, that the States General decided to increase the level of industrial protection marginally with a revised tariff list, the first to be introduced since 1655. The main purpose of the 1725 *Placaat* was to stem the evasion of customs duties, the *convooien en licenten*, and where possible to simplify and facilitate their collection. For many commodities, including woollen goods, the earlier specific duties were replaced by ad valorem rates. Low duties on raw materials were retained and extended, and agriculture, fisheries and the processing industries were given stronger protection.[26] The prohibition against dyed and finished English textiles was reaffirmed and, on paper at least, extended. The provisions of the new *Placaat* in relation to woollens are summarised in Table 4.1. The main changes were twofold. Firstly, the prohibition of dyed stuffs (in addition to dyed cloths) was made more explicit: previously, only dyed cloths and kersies had been specifically named. Secondly, specific duties were replaced by a simpler uniform 'ad valorem' duty of 2–3%, in addition to which a now-reduced *veilgeld* or premium of 1% on import and $\frac{1}{2}$% on export was charged, making 4% and $3\frac{1}{2}$% respectively.[27] The one-third additional duty was abolished. It is difficult to make exact comparisons between specific duties charged on notional values and true 'ad valorem' duties, but it is clear that the difference between the new and the old rates was very marginal in the case of woollens. If anything, the new rate was from $\frac{1}{2}$% to 1% higher than the old.[28] Compared to the English duty increases placed on Dutch and other imported linens during the period, the change was negligible. As

---

[25] Posthumus, *Leidsche Lakenindustrie*, vol. III, pp. 1114–23.

[26] Engelhard, *Het generaal-plakaat van 1725*, ch. 3; Joh. de Vries, *Economische Achteruitgang*, pp. 46–51.

[27] Certain new species of stuffs not listed, it will be noted, could be entered at value.

[28] Before 1725, shortcloths rated at 100gl (or approximately £9 1s 9d at the rate £1:11gl) paid 3gl. The Inspector General's official value for the shortcloth, which remained unchanged from 1700 to 1760, was £12 10s 0d and this was probably an overvaluation. If we take a figure between the two, this gives a true ad valorem rate of duty of about 3%. Similarly, callimancoes rated at 24gl (or about £2 3s 7d) paid $17\frac{3}{5}$ stivers. The official values of these were related to pounds in weight rather than pieces; from the correspondence of J. Reeve and J. Morter in the Archief Brants (928), it is evident that medium-quality callimancoes sold in Holland from £2 0s 0d to £2 5s 0d per piece, so that the official Dutch rate would be fairly accurate as a real valuation. This gives an ad valorem rate of duty of about $3\frac{3}{4}$%.

Table 4.1 *Dutch import and export duties, 1581/4–1725*

A. *Convooien & Licenten*, or CUSTOMS DUTIES levied on	1581/84		1603		1609		1625		1651/55		1725	
	Import	Export	Import	Export	Import	Export	Import	Export	Import	Export	Import	Export
English Woollen Manufactures: Pre-1725: gilders per piece. Post 1725: percentage ad valorem.												
1 Cloths, white (undyed), long: 44–50 ells	–	1.0	–	1.75	–	1.0	–	1.75	1.0	1.9	3%	0.5%
2 Cloths, white (undyed), short: 37–8 ells	–	1.0	–	–	–	–	–	–	1.0	1.25	3%	0.5%
3 Cloths, dyed in the wool, long	–	1.0	–	–	–	–	–	–	1.0	1.5	3%	0.5%
4 Cloths imported for finishing & dyeing	–	0.5	–	–	–	–	–	–	–	–	–	–
5 Cloths, finished & dyed overseas	–	1.0	–	–	prohibited		prohibited		prohibited		prohibited	
6 Kersies, white, single, 15–16 ells	0.1	0.1	0.15	0.15	0.15	0.15	0.15	0.15	0.15	0.15	2%	1%
7 Kersies, dyed in the wool, single	?	–	–	–	–	–	–	–	0.2	0.2	2%	1%
8 Kersies, dressed & dyed	?	–	–	–	prohibited		prohibited		prohibited		prohibited	
9 Stuffs, Callimancoes, Bays etc., 36 ells	0.6	0.6	0.3	0.3	0.3	0.3	0.3	0.3	0.3	0.3	2%	1%
10 Perpetuanas, broad, 36 ells	–	–	–	–	–	–	–	–	0.5	0.3	2%	1%
11 Serges	–	–	–	–	–	–	–	–	0.3	0.1	2%	1%
Extraordinary Revenue												
B. *Last & veilgeld* (from 1599) ad valorem									$2\% +\frac{1}{3}$	$1\% +\frac{1}{3}$	1%	0.5%
C. *Derde verhoging* (from 1651) Specific, based on the addition of one-third of existing customs duties											duty abolished	

Source: Posthumus, *Leidsche Lakenindustrie*, III, p. 835.

one observer remarked in 1730, 'Does not England put 8d an ell duty on their linen of all prices? And do they [the Dutch] put any more than 2d an Ell on our Cloth, of much greater value?'[29] More threatening to English interests was the extension of the prohibition.

In trying to evaluate the impact of the new edict, historians have traditionally relied on a memorial (*Consideratien*) drawn up by a group of Amsterdam and Rotterdam woollen merchants shortly before April 1752, at the time when De Larrey was collecting evidence to compile the *Propositie*.[30] The memorialists clearly distinguished between three categories of foreign woollens: white goods, the import of which provided employment for large numbers of dyers and finishers; mixed goods, which were dyed in the wool or yarn, and, although they brought no benefits to native workmen, were nevertheless vital for a healthy transit and re-export trade; and goods dyed in the piece, which were prohibited, but were 'nevertheless truly imported'.[31] Even this third category, they stressed, was not uniformly damaging to domestic dyers and finishers, as many varieties were re-exported and not consumed at home. Only certain types of goods dyed in the piece, they judged, should be prohibited, including bays, says, serges, broadcloths and kerseys.[32] With the exception of fabrics such as these, the memorialists implied that woollens dyed in the piece were freely imported on the grounds that they were mixtures.[33] 'Had no means been contrived to moderate these heavy taxes', they insisted, and had 'the Placaat of 1725 been enforced with strict and uniform attention in the proper way, the entire trade in and through these provinces...would have been ruined and lost'.[34] Opinion was not undivided, however. One

[29] Answer to a letter from 'Peregrine English' to the author of Fog's Journal (7 Nov. and 12 Dec. 1730) in Forman, *Letter to the Merchants of Great Britain, by Peregrine English*, p. xviii.

[30] Printed in E. Luzac, *Hollands Rijkdom*, Amsterdam, 1783, vol. IV Bijlage D., pp. 35–43; see also Posthumus, *Leidsche Lakenindustrie*, vol. III, p. 1117, and Hovy, *Voorstel van 1751*, pp. 494–6, and H. R. C. Wright, *Free Trade and Protection*, pp. 62–3.

[31] Although mixtures were produced only on a small scale in Holland, and did not compete seriously with native Dutch products.

[32] See the 'Consideratien', as printed in Hovy, *Voorstel van 1751*, p. 40: all sorts of bays, crown rashes, broad and short cloths (*lakens*), stammells, dozens imperials, cloth rashes, perpetuanas, kerseys, serge *de dames*, duffels, Scottish says, rugs, Sterling says, frises, pleats, flanells, Kilmarnock serges, *Chalons amens*, Siberian says, sempiternas, Liège says, everlasting, raincoats, *serge de Nîmes*.

[33] Posthumus, *Leidsche Lakenindustrie*, vol. III, p. 1117. On the method of distinguishing between mixtures and goods dyed in the piece, see the 'Consideratien', p. 41. A mixture was defined as a fabric in which 'the front edge or selvedge, or one of each (provided that neither is split) has one other colour besides that of the piece' (Hovy, *Voorstel van 1751*, pp. 495–6, explains how this definition could be abused: cords or threads were sewn along the selvedge before the fabric was dyed, which were then removed leaving white stripes).

[34] 'Consideratien', p. 38.

Rotterdam woollen merchant wrote in November 1752, for instance, that, before the publication of the 1725 edict, a lively transit trade had existed from England to Germany, via Holland, which was since 'more than half declined' because of the stringency with which the *Placaat* had been applied.[35]

What light do the English customs figures throw on these conflicting reports? A glance at Figure 4.1 shows that, rather than declining after this date, English woollen exports to Holland actually began to assume a rising trend, suggesting that the *Placaat* had no lasting effects. The trade in stuffs, which in the dyed state had been specifically prohibited by the *Placaat*, seems to have continued in its steady and slightly rising course, without interruption. Annual figures show the late 1720s as a period of short-term decline in the woollen trade, but this recurs in the late '30s and again in the late '40s, and appears to be in the nature of a short inventory cycle. Indeed, a search through the papers of the Commissioners for Trade, State Papers Holland, and the Calendar of Treasury Papers shows that English merchants were largely indifferent to the new Dutch edict. It seems that only one minor protest was made on the English side, and this not particularly in connection with the woollen trade. James Dayrolle, English Resident at the Hague, reported in November 1725:

In execution of the new Tariff there has been at Rotterdam some English goods belonging to the people of this town confiscated for not having declared the just value of them, and as the same thing has happened to some merchants at Amsterdam who have not been used to that rigidity, they begin to cry very much against the said new tariff.[36]

The imposition of a new administrative procedure clearly generated some disquiet, but the new ad valorem principle could hardly be thought of as damaging at a time when prices were generally stable or falling. This relative lack of English reaction is further explained by important structural changes, discussed later in this chapter, whereby the bulk of English woollens exported to Holland were by this time sent on the account of the Dutch merchant whose task it was to attend to Dutch customs procedure and himself pay duties. It is generally known that Dutch merchants tacitly acknowledged the 'spirit of the *placaat*', in the eighteenth century, as one which enabled them to handle a lax customs administration with a certain degree of latitude in order to gain a concealed preference over foreigners.[37] It seems, then, that the course of the woollen trade was virtually unaffected by the provisions of the 1725 tariff reform.

[35] Quoted in Hovy, *Voorstel van 1751*, p. 499.
[36] PRO SP84/285, J. Dayrolle to Lord Townshend, The Hague, 10 November 1725.
[37] H. R. C Wright, *Free Trade and Protection*, pp. 71 3.

This is not to say, however, that the 1614 restrictions on the import of dyed woollens did not have an important long-term influence. They had given the Dutch dyeing industry a measure of protection which was in some degree responsible for maintaining Dutch superiority in this field.[38] Apart from Spanish or medley cloths, it is almost certain that a high proportion of English cloths exported to Holland in the seventeenth century were still sent in an undyed state. Pressed by the financial demands of war, parliament in 1707 thought it necessary to lay a duty of 5s on each white broadcloth exported so that 'such exportation may not be prejudicial to the Dressing or Dyeing of Woollen Cloths within this kingdom'.[39] It seems that the meaning of this legislation was misunderstood, for it was immediately followed by another which clearly stated that the export of white cloth was by no means prohibited.[40] The tone of the preamble is that of a concession to reality: 'whereas there are great quantities of white woollen cloth now ready to be shipped off and exported into parts beyond the seas, where there is a great demand for the same, and it hath been the wisdom of this nation in all ages, to give all due encouragement to the Woollen Manufacture thereof'. In other words, a revival of the Cockayne project was not envisaged.[41] Merchants' correspondence indicates that it was the Dutch market for which the majority of such cloths were destined in the earlier decades of the eighteenth century.

Yorkshire kersies were exported to Holland as both whites and yarn-dyed mixtures by Halifax and Leeds merchants such as Joseph Holroyd, Robert Allenson and William Denison.[42] Perpetuanas and serges were sent from Devon as both whites or mixtures, and the Exeter merchant Sir John Elwill wrote in 1715, 'mixed serges are much demanded but white goods are less in esteem'.[43] Serges were even occasionally exported from Exeter in the white to be dyed in Holland and then re-imported.[44] Tiverton merchants such as John Andrews and William and Samuel Lewis regularly exported shaded and bastard serges in accordance with patterns sent by their Dutch correspondent. A surviving sample shows the type of serge which the Lewises judged suitable for the Dutch market;

[38] See above, p. 111.
[39] 6 Anne c. 8, An Act for Encouraging the Dressing and Dyeing of woollen Cloths, Section I.
[40] 6 Anne, c. 9, An Act for the Exportation of White Woollen Cloth (and to prevent doubts which have arisen over this).
[41] The statute in fact made reference to this piece of seventeenth-century legislation.
[42] F. Atkinson (ed.), *Some Aspects of the Eighteenth Century Woollen and Worsted Trade in Halifax*, Halifax, 1956 (Letter Book of Joseph Holroyd), p. 45; Brants 1341, Robert Allenson, Halifax, to J. I. de Neufville, Amsterdam, 6 August 1742; from W. M. Denison, Leeds, 18 June 1759 (Brants 1343).
[43] Brants 924, J. Elwill to D. Leeuw, Amsterdam, 30 July 1715.
[44] PRO Cust. 64/2 (Exeter) Collector-Board, 14 Jan. 1748; March 1750.

woven from a brown weft and a yellow warp, the result was a speckled golden effect.[45] It was presumably this type of cloth which Burrish had in mind when he commented on Dutch inferiority in certain branches of the woollen manufacture, 'particularly in mixing their colours', a practice which gild regulations discouraged.[46] Information relating to the trade in East Anglian stuffs is more sparse, but Benjamin Andrews, John Reeve and John Morter were perhaps typical Norwich clothiers who at different times advised their Amsterdam correspondents of the types of manufacturers most suitable for their market. All three quoted similar assortments of flowered callimancoes and damasks, both coloured and white; figured, striped and plain estamines and satinetts; and 'toys of all sorts'.[47]

It can therefore be seen that, although the 1725 *Placaat* had a very limited impact, the character of the eighteenth-century woollen trade to Holland reflected in some degree the earlier Dutch legislation which had encouraged the import of white woollens and mixtures. The former received a new value in the hands of skilled Dutch dyers, while the latter supplied a fabric for domestic consumption and, more important, the transit trade, which could be less easily produced by Dutch manufacturers. As a pamphleteer of the 1730s wrote 'The Dutch do wisely allow our medleys, because it keeps them forward in the trade to the Empire.'[48] How much value, in fact, was added by the dyeing process, and how serious a problem was Dutch inferiority in cloth finishing, as some contemporaries alleged?[49]

By 1700, English clothiers appear to have established a margin of superiority in the finishing processes, especially shearing. It was in the 1670s that new finishing methods were introduced into England by Dutch immigrants settling at Trowbridge and Bradford-upon-Avon. Within a generation, West Country clothiers had perfected the technique of shearing their superfine cloth in the wet state, whereas the Leiden clothiers invariably cut theirs dry.[50] In 1718, a group of Leiden clothiers and cloth-finishers attributed the success of English fine cloths in Dutch domestic

[45] Brants 929, J. Andrews to D. Leeuw, 4 Jan. 1706, and invoices of 35 pieces of serge (13 May 1710), and 12 ends of serge (Jan. 1713), from W. & S. Lewis, 21 and 18 Aug. 1714.

[46] Burrish, *Batavia Illustrata*, p. 374. See also Hovy, *Voorstel van 1751*, p. 498.

[47] Brants 928, B. Andrews, Norwich, to D. Leeuw, Amsterdam, 4 March 1701/2; from J. Reeve, Norwich, 1704 [*sic*] and J. Morter, Norwich, 7 Sept. 1707.

[48] Answer to the letter from 'Peregrine English' to the author of Fog's Journal (7 Nov. & 12 Dec. 1730) in C. Forman, *Letter to the Merchants of Great Britain*, p. xviii.

[49] Burrish, *Batavia Illustrata*, p. 374.

[50] J. de L. Mann, *The Cloth Industry in the West of England, from 1640 to 1880*, Oxford, 1971, pp. 12–14; J. de L. Mann, 'A Wiltshire Family of Clothiers: George and Hester Wansey, 1683–1714', *EcHR*, 9 (1957–8), p. 244.

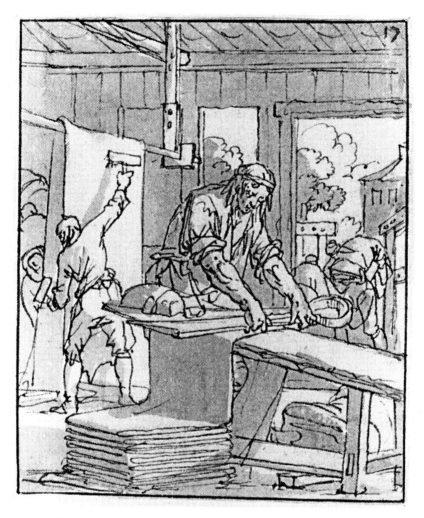

Illustration 4.3 J. Luiken, sketch for *De Droogscherder* (the cloth shearer), for the *Spiegel van het Menselijk Bedrijf*, Amsterdam, 1718, pen and wash.

and re-export markets to English finishing skills, especially wet shearing and close-cutting (shearing).[51] The Leiden clothiers failed in their attempt to imitate finishing in the 'English manner', it seems, because

---

[51] N. W. Posthumus, *Bronnen tot de Geschiedenis van de Leidsche Textielnijverheid*, vol. VI, *1703–95*, 's-Gravenhage, 1922, pp. 378–9, no. 220, 11 January 1718. The petitioners referred to the use of the crook, a wooden device attached to the upper blade of the shears which facilitated a smoother and closer cut; and the use of the brush rather than a blade for raising the fibres in the same direction (mozing).

of the opposition of the journeymen finishers. When a similar dispute arose in 1741 between masters and journeymen, the latter refused to handle cloth shorn abroad, while the former insisted that foreign shearing was cheaper.[52] Cloth-finishing was a highly labour-intensive process, and high Dutch labour costs and gild restrictions, it seems, presented an insurmountable problem.

The profitability of dyeing, on the other hand, was largely determined by the cost, quality and availability of dyestuffs, an area where the Dutch enjoyed major advantages. In the late 1720s, the governors of the Leiden orphanhouse were purchasing white English kersies, which they had dyed and pressed by native workmen. Dyeing charges, in this case, represented around 10% of the final value of the cloth.[53] The orphanhouse no doubt occupied the cheaper end of the market, and such a figure is open to the usual objections common to institutional price series. It is possibly more reliable, however, than those quoted over a century earlier at the time of the Cockayne project when inflated figures of 50–100% were in circulation. At this time, reference was also made to a sixteenth-century Dutch schedule in which dyeing accounted for 47% of total manufacturing costs, which has since been uncritically accepted by modern historians.[54] Unless the proportions had dramatically changed during the seventeenth century, the figures quoted by the Leiden governors suggest that the profits which the Dutch were said to draw from the dyeing of English textiles, for the cheaper colours at least, have been much exaggerated.

If Dutch industrial interests supported prohibitions and restrictive policies to maintain their position, the Merchant Adventurers were equally willing to trade 'in the spirit of the *placaat*', on a basis which perpetuated their own grip on the trade in undyed and undressed fabrics. Between 1624 and 1634, when parliament permitted free trade in coloured cloths and new drapery, the company confined its exports to white cloths with surprisingly little complaint.[55] In 1634, when the Privy Council agreed to reinstate full monopoly powers, to include all kinds of coloured as well as undyed cloths, the Adventurers effectively reconstituted themselves

---

[52] Posthumus, *Leidsche Lakenindustrie*, vol. III, p. 1107. See also H. R. C. Wright, *Free Trade and Protection*, p. 64.

[53] Posthumus, *Bronnen tot de Geschiedenis van de Leidsche Textielnijverheid*, vol. VI, p. 418, no. 249.

[54] Supple, *Commercial Crisis*, p. 33, suggests that the Privy Council was aware of this estimate, as Sir Julius Caesar in his notes taken at Privy Council meetings gives figures which exactly reproduce this percentage (Add Mss 14,027, fols. 265–6, printed in Friis, *Alderman Cockayne's Project*, pp. 461–3; see also F. Niermeyer, *De Wording van onze Volkshuishouding*, 's-Gravenhage, 1946, p. 76, and C. H. Wilson, *England's Apprenticeship*, p. 71).

[55] Below, p. 124; Supple, *Commercial Crisis*, pp. 69–70.

in Rotterdam with a more inclusive membership. The company and its factors, however, still operated as an Anglo-Dutch consortium, sensitive to Dutch interests, trading in white and mixed coloured cloths and new draperies which did not compete with Dutch woollens. Not until the 1660s did the mart town system break apart, with the challenge of the English Navigation Acts and the activities of interlopers trading in an increasingly diverse range of fabrics.

The demise of the Merchant Adventurers in Holland, 1600–1689

During the later seventeenth century, the English woollen export trade to Holland underwent fundamental reorganisation until, by about 1700, it could be more accurately described as a Dutch import trade. The basis of this change lay in the declining role of the Merchant Adventurers, whose monopoly of the woollen trade was lifted, modified and reinstated at intervals throughout the seventeenth century. The demise of the most prestigious of the regulated companies forms an important episode in English commercial history, the neglect of which can be explained only by the disappearance of the company's official records. To some extent, however, it is possible to reconstruct the process of decline from surviving business correspondence. The papers of the London merchant and company member, William Attwood, cover the period 1649–93 and include material relating to cloth exports to Holland during the mid-1650s following the conclusion of the first Anglo-Dutch War, and to Hamburg during the 1660s and early '70s, when trade through the Dutch staple had reached a standstill.[56] His trade to Holland was handled by two of the company's resident factors, Robert Gay and Thomas Bale, who made the move from Rotterdam to Dordrecht in June 1656. Attwood also traded to Portugal and the Levant: in the 1660s, he was sending cargoes of lead and pepper to Leghorn on half-account with Josiah Child, taking sugar and currants as return cargoes.[57] For the 1670s, the activity of interloping merchants can be followed in the letter book of the Norwich merchant Thomas Baret, who also emerges as one of Child's correspondents – though there is no evidence that they were business partners.[58]

Attwood's correspondence with Gay and Bale begins in 1655 by which time interlopers had already made great inroads into the company's trade, and Gay and Bale wrote

---

[56] C109/19–24, Letters and Accounts of William Attwood of Hackney, merchant, 1649–93.
[57] C109/19, J. Gould & Company, Leghorn, to W. Attwood, London, 5 January 1663.
[58] NRON, Ms 6360/6B8, Letter book containing copies of 'all letters sent beyond the seas', by Thomas Baret, Norwich, 1672–5.

you will finde it [trade] but meane as it stands at present; for other places as Amsterdam, Middbr. & moste of our haven towns in Holland not this excepted are soe furnished with all sorte of clo[th] & cr[edit] by those that are not free brethren of our Compa[ny]; that know not how to sell, nor whether they winne or loose & soe undersell to theire owne & our disadvantage.

Underselling, it appears, was not restricted to interlopers, since, they continued, 'some of our brethren of our company being willing to engross all the sales by underselling (as Mr Raphe Bresy), as we are informed'.[59] Complaints of interloping continue throughout the correspondence, and, with it, the related evil of an overstocked or 'overburdened' market which allowed customers to 'pick and chuse'.[60] Gay and Bale themselves estimated their annual turnover at 500 cloths or more, since the peace of 1654, doing 'business for several men' and charging a commission of 2%.[61] Their business methods emerge fairly clearly from the (single-entry) accounts relating to the sale of Attwood's cloths and kersies.

Attwood's first consignment arrived in Rotterdam in May 1655 and consisted of 63 Spanish cloths and 6 northern kersies. Six months later 36 of the cloths and all 6 kersies had been sold, while, twelve months later, only 10 cloths remained unsold.[62] A further 70 cloths were then despatched. The usual pattern was for small sales of 1 or 2 cloths, to the value of between £20 and £30 each, to a large number of presumably small customers. It seems likely that several were drapers and shopkeepers, or *koopman-winkeliers*, and Gay and Bale described their business thus: 'what we sell are in pedling parcells to those that sometimes rebate & sometimes runne out'. During the first six-month period of trading, Attwood's cloths and kersies were taken by twenty-five separate customers from seventeen different towns or cities, mostly in the Low Countries. Credits of up to six months were given and, if payment was made within three, four or even five months, rebates of around 5% were made for prompt payment. Gay and Bale's correspondence shows that most customers settled their accounts within three months, but they lamented 'we are forced to stay 12 mo[nths] & above for some men's money & cannot obtain a farthing for interest'.[63] These generous credit terms were only given, it was explained,

[59] C109/19, R. Gay and T. Bale, Rotterdam, to W. Attwood, London, 30 April 1655. It is likely that this was Raphael Brassey, who became Deputy Court Master in 1674 (Te Lintum, *De Merchant Adventurers*, p. 217).
[60] C109/19, R. Gay and T. Bale, Rotterdam, to W. Attwood, London, 8 Oct. 1655.
[61] Ibid., 4 June 1655.
[62] Ibid., 7 Jan. 1656: 'Copy of Journall for acct of Mr William Attwood of London, Merchant, beginning 24 May to the last of December 1655'; and succeeding journal for 14 July 1656.
[63] 'Copy of Journall', 24 May   31 Dec. 1655; C109/19, R. Gay and T. Bale, Dordrecht, to W. Attwood, London, 11 Jan. 1658.

because the market was oversupplied – in Gay and Bale's words, because of the 'encroachments which are daily put upon us'. Attwood was remitted whenever bills were available, purchased from German or Dutch merchants involved in trade with London. By 15 October, just over half the proceeds of Gay and Bale's commission sales to date had been remitted. Payment was slow, generous rebates were expected and provided, and 'the prices wee sell at but meane'.[64]

A high level of stocks was maintained in accordance with the principles of the company, as Gay and Bale explained:

we have need to have at least 200 clo[ths] in packhouse from time to time and those to be very well sorted otherwise little good to be done. Some times if we have not cloths of just such prices and colours as some men would have they will not buy a clo[th] . . . we have now more than 250 clo[ths] in packhouse and yet we find ourselves unsorted of some prices and colours.[65]

Patterns were sent of the colours most in demand: 'sad musts & white & some of very sad greys & some light' were most likely to 'do well'. For a good sale it was deemed that cloth should have these properties: 'culler[d] & well mixed, thick substantial, fast clo[th]: small spinnings, well dressed, wool lying smooth, not curly, nor thready, & well measured'.[66] The traditional custom of 'show days' was still followed, and in September two show weeks were held. It was during this month that the largest single quantity of Attwood's cloth was disposed of. In September 1656, for example, 11 Spanish cloths and 2 northern kersies were sold to nine customers, while, in September 1657, 16 cloths and 6 northern kersies were sold to nine customers.[67]

The trading etiquette followed by Gay and Bale in Rotterdam and Dordrecht represented an effort to maintain the Merchant Adventurers' ideal of a 'well-ordered and ruled trade' in the difficult circumstances which followed the commercial crisis of 1621–4, and, as such, involved more than the application of a series of crude restrictive mechanisms. It was in 1621 that the company moved from Zeeland to Holland, and, by so doing, hoped to stabilise and strengthen a declining trade by dealing directly with the smaller Dutch retailers and merchants of that province –

[64] C109/19, R. Gay and T. Bale, Rotterdam, to W. Attwood, London, 30 April 1655.
[65] Ibid., 4 June 1655.
[66] Ibid., from Dordrecht, 15 Sept. 1656. Kerseys and northern dozens, of course, were cheap and sold in large quantities: to achieve good results, the former 'must be the best to be gotten . . . & Dozens of all prices if very good . . . must be well dresst. & not too fatty, but your factors in the North must have good skill & bee exceeding careful to buy of best makings'.
[67] Lipson, *Economic History of England*, vol. II, p. 234. 'Copy of Journall', and 'Particulars of Sales for account of Mr W. Attwood for first and 2nd show week', 22 Sept. 1656.

individuals, that is, who had previously obtained their goods from the handful of large Dutch wholesale merchants. The latter, the so-called 'royal merchants', in turn obtained their cloths, in large quantities, from a handful of large Merchant Adventurers at Middleburg.[68] The deal which was struck in 1621 between the States of Holland and the Adventurers involved an agreement whereby the latter would abide by the *Placaat* of 1614, which allowed only the import of unfinished or undressed and undyed English woollen stuffs (*stoffen*) and of mixed coloured cloths (*lakens*), in return for which the Adventurers would be enabled to deal directly with the small traders of Holland. The last-mentioned was achieved by the approval of a court regulation whereby the membership limited itself to acting as wholesale dealers, thus preserving the retail trade in finished cloths for Dutch merchants and producers.[69] If one compares the scale of Lionel Cranfield's earlier operations from Middleburg in 1601–3 with those of William Attwood, it is obvious that the company was operating a much more broadly based trade, albeit smaller in overall terms, by the 1650s. Cranfield's agent in Middleburg, Daniel Cooper, turned over £10,035 in woollens during an average year, 1601, and acted solely for Cranfield.[70] The latter was, admittedly, one of the largest cloth dealers in London during the first decade of the seventeenth century. In 1606, for instance, an Antwerp correspondent asked him to supply 6,500 pieces, while the majority exported up to 400 pieces each. Nevertheless, Gay and Bale were clear that, in the 1650s, the sale of 500 cloths per year was 'not to be expected for one man's account', and themselves acted for several merchants, supplying small quantities to numerous small dealers.[71] Attwood's correspondence with his agents suggests that the Dutch protectionist legislation of 1621 which encouraged the export of white cloths and mixtures continued to influence the overall character of the woollen export trade. Although the *Placaat* was evaded, it seems that the obstacles to trade in prohibited goods discouraged many: 'whatever is dyed in the clo[th] there [England] is alsoe prohibited heere, soe that wee sell such goods by conievence, & for low price'.[72]

There is little doubt that Gay and Bale regarded competition and a well-stocked market as a threat to their trade. Interloping merchants such as Thomas Baret traded with only a small stock and sold at low prices by instructing their Amsterdam correspondents to communicate

[68] Friis, *Alderman Cockayne's Project*, pp. 389–90.
[69] Bijlsma, *Rotterdams Welvaren*, p. 144.
[70] R. H. Tawney, *Business and Politics under James I. Lionel Cranfield as Merchant and Minister*, Cambridge, 1958, pp. 62–7.
[71] C109/19, R. Gay and T. Bale, Rotterdam, to W. Attwood, London, 4 June 1655.
[72] Ibid., 14 May 1655.

their immediate requirements, and by ordering small parcels from the clothiers.[73] The remedy was seen unambiguously in terms of 'restriction' and enforcement of the Adventurers' monopoly: 'wee wish our establishment heere & a powe[r] there [in London] to stopp our pedling & wandring interlopers or wee shall have little incouragement'.[74] Against their own perception of the advantages of monopoly, in terms of high prices, buoyant sales and predictability, however, they clearly maintained a genuine concern for the quality of the product and what they regarded as fair and well-ordered trade. Long credit with generous rebates, the maintenance of a good and 'well-sorted' stock, the provision of show days, and a scrupulous concern for providing good measure were fundamental to their way of doing business. The company's agents fulfilled the obligations of the 'tare', the system by which purchasers might be compensated for faults and short measure. Gay and Bale recommended good measure 'soe much the better to keep them out of our sworne measurers hands', and agonised over the tendency of some cloths to shrink excessively during finishing: 'sometimes indeed wee are ashamed of their complaynte'.[75] The company's avowed aim, then, was to provide a quality product in a stable and well-regulated market, whilst maintaining good prices for English producers. The interests and advantages of the membership, it seems, were conceived in terms of predictability and control of fluctuating markets which regulated trade, ideally, might achieve.

The commercial correspondence of the Norwich merchant, Thomas Baret, shows that, during the early 1670s, some interloping merchants were prepared to compromise by dealing in new types of woollens lying outside the company's monopoly, whilst utilising the services of its factors. In 1672, Baret had consigned a pack of goods to one of the company's factors in Hamburg, Thomas Shepherd. In the event, Shepherd was 'not free to sell stuffs in that place although these are not commodities which our English merchants or any others that I [Baret] have heard of [or] ever dealt in'.[76] Accordingly the goods were shipped to Amsterdam for sale there. Baret continued to correspond with Shepherd, however, and attempts were made to persuade the company to permit dealings between them; but in the following year Baret noted 'I perceive they are resolved in their way . . . they will force me to steer another course than I intended . . . if ever they did see any of the commodities must acknowledge

---

[73] Ibid., 8 October 1655. NRON, Ms 6360/6B8, Thomas Baret, Norwich, to R. Cockey, Amsterdam, 19 February 1673.

[74] C109/19, R. Gay and T. Bale, Rotterdam, to W. Attwood, London, 14 May 1655.

[75] Ibid., 30 April 1655, and, from Dordrecht, 10 November 1656.

[76] NRON, Ms 6360/6B8, T. Baret, Norwich, to Jacomo Lemo, Amsterdam, 10 March 1673.

them to be of new invention and differing materially from what commodities they ever had before.'[77] As a footnote, he added defiantly: 'The
Pliament of England are great incouragers of the trade of the nation: as is
manifest to the liberty granted to the Eastland trades, whale fishing and
other such like trades . . . I am now drawing up reasons and stating the case
to several members in Pment.'[78] In the meantime, Baret concentrated his
energies on the free-trade outlets of Amsterdam and Rotterdam. In 1673,
parliament removed the aliens' duty on woollen exports, and, three years
later, a further twelve-month period of free trade was approved.

For a variety of reasons, therefore, monopolistic trading on the traditional pattern had become difficult to manage by the third quarter
of the seventeenth century, in the highly competitive and increasingly
well-supplied markets of northern Europe. In the first place, it is clear
that as English and European woollen textile production became more
diversified, the scope of the Adventurers' monopoly became, in effect, a
constantly shrinking one; and it became correspondingly more difficult to
define the exact scope of permitted trade. Secondly, the legal and political conditions underlying monopoly privileges had to be maintained and
enforced at both ends of the chain, at home and abroad, for the system to
work. In a period marked by war and political instability, this was difficult
to achieve. Thirdly, there was an inevitable tension between the interests
of monopoly exporters in London and their factors abroad: the former
were anxious to maintain high prices, while the latter were more inter-
ested, as commission agents, in securing a high turnover. Finally, as the
interlopers' trade met with increasing success in Holland and Germany,
and as parliament and Privy Council tended to intervene in their favour
during the depressed conditions then facing the woollen industry in the
post-Restoration period, the elements of predictability which regulated
trade was intended to promote were replaced, instead, by instability and
uncertainty.

The position of the Merchant Adventurers was thus weakening until, in
1689, the woollen trade was thrown open by statute (rather than proclamation), on a basis which proved to be permanent.[79] By 1711 it was said
that the company's residence at Dordrecht was ruined 'and not an English
merchant left there'.[80] In both a practical and a symbolic sense, the manner in which change was effected reflected a decisive shift in the shaping

---

[77] They were possibly a new type of 'orange mixtures' of which Baret was building up
stocks from August 1673 onwards.
[78] NRON, Ms 6360/6B8, T. Baret, Norwich, to T. Shepherd, Hamburg, 23 January 1674.
[79] By 1 Wm. & M. c. 32. The Act is dated 1688 in the statute book but the correct date is
1689; see Lipson, *Economic History of England*, vol. II, p. 266, n. 4. The monopoly of
the Levant, Eastland, Russian and African companies remained.
[80] CO388/14, Letter received from the Hamburg Company, 22 April 1711.

of commercial policy, of the kind which had produced the first Navigation Act of 1651: the basis was parliamentary initiative in place of the exercise of royal prerogative and court patronage. As Horwitz has pointed out, the greater recourse to parliamentary legislation after 1689 to some extent reflected the enhanced authority of statute; and this, he suggests, was most apparent in the case of the chartered trading companies.[81] The Glorious Revolution, of course, provided a new context highly conducive to the liberalisation of trade. The Lockean emphasis on natural liberty and individual freedom was paralleled by a more liberal and inclusive approach to economic matters, in both thought and practice, a development which has sometimes been obscured by a one-sided emphasis on the rise of protection during the 1690s. The task of promoting employment, it can be shown, 'gained priority over the accumulation of a national stock of money' and consumption gained an importance in its own right.[82]

The Hamburg trade, and the decline of the transit trade through Holland

It remains to analyse the transit trade in woollens, and the extent to which the growth of what had been called 'direct trade' between England and the countries of the Republic's hinterland, particularly Germany, affected the commercial relations between England and Holland. Charles Wilson emphasised the growth of Hamburg's and Bremen's trading connections with England in the early part of the eighteenth century, which enabled the English merchant to dispense with his Dutch agent, particularly, he noted, in the linen and woollen trades.[83] One weakness of this explanation is that it regards the German market as a single entity, which it was not, and Holland and Hamburg as substitutes, when they were rather distinct alternatives serving sometimes different markets. An imaginary line from, say, Ratisbon to Zwolle divides the markets of the Empire into two, if not entirely separate units, at least physical regions which were sufficiently distinct to enable contemporaries to speak of the South German and North German markets. The former was served by the Rhine and the Main river systems terminating their courses at Rotterdam with the Maas and Waal estuaries, and was spoken of by some as 'Upper Germany'; while the latter was served by the Elbe and its tributaries

---

[81] Horwitz, *Parliament, Policy and Politics*, p. 315.
[82] Gunn, *Politics and the Public Interest in the Seventeenth Century*, p. 245; C. H. Wilson, 'Other Face of Mercantilism'.
[83] Wilson, *Anglo-Dutch Commerce*, pp. 40, 51–3, and 'The Economic Decline of the Netherlands', *EcHR*, 9 (1939), and reprinted in E. M. Carus Wilson (ed.), *Essays in Economic History*, vol. I, 1954, p. 257.

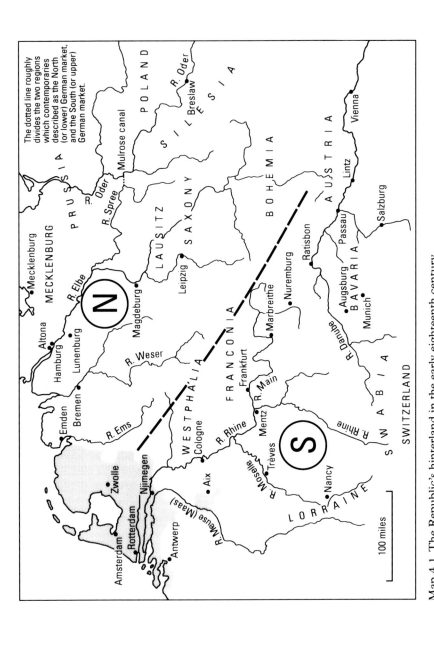

The dotted line roughly divides the two regions which contemporaries described as the North (or lower) German market, and the South (or upper) German market.

Map 4.1 The Republic's hinterland in the early eighteenth century.

terminating at Hamburg, and was sometimes termed the 'Lower Parts' of Germany (see Map 4.1). Charles Whitworth, when plenipotentiary to the imperial Diet at Ratisbon in 1716, prepared a detailed and revealing report on the trade of Germany which makes this distinction plain.[84] The other arteries of trade into Germany consisted of Emden, at the head of the Ems, and Bremen, at the head of the Weser, both of which, according to Whitworth, served 'little more than their own neighbourhood'. By contrast, the Hamburg Company, as the remnant of the former Merchant Adventurers company was now known, had, for several years, furnished many parts of the Empire with woollens, stuffs and other goods which were carried along the Elbe to Magdeburg, Leipzig, Bohemia or Silesia. From the last-mentioned they were again dispersed in smaller quantities to Poland, the Ukraine, Hungary and Vienna. The chief returns were linen, flax yarn and thread. Furthermore, the three-mile-long Mulrose canal joining the Oder with the Spree made possible water communication from Breslaw to Hamburg. 'Direct trade' of this sort to Germany, therefore, was hardly a new phenomenon. The other great entry of goods into Germany, as Whitworth noted, was by Holland up the Rhine as far as Switzerland, and by the Main into Franconia, the latter being navigable 'For boats of considerable burthen' as far as Marbreithe. Thus, a Customs-House official noted three years later that 'the German trade is not confined to the ports in Germany...but that the same is also brought through the Netherlands by the following ports vizt. Amsterdam, Rotterdam, Middleburgh, Helvoetsluice, Dort, Ostend, Neuport, Bruges, and Dunkirk'.[85]

When pleading for the restoration of their privileges in 1715, members of the former Merchant Adventurers Company made this important distinction and demanded that monopoly trading rights in woollens should be restored only to cover their dealings in the 'North Part of Germany'. These were doubtless under-estimated at 'not a fourth part of the whole German trade'.[86] They were satisfied that the English trade to Holland and the south part of Germany should remain free and open, for this was a 'vast extent of country where there is room enough for a most considerable trade to be carried on by all persons'. In accordance with this view

[84] CO388/18, fo. 68, 'Enquiries into the trade of Germany' addressed to Lord Townshend, Ratisbon, 29 April 1716. Charles Whitworth, created Baron Whitworth in 1721, was said to have understood the politics of the Empire better than any Englishman of his time, apart from Stepney (*DNB*).

[85] CO388/21 Q7, Letter from Mr Carkesse concerning the German trade, 30 Dec. 1719, Customs House, London. The German ports listed were Hamburg, Bremen, Altona, Gluckstadt, Stetin, Stade, Emden and Lubeck.

[86] CO388/18, fo. 47, Memorial of the Hamburg Company relating to the state of their trade, Hamburg, 3 May 1715.

was that expressed by Whitworth in his 'Enquiries' and also in a letter written to Townshend four months later, which spoke of 'the upper parts of Germany [ie the 'south German' market] in which alone I believe our trade is now improvable, since the consumption of English commodities in the lower circles must lessen everyday, by the frequent manufactures erected in several places, and the very high duties laid on all foreign goods for their encouragement'.[87] The 'Enquiries' elaborate this point at greater length. By 1716, it was said that the call for English manufactures in the 'lower circles', particularly woollens and mixed stuffs, was at its height 'if not already declined'. For several towns in Silesia, the Lausitz and the frontiers of Poland made:

such quantities of woollen goods, stuffs, fustians, stockings &c as not only to sup-ply their own wants, but in a great measure furnish Franconia, Swabia, Bavaria, Austria, Tyrol &ca. For common use several thousand pieces, go to Poland and Russia yearly, and some are even sent from Oltz and Zullico, which are so good that when pressed and prepared, particularly in Magdeburg they pass for ordinary English.[88]

Silesian wool, Whitworth added as a partial explanation, was the best in Germany.[89] The growing success of the Silesian industry is also attested by the comments of a group of British merchants reporting on the state of the British trade to Danzig in 1715. They attributed the decline in the export of northern cloths there to the Silesian coarse cloth which was being brought overland free of custom in such quantities as to supersede the English equivalent.[90] (Comments such as these follow the general tone of the 1715 investigation into the state of the woollen trade which emphasised the exposure of the English industry to foreign competition on the conclusion of peace.)[91] Thus, the German market should not be regarded as a single unit, more particularly since one section of it seems to have been developing an economic life of its own.[92] 'Direct trade' to the north German market at this time, far from increasing, was actually declining from the levels reached during the heyday of the Merchant

---

[87] CO388/18, fo. 102, Extract from a letter from Whitworth (Envoy Extraordinary and Plenipotentiary to the King of Prussia) to Lord Townshend, Berlin, 22 August 1716.

[88] 'Enquiries', fo. 68.

[89] See also W. O. Henderson, *The State and the Industrial Revolution in Prussia, 1740–1870*, Liverpool, 1958, p. 2.

[90] CO388/20 P 63, 'A State of the British Trade in Dantzig, Anno 1715' received from Richard Vernon, British envoy to the King of Poland, and signed by twelve British merchants, 29 Feb. 1716.

[91] See above, p. 88.

[92] See Henderson, *State and the Industrial Revolution*, pp. 3–4, and W. O. Henderson, *Studies in the Economic Policy of Frederick the Great*, 1963, pp. 143–6.

Adventurers' trade, and for reasons quite unconnected with the structural changes taking place within the Dutch economy.

That part of Germany most capable of absorbing increased quantities of woollens, whether Silesian, Dutch, Dutch-dyed English, or English mixtures, was therefore the South German market in which the chief trading towns were, as Whitworth said, Frankfurt, Nuremburg, Augsburg and Ratisbon. Geographically speaking, it was most accessible along the Rhine, but a number of factors existed to render 'this noble tract of water carriage... almost useless to England'. Firstly, transit duties had to be paid in Holland; secondly, the towns of Cologne, Mentz and Frankfurt each enjoyed rights of staple which involved relanding goods and thus wasted time as well as porterage and commission charges; and thirdly, goods passing between say, Holland and Frankfurt entered five different principalities each involving 'a multiplicity of tolls with the vexations and delays of the customs officers'. Similarly, water carriage along the Danube from Ratisbon to Vienna was good, but involved nineteen tolls. At this point, however, Whitworth commented, 'tis true the factors have their methods of eluding in a great measure these as well as all the other tolls; but as the risk is theirs they take the profit wholly to themselves'.[93] As late as 1772, Joseph Marshall testified to the Dutch monopoly of the Rhine navigation: 'the Dutch alone have this trade, and they regard themselves almost as the proprietors of the navigation of that river'.[94] To the English merchant, less able to cope with Dutch and German customs procedures, freight by land was almost as cheap as water carriage.

The most serious hindrance was that of transit duties through Holland. On the Dutch side the question of the transit was much discussed by contemporaries, as in 1716 when the States of Holland were considering the decay of their trade.[95] It was then pointed out that the transit of British manufactures was likely to be lost through high duties, but no alteration was made. Nor, in 1725, with the general tariff reform, was any perceptible change effected.[96] The difference between the new and the old rates was marginal, perhaps by 1% either way depending upon the type of fabric and the extent to which its pre-1725 rate had approached real prices. The transit question again came into prominence during the discussions

---

[93] 'Enquiries', fo. 68.   [94] Marshall, *Travels*, vol. I, p. 110.

[95] For a short general discussion, see H. R. C. Wright, *Free Trade and Protection*, pp. 73–7; CO 388/18, fo. 102.

[96] Referring to Table 4.1 above, the transit rate on say, one piece of English white cloth of 37–8 ells passing into any part of the hinterland, other than the southern Netherlands, amounted to 6% of the *rated* value before 1725 (adding together outwards and inward rates), and 5% thereafter. The divergence between real prices and the official Dutch rates, however, by the early eighteenth century, worked in favour of the importer, so that the pre-1725 value was closer to 4% than a formal 6% rate (Whitworth, 'Enquiries').

centring round the proposals for a limited free-zone in 1750–1, when Thomas Hope proposed a free transit to counterbalance the protection which was to be applied to industry and agriculture. In spite of the support which this received in Rotterdam, negotiations ended in deadlock through a variety of reasons: the untimely death of Willem IV, the opposition of the industrial towns and the non-seafaring provinces, Zeeland's desire to protect her smuggling trade and the outbreak of the Seven Years' War.[97] The transit duties remained therefore. In order to avoid these and the river dues and other exactions of the German principalities, English woollens destined for the South German market could take the alternative route overland from Bremen, Hamburg or Altona, where duties were $1\frac{1}{2}$%, 1% and zero, respectively.

Whitworth agreed that the South German market was partly supplied by this overland route, the largest quantity of English woollens received in this way being taken by Frankfurt – that is, the major part of the £100,000-worth of English woollens which the town annually received at this time. This consisted of 'bays, kersies, serges from Exeter and Tiverton, flannels from London, and cloth from Leeds'. Nuremburg had a 'small' trade with England while Augsburg took off 'very few English goods' and those only at second and third hand from Amsterdam or Frankfurt.[98] In the Austrian market, English woollens competed with those of Silesia and the Lausitz, so that few were sold; in any case, Whitworth noted, Ratisbon (and presumably those Austrian cities to the east of it) had always received English woollens from either Leipzig or Hamburg rather than Holland.

In fact, trade was hardly any more 'direct' when an English merchant corresponded with a Hamburg or Bremen house, from which goods then had to be sent overland, than if the same merchant corresponded with a Dutch house which was more capable than himself of evading Dutch transit duties and manipulating German river tolls and staple rights. Moreover, the north German market, more conveniently situated for trade with Hamburg, was gradually shrinking as native woollen manufactures expanded. Trade to Germany might have become more 'direct' in an organisational sense if English traders had begun corresponding with, say, Frankfurt houses to the exclusion of the Hamburg or Amsterdam middleman. Whitworth noted that a Ratisbon merchant had '2 or 3 years ago begun a correspondence directly to Leeds and has his goods sent from Bremen by land carriage, most whereof go to Vienna'.[99] This, however, had eliminated a Hamburg rather than a Rotterdam merchant. The Inspector General's commercial statistics suggest that the course of English woollen exports to both Germany and Holland followed a remarkably

[97] Hovy, *Voorstel van 1751*, pp. 656–8.   [98] 'Enquiries', fo. 68.   [99] Ibid.

similar pattern until at least 1740 (Figure 4.2). After about 1708, while total English woollen exports were still increasing, those to Germany and the Dutch staplemarket declined together at comparable rates and continued to do so until the mid 1720s. Throughout the late '20s and '30s, woollen exports to Germany increased at a slightly more rapid rate than those to Holland at a time when total woollen exports to all markets were growing. During the '40s, however, while exports to both markets were expanding, those to Germany increased at a far more rapid rate than those to Holland, the former exceeding the latter for the first time in 1743. During the '50s and early '60s Germany continued to take a higher proportion of English woollens than Holland. The remarkably similar movement of these two trades up to *c.* 1740 suggests that perhaps both were affected by the same source of demand, namely, that of the South German market. There are no statistics available to indicate the size of the Dutch transit trade in woollens, though in 1765 it was estimated that one-third of English woollens exported to Holland were ultimately destined for Germany, a sufficiently high proportion to determine the course of total trade in English woollens to the Dutch staplemarket.[100] This indicates that 'direct' trade to Germany at the expense of Holland did not take place on a significant scale until at least 1740. Had this been otherwise, it might be expected that movements in the two trades would be inverse to one another. Furthermore, it is conceivable that the rapid expansion of woollen exports to Germany from 1740 onwards is to be attributed in some measure to a slight revival in the north German market rather than by an increased amount of 'direct trading' to southern Germany. The outbreak of the War of the Austrian Succession caused some disruption of continental trade, particularly that of Silesia which assumed a role of strategic importance during the first two years of the conflict. This should not be overstressed, however, for the Silesian economy showed a remarkable degree of resilience against wartime dislocation, her woollen manufactures reaching record heights in 1748–9.[101] The overall expansion of the trade in woollens direct to Germany after *c.* 1740 is largely accounted for by increased exports of stuffs, which were subject to a sudden increase in the two years immediately following the annexation of Silesia in 1742. By the late '40s, however, exports were declining from these high levels as the Silesian economy recovered.[102]

[100] CO388/95, R. Wolters, 'Particulars of the Trade carried on between the different ports of HM Dominions and Rotterdam, and the other ports of the Mase', 16 July 1765.
[101] Henderson, *State and the Industrial Revolution*, pp. 3–4.
[102] PRO Cust. 3/45–50.

In the absence of satisfactory export statistics which make the distinction between, on the one hand, woollens destined for consumption in Holland and those entering into the transit trade to Germany, and, on the other, between the north and south German markets, it is impossible to indicate with any degree of certainty the extent to which the Dutch staplemarket was being circumvented by an expansion of English woollen exports 'direct' to Germany. It seems likely, however, that this occurred on a smaller scale than has been supposed. At least one well-informed contemporary noted that, even in the 1770s, the central and southern parts of the Empire were still supplied 'in a great degree' by the Dutch.[103] On the whole, the English export of woollen textiles to nearby Europe was fairly stagnant during the eighteenth century; the steady growth of the woollen trade at this time is explained rather by the growth of southern European markets, of which Portugal was a notable example, and by the expansion of extra-European demand.[104]

The influx of foreign buyers into London and the decline of the wholesale merchant

The withdrawal of the Merchant Adventurers' monopoly in 1689 was followed by a minor flurry of pamphleteering in which the company rehearsed a number of well-tried arguments about the advantages of regulated trade, stressing its ability to maintain large stocks of textiles abroad and to provide long credits. It also claimed that earlier periods of free trade had failed to generate a larger and 'more liberal vent' for English cloths abroad. In addition, however, a more novel argument surfaced, which seems to have first emerged as a serious issue during the company's discussions with the Committee for Trade and Plantations in 1683, when the company was successful in obtaining a proclamation against the infringement of its charter.[105] This was the claim that foreign merchants (aliens) were participating in the Adventurers' commerce alongside native interlopers. By 1711, the company reported to the Commission for Trade that, since the 'liberty of trade' of 1689, foreign merchants in Germany and Holland who were previously its customers were now supplying themselves directly from England: even foreign shopkeepers, it was said, commissioned Dutch factors to make their purchases in England. In short, foreigners had 'found means almost totally to exclude the English merchants from the trade to Holland, Zealand, Brabant and Flanders'

---

[103] Marshall, *Travels*, vol. I, p. 110.
[104] Davis, 'English Foreign Trade, 1700 1774'; figures for woollen exports to Portugal kindly supplied by Dr H. E. S. Fisher.
[105] The aliens' duty on woollen exports was withdrawn in 1673 by 25 Chas. II c. 6.

as well as from 'the several parts of Germany'.[106] Foreign factors, the company continued, were being sent into England and recommended to English factors, 'and when those have got acquaintance and knowledge in the way of buying, the English factors are turned off'. Unlike the Merchant Adventurers, the committee appointed to enquire into the declining state of the woollen manufactures in 1715 had no particular axe to grind. Yet it too noted that foreign merchants now had a 'very considerable share' in the woollen trade to Germany, 'and a much larger in the Holland and Flanders Trade'.[107] In the 1720s, Onslow Burrish recalled how the English formerly kept warehouses for their woollen manufactures at Dordrecht; at present, he wrote, 'the Dutch commission their factors in England to buy up what they have occasion for... and the goods are consigned directly to themselves'.[108]

The foreign takeover of the most valuable branch of England's export trade to Europe, in fact, represented only one aspect of a larger process involving the channeling of Dutch, Huguenot and German capital into the commodity trade and financial markets of London during the Williamite revolution, and beyond. The influx of Dutch capital into the English national debt is, of course, a familiar aspect of the financial revolution and the enhanced role of the City's ultra-protestant business community during the 1690s, but there was also a substantial movement of Dutch and other foreign capital into English commodity trade, including London's re-export trade with nearby Europe.[109] There is some evidence that Dutch investors were lending substantial sums to British merchants as early as the 1660s, at relatively low interest rates.[110] Three decades later however, much larger sums were clearly involved. The most reliable estimate available suggests that foreign capital financed over one-third of English domestic exports in 1695, a major commitment which was reflected in the growing 'cosmopolitanisation' of the London mercantile community during William's reign.[111] Unsurprisingly, extreme Tory pamphleteers made much of this, suggesting that richer citizens, 'must now give up their Shops and Warehouses to every Dutch petty tradesman. The Richer Merchants, who, under the King's protection fetched the wealth of the Indies to the Royal Exchange, must now think themselves happy if they can be Factors or very Journey Men to a Dutch

---

[106] CO388/14, Letter received from the Hamburg Company, 22 April 1711.
[107] See also Add Ms 15,766, Diary of the Revd J. Milles, Hamburg, 1736, fo. 57; CO 390/12, fo. 37, Representation, 1715.
[108] Burrish, *Batavia Illustrata*, p. 375.   [109] See below, ch. 10, pp. 322–8.
[110] HMC, *Eighth Report, and Appendix* (Part 1), 1881, item 215 (134b).
[111] Jones, *War and Economy*, p. 256 and Tables 8.3 and 8.4; Chapman, *Merchant Enterprise in Britain*, pp. 29–35; C. H. Wilson, 'Anglo-Dutch Establishment', pp. 11–32.

Pedlar.'[112] The recovery of the woollen export trade to Holland and Germany during the Anglo-French wars of 1689–1713, under the stimulus of a falling exchange rate and the disruption of continental cloth production, did indeed provide enhanced opportunities for both English and foreign merchants. There is, however, some evidence that several members and former members of the Merchant Adventurers Company actually chose to withdraw from their traditional markets in the wake of de-regulation, and to 'launch out into other trades', before the foreign presence reached substantial proportions.[113]

Nevertheless, the fact remains that foreign merchants gained a firm foothold in the formerly privileged areas of regulated trade, which they retained after 1713, when woollen exports to nearby Europe declined for almost two decades. The operations of merchants such as John d'Orville of Amsterdam became legendary, of whom it was said, in 1714, he 'hath ware-houses like Blackwell Hall; he deals vastly upon his own account, in woollen goods'.[114] In 1706, Michael Bovell, a London woollen factor wrote to David Leeuw of Amsterdam, 'I have the honour to serve Mr John Orville & some other: and one merchant who I believe to [be] the most considerable dealer in druggetts in Amsterdam who I am obliged not to name.'[115] Leeuw himself was a merchant of some substance, taking woollens from West Country merchants to the value of several thousand pounds annually, while d'Orville received woollens to the annual value of over £10,000 from Joseph Holroyd alone.[116] Holroyd, a Yorkshire woollen factor, also dealt with other considerable Dutch correspondents such as Adrian Deynoot who is later to be found insuring cargoes, presumably woollens, from Topsham to Rotterdam valued at 10,000 and 8,000 gilders.[117] Those English observers therefore, who

[112] Goldsmiths Library 2697, Anon., 'The Dutch Design Anatomised . . . or, a Discovery of the Wickedness and Injustice of the Intended Invasion . . . written by a True Member of the Church of England, and lover of his country', 1688, p. 20.

[113] Goldsmiths Library 2968, Anon., 'Reasons humbly offered against the Continuation of a General Liberty for Exporting the Woollen Manufactures of this Kingdom by Foreigners, into the Privileges of the Merchants Adventurers of England', 1693, p. 3.

[114] The reference comes from the contemporary comedy, author unknown, *The Beaux Merchant, a Comedy written by a Clothier*, 1714, p. 26.

[115] Brants 927: M. Bovell, London, to D. Leeuw, Amsterdam, 18 March 1706. Bovell added, 'I beg . . . of you would not mention my name to Mr John Orwill who I am sure would not give me anymore commission if he knew I dealt with any but himself.'

[116] Brants 924, G. Poe to D. Leeuw, 27 Jan. 1705; Brants 929, J. Andrews to D. Leeuw, January 1714. During the period 1701–22, Leeuw had sixteen correspondents in Exeter and five in Tiverton, besides a much larger number in London. For Holroyd's dealings, see Atkinson (ed.), *Woollen and Worsted Trade*, Introduction, p. xii, and the Letter Book of Joseph Holroyd reprinted therein, p. 48, Letter to Samuel Clark, 8 Oct. 1706. J. and P. d'Orville were insuring cargoes valued at 3,000 and 4,000gl. on voyages from Hull to Amsterdam (MADBR, Assurantie Boek 1735).

[117] MADBR Assurantie Boeken, 25 February 1721 & 23 March 1725.

claimed that the Dutch were now drawing their woollens 'directly' from England on their own accounts, were correct only in a limited sense. The English Merchant Adventurer or commission agent had been replaced by a Dutchman, and the small Dutch country trader or chapman was still at the same remove from the original source of supply. The credit risk had been transferred from an English to a Dutch account, enabling trade to continue on the basis of lower profit margins. One of the more reliable pamphleteers of the 1730s pointed out that 'the Dutch ordering... [woollens] over from England for their own account, are satisfied with a small profit, because they can borrow money to trade with, or upon goods, at the rate of $2\frac{1}{2}$ per cent per annum, and think 5 per cent a good profit; whereas our interest being 5 per cent we must have a larger profit'.[118] The deregulation and restructuring of this important branch of English overseas trade, therefore, may be understood as a strategy in which low risks were balanced by low returns.

The elimination of corporate control and the increasing importance of 'direct orders' from continental buyers, however, opened up new possibilities for increasing profit margins in the long run, in a way which circumvented the London wholesale market. It was during the 1730s that a tendency which had become apparent early in the century assumed a new importance. As early as 1706, a somewhat alarmed Joseph Holroyd had remarked that two manufacturers, James and John Maude, 'sends their goods into Holland themselves'.[119] Some weeks later, he elaborated this point to John d'Orville: 'so far as I can find by the clothiers they get more for their goods that they send to be sold than by selling here. But I hope that they may be weary of it in a little time.'[120] Low prices caused by the overstocking of the Dutch market in wartime strengthened this tendency, and the practice slowly spread. By the 1730s, an innovative manufacturer such as Sam Hill of Soyland, near Halifax, was exporting his own woollens to John and Peter d'Orville, Hendrick and Pieter Kops, Abraham van Broyel, the van der Vliets and other merchants in Holland.[121] The last three houses were signatories to the *Consideratien* drawn up by a group of Amsterdam and Rotterdam woollen merchants *c.* 1752, and their trade was presumably sizeable.[122] Hill worked largely on the basis of regular orders – in his own words, 'most Gentlemen that

---

[118] Charles Forman, *Letter to the Merchants of Great Britain*, p. xix.
[119] Atkinson, *Woollen and Worsted Trade* (Letter Book of Joseph Holroyd), p. 50, J. Holroyd to James Baden, 1 November 1706.
[120] Ibid., J. Holroyd to J. d'Orville, 19 November 1706.
[121] Atkinson, *Woollen and Worsted Trade*, pp. 2–16 and Introduction, p. xii; see also H. Heaton, *The Yorkshire Woollen and Worsted Industries from the Earliest Times up to the Industrial Revolution*, Oxford, 1920, pp. 387–8.
[122] See n. 30 above.

I serve have agreed to take a certain quantity every year, and they fix the months wherein they desire them and then they are seldom or ever disappointed, but never any price fixed but a market price when ready'.[123] By mid-century, Hill's turnover was £30,000 per annum, equivalent to that of the largest merchant houses in Leeds.[124] This was clearly an arrangement which would work best in the case of the large Dutch merchant importer. Similarly, Robert Allenson of Halifax wrote to J. I. de Neufville of Amsterdam, in 1742, 'being told you trade in white kerseys, I take the liberty to advise you the marks and prices of my sorts . . . also to inform you that I am the maker, & that you may save commission by ordering 'em directly from me'.[125] A trial consignment of kerseys and shalloons was made, and Allenson requested that secrecy be maintained 'for it would be a prejudice to me wth my other friends', adding, 'I deal with Messrs Vliets and Mr Cops therefore desire you will not make any offers to them of my goods.'[126] In fact these two houses were also supplied by Sam Hill, suggesting that direct dealings with manufacturers were becoming common. Several similar examples occur in the Archief Brants. In the early 1740s, Birmingham manufacturers were supplying 'Cambletts, Cublettees, Striped Callamancoes, Tammays, Shalloons &c, figured stuffs called Everlasting' to Dutch customers, while Derbyshire stocking manufacturers were seeking out direct orders from Holland some years later.[127] By the 1750s, a woollen *merchant* like William Denison of Leeds explained that he was only able to compete effectively by dealing in large quantities of goods, and 'the manner I pay, [which] entitles me to a preference amongst the manufacturers'.[128]

It is not always possible to draw an exact dividing line between manufacturer and merchant in the eighteenth-century woollen trade. John Powys of Shropshire for instance was a 'merchant clothier' who in the 1730s bought Welsh 'Plains' (white milled cloths) which he subsequently dyed and finished: clearly, he was an important intermediary between the manufacturing and finishing processes.[129] As the century progressed and direct contacts between manufacturer and overseas buyer developed, the

[123] Atkinson, *Woollen and Worsted Trade*, pp. 3 4, S. Hill to H. and P. Kops, Amsterdam, 31 January 1737.
[124] J. Smail, *Merchants, Markets and Manufacture. The English Wool Textile Industry in the Eighteenth Century*, 1999, p. 34.
[125] Brants 1341, Robert Allenson, Halifax, to de Neufville, Amsterdam, 6 August 1742.
[126] Ibid., 14 September 1742; and Brants 1347, from Samuel Powel, Rochdale, 16 November 1750.
[127] Brants 1330, from T. and J. Roe, Birmingham, 7 May and 26 Nov. 1743, Brants 1334, from H. Peckham, 8 April 1763.
[128] Brants 1343, from W. Denison, Leeds, 21 August 1754.
[129] Brants 1348, from John Powys, Shropshire, 6 June 1735.

distinction becomes more obscure. During the first decade of the century, Norwich men like John Morter, Dan Smith, John Gooch, John Reeve and Benjamin Andrews were clearly acting as cloth factors buying stuffs, callimancoes and estamines for the account of Dutch merchants. Morter for instance had 'a very good acquaintance amongst the makers', and obviously did not regard himself as a clothier.[130] By the late eighteenth century, however, the Norwich trade was in the hands of a few large merchant manufacturers who performed both functions. The same is true in the case of the Yorkshire industry, first in the worsted branch and later in the woollen cloth branch.[131] These developments have normally been seen in the context of the merchant taking over the activities of the manufacturer. In the restructuring of England's relationship with the Dutch staplemarket, it seems that the reverse process of manufacturer becoming merchant was prominent in the early stages.

A sequence of organisational changes in the woollen export trade thus emerges. The decline of the Merchant Adventurers and the English factor in Holland undertaking sales on commission made way in the late seventeenth and early eighteenth centuries for the Dutch merchant who took woollens on his own account. By the 1730s, evidence of commission sales in Holland which led to prolonged dealings is scarce and those who continued to trade on this basis, such as the Yorkshire merchant clothier George Stansfield, found themselves in growing difficulties.[132] Traditional methods of dealing and foreign commission sales persisted in more distant and less predictable markets, such as Portugal and the Levant, each with its own colony of merchants and factors.[133] But in the trade with Holland and nearby Europe, the new pattern of trading involved the transfer of risk to the Dutch side, with the consequent tying-up of Dutch capital in stocks. It may further have involved a narrowing of profit margins. Low or falling woollen prices and an overstocked market may account for the apparent need of the Dutch woollen merchant to reduce costs. In any event, it is clear that he increasingly tended to correspond directly with manufacturers to the exclusion of the general merchant or wholesale dealer, and, in a real sense, this represents the logical conclusion of the deregulation process.

[130] Brants 928, John Morter, Norwich, to D. Leeuw, Amsterdam, 7 September 1707.
[131] J. H. Clapham, 'The Transference of the Worsted Industry from Norfolk to the West Riding', *Economic Journal*, 20 (1910), p. 198, n. 2; H. Heaton, *Yorkshire Woollen and Worsted Industries*, pp. 300, 388; Smail, *Merchants, Markets and Manufacture*, ch. 3.
[132] Smail, *Merchants, Markets and Manufacture*, pp. 15–16, 25–6.
[133] H. E. S. Fisher, *Portugal Trade*, p. 98; R. Davis, *Aleppo and Devonshire Square. English Traders in the Levant in the Eighteenth Century*, 1967, chs. 5 and 6; R. G. Wilson, *Gentlemen Merchants*, p. 47.

The new pattern of marketing, of course, had important, even crucial, implications for industrial development in the long term. Changes in the 'mode of marketing', as John Smail suggests, prepared the way for changes in the mode of production in the late eighteenth century, in the shift from Smithian to Schumpeterian growth. Direct contacts between producers and overseas buyers and the rationalisation of merchant networks led to aggregate capital saving, the development of more rigorous production standards and supply schedules, and the tightening of entrepreneurial control in general.[134] Closer relationships between producers and merchants became especially marked in Yorkshire, whose merchant–entrepreneurs were much more ready to explore new market opportunities than their London counterparts.[135] The manufacturers of Norwich, although responsive to changes in fashion, depended too much on London wholesalers to match orders with production successfully.[136] The disintegration of the older nexus of company trading, metropolitan control, and dependence on the Dutch staplemarket released powerful energies for change, but not before Dutch capital and financial expertise had entered the mainstream of London's commercial life.

[134] Smail, *Merchants, Markets and Manufacture*, chs. 2, 3, 8. Samuel Hill, a pre-eminent merchant manufacturer, produced kerseys in nine different grades to facilitate his correspondents' orders (p. 34).
[135] Ibid., pp. 150–1; R. G. Wilson, 'The Supremacy of the Yorkshire Cloth Industry in the Eighteenth Century', in Harte & Ponting (eds.), *Textile History and Economic History*, p. 245.
[136] Smail, *Merchants, Markets and Manufacture*, p. 128.

5 Import substitution and European linen imports

The main stimulus behind commercial growth and restructuring during the long seventeenth century, it has been argued, was an increase in demand, especially for the products of the New World and Asia. Amongst other things, it was the growing demand for imports, as we have seen, which undermined the traditional model of regulated company trading typified by the Merchant Adventurers and their export trade with Europe, and generated major political tensions in the pre-Civil-War decades.[1] The inevitable balance of payments problems which followed in the wake of rising imports generated a search for radical solutions, including the expansion of re-exports and the provision of shipping services under the stimulus of the Navigation Acts. In effect, both involved a novel form of import substitution in which English colonies were substituted for foreign countries as sources of supply, and English ships and commercial services replaced those of foreigners, principally the Dutch.[2]

The conventional response to problems of import-led growth, however, was a rising demand for the protection and encouragement of home industry. A strong emphasis on protectionism was already apparent in the revisions carried out to the 1660 Book of Rates, but the years 1670–1 seem to mark a turning point in parliament's attitude to the balance of trade. Hitherto, fiscal and commercial interests had run parallel, but henceforth, the Commons became more concerned with the balance of trade and the encouragement of native manufactures.[3] The post-Restoration

---

[1] K. N. Chaudhuri, *Trading World*, p. 3; R. Brenner, 'The Social Basis of English Commercial Expansion, 1550–1650', *JEH*, 32 (1972).

[2] In Fisher's words, 'the great import substitution measures of the seventeenth century were not protective duties but the Navigation Acts'. The protection of shipping against Dutch competition preoccupied the Committee for Trade during the commercial crisis of the 1620s, but it was Dutch penetration of the West Indian and colonial carrying trades during the 1640s, when the English were otherwise distracted, that brought matters to a head, in the Act of 1651 (F. J. Fisher, 'London as an "Engine of Economic Growth"', pp. 190–1; Harper, *English Navigation Laws*, p. 36; Brenner, *Merchants and Revolution*, pp. 600, 625–8).

[3] Chandaman, *English Public Revenue*, pp. 12, 16.

surge in colonial and Asian imports coincided with a marked decline in population, and complaints were heard of the underconsumption of home-produced goods, especially of farm products and textiles, as imports increased. In 1669, the House of Lords Committee on the Decay of Rents and Trade noted that 'The gentry and generality of people [were] living beyond their fortunes by which the consumptive trade is greater than that of the manufacture exported.'[4] Cloth exports were reduced to one-third of the value exported in 1630. The increased consumption of French luxuries and imported groceries thus took on a particularly menacing aspect, and, in 1678, imports of French wines, brandies, silks and linens were prohibited. In the longer term, strategic adjustments were made to the structure of Anglo-Irish trade to compensate for the loss of French linens, to reduce imports of Irish woollens, and to encourage the export of raw wool to England alone, a policy which was 'in some respects colonial'.[5] Imports of Irish linen and yarn were exempted from duty from 1696, and, in 1699, the export of Irish woollens was banned, except to England, where they incurred a prohibitive duty. By the end of the decade, import duties on a wide range of manufactured imports from Europe had been raised to new high levels.[6] It was the flood of imported Indian calicoes in the 1680s and '90s, however, which crystallised views in England on the issue of industrial protectionism. It was out of these debates, and the woollen industry's campaign for a prohibition, that the disadvantages of commercial monopoly were widely canvassed. By 1700, mercantilist policy had moved from an obsession with the balance of trade towards industrial protectionism.[7]

As we have already noted, the substantial raising of the general tariff level during the 1690s was an integral part of a piecemeal policy of import substitution which matured over a much longer period, which was governed by more than fiscal necessity.[8] In an economy subject to serious balance of payments constraints, such as those operating during the Anglo-French wars of 1689–1713, import savings or a major boost to export earnings were needed.[9] Adam Smith, indeed, referred to both policy objectives as the 'twin engines' of political economy under the mercantile

---

[4] J. Thirsk & J. P. Cooper, *Seventeenth Century Economic Documents*, Oxford, 1972, p. 68.

[5] Cullen, *Anglo-Irish Trade*, p. 2.   [6] Davis, 'Rise of Protection', pp. 306–7.

[7] P. J. Thomas, *East India Trade*, ch. 1.

[8] See above, chapter 2, pp. 49–52. The word 'policy' is used here to indicate a series of measures, usually discrete or disconnected legislative acts, which nevertheless possess a degree of underlying coherence in their acceptance of some of the central tendencies of mercantilist thought; it does not refer to a pre-existing 'Industrial Policy' formulated by ministers, which clearly did not exist.

[9] On the theory of import substitution, see J. Eatwell, 'Import Substitution and Export-led Growth', in J. Eatwell, M. Milgate and P. Newman (eds.), *The New Palgrave. The World of Economics*, 1987, pp. 345–8.

system.[10] Falling woollen prices and increased competition amongst European textile producers made the latter an unlikely prospect during the late seventeenth and early eighteenth centuries, but, although the chief emphasis during these years fell on import saving, this was increasingly linked with complementary measures designed to promote exports, where appropriate.

Import substitution involved the development of home industries within the three kingdoms which would replace imported products so that 'the monopoly of the home market is more or less secured to [them]'.[11] The most important were linen, paper, silk and, of course, cotton, but others included ceramics, glass, dyestuffs and several branches of the luxury trades. Duty increases, embargoes and prohibitions might be imposed against the rival foreign product, while efforts were made to attract foreign craftsmen and technical knowledge from Europe. At the same time, appropriate export promotion policies or controls might be applied, including direct subsidies or bounties on manufactured exports as well as export prohibitions and other restrictions designed to retain local raw materials for domestic use.[12] Linen, canvas and sailcloth formed perhaps the most important single group of import substitution industries, to which this entire range of policy instruments was applied. Although the framing of protectionist measures owed much to a variety of contingent circumstances including revenue needs, the interests of rival commercial and industrial interest groups, and the politics of the British internal market, it is nevertheless possible to identify several coherent elements in parliament's adoption of a strategy of import substitution after 1689.[13] Although a majority of statesmen may have taken no interest in economic policy as such, there is clear evidence that the first Chairman of the Commission for Trade and Plantations, Lord Bridgewater, was exploring plans to develop home industries while composing his report on the 'State of the Trade of the Kingdom' in 1697.[14]

Commercial writers were quick to point out that linen-based products constituted the most valuable item on the import account from Europe, with a significant potential for import-saving.[15] The bulk were imported from Holland and Germany, although, as Defoe noted, 'England does as

[10] A. Smith, *Wealth of Nations*, p. 197.   [11] Ibid., p. 198.
[12] Gomes, *Foreign Trade*, pp. 82–3.
[13] O'Brien, Griffiths and Hunt, 'Political Components of the Industrial Revolution', pp. 397, 416.
[14] See below, p. 173. O'Brien, Griffiths and Hunt have made a careful survey of statesmen's papers for the early eighteenth century, and find no evidence of ministerial involvement in economic policy; but perhaps it would be unwise to turn this into a generalisation ('Political Components of the Industrial Revolution', p. 416, n. 92).
[15] See, for example, J. Gee, *The Trade and Navigation of Great Britain Considered*, 1738, pp. 112–13; Defoe, *Plan*, pp. 154–9.

it were ravage the whole spinning world for linen.'[16] On the basis of the official values, over one-third of English imports from Holland consisted of linens of various types, but the true proportion may have been higher, bearing in mind the tendency for linens to be underrated.[17] Furthermore, the overall trend in total imports from Holland closely follows that exhibited by this particular branch of trade during the eighteenth century. It is therefore with some justification that the fortunes of the Anglo-Dutch linen trade have been seen as symptomatic of those of England's imports from the Dutch staplemarket in general, and, more than this, of the changing position which the Republic came to occupy in European commercial affairs.[18]

The consumption of household linens also reveals much of interest to the social historian. Their possession offered scope for accumulation, social differentiation and the 'construction of particular styles of domestic environments, capable of translating discourses of manners, cleanliness, and diet...into material form'.[19] Linen goods were frequently handed down from one generation to the next, and the second-hand market served to link poorer consumers with the tastes of the better-off. In many parts of Britain, country people produced a coarse, heavy fabric for their own use, as John Marshall noticed while touring Scotland, where they 'dress it, spin it, weave it and bleach it, all in their own families'.[20] The same was true of several English counties and regions, including East Anglia, Kent, the south-west, Lancashire, Yorkshire and the north-east.[21] The range of types and qualities, however, was extremely wide and, in 1700, the better grades were obtainable only as European imports. During the course of the eighteenth century, it seems that the replacement demand for linens increased, while falling prices, at least before the 1740s, may have widened their consumption. Paradoxically, the evidence of probate inventories shows that the proportion of wealth represented in household linens declined between the late sixteenth and

---

[16] Defoe, *Plan*, p. 207. [17] Clark, *Guide*, p. 17. See also below, Table 5.1 and its notes.
[18] Outlined in Part I of C. H. Wilson, *Anglo-Dutch Commerce*.
[19] P. Glennie, 'The Social Shape of the Market for Domestic Linens in Early Modern England', unpublished working paper presented to the Conference on 'Clothing and Consumption in England and America, 1600 1800', Victoria and Albert Museum, London, June 1992, p. 3; L. Weatherill, *Consumer Behaviour and Material Culture in Britain, 1660–1760*, 1988, p. 156.
[20] Quoted in W. G. Rimmer, *Marshall's of Leeds, Flax Spinners, 1788–1886*, Cambridge, 1960, p. 1.
[21] N. Evans, *The East Anglian Linen Industry. Rural Industry and Local Economy, 1500–1850*, Aldershot, 1985, ch. 1; N. B. Harte, 'The Rise of Protection and the English Linen Trade', in Harte & Ponting (eds.), *Textile History and Economic History*, pp. 102 3; D. J. Ormrod, 'Industry: 1640 1800', in W. A. Armstrong (ed.), *The Economy of Kent, 1640–1914*, Aldershot, 1995, pp. 98 100.

the early seventeenth centuries, at a time when other sources indicate that their consumption was clearly growing.[22] In 1738, a London dealer told a House of Commons committee that English consumption had doubled since 1700.[23] The most plausible interpretation of these trends would suggest that people were purchasing new linen in greater quantity and discarding it more readily, as the second-hand market contracted. The contemporary case for import-saving must be understood in the light of these developing consumption patterns.

The linen trade anatomised

Linen products met a variety of needs, as clothing, bedding, tabling and upholstery, while the coarser types were used for sacking and as wrappers for trade goods. Canvas was used for ships' sails and bagging, and during the seventeenth century replaced wooden panels as a painting support for artists' work. Unsurprisingly, the 1660 Book of Rates listed over fifty-four different varieties, of which a number could be further subdivided, particularly the category known as 'narrow Germany'. By the early eighteenth century, the number had expanded to take account of the 'striped, spotted and flowered lawns and cambrics, which are imported here in considerable quantities, and sold at great prices', and the 'striped linens for wastcoats and breeches' which the perplexed Commissioners of Customs noted were increasingly being brought from Holland.[24] These shifts in demand, of course, were partly a consequence of the spread of East Indian textiles which transformed European tastes in dress and furnishings. In England, as elsewhere in Europe, the attempt to ban the use of the offending textiles encouraged local producers to develop calico substitutes, including linens, cottons and mixtures.[25]

Customs officials and administrators were indeed faced with an intricate problem (which has been passed on to historians attempting to reconstruct the trade) when confronted with new types of linens and

---

[22] C. Shammas, *The Preindustrial Consumer in England and America*, Oxford, 1990, pp. 172–3; Glennie, 'Market for Domestic Linens', pp. 6–11; L. Weatherill, 'Consumer Behaviour, Textiles and Dress in the Late Seventeenth and Early Eighteenth Centuries', *Textile History*, 22 (1991), Table 2A, p. 302.

[23] Harte, 'Rise of Protection', p. 102.

[24] PRO T1/106, Presentment touching the duties on thread and tape, and Holland and Germany Linen. From the Commissioners of the Customs to the Lord High Treasurer, 1707/8. Reprinted in Clark, *Guide*, p. 59.

[25] B. Lemire, 'East Indian Textiles and the Flowering of European Popular Fashions, 1600–1800', in S. Cavaciocchi (ed.), *Prodotti e Techniche d'Oltremare nelle Economie Europee secc. XIII–XVIII*, Prato, 1998, p. 523; B. Lemire, *Fashion's Favourite. The Cotton Trade and the Consumer in Britain, 1660–1800*, Oxford, 1991, ch. 1.

changes in the quality of the older varieties which had to be accommodated within the existing categories. The former presented fewer problems as new labels could be created retrospectively with little difficulty.
The Customs Ledger for 1700 contains entries for only three different
types of Russian linen but, by 1726, entries had expanded to include
broad, narrow, striped and stained varieties of 'Russia' and 'Muscovia'
linen as well as Russian Diapers and Sailcloth. The latter problem, that
of quality changes, is less straightforward, particularly as it is connected
with the incidence of import duties. Because the amount of duty to be
paid was calculated as a percentage of a commodity's 'value' as laid down
in the Book of Rates compiled in 1660, which remained in use throughout the eighteenth century, importing merchants could use the pretext
that the quality of a particular type of linen had declined since 1660 in
order to obtain a reduction of the percentage duty. It is therefore difficult
to identify genuine quality changes. Furthermore, comparison of prices
for different types of linen is complicated by the fact that merchants usually priced their linen by the piece rather than the ell, and the former
unlike the latter was not a constant unit of measurement.[26] Several other
measures were also in use. Historians wishing to analyse and quantify the
trade must therefore rely on the official values drawn up in the 1690s.
Although these do not truly represent current prices, they approach them
more closely than those laid down in the Book of Rates (see Table 5.1).[27]

Imported linens ranged from fine-quality Dutch and Flemish damask
which might cost as much as twelve shillings per ell down to the coarsest
borelaps which might be had for a few pence.[28] Table 5.1 shows that the
official values constitute only a rough guide to real values, and underestimate the latter in many instances.[29] The implications of this will be
discussed later, but for the moment the table may be useful in showing
the different types and prices of linen imported.[30] Little is known of the
Dutch linen industry. Haarlem had its linen tape and thread manufactures, and linen cloth was produced in Alkmaar and Amsterdam, and in
the provinces of Overyssel and North Brabant, but in what quantities it
is impossible to say.[31] Relative insignificance may explain the elusiveness

---

[26] H. Crouch, *Complete View of the British Customs*, 1746, vol. II, pp. 122–57, 321.
[27] Clark, *Guide*, p. 10.   [28] Defoe, *Plan*, p. 208.
[29] In the case of linen, the official values and prices given in Table 5.1 represent the price
in the country from which the linen was imported, rather than retail prices in England
(see notes to table).
[30] This is not exhaustive but shows a cross-section of types and prices.
[31] Treated in J. G. van Bel, *De Linnenhandel van Amsterdam in de XVIII Eeuw*, Amsterdam,
1940; Teylers Museum, *Textiel aan het Spaarne. Haarlem: van linnen damast tot zijden
linten*, Amsterdam, 1995, especially the essay by D. M. Mitchell, 'The Linen Damask
Trade in Haarlem. Its Products and its Markets', pp. 5–33. In Overyssel, linen

Illustration 5.1 J. van Ruisdael, view of Haarlem (detail), 1670s, showing the bleaching fields (oil on canvas).

of the industry, and, in comparing the linen manufactures of Germany with those of Holland, the Commissioners of Customs wrote in 1708 of 'the great extent of territory in Germany, beyond the Netherlands, and the vastly exceeding number of manufactures in the linen trade of one country the beyond the other, for quantity'.[32] The European linen trade of the early eighteenth century was perhaps similar to the woollen cloth trade of the previous century in that it formed 'something like a single theatre of economic operations' based on a degree of international specialisation.[33] Holland concentrated on the bleaching of linen rather

manufacture was established at Kampen and Zwolle, but these centres, like Haarlem, were in decline before the opening of the eighteenth century. In the Twentse region, however, the manufacture experienced considerable growth up to about 1725. In Brabant, production was carried on at Helmond and Eindhoven, and the eighteenth-century situation here was one of sharp decline (Joh. de Vries, *Economische Achteruitgang*, p. 119).

[32] T1/106 Presentment. Printed in Clark, *Guide*, p. 60.

[33] C. H. Wilson, 'Cloth Production', p. 209.

Table 5.1 *Imported linens, types and quantities, 1700–1761 (prices per English ell)*

	Official values	Real (wholesale) prices						
	1700	1700s	1710s	1720s	1730s	1740s	1750s	1761
Hollands								
striped	3s 4½d		3s 4d – 5s					
plain, unspecified	3s				*4s 6d – 5s*			
menage					*2s 8d*	*2s – 4s 6d*		
freeze					*3s 4d – 6s 8d*	*4s 6d – 7s 6d*		
gulix					*4s – 6s*	*3s – 8s 4d*		
Tabling								
Holland damask	3s 5¼d							
Holland diaper	2s 8d	1s 10½d						
Silesia damask	2s 8d							
Silesia diaper	2s 2¼d							
Flanders	1s 11¾d							
Ghentish	1s 6d				3s 6d – 5s			
Cambrics	1s 5d			*4s 2d – 5s 5d*				
Lawns (Silesia)	1s 4¼d							1s 9d
Sailcloth								
Hollands duck	1s 1d		1s 6½d – 2s 1¾d		*2s 4s 4d – 4s 10d*			
Russia duck	10d							
Middle grades								
Germany broad	1s							
dowlas	11½d		11½d – 1s 6¼d					1s 2d, 1s 7d
Germany narrow	9d	8½–8¾d	8¼–8½d					10¾d, 1s 2d
ozenbriggs	7d	8–8¼d						11½d
Napkining								
Holland damask	1s 6¾d							

Holland diaper	$11\frac{1}{4}$d			
Silesia damask	$11\frac{1}{4}$d			
Silesia diaper	$7\frac{1}{2}$d			
Canvas				
drilling	10d			...... 1s 5d
hessens	$5\frac{1}{2}$d	$7\frac{3}{4}$–11d	...... 6–7d	$9\frac{1}{2}$d
spruce	4d			...... $4\frac{1}{4}$–6d
Lower grades				
E. Country narrow	6d			
ticks, E. Country	$7\frac{1}{2}$d			
Muscovia narrow	$4\frac{1}{4}$d			
borelaps	4d			

Notes to accompany Table 5.1

1 *Official values*

These are taken from the Customs Ledger for 1700 (Customs 3/4) from entries relating to Holland, where possible. Two limits of value were set in the ledgers, but, in practice, the middle value was always taken as the basis for the commercial statistics which they were used to provide; it is this which is shown here. The values were said to represent the first cost of imports in the country of origin, and indeed it is this which they approach most closely. (See Clark, *Guide*, pp. 9–10, 17, s.9.) Those linens valued by the 'Hundred' have been converted to value per ell on the basis of the 'Hundred' = 120 ells, except for Dowlas which contained 106 per 'Hundred'.

2 *Wholesale prices, 1707–43, taken from the Archief Brants, Gemeente Archief, Amsterdam*

Unless italicised, these consist of the importing merchant's selling price in England. They rarely represent the final retail price, as merchants often sold to linen drapers who in turn supplied final consumers. Italicised prices represent the wholesale price in Holland, being taken from English importing merchants' and drapers' orders placed with J. I. de Neufville of Amsterdam. Prices have been taken from the correspondence of the following merchants:

1707–9 & 1714–15, Sir John Elwill, Exeter; Edmund Cock, Exeter; Peter Southey, Exeter (Brants 924).

1726, Thomas Watson Jr, Berwick on Tweed (Brants 1329).

1730–2, Coulter and Townshend, Harry Gough, Christian Levie, Allix and Le Conte, London (Brants 1344).

1734, John Eccleston, London (Brants 1344).

1740, Nash & Eddowes, John Antrobus, London (Brants 1344).

1743, Edmund Barham, Thomas & John Roe, Birmingham (Brants 1330).

3 *Wholesale prices, 1761, taken from the House of Commons Report on the State of the Linen Trade (1773)*

These are taken from Appendix 8 of this report, 'Invoice of Samples of Foreign Linens bought by John Ellis Esquire, from Messrs. Nash, Eddowes, and Petrie, in 1761, for the Linen Board of Ireland'. These must represent a wholesale price in England. Nash, Eddowes, and Martin are listed in J. Mortimer's *Universal Director* (1763) as 'wholesale linen drapers'.

than its manufacture, and Dutch merchants brought linen from West-phalia, Silesia, Juliers, Flanders and Brabant to be bleached at Haarlem. As Joseph Marshall put it, these were then 'produced in commerce under the name of Dutch linens; for this whitening adds a new price to the linnen when it is of a good fabric'.[34] Thus merchants paid particular attention to the quality of the bleach, and one wrote, typically, 'as the well bleaching is a great addition to the value of linnen, would not have the lawns so hurried as to hinder their being done in the best manner'.[35] These Haarlem bleached linens are the 'Hollands' listed in Table 5.1, which were used for high-quality shirts and 'for shifts and sheets and such like fine uses'.[36] They constituted the bulk of the English linen import trade from Holland. Diapers, damasks and lawns came from Silesia, Lusatia and Saxony, and either came to England directly from Hamburg or via Holland if they had been bleached at Haarlem. The higher grades of these were used for shirts and tablecloths, the lower for napkins and towelling.

Similar use was made of fine linens from Flanders – the cambrics from Lisle, Brussels and Valenciennes, and those which, after passing through Haarlem, were known as Ghentish Hollands. The import of cambrics from France was banned and prohibitive duties had been placed on other French linens in 1685, but a sizeable smuggling trade in these existed, and Defoe declared that England and Ireland imported above £200,000-worth of cambrics from Europe per year.[37] The best sailcloth came from Holland under the name 'Hollands duck', but increasing quantities were supplied by Russian and Baltic producers. The latter specialised in canvas which was imported from Danzig, Konigsberg, Stettin and Stralsund.[38] The bulk of English linen imports, however, consisted of what Defoe called 'sorts of middling fineness' produced in the Elbe region and entered in the customs ledgers as 'Germany narrow'. These were known to the trade under a variety of names such as tecklenburghs, hamborough, dowlas and ozenbriggs (which sometimes passed as a coarser sort) and were purchased by 'the meanest sort of people'.[39] Finally came the coarsest linens such as hinderlands, borelaps, East Country narrow, ticking which was used for covering mattresses and crocus for making sacks.[40] Linen imported from continental Europe was supplemented by the growing manufactures of Ireland and Scotland, providing linens of the

[34] Marshall, *Travels*, vol. I, p. 232.
[35] Brants 1344, J. Badcock, London, to J. I. de Neufville, Amsterdam, 19 March 1745.
[36] Defoe, *Plan*, p. 208.   [37] Ibid., p. 209.   [38] Ibid., p. 208.
[39] PRO CO388/1OH57, Some considerations relating to the customs upon Holland Linen; Memorial from Mr Beck, 10 December 1706.
[40] *RHC*, vol. II, Report from the Committee relating to the Linen Trade, 11 March 1744, p. 68.

Illustration 5.2 J. Luiken, sketch for *De Bleeker* (the bleacher), for the *Spiegel van het Menselijk Bedrijf*, Amsterdam, 1718 (pen and wash).

middle grades. The Irish and Scottish bleacheries could not equal those of Haarlem for whiteness, however, and Joseph Marshall claimed that 'whole shiploads' of the finer cloths were brought to Holland for bleaching.[41] Nonetheless, Irish and Scottish fabrics were to prove highly competitive

[41] Marshall, *Travels*, vol. I, p. 48.

with continental linens in the middle and lower price ranges, particularly German 'osnaburghs' or ozenbriggs, which formed the bulk of the re-export trade.[42] As early as 1719, we hear of a merchant who 'lives in Ireland & comes over here [to England] to sell linnens two or three times in a year'.[43]

Re-export markets in the American mainland colonies and plantations were expanding vigorously during the eighteenth century. It was initially the cheaper grades of German linen which were used to clothe the slave population, in a trade which benefited from the stimulus of drawback payments. British and Irish linen producers much resented their lack of protection in colonial markets, but the situation was rectified when bounties were granted on the export of various types of linen in 1743 and 1745.[44] The drawback was retained, partly because of anxieties about the possible loss of German markets for English woollens and other manu-factures sent in exchange, and partly because too high a level of duty and other charges would encourage the colonial population to produce their own fabrics, to the detriment of merchants and manufacturers at home.[45] As the plantation system expanded, supplies of European linens were increasingly supplemented by English, Scottish and Irish substi-tutes, before cheap English cottons became available in the later part of the century.[46] By 1750, exports of English linen together with re-exports of Irish linen were valued at over £200,000, the bulk of which were sent to America. Fifteen years later, the figure was close on £500,000.[47] The process of import substitution in the linen trade cannot be understood in isolation from re-exports and the conflicting needs of producers and consumers within the imperial trading system.

Like the re-export market, the home market for linen was rapidly ex-panding throughout the greater part of the eighteenth century, as many contemporaries realised. 'No People in Europe', wrote Defoe, 'wear and consume so great a quantity of linen, and that quantity so fine in its qual-ity, as the English do.'[48] In spite of this, he added, there could be few countries which manufactured less than England. It seems that Defoe was not merely eulogising on the superior advantages of being an Englishman – he was, in the late 1720s, noting the visible results of

[42] *RHC*, vol. II, Report . . . relating to the Linen Trade, pp. 67–8.
[43] Brants 927, M. Bovell, London, to David Leeuw, Amsterdam, 4 August 1719.
[44] *RHC*, vol. II, Report . . . relating to the Linen Trade, p. 67.
[45] O'Brien, Griffiths and Hunt, 'Political Components of the Industrial Revolution', pp. 410–11; J. Horner, *The Linen Trade of Europe during the Spinning-Wheel Period*, Belfast, 1920, p. 227.
[46] Cullen, *Anglo-Irish Trade*, pp. 62–3.   [47] Horner, *Linen Trade*, pp. 231–3.
[48] Defoe, *Plan*, p. 212; PRO Chatham Papers, 30/8, *c.* 1755, fo. 137, 'The people of this country in general wear finer linens than any nation in Europe.'

what many economic historians have long regarded as a key characteristic of the eighteenth-century economy: that the combination of low food prices and a slackening in the rate of population growth during the period *c.* 1680–1750 had created a 'rise of internal demand which permanently affected the level of expectation of most classes in English Society'.[49] The most substantial growth of the domestic market occurred after 1700, and, after food, 'there was no product more likely to reflect an increase in real wages than textiles'.[50] Clearly, it might be expected that the consumption of linens would rise. The English linen industry, it was stated in a Parliamentary Report of 1756, produced about 25.8 million yards.[51] The home industry, however, produced very poor-quality linens known as 'huccabacks' which did not seriously compete with imported linens.[52]

The changing course of linen imports

Defoe, whose enthusiasm for quantification normally ran high, had to admit that 'it is indeed impossible to make an estimate of the quantity of linen imported from all these places [in Europe] into Great Britain and Ireland'. The task is indeed difficult, as linens were entered in a variety of measurements – yards, ells, bolts, pieces and by weight. The Inspector General's official values, on the other hand, tend to underestimate wholesale prices, as we have seen.[53] Hollands linen and cambrics are the categories most seriously affected, while Germany narrow linen may be most accurate. Total linen imports from Holland therefore appear smaller than their true level by perhaps as much as two-thirds, while those from Germany are probably more authentic.[54] However, the official values do possess the merit of reducing a number of non-comparable quantities into a single unit of measurement – the constant price. This is particularly useful for indicating changes in the volume of trade and enables us to make rough comparisons between the quantities of linen imported from different European suppliers.[55] Although the Inspector General's

---

[49] A. H. John, 'Aspects of Economic Growth in the First Half of the Eighteenth Century', *Economica*, 28 (1961), and reprinted in Carus-Wilson, *Essays*, vol. II, p. 373.

[50] John, 'Aspects of Economic Growth', in Carus-Wilson, *Essays*, vol. II, p. 368.

[51] Quoted by Horner, *Linen Trade*, p. 233, and C. Gill, *The Rise of the Irish Linen Industry*, Oxford, 1925, p. 11 (compared to the 30m. yards imported from the continent, 12.2m. yards from Ireland, and 12m yards from Scotland).

[52] *RHC*, vol. II, Report . . . relating to the Linen Trade, p. 67.

[53] See above, pp. 148–9.

[54] On the valuation of Dutch linen, see also T1/106 Presentment, printed in Clark, *Guide*, p. 69.

[55] Minor adjustments were made in the valuations over the period covered, affecting the categories Germany broad and narrow, and these are practically self-cancelling.

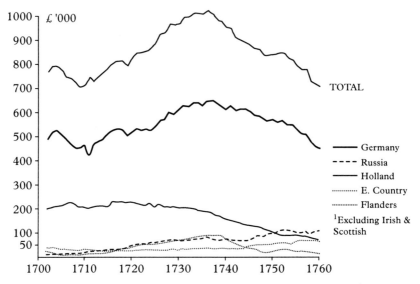

Figure 5.1 English imports of European linens, 1702–1760[1] (Official values, £'000: nine-year moving averages)

figures do not lend themselves to refined measurement, they nevertheless highlight the general trends involved, which are indicated in Figure 5.1 and Table 5.2.

These figures, when set alongside estimates for Scottish, English and Irish production, confirm the general picture of an expanding domestic and colonial market for linens which emerges from other sources. Imports from continental Europe increased rapidly up to the mid 1730s, after which a marked decline sets in. The shortfall in foreign imports, which was of the order of about 10 million yards for the period 1731–80, was more than made up by an increased contribution from the Irish and Scottish industries. English imports of Irish linen increased from 3.8 million yards in 1730 to 13.1 million yards in 1760 which alone was sufficient to offset any decline in total linen imports.[56] Although English consumption of Scottish linen cannot be precisely measured, the great bulk of 'stamped' Scottish linen was sold in England, and the available figures suggest a rate of growth only slightly less impressive than that of Irish production during the same period, from 3.8 to 11.7 million yards. English linen production and sales are not recorded, but minimum estimates for these decades suggest that production almost doubled, rising from 14.4

[56] Cullen, *Anglo-Irish Trade*, p. 60, and, below, Table 5.5.

Table 5.2 *Retained imports and re-exports of foreign linens, 1700–1765 (£'000 official values)*

	Foreign linen imports	retained imports	re-exports	re-exports as a % of total linen imports	% of re-exports comprised by:	
					'Germany' linen	'Hollands' linen
1700	887	698	189	21.3	45.6	10.9
1706	581	488	93	16.0	54.9	7.1
1710	620	476	144	23.2	53.4	7.9
1715	834	639	195	23.4	64.4	8.2
1720	669	526	143	21.3	61.9	8.2
1725	1,030	681	349	33.9	64.5	6.4
1730	1,016	733	283	27.9	72.7	5.2
1735	1,157	853	304	26.3	67.4	4.9
1740	1,001	668	333	33.3	73.7	4.7
1745	790	609	181	22.9	75.0	4.6
1750	905	654	251	27.7	69.8	3.2
1755	812	536	276	34.0	74.3	2.1
1760	687	251	436	63.5	66.4	1.7
1765	655	406	249	38.0	59.1	1.3

Source: Cust. 3.

to 26.8 million yards (Table 5.5). Clearly, the market was an extremely buoyant one.

On average, the colonial market absorbed around one quarter of the foreign linens imported during the first half of the eighteenth century, although the proportion was a fluctuating one. The available statistics suggest a clear pattern of growth up to the 1740s followed by a marked setback before an upsurge in the later 1750s. Re-exports, it seems, were growing at a more rapid rate than imports of foreign linens, consisting mainly of German 'ozenbriggs', destined for the plantations.[57] German fabrics came to form an increasing proportion of all linen re-exports, while Hollands linen declined – according to the official statistics. However, the dwindling volume of this latter branch of trade may have been balanced by illegal shipments. Sir William Yonge, one of the Commissioners for Trade, received notice from an informant in Exeter, in 1737, that 'linens are sent from Holland to our Colonies in America without touching at any port in England, by which the Crown is defrauded of $2\frac{1}{2}$ per cent back upon exportation'.[58] As far as the cheaper grades were concerned, West Indian planters claimed before a Commons Committee in 1744 that the majority of plantation owners took linens on their own account from English correspondents in exchange for sugar and rum, and it was therefore in their interests to prevent a clandestine trade.[59] However, the illegal shipment of high-priced linens to the mainland colonies was a different matter, as witnesses before the 1751 Commons Committee on the Linen Trade testified. John Fell, a Lancashire linen merchant lately returned from America, insisted that colonial vessels commonly imported checked and striped linens directly from Holland to New York, and had been prevented from selling British checks by the quantity of Dutch linen thus brought in. This trade, he thought, had increased in recent years.[60] Allowance must be made for the interest of the petitioners in extending the bounty granted on the export of British and Irish linens to checked and striped varieties.[61] Nonetheless, it appears that a sizeable unrecorded transatlantic trade in medium-priced Dutch linens existed alongside the more substantial export of cheaper goods, mainly German, to the plantation colonies.

It is only against the background of growing home and re-export markets for linen that changes in Holland's role as an intermediary supplier

[57] Ibid., pp. 67, 71.
[58] PRO CO388/38 Y83, Letter from anonymous writer from Exeter, 27 April 1737; PRO 30/8, Chatham Papers, vol. 81, fo. 138, n.d. ('1755' pencilled in margin).
[59] RHC, vol. II, Report . . . relating to the Linen Trade, p. 71.
[60] RHC, vol. II, Report from the Committee relating to Chequed and Striped Linens, 26 April 1751, p. 292.
[61] JHC, 26, 26 April 1751, p. 198.

can be properly explained. Charles Wilson and subsequent writers identified the forging of 'direct trade' links between England and Germany, together with increasing competition from the growing Irish and Scottish industries, as the principal elements in the weakening of the Dutch linen trade and the intermediary role of the staplemarket.[62] Taken by themselves, however, these factors provide an insufficient explanation of the changes that were actually taking place. The expansion of 'direct trade' between England and Hamburg was hardly a novel development in the 1720s and '30s, and a House of Lords report of 1714 indicated that imports of linen from Hamburg alone were clearly greater than those from Holland as early as 1681–8. It is necessary to go back to the 1660s for evidence that linen imports from Holland exceeded those from Germany (Table 5.3). By the opening of the eighteenth century, as Figure 5.1 shows, English linen imports from Germany were already significantly higher than those from Holland, even making allowance for an undervaluation of Hollands linen relative to narrow Germany linen of the order of two-thirds. Imports from Holland stagnated around a level of £200,000 until 1730. A slow decline set in thereafter, such that the 1760 level was almost exactly half that of 1730.

The increased demand for linen called forth an expansion of German imports, but not at the expense of Holland until after 1730, nor by the forging of 'direct trade links' which were in any sense new; for this, one must look to the 1670s and '80s. By the time that effective competition arose from the growing Celtic industries, imports from Germany, like those from Holland a few years earlier, began to decline. Of the improvements made to the Irish manufacture, however, merchants were in no doubt. In 1744, a London dealer wrote, 'the Holland trade at present in England is pretty much at a stand on account of large quantities of Irish linen which exceed the Hollands in every respect except the colour'.[63] The same observations were made in connection with German linen. 'I hope they will come cheaper than they were last year or else our Irish linen will soon ruin the German trade in these parts', wrote John Powys from Shropshire to his Dutch correspondent.[64] Complaints of this kind grew in volume during the 1730s and '40s, and by mid-century it was said that Irish linen cost one third less than linen of an equivalent quality imported from Holland, and that bleaching, previously thought to be

[62] C. H. Wilson, *Anglo-Dutch Commerce*, pp. 11–12, 61. This was also the view of S. C. Regtdoorzee Greup-Roldanus, *Geschiedenis der Haarlemmer Bleekerijen*, 's-Gravenhage, 1936, p. 281. Wilson's account has been repeated by Cullen, *Anglo-Irish Trade*, p. 61; K. H. D. Haley, *The British and the Dutch*, 1988, p. 161; and F. Braudel, *Perspective of the World*, p. 261, amongst others.
[63] Brants 1344, J. J. Battier, London, to de Neufville, Amsterdam, 23 May 1744.
[64] Brants 1348, from J. Powys, Salop, 24 Dec. 1744.

Table 5.3 *Comparison of European sources of imported linen, 1662–1686*

(a) Linen imported into London (£'000, official values), 1662–3 and 1668–9

	1662 3	% of total	1668 9	% of total
France	188.2	35	184.6	32
Holland	160.1	30	162.0	28
Germany	91.3	17	121.6	21
Flanders	85.4	16	99.5	17
Eastland	3.7	1	7.5	2
Russia	0.5	>1	0.5	>1
TOTAL	529.5		576.0	

(b) Linen imports from Holland and Hamburg (London & outports), 1685–6

Holland	Hamburg
1,497,584 ells	1,827,971 ells
2,540 cwt	35,613 cwt
791 bolts	
89 rolls	

Sources:

(a) BL Add Mss 36,785.

(b) *Calendar of House of Lords Mss*, vol. X, new series (1712 14), Historical Manuscripts Commission, 1953, p. 537.

(Pieces converted to ells at the rate 30 ells to the piece, the ell at 45 inches.)

It should be noted that these figures relate to the import trade of London only, but, after 1696, the Customs ledgers show that the metropolis handled the bulk of the linen trade throughout the period, that is, over 75%. This was doubtless true of the seventeenth century when London's predominance was even more marked.

inferior to that of Haarlem, had attained a degree of perfection comparable to the Dutch.[65] A doubtless biased correspondent of the *Gentleman's Magazine* claimed in 1742 that '£5 laid out in Scotch Hollands will go as great a length in wear as £10 or £15 laid out in Dutch Hollands.'[66] The superior wearing qualities of the former were ascribed to the fact that the warp and weft were of the same type of yarn (of 'Home Flax' or the best-quality foreign) whereas the latter contained only a warp of good-quality Flemish yarn and a weft of inferior Silesian yarn 'for cheapness sake'.

Damaging in some degree to the Dutch linen export trade, in that it reduced German dependence upon Holland, was the development, under the guidance of Frederick II, of German bleacheries at Bielefeld and

---

[65] Ibid., from L. Bowles, London, 22 Aug. 1749; Brants 1344, from Nash and Eddowes, London, 12 Mar. 1750.

[66] *Gentleman's Magazine*, 12 (April 1742), p. 192.

Ravensburg. The quality of the bleach produced by these German centres was far inferior to that of Haarlem, however, because of the deficiencies in the lactic acid content of the milk used, and the poor quality of the water supply compared to that of the Haarlem dunes.[67] In fact some bleaching of the cheaper types of linen was undertaken in England, and it seems that this practice was growing and improving.[68] Thomas Lowndes, that vigorous projector and keen observer of commercial affairs, could write optimistically in 1742: 'a great bleaching yard, made last year opposite to Richmond in Surrey proves beyond all manner of doubt that the Thames-Water, in giving linen a fine colour is no way inferior to that of Haarlem, and that we can in every respect equal the Haarlem Bleach'.[69] The growth of rival linen-producing and bleaching industries thus constituted a powerful factor in the decline of the Dutch linen export trade to England after 1730, but one which began to take effect only when German exports of linen were already falling off.

Deserving equal consideration is the gradual expansion of sailcloth and canvas imports from the Baltic, and of coarse linens from Russia throughout the period. The official values show that the latter began to exceed imports from Holland around 1750, while, by 1760, imports of linen from the East Country were about equal in volume to those from Holland. The undervaluation of Hollands linen may, however, exaggerate the rapidity of this convergence, though the movements themselves are clear. This does not represent the growth of direct trade links between England and these countries at the expense of Holland, for Muscovia and East Country linen had never been imported via Holland in quantities of anything more than a few hundred pounds'-worth.[70] Rather it reflects the growth of home industries, especially those of Russia fostered by Peter the Great and his successor, Catherine, during whose reigns skilled foreign craftsmen were encouraged to settle.[71] The statistics of the College of Manufactures for 1761–3 indicate that the Russian linen industry made most progress after 1745; of the fifty-three establishments manufacturing linen in 1763, five had been set up prior to 1731, thirteen during the period 1731–45, and the remaining thirty-five after 1745.[72]

[67] Regtdoorzee Greup-Roldanus, *Haarlemmer Bleekerijen*, p. 280.
[68] See above, p. 144. Significantly, the theft of linen from bleaching grounds was declared a felony without benefit of clergy, in 1731, by 4 Geo. II c. 18.
[69] CO388/40 Aa 61, 'A state of the Cambrick Trade between Great Britain and Flanders', 18 May 1742, memorandum of Thomas Lowndes.
[70] Table 5.3 shows the negligible levels of linen imports from these countries in the 1660s.
[71] Horner, *Linen Trade*, pp. 457–72. Foreign craftsmen were first introduced into linen manufacture in 1697.
[72] R. Portal, 'Manufactures et classes sociales en Russie 18e siècle', *Revue Historique*, 201 (July & Sept.,1948), p. 176.

It is certainly noticeable that Russian linen imports show a marked up-turn after the mid-1740s, following a period of relative stagnation in the late 1720s.

Linens imported from Flanders show a steady growth up to the late 1730s. Thereafter, decline set in, though at an uneven rate, and the over-all pattern is similar to that of German imports, but at a much lower level. However, the true level of Flemish imports may have been significantly higher for two reasons. First, cambrics, which by 1730 formed the bulk of linen imports from Flanders, probably constituted the most undervalued category of linens at a mere 1s 1d per ell. Thomas Lowndes, pleading for an increase in the duty on cambrics, claimed that an ell of cambric was frequently worth 14s or more on import.[73] Second, when linen was smuggled at all, it consisted of the higher-quality French varieties run from France and Flanders. The English vice-consul at Ostend observed that the Flemings 'let no opportunity creape of smuggling into England both linnen & lace. The masters and mariners of British ships constantly load their pockets with lace every voyage and make up two or three pieces of linen each in shirts, which they carry over on freight & even have the boldness to insure their delivery at any house in London.'[74] In fact cambrics were subject to significant duty increases in the 1740s, and this would seem to account for this falling off in the legal Flemish trade.[75] Whether or not the previous rate of growth was maintained by an expansion of the illegal trade is impossible to say, but in view of the comments of Defoe and Mortimer, this is likely.

The impact of duty increases

It is well known that the war years of the 1690s formed the critical pe-riod which saw the transformation of the English tariff structure 'from a generally low-level fiscal system into a moderately high-level system which, though still fiscal in its purposes, had become in practice protec-tive; and which was then endlessly and minutely modified in ways that added marginally to this protective element.'[76] But as Davis himself em-phasised, this general rise exposed, in particular trades, problems which were unimportant when duties were low. It was often these 'minute' modi-fications, as the case of the linen import trade shows, that eroded the small remaining profit margin and set in motion a process of slow decline.

---

[73] CO388/40 Aa 81, State of the Cambric Trade.
[74] CO388/95 I14, Thomas Mortimer, English vice-consul in Ostend, to the Commissioners for Trade, 28 Feb. 1763.
[75] See below, p. 162.   [76] Davis, 'Rise of Protection', p. 307.

The duty increases as they affected linen are shown in Table 5.4. In 1660, all linens were paying a $7\frac{1}{2}$% customs duty. The new Impost of 1690 discriminated between different types, but narrow linens made or bleached in the Low Countries escaped the increase, and the 1692/3 Impost did not affect linens of any type. It was not until 1697 that linen duties were again raised with the New Subsidy, by 5%, whatever their country of origin. The War of the Spanish Succession brought further increases: the One-Third and Two-Thirds Subsidies of 1703 and 1704 added a further 5%. Not surprisingly, this string of Acts provoked consternation amongst foreign suppliers and producers, which was aggravated by a short-term commercial depression affecting English importers. One English merchant ascribed the outcry from Dutch linen suppliers not so much to the actual duty increases which they complained of, but rather to 'a great dulness of trade at present, perceived all over England, and the slow and miserable returns from the country made to the drapers in London'.[77] The re-export trade in linen, he added, was also affected because of the low prices obtained for returns, mainly groceries, made against linens exported to the plantations. To the linen producers of Holland and Overyssel, however, it appeared that the new duty increase was the sole cause of their distress, and the States General sent a special envoy to London to put their case, in December 1706.[78]

By this time, most Dutch linen measured less than $1\frac{1}{4}$ yards in breadth and was paying a nominal duty of $17\frac{1}{2}$% calculated on the basis of values laid down in the 1660 Book of Rates. Although real prices for linen had risen significantly since then, however, relative prices of the Dutch and German product had altered to the disadvantage of the former. In particular, the quality of imported Dutch linens had in general declined, while that of imported German narrow linen was much improved. As the petitioners put it, 'the Germans have quitted their former manufactures of these coarse linens and turned themselves to the fabrique of the finer, which has been a manifest loss to those of the United Provinces'.[79]

---

[77] CO388/10 H57 Mr Beck's Memorial . . . relating to linen duties, 20 Dec. 1706.

[78] *JCTP*, I (1 April 1714), pp. 300, 305, 307, 311, 312, 321.

[79] Dutch manufacturers pointed out in 1707 that in 1640, 'there was scarce any other linen transported from Holland to England but fine linens. But in succeeding years great quantities of coarse linens have been transported from thence so that counting the coarse with the fine and estimating both together they are not worth more than half-a-crown the ell [as distinct from 5s in the Book of Rates] . . . the linens brought from Hambourgh, Salasia, and other parts of Germany were rated only at the value of one shilling and some sorts as sixpence per ell, that the manufacturers of Germany did at that time only fabrique a coarser sort of linen, the finer sort then being brought from Holland and Flanders upon which this disposition in the duties was founded' (Add Mss 10,413, Treasury Papers, vol. I, fo. 77; this is a summary of the memorial from the

Table 5.4 *Duties on foreign linens, 1660–1760*

Act and date passed	duty	%
12 Chas. II c. 4	1660 OLD SUBSIDY	5
	1660 ADDITIONAL DUTY	$2\frac{1}{2}$
2 Wm. & M. s.2 c.4	1690 IMPOST on Linen:	
	– manufactured in the Spanish Netherlands or	
	United Provinces, of 2–3 ells breadth,	
	1s 6d per £ value	$7\frac{1}{2}$
	– ditto, 3 ells or more in breadth, 4s 6d per £ value	$22\frac{1}{2}$
	– other than that manuactured in the Spanish	
	Netherlands or United Provinces, not exceeding	
	$1\frac{1}{8}$ ells in breadth, 9d per £ value	$3\frac{3}{4}$
9 Wm. III c. 23	1697 NEW SUBSIDY	5
2 & 3 Anne c. 9	1703 ONE-THIRD SUBSIDY	$1\frac{2}{3}$
3 & 4 Anne c. 5	1704 TWO-THIRDS SUBSIDY	$3\frac{1}{3}$
7 Anne c. 9	1708 European Linen exempted	
	from Two-Thirds Subsidy	
10 Anne c. 19	1711 NEW DUTY On chequered, striped,	
	printed, painted and stained linen only,	
	3s per £ value	15
12 Anne s.1 c.16	1713 DUTY ON FOREIGN SAILCLOTH	
	1d per ell	10
12 Anne s.2 c.9	1713 ADDITIONAL DUTY On chequered,	
	striped, printed, painted and stained linen only,	
	3s per £ value	15
15 Geo. II c.29	1742 DUTY ON FOREIGN CAMBRICS	
	1s 5d per $6\frac{1}{2}$ ells	$7\frac{1}{12}$
19 Geo. II c. 27	1746 DUTY ON FOREIGN-MADE SAILS	
	1d per ell	10
21 Geo. II c. 2	1747 ADDITIONAL DUTY	5
32 Geo. II c. 10	1759 ADDITIONAL DUTY	5

The Commissioners of Customs were aware of this, and indeed the Inspector General's own commercial statistics incorporated a valuation for Hollands linen 40% lower than that set out in the 1660 Book of Rates, while that for German narrow linen, the staple of the import trade from Germany, was raised by $12\frac{1}{2}$%. But the Customs authorities were unable to persuade the Treasury to revise the Book of Rates, and duties continued to be collected on the basis of out-of-date valuations.

It was to remedy this situation that Dutch linen had been exempted from the 1690 Impost, but, after the increases of 1687–1704, Dutch

merchants and manufacturers of linen in the provinces of Holland and Overyssel by the Commissioners for Trade and Plantations in their 'Memorial relating to linen duties', 17 Jan. 1707).

suppliers claimed that the duties which they were now paying were still disproportionately high compared to the more lightly taxed German equivalent. On Hollands linen, they claimed the duty represented 'One-third of their value which amounts to a prohibition'.[80] This was an exaggeration: even on the basis of the first cost of the product, the 5s. valuation laid down in the Book of Rates did approximate to real prices.[81] For the cheaper varieties, however, the Dutch representations were justifiable: Alkmaar linens which were 'generally used for sheeting and other common uses', for example, were bought for export at sums equivalent to 1s 8d – 2s 7d per ell, and were liable to a duty of $10\frac{1}{2}$d, amounting to 50% of their real value. It was in these goods that the bulk of the trade from Holland consisted, according to the petitioners.[82]

The remedy proposed by the Dutch envoy was that Hollands linen pay an ad valorem duty of one-sixth of the real value to take account of variations in the quality and price of the product.[83] Objections followed from the Hamburg Company and from the Commissioners of Customs, who retorted that merchants could not be trusted to make honest declarations of value: 'very eminent merchants have valued a parcel of goods at the Custom House at £800 for payment of dutys, and have sold the same for £3,000'.[84] The demands of the Envoy Extraordinary for an ad valorem duty, unsurprisingly, met with little success. It was not until the States General sent a second representative, armed with a mild ultimatum, that an impression was made. The States General, he suggested, might be obliged to lay a larger duty on English goods entering the United Provinces, which currently paid less than 5%. English corn and woollen imports into Rotterdam alone, he reminded the government, amounted to 'above £800,000 a year, besides what is imported of lead, tin, East India, Plantation and other goods'.[85] Davenant, when in Holland, had previously reported to Godolphin how the Dutch 'complain very grievously of the high duties laid upon their linens in England... and the People 'tis said are hardly kept from urging for a retaliation by laying high duties upon English Grain, especially malt'.[86] In the event, a compromise was reached: *all* European linen imports were exempted from the

[80] Ibid.
[81] See Table 5.1 and CO388/10 H57 (20 Dec. 1706). Beck stated that 'The linen which is mostly imported, vended and consumed here is bag-hollands and Gulicks, the same sorts being sold at 4s.6d to 7s. per ell.'
[82] CO388/10 H64, Memorial from Mr Taverner, 16 Feb. 1707.
[83] Add Mss 10,453, fo. 77.
[84] PRO T1/160, printed in Clark, *Guide*, p. 61, 19 March 1708.
[85] CO388/10 H64, Memorial from Mr Taverner, 16 Feb. 1707.
[86] CO388/18, Davenant's Memorial to the Lord Treasurer concerning the Free Trade now carried on between France and Holland, 17 Dec. 1705, fols. 122–3.

Two-Thirds Subsidy in 1708. The disparity between the duties on Dutch and German linen remained, and the ad valorem proposal was rejected out of hand.[87]

This scale of duties on plain foreign linen, with the exception of sail-cloth, remained unaltered until 1747, as the War of the Austrian Succession was drawing to a close.[88] In that year, a general increase in import duties of 5% was voted by the Additional Duty. Further increases came in the midst of war: in 1759, a further Additional Duty of 5 per cent brought the total duty paid on plain Hollands linen to $24\frac{1}{6}$%, and on plain Germany narrow linen to $28\frac{11}{12}$%. The waging of war obviously necessitated increased revenue. At the same time, however, it provided the occasion for limiting imports and encouraging import substitution policies, which could be adjusted to take account of diplomatic representations and the pressures exerted by different commercial and industrial interest groups. Petitioners naturally argued their case in fiscal terms when it suited them, and the customs authorities carefully scrutinised the arithmetic, alongside the merits of the case, for the benefit of the Treasury. During the Anglo-Dutch disputes over the duty increases of 1706–7, for example, the Customs Commissioners pointed out that the Dutch arguments were 'very rational' and, if accepted, 'three times the quantity of linen would vend here to what is sold now of the sorts of 4 and 5 shillings an ell . . . it is believed that the Crown would rather gain than loose by it'.[89] It was the job of the Customs Commissioners to provide advice on the revenue implications of changes in the tariff structure; but parliament and the Commissioners for Trade and Plantations tended to take a wider view, in which the balance of trade, the maintenance of employment, and strategic considerations played equally important roles. Thus, the 1708 exemption of European linen from the Two-Thirds Subsidy was granted mainly under the threat of reciprocal duty increase by the States General against English woollen and grain exports, rather than on fiscal grounds.

How and in what ways did changes in the tariff structure influence the course of imports? Figure 5.2 shows that imports of Hollands linen grew in volume up to 1729, and thereafter declined at an uneven rate.[90] Insofar as duties had any effect on the types of linen imported, they discouraged the import of the cheaper and coarse linens from Holland, such as those from Alkmaar, thus reversing a tendency which had been

---

[87] By 7 Anne c. 7.   [88] Table 5.4.
[89] CO388/10 H57, Mr Beck's Memorial . . . relating to linen duties, 20 December 1706.
[90] It should be emphasised that this data is most useful as an index of volume rather than value, because of the possible undervaluation of Hollands linen.

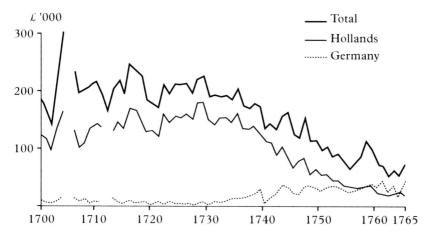

Figure 5.2 English linen imports from Holland, 1702–1760 (Official values, £'000: annual figures)

growing in the years before 1706.[91] It was those Hollands which reached selling prices near or above the rated value of 5s per ell which could best bear a heavy duty. Of the 1747 duty, a linen merchant wrote typically, 'upon fine linens, it will not fall so heavy', and, in practice, this meant the category of linen known as 'gulix' or 'gullick' Hollands.[92] 'You'll please to observe low prixed Gulicks generally produce the best profits' wrote Nash and Eddowes to their Dutch suppliers, by which they meant linens which they sold on commission for between 6s 7d and 7s per ell.[93] Similarly, Leonard Bowles wrote 'would advise you to keep up your fabrick of Gulix to an even good make and fine colours', and some years later complained 'those Courtrays are most prodigious course, could I have imagined they was so bad would not have brought them here to pay our high duty'. In fact he normally dealt in gulix which would sell for around 4s 8d per ell.[94] In December 1738, J. I. de Neufville and Company, probably the largest linen house in Amsterdam, drew up a detailed inventory of all their linen in stock which still remained unsold.[95] This indicates that linens within the wholesale price range 10–20 stivers per Dutch ell (1s 8d – 3s 4d per English ell) were selling badly compared to those within the range 25–40

[91] See above, p. 161.
[92] Brants 1344, Thomas Hill, London, to de Neufville, Amsterdam, 4 March 1747.
[93] Ibid., from Nash and Eddowes, 12 March 175; 17 Oct. 1749.
[94] Ibid., from Leonard Bowles, 30 April 1742; 22 Aug. 1749; 22 Dec. 1741.
[95] Brants 1103, J. I. de Neufville and Comp., 'Specificatie van de linnen die op Ultimo December 1739 onder ons onvercogt syn overgebleeven'. The title strongly suggests that this was linen which the owners were unable to sell, rather than a routine piece of stocktaking. The majority of pieces contained 49–50 Dutch ells.

stivers (4s 2d – 6s 8d per English ell). Presumably few linens were kept or sold above 45 stivers.

If the import of relatively highly priced Hollands was a natural response to a trade burdened with heavy duties, however, it made merchants vigorous critics of the quality of their product. 'Not only the bleach of the cloths...was good for nothing but likewise the make'; 'too much blew put in them, it lay on them in so gross a manner that it looked as if it had been plastered on'; 'many of them yellow within and numbers of large yellow stains like buttermilk not washed out'; 'full of small holes like pins heads'; 'wretched stuff'; 'have bought in London as fine for the money' – complaints were both graphic and extravagant.[96] After making due allowance for the natural tendency of merchants to complain to their suppliers, it seems clear that high duties made importers more conscious of quality when increasingly acceptable duty-free alternatives were becoming available. It also appears that foreign manufacturers and bleachers were attempting to cut costs in a trade suffering from declining profit margins. The imposition of the Additional Duty of 1747 strengthened these tendencies, as more than one linen importer testified: 'The Irish...have been getting ground of you for some years, & as this further duty is laid upon Hollands, the sale of Irish linens must necessarily increase.'[97] A year later, after merchants were 'reconciled to this new duty', Ciprien Rondeau wrote, 'all goods are out of their channel at present by their dearness and the new duties laid on them last year of 5 p. ct. – all Holld. pays 3d more [and] 8d before is 11d per ell besides charges, these Irish and Scotch Hollands sell a great deal more'.[98] By 1759, the Holland trade was already at a very low ebb, but when the Additional Duty of 5% was imposed, any chance of revival was rendered impossible. Jones and Cross commented 'hope you'll send them [gulix] good at these prices or we shall intirely loose this article, as we have lately had another duty laid on them of three pence sterling p. ell English'.[99] In 1765, the English Consul at Rotterdam wrote of linen exports from that port to England, which 'in former times were very considerable', as 'decreasing every day'.[100] In spite of pressures from domestic linen producers, the drawback remained

---

[96] Brants 1344, de Neufville's correspondence with the following London merchants: G. Allix, 28 Feb. 1735; R. Chauncey, 8 June 1736; G. Maynard, 11 June 1754; C. Rondeau, 27 June 1755; B. Cazalar, 24 Oct. 1749; and Brants 1330, with his Birmingham correspondents T. and J. Roe, 27 Aug. 1743.

[97] Brants 1344, Thomas Hill, London, to J. I. de Neufville, Amsterdam, 4 March 1747.

[98] Ibid., from John Manship and Son, London, 22 March 1748, and Ciprien Rondeau, 19 Aug. 1748.

[99] Ibid., from Jones and Cross, London, 27 July 1759.

[100] CO388/85 LI, Consuls' Reports, Report on the trade between Rotterdam and England, R. Wolters, Rotterdam, 16 July 1785.

on re-exports of foreign linens, unlike those of foreign paper, sailcloth, iron and steel wares, and certain other manufactures, where competition from colonial producers was unlikely.[101] These discouragements hardly applied to American and West Indian markets therefore, but as colonial demand was directed towards the cheaper grades of linen (mainly German ozenbriggs), this was of little consolation to Dutch suppliers. As Table 5.2 shows, 'Hollands' linen formed a declining proportion of linen re-exports.[102]

Apart from any secular movements which duty increases may have induced, a number of short-term responses are evident. Both total linen imports and imports of Hollands decline shortly after the increases of 1704, 1747, and 1718, while marked increases occur after the reduction of 1708. Those short-term responses are also visible in the case of imported sailcloth and canvas, and cambrics and lawns. In addition to the duties already discussed, these categories were also subject to specific increases.

Protectionism and import substitution

The English demand for linen was expanding steadily during the period 1700–60, not least for striped and checked varieties which provided acceptable alternatives to prohibited printed Indian calicoes, many of which were imported from Germany. Imports of Hollands linen, the staple of the Dutch industry, increased only slightly during the first three decades of the century, while imports of Germany narrow linen grew more rapidly and sustained their increase for another decade or so. It is unacceptable, however, to explain the decline of the Dutch linen export trade merely in terms of the build-up of new direct trade links with Germany at the expense of Holland; from 1730 to 1760 in fact, the export of Germany narrow linen to England via Holland actually increased.[103] The popularity of narrow German linens is explained by the fact that this relatively cheap category of linen, unlike Hollands, was by 1700 underrated in the Book of Rates, so that it bore a proportionately lighter burden of duty.[104] This was not an altogether artificial advantage, for contemporaries were

---

[101] See, for example, PRO 30/8 (Chatham Papers), vol. LXXXI, fols. 136–7, c. 1715.
[102] See above, p. 152.   [103] See Figure 5.2.
[104] *RHC*, vol. III, Report from the Committee appointed to enquire into the state of the Linen Trade (25 May 1773), p. 102: (evidence of W. Beggar), 'Dutch Holland is rated at or near its real value, but the fabricks of the others [i.e. German linens], having been altered, are now more valuable than they were when the rates were laid.' John Colvill remarked on the 'improvement of the manufacture in Germany, since the time when the Book of Rates was formed...agreeable to which Book all Duties have been laid' (p. 102).

agreed that its quality was constantly improving in relation to other types of linens. Great strides were also being made by Russian and East Country producers, providing additional competition against Dutch sailcloth and canvas, if not against finer linens; and the import of cambrics from Flanders grew moderately up to 1742.

Leaving aside their obvious short-term influences, the long-term effects of changes in the structure of tariffs are fairly clear. Duty increases served to protect British and Irish producers of linen at the lower end of the large category of medium-priced fabrics, those which might be compared with cheap Hollands priced at around 3s per ell. The demand for cheaper linens in the price range 8d–1s per ell was satisfied by German imports, helped by a mildly preferential duty, while coarse linens and homespun fabrics, costing a few pence, had long been produced by the English industry and lay outside the scope of protectionist intentions. Colonial markets for both foreign and British and Irish linens became increasingly important from the 1720s, and the refusal of the state to bow to pressure from home producers to abolish the drawback on foreign linens has been seen as evidence of the non-protective intentions underlying the duty structure; but the rationale here was to discourage colonial consumers from developing home manufactures of their own in this sphere, and hence to protect the carrying trade.[105]

The slow decline of foreign linen imports was more than compensated for by the growth of the Irish, Scottish and English industries, which were carefully fostered by bounties, subsidies and the establishment of Boards of Trustees in Ireland (1711) and Scotland (1727). The situation, it must be stressed, was one in which demand was increasing, both quantitatively and qualitatively, for an increasing range of types and varieties of fabric. The quantity of linen sold in England probably doubled during the period 1700–60, and British and Irish production was, to some extent, opening up new areas of demand (Table 5.5). 'Import substitution' did not, in this case, involve the direct replacement of domestic for foreign sources of supply, but enabled the demands of an expanding consumer society to be satisfied at a number of social levels. The state possessed no predetermined industrial policy to generate growth of this sort, but the underlying strategy of import saving was one which looked favourably on 'the increase of the product of our native growth and manufacture'. The encouragement of Celtic linen manufacture was entirely consistent with this outlook, but its origins lay in the anxieties about import saving and the balance of trade, rather than the desire to mount a consumer-oriented industrial policy. Measures to promote Irish linen production, in fact, were devised as a counterweight to the high-handed prohibition on the

[105] Horner, *Linen Trade*, p. 227; Davis, 'Rise of Protection', p. 312.

Table 5.5 *Sources of linen consumed in England, 1700–1770 (million yards)*

	1 retained imports from Europe	2 Irish exports to England	3 Scottish production	4 columns 2+3	5 total 1+4	6 estimated minimum English production	7 contemporary English production estimates
1700	22.1	0.3				12.9	
1710	15.1	1.5	(1.5)	(3.0)	(18.1)	9.9	
1720	16.7	2.6				12.4	
1730	23.1	3.8	3.8	7.6	30.7	14.4	(21.0)
1740		6.4	4.6	11.0	} 32.0	16.4	
1741	21.1						
1750		10.9	7.6	18.4	} 39.1	27.1	
1752	20.7						
1752–5							(25.8)
1760	17.9	13.1	11.7	24.8	52.8	26.8	
1770	18.6	19.7	13.0	32.7	59.8	42.8	

Sources: Column 1. 1700–20 (italics): Customs 3. Imports were initially extracted on the basis of the official values, and converted into an equivalent measure for square yards (on the basis of a mean Official Value of 7.611d per yard, based on 1730); 1730, 1741: 'Account of Foreign Linens Imported', presented to the House of Commons by the Commissioners of Customs, 28 January 1756, *JHC*, 27, p. 408, and printed in Horner, *Linen Trade*, p. 234; 1752, 1760, 1770: *Reports from Committees of the House of Commons*, vol. III, 'Report relative to the Linen Trade in Great Britain and Ireland', 23 May 1773, Appendix 12, pp. 119–24.
Column 2. Cullen, *Anglo-Irish Trade*, p. 60 (from PRO Customs 15).
Columns 3 & 7. H. Hamilton, *An Economic History of Scotland in the Eighteenth Century*, Oxford, 1963, Appendix IV, pp. 404–5. The figures in brackets in columns 3, 4, 5 and 7 represent or include various contemporary estimates assembled by A. J. Warden, *The Linen Trade, Ancient and Modern*, 1864, and discussed by W. A. Cole and P. Deane, *British Economic Growth, 1688–1959*, Cambridge, 1964, pp. 52–3, 201–3.
Column 6. Harte, 'Rise of Protection', p. 104.

export of Irish woollens in 1699, secured by pressure from the clothing districts of the south-west. Although the initiative came from merchants and manufacturers, it was the Commission for Trade which, in proposing to end Irish competition in overseas woollen markets, suggested that the king's subjects in Ireland should be diverted to linen manufacture. Already, from 1696, linen, flax and yarn imported from Ireland had been exempted from duty. In essence, English policy towards Irish industry was of a colonial type, reflected further in the unilateral tariff preferences secured for English goods exported to Ireland.[106]

[106] H. F. Kearney, 'The Political Background to English Mercantilism, 1695–1700', *EcHR*, 11 (1959), p. 487; Cullen, *Anglo-Irish Trade*, ch. 1.

The establishment of the Linen Corporation followed in 1700, supported by generous state subsidies, and the success of Louis Crommelin's Huguenot colony in developing Ulster's linen industry became legendary. The progress of the Scottish linen industry lagged well behind that of Ireland. At the time of the Act of Union it had acquired a reputation for poor quality, and the rapid growth of production from 1730 to 1760 was based on sales of the lower-priced varieties.[107] The Celtic industries, however, benefited greatly from duty-free access to the growing English market, and their freedom to trade directly with the Atlantic colonies.[108] A string of direct measures to stimulate production included bounties for preparing kelp used in bleaching and for the import of hemp seed, approved in 1707, and the removal of duties on foreign linseed imports (1717) and undressed flax (1731). Not until 1756 were duties on foreign yarn imports removed, an anomaly explained by the fact that Irish flax and yarn had been available as duty-free alternatives since 1696.[109] Bounties on exports of British and Irish linen were granted in 1743 and 1745, partly to compensate home manufacturers for the state's refusal to withdraw drawbacks on re-exported fabrics, and partly to reduce direct export from Ireland to colonial markets.[110] As we have seen, the improvements made by these carefully fostered industries were only too clear to merchants engaged in the trade, as they became increasingly critical of the foreign alternatives.

The English linen industry is less well documented than those of Ireland and Scotland, although its output probably exceeded both combined (Table 5.5). The examples of East Anglia and Kent suggest that linen production could become a vital source of employment in areas characterised by a declining woollen textile industry, something 'much more highly developed and important than a localised, peasant and

---

[107] Gill, *Irish Linen Industry*, pp. 16 20, 64, 202 5; T. C. Smout, *Scottish Trade on the Eve of Union 1660–1707*, Edinburgh, 1963, pp. 232 4; Harte, 'Rise of Protection', p. 92; H. Hamilton, *Economic History of Scotland in the Eighteenth Century*, Oxford, 1963, ch. 5; A. J. Durie, *The Scottish Linen Industry in the Eighteenth Century*, Edinburgh, 1979, p. 27, and ch. 8; R. H. Campbell, Introduction to Campbell (ed.), *States of the Annual Progress of the Linen Manufacture, 1727–54*, Edinburgh 1964; T. S. Ashton, Introduction to E. B. Schumpeter, *English Overseas Trade Statistics, 1687–1818*, Oxford, 1960, p. 12; Cullen, *Anglo-Irish Trade*, pp. 47, 62 3.

[108] From 1705 in the case of Ireland, and from 1707 for Scotland.

[109] English flax and hemp growers lost their protection by this measure, and in 1767 were provided with subsidies from a fund of £15,000 per annum set aside from duty increases introduced in that year (Harte, 'Rise of Protection', p. 99). Harte, oddly, ignores the state's intention to protect British and Irish flax and hemp cultivation and processing, in an argument which considers the protective apparatus largely from the standpoint of the weaving sector.

[110] Gill, *Irish Linen Industry*, p. 71.

predominantly part-time occupation'.[111] As early as the 1630s, flax growers in Somerset improved their skills 'in sowing and ordering of flax and
flax seed' by applying the best Kentish practice.[112] As the Wealden cloth
industry declined during the decades from 1660 to 1720, the appearance of linen weavers, flax- and hemp-dressers, and linen drapers became increasingly common in Quarter Sessions records.[113] By the 1780s,
however, the bounty returns on flax production suggest that Somerset,
Dorset, Lincolnshire and Yorkshire sustained larger linen industries than
either Kent or East Anglia. English production as a whole probably
experienced its most concentrated burst of growth between 1740 and
1790, and, by mid-century, was greater than the quantity imported from
continental Europe.[114] The export bounties of the 1740s clearly gave
the industry a major boost: the official value of linens exported from
England rose from £87,000 in 1740 to over £200,000 in 1750.[115]

The government's policy of import substitution in the linen trade, however, was directed less at the mass of small producers within the kingdom
itself than towards fostering the Huguenot Irish industry, and addressing
the need to reduce dependence on Baltic linen, flax and hemp imports
during wartime. The new Commission for Trade was preoccupied with
precisely these problems in its early years.[116] A major strategic priority
was to develop England's sailcloth production, especially for the Commissioners of the Navy who, since 1696, were required to pay a premium to home producers. In the same year, export duties were removed
from English-made sailcloth in the same statute which exempted Irish
linen products and raw materials from import duties. In 1713, an export
bounty of 1d per ell (roughly 8%) was granted, which was doubled in
1730. The preamble to the 1696 statute noted that sailcloth manufacture was of 'great Use and Benefit to the Nation, and will employ many
Thousands of the Poor'. The other specialised area of English linen production which was singled out for particular encouragement was that of
printed, stained, striped and chequered fabrics, in an equally clear case
of import substitution – in this case, to replace the enormously popular
patterned Asian calicoes which had been prohibited in 1700. The makers
of printed fustians and linens, along with textile printers themselves, were

---

[111] Evans, *East Anglian Linen Industry*, p. 60, and chapter 4.
[112] W. Page (ed.), *The Victoria History of the Counties of England*, vol. III, *Kent*, 1932,
p. 378.
[113] Linsey woolsey was made in Maidstone and Sandwich, and hop-bagging at Maidstone
and Cranbrook (D. C. Coleman, 'The Economy of Kent under the Later Stuarts',
University of London Ph.D. thesis, 1951, pp. 158–60).
[114] Harte, 'Rise of Protection', pp. 96–110.
[115] Schumpeter, *English Overseas Trade Statistics*, Table X.
[116] Kearney, 'English Mercantilism', p. 488.

forced to defend their expanding share of the market against repeated attacks from the woollen and silk industries, but succeeded in maintaining the high levels of protection embodied in the prohibitive import duties of 1711 and 1713. The freedom to wear and use domestically manufactured printed linens and cottons, in some doubt since the second prohibition of printed East Indian calicoes in 1721, was clarified in the 'Manchester Act' of 1736. Although it could hardly have been foreseen, this group of import saving measures played a central role in establishing a niche for England's future leading industry, the cotton manufacture.[117]

The duties on sailcloth and printed linens seem to have been particularly effective in curtailing these respective branches of the import trade from Holland and nearby Europe. The state had little interest in protecting English producers of coarse linen, a long-established rural manufacture which faced no obvious threat from foreign producers. In 1696, when the proposed New Subsidy was under discussion, the government abandoned its plans to impose duty increases on borelaps, a type of coarse linen imported from Holland rather similar to that made by English country producers. Low-priced linen, it was claimed, could not bear a duty equivalent to over one-third of its value: 'the trade is not only likely to be lost but the customs thereby much abated'. Borelaps were accordingly admitted on an ad valorem basis. N. B. Harte describes this as especially clear evidence of the 'exclusively fiscal intentions' of the duty increases.[118] In fact the quantities and values involved were extremely small: annual imports of borelaps from Holland were valued, on average, at only £3,600 during the 1700s, and £1,400 during the 1710s. The revenues involved amounted to a mere £600 per year, at most, even before the duty reductions of 1708.[119] There were no serious opportunities here for import saving, no obvious strategic advantages, nor did cottage production of this type stand in need of strong parliamentary support. The purpose of high duties on linen, as the Commissioners for Trade explained in 1697, was primarily to 'prevent the importation of great quantities of linen now imported on us from France and other foreign countries'.[120]

The government's protectionist intentions are best judged in the context of the comparative advantages attaching to different branches of

---

[117] O'Brien, Griffiths and Hunt, 'Political components of the Industrial Revolution', pp. 408, 409–10; A. P. Wadsworth and J. de L. Mann, *The Cotton Trade and Industrial Lancashire. 1600–1780*, Manchester 1931, ch. 6.

[118] Harte, 'Rise of Protection', p. 97.

[119] Borelaps were given a rating (of 10d per ell) in the supplement to the Book of Rates approved in 1724, and they were probably undervalued beforehand, at around 4d. But the sums involved were still trivial, especially by the early 1720s.

[120] *Calendar of House of Lords Mss*, new series, vol. X, 'Report from the Commissioners of Trade and Plantations on the State of Trade of the Kingdom in 1697, 23 December 1697', p. 160.

textile production across the three kingdoms, the possibilities offered by expanding home and colonial markets, the strategic needs of the state, and, above all, the possibilities for easing pressure on the balance of trade during wartime. The state's need for revenue was, of course, paramount in bringing about the general rise of tariffs in the 1690s, as Ralph Davis emphasised. But this alone explains very little about the direction of policy and the force of intention in an age when trade and warfare went hand in hand. Protectionism was more than 'the incidental result of actions taken to meet the financial needs of government'.[121] Nowhere is this more evident than in the work of the newly established Commission for Trade and Plantations which *inter alia* played a key role in mediating between mercantile interests and parliament during the restructuring of Anglo-Irish commercial relations during the 1690s and the Anglo-Dutch disputes over linen duties in 1706–7. The papers of its first chairman, John Egerton, third Earl of Bridgewater, contain numerous pages of personal notes and memoranda including several written to amplify the Commission's role, on, amongst other things, general maxims of trade and the scope of parliamentary authority in regulating trade. Other notes contain observations on violations of the Navigation Acts, the encouragement of the linen manufacture in Ireland, the trade in imported paper and measures to improve home production, possibilities for developing colonial sources of pitch and tar, and so on. Using his influence as Speaker of the House of Lords, Bridgewater presented an important report on the State of Trade of the Kingdom in 1697, which, in addition to describing the state of each individual branch of foreign trade, also discusses the case for encouraging the silk, linen and paper industries, 'that we may improve to make as good as what comes from abroad'.[122] Like other members of the Commission, including Blathwayt, Pollexfen and Locke, Bridgewater concerned himself with both the details of economic policy and general precepts.[123] None of this points to the existence of an 'industrial policy', but it is difficult to ignore the influence of a core of 'central tendencies' influencing policy which derived from the balance-of-trade theory.[124]

Dutch linen producers held out against this rising tide of protectionism with great difficulty during the first three decades of the eighteenth

[121] Davis, 'Rise of Protection', p. 317.

[122] *Calendar of House of Lords Mss*, 'Report . . . on the State of Trade of the Kingdom in 1697', p. 160.

[123] Huntington Library, California, Ellesmere Mss, EL 9625–6, 9657, 9814, 9839–54, 9873–81. On Bridgewater's career and the early history of the Commission, see Steele, *Politics of Colonial Policy*, chs. 1 and 2; Laslett, 'Origins of the Board of Trade'.

[124] I owe this phrase to Dr N. Zahedieh. For an interesting discussion of the attributes of 'strong' and 'weak' balance-of-trade theories at the time of the founding of the Commission, see K. A. A. Kwarteng, 'The Political Thought of the Recoinage Crisis, 1695–7', unpublished University of Cambridge Ph.D. thesis, 2000, pp. 191–212.

century, and relied on their reputation for supplying a fabric of high quality. Essentially, this was based on the excellence of the Haarlem bleacheries, and the quality of its finest product, the white figured damask. By the late seventeenth century, however, German producers in Silesia and Saxony were perfecting acceptable variants of Dutch damask, and, by the 1720s, Irish producers were following suit.[125] The most disruptive change for the Dutch industry was the growing demand for printed, striped, checked and patterned linens, which shifted the emphasis away from the quality of the bleach alone. Dutch finishers also began to produce printed linens but failed to develop a clear lead over their competitors. In the final section of this chapter, the reactions of the individual traders will be examined, particularly those of the Dutch linen merchant, who, faced with a declining trade, was forced to adopt changes in commercial organisation in order to cope with narrowing or disappearing profit margins.

Commercial organisation

The best surviving evidence for the changing fortunes of the Anglo-Dutch linen trade comes from the correspondence of Jan Isaak de Neufville and Company.[126] It was in the late 1720s that Jan Isaak, the youngest of four brothers, set himself up as a general import and export merchant in Amsterdam. His eldest brother Mattheus had meanwhile established himself in London in 1722 in partnership with a nephew, John de Neufville; and, by 1730, they are to be found making very substantial purchases of cossacs, mullmulls, chintz and other Asian textiles at the East India Company's London sales, side by side with Loubier and Sons, van Hemert, Claude Fonnereau, Joseph Solomons, John Higden and Giles Bullock who were later to become customers of Jan Isaak.[127] The London house proved invaluable in the early stages in recommending Jan Isaak to English correspondents, and not surprisingly the early business consisted of commission trade in Asian textiles sent from London. The export of linen from Holland quickly followed, however, and, in June 1730, Jan Isaak took into partnership Johan Ter Meulen who had just completed six

[125] Mitchell, 'Linen Damask Trade', pp. 22–5.
[126] Analysed by Veluwenkamp, *Ondernemersgedrag*; E. E. de Jong-Keesing, *De Economische Crisis van 1763 te Amsterdam*, Amsterdam, 1939; Wilson, *Anglo-Dutch Commerce*, ch. 2(v).
[127] I. H. van Eeghen, *Inventaris van het Familie-Archief Brants*, Amsterdam, 1959, p. 13. The other two brothers were Issak and Pieter who set up their own house in Amsterdam, which flourished *c.* 1721–40, dealing, amongst other things, in velvets. (See Brants 1155, letters from Wm Wood; C108/132, papers of Henry Gambier, Bundle 2 (i) list of purchases, Nov. 1730: de Neufvilles were the largest single purchasers.)

years' apprenticeship with the 'Greatest linen marchand in Amsterdam', Peter Graver, at the moment when Graver retired from trade.[128] It seems likely that de Neufville was hoping to develop some of the business which was formerly Graver's. At any rate, vigorous attempts were made to acquire new English correspondents with the help of the London house; and in August 1730 a list of twenty-four linen drapers of London was obtained from Nathaniel Adams, himself a draper. 'We shall use our endeavour to gett them for our Customers', replied de Neufville to Adams, and those with whom they were not already in correspondence were invited to make a trial order of 20–30 pieces of gulix.[129] The advantages were carefully explained; 'you pay no more for them as they cost our selft in brown and for the & p.ct Prov[ision] & Proffit we must lay out our money and buy sortes thens and stay our ad vantur by the bleaching and derect them further, all which is a Great Matter for such a small proffit', and, by December 1732, de Neufville was able to inform his customers: 'we have our own house at Haarlem from which we direct our goods to the bleach'.[130]

Significantly, de Neufville entered the linen trade at the moment when the export of Hollands linen to England was at its eighteenth-century peak.[131] From 1731, as we have seen, decline set in swiftly, so that the timing of this particular venture was obviously unfortunate. De Neufville was doubtless alarmed at the disappointing response of the London drapers, and in 1731 again appealed to at least eleven drapers and linen merchants: 'For some time we had the honour to write you in expecting that you should have made tryall with us in our linen trade, but as yet none recd.'[132] Of the twenty-four drapers mentioned by Nathaniel Adams, replies were received from at least nine, and de Neufville was already in correspondence with another three. Eight of these took trial consignments of gulix, but only three pursued the trade any further. In total, at least twenty trial consignments sent to English correspondents resulted in failure during the years 1730–2. Only a handful were successful.

---

[128] The house became known as J. I. de Neufville and Company, however, and Ter Meulen died in April 1750 (van Eeghen, *Inventaris*, p. 13).

[129] Brants 1344, N. Adams to de Neufville, Amsterdam, 21 Aug. 1730, and reproduced in Wilson, *Anglo-Dutch Commerce*, p. 54; Brants 1402 (Copieboek), letter to N. Adams and Comp., 19 Sept. 1730. Some, such as Thomas Smith and Son, Jasper Waters and Son, and John Higden Jr were already well known to de Neufville who received their Asian textiles to sell on commission in Amsterdam.

[130] Brants 1402 (Copieboek), letter to Chase and Harvey, 11 Sept. 1730; ibid. letter to Payne, Swayne and Payne, 30 Dec. 1732.

[131] Figure 5.2. In 1729, a peak was reached. Total linen imports had been higher in 1704 and 1716, the abnormally high import of 1704 being accounted for by the Royal Navy's demand for sailcloth.

[132] Brants 1402 (Copieboek), 21 May 1731.

At this stage, the English correspondents of de Neufville and Company were taking linen on their own accounts, but as profit margins on Dutch linen gradually narrowed during the 1730s and '40s, this method of trade became increasingly difficult. At the outset, the house was already dealing direct with linen drapers who would in any case take linen on their own accounts; but for the importing merchant who in turn supplied the London drapers, this method of trade was by 1730 becoming impossible. Claude Fonnereau replied to de Neufville's offer to open trade in 1730, 'we are not disposed to order any linen on our own account, if you please to send us some on your account, we shall pay all duties', as did Alexander Forbes who reported, 'I have always followed the commissions in the linen business without doing anything on my own account', and 'every draper who formerly were my customers for Hollands linen hath now his correspondent at Amsterdam and other parts of Holland'.[133] In spite of this advice, de Neufville refused to alter his method of dealing. In 1733, Peter Teage of Falmouth complained, 'I take notice you never deal on your own accounts for which reason I would not be concerned in the Hollands I wrote you about.'[134] In the following year, Thomas Church offered to sell on commission to linen drapers in London, but de Neufville politely refused.[135] In 1736, Gilbert Allix put the position in a nutshell:

am much in doubt whether or no I could not frequently make better bargains here in Town, than I do abroad . . . you must give me leave to tell you there are so many persons in Holland that send their linnens over for their own account, that we are overstocked, and at present I find it a Branch of Trade scarce worth my while to meddle in.[136]

Shortly afterwards, Allix and Crespin terminated their orders.[137] By the late 1730s and early '40s, the only customers regularly ordering linen on their own accounts from de Neufville were linen drapers, such as J. N. Badcock, William Pomeroy and Sons, and Chauncey and Brown. Even this business had to be carefully fostered by regular presents of hams, cheeses, tulip bulbs and the like.[138]

---

[133] Brants 1344, Claude Fonnereau to J. I. de Neufville, Amsterdam, 8 Dec. 1730; and from Alexander Forbes, 21 May 1731 and 8 Jan. 1733.

[134] Brants 1339, from Peter Teage, Falmouth, 27 Aug. 1733.

[135] Brants 1344, from Thos Church, London, 28 June 1734.

[136] Ibid., from Gilbert Allix, London, 22 June 1736; also from J. and N. Knight, 19 Feb. 1741.

[137] Ibid., from G. Allix and Crespin, London, 5 Sept. 1738.

[138] Badcock and Pomeroy are listed in Mortimer's *Universal Director* of 1763 as linen drapers; Chauncey and Brown appear in Nathaniel Adams's 'List of Linen Drapers' (Wilson, *Anglo-Dutch Commerce*, p. 14).

The longer credit available in Holland, however, might occasionally tempt merchants to take a consignment of linen on their own account, from a Dutch house. As one importing merchant, who had earlier supplied the draper, explained in 1732, 'I am sure I should be glad if our customers [the drapers] would pay as punctually in 8 months; but instead of that they often take 16; such is the difference betwixt your trade and ours.'[139] Six months' credit was thus commonly demanded and obtained by merchants trading on only a moderate capital stock. Such was Henry Palmer of London, who wrote, 'I have often occasion to make use of my friends in Amsterdam in order to gain a little time. The credit we are obliged to give here being very long, it is of service to a man except he has a very large fortune indeed.'[140] Witnesses before the 1744 Commons Committee on the Linen Trade confirmed that importers of foreign linens were obliged to give long credits to the drapers, and that this was detrimental to home linen manufacturers, 'who for want of a stock sufficient could not give such long credit'.[141] For the merchant, however, as distinct from the draper, long credit alone was an insufficient attraction to trade on one's own account, when commission sales provided a small but steady return for a trade in which profits were neither large nor fluctuating. Commission trade in fact took the process to its logical conclusion, with the Dutch linen merchant bearing the whole burden of credit.

By the early 1740s, a little of this must have become clear to de Neufville, for attempts were made to obtain new customers, if necessary on a different basis from before. From 1741 to 1743, circulars were sent to merchants and drapers, as had been done ten years earlier. At least twenty replies were received, of which eight led to a continuing correspondence. One of the more successful of these new arrangements was with Leonard Bowles (a merchant rather than a draper), who indicated the terms upon which he was willing to trade:

I sell a pretty large quantity of Flanders linnen which I buy brown at Courtray, Menin, &c. and have them bleached at Haarlem . . . as my friends who buy them brown and the persons under whose care they are bleached take a part therein, it is more incouragement for me to continue on this footing than to order for my intire account . . . if you are willing to be half concerned with me in 30 or 40 whole ps. of a low sortment [of menage]; on your answer advise you how to have them made up.[142]

De Neufville reluctantly agreed to trade on this new basis, and the precedent soon became general in de Neufville's dealings with English

---

[139] Brants 1344, Thos Church, London, to J. I. de Neufville, Amsterdam, 10 Oct. 1732.
[140] Ibid., from Henry Palmer, London, 31 Aug. 1731.
[141] *RHC*, vol. II, Report . . . relating to the Linen Trade, p. 70.
[142] Brants 1344, L. Bowles, London, to J. I. de Neufville, 24 March 1741.

merchants. The move towards trade on joint account was encouraged by the imposition of an Additional Duty of 1747, since the burden of duty was henceforth shared. As Thomas Hill remarked in 1748, 'I should be glad if you would charge commission on the linnens & let me do the same (as all my other friends do), because as the duty is now so very high upon them, the amount when sold is much higher than the first cost, by which means we are not quite upon an equal footing.'[143] These demands were complied with, and Hollands were now sent on half account. By 1750, however, Hill was complaining that wholesale drapers were importing their own Hollands, 'so that we have only an opportunity of selling now and then a lot or two to a retail draper, which is hardly worth our while'.[144] Commission business only partially eased the difficulties of a declining trade, it seems.

Nonetheless, readjustment was made which meant that the initiative in buying German or Flemish linen ceased to come from de Neufville, who now merely attended to the bleaching and took his commission for this, and passed to the English merchant or wholesale draper and his German or Flemish agent. De Neufville would take a half, or sometimes a one-third share in the ownership of the linen, in which case the third party involved would be the German agent or producer. Linen in which ownership was thus split was sold on commission by the English merchant or wholesale draper. In this way, de Neufville's linen trade with England continued for another twenty years or so, but at much lower levels than hitherto. The firm's highest trading profits were recorded in the early 1750s, but, by this time, de Neufville had already begun to shift his interests towards the home market. Turnover declined by about one-fifth between 1745 and 1760, and the earlier commitment to the Anglo-Dutch linen trade gave way to a more diverse pattern of trade which essentially involved supplying industrial raw materials to Dutch domestic producers.[145] In the later 1740s, the firm moved into the trade in ash, an important material used in the bleaching process. The same forces that were undermining the linen trade, however, also operated against the bleacheries, and, by 1760, the firm was supplying only one major buyer of this commodity.[146] In its early years, nearly 90% of de Neufville's commodity trade had been directed to the English market. By 1745, the proportion had fallen to 52%, and, by 1760, to a mere 22% of a trade which had moved into rapid decline.

The extent of the reorganisation of de Neufville's linen business is indicated in the debit balances of the company's English correspondents,

[143] Ibid., from Thomas Hill, 16 Sept. 1748.
[144] Ibid., from T. Hill and Hake, 13 April 1750.
[145] Veluwenkamp, *Ondernemersgedrag*, pp. 72–90, 109–12.   [146] Ibid., p. 136.

which fall into two clearly defined groups. Amongst the first group with whom business continued to increase after 1738, six out of eleven correspondents were trading on half or one-third account with de Neufville.[147] A further four appear to have been linen drapers ordering on their own account, one of whom was dealing in prohibited 'Dresden work' (fine-quality lace) and velvets. The second group, consisting of those whose business was declining by the early 1740s, were all dealing on their own account.[148] It is thus quite clear that de Neufville was only able to continue in the linen trade by, on the one hand, trading on his own account in some measure, which entailed making use of English commission agents, and, on the other, corresponding directly with linen drapers. Commission trade was at best a compromise, an expedient for reviving or prolonging a dying trade, and for this reason it was resorted to with reluctance.

Just as Charles Wilson saw the experience of de Neufville as epitomising the decline of the Dutch intermediary trade, J. W. Veluwenkamp has interpreted the firm's history to illustrate another paradigmatic aspect of the staplemarket economy: the tendency to reduce competition through 'niche marketing'. Recognising that very few commodities lent themselves to thorough monopolisation in the manner described by Klein, Veluwenkamp argues that monopolistically competitive practices were much more common, in which each supplier tried to create and control his 'own' market through specialisation, product differentiation and the development of customer loyalty.[149] De Neufville's share of the English linen market was clearly a small one, and the firm operated in an essentially competitive environment. Nevertheless, great care was taken

[147] *Viz.*, L. Bowles, Thomas Hill, Philip Milloway, Nash and Eddowes, J. Manship and Co., and John Dupré. Philip Milloway: traded in German lawns on one-third account with 3 Hirschberg merchants (John Hartman, Videbants Bros and John Barnhard Linckh) and de Neufville and Company. See Brants 1344, 11 Dec. 1753. Nash and Eddowes: de Neufville proposed trade on one-third account in lawns, and himself suggested a German house. On 13 Nov. 1750 (Brants 1344) they agreed to this, for 'as a very great part of the Germany goods sent to England are for foreign acct. we presume a proposal of this kind will be readily accepted'. J. Manship and Comp.: similarly traded on half account with de Neufville in Hollands; and on one-third account in lawns with Messrs Luhler and Scheffer of Hirschberg, and de Neufville and Co., the latter taking commission for bleaching. Trading on this basis began 28 Nov. 1741 (Hollands) and 10 Jan. 1750 (lawns). John Dupré began trade on half account with de Neufville on 3 April 1741 (Brants 1344).

[148] Business with the following was in serious decline: Bullock and Moller; Chauncey, Brown and Chauncey; H. Combauld; A. F. Pigou and Son; W. Pomoroy and Son; C. Yonge and Comp.; and Payne, Swayne and Payne. Other customers whose business similarly tailed off were Allix and Crespin, Silvanus Grove, Peter Teage, Christian Levie and Thomas Church.

[149] Veluwenkamp, *Ondernemersgedrag*, ch. 1 and summary, pp. 129–37. See above, ch. 2, p. 53. As Veluwenkamp points out, only staple goods coming from a single production area, such as Swedish copper and tar, could be thoroughly monopolised.

to maintain continuity of correspondence with an established group of clients in a specialised market: the average trading life of the firm with its fifteen most important customers was eighteen years, taking the cohort centred on 1745.[150] Such a strategy became increasingly difficult to maintain as alternative sources of supply became more widely available, particularly the protected industries of Ireland and Scotland, and, to a minor degree, those of Russia and the Baltic. The discouraging effect of rising tariffs played a critical role in undermining de Neufville's commitment to the English market – especially the increases of 1747 – for it seems that he had little choice but to accept an increasing burden of the costs and risks involved. Ultimately, the firm was forced to contract its international trading operations and concentrate on the internal market.

[150] Ibid., p. 134.

6   The Dutch staplemarket and the growth of English re-exports

For centuries, England's traditional trading relationship with the Low Countries was based on the bilateral exchange of woollen manufactures for European linens. R. H. Tawney expressed something of the self-limiting possibilities of such a commerce when he commented, 'one's first feeling, when one looks at the figures, is surprise at the persistence with which all countries strain every nerve to force the produce of their looms on to a world already wallowing in superfluous fabrics'.[1] Long-distance trade to America and India broke this old pattern apart. The new phase of commercial growth which unfolded after 1660 was driven by two distinct patterns of demand: on the one hand, the desire for new or exotic goods – colonial tobacco, sugar, Asian textiles, spices, coffee and tea – and, on the other, the demand for larger supplies of traditional luxury goods imported from Europe, especially France, including wines, brandy, silks, paper, fine linens, clothing and 'numberless nameless toys'. The distinction, of course, was one which was repeatedly made by mercantilist writers of Whiggish inclination, such as Charles King.[2] The commercial expansion of the post-Restoration period, it has often been stressed, was essentially import-led; and import-led growth produced serious balance of payments problems, intensified, after 1689, by prolonged warfare.[3] Rising consumer demand for goods of the latter type – for traditional, European luxury or semi-luxury items – could be limited by traditional restraints such as prohibitions and the raising of duties, which might also serve as instruments of commercial warfare.[4] In the long run, as we have

---

[1] British Library of Political and Economic Science, Tawney Papers, 1/12, p. 6. For a recent survey which stresses the transformative impact of plantation goods on traditional consumption patterns, see C. Shammas, 'The Revolutionary Impact of European Demand for Tropical Goods', in K. Morgan & J. J. McCusker (eds.), *The Early Modern Atlantic Economy*, Cambridge, 2000.
[2] King, *The British Merchant*, vol. II, pp. 143–7, 273.
[3] Fisher, 'London as an "Engine of Economic Growth"', pp. 7–9.
[4] Significantly, the more fundamentalist strands of mercantilist thought, focusing on 'particular balances' with individual countries, were often associated with the older branches of trade with nearby Europe; it was the problems of the newer long-distance

seen, a successful import substitution strategy was devised. The mounting pressure for colonial and Asian goods, however, soon gave rise to a more novel solution to the problems of import-led growth: the re-export of goods surplus to domestic requirements.

To locate the rise of the English re-export trade in the post-Restoration decades is to recognise that English merchants, with the added protection of the Navigation Acts, were learning to apply the long-established methods of their Dutch counterparts. It became a major policy objective to make Britain, in Tucker's words, 'the common depositum, magazine, or storehouse for Europe and America, so that the medium profit might be made to centre here'.[5] Unlike that of the Dutch Republic, however, the economy of early modern England was not primarily dependent on the carrying trade, and the growth of re-export business was a secondary consequence of a large and growing domestic market for new and semi-exotic consumer goods. By 1750, the home market in Britain was almost three times as large as the Republic's. Thus, the bulk of West Indian sugar imported into England was retained for home consumption (over 80% from 1720 to 1770), and the same was true of tea. The voracious appetite for imported Indian fabrics was only restrained by sumptuary legislation, approved by parliament in 1701 and 1721, which diverted the flow to Europe and the plantations.[6] Imported coffee was mostly retained for home consumption before 1718, but entered the re-export trade in increasing though sharply fluctuating quantities thereafter, as new sources of supply in the Yemen were opened up.[7] Tobacco was something of an exception to the general pattern, in that around two-thirds of English imports were re-exported during the first half of the eighteenth century. Holland's commercial economy, by contrast, functioned pre-eminently as a re-export system. According to Posthumus, about half the Dutch

---

trades, especially with Asia, which stimulated new thinking about the general balance of trade.

[5] J. Tucker, *A Brief Essay on the Advantages and Disadvantages which Respectively Attend France and Great Britain with Regard to Trade*, 1750, p. 72.

[6] The customs ledgers indicate the following figures for retained imports:

	sugar	tea	tobacco	coffee
1701	70%	31%	34%	91%
1720	83	82	32	−13
1750	88	92	35	40
1770	91	92	19	−3

(Schumpeter, *English Overseas Trade Statistics*, Table XVIII)

[7] Chaudhuri, *Trading World*, pp. 373–7.

East India Company's (VOC's) imports of Asian goods were re-exported at mid-century.[8]

The Dutch and English economies as re-export systems

During the century following the Restoration, the course of English commercial development began to resemble the Dutch pattern more closely: both economies were sustained by new and varied forms of re-export business. The differences, however, were more marked than the similarities. Above all, it is clear that the development of the English entrepôt involved a large investment in commerce which was not accompanied by industrial investment.[9] One of the few exceptions to this state of affairs was the establishment of an English calico-printing industry, which by the mid eighteenth century had reached a high degree of technical excellence. The closure of the home market to printed Asian textiles in 1701 gave a sudden boost to the industry, which was only partially restrained by subsequent legislation designed to placate the woollen and silk industries. Although the wearing of printed calico was banned in 1721, muslins, fustians and linens were exempted. In 1751, a firm of London linen drapers, Nash and Eddowes, wrote to an Amsterdam correspondent:

[we] desire the favour of you to get some drawer to copy that curious fine pattern of India Chints which you were pleased to show Mr & Mrs Nash when they were at your house, & to ask your opinion, whether if it was well cut here & printed on a fine cotton or calico, it would not be saleable; because your printers cannot possibly execute those fine patterns like ours.[10]

Apart from this new industry, the extent of processing prior to re-export was relatively small before 1750, if we exclude the enterprise of Glasgow merchants. Most of the tobacco leaving England in the early eighteenth century was leaf tobacco which was exported to Holland where it was cut and mixed with the Dutch-grown (inland) product. A witness before the 1733 Commons Committee on the Frauds and Abuses in the Customs claimed: 'It is very seldom the Merchants re-pack any Hogsheads of Tobacco for Exportation (and when they do, it is such on which are

---

[8] Steensgaard, 'Growth and Composition', p. 151.
[9] Minchinton (ed.), *Growth of English Overseas Trade*, p. 44 (editor's introduction).
[10] Brants 1344, Nash and Eddowes, London, to J. I. de Neufville, Amsterdam, 31 July 1751; on the nature of printers' demands for Indian textiles, see D. Rothermund, 'The Changing Pattern of British Trade in Indian Textiles, 1701–1757', in S. Chaudhuri & M. Morineau (eds.), *Merchants, Companies and Trade. Europe and Asia in the Early Modern Era*, Cambridge, 1999.

very large damages).'[11] The same was true of Indian printed cottons and silks, which were the first commodities to fall within the scope of the bonded warehousing system – which, together with the tariff structure itself, greatly inhibited the development of processing industry. Matthew Decker, one of the most perspicacious opponents of high tariffs, argued that, 'Because our duties being so great an additional disbursement to the first cost of the goods, no merchant will let so much of his capital lie dead for duties here when he can have it all circulating in commodities in other countries', thus, 'high customs prevent our country's being an universal storehouse'.[12]

In fact the 'drawback' system was intended to overcome this problem. Either the whole or a part of the duties paid on import could be repaid (or 'drawn back') when goods were re-exported, provided they were re-exported within a specified time – usually within three years of import. By the end of the seventeenth century, however, duties on colonial and Asian goods had in many cases risen to prohibitively high levels, and the method of claiming drawbacks had become increasingly complicated. Both developments enlarged the scope for making fraudulent claims to such a degree that it became necessary to devise an alternative system. At its inception in 1700, the new system was applied only to Indian and Persian wrought silks, which formed one of the more valuable components of the re-export trade, but in 1709 it was extended to include pepper, in 1714 tobacco, and, at later dates, rum, coffee and rice were covered.[13] That system was the so-called 'warehousing system' by which imports were stored in warehouses under the joint locks of the Crown and the merchant, and paid duty only when they were delivered out for home consumption.

The drawback system therefore postulated the actual payment of duty, whereas the warehousing system postponed or waived payment of duty, or in some instances required only the payment of half duties. The temptation to re-land goods and make fraudulent drawback claims was much reduced, to the benefit of the public revenue, and the system was simpler and more convenient, which suited both merchants and customs officers. Most interesting to the historian, however, are two important long-term effects which influenced the course of the already well-established re-export trade, and which must have assumed a greater weight in proportion

[11] *RHC*, vol. I, Report from the Committee appointed to inquire into the Frauds and Abuses in the Customs, June 1733, p. 618 (no. v, Mr Gilbert Higginson's Examination, 8 May 1733).

[12] M. Decker, *An Essay on the Causes of the Decline of the Foreign Trade of Great Britain*, 1744, p. 10.

[13] Hoon, *English Customs System*, pp. 262–4.

to progressive increases in the level of duties. They have been curiously overlooked by commercial historians. The first was the tendency of the new system to divert imported colonial and Asian products away from home consumption and towards re-export markets; and the second was its discouragement of any form of processing prior to re-export. Goods simply went directly into the warehouses and out again. In the case of those goods purchased by brokers at public sales, they often remained unseen and untouched by those merchants on whose accounts they were re-exported. When the firm of London linen drapers Jasper Waters and Sons heard from their Amsterdam correspondent that two bales of chintz had been received in poor condition, they replied:

as to what you mention about the damage, we have no notion of it, they being sent in good condition out of our Company's warehouse; and if there be any damage upon them, it must have been received on board of Bredemos, and therefore he ought to be accountable for it, and we depend upon our being clear from any charge upon that account.[14]

If the English fiscal system actually discouraged the growth of processing industries dependent upon imported goods, the Dutch system of low duties, low interest rates and cheap freight rates clearly had the reverse effect. The Dutch *verkeersindustrien* (literally 'traffic industries') overshadowed the rest of the Republic's industrial sector, and England's commercial relations with Holland during the first half of the eighteenth century were conditioned as much by the capacities of these industries as by the declining importance of the Dutch entrepôt.[15] A significant part of England's export surplus was chanelled towards the finishing industries of Holland, providing a flow of raw materials and semi-finished goods which reversed the mercantilist's ideal of a beneficial trade. A sizeable proportion of English woollens exported to Holland were sent in a white state to be dyed and finished at Leiden, though mixtures were sent chiefly for the transit trade to Germany and the Empire. 'The more they bought from hence', Davenant lamented in 1711, 'the better opportunities they had to enlarge their general trafficks.' The bulk of the English grain export trade consisted of the malt required by the Dutch brewing and distilling industries; whilst coal exports likewise served the needs of those industries in Rotterdam and Schiedam, together with those of sugar bakers, smiths and others. And much of the English lead and tin exported entered into the largely Dutch-controlled international arms trade. On the

---

[14] Brants 1344, Jasper Waters and Sons, London, to J. I. de Neufville, Amsterdam, 12 March 1730.
[15] C. Visser, *Verkeersindustrien te Rotterdam in de tweede helft der achttiende eeuw*, Rotterdam, 1927, pp. 23–4.

import side, most of the Holland linens shipped to England had been manufactured in Germany prior to bleaching and finishing at Haarlem.

Most significant, however, was the fact that Holland remained the initial destination for the bulk of English re-exports in the earlier decades of the century – from whence they were re-exported a second time by the Dutch, in some cases after processing. This is the real measure of the success of the Dutch re-export system in the late seventeenth and early eighteenth centuries. As late as 1773, Wyndham Beawes complained that 'our products and manufactures, Plantation and East-India goods furnish materials for a great part of their trade [*viz.* of the Dutch] with other nations; by which they are so far from being sufferers, that, on the contrary, the more they take from us, the more they enlarge their universal traffic, and consequently increase their riches.'[16] By this time, such a view was anachronistic, but it illustrates the persistence of exaggerated fears of Dutch commercial strength in some quarters.

The Dutch staplemarket and English re-exports

When, in fact, did the Dutch entrepôt begin to lose its importance as a market for English re-exports, and how did competition between the Dutch and English East India companies shape the flow of re-exported goods consumed in Europe? The official statistics on which we depend for answers to these questions are unfortunately more difficult to interpret for re-exports than the other main branches of English overseas trade. Colonial and Asian goods were usually less familiar to the Inspectors General than European products, and were therefore difficult to value. Identification and description of the proliferating varieties of exotic silk, cotton and mixed fabrics entering the East India Company's warehouses posed a particularly intractable problem for customs officers. Merchants' valuations (or entries ad valorem) were therefore accepted for these and for several other categories of re-export goods in the early eighteenth century, in place of the official, fixed values. Defoe, a fairly resourceful commentator, had to admit that the value of re-exported groceries was 'hard to determine', though 'exceeding great'. The question of re-export valuations is one which continues to perplex historians.[17]

---

[16] W. Beawes, *Lex Mercatoria or The Merchant's Directory*, 6th edn, Dublin, 1773, p. 521.

[17] Defoe, *Plan*, p. 182. T. S. Ashton believed that the official statistics were 'too unreliable to make it possible to give even approximate estimates of the value (or "volume") of re-exports'. Ralph Davis conducted a careful investigation of valuations in the 'Book of Tables' for London's trade in the 1660s, but not of the customs ledgers, and more recent writing has not advanced beyond Ashton's erroneous assumption that the only substantial revaluation was that of coffee, in the late eighteenth century. Although the

In fact two separate problems present themselves, involving changes in the official values and authenticity, that is, the extent to which they represented real selling prices. Table 6.1 attempts to throw some light on these questions by comparing the official values with real wholesale prices taken from merchants' correspondence. This indicates that a firm list of valuations for Asian textiles emerged after the first decade of the eighteenth century. As in the case of tea, coffee and diamonds, Asian textiles were entered in the ledgers at the merchant's valuation; but, in practice, a list of official values seems to have fossilised by 1711, certainly by 1716, in the case of textiles other than calicoes, which had always been valued at 12s per piece.[18] Tea, on the other hand, seems to have been entered at a variable valuation, presumably approaching its real value.[19] The practical implication of this is that the Inspector General's statistics can be used to give a fairly reliable indication of changes in the *volume* of re-exports of Asian textiles, since the trade was dominated by calicoes, the value of which remained fixed. During the first decade of the century, however, the upward drift of valuations for other fabrics gives a slightly exaggerated impression of the true rate of growth overall.[20] Furthermore, when the official values are compared with wholesale prices, it appears that the later, post-1711 valuations probably overestimated the real value of Indian textile re-exports. The official values current at the start of the century appear to be more authentic, and the exaggerated 'ad valorem' entries in the ledgers are doubtless explained by the efforts of merchants to obtain enhanced drawback payments. High valuations, on the other hand, are to some extent counterbalanced by the tendency of traders to describe a large proportion of textiles as low-valued 'calicoes', in order to save duties on goods which may have originally been intended for home consumption. These qualifications must therefore be borne in mind when reading the statistics of the re-export trade, assembled in Table 6.2.

At least two major conclusions emerge from these figures. In the first place, it is clear that Holland retained its position as the primary European market and distribution point for English re-exports, both during and well beyond the War of the Spanish Succession. After the war, and during the

---

issue cannot be resolved in a simple formula, we will nevertheless attempt to unravel its main outlines below. See Davis, 'English Foreign Trade, 1660–1700'; T. S. Ashton, Introduction to Schumpeter, *English Overseas Trade Statistics*; Ashton, *Eighteenth Century*, p. 161.

[18] Clark, *Guide*, pp. 86–7.

[19] Tea was entered 'at value' in the customs ledgers as follows (per lb), 1700, 3s 2d; 1706, 19s; 1711, 6s 2d; 1716, 11s; 1721, 12s 6d; 1731, 10s.

[20] Chaudhuri shows that, for the second quarter of the eighteenth century, the customs ledgers underestimate the rate of growth of English imports from Asia because of inflation, and overestimate real values (*Trading World*, p. 14).

Table 6.1 Official values of Asian textiles compared with wholesale prices, 1727–1749

	official values					real wholesale prices				
	1700	1706	1711	1716	1721	1727	1728	1730	1731	1749
'calicoes'	12s	12s	12s	12s 6d	12s					
plain cottons										
romalls	18s 8d	10s	21s 6d	28s	28s	9s–10s	10s 1d	9s 3d		8s 4d
cossacs			20s	55s	49s	54s 6d – 55s 6d	17s 8d – 59s	31s – 54s 6d	52s 6d – 55s 6d	37s 6d – 44s 6d
humhums		10s					32s–34s	29s 6d – 32s 6d		
mulmulls	20s 4d		40s	41s	41s	49s	40s 6d	32s 6d – 57s 6d		65s 6d
tanjeebs	54s 6d		101s 1d	55s 4d	55s 6d	33s–44s	31s 6d – 34s 6d	31s 6d		
striped, dyed or printed cottons										
photaes	22s 2d	15s	10s	10s	10s	9s 2d		9s 2d	7s 7d – 8s 5d	
chelloes		15s	17s		17s		8s 1d – 12s 4d – 13s 2d			
chintzes	12s 5d	20s	16s 6d	26s 6d	26s 6d			17s 9d – 19s 2d		
silk and cotton mixtures										
nilleas	13s 2d	20s	25s 6d	25s	25s			13s 2d – 13s 10d		
chucklees	40s	40s	45s	45s	45s	32s				
seersuckers	21s 2d			24s 6d	52s	18s – 19s 2d	14s 8d – 17s 2d			
soosaies	38s 1d	40s	48s 3d	52s	52s			41s		32s–34s
tepoys	16s 6d		36s	36s			17s 8d			

Sources: Official values, Cust. 3 3/4, 9, 14, 18, 23. Real prices represent wholesale prices of textiles re-exported to Amsterdam by English merchants, taken from Archief Brants 1344, J. Waters and Sons, London, January–December 1727 and May–June 1728; ibid., C. Bosanquet, London, February and October 1749; and PRO C108/132, H. Gambier, London, November 1730 and October 1731.

Table 6.2 *The English re-export trade, 1700–1760 (£'000 official values)*

	total re-exports from England and Wales	total re-exports to Holland	re-exports to Holland as % of total	re-exports to Holland of			
				Asian textiles	groceries	tobacco	other
1700–5	1,822.4	781.9	42.9	234.6	165.2	157.5	224.6
1706–10	1,539.6	605.4	39.3	209.3	121.7	164.8	109.6
1711–15	2,072.3	938.2	45.3	387.1	251.7	116.9	182.5
1716–20	2,291.4	820.2	35.8	277.3	265.1	138.8	139.0
1721–5	2,278.2	941.6	34.5	413.5	294.0	118.4	115.7
1726–30	3,096.2	1,075.0	34.7	463.2	182.1	199.3	230.4
1731–5	3,058.4	981.6	32.1	548.9	137.7	148.8	146.2
1736–40	3,314.2	902.9	27.2	451.9	113.7	195.5	141.8
1741–5	3,722.0	1,059.4	28.5	448.3	242.4	250.8	117.9
1746–50	3,448.8	933.3	27.1	393.8	123.9	248.3	167.3
1751–5	3,448.8	843.8	24.5	376.1	142.7	240.8	84.2
1756–60	3,656.4	678.3	18.6	270.2	142.6	183.4	82.1

Source: Cust. 3.

Table 6.3 *Comparison of the Dutch and English East India companies' import trades, 1668–1670 and 1738–1740**

	1668–1670		1738–1740	
	VOC Amsterdam %	EIC London %	VOC Amsterdam %	EIC London %
pepper	29.0	17.5	11.0	3.3
textiles	24.0	67.9	28.5	80.6
tea & coffee	0.03	1.1	25.0	14.0
other goods**	47.0	13.5	35.5	2.1

* VOC figures relate to the Amsterdam Chamber's sale of each commodity expressed as a percentage of its total sale of Asian goods (annual average). The Amsterdam Chamber's sales amounted to around half the VOC's total imports in the century after 1650. EIC figures relate to the company's imports of each commodity expressed as a percentage of its total Asian imports.
** Includes indigo, copper, saltpetre, fine spices, sugar. In the Dutch case, fine spices predominated, accounting for 28.5% in 1668–70 and 23.5% in 1738–40.
Sources: F. S. Gaastra, *De Geschiedenis van de VOC*, Haarlem and Antwerp, 1982, pp. 122–3; K. Glamann, *Dutch-Asiatic Trade, 1620–1740*, Copenhagen and The Hague, 1958, p. 14; Chaudhuri, *Trading World*, Appendix 5, pp. 507–48.

1720s, the proportion of re-exports absorbed by the Dutch declined to just over one third of the total, and by the early 1750s it had fallen to about one quarter. If we look at the absolute figures involved, however, and take account of the overvaluation of some types of Indian textiles during the first decade of the century, we can see that the trend is a fairly stable or stagnant one, rather than a case of absolute decline. This is a state of affairs which is reflected in so many other areas of Dutch economic life – one of relative economic decline – that it has become a commonplace amongst Dutch economic historians.[21] Hamburg competed with the Dutch ports for a share of the English re-export trade, but not until the 1750s did the German entrepôt overtake Holland in this important role.

The second striking feature to emerge is the overwhelming dominance of Asian textiles over other categories of re-export products, which, in an important sense, represented the outcome of a protracted process of competition between the English and the Dutch East India companies. By the 1660s, the VOC's concentration on the import of pepper and fine spices from Asia was matched by a corresponding focus on textiles by the EIC (Table 6.3). Although the Dutch company increased its commitment to the coffee and tea trades to a greater degree than its English counterpart

[21] The underlying argument of Joh. de Vries, *Economische Achteruitgang*, pp. 30, 83.

as time went on, the latter concentrated the bulk of its resources on meeting the enormous European demand for light Indian textiles. By the late 1730s, 80% of the EIC's Asian imports consisted of textiles, and the bulk of these were disposed of, at least initially, in Holland. It was indeed the trade in these fabrics which determined trends in the re-export trade to Holland as a whole, since the decline in re-exports of groceries from the 1730s was partly counterbalanced by a subsequent rise in tobacco re-exports. When we place the Inspector General's statistics alongside those of the EIC's own figures for total imports of textiles from Asia into Britain, and make correction for the undervaluation of the latter so as to make the two sets of figures roughly comparable, it is evident that a very high proportion of the Indian fabrics imported into Britain, usually around two-thirds or above, were re-exported to Holland up to the 1740s.[22] Those contemporaries who complained that the Dutch controlled the most lucrative part of the English re-export trade spoke with some truth. Davenant, as one of the early Inspectors General, was well aware of the direction in which the statistics pointed when he wrote, in 1711:

As the case now stands, Amsterdam and Rotterdam are in a manner the magazines for the wrought silk, Bengal stuffs mixed with silk, or herba of the manufacture of Persia, China, or East India, and of all callicoes painted, dyed, printed, or stained there, the use of which commodities being prohibited here, are chiefly sent to Holland. Which goods being bought cheap in the Indies, and sold dear in Europe, ought to turn richly to the importers account; but it is to be feared our neighbours make a greater profit from them than England, which sends out its bullion, runs all the hazards of the sea and by-captures, and is at the expense of forts, castles and factories to support this traffic.[23]

Davenant was right in claiming that the most valuable sector of the English re-export trade to Europe arose as a secondary consequence of the prohibitions secured by the woollen industry in 1701 and 1722, in an attempt to protect itself from the rising tide of Asian imports.[24] Additional duties on imported Indian calicoes, wrought silks and mixtures had been imposed in 1685 and 1690, but these failed to reduce the popularity of the new fabrics. Imports grew particularly fast during the 1690s and the 1710s. Rioting and unemployment in the weaving districts, especially Spitalfields, forced parliament to pass the Prohibition Acts, in situations which called for 'crisis management' rather than parliamentary inquiries and the careful balancing of commercial and industrial interests.

---

[22] Statistics of total imports of textiles from Asia by the English East India Company are provided in Appendix 5 of Chaudhuri, *Trading World*, pp. 547–8.
[23] Davenant, 'Second Report', p. 430.
[24] A. Plummer, *The London Weavers' Company, 1600–1970*, 1972, pp. 292–311.

As Chaudhuri concludes, 'the significance of re-export trade was generally forgotten in the fears that England was importing and consuming too many foreign goods'.[25]

The inadequacies inherent in the prohibition policy are reflected, amongst other things, in parliament's repeated effort to draft a workable piece of legislation.[26] The first Act, passed in 1700 but taking effect from 29 September 1701, prohibited the wearing and household use of all wrought silks, Bengals (Bengal silks), stuffs mixed with silk from Persia, China or India, and all calicoes painted, dyed, printed or stained abroad; these goods were to be warehoused and accounted for by warehouse keepers; any unwarehoused goods were liable to seizure and their owners to fines; and no duties were to be paid on import, apart from the half subsidy. The second Act, passed in 1720 but taking effect from 25 December 1722, prohibited the wear and household use of painted, dyed, printed or stained calicoes, whether coloured at home or abroad, and established a £5 penalty to be paid by the wearer to the informer. Muslins, neckcloths, fustians and calicoes dyed blue were exempted from the provisions of the Act, while the import of white calicoes was permitted throughout. It will be seen at once that the 1720 Act was a much more direct attempt to impose a piece of sumptuary legislation than that of 1700; the earlier Act concentrated mainly on controlling and diverting the import trade, whilst the later Act introduced a simple and practicable means of limiting the consumption of the offending textiles. It also attempted to restrain the developing textile-printing industry.

In fact the prohibitions had a double-edged impact, which proved to be more damaging to home industry than their promoters had first imagined. In diverting Indian fabrics overseas which otherwise would have been consumed at home, competition in the home market was simply transferred to export markets. The enlarged flow of Asian goods into Europe, especially Holland, would reduce foreign demand for English woollens, particularly as Holland remained the principal market for these goods too. Opponents of the prohibition had already pointed this out at the turn of the century, and Davenant noted how, after returning from Holland in 1705, he

found the Dutch universally pleased with our Prohibition to wear East India and Persia wrought silks, Bengalls, dyed, printed or stained callicoes. And, whereas we expected it would advance our woollen manufactures, they affirm the contrary, and that these Indian goods are worne by their own people, and sold by the Hollanders to other countries with whom they deale in the very room of our

---

[25] Chaudhuri, *Trading World*, p. 12.
[26] 11 and 12 Wm. III c. 10 (1700); 7 Geo. I c. 7 (1720).

Woollen Manufactures which they dayly beat out abroad by being as well cheaper as finer to the eye.[27]

The two categories of textile were not, of course, close substitutes, but the growing trend towards the production of lighter fabrics within the English woollen industry, especially mixtures such as the East Anglian 'stuffs mixed with silk', meant that there was a strong element of competition between them. It was one which was largely absent from the Dutch woollen industry, which, as Posthumus showed, shifted gradually towards the production of *lakens* (the heavier broadcloths) during the course of the seventeenth century, at the expense of new drapery manufacture.[28]

Davenant, of course, was a spokesman for the EIC and the deceptively uncommitted and informed tone of his remarks is belied by his role as a leading Tory pamphleteer.[29] Impartial comments on any aspect of the EIC's activities are indeed difficult to find, and it is therefore worth setting contemporary comments against the evidence of the statistics for overseas trade. Some allowance must be made for the smuggling of prohibited goods between Holland and the eastern ports of England. Entirely reputable merchants engaged in occasional smuggling ventures at times when opportunities for profitable legal trade were few. During the 1750s for example, Jones and Cross, linen drapers of London, placed regular orders with de Neufvilles in Amsterdam for prohibited goods – French and Flemish lace and russells and Indian goods – although their main business was the import of linen through legal channels.[30] Another importer of linen, Ciprien Rondeau, suggested that 'one might have a case made pretty strong and a dubb bottom, the vacancy not to exceed three-quarters of an inch and the inside bottom to be thin and nailed also with paper as usual at the bottom of the case' for the handling of prohibited goods.[31] Ventures such as these, however, would not have been worth the great trouble and expense involved for any but the most expensive silks and laces. When we turn to the commercial statistics, there seems to be little doubt that the prohibitions greatly reduced the consumption of Indian goods, though some illegal trade was carried on.

The figures assembled in Table 6.4, which show the extent to which Indian textiles were diverted from home consumption to the chief

---

[27] O'Brien, Griffiths & Hunt, 'Political Components of the Industrial Revolution', pp. 404–5; CO 389/18, fo. 523.

[28] Posthumus, *Leidsche Lakenindustrie*, vol. III, pp. 929–32.

[29] D. Waddell, 'Charles Davenant (1656–1714): A Biographical Sketch', *EcHR*, 11 (1958), p. 286; Coleman, 'Politics and Economics', p. 190.

[30] Brants 1344, Jones & Cross, London, to J. I. de Neufville, Amsterdam, 29 October 1756, 26 August 1757, 5 May 1758, 31 January 1759.

[31] Ibid., C. Rondeau, London, to de Neufville, Amsterdam, 8 November 1745.

Table 6.4 *Re-exports of Asian textiles to Holland*
following the Prohibition Acts (£'000 official values)

year		year	
1697 8	63.6	1717	194.0
1699	123.0	1718	120.2
1700	243.7	1719	333.4
1701	228.8	1720	470.2
		1721	540.1
1702	181.3		
1703	255.4	1722	485.9
1704	210.5	1723	213.4
		1724	376.0

Source: Cust. 3.

re-export markets in Holland, are reasonably clear. Although the Acts did not take effect until September 1701 and December 1722, the controversy and uncertainty surrounding their passage through parliament might be expected to produce changes in the direction of trade at earlier moments – since the trade in these and indeed in all re-export commodities was highly speculative. The so-called 'calico controversy' was especially acute during the period 1719–21, and the expected change in the course of trade can be identified with little difficulty. The longer-term effects of the second prohibition may well be reflected in the data of Table 6.2, although it is difficult to say what other influences were at work. As P. J. Thomas explained, contemporaries were by no means agreed even on the immediate effects of the prohibitions, although there was some acknowledgement that the second Act was more effective than the first, if only because of its greater simplicity and the extent to which it allowed the woollen and silk weavers to take the law into their own hands – which indeed they did.[32] Norwich weavers instituted prosecutions under the 1720 Act and inserted notices in the local press pointing out that the wearing of printed fabrics was illegal. At the same time, the use of calico was similarly prohibited in all parts of Europe except, significantly, Holland.[33]

Perhaps the most suggestive evidence lies in a comparison of trends in the re-export trade to Holland with the course of exports of woollen manufactures to that market, shown in Figure 6.1. It is fairly clear that there is an inverse correlation between the two. As re-exports of Indian textiles increased, it seems that exports of woollens declined, and vice

[32] Thomas, *East India Trade*, pp. 118 21, 159 65.   [33] Ibid., pp. 164, 86–7.

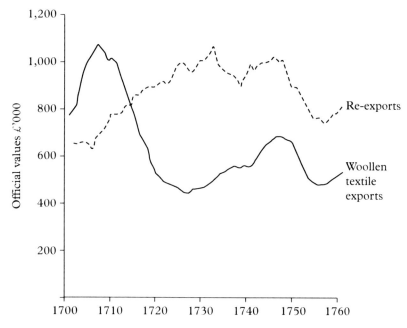

Figure 6.1 Anglo-Dutch trade, distinguishing re-exports and woollen exports, 1700–1760 (Official values, £'000; nine-year moving averages)

versa. This is not to say that independent influences did not affect the course of the woollen trade – such as conditions of wartime trading, clothing contracts for troops, and movements in the exchange rate – but simply to suggest that, in a period of stagnant population and overstocked markets (a favourite phrase bandied about by merchants in the 1720s and 1730s), there were certain limits to the demand for all types of textile taken together, so that buoyancy in one area of the market was liable to produce depression in another.

This inverse relationship between movements of woollen manufactures and of Indian goods seems to hold until at least 1740. It is linked with an unmistakable tendency, which emerges from contemporary merchants' correspondence, for European markets to become saturated with re-exported products of all kinds, but particularly textiles, during the 1720s and early 1730s. This state of affairs was admirably summarised by an English merchant resident in Amsterdam in 1730, Diederick Smith: 'Nobody can imagine him the poor and miserable state of trade of all India goods; almost a man doth not know which way he shall turn himself and on what article he shall touch.'[34] Similarly, Jasper Waters and Sons, who exported chintzes, muslins and Bengals from London to Amsterdam, complained by 1734 that: 'you reap a certain profit by this correspondence, which is more than we do; this trade is indeed not worth our carrying on'.[35] Such instances and comments could be multiplied to show that individual merchants gradually abandoned the London–Amsterdam trade in these goods during the 1730s. Jasper Waters, for example, turned increasingly to the African trade which absorbed the cheapest Indian fabrics. In 1733 he wrote

Our company have gone a great way in selling their Bengal goods. Last week they sold their seersuckers; there was but 26 bales of them of which we bought 18–16 of them in our own names, and two by brokers. We must own they are ordinary goods but much wanted for our Guinea trade. We have sold lately some bales of a former buying for a very great profit to those who trade for Africa, and an inferior sort will serve for them. We know they won't do for your market [Amsterdam], and indeed not one bale of this sale is bought for any market in the world besides Africa; all ours are designed for the same.[36]

In the case of tea, coffee and other groceries, it was clear that too many were participating in the Amsterdam trade – as Sir Jacob Senserf put it, business was 'overdone on all sides'.[37] The margin between selling prices in England and in Holland was too narrow to sustain trade at this level, and during the later 1730s the volume of re-exports sent to Holland contracted. It was during the 1720s that tea drinking reached enormous proportions in Europe. 'The consumption of tea', wrote one merchant in 1733, 'is become an epidemical distemper, and even the Northern People who used to drink brandy begin to drink tea'; and, later, 'We believe our common people [in Holland] would rather want bread than tea.'[38] Coffee drinking had likewise affected all levels of society: 'The world is so debauched here that all people from the highest to the lowest drink regularly their coffee in the morning and tea in the afternoon.' Yet by 1739 the same merchant wrote: 'What will become of these articles [tea and coffee] God knows, but it is impossible to consume them.'[39] A

[34] PRO C103/131, bundle 5, Diederick Smith, Amsterdam, to Thomas Hall, London, 5 May 1780.
[35] Brants 1344, J. Waters and Sons, London, to J. I. de Neufville, Amsterdam, 4 June 1734.
[36] Ibid., J. Waters and Sons, London, to J. I. de Neufville, Amsterdam, 30 October 1733.
[37] C103/133, bundle 17, J. Senserf and Son, Rotterdam, to Thomas Hall, London, 23 September 1735: 'We seldom encourage our friends to engage in any commodity because we daily finde by experience how little there is to be depended upon, trade being overdone on all sides.'
[38] Ibid., J. Senserf and Son, Rotterdam, to Thomas Hall, London, 2 October 1733, 2 February 1734.
[39] Ibid., J. Senserf and Son, Rotterdam, to Thomas Hall, London, 8 November 1735, 15 September 1739.

fairly high elasticity of demand for groceries, and the almost unlimited possibility of bringing increased supplies to Europe, had greatly extended their markets in the 1720s and 1730s; but by the later 1730s it seems that lower prices meant disappearing profits.

The problem facing merchants was undoubtedly one of over-supply, particularly as the hitherto monopolistic market situation governing Asian products became an oligopolistic one in the 1720s. It was in 1718 that the VOC's favoured position in China collapsed, following the refusal of the Chinese to accept the low prices fixed for tea by the Governor General.[40] The result was the opening up of the tea trade, and enlargement of opportunities for 'comprehensive interloping' already being seized by the Ostend Company and its Danish and Swedish successors.[41] Before the rise of the Ostend traders during the 1710s, it was the buying policies of the English and Dutch East India companies which determined world prices for Asian goods. The English company, from the mid seventeenth century, auctioned its imports at quarterly sales held in London, though the September/October sale seems to have been the most notable. The prices obtained at these sales provided the Directors with the information they needed to determine buying strategies in Asia, and both buyers and sellers kept a close watch on the level of prices reached in Amsterdam and Middelburg where the Dutch East India Company's sales were held.[42] India goods were increasingly auctioned at private sales, and, with the passage of the Prohibition Acts and the rising level of import duties, sales of seizures and 'damaged goods' were held more frequently by the customs authorities. The circulation of printed lists and sale notices was common.[43]

It was the progress of the Ostend Company, however, which disturbed the entrenched positions of the English and Dutch companies more than anything else. In one respect, the formation of the Ostend Company was part of the southern Netherlanders' protracted struggle to break the economic stranglehold established over them by England and Holland during the seventeenth century and confirmed in the Barrier Treaty of 1715. But it was more than this; it represented a wider offensive, attracting discontented merchants from all over north-western Europe, against the commercial chauvinism practised by the great monopoly India companies of England and Holland. Amongst the Ostend traders were to be found

[40] Glamann, *Dutch Asiatic Trade*, pp. 216–18; H. Furber, *Rival Empires of Trade in the Orient, 1600–1800*, vol. II, Minnesota, 1976, p. 129.
[41] The phrase is Glamann's, *Dutch-Asiatic Trade*, p. 10.
[42] Chaudhuri, *Trading World*, pp. 131–5.
[43] Hoon, *English Customs System*, pp. 281–6; Brants 1344, C. Bosanquet, London, to de Neufville, Amsterdam, sale notices of 26 September 1750, 10 December 1750.

not only Flemings but also Dutchmen, French, English, Scots and Irish.[44] Their impact on European commerce has not been fully recognised by English historians.

From about 1715 to 1722, the Ostend Company's activities took the form of unorganised individual ventures which were licensed by the imperial authorities in Brussels. In 1722 it was formally established by imperial charter, and there followed five years of rapidly growing trade with Bengal and China, until its activities were suspended in 1727 before dissolution in 1731. The vigour of the Ostend tea sales during this period was attested by several merchants, such as Isaac and Willem Kops of Amsterdam, who wrote in 1719 that they were resorted to by great numbers of Dutch, French and English buyers, who would 'fetch their belly full at Ostend'.[45] By the early 1730s, Ostend had been eclipsed by the markets of Middelburg and Rotterdam, especially the former, where port charges were low and duties non-existent, which, as one merchant said, was 'a vast encouragement for them to resort thither and abandon Ostend as they have all done'.[46] Although the company's formal organisation fell apart in 1731, however, the Ostenders found ways of continuing their trade – by sailing under Polish or Prussian colours, by using other ports, such as Hamburg or Cadiz, or by transferring their allegiance to other companies of a similar kind newly established in Sweden (1731), Denmark (1732), Spain (1733) and Prussia (1750).[47] In 1737, Sir Jacob Senserf of Rotterdam wrote: 'There is little prospect that tea will ever bear a high price; those Danish and Swedish ships knock down at speculation in these parts, because they furnish now what this country [Holland] used to do formerly.' And three years later: 'The article of tea is very bad and will hardly mend as long as so many European nations trade to China.'[48]

Various efforts were made by the English and the Dutch to put these companies out of business, either through conventional diplomatic channels, through bribery or by commercial strategies such as flooding the market and depressing prices.[49] Their failure stemmed largely from the very limited degree of co-operation between the British and Dutch governments and the two East India companies. Hugh Dunthorne suggests that 'The undoubted community of interest among ordinary British and Dutch merchants seems to have been rather less in evidence at the higher

[44] H. Dunthorne, *The Maritime Powers, 1721–1740. A Study of Anglo-Dutch Relations in the Age of Walpole*, New York and London, 1986, ch. 3.

[45] Ibid., p. 58; C108/132, I. & W. Kops, Amsterdam, to Henry Gambier, London, 8 August 1719.

[46] C103/131, Charles Pike, Amsterdam, to Thomas Hall, London, 14 December 1731.

[47] Dunthorne, *Maritime Powers*, p. 58.

[48] C103/133, bundle 22, J. Senserf and Son, Rotterdam, to Thomas Hall, London, 20 December 1737, 22 July 1740. See also Chaudhuri, *Trading World*, pp. 391–2.

[49] Dunthorne, *Maritime Powers*, pp. 62–5.

level of government ministers and East India directors.'[50] The British government's half-hearted concern over the Ostend question no doubt stemmed from a mild suspicion of the East India interest, and possibly from a feeling that the Dutch were a greater threat than the Ostenders who were perhaps serving a useful function in undermining the Dutch East India Company.

There seems to be little doubt that these developments, which evidently lay outside the control of the British and Dutch governments and the two great India monopolies, go far in explaining the 'dullness' of the re-export trade in groceries during the 1720s and 1730s which is depicted in the data of Table 6.2 and Figure 6.1. As a result of the new trading ventures to Asia, European and particularly Dutch markets were swollen with additional supplies producing low prices and profits and sluggish returns. Merchants' correspondence suggests that a profit of 4 or 5% was considered to be an 'advantageous' return on the sale of re-export goods.[51] It seems that conditions of overstocked markets produced a declining trend in re-exports of Indian textiles from about the mid 1730s. Up to this point, the effect of the prohibitions had been to encourage the growth of a re-export trade in these fabrics to the Dutch staplemarket, which appears to have been competitive with exports of English woollen manufactures.

To some extent, the revival of the tobacco trade after 1723 provided some compensation for the otherwise languishing position of the Dutch re-export market during the 1730s and '40s. In 1700, almost 40% of British colonial tobacco was sent to Holland, where it was mixed with the cheaper inland Dutch and German varieties. During the wars against Louis XIV, however, deliveries of Virginia tobacco were interrupted and prices rose by at least 50% in Amsterdam, which encouraged a massive shift to inland supplies.[52] For the first quarter of the eighteenth century, European markets stagnated, and not until Walpole's customs reforms of 1722 did the trade spring back into life when drawback payments on tobacco re-exports were increased to refund the whole of the import duty.[53] The resulting fall in prices was less serious than that facing other re-export goods, as the Dutch switched from processing to the re-export of unmanufactured leaf tobacco from Rotterdam to other European consumers. 'We very well know', wrote a Glasgow merchant, 'that

---

[50] Ibid., pp. 73–4.

[51] Brants 1344, John Eccleston, London, to de Neufville, Amsterdam, 19 June and 7 December 1733; and from Claude Bosanquet, London, 2 March 1749.

[52] J. M. Price, 'The Economic Growth of the Chesapeake and the European Market, 1697–1775', *JEH*, 24 (1964), pp. 500–1; J. M. Price, 'Economic Activity', ch. 23 in J. S. Bromley (ed.), *The New Cambridge Modern History*, vol. VI, 1970, pp. 851–3; H. K. Roessingh, *Inlandse Tabak (AAG Bijdragen 20)*, 1976.

[53] 9 Geo. I, c. 21 s.6; Hoon, *English Customs System*, p. 257.

overpressed and cutt tobacco do not answer at Rotterdam.'[54] During the second quarter of the century, the trade remained fairly buoyant, overtaking the re-export trade in teas and groceries. After 1730, however, France emerged as the primary European market for colonial tobacco, where the trade was in the hands of a national monopoly company whose strategy was to buy from Britain to combat the trade in smuggled continental varieties. The same Glasgow merchant informed his Dutch correspondent at mid-century, 'You must know the French agents take all Virginia Toba[cco]after wch. we draw what's fit for other markets.'[55]

The marketing of colonial tobacco in Europe was of course radically altered by the Navigation Acts, which both added the cost of trans-shipment via England and virtually eliminated Dutch transatlantic participation in the trade.[56] From c. 1660 to 1700, tobacco was generally re-exported from England to Holland on English account, to be consigned to Dutch merchants for sale on commission. In this sense Holland became, in Jacob Price's view, a 'passive market' for colonial tobacco, and, from c. 1689, control of the trade passed into the hands of a small group of merchants who ceased to be connected with importing. By the 1690s, for example, John Cary controlled about one-third of London tobacco re-exports, while a handful of other leading exporters emerged such as Josiah Bacon and Richard Booth.[57] The growing separation of imports from re-exports, however, gave Dutch merchants a foothold in the trade, especially when Amsterdam's role as a processing centre declined and Rotterdam became purely a shipping centre for leaf tobacco. The records of Rotterdam's municipal insurance company record numerous instances of Dutch and Hollando-British merchants in that port importing shiploads of tobacco from London on their own accounts during the 1720s and '30s, including Jacob Senserf, Bastiaan Molewater, Allan and Roycroft, and Pickfatt and Foster.[58] In the 1740s, Coutts and Company of Edinburgh were purchasing substantial amounts of Virginia and Maryland tobacco for the accounts of Amsterdam merchants such as Conrad Zetsma and Jan Isaak de Neufville, while Clifford and Sons of Amsterdam were chartering vessels to bring their own cargoes of tobacco from Glasgow. The Amsterdam notarial archives still contain isolated instances of illegal direct trade

[54] Brants 1340, Colin Dunlop, Glasgow, to J. I. de Neufville, Amsterdam, 19 November 1750.
[55] Ibid.; J. M. Price, 'Economic Growth', pp. 501 5.   [56] See below, pp. 310–12.
[57] R. C. Nash, 'English Transatlantic Trade, 1660 1730: A Quantitative Study', pp. 167 89; J. M. Price, 'Economic Growth', pp. 500 1.
[58] GAR MADBR, Assurantie Boeken: J. Senserf (1 Dec. 1721); Allan and Roycroft (30 Dec. 1721; 2 and 13 Jan. 1725; 24 Jan. and 4 Feb. 1730); Pickfatt and Foster (18 Feb., 17 Mar., 5 and 8 April, 23 May, 15 Sept., 5 Nov. 1721); R. Pickfatt (4 Apr. and 27 June 1730; 19 Feb. 1735); B. Molewater (27 May 1721).

between the Chesapeake and Dutch ports, but most Dutch importers relied on British associates and touched at English ports such as Cowes before proceeding to Holland.[59]

With the exception of tobacco, the English re-export trade was characterised by poor returns and damaging side-effects affecting the consumption of English woollens abroad. Moreover, such profits as it produced did not accrue wholly to English merchants, since a large proportion of the trade was carried on Dutch accounts including groceries and Asian goods, as well as tobacco. Many of the buyers at the English East India Company's sales were either visiting or resident Dutch merchants, or agents and brokers acting for Dutch buyers. Henry Gambier, a London merchant and broker whose bankruptcy in the 1730s caused his papers to acquire the doubtful status of Chancery Masters' Exhibits, was one of the largest brokers attending the London sales, and his most substantial purchases were those for two Dutch houses established in London, John and Mattheus de Neufville and Francis and John van Hemert.[60] Mattheus established the London firm with his cousin John in 1722, and the correspondence ends ten years later, when Mattheus returned to live in Amsterdam, though no longer as a merchant; John de Neufville remained in London until at least 1743.[61] The van Hemerts appear to have been established in London for a longer period.[62] As well as making purchases on behalf of Dutch customers or resident Dutch merchants such as these, Gambier also purchased teas, chinaware and Indian textiles on his own account and seems to have developed two major outlets for these commodities: North America, mainly S. Carolina, supplied via wholesale merchants; and provincial grocers in places such as Newbury, Epsom, Wantage, Poole and Tonbridge.[63] Apart from illustrating the extent to which it was possible to combine trade on one's own account with commissions, Gambier's interests indicate the tendency of merchants engaged in the re-export trade to avoid specialisation. Trade in tea, for example, generally led to trade in other groceries, and this was usually combined with dealings in Indian textiles, and sometimes chinaware, spices and

[59] Brants 1337, J. Coutts and Comp., Edinburgh, to J. I. de Neufville, Amsterdam, 19 Jan., 9 Feb., 15 and 26 Mar., 27 Aug., 19 Nov. 1748. GAA; NA 10232/316 (B. Phaff) 30 Apr. 1745; NA 874/374 (J. Hoekeback) 6 Feb. 1700; NA 6110A (P. Schabaalje) 18 Mar. 1718; NA 8569 (A. Baars) 17 and 21 Aug., 1 Sept. 1719; NA 8621/1782 (A. Baars) 26 Nov. 1726; NA 10361/1291 (D. van der Brink) 17 Aug. 1744.
[60] PRO C108/132 (Gambier Papers), e.g. list of purchases, November 1730, 20 October 1731. On de Neufville, see van Eeghen's editorial introduction to her *Inventaris*, pp. 13–14, and Veluwenkamp, *Ondernemersgedrag*.
[61] Van Eeghen, *Inventaris*, p. 13.   [62] Brants 1344, van Hemert correspondence.
[63] C108/132, correspondence with David Compigne, S. Carolina (bundle 3); Edward Crisp, Epsom; J. Lipyeatt, Newbury; J. Rosfield, London and Poole; C. Weekes, Dorchester.

dyestuffs. The prevailing impression is that the larger dealers and brokers were likely to be most successful in the often speculative East India trade. The London linen drapers, on the other hand, who imported Dutch and German linen on their own accounts from Amsterdam and exported Indian cottons and silks from time to time to be sold on commission by Dutch houses, obtained low returns and consistently disappointing results.[64]

It is difficult to say what proportion of the re-export trade in Indian textiles was carried on the accounts of Dutch houses, but the impression given by the London merchant Claude Bosanquet was that it was considerable, when he wrote to an Amsterdam correspondent in 1751: 'Can it be worthwhile for so many of your Gentry and others to cross the seas to continue from sale to sale such a trade? Surely they must have ways of disposing of their goods at some what better prices than you do.'[65] Since the late 1740s, Bosanquet had been trading on joint account with de Neufville in East Indian goods, and he continued to do so until 1753 when the correspondence peters out. Certainly, Davenant indicated early in the century that there were 'two sorts of buyers at the candle of these [Indian] goods, viz. those who bid by commission from Holland, and our own linen drapers and other dealers in those commodities'. The former, he suggested, predominated; for, if the prohibition against Indian goods were lifted, 'the Dutch will not have it so much in their power to set their own price upon them and London, instead of Rotterdam and Amsterdam, will be the great magazine for East India wares, as heretofore it was'.[66] In terms of commercial organisation, therefore, the re-export trade was characterised by strong tendencies towards quasi-monopolistic and monopolistically competitive practices affecting both sources of supply and control of the London–Amsterdam trade by Dutch houses. It was precisely the undermining of the English and Dutch East India monopolies in the 1720s and 1730s by the Ostend traders which destabilised the trade, but the benefits to consumers in the shape of lower prices were real enough.

Competition and monopoly

The course of the re-export trade throws a good deal of light on the relative progress of the maritime powers during the early eighteenth century, and the role of monopolistic practice as an attempt to optimise profits.

[64] Brants 1344, correspondence of J. Eccleston; J. Higden, Jr; T. Smith and Son; R. Peckham; J. Waters and Sons.
[65] Ibid., C. Bosanquet, London, to J. I. de Neufville, Amsterdam, 1 January 1751.
[66] Davenant, 'Second Report', p. 434.

Several historians have perceived significant advantages in the exercise of monopoly power by the two great East India companies. By controlling import flows and the level of buying prices in Asia, the VOC, according to Klein, was able to pursue a risk-reducing strategy of stabilising prices and lowering transactions costs.[67] In addition, the company was able to combine the functions of a sovereign state with those of a large-scale business enterprise which, according to Steensgaard, lowered and 'internalised' the costs of protecting trade in distant markets.[68] In these ways, the market was rendered more predictable or 'transparent'. Less has been claimed for the EIC's monopoly status, which in any case was broken down during the 1690s. A new company, formed in 1698, merged with its predecessor in 1709 and, in general, the English company was characterised by a greater degree of public accountability than its Dutch counterpart, as the calico controversy indicates.[69] The strength of the EIC has been identified with its business methods rather than with monopoly powers as such. It functioned, in Chaudhuri's view, as an efficient bureaucracy, whose managers had 'very little to learn from modern systems theorists'.[70]

Large-scale corporate organisation may have conferred certain operational advantages, but the 'transparency thesis' is obviously weakened by the extent to which monopoly arrangements were, in practice, undermined by competition in Asia between the Dutch and English companies and their rivals, and by a market situation in Europe where the resale of oriental goods lay outside their formal control. During the 1620s and '30s, the VOC often disposed of its cargoes of pepper, spices and silk to various consortia, either at fixed prices or by contract, but this practice was halted in 1642.[71] Thereafter, the bulk of Asian imports were sold at auction by both companies to individual merchants in London, Amsterdam and Middleburg. It seems likely that the stabilising effect of monopoly purchasing powers must have operated to greatest advantage in the early decades of the companies' existence when the need for protection was greatest, in the manner described by Steensgaard, and the

[67] P. W. Klein, 'The Origins of Trading Companies', in Blussé & Gaastra (eds.), *Companies and Trade*, p. 22.
[68] By 'protection costs', Steensgaard had in mind extortion by local rulers and armed robbery which had hindered the caravan trade, supplanted in the seventeenth century by the VOC (N. Steensgaard, 'The Companies as a Specific Institution in the History of European Expansion', in Blussé & Gaastra, *Companies and Trade*, pp. 245–6).
[69] L. Neal, 'The Dutch and English East India Companies Compared; Evidence from the Stock and Foreign Exchange Markets', in J. D. Tracy (ed.), *The Rise of Merchant Empires. Long Distance Trade in the Early Modern World, 1350–1750*, Cambridge, 1990, pp. 221–3; Chaudhuri, *Trading World*, p. 448.
[70] Chaudhuri, *Trading World*, pp. 22–39.   [71] Glamann, *Dutch-Asiatic Trade*, pp. 30–9.

range of Asian imports rather limited. By the early eighteenth century, Anglo-Dutch competition in Asia had become intense, involving private merchants and interlopers as well as formal company trade. As we have seen, it was during the 1720s that English competition supplemented by the activities of the Ostend Company and its Danish and Swedish successors forced open the trade in tea and other groceries.[72] The huge expansion of the calico trade from the 1670s and '80s likewise left the Dutch behind, in the face of English and northern European competition.[73]

There can be little doubt that the multiplying demands of western European consumers for new commodities, especially cotton textiles, reduced the scope of the VOC to generate monopoly profits. Although it moved quickly into tea and coffee, the Dutch company still maintained a predominant interest in fine spices and pepper, the areas in which its monopoly had initially been most effective (Table 6.3).[74] These, however, were commodities with a lower elasticity of demand than tea, coffee and Indian textiles, which formed the mainstay of the EIC's trade – particularly the latter. Steensgaard, indeed, suggests that the consumption of spices and pepper were subject to 'the law of saturation'.[75] As competition from rival suppliers increased and prices of re-export goods in general tended to fall, the Dutch position looked increasingly vulnerable in the newer trades where the final resale price was beyond the seller's control. The logic of the situation – an oligopolistic market governed by falling prices – suggests that the weakening of monopoly trading powers in Asia must have impacted more seriously on the Dutch than the English.

Much of the reasoning behind the 'transparency thesis' rests on supply-side arguments involving the stability of buying prices in Asia. But the growth of long-distance trade and the marketing of new products depended increasingly on the readiness of the companies to respond to changing consumption habits and preferences. In broad terms, the increased competitiveness of European trade during the seventeenth century involved a shift from a seller's to a buyer's market. After extensive reorganisation and liberalisation in 1650, the English company

---

[72] Ibid., pp. 216–18; Furber, *Rival Empires*, p. 129.

[73] The Dutch may have been reluctant to enter the calico trade because it competed with their own home-produced linens and Dutch-bleached German linen (Glamann, *Dutch-Asiatic Trade*, p. 138).

[74] In the cloves, nutmegs, and mace of the Moluccas and the cinammon of Ceylon, the VOC retained an effective monopoly; English competition in the pepper trade was serious, though to a lesser extent than in the Chinese trade, especially in tea, and the Indian textiles trade (C. R. Boxer, *Dutch Seaborne Empire, 1600–1800*, p. 94).

[75] Steensgaard, 'Growth and Composition', p. 152. On the commodity composition of the VOC's trade, see J. R. Bruijn, F. S. Gaastra & I. Schoffer, *Dutch-Asiatic Shipping in the Seventeenth and Eighteenth Centuries*, vol. I, The Hague, 1987, pp. 189–94.

was quick to develop a more broadly based Asian trade, including Indian textiles, Chinese silks and tea. It responded more readily than the VOC to the craze for chintz, and established a firmer and earlier foothold in the Chinese market.[76] The movement towards greater freedom of trade after 1689 ushered in a new period of reorganisation, the outcome of which was a much broader participation in English trade with the Far East.

The Achilles' heel in this long-term strategy was, of course, the vulnerability of the English woollen industry to imported Asian products. The prohibition policy and the diversion of forbidden textiles into the re-export trade, principally to Holland, provided something of a compromise solution, albeit one which did not fully meet the woollen industry's demands for comprehensive protection. As Chaudhuri has shown, imported Indian textiles were marked by extraordinary product differentiation, so that when one type of fabric was banned, the company could easily turn to another variety.[77] As we have already noticed, the diversion of prohibited goods to Holland in some degree reduced the capacity of the Dutch staplemarket to absorb English woollens. In the long term, moreover, protection of home-produced woollens and, to a lesser extent, wrought silks merely served to encourage the consumption of Scottish and Irish linen in place of imported calicoes. The woollen interest failed in its campaigns to include the use of printed celtic linens within the terms of the prohibition, and, in 1736, parliament expressly exempted fustians (linen and cotton mixtures) from the provisions of the 1721 Act.[78] It has been persuasively argued that the long-term result of the prohibition of Asian calicoes was to encourage a protracted process of import substitution, the final result of which was the flowering of the English cotton industry. In a series of distinct stages, most of them unforeseen and unplanned, the import and re-export of Asian textiles helped to undermine production of the staple textile industries, while encouraging a taste for new, lighter fabrics.[79]

The re-export of Indian fabrics to the unprotected Dutch staplemarket thus enabled the English East India Company to develop its trade and remain on a competitive footing with the VOC, while permitting parliament to experiment with a series of protective measures designed to promote various branches of domestic textile manufacture. Profits obtained from the disposal of re-exports in Europe may not have been high, and indeed a major share of them accrued to the Dutch, who controlled not only a part of this branch of English trade but also a large slice of the English woollen

---

[76] Furber, *Rival Empires*, pp. 130–1.   [77] Chaudhuri, *Trading World*, pp. 278–9, 292–9.
[78] O'Brien, Griffiths & Hunt, 'Political Components of the Industrial Revolution', pp. 409–10.
[79] Ibid., pp. 413–18.

export trade.[80] The available price-materials suggest that the largest profits accrued to the East India Company on import rather than to merchants involved with the disposal of re-exports, who sustained themselves with the hope of an occasional speculative windfall.[81] Although re-exports provided a valuable source of foreign earnings for the British economy, re-export business was a residual activity which developed in the wake of an expanding home market. As an object of commercial policy, the encouragement of the re-export trade took second place to the protection of a domestic industrial sector which relied on home-produced raw materials and energy sources rather than the processing of imports, as in Holland.

[80] As we have seen, wholesale cloth merchants in Amsterdam and Rotterdam were drawing supplies of woollens on their own accounts from the late seventeenth century onwards, and in the 1730s were corresponding directly with English manufacturers. There was thus an organisational connection between flows of English woollens and Anglo-Indian textiles to Holland, which helps to explain the 'compensatory movements' between both branches of trade.

[81] In 1719, the Inspector General, Henry Martin, suggested that calicoes, 'much the greatest part of the whole value imported from the East Indies', were correctly valued on re-export at 12s, but overvalued 'clear on board from East India' (i.e. at import), by between 2s and 3s. The correct import valuation, he judged, was 5s rather than the EIC valuation of 7s 6d. As far as other categories of East Indian textile are concerned, it seems that these were overvalued both on import and at re-export. It seems that goods were indeed bought cheap in Asia and, if not exactly sold dear in Europe, were sold at prices which only could be described as 'moderately expensive' (H. Martin, 'An Essay Towards Finding the Balance of our Whole Trade Annually from Christmas of 1698 to Christmas 1719', CO390/14, reprinted in Clark, Guide, p. 86).

7   England, Holland and the international grain trade

In emphasising the modernity of the Dutch economy, historians have rightly stressed the key role of a specialised and highly productive agricultural sector. Large-scale grain imports from the Baltic freed the cities from the vicissitudes of the domestic harvest cycle, and released resources for the development of dairy farming, market gardening and specialised industrial crops. The English, on the other hand, moved much closer to agricultural self-sufficiency and, after 1689, opted for protectionism, the abandonment of customary and social controls over food supply, and the manipulation of prices in the interests of producers by means of subsidised export. The place of grain exports in the structure of the English economy was entirely different from the more dominant position which the Dutch Republic's grain trade occupied in relation to its more specialised agriculture and to its economy as a whole. East Anglian producers were most directly affected by overseas markets, but the impact of grain exports on the farming regions of England as a whole has been described as modest and uncertain.[1] Although England's grain surplus was at times sizeable before the early 1760s, it was nonetheless a marginal one, representing about 8% of total domestic production. Yet there is little doubt that it played a major role in undermining Amsterdam's traditional role as north-west Europe's principal grain entrepôt.

From an irregular export of a few shiploads in the 1680s, English grain exports to Holland came to exceed half a million quarters after the good harvest of 1750; and to the rest of Europe and the colonies, over a million quarters. A regular trade in grain, of considerable magnitude, had been built up over the preceding half-century. England, in brief, became a principal supplier of grain to Holland and the rest of Europe on a scale equal to and at times greater than the Baltic countries. In 1711, Davenant noted that, 'in this branch of trade, we have in a great measure supplanted those

---

[1] J. Chartres, 'The Marketing of Agricultural Produce', in J. Thirsk (ed.), *The Agrarian History of England and Wales, 1640–1750*, vol. V(II), *Agrarian Change*, Cambridge, 1985, p. 452; M. Overton, *Agricultural Revolution in England. The Transformation of The Agrarian Economy, 1500–1850*, Cambridge, 1996, pp. 88–9.

northern countries from whence Holland was heretofore furnished with grain'. But Amsterdam rather than London, he realised, still remained the international corn market of Europe. England was indeed shipping its own corn directly to every country or region listed in the customs ledgers, except India and Turkey. Over half the English grain surplus, however, still went to Holland from whence Davenant supposed the greater part was re-exported. 'In years of scarcity', he complained, 'they bring us back our own wheat, because of the premium we give upon exportation, and which they are enabled to do, by having large granaries almost in every great town... As the case now stands, the Dutch have too great a share in a plentiful year of corn here.'[2] The Baltic countries, it seemed, had been displaced by England as the cornfield of Europe, while Holland still remained its granary.

Unease about the Dutch intermediary role in this new branch of trade was increased in some quarters by the system of subsidised export, referred to by Defoe and others as 'forced export'. The bounty policy was inaugurated with the experimental Corn Law of 1672, which was made permanent in 1689 and remained in force, apart from temporary suspensions, until 1815. Ceiling prices were set, below which export was permitted, and bounties were paid to the exporter of 5s per quarter for wheat, 3s 6d for rye, and 2s 6d for malt and barley.[3] Merchants generally regarded the bounty as covering freight and handling charges involved in overseas shipment. In addition to the bounty, the export of malt was encouraged by a drawback of the malt duty during the first quarter of the eighteenth century, and by exemption from duty after 1726, of which more will be said later. Debate about the bounty system was vigorous during the years after 1750, marked by rising grain prices, but surfaced at other times, especially during poor harvest years. It was in 1728, when wheat prices at Oxford exceeded 50s per quarter, that Defoe launched his criticisms of the bounty system: 'It is true that dear or cheap, corn always finds a market in Holland; but then, 'tis as true, that if the Dutch find a forced exportation, they, like all expert merchants will buy cheap and perhaps to loss... in short, it is no market at all.'[4] Britain's brief involvement in the international grain trade thus raises several distinct issues bearing on the restructuring of what many contemporaries and modern historians regard as a vital sector on which Dutch prosperity depended. To what extent were British grain surpluses actually replacing Baltic grain previously handled by the Dutch? What was the role of subsidies in stimulating

[2] Davenant, 'Second Report', pp. 425–6.
[3] 1 Wm & Mary c. 12; D. G. Barnes, *A History of the English Corn Laws from 1660 to 1846*, 1930, ch. 2.
[4] Defoe, *Plan*, p. 234.

the trade compared with other influences such as agrarian improvement and extraneous factors such as changes in population size and the level of home demand? In what respects did subsidised British grain export damage or benefit the Dutch economy?

English exports and the decline of the Baltic grain trade

With few exceptions, historians have emphasised the vital role played by the Baltic grain trade in stimulating several key sectors of the Dutch economy, and writers such as van Dillen and Faber noted a close connection between the recession of the grain trade in the second half of the seventeenth century and Dutch economic decline in general. J. A. Faber, in a classic article, argued persuasively that rising cereal production in southern and western Europe, together with demographic stagnation, accounted for the decline of Baltic grain shipments, and we will indeed go on to show that the substantial English grain surplus played a major part in making good the continuing shortfall which existed.[5] Some have taken the argument a stage further to suggest that agrarian improvement and the 'highly competitive' position of English agriculture, bolstered by subsidies, caused English grain actually to displace Baltic supplies in European markets.[6]

However, in recent years, this picture has been re-examined and modified. Israel has disputed the centrality of Baltic trade to Dutch prosperity, arguing that Dutch commercial hegemony depended increasingly on the 'rich' non-Baltic trades, after 1647.[7] Lindblad, on the other hand, has re-confirmed the traditional view of the northern trades as the fundamental element in the Dutch commercial system, but provides a more optimistic view of their buoyancy during the second half of the seventeenth century. His investigations have corroborated Faber's view of the decline of aggregate grain shipments through the Sound during the seventeenth century, from around 68,000 lasts per year before mid-century to 55,000 lasts per year thereafter. But Lindblad shows, crucially, that the Dutch share

[5] J. A. Faber, 'Het probleem van de dalende graanaanvoer uit de Oostzeelanden in de tweede helft van de zeventiende eeuw', *AAG Bijdragen*, 9 (1963), and translated as 'The Decline of the Baltic Grain Trade in the Second Half of the Seventeenth Century' in *AHN*, 1 (1966), revised version in Heeres *et al.* (eds.), *Dunkirk to Danzig*, to which future references relate. Faber subsequently put greater stress on the significance of English grain supplies in compensating for the decline in Dutch-Baltic imports, in 'De Sontvaart als spiegel van der structuurveranderingen in de Europese economie gedurende de achttiende eeuw', *Tijdschrift voor Zeegeschiedenis*, 1 (1982), translated and repr. in Heeres *et al.* (eds.), *Dunkirk to Danzig*, as 'Structural Changes', p. 88.
[6] A. H. John, 'English Agricultural Improvement and Grain Exports, 1660–1765', in Coleman and John (eds.), *Trade, Government and Economy*, pp. 56–7.
[7] Discussed in chapter 9.

of this trade actually rose after *c.* 1650, so that the annual average of Dutch grain shipments fell by only a small margin.[8] Furthermore the tendency towards a slight contraction in the Dutch grain trade was counterbalanced by expansion in other branches of Dutch-Baltic trade, such as wood, iron, textiles and colonial goods, although these newer trades involved serious competition with other trading nations. Lindblad's revisions provide a more dynamic view of Dutch trade with the Baltic than those of either Faber or Israel, but the contraction of the grain trade is still understood in structural rather than competitive terms. How competitive, in fact, was English agriculture during the late seventeenth and early eighteenth centuries, and to what extent did English grain actually displace Baltic supplies during these years, especially during the period 1690–1760, when the Dutch-Baltic grain trade experienced a recession even more serious than that of the 1660s and '70s? The likely extent of these supply changes is indicated in the figures assembled in Table 7.1.

It is clear that total English grain exports were comparable in magnitude to shipments through the Sound from the very early years of the eighteenth century, and greatly exceeded the latter during the period 1730 to 1760. The greater proportion of Baltic grain cargoes, however, consisted of wheat and rye, with malt and barley occupying a fluctuating but usually minor position in the trade. In 1667, a year for which information is readily available, malt and barley accounted for as much as one third of Amsterdam's grain imports; in 1692, the figure was one-seventh.[9] While English exports of malt and barley replaced these Baltic imports in some degree, the massive trade in these grains from East Anglian ports in the eighteenth century was largely opening up a new area of demand in Holland – that of the distiller.[10] Bearing this in mind then, it is apparent that English exports of bread grains only began to displace Baltic shipments on a substantial scale during the period *c.* 1730 to 1760. Furthermore, there is a clear interval from the 1680s, when Baltic shipments begin to decline, to the year 1703 when English exports began to increase.

It seems therefore that there is no immediate chronological connection between the decline of the Baltic grain trade and the growth of English exports. Throughout this period of course, international grain movements were extremely marginal to the food requirements of Europe as a whole, and Faber's suggestion of a slight downturn in the demand for Baltic grain

---

[8] From 50,000 to as much as 45,000 lasts (Lindblad, 'Foreign Trade', p. 236; Lindblad, 'Structuur en Mededinging in de Handel van de Republiek op de Oostzee in de Achttiende Eeuw', *ESHJ*, 47 (1984), pp. 79–88).

[9] J. G. van Dillen, 'Stukken betreffende den Amsterdamschen graanhandel omstreeks het jaar 1681', *EHJ*, 3 (1917), p. 80.

[10] See below, pp. 221–5.

Table 7.1 *Grain shipments through the Sound, compared with English grain exports, 1680–1689 to 1760–1769*

(Decennial averages, '000 quarters)

	Grain shipments through the Sound[1]	English exports of wheat, rye and oatmeal[2]	English exports of malt and barley
1680–9	905.1		
1685–6		17.4	1.0
1690–9	587.2	3.9	46.8
1700–9	316.1	153.8	128.7
1710–19	283.7	137.2	231.5
1720–9	431.9	129.7	286.1
1730–9	336.4	312.9	221.4
1740–9	337.2	361.2	304.6
1750–9	393.0	372.2	285.2
1760–9	587.6	259.1	187.0

[1] Shipments through the Sound have been converted into quarters on the basis 1 Dutch Last = 10.75 Imperial Quarters, from data kindly supplied by Prof. J. A. Faber. In reading these figures, it should be remembered that the proportion of the Baltic grain trade handled by the Dutch increased from 78% during the first half of the seventeenth century to 85% from 1660 to 1690, falling to 70% from 1690 to 1700. From 1722 to 1740, the Dutch share was 77%, from which point it declined continually to 1741–60, 66%, and 1761–80, 55% (Lindblad, 'Foreign Trade', p. 243; 'Structuur en Mededinging', p. 90).
[2] English exports = gross exports throughout. No account is taken of the substantial wheat imports of the years 1765 to 1769.

in the later seventeenth and early eighteenth centuries remains a plausible explanation for the sustained decline of these years. Demographic stagnation, together with increasing self-sufficiency in grain production in certain parts of western and southern Europe, do indeed emerge as the major determinants of this reduced demand.[11] France, Germany and the southern Netherlands, especially Brabant, began to produce sizeable surpluses from the later seventeenth century, and de Vries identified a revival of domestic grain production in Holland in the 1690s. Zeeland in the south-west and Groningen in the north-east began sending regular shipments to the traditional grain deficit areas and to the cities.[12]

These changes not only reduced the demand for Baltic grain for international redistribution from Amsterdam but also made the Dutch

[11] Faber, 'Baltic Grain Trade', pp. 44–51.
[12] M. Morineau, 'La balance du commerce franco-néerlandais et le resserrement économique des Provinces-Unies au XVIIIème siècle', *EHJ*, 30 (1965), p. 197; K. Glamann, 'European Trade, 1500–1750', in C. M. Cipolla (ed.), *The Fontana Economic History of Europe*, vol. II, 2nd edn, 1974, pp. 464–5; J. de Vries, *The Dutch Rural Economy in the Golden Age, 1500–1700*, New Haven, 1974, p. 171.

themselves less dependent upon Baltic supplies. During the second half of the seventeenth century, on average, over half Amsterdam's grain imports were retained for domestic consumption.[13] At the same time, it seems that supply conditions in eastern Europe were beginning to alter. Wyczanski has shown that productivity, as measured by the level of the harvest, was declining in some areas of Poland between 1660 and 1765 due to soil exhaustion, the fragmentation of peasant holdings and loss of population.[14] To falling yields should be added the widespread devastation caused by the Great Northern War of 1700 to 1721, which coincided with a particularly severe outbreak of plague from 1706 to 1713. The survey of Polish crown lands undertaken from 1710 to 1715 constantly reported heavy losses of population, destruction of buildings, untilled fields, absence of estate inventories, and lack of corn for sowing. In parts of Lithuania and Western Galicia, up to 90% of farms had been deserted.[15] It is likely therefore that the tailing-off of Baltic grain supplies was largely independent of England's entry into the European grain trade until perhaps the 1730s, although English exporters doubtless took advantage of the situation. Davenant realised much of this when he wrote in 1711, 'corn is in a manner a new exportation arising to us from the war, which has in other countries so employed the hands of their people that they could not till the ground; or from deaths or plagues, wherewith divers nations have been afflicted for these last 23 years'.[16]

From about 1730 onwards, however, European demand for cereals revived. After a long period of stagnation, population began to increase, especially in southern Europe. The most dramatic growth occurred in Spain's population which increased by one third over roughly a forty-year period – from 7 millions in 1712–17 to 9.3 millions in 1756–8 – while that of Portugal increased from 2.1 to 2.5 millions between 1732 and 1770. Significant increases also occurred in France and some of the Italian states. Although the population of Holland was declining during this period, Dutch demand for overseas bread grains increased during the 1740s when Brabant was no longer in a position to export its surplus rye and buckwheat.[17] The shortages of these years were doubtless

[13] J. de Vries, *Dutch Rural Economy*, p. 172.

[14] A. Wyczanski, 'Le Niveau de la récolte des céréales en Pologne du XVIe au XVIIIe siècle', in *Contributions and Communications, First International Economic History Conference, Stockholm*, Paris, 1960, pp. 585 90.

[15] J. Gierowski and A. Kaminski, 'The Eclipse of Poland', in J. S. Bromley (ed.), *New Cambridge Modern History*, vol. VI, Cambridge, 1970, pp. 704–5.

[16] Davenant, 'Second Report', p. 424.

[17] C. H. Wilson and G. Parker (eds.), *Sources of European Economic History*, p. 37; Fisher, *Portugal Trade*, p. 29; K. F. Helleiner, 'The Population of Europe' in Rich & Wilson (eds.), *The Cambridge Economic History of Europe*, vol. IV, pp. 63–7; Faber,

exacerbated by the high prices and scarcity of meat and dairy products which followed the prolonged outbreak of cattle plague in the Netherlands from 1744, one of the most serious aspects of what van der Woude has called a 'crisis situation' in the agriculture of North Holland.[18] The late 1740s and early 1750s were marked by dearth in both France and Holland. In 1747, mobs plundered grain vessels at Rotterdam and Brielle, the cargoes of which were destined for France, though the most serious shortages occurred from 1749 to 1751.[19]

In broad outline therefore, it seems that a variety of somewhat adventitious circumstances provided English farmers with exceptionally favourable overseas market opportunities in the first half of the eighteenth century. During the initial phase of export prior to c. 1732, changes on the supply side predominated with the dislocation of east European agriculture and the trade of the Baltic ports, while European demand remained moderate. The demand for malt and barley, however, was much more elastic than that for bread grains. As we shall see, the substantial fiscal advantages associated with this branch of trade largely explain its rapid growth. In the second phase of export from c. 1732, demand for bread grains in Europe increased substantially and English producers, experiencing a run of exceptionally favourable seasons, were able to respond. In these circumstances, the role played by agricultural improvement was probably rather modest, and the suggestion that grain exports might be regarded 'in a very approximate way as the measurement of investment in agriculture' in the improved areas must be viewed with scepticism.[20]

How competitive in fact was English agriculture during the first half of the eighteenth century? It is now widely accepted that, for much of the period 1650 to 1750, agriculture in many parts of Europe was in a depressed condition, characterised by a low and falling level of grain prices. Although the complaints of farmers and landlords sometimes give a contrary impression, the extent of the price fall in England's case was only moderate and, perhaps more important, the absolute level of English cereal prices was high by European standards from the late seventeenth

Roessingh et al., 'Population Changes', pp. 60, 110; PRO CO388/95, 'Particulars of the Trade carried on between the different Ports of his Majesty's Dominions and Rotterdam, and the other Ports of the Maas, and vice-versa', by Richard Wolters, Agent at Rotterdam, 16 July 1765, unpaginated.

[18] A. M. van der Woude, Het Noorderkwartier. Een regionaal historisch onderzoek in de demografische en economische geschiedenis van westelijk Nederland van de late middeleeuwen tot het begin van de negentiende eeuw (AAG Bijdragen, 16), (1972) vol. II, pp. 585–6, 593–6; vol. III, pp. 840–1.

[19] PRO SP84/429, R. Wolters to Wm Chetwynd, 30 May 1747; see also SP 84/430, ibid., 1 and 22 Sept. 1747; Morineau, 'La Balance du commerce franco-néerlandais', pp. 196–8.

[20] John, 'English Agricultural Improvement', p. 63.

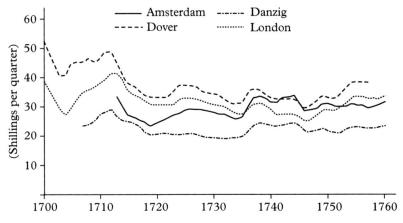

Figure 7.1 European wheat prices, 1700–60 (nine-year moving averages)

century onwards. The cereal price index constructed by Abel illustrates the first of these points: taking the first half of the period (1650–1700) as a base of 100, the index falls in the second half-century (1701–50) to 84 for England, 75 for France, 73 for the southern Netherlands, 70 for the United Provinces, and 60 for Poland. In the case of Germany and Austria, the index rises (104 and 103 respectively), and for Denmark and northern Italy it shows a moderate fall to 90 in each case.[21] On the second point, relating to the absolute level of English grain prices, Braudel and Spooner have shown beyond reasonable doubt that English wheat, measured in silver prices, was the most expensive in Europe during most of the years from 1690 to 1760, with the exception of the 1740s.[22] This is hardly surprising when we consider the nature of the unique agrarian structure which was developing in England during the early modern period, and especially after the Civil War: one of large estates divided into compact tenanted farms, highly capitalised and worked by free wage labour. The contrast with the more labour-intensive peasant farming of France and Spain, or the serf agriculture of eastern Europe, is obvious enough, and the differences were reflected in relative price levels.

Exact comparison of international wheat prices is difficult for the eighteenth century, when qualitative differences were rarely specified, but some indication of the competitive position of English wheat in relation to east European supplies may be obtained from the material assembled

[21] W. Abel, *Agrarkrisen und Agrarkonjunktur im Mitteleuropa vom 13. bis zum 19. Jahrhundert*, Berlin, 1966, pp. 152–3.

[22] F. P. Braudel & F. Spooner, 'Prices in Europe from 1450', in Rich and Wilson (eds.), *The Cambridge Economic History of Europe*, vol. IV, pp. 470–1.

Table 7.2 *European wheat prices, 1700s–1750s*

(Decennial averages, shillings per quarter)

	Eton	Dover	London	Amsterdam	Dordrecht	Polish wheat, Amsterdam	Konigsberg wheat, Amsterdam	Danzig
1700–9	36.07	44.10	29.58	–	37.69*	34.71*	29.77*	21.90
1710–19	44.89	39.01	38.11	29.05	35.50	–	–	26.47
1720–9	38.45	37.32	32.68	28.22	28.78	–	–	20.23
1730–9	32.78	31.60	27.86	26.26	26.48	26.63*	22.28*	19.48
1740–9	32.61	32.78	27.71	33.62	33.98	36.62*	30.75*	24.23
1750–9	38.50	37.74	32.74	30.80	32.73	29.52*	27.74*	22.91

Sources:

Eton, Dordrecht, Danzig	J. Marshall, *A Digest of all the Accounts*, 1833, pp. 98–9
Amsterdam	BPP, 1826–7 (Consuls' Returns)
Dover	D. A. Baker, 'The Agriculture of Kent, 1660–1760' (University of Kent Ph.D. thesis, 1976)
London	M. Combrune, *Enquiry into the Prices of Wheat, Malt &c*, 1768, p. 74
Amsterdam (Bourse)	N. W. Posthumus, *Nederlandsche Prijsgeschiedenis*, vol. I 1943, pp. 2–6

* fewer than ten quotations available

in Table 7.2. London (Bear Quay) prices are substantially lower than any other recorded English series, including Dover, yet remain well above Danzig prices throughout the period, except for the 1740s. The only means therefore by which English grain could compete with Baltic grain in European markets were through either lower transfer costs or a more advantageous timing of despatch. It is certain that the English grain trade was fairly active during the winter months when the Baltic ports were frozen up. Ralph Carr, for example, sometimes asked his correspondents for information on grain prices 'in the spring, before the Baltic is open'.[23] It was, however, mainly through lower transfer costs that English merchants were able to compete with Dutch suppliers of Baltic grain who faced the additional expense of trans-shipment via Amsterdam. Voyages from London and the east coast ports to southern Europe were obviously shorter and cheaper than those from Danzig and Konigsberg and, above all, English exporters enjoyed the advantage of the bounty which they often regarded as covering handling and freight charges. In 1738, Carr wrote to his Dunkirk agent 'I could have any quantity [of barley] at 14s p. qr. besides getting the bounty [of 2s 6d] which wd. pay a great part of the fraught and other charges.'[24] At that time, the Maisters were chartering vessels to carry wheat to Cadiz at 4s per quarter which, together with handling and port charges, was exactly covered by the bounty.[25] It is abundantly clear that without the benefit of the bounty to absorb transfer costs, English grain would not have found a market in Europe – and, in this sense, Adam Smith and others were correct in referring to the corn trade as a 'forced export'.[26] Significantly, the trend of Amsterdam wheat prices rose to reach the higher levels prevailing in London and southern counties from the 1720s, suggesting that it was the growth of European demand, rather than English competitiveness, which provided the main stimulus.

The course of trade and the impact of subsidies

Writing in the *Farmer's Magazine* for 1802, Dr George Skene Keith, author of one of the Board of Agriculture's county reports, surveyed the rise, progress and decline of the English grain trade during the previous

---

[23] NRO ZCE10/11, R. Carr to R. Hayes, Konigsberg, 2 Nov. 1738.
[24] Ibid., R. Carr to Wm Norton, Dunkirk, 24 Nov. 1738.
[25] Maister Letters, N. Maister to H. Maister, London, 4 Feb. 1738; H. Maister to N. Maister, Hull, 28 Feb. 1738.
[26] Comparison of the data contained in Table 7.2 confirms that transfer costs were wholly absorbed by the bounty, since prices of English grain sold on the Amsterdam Bourse were rarely higher than London prices.

Table 7.3 *The English grain trade, 1697–1801*

(million quarters)

		exports	imports	excess exports (+) / imports (−)
1697–1731	wheat	3.59	0.13	+3.46
	malt & barley	7.47	0.04	+7.43
	oats & rye	1.32	0.61	+0.71
1732–66	wheat	11.54	0.29	+11.25
	malt & barley	10.26	0.05	+10.21
	oats & rye	1.80	1.07	+0.73
1767–1801	wheat	3.06	10.54	−7.48
	malt & barley	2.61	1.96	+0.65
	oats & rye	0.90	16.04	−15.14

Source: Cust. 3

century.[27] The course of that trade, he considered, fell naturally into three equal and distinct periods, as the statistics of the Inspector General of Imports and Exports showed. The first period of moderate exports, from 1689 to 1732, coincided with a 'period of national economy [when] our agriculture had a much inferior population to support; and . . . the bounty which had recently been given by Parliament no doubt stimulated our exportation, which had formerly been loaded with a duty'. During the second phase, one of sustained growth from 1732 to 1766, 'the population was not much increased; only a small quantity of oats was consumed on horses; and not a great demand for barley, either by the distiller or the common brewer . . . the seasons in general had been more favourable, and crops more abundant'. During the 1760s, grain exports were overtaken by imports and the last three decades of the century formed a period of substantial net imports. This third period, the writer emphasised,

was distinguished by a great increase of population, a very improved mode of agriculture, and a high degree of national exertion stimulated by a national spirit of enterprise, a great accumulation of capital, and also by our national luxury and profusion. Notwithstanding which, we have imported an immense quantity of corn (nearly one year's supply), in the course of the last 35 years.[28]

The interest of Skene Keith's account lies in the weight which it places on the bounty system and the absence of population growth in encouraging exports, together with the added stimulus of good seasons during the years of most substantial export. Gains in productivity play a minor

[27] G. S. Keith, 'A General View of the Corn Trade and Corn Laws of Great Britain', *Farmers' Magazine*, 11 (1802), pp. 277–96.
[28] Ibid., pp. 278–81.

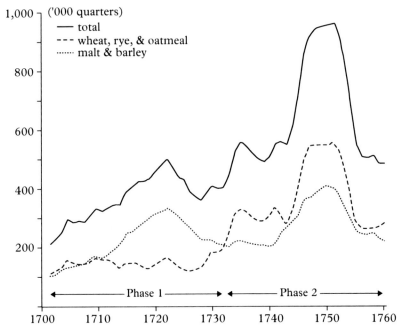

Figure 7.2 English grain exports, 1700–1760 (nine-year moving averages)

role, and are associated with the later years of the century in the shape of 'a very improved mode of agriculture'. In pursuing the analysis further, with its emphasis on the impact of subsidies, we must disaggregate the trade into its component parts, as different grains were affected by different sources of demand. The bread grains wheat, rye and oatmeal were exported as foodstuffs either to the granaries of Holland for both domestic consumption and international redistribution, or directly to European markets, particularly those of the south, during periods of scarcity. Malt and barley, however, were exported as industrial raw materials for the supply of brewers and distillers, especially those of Holland. This important distinction, which is also reflected in the organisation of the grain trade, emerges strikingly from the Inspector General's commercial statistics (Figures 7.2–7.4).[29]

[29] Given the wide extent of annual fluctuations in the grain trade, depending largely on the state of the harvest, objection can legitimately be made against the use of a moving average. It has been undertaken in order to facilitate visual comparison of various sets of figures, and because the trade can arguably be seen as a regular trade supplied by a growing surplus; but the trends shown in Figures 7.1–7.3 should be read in conjunction with the annual grain export figures given in Appendix 7, pp. 360–1.

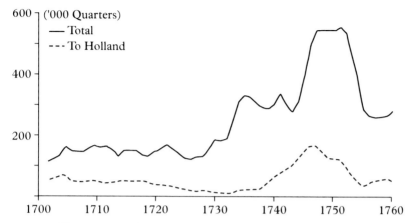

Figure 7.3 English exports of wheat, rye and oatmeal, 1700–1760 (nine-year moving averages)

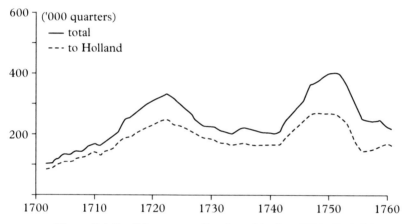

Figure 7.4 English exports of malt and barley, 1700–1760 (nine-year moving averages)

The official statistics provide a reasonable indication of the real volume of grain shipments, though a margin of error arises due to merchants' over-entries made in order to claim excess subsidies. The Customs Letter Books suggest that this became more common in the 1740s and early 1750s, when supervision of a rapidly growing volume of shipments became more lax.[30] Figures for these years may therefore be somewhat exaggerated, though this is unlikely to affect the relative proportions of

[30] PRO Cust. 97/1 16 (Yarmouth, Collector-Board). By 1744, complaints begin to appear on this score together with requests for additional officers.

the different grains exported. The first two phases identified by Skene Keith in the history of the eighteenth-century grain trade are clearly reflected in the trends shown in Figure 7.2. The first phase of export, it is clear, was dominated by a growing volume of malt and barley exports, while exports of cereal grains remained at a modest level. During the second phase of more substantial export, the position was reversed, with the overall trend determined by a much larger volume of wheat, rye and oatmeal shipments. As we shall see, it was adjustments to the system of subsidised export which played a major part in shaping changes in the composition of the trade between these two sub-periods.

The figures also show that Holland's apparent predominance as a market for English grain was largely confined to the first phase of export prior to 1731, during which malt and barley dominated the trade, since the Dutch market always absorbed a far higher proportion of English malt and barley than cereals. More precisely, between 10% and 45% of England's surplus wheat, rye and oatmeal was sent to Holland annually, while over 75% of malt and barley exports were annually disposed of in this way until the proportion fell in the late 1740s and early 1750s. In 1751, this represented one third of Holland's total wheat and rye imports, one half of its total barley imports and almost all its total malt imports.[31]

As one might expect, the export of cereals to Holland was more sensitive to wartime conditions than was the case with the malt and barley trade, and, during periods of peace, the former was only of marginal significance. During the first twenty years of the eighteenth century, around 50,000 quarters were sent annually to the Low Countries; exports declined steadily thereafter to the low levels of the 1730s. During the War of the Austrian Succession, however, the Dutch market revived considerably when exports of bread grains reached levels of over 150,000 quarters. At this time, the British army was supplied from Holland and this situation, together with trading difficulties brought about by war, goes some way towards explaining why the proportion of bread grains exported to Holland rose substantially.[32] Various circumstances unconnected with wartime conditions also had a bearing on the situation, such as the short-term difficulties facing Dutch farmers and the availability and prices of alternative supplies, especially from the Baltic. Nonetheless, it remains true that in the grain trade, as in a number of other branches of Anglo-Dutch trade, the redistributive functions of the Dutch market revived during wartime as direct trade between England and southern Europe became difficult. In 1739, for example, a Newcastle merchant wrote to

[31] Barnes, *English Corn Laws*, p. 46, n. 24.
[32] CO388/95, 'Particulars of the Trade ... [with] Rotterdam'.

his Rotterdam correspondent: 'We would have a very brisk corn export for the Portugal and Spanish markets, but since our masters have got a notion of Spanish privateers being out they won't go any way to the southward.'[33] When peace returned, the markets of southern Europe, principally Spain, Portugal and the Straits of Gibraltar, regained their previously predominant position in this branch of the trade.[34]

The export of malt and barley to Holland, being less subject to the artificial stimulus of war, followed a more stable course than exports of bread grains. While malt and barley exports to Europe as a whole indeed rose significantly during the War of the Austrian Succession, the proportion sent to Holland actually declined, emphasising that these grains were sent to Holland for industrial use rather than for storage and redistribution to other European markets, as was the case with bread grains. Two constant features of this branch of trade should be emphasised at the outset. First, malt was always exported in greater quantities than barley for fiscal reasons, usually in proportions greater than 4:1. Secondly, Norfolk and the ports of Yarmouth, and to a lesser extent Wells and Lynn, were of overwhelming national predominance in the trade because of the extent of the grain-producing hinterland and the accessibility of the Dutch market.[35] As some of the opponents of the bounty system were later to argue, the temptation to ship grain to Holland in preference to the home market was strong in view of the short sea voyage and the low cost of water transport for a bulky commodity sensitive to handling charges.[36] Carriage by sea, it was estimated in the late seventeenth century, was generally twenty times cheaper than carriage by land, a calculation which was probably 'little exaggerated'.[37] Of the two groups of Dutch consumers of English malt and barley, the brewers and the distillers, the latter took by far the larger share since most brewers already operated their own malt houses; and the Dutch distilleries were indeed highly accessible to the East Anglian ports. By 1771, when the location of the mature distilling industry had been fully worked out, it was apparent that of the 200 distilleries in Holland, 122 were located at Schiedam, 22 at Rotterdam and 22

[33] ZCE10/12, Carr Ellison Mss, R. Carr to T. M. Liebenrood, 29 Sept. 1739.
[34] Spain, Portugal and the Straits of Gibraltar received on average 51% of English exports of wheat, rye and oatmeal during the period 1749–51 as compared to Holland's 20%; during the period 1744–6, the respective figures were 15% and 39% (BL Add Ms 38387, fols. 31–52). On the course and organisation of the grain trade to Portugal, see H. E. S. Fisher, *Portugal Trade*, pp. 64–71, 115–16.
[35] The East Anglian ports handled over three-quarters of total malt and barley exports during much of the period – see Table 7.5; see also Defoe, *Plan*, p. 236, and Burrish, *Batavia Illustrata*, p. 373.
[36] Combrune, *Enquiry*, pp. 95–6.
[37] By Sir Robert Southwell in a paper read before the Royal Society in 1675, and referred to in T. S. Willan, *The English Coasting Trade, 1600–1750*, Manchester, 1938, pp. xiv–xv.

at Delftshaven.[38] In other words, 83% of all distilleries in Holland were to be found in the Maas region where the bulk of English trade was already concentrated. The malt and barley trade therefore possessed a notably regional character, connecting two well-defined areas on either side of the North Sea. During the second and third decades of the century when the business of malting and malt export was subject to much discussion, the arguments of maltsters and merchants emerged as a distinctly regional issue.

If English merchants and maltsters were encouraged, under the stimulus of bounties and other inducements, to export to the nearby market of Holland, Dutch distillers were equally keen to take a subsidised product. In addition to the bounty, the export of malt was further encouraged by a drawback of the malt duty during the first quarter of the eighteenth century, and by exemption from duty after 1726.[39] Modern writers on the grain trade have consistently emphasised the stimulating effects of the bounty system on exports, particularly wheat, but have failed to recognise the twofold stimulus which lay behind the growing volume of malt exports from the early years of the century. This is all the more surprising since the bounty represented a less substantial fiscal incentive than the drawback, which cancelled out a heavy duty. From 1697 to 1760, a duty of 6d was to be paid by the maltster for every bushel of malt made (i.e., 4s per quarter); but the whole of this sum could be 'drawn back' or reclaimed if the malt was exported overseas. The purpose of the drawback, as one reliable commercial writer suggested, was to 'enable the English merchant to furnish the Southern parts of the Province of Holland, and other countries as cheap, or cheaper, than those of Amsterdam could do with the malt they make of the barley imported from the Baltic'.[40] The extent to which the provisions of the Act achieved this result was as much due to evasion and manipulation of the excise regulations by exporting maltsters, as to anything which parliament had been able to devise.

Because bounties and drawbacks were paid on the basis of bulk rather than weight, exporting maltsters contrived to produce a bulkier product than they otherwise might have done, by manipulating the excise regulations which attempted to control the extent to which barley was allowed to swell and germinate during the malting process.[41] The Excise Office claimed in 1717 that it had become a common practice for

---

[38] Visser, *Verkeersindustrieen*, p. 97.
[39] 9 Wm III c. 12; the duty was halved in 1725 by 11 Geo. I c. 4; 12 Geo. I c. 4 granted exemption from duty.
[40] Burrish, *Batavia Illustrata*, p. 376.
[41] For details of the malting process, see P. Mathias, *The Brewing Industry in England, 1700–1830*, Cambridge, 1959, pp. 406–11. After steeping in a cistern for three to four days, the water was drained off, and the barley was placed in a wooden 'couch' for

exporting maltsters to allow their barley to sprout and grow 'excessively' as it lay on the malthouse floor, following the steeping and germination stages. In this way, it was alleged, maltsters were able to convert twenty bushels of barley into thirty bushels of malt and obtain a 'bonus' drawback on the excess ten bushels. The excise officers were obliged to grant an allowance of ten bushels in every twenty to account for shrinkage, but maltsters were able to 'almost entirely prevent' shrinkage taking place.[42] Furthermore, bounties were claimed, and paid, in proportion to the amount of drawback. This practice, it was said in 1717, was chiefly carried on in Norfolk where it was 'much increased of late years', but was beginning to spread to other counties.[43] The predominance of Norfolk was reflected in the drawback figures quoted by the Excise Office two years later. Around 90% of all drawbacks paid on malt exports were claimed by Norfolk exporters during the years 1716 to 1719.[44] Similar accusations were made of a more exaggerated kind by the brewers who were to a limited extent competing for the same raw materials as maltsters.[45] 'Barley was steeped so as to increase eight or ten times in measure', it was alleged, 'and being exported under the name of malt, received bounty on that quantity.'[46] This was the 'bogus-malt' which probably figured more prominently in the polemical literature surrounding the conflict between the revenue authorities and the maltsters than it did in reality.

In their anxiety to protect the revenue, the customs and excise authorities tended to ignore the technical requirements of the Dutch distillers for whom the bulk of Norfolk malt exports were destined. Indeed, the Excise Office described the latter as a 'commodity of little or no value, which can make little or no returns from foreign parts'.[47] But in fact the 'blowing-up' of barley by East Anglian maltsters produced the 'long-malt' with a high enzyme content which was necessary for the distilling

---

twenty-four hours when swelling took place. It was then spread on the malthouse floor for germination, for 12–15 days. According to the type of malt being produced, the shoot of the grain (the 'acrospire') was allowed to grow to varying lengths, and vigorous 'acrospiring' could be encouraged by sprinkling with water. Finally, the germinated grain was dried on the kiln.

[42] PRO Cust. 48/11 (Excise and Treasury), 9 Nov. 1717. See also Mathias, *Brewing Industry*, p. 431.

[43] Cust. 48/1. These practices were facilitated by the fact that bounties were payable in London as well as the port of export.

[44] Cust. 48/11, 8 Dec. 1719.

[45] By the early eighteenth century, it had become a common practice for brewers to undertake their own malting, but malt produced for the export trade generally used poorer-quality barley than that produced for the inland trade. See below, p. 235.

[46] W. T. Comber, *An Inquiry into the State of National Subsistence*, 1808, pp. 142–3; Combrune, *Enquiry*, pp. 83–4.

[47] Cust. 48/11.

of Dutch genever.[48] The composition of long malt was such that it broke down the large quantities of unmalted grain with which it was mixed in the initial stages of production. Some Yarmouth exporters, it seems, were in effect undertaking this preliminary stage of production by exporting a mixture of long malt and unmalted grain which, because of the extra bulk created, could be a highly profitable operation through the additional bounties claimed.[49] In 1714, for example, the Collector of Customs at Yarmouth sent a sample of Norfolk malt to the Commissioners of Trade in London, asking them to note the 'foulness and dross therein, whereof there is great quantities shipd from hence, tho' some shipd off is of a better sort'.[50] From a mixture of malted and unmalted grain, crude malt spirits (*moutwijn*) were produced which were redistilled (or 'rectified') with the flavour of juniper berries. These two basic processes were in fact separately organised: malt was purchased by the distillers of Schiedam to be converted into crude spirits, which was then sold on the *Moutwijnbeurs* at Schiedam (established, significantly, in 1718) to the wine merchants of Rotterdam who undertook redistillation and organised export to France, England and Spain.[51] As Combrune explained, the Dutch were able to make good the defects of cheap English malt and 'ever attentive to their interests, soon found on what easy conditions their distilleries might be maintained'.[52] Here, it seemed, was the mercantilist's case of a damaging trade: one which resulted in the loss of potentially useful raw materials to the advantage of a competitor's manufacturing industry. Certainly, the cheapness of subsidised English malt and barley was its prime attraction, and one of the government's diplomatic agents had seen these grains sold in Rotterdam 'for little more than an honest maltster in England could prepare it, or the farmer get it into his barn', and ascribed this to the unintended effects of the drawback.[53] No doubt the exporting maltster obtained his profit chiefly at the expense of the public revenue, but the point could be made that the trade opened up a market for inferior

[48] Mathias, *Brewing Industry*, pp. 408, 430. Malt with a long 'acrospire' was commonly described as 'long malt'.

[49] Cust. 97/3, 27 Oct. 1714.

[50] Ibid.; see also Cust. 97/5, 12 Sept. 1726, when samples were again taken of malt intended for Holland which was said to be 'little better than screening of malt . . . the officers seeing the corn rise badly out of the lighter . . . stopped the shipping that part of which was very bad and lay at the bottom of the lighter'.

[51] Visser, *Verkeersindustrieen*, p. 93; Lord Kinross, *The Kindred Spirit. A History of Gin and the House of Booth*, 1959, p. 1.

[52] Combrune, *Enquiry*, p. 68. The Excise Office acknowledged that 'Distillers in Holland can make spirits much cheaper than the distillers here can do', on account of the cheapness of English malt, although this was inconsistent with its basic argument that the malt export trade was of 'little or no value' (Cust. 84/11, 9 Nov. 1717).

[53] Burrish, *Batavia Illustrata*, p. 376.

barleys which were most suitable for 'blowing-up' and, in the words of the maltster, were 'fittest for a foreign market'.[54]

As far as the revenue authorities were concerned, however, a situation had arisen in which maltsters were obtaining higher drawback and bounty payments than the legislature had intended and, in many instances, this actually amounted to fraudulent practice.[55] An attempt was made in 1720 to remedy these abuses with the passage of an Act which was possibly drafted by the Excise Office and which attempted to prohibit excessive 'acrospiring', that is, the swelling of the acrospire or shoot of the grain.[56] This was apparently difficult to define or enforce, particularly in view of the fact that long malt (malt with a long 'acrospire') was technically necessary for Dutch distillers. Six years later, therefore, the drawback was totally withdrawn and all malt intended for export was in future to pay no duty in the first place.[57] In spite of the degree of forward planning on the part of maltsters and exporters which this necessitated, the 1726 Act seems to have worked reasonably well. Complaints were occasionally received from the Commissioners of Customs that the quantity of malt entered on an excise certificate did not agree with the quantity entered on the debenture (relating to malt actually exported), but this could easily be explained by local conditions. Each maltster might make thirty, forty or fifty steepings of malt in a season, all of which would be placed in his warehouse under a joint lock with the excise officer.[58] Although individual withdrawals from this stock might not tally with the excise certificates, the officers were satisfied provided that an overall balance was obtained at the end of the season. This appears to have been well understood at Yarmouth which handled a high proportion of all malt exports. Malt and barley exports to Holland show a sharp decline from 276,000 quarters in 1726 to 186,000 in the following year, reaching 128,000 quarters in 1729, suggesting that the legislation was fairly successful in curtailing the worst excesses of exporting maltsters. The years 1728 and 1729 were marked by dearth and high prices so that we would in any case expect some decline in exports, but it is clear that this was already under way in 1727.

[54] Cust. 48/11, 8 Dec. 1719; see also Cust. 97/11, 1 Mar. 1741; Cust. 97/2, 31 Oct. 1740; and Mathias, *Brewing Industry*, pp. 405, 408.
[55] That is, whenever the drawback claimed exceeded the original amount of duty paid, or when unmalted was mixed with malted grain, and the malt bounty claimed for the whole amount.
[56] 6 Geo. I c. 21, taking effect from 1 June 1720. A draft appears in Cust. 48/11, 5 Jan. 1720.
[57] From 24 June 1726 by 12 Geo. I c. 4. Maltsters intending to produce malt for export were in future obliged to give written notice before steeping began.
[58] Cust. 97/7, 25 Aug. 1731; Cust. 97/9, 31 Dec. 1735.

The Act of 1726, therefore, made that of 1720 (attempting to control 'acrospiring') somewhat redundant. The bounty on exported malt still continued so that some incentive remained to 'blow-up' barley, but withdrawal of the drawback had reduced this considerably. In 1730, the provisions of the 1720 Act relating to 'acrospiring' were repealed, and a fixed ratio was statutorily established between the quantity of barley steeped and the output of malt produced.[59] There is no evidence, however, to suggest that these proportions were strictly adhered to. By 1738, it was reported that 'malt for Holland markets... in making is suffered to run out to a very great length on the floors', and, in 1741, that 20 quarters of barley were made into 38 or 40 quarters of malt.[60] It seems, therefore, that the remarkable growth of English malt exports during the first quarter of the eighteenth century (and possibly beyond) owed little to the natural competitiveness of the malting industry, but proceeded rather from quite adventitious circumstances, namely, the manipulation of fiscal incentives which in some instances involved fraudulent practice. However, the conjuncture of the English malt legislation with the technical requirements of Dutch distillers produced, on the supply side, a flow of heavily subsidised raw materials whose expansion was self-reinforcing given that the demand for Dutch spirits was highly elastic. Certainly, the English agent in Rotterdam had no doubt that Dutch distillers had a 'constant vent for as much spirits as they could make' during the first half of the eighteenth century when 'almost all the distillers and most part of the brewers used to depend upon England for malt'.[61] It is hardly surprising, then, that the period which saw the most rapid growth of the Dutch distilling industry coincided with that of the English bulk export of malt and barley.

English grain exports and the Dutch economy

While it would be inaccurate to suggest that English grain exports actually undermined the Dutch-controlled Baltic trade, English exporters were quick to exploit the opportunities arising from its decline. It is important, however, to avoid the mistake of those contemporaries who suggested that a profitable trade must necessarily be driven at the expense of competitors. The notion that English grain exports damaged the Dutch economy and that 'Holland's loss was England's gain' would be misleading

---

[59] By 3 Geo. II c. 7, taking effect from 24 June 1730.
[60] Cust. 97/6, 31 July 1730; Cust. 97/11, 18 Nov. 1738; ibid., 1 Mar. 1741.
[61] CO388/95, 'Particulars of the Trade ... [with] Rotterdam'.

in several respects.[62] The advantages enjoyed by English landowners and farmers in the form of higher prices were obtained, if anything, at the expense of domestic consumers rather than the Dutch, whose prosperity depended on a steady supply of imported grain to supplement home production.

It is clear that the shift in European demand from Baltic to English sources did indeed reduce the derived demand for Dutch shipping in this important branch of trade. Yet, on balance, it is probable that the Dutch economy benefited from the import of subsidised English grain. We have already seen that England's entry into the international grain trade was facilitated if not actually brought into being by the dislocation of Baltic supplies so that, in reality, English grain shipments provided the only alternative to shortages and higher prices.[63] Shipping from the Baltic to Holland suffered not only during the Great Northern War from 1700 to 1721, but also as a result of the Nine Years' War and the War of the Spanish Succession. In each successive decade from 1688 to 1721, Baltic shipping to Holland declined by about one third. When peace was restored in 1721, Dutch-Baltic shipping recovered to such an extent as to exceed the previous high level of the 1680s.[64] With the outbreak of the War of the Polish Succession in 1731, however, Dutch-Baltic trade was again dislocated for several years. In 1734, William Stout explained that great quantities of grain were being shipped from London and southern England, 'there being now heavy wars in Poland upon the election of a King; Dantzig besieged, and much destroyed, from whence most of Europe was supplied with corn; and now the country is so ruined that they fear a famine there, as also in Germany'.[65] Without these substantial grain shipments from England to make good the continuing shortfall of imports from the Baltic, Holland's domestic economy as well as her international trading position would have faced added strains. Wages in the Dutch Republic were already higher than those of its competitors, and high food prices would have widened the gap still further.[66] With a small and specialised agricultural sector and a substantial industrial base, which remained tied to overseas markets, the Dutch were extremely vulnerable to increases in the price of imported grain. Jan de Vries has shown how

---

[62] John, 'English Agricultural Improvement', p. 57.   [63] See above, pp. 209–13.

[64] J. Knoppers, 'Dutch-Baltic Shipping from the late Seventeenth to the early Nineteenth Century' (Papers presented to the Fifth Conference on Baltic Studies, Columbia University, May 1976), pp. 8–9.

[65] J. D. Marshall (ed.), The Autobiography of William Stout of Lancaster, 1665–1752, Manchester, 1967, pp. 217–18.

[66] Joh. de Vries, Economische Achteruitgang, p. 107.

the functioning of the entire Dutch economy depended upon its ability to obtain regular supplies of overseas grain: by the mid seventeenth century, foreign grain fed well over half of the million inhabitants of Holland, Utrecht, Friesland and Groningen, and the position changed little over the next century.[67] Over a long period, the Dutch had freed themselves from the necessity for extensive arable cultivation which enabled them to devote resources to more productive activities. The labour and capital thus released found employment in industry and commerce, and a highly specialised form of agriculture developed on the basis of dairying and the production of industrial crops.[68] Only when harvests failed over large areas of Europe did Dutch farmers temporarily revert to a more balanced system of mixed farming, as in 1709, when a Rotterdam correspondent reported that: 'At present, corn being so dear, it is the opinion of most people that instead of sowing flax, the country people will sow corn.' The price of rapeseed, he added, would probably rise for the same reason.[69]

In his survey of food crises in the pre-industrial Netherlands, J. A. Faber concluded that, in the seventeenth and eighteenth centuries, scarcity was less severe and price rises less extreme than in most other European countries.[70] This favourable situation, he observed, arose from Holland's position at the centre of the world market for grain, together with a relatively high level of real wages which implied a higher elasticity of demand for grain than was the case elsewhere.[71] Although Faber insisted that these conclusions were based on impressionistic evidence, the relatively moderate extent of fluctuations in the price of wheat in Holland as compared with other parts of Europe is borne out by the evidence of price fluctuations on the grain markets of Europe.[72] Fluctuations on the Amsterdam market seem to have been less marked than those in London from 1713 to 1760, with the exception of 1740–1. On the other hand, the instability of French grain markets (against which Faber compared the position of Holland) seems to have been somewhat exceptional in the eighteenth century.[73] Nevertheless, the relatively small size of the United Provinces and its population together with the excellence of internal communications meant that dearth in any part of the country could easily be

---

[67] J. de Vries, *Dutch Rural Economy*, pp. 172–3.   [68] Ibid., p. 10.

[69] NRO ZBL192 (Blackett (Matfer) Mss, Blackett Letter Book), John Blackett to Ralph Hael, 12 Mar. 1709.

[70] J. A. Faber, *Dure tijden en hongersnoden in preindustrieel Nederland*, Amsterdam, 1959, p. 9.

[71] Ibid., p. 10.   [72] Ormrod, *Grain Exports*, pp. 84–8.

[73] J. Meuvret, 'Les Oscillations des prix des céréales aux XVIIe et XVIIIe siècles en Angleterre et dans les Pays du Bassin Parisien', *Revue d'Histoire Moderne et Contemporaine*, 16 (1969), and reprinted in Meuvret (ed.), *Etudes d'Histoire Economique* (Cahiers des Annales, 32, 1971), p. 123.

relieved in all but the most severe years of shortage.[74] The granaries of Amsterdam seldom held less than 200,000 quarters of grain, and during years of scarcity, overseas export was prohibited by the States General.[75] Although the level of duties on imported grain was frequently disputed amongst the Admiralty Colleges, with those of Zeeland and Friesland demanding stronger protection for their own agriculture, the opposition of the Admiralties of Holland prevailed, and duties remained low. The tariff reforms of 1681 and 1725 abolished export duties on grain, and import duties on wheat and rye amounted to no more than 3 or 4% of real values.[76]

Although figures are not available to indicate the quantity of grain imports retained for domestic consumption, the course of prices suggests that the Dutch were successful in maintaining an adequate supply of imported grain which, given the specialised nature of Dutch agriculture, was essential to feed a relatively large urban population. By subsidising the export of surplus grain to Holland and other markets, English landlords were passing on the advantages of low food prices at a time when alternative supplies from the Baltic were interrupted. As consumers of imported grain, the Dutch could hardly fail to benefit from this situation.[77] As merchants and carriers of grain, however, it is likely that the Dutch suffered from English competition in this extremely important branch of trade, which in the seventeenth century had provided the basis for Amsterdam's prosperity. To what extent was this the case?

From time to time, Dutch corn merchants did indeed complain of English competition in the international grain trade. In the discussions preceding the *Propositie* of 1751, when the Admiralties of Holland came into conflict on the question of grain import duties, the Maas College argued for the total abolition of import duties on wheat, rye and barley, on the grounds that English merchants were underselling the Dutch in Mediterranean markets.[78] The Amsterdammers, however, anxious to maintain their income from the existing duties, put forward a more

[74] Such as 1698; see J. G. van Dillen, 'Dreigende hongersnood in de Republiek in de laatste jaren der zeventiende eeuw', in van Dillen, *Mensen en achtergronden, studies, uitgegeven ter gelegenheid van de tachtigste verjaardag van de schrijver*, Groningen, 1964, pp. 193–226; J. G. van Dillen, 'Amsterdams's Role in Seventeenth-Century Dutch Politics and its Economic Background', in J. S. Bromley and E. H. Kossman (eds.), *Britain and the Netherlands in Europe and Asia*, vol. II, Groningen, 1964, pp. 145–6.

[75] J. Arbuthnot, 'A Short Account of the Corn Trade of Amsterdam' (1773), *Annals of Agriculture* XXVII (1796) p. 370; W. D. Voorthuijsen, *De Republiek der Verenigde Nederlanden en het Mercantilisme*, 's-Gravenhage, 1965, pp. 65–7.

[76] Hovy, *Voorstel van 1751*, pp. 131, 483–5.

[77] See the 'Commentary' by Jan de Vries in Krantz and Hohenberg (eds.), *Failed Transitions*, p. 55.

[78] Hovy, *Voorstel van 1751*, p. 484, n. 234.

confident position, arguing that the trade could easily bear a low duty and that their long credit was indispensable.[79] Earlier in the century, Davenant had warned that the Dutch were pressing for high duties on imported English grain, especially malt, in retaliation against the English duty increases on Dutch linens.[80] These complaints, however, were made by specific interest groups arguing particular cases; they did not represent English competition as an urgent threat and in fact they were not acted upon.

The impact of English competition in the carrying trade was modified by two sets of circumstances. In the first place, it is clear that a certain amount of Dutch capital and shipping was in any case employed in the English grain trade. While Dutch agents were frequently used by English exporters, Dutch merchants are known to have exported English grain on their own accounts, and some Dutch capital was certainly employed in the East Anglian malt trade.[81] Recourse was made to Dutch and other foreign shipping during wartime and, when the flow of grain exports was reversed, as in 1728, 1740 and the later 1760s, shortages were relieved by wheat and rye imported from Dutch ports in Dutch ships.[82]

In the second place, it appears that Dutch merchant capital found more profitable employment in trades other than the carriage of Baltic grain, given that the domestic market was now adequately supplied with English grain. A number of writers have drawn attention to the fact that activity in the Dutch-Baltic grain trade corresponded closely to the level of grain prices prevailing in Danzig and Amsterdam, with falling prices producing stagnation or decline. This relationship seems to apply in the case of secular trends as well as short-term movements. Thus, van Dillen accounted for the decline of the period 1650 to 1680, the revival of the 1680s and '90s, and the stagnation of the period 1720 to 1750 by reference to price movements, while Knoppers explains annual Dutch-Baltic shipping movements in similar terms during the first half of the eighteenth century.[83] Certainly, contemporaries were well aware of this. 'The importation of foreign corn [is] very considerable' wrote the English agent in

[79] Ibid., pp. 483–4.

[80] PRO CO389/18, Davenant's 'Memorial to the Lord Treasurer concerning the free trade now carried on between France and Holland', 17 Dec. 1705.

[81] See above, p. 00.

[82] SP84/517, R. Wolters to Wm Frazer, 12 Dec. 1767, 'All most all the wheat that comes to this market [Rotterdam] is bought up, to be sent to some part of England.' See also R. B. Westerfield, *Middlemen in English Business, particularly between 1660 and 1769*, New Haven, 1915, p. 163.

[83] J. G. van Dillen, 'Economic Fluctuations and Trade in the Netherlands, 1650–1750', in P. Earle (ed.), *Essays in European Economic History, 1500–1800*, Oxford, 1974, p. 202; Knoppers, 'Dutch-Baltic Shipping', p. 9.

Rotterdam, 'this is all laid upon store which is a sign that the Dutch, who understand this trade as well as any nation whatsoever, expect that there will be a great demand from abroad'.[84]

During the first half of the eighteenth century therefore, and especially in the period 1720 to 1750, it is hardly surprising that the Baltic grain trade stagnated when a period of low grain prices coincided with several other restraining influences, notably, political disturbances and disruption of trade, increasing self-sufficiency in grain production in southern and western Europe, and a growing preference for wheat in place of rye, which implied a shift away from Baltic suppliers. Not only did the Baltic grain trade as a whole stagnate, however, there was an absolute and relative decline in the share of that trade handled by the Dutch from the 1690s onwards. During the years from 1660 to 1690, the Dutch share stood at around 85%, falling to 70% during the 1690s. Following a marginal improvement during the 1720s and '30s, decline was continuous after 1741, so that, by the 1780s, Dutch shipping carried no more than 55% of the rye and 49% of the wheat passing through the Sound.[85] A larger share of the trade was now being handled by Scandinavians and Hansards. By itself this substantial decline in Dutch-Baltic grain shipments would have proved extremely damaging to the Dutch economy; but in fact Dutch merchants merely shifted their interests from grain to other products, especially timber. In the 1660s, no more than a million 'pieces' of Baltic timber were imported into Holland. By the 1730s, the figure had risen to 10 million pieces, a level which was maintained until 1780.[86]

While the English and the Swedes participated in the rapid expansion of the Baltic timber trade which occurred after 1720, the Dutch retained the lion's share throughout the period. The great upsurge in the export of colonial goods to the Baltic also occurred after 1720, and although the Swedes, the Danes and the Hansards succeeded in increasing their share of this trade at the expense of the Dutch and the English, that of the last two nevertheless showed substantial absolute increases.[87] It is largely because of these adjustments within the structure of Dutch-Baltic trade that the number of ships that sailed from the Baltic to Holland more than doubled between 1710–19 and 1750–9 in spite of the tailing-off of grain shipments.[88]

[84] SP84/527, R. Wolters to R. Sutton, 7 Sept. 1770.
[85] See above, n. 8, and Table 7.1, and W. S. Unger, 'Trade through the Sound in the Seventeenth and Eighteenth Centuries', EcHR, 12 (1959), pp. 213–14.
[86] Van Dillen, 'Economic Fluctuations', p. 203; van Dillen added that these changes in Dutch-Baltic trade did not completely compensate for the decline of the grain trade.
[87] Unger, 'Trade through the Sound', pp. 212, 215.
[88] Knoppers, 'Dutch-Baltic Shipping', p. 6. It must be emphasised, however, that the Dutch share of the Baltic trade declined.

Around 1760, however, Baltic grain prices began to rise and the Baltic grain trade revived just as the period of massive English grain exports was drawing to a close.[89] The most substantial demands to be placed on Amsterdam's granaries during these years came from the growing markets of France and the southern Netherlands.[90] At the same time, with the rising level of cereal prices, the earlier protracted depression of Dutch farming came to an end. Against these improvements in the economic situation, however, must be set the detrimental consequences of higher food prices, especially in so far as these affected the level of internal purchasing power. Faber has suggested that the cost of living began to rise as early as 1740, but points out that the discrepancy between rising prices and the stationary level of wages became substantial only after c. 1770.[91] Nevertheless, it is clear that, from about mid-century, the fortunes of Dutch industry and agriculture began to diverge considerably and if, as Schama maintains, the rural background to the political upheavals of the later eighteenth century was one of steadily accumulating well-being, there is little doubt that the position of the urban wage-earner deteriorated.[92] The widespread extent of poverty in Amsterdam in the later eighteenth century has been well documented, together with the close correlation which existed between the level of mortality, the number of marriages, and the price of bread during a period in which the trend of rye prices was moving steadily upwards.[93] Jansen's investigations demonstrate clearly the 'pre-industrial character' of economic crises in Holland at the end of the eighteenth century, and indicate that, 'apart from increasing foreign competition, high grain prices must have played a significant role in the Republic's rapid economic decline during the last quarter of the eighteenth century'.[94]

There is little doubt that the decline of the Baltic grain trade harmed the Dutch trading system, but the extent of the damage should not be exaggerated, given the readjustments which were taking place within the structure of Dutch-Baltic trade. Moreover, the revival of that trade offered little that was propitious to general economic recovery. More important than the source of grain imports was the price at which that grain could be imported. In this context, the period of bulk import of subsidised

[89] J. G. van Dillen, *Van Rijkdom en Regenten: Handboek tot de economische en sociale geschiedenis van Nederland tijdens de Republiek*, 's-Gravenhage, 1970, p. 560.

[90] Ibid., p. 562.   [91] Faber, *Dure tijden*, pp. 7–8.

[92] S. Schama, *Patriots and Liberators: Revolution in the Netherlands, 1780–1831*, 1977, p. 29.

[93] P. Jansen, 'Armoede in Amsterdam aan het eind van de achttiende eeuw', *TvG*, 88 (1975), pp. 613–25; P. Jansen, 'Het ritme van de dood: sociale conjunctuur in Amsterdam, 1750–1800', *Ons Amsterdam*, March 1973, pp. 24–7.

[94] Jansen, 'Het ritme van de dood', pp. 26–7. The first economic crisis in the Netherlands which did not coincide with high grain prices was that of 1857.

English grain should be seen as a positive one for the highly vulnerable Dutch economy, particularly in what might be termed the 'second phase' of export from *c.* 1732 to 1760.

Not only, of course, did this price-vulnerability encompass food imports, it also extended to imports of industrial raw materials, and here it is evident that the import of heavily subsidised English malt provided the basis for the rapid expansion of the Dutch distilleries during the early eighteenth century. We have already seen how the conjuncture of the English bounty legislation and excise regulations with the technical requirements of Dutch distillers produced an irresistibly cheap raw material which gave rise to a period of exceptionally rapid growth in the distilleries of the Maas region.[95] At Schiedam, the centre of the industry, the number of distilleries increased from 34 in 1700 to 121 in 1730, reaching 122 by 1771.[96] As a result, Schiedam was one of the few industrial towns in Holland to experience any increase in population during the eighteenth century.[97] In Rotterdam, the *Vroedschap* passed a resolution in 1718 setting aside the Baan for the distillers, and the industry also flourished in Delfshaven. It is thus not surprising that, by mid-century, grain-spirits formed one of the principal exports of the Maas region, finding markets in England, France and Spain, the East and West Indies, and North America. By the early 1770s, 85% of total output was exported.[98] The remarkable growth of this export-oriented industry must therefore be seen as one of the most conspicuous exceptions to the Republic's industrial history in the eighteenth century, and it is perhaps significant that this was due to circumstances external to its own economic situation – the cheapness of imported raw materials – rather than to the unique quality of the product, as Joh. de Vries suggested.[99]

The Dutch brewing industry also received a proportion of its malt and barley from England during the same period but was not nearly as dependent upon English supplies as the distilleries, since English maltsters and merchants found it most profitable to export 'long malt' which could only be used in the latter. In any case, the brewing industry in Holland was one of the oldest of the processing industries and for most of the eighteenth century was in a state of decline in the face of contracting markets. The growth of foreign competition, increasing consumption of coffee, tea and spirits, and heavy internal taxation – there were no less than seven taxes on beer – were the main elements in the situation.[100] While distillers and, to a small extent, brewers obviously benefited from

[95] See above, pp. 223–5.   [96] Visser, *Verkeersindustrieen*, pp. 93–7.
[97] J. A. van Houtte, *An Economic History of the Low Countries, 800–1800*, 1977, pp. 255–6.
[98] Joh. de Vries, *Economische Achteruitgang*, pp. 91–2.   [99] Ibid.
[100] Visser, *Verkeersindustrieen*, pp. 59–61.

imports of English grain, the Dutch malting industry was adversely affected by English competition. Dutch maltsters continually pressed for increased protection against English malt exports and, in 1725, an already low duty of 3.15 gilders per last was increased to 5.0gl. Even the Amsterdam Admiralty supported the maltsters in their attempt to secure a tariff reduction on imported barley, although this was not implemented until 1751.[101] Since the level of import duties was, by English standards, extremely low, it is likely that these adjustments had only a marginal effect. If, however, as has been argued, the expansion of the Dutch distilleries was itself a consequence of the growth of heavily subsidised East Anglian malt exports, it cannot be said that the Dutch malting industry suffered unduly. When English malt exports were cut off during the years of harvest failure in 1757-8, the industry revived. Contemporaries noted that Dutch producers 'set upon building a number of malt houses all over the country, which they continue to keep at work with success'. By 1765, Dutch distillers and the majority of brewers were 'almost wholly supplied with their own inland malt'.[102]

On balance therefore, Dutch industry can only have benefited from the import of subsidised malt and barley, while the import of English cereals probably helped to sustain the specialised rural sector at a time when other influences were tending to depress Dutch agriculture. The substitution of English for Baltic grain supplies, on the other hand, clearly involved a major loss of shipping earnings for the Dutch and it was in this critical area that the Dutch economy was most vulnerable to the rise of English competition.

Commercial organisation

As industrial raw materials, malt and barley were subject to different sources of overseas demand than was the case with the bread grains. In addition, malt was affected by its own peculiar supply characteristics in the shape of processing. Not surprisingly, these distinctions between the two branches of the grain trade were reflected in its organisation. As far as malting for the domestic market is concerned, the industry during the eighteenth century was substantially dominated by the common brewer, with the exception of London where the size of the market and lack of space encouraged specialisation between brewers and maltsters. In the provinces, malting and brewing were undertaken together, although some independent maltsters carried on their trade by supplying a variety

---

[101] Hovy, *Voorstel van 1751*, pp. 484 n. 235, 485.
[102] CO388/95, 'Particulars of the Trade ... [with] Rotterdam'.

of customers, especially household brewers.[103] In Norfolk, malting and brewing had already become integrated by the end of the seventeenth century, as the Norwich merchant Thomas Baret explained to Sir Josiah Child: 'Malting and grazing were very Genteele imployments for Gentlemen's younger sons . . . both which ways are now quite lost as to the profit of them, viz. the brewers have joined malting to their other trade & now will buy no malt but use what [they] makes & so the maltsters for want of customers was forced to give over.' In the face of a contracting demand from local brewers therefore, Norfolk maltsters producing for the export trade would be relieved of the need to compete with the organised brewing maltsters for raw materials, since the 'long malt' required by the Dutch distillers could be made from the cheapest and inferior grades of barley. As Thomas Baret went on to explain, the brewing maltsters 'combine together & give but what price they please, & when they have a little before hand will bring corn from 10s to 6s p. coomb & under in less than two months time by pretending they want none, when if their chambers were examined, they are not half stockt for the year'.[104] The terms of trade were thus becoming increasingly disadvantageous for independent maltsters, and while market conditions did not amount to those of complete monopsony (domination of the market by a single buyer), this was clearly the direction in which change was occurring.

It seems, therefore, that structural changes were taking place in the malting industry which, together with the attractions of bounties and drawbacks, must have made the export trade irresistible to independent maltsters, and some of them became heavily committed to it. In the 1730s, for example, John Wright of Honingham, near Norwich, kept five malt houses employed for the export trade alone.[105] In this case, and probably in the majority of instances, production and export were organised separately. In 1730 the Collector of Customs at Yarmouth reported that 'a good deal of malt is sent out of the country by the country maltsters to our merchants to export for them' – merchants such as Joseph Cox who a few years later was described as agent for several maltsters, some of whom lived more than twenty miles from the port.[106] At the same time, however, it seems that a certain proportion of the malt trade was handled by merchants exporting on their own accounts. Norwich merchants in the 1750s, for example, were themselves buying barley and making the arrangements for malting, in which case they remained the

[103] Mathias, *Brewing Industry*, pp. 465–6.
[104] NRON, Ms 6360/6B8: copy of all letters sent beyond the seas by Thomas Baret, Horshead, nr Norwich (Thomas Baret to Josiah Child, 5 Apr. 1695).
[105] Cust. 97/10, 11 Nov. 1737.
[106] Cust. 97/6, 21 Sept. 1730; Cust. 97/3, 31 Dec. 1735.

Table 7.4 *Merchants and agents exporting malt from Yarmouth, 1737*

	quantity exported ('000 quarters)	percentage shipped to Rotterdam	percentage of Yarmouth's total malt export
J. Cox	8.14	89.4	14.1
T. Martin	7.52	84.9	13.0
R. Jarvis	7.00	68.5	12.1
R. Boyce	8.47	55.7	14.6
G.Ward	5.26	66.1	9.1
C. Benard	3.27	70.8	5.6
nine others	18.22		31.5

Sources: PRO E190/551/13 (Exchequer, K. R., Port Books)

owners of the grain during the malting process.[107] It is not possible to be much more precise as to the relative proportions of the trade handled by merchants exporting on their own accounts and by maltsters' agents, and it seems likely that some individuals combined both activities. Nevertheless, the numbers engaged in the trade, whether as agents or exporters, were fairly small, and one or two names dominate the Yarmouth Port Books. In 1737, for example, fifteen people entered quantities of malt for export overseas but only six of these entered more than 3,000 quarters (Table 7.4). It is likely that this handful of men were agents for country maltsters (and Cox at the head of the list appears in the Customs Letter Books as such, though Jarvis was referred to in 1731 as a merchant shipping *his* malt directly from the kiln).[108] The trade of this small group of Yarmouth exporters and agents accounted for almost one third of total English malt exports, and just over two-thirds of Yarmouth's malt trade. This concentration of mercantile operations in the grain trade, it seems, was common to several provincial markets including Maldon, Faversham and Sandwich. John Chartres describes it in terms of the emergence of 'mercantile oligopsony', a response conditioned by the growth of urban demand.[109]

The Yarmouth Port Books indicate another salient characteristic of the grain export trade: the marked specialisation which existed between exporters of malt and bread grains. The above-named agents and merchants were concerned almost exclusively with malt. Wheat and rye were handled by a different group of exporters (or agents), chiefly Messrs White, Olier and Palgrave. The last-mentioned, for example, shipped 13,205

---

[107] Cust. 48/15, 10 Feb. 1758.   [108] Cust. 97/3, 25 Aug. 1731.

[109] 'City and Towns, Farmers and Economic Change in the Eighteenth Century', *Historical Research*, 64 (1991), pp. 151 3.

quarters of wheat to overseas markets in 1737 (of which 5,810 quarters went to Rotterdam), while he shipped only 432 quarters of malt.[110] This further emphasises the distinction between these two groups of grains: not only were they absorbed by different markets and put to different uses, they might be handled by virtually separate groups of exporters within a single region.

The trade in bread grains was much less regionally concentrated than the malt trade, with supplies drawn from the southern and eastern counties, often by way of London, and distributed to a wider range of European markets. Some idea of the regional origins of grain exports may be gained by comparing the contributions of the outports, shown in Table 7.5. The fact that a high proportion of bread grains passed through the wholesale markets of London means that comparisons based on the export statistics alone tend to obscure the real contributions of the grain-producing areas. Nevertheless, the increasing role of London in the handling of cereal exports between the 1730s and the succeeding two decades deserves notice, paralleled only by the increasing contribution of the East Anglian ports. Organisation of the wholesale grain markets of London was rationalised at mid-century when the corn factors abandoned their Monday, Wednesday and Saturday markets by the waterside at Bear Quay and entered the fine new Corn Factors' Exchange in nearby Mark Lane. Completed in 1751, the new Exchange was open for daily business: 'There they fingered their little palmsful of grain and bargained under less draughty circumstances in the coffee houses on the upper floor.'[111] These new arrangements, more commodious but less democratic than the old, would scarcely have been possible without a prior series of accumulated improvements in internal marketing which made the metropolitan market more accessible to provincial suppliers: the growing practice of selling on the basis of samples, the regular publication of London prices in the provincial press, and intensified competition among the owners of coasting vessels, the corn hoys, which lowered freight charges.[112]

From the standpoint of commercial organisation, it must be emphasised that London merchants and factors exercised an even more dominant influence over the trade in bread grains than Table 7.5 would indicate. While much grain was indirectly exported to Europe via the granaries of London, substantial amounts were also exported from the outports on the accounts of London merchants. In 1714–15, for example, the prominent Hull merchants Nathaniel and Henry Maister were

[110] PRO E190/551/13.   [111] H. Phillips, *The Thames about 1750*, 1951, p. 39.
[112] D. A. Baker, 'The Marketing of Corn in the First Half of the Eighteenth Century: North East Kent', *Agricultural History Review*, 18 (1970), pp. 126–50.

Table 7.5 *Grain exports from English and Welsh ports, 1736–1763*

Percentage exported from:	1736–9		1744–8		1749–53		1754–8		1759–63	
	malt & barley	wheat, rye & oatmeal	malt & barley	wheat, rye & oatmeal	malt & barley	wheat, rye & oatmeal	malt & barley	wheat, rye & oatmeal	malt & barley	wheat, rye & oatmeal
North East	3.9	17.7	2.4	14.7	2.4	15.5	0.7	5.8	3.3	12.2
East Anglia	81.9	17.1	83.6	38.4	77.6	28.4	79.3	31.2	84.9	32.4
London	3.9	35.3	0.8	23.5	3.1	30.7	0.6	27.7	1.9	32.2
South East	1.9	12.0	4.4	7.3	6.5	9.2	8.2	11.3	3.6	5.3
South	2.1	9.0	2.2	8.3	5.6	8.1	9.5	7.6	4.9	13.8
South West	5.3	7.4	4.3	5.4	3.4	5.4	1.5	14.7	0.4	3.0
Wales	0.8	0.6	1.6	1.6	1.0	1.3	0.1	0.5	0.7	0.6
North West	0.2	0.9	0.7	0.8	0.4	1.4	0.1	1.2	0.3	0.5

Sources: 1736–9, *Gentleman's Magazine*, 12 and 13
1744–63, BL, Add Ms 38387

engaged as factors to several London merchants, completing wheat cargoes of between 400 and 900 quarters (each for the account of a single merchant) to be shipped from Hull and consigned to agents in Amsterdam, Lisbon and Hamburg, for which the customary 2% commission was charged.[113] During the 1730s, while representing Hull in parliament, Henry took advantage of his business connections in the Commons to secure large commissions from London merchants which were passed on to Nathaniel in Hull to be completed with northern grain.[114] Since it was acknowledged that 'if a man ingages [in corn] by way of commission, it will infallibly take up his whole attendance upon Bear Key', we might suppose that Henry Maister devoted more attention to the corn trade than he did to politics.[115] Early in 1738, for example, he had obtained a commission for 6,500 quarters of wheat to be shipped from Hull to Cadiz on the account of John Bance, MP for Westbury in Wiltshire. At the same time, the Maister brothers were exporting grain on their own accounts chiefly to Lisbon, Cadiz and Amsterdam. Given the combined extent of their own business and their substantial commission sales, it is hardly surprising that they encountered difficulties in obtaining sufficient shipping and in assembling bulk shipments of uniform quality and price. In March 1738, for example, Nathaniel wrote from Hull:

It comes in prodigious slowly; tho' I have given 2 or 3 of the factors permission to go along with the market price, I don't find they buy any. I have got about 70 quarters since my last advice that the whole of what we have bought is about 5,500 [quarters]. If the price was one fixed, it would come in plentiful enough as there are great quantities yet in the country.[116]

During an earlier year for which information is available, 1714, it appears that the Maisters obtained their grain from at least twenty-three separate farmers and country factors.[117] Success rested among other things on purchasing at the beginning of the year before 'the buyers begin to stir', or just after harvest when farmers needed cash to purchase livestock.[118] As one merchant wrote during October, 'our fair is just now and country men must have their money to buy their cattle'.[119]

---

[113] Hull University Library, Ms DP/82, Maister Ledger, entries for 12 Nov. 1714, 17 Dec. 1714, 15 and 18 Mar. 1715.

[114] Maister Letters, consulted by kind permission of the late Col. R. A. Alec-Smith, Winestead, Hull.

[115] ZCE10/11, R. Carr to J. G. Liebenrood, London, 2 Nov. 1738.

[116] Maister Letters, N. to H. Maister, London, 13 Feb. 1738; N. to H. Maister, London, Mar. 1738.

[117] Hull University Library, Ms DP/82, Maister Ledger dates same as n. 114, above.

[118] Maister Letters, N. to H. Maister, London, 13 and 15 Feb. 1738.

[119] ZCE10/11, R. Carr to Win. Norton, Dunkirk, 20 Oct. 1738.

Ralph Carr of Newcastle provides another example of a provincial merchant who was 'pretty deeply engaged...in the corn trade for export', and who maintained close links with the London grain market, chiefly, it seems, to supply its factors at times when the difference between home and overseas prices did not encourage export. To a correspondent who had recommended Messrs J. and T. Simpson of London, Carr replied, 'they shall have a large share of my business at Bear Key for tho' I am pretty closely attached to some factors there, yet I am under no considerable obligation to any of them'.[120] As well as exporting grain on his own account and supplying the London export market, Carr also undertook commissions for overseas buyers. 'We have at present a very large demand from France, Spain, Portugal and Barbary', he wrote in November 1738, and 'I have very large quantities of wheat bought up and fresh orders arriving every day'.[121] Although documentation is sparse, the indications are that the larger exporters did not adopt a uniform method of trading, but combined the functions of exporting merchant with that of corn factor as occasion demanded. Even the smaller country factors might export on their own accounts. In 1740 the customs officers noticed a quantity of wheat shipped from Sunderland to Amsterdam which was the joint property of a coal fitter and a corn factor.[122]

The scale of operations could vary enormously within the trade from the small and usually speculative shipments of general merchants to the substantial quantities of grain handled by the navy victualling contractors (assembling 4,000 quarters of wheatmeal alone per month in the 1750s) or by the London factors such as Thomas Farrer, who claimed to have shipped off 40,000 quarters in one year.[123] The 'largest and most adventurous corn dealers' in the kingdom, however, were said to be the Coutts brothers of London and Edinburgh who established an elaborate network of factors throughout Scotland and England to supply their extensive export trade. It is described in some detail by the firm's nineteenth-century historian:[124]

They had a settled agent in Northumberland, residing at Fenwick, who was employed to make purchases of corn for the house, and for none else, in that country. Others at Aberdeen, at Portsoy, and at Dundee, made purchases for the house in the fertile corn countries of Perth, Forfar, Kincardine, Aberdeen, Banff and

---

[120] ZCE10/12, R. Carr to J. A. Crop, Amsterdam, 7 Aug. 1739; R. Carr to T. M. Liebenrood, Rotterdam, 14 Oct. 1739.

[121] ZCE10/11, R. Carr to R. Hayes, Konigsberg, 2 Nov. 1738.

[122] Cust. 85/2 (Sunderland, Collector-Board), 13 June 1740.

[123] PRO 30/8 (Chatham Papers), 81, fo. 187 (undated).

[124] W. Forbes, *Memoirs of a Banking-House* (1803), Edinburgh, 1859, p. 7.

Moray; and two others again, in Caithness and in Ross-shire, both of them gentlemen of landed property, but also men of business, though not, strictly speaking, merchants, made purchases for the house on their joint account in those northern counties. In England the house had large quantities of corn shipped for them at Yarm and at Stockton in Yorkshire; at Lynn Regis, Fakenham, and Yarmouth all in the rich county of Norfolk; at Haverfordwest, in South Wales; and by the noted Cooper Thornhill, who at the time kept the Bell Inn at Hilton, and was one of the most considerable corn factors in England.

None of these specialist exporters was wholly committed to the grain trade, however. The unpredictability of harvests and the level of prices, the possibility of overheating and damage during storage and transit, and the relatively high cost of handling and therefore of trans-shipment meant that the trade was extremely risky and speculative. During periods of harvest failure, exports could be reduced to low levels or could disappear altogether following an embargo. Thus the Couttses combined their primary interest in grain with trade in lead, salt and tobacco before their banking activities grew to predominance in the later part of the century.[125] Ralph Carr exported flax, lead, litharge and coal as well as grain, and the Maisters operated a very extensive trade with Scandinavia and the Baltic.[126] Just as these large grain exporters tended to diversify their interests, however, so the general merchant might occasionally enter this somewhat specialised branch of trade, in which case his consignment would probably be sent to Amsterdam to be sold on commission by a Dutch house. The Amsterdam grain market with its weekly quotations of English wheat, rye, barley and malt prices published in the Amsterdam *prijscouranten* was probably less unfamiliar than the fluctuating markets of southern Europe.[127] Small and irregular shipments, however, were unlikely to yield satisfactory returns and it seems that the greatest profits would be made by those merchants shipping grain in bulk directly to final markets. Apart from tending towards reduced unit handling charges, bulk shipment permitted the exporter to charter a vessel and thus to secure a quick despatch and retain complete discretion over the final disposal of the cargo, which would eliminate some of the risk caused by fluctuating markets. Charterparties in the Rotterdam notarial archives relating to English grain shipments show that masters trading to southern Europe were frequently given instructions to lie for twenty-four hours at either Lisbon or Cadiz 'to await orders whether to sail to Gibraltar, Malaga,

[125] Ibid., p. 12; Brants 1337, Letters of John Coutts and Comp., Edinburgh, and Coutts Bros. and Comp., Edinburgh, 1748–9 and 1755–8.
[126] ZCE10/11–17; G. Jackson, *Hull in the Eighteenth Century*, 1972, pp. 28, 31, 52.
[127] See above, p. 228.

Cartagena, Alicante, Barcelona, Cette, Marseilles, Toulon or Genoa'.[128] Specialist exporters usually received fairly precise reports of price changes and differentials in various markets. In 1740, for example, Ralph Carr was expecting to load five grain ships for Holland and 'sundry more' for southern Europe and at this time was corresponding regularly with agents in a number of grain markets: T. M. Liebenrood in Rotterdam and J. A. Crop in Amsterdam providing information on the state of the Dutch market; William Hayes in Konigsberg on Baltic supplies; William Norton in Dunkirk on western and northern French markets (Nantes, La Rochelle and Rouen) and unnamed correspondents in southern France and Lisbon.[129] The most important of these correspondents was undoubtedly Liebenrood in Rotterdam who also provided information on the extent and direction of Baltic supplies, particularly those destined for Holland. In May 1738, for example, Carr wrote to Liebenrood 'please inform me how the demand & prices of corn goes with you & your opinion. Barley as well as wheat is much advanced and there is like to be an export of that grane for the Spanish and Portugal marketts... please likewise to let me know if there is much corn either already come or exported to your parts from the Baltic.' Liebenrood's reply that large quantities of Baltic grain were expected caused Carr to look towards the Spanish and Portuguese markets rather than Holland.[130] In the later part of 1740 when scarcity at home had transformed the grain export trade into an import trade, Carr circumvented the Dutch granaries and despatched ships direct to Danzig; in addition, he called upon his Dutch intermediary to supply information as to grain already in transit from the East country, but explained that he was unwilling to purchase such grain after it had been landed in Holland.[131] Carr was obviously anxious to avoid excessive handling and reshipment charges which import via Holland would involve: handling charges, commission and import fees on foreign grain imported into Amsterdam could in fact amount to over 9%.[132]

When possible therefore, the larger specialist exporters would attempt to circumvent the Dutch granaries for both export and import, and the official statistics indicate that, as far as exports of bread grains were concerned, they were largely successful in doing so during the 1720s and 1730s. A striking example of an English exporter completely by-passing the Dutch entrepôt is provided by George Radcliffe of London. After his return from the Levant in 1724, he decided to enter the grain trade and

[128] GAR NA2332/74 A. I. and Z. Hope and B. Lowes, 25 Mar. 1738; see also ibid., 2332/43 24 Feb. 1738; 2328/657 28 Sept. 1734; 2345/350 25 Aug. 1750.
[129] ZCE 10/12, R. Carr to Wm Norton, Dunkirk, 24 Apr. 1740.
[130] Ibid., R. Carr to T. M. Liebenrood, Rotterdam, 11 May 1738, 5 June 1739.
[131] Ibid., 25 May 1740.   [132] ZCE10/11, Charges on barley sold at Amsterdam, 1738.

established one of his partners, Henry Croston, at Mahon on the island of Minorca, which was to serve as a granary from which English grain was to be shipped to Mediterranean markets. Croston received information as to the state of the grain market in France, Spain and Portugal, which was then transmitted to Radcliffe in London. In February 1726, for example, Croston reported:

Hitherto, the prices on the coast of Spain have been low, but now the time draws on they may be expected to rise; but by all accounts I have, Lisbon is the most promising market which probably the demand in France may still effect. You know best whether it will answer going farther, though we have it that corn bears a great price in the West parts of France.

Croston in turn received very exact information on the state of the Spanish market from an English house in Alicante, Merrett Hall and Company, which itself dealt in English grain.[133]

A certain proportion of the trade in English bread grains, however, was handled by the Dutch both as agents acting for English principals and as merchants exporting on their own accounts. The Rotterdam notarial archives contain numerous instances of Rotterdam merchants chartering English vessels lying in that port for grain voyages, usually sailing in ballast but sometimes with mixed cargoes from Rotterdam to an English port to load a cargo of wheat, and then back to Rotterdam or on to a European port for disposal of the grain. Some of these voyages were doubtless made on the instructions of English principals. Ralph Carr's Dutch agent T. M. Liebenrood, for example, is frequently named in the agreements.[134] But others were clearly undertaken by Dutch merchants on their own accounts, such as those of William Konink exporting English coal and grain to Norway and returning to Holland with timber, or J. P. Charron, who regularly imported his own grain from England and was quick to complain of its quality. The most frequently recurring name is that of the famous Rotterdam house, Archibald and Isaac Hope, trading in wheat and barley to southern Europe.[135]

At the same time the Hopes were deeply involved in the Anglo-Dutch malt trade, and the will of Archibald Hope, Sr, dated 1720, shows him

---

[133] Guildhall Library: Ms 6645/1, Radcliffe Papers, H. Croston to E. Radcliffe and C. Barnardiston, 11 Feb. 1726.
[134] GAR NA2332/70 T. M. Liebenrood and J. Moore, 24 Mar. 1738; 2335/420 T. M. Liebenrood and S. Prockter, 22 Apr. 1741.
[135] Ibid., 2345/350 W. van Rykevorsel and Son and R. Jeddere, 25 Aug. 1750; 2337/636 D. van der Leven and R. Lindsay, 16 Nov. 1743; 2328/567 Wm Konink and J. Roxby, 21 Aug. 1734; 1509/509 Declaration of J. and P. Charron, 18 Dec. 1719; 1509/356 A. Hope and E. Seaman, 5 Nov. 1719; 2344/393 I. and Z. Hope and J. Melbourne, 4 Nov. 1749.

to have been the owner of malting houses in Ipswich, Stowmarket and Bury St Edmunds and of two vessels used specially for the transport of malt.[136] It seems therefore that Dutch capital played an important part in the English grain export trade though the precise amount cannot be specified. Some contemporaries alleged that French capital was employed in the trade, with English exporters contracting to deliver wheat at fixed prices to French importers, but the evidence here is less reliable.[137] It is not clear whether bounty payments were actually received by foreign importers though in 1714 we find the Maisters, as agents for London merchants, collecting bounty money in Hull and remitting the proceeds to London.[138] Presumably such remittances could equally well be sent abroad or balanced against freight charges and commission.

Disposal of the English grain surplus became a highly commercialised activity during the first half of the eighteenth century, with a marked degree of specialisation between the two groups of grains, the 'industrial' grains, malt and barley, and the bread grains, wheat, rye and oatmeal. The state of overseas demand and a range of commercial imperatives, including the availability of shipping space, commercial intelligence and the level of Baltic supplies were no less important than the state of the home market in determining whether grain would be exported or retained for home consumption, particularly that of the metropolis. Although the momentum behind the trade was largely generated by the merchant, its rationale was provided by the temporary convergence of landed and mercantile interests.

[136] M. G. Buist, *At Spes Non Fracta: Hope & Co. 1770–1815*, The Hague, 1974, p. 5.
[137] Barnes, *English Corn Laws*, p. 15; Comber, *Inquiry*, pp. 144–5.
[138] Hull University Library DP/82, Maister Ledger, Mar. 1715, 'Hugh Mason, Dr. to sundry accounts for Bounty Money on corn'.

8   The coal trade and energy resources

One of the consequences of seventeenth-century commercial expansion, which affected England and the Dutch Republic alike, was an unprecedented rise in the demand for timber, iron and naval stores. In both countries, deforestation, coupled with the competing requirements of the shipbuilding, construction and processing industries, meant that wood had become an increasingly scarce resource compared to other consumables. In the case of England, the extent of the sixteenth-century 'timber crisis' has undoubtedly been exaggerated, but for the period from the 1630s to the 1680s, the evidence of an energy shortage is clearly reflected in the available price-materials. While population declined slightly and the price of consumables fell by 6%, the price of charcoal more than doubled.[1] In Holland during the same period, the price of consumer goods fell by over 10%, while the cost of firewood rose by about one third. By 1640, Dutch stocks of renewable woodland were virtually non-existent.[2] Each country was forced to break through the ceiling imposed by replaceable energy resources, and in doing so moved gradually away from the old photosynthesis regime. In different ways, the advanced preindustrial economies came to rely on their stocks of geologically formed energy reserves, on carbonaceous fossil fuels.

British coal and Dutch peat provided an escape route from the age-old dependence on a restricted flow of energy resources, but with a vastly different range of possibilities in each case. Wrigley, in particular, has elaborated on the differences between these two energy regimes, emphasising the enormous growth potential inherent in the embryonic mineral-based energy economy.[3] Although the use of peat greatly expanded the energy

[1] B. Thomas, 'Britain's Energy Crisis in the Seventeenth Century', in Thomas (ed.), *The Industrial Revolution*, p. 6.
[2] Posthumus, *Inquiry into the History of Prices in Holland*, vol. II, pp. LXXXVIII, XCIII (Amsterdam Municipal Orphanage series); J. W. de Zeeuw, 'Peat and the Dutch Golden Age. The Historical Meaning of Energy Attainability', *AAG Bijdragen*, 21, 1978, pp. 5, 25.
[3] E. A. Wrigley, *Continuity, Chance and Change. The Character of the Industrial Revolution in England*, Cambridge, 1988, chs. 2 and 3.

Illustration 8.1 J. Marci, peat dredging, engraved for *Deliciae Bataviae*, 1618.

resources of the 'advanced organic economy', it was in itself an organic fuel whose exploitation placed conflicting demands on the traditional rural economy – in ways that coal mining did not. The destructive impact of peat workings during the Golden Age was intense, resulting especially in the loss of farmland and the phenomenon of deserted villages.[4] It was in the early years of the seventeenth century that the rapid expansion of canal building in the high peat areas of Groningen and Eastern Drenthe opened up the peat fields there, while in the low peat (*laagveen*) regions of Holland and Utrecht, the commencement of deep dredging after *c.* 1550 made possible a greatly enhanced rate of peat extraction during the next two centuries. But peat reserves were used up at a much faster rate than British coal: on average, between 3 and 5% of the workable stock was consumed during each decade of the seventeenth century. By the third quarter of the eighteenth century, the pace of exploitation had slowed down.[5] Production of British coal, by contrast, continued to expand throughout the modern period, down to 1920. Between the 1560s and the 1690s, output multiplied twelve-fold, reaching 3 million tons by 1700, while the eighteenth century saw a five-fold increase.[6]

Holland's energy crisis and coal imports

Large claims have been made for peat production, as a highly accessible and relatively cheap energy source. De Zeeuw argues that the Dutch Golden Age was 'born of turf', but, on several grounds, this is a serious overstatement – particularly when comparisons are drawn with Britain. In the first place the amount of thermal energy available from peat during the seventeenth century was much less than that estimated by de Zeeuw. The high moisture content of the *laagveen* turfs meant that shrinkage was considerable, and R. W. Unger's revised figures suggest a calorific content around one-fifth of that estimated by de Zeeuw.[7] Secondly, Dutch peat stocks were much less extensive than British coal reserves, and the latter

---

[4] A. M. Lambert, *The Making of the Dutch Landscape*, 1971, pp. 208–12; de Zeeuw, 'Peat and the Dutch Golden Age', p. 11; J. de Vries, *Dutch Rural Economy*, pp. 31, 68, 194.

[5] Wrigley, *Continuity, Chance and Change*, p. 58, n. 60; J. Hatcher, *The History of the British Coal Industry*, vol. I, Oxford, 1993, p. 550; de Zeeuw, 'Peat and the Dutch Golden Age', pp. 9–14.

[6] Hatcher, *Coal Industry*, vol. I, table 4.1, p. 68; M. W. Flinn, *The History of the British Coal Industry*, vol. II, Oxford, 1984, p. 26.

[7] R. W. Unger, 'Energy Sources for the Dutch Golden Age', *Research in Economic History*, 9 (1984). De Zeeuw estimates that peat produced 6×10^{12} kilocalories of energy during the seventeenth century, in the Republic. Unger's criticisms are based on four sets of arguments: not all the peat in the zones identified was commercially viable; exports are ignored; the calorific content of peat is overestimated by a factor of 2; and the extent of shrinkage is underestimated by a factor of 3.

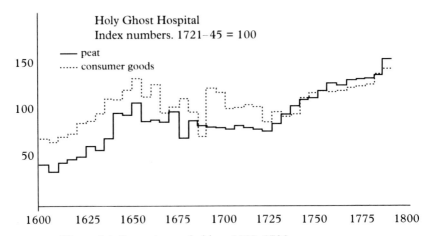

Figure 8.1 Peat prices at Leiden, 1600–1790
Source: Posthumus, *Nederlandse Prijsgeschiedenis*, vol. II, Table C, pp. lxxxiv–lxxxv, Table E III, pp. xciii–xciv.

in any case generated about four times as much energy as peat for a given weight. Wrigley calculates that the English coalfields were producing between 3 and 3.5 times the thermal equivalent of the Dutch peat zones in 1700, with a capacity to sustain production for centuries to come.[8] Coal mining, furthermore, with its accompanying drainage problems, compelled mineowners to develop a technology which converted heat energy into kinetic energy – that is, motion.[9] The steam engine was quintessentially the product of the mineral-based energy economy. Its Dutch equivalents were the windmill and the hand-operated *baggerbeugel*, or dredging tool. Thirdly, both de Zeeuw *and* his critics have greatly underestimated the extent of Dutch dependence on British coal, which perhaps more than anything else indicates the limitations of the notion of an energy revolution based on peat.

By the late seventeenth century, the rate of peat exploitation in the Holland–Utrecht producing zone was beginning to level off. Rising fuel prices during the first half of the century had stimulated the industry, particularly through the building and extension of feeder canals, and, by mid-century, the gap between the price of peat and that of consumer goods in general had narrowed considerably. During the late seventeenth and early eighteenth centuries, a period of generally low prices in the northern Netherlands, the price of peat seems to have fallen at a rate well

---

[8] Unger, 'Energy Sources', p. 232; Wrigley, *Continuity, Chance and Change*, p. 59.
[9] J. Mokyr, *Lever of Riches*, Oxford, 1990, pp. 62, 85.

below that of the general level of prices. During the 1720s, however, the position was reversed and peat prices climbed steadily upwards, keeping well ahead of the inflationary trend for the rest of the century. In 1728, Onslow Burrish predicted that the English coal trade would 'increase and grow more advantageous to us every year, in proportion, as the marshy lands in Holland are wasted, which now afford an immense quantity of turf'.[10] Although peat still remained the 'chief article of fewel to the inhabitants', the habit of using coal for domestic burning increased, as many came to realise that smoke from coal fires was not, after all, a health risk.[11] One writer claimed that the splint coals of eastern Scotland were favoured by Dutch housewives, as they were clean and easy to use.[12] In 1765, the English consul at Rotterdam reported that

the demand for coals in this country increases every year as by the yearly advance of the price of turff [peat] . . . and the scarcity and dearness of wood, the Dutch people get more and more into burning of coals; and a time will even come when it will be dangerous (by the consequence of encreasing the lakes by this operation) to cut peat at all.[13]

Domestic burning of coal extended the market in the eighteenth century, but the chief consumers remained the processing industries of Rotterdam and its region, particularly sugar refiners, brewers, distillers, dyers and bleachers, as well as blacksmiths and bakers.[14] Although domestic and industrial demand overlapped, coal was not a homogeneous commodity, and buyers and sellers were aware of distinct qualities and properties which were reflected in prices. The largest and most expensive coals burned slowly, and were considered most suitable for domestic burning, as well as for the brewing industry, glass making and soap boiling. These were generally reserved for the London and home markets. The smaller, sulphurous coals burned with a more intense heat, and were suitable for several industrial uses including brickmaking, lime-burning, dyeing and forging – indeed, they were often referred to as smiths' coals.[15] The disposal of smaller-grade coal, as Nef emphasised, constituted one of the mineowner's chief problems. The solution was to ship it abroad, primarily to Holland, and, to a lesser extent, France and Germany.[16]

[10] Burrish, *Batavia Illustrata*, p. 377.
[11] T. Lowndes, *A State of the Coal trade to Foreign Parts, by way of a memorial to a supposed very great assembly*, 1744–5 (Hanson 5897). An identical version occurs in CO 388/43, Bb 103.
[12] T. S. Ashton & J. Sykes, *The Coal Industry of the Eighteenth Century*, Manchester, 1929, p. 227.
[13] PRO CO388/95, 'Particulars of the Trade . . . [with] Rotterdam'.
[14] J. U. Nef, *The Rise of the British Coal Industry*, 1932, vol. I, pp. 112–14.
[15] Ibid., pp. 109–22.   [16] Ibid., pp 113–14.

Ralph Carr, a prominent export merchant, distinguished between three different 'sorts' of coals sent overseas from the north-east in the 1740s: 'small ones at 9s 6d, better sort at 10s 6d & largest of all at 11s 6d p cha.', with an additional 10d–1s charged on those which had been preserved from the rain.[17] These were net prices representing the prime cost in Newcastle for January 1745. In April 1740, prices had been higher at 11s, 12s and 13s. When a new Rotterdam customer requested 'pretty round coals fit for brewers and distillers', Carr recommended the cheapest and smallest sort, although the customer had expressed a preference for the medium grade then priced at 12s. Carr, however, insisted: 'if for Holland, will ship those at 11s. which assume will be most for yr. interest & doubt not will meet with yr approbation'.[18] This cheapest grade was also sent to the Bay of Biscay; to Rouen and Le Havre, the medium grade was sent; whilst to Dunkirk and Calais, the very largest sort at 13s usually sold best.[19] Even the cheapest grade, however, could be supplied with particular firing or caking properties as desired.[20] The very largest coals were rarely sent to Holland, being suitable for 'the light-houses or some such purpose; besides they are dearer and so fit for common uses', that is, for domestic burning.[21] The British consul in Rotterdam noted that large, expensive coals, 'the sort of coals that is used for the London market, is never sent abroad'.[22] Carr, whose father was a substantial coal owner, was clearly pursuing his own logic in directing the cheaper grades towards the Dutch market, and in recommending small coals for Rotterdam brewers and distillers was neglecting their best interests.[23] In the early years of the eighteenth century too, Dutch complaints of the 'badness' of English coal were common.[24] Because the best-quality fuel was conserved for English use, pamphleteers regarded the export of coal to Holland less unfavourably than the trade to Dunkirk. Taking only the largest coals, it was said that the manufacturing industries of Dunkirk used British coal to too great an extent.[25] As was also the case with English

[17] NRO ZCE10/16, R. Carr to Dirk van Dam, Rotterdam, 10 Jan. 1745. This process had become general in most colliery districts during the seventeenth century (Nef, *British Coal Industry*, vol. I, p. 112).

[18] ZCE10/12, R. Carr to Anna Brouwer, Rotterdam, 13 April 1740.   [19] Ibid.

[20] ZCE10/2, Wm Cotesworth, Gateshead, to R. Bewicke, Amsterdam, 14 June 1715. Cotesworth was also supplying a cheap grade at 8s 6d.

[21] ZCE10/16, R. Carr to Dirk van Dam, Rotterdam, 15 Oct. 1745.

[22] CO388/95, 'Particulars of the Trade ... [with] Rotterdam'. Unger's figures for 1784–93 show that virtually all the coal imported into the Maas Admiralty District consisted of small, or 'smiths' coal, rather than large coal ('Energy Sources', p. 243).

[23] ZCE10/11, R. Carr to Edmund Wortley, 23 March 1738/9.

[24] NRO ZBL192, J. Blackett to J. Kelley (?Hull), 5 May 1711.

[25] Lowndes, *State of the Coal trade*: 'It is most truly affirmed, that almost every commodity, wherein Dunkirk interferes with Great Britain, is manufactured with our coals.'

malt, it seems that the industries of Rotterdam were absorbing an inferior product.[26]

Although this pattern of trade largely served the coalowners' interests, the quasi-monopsonistic position of Dutch industrial users was one which worked to the latter's advantage from time to time. In May 1709, for example, the informal decision of the Rotterdam sugar bakers and brewers to withhold their purchases of coal in expectation of peace and falling freight costs caused prices to drop from 16 to 13gl. per hoed.[27] A specialised market and a relatively inelastic demand shaped the pattern of price movements, and Dutch consumers benefited from the conditions under which coal was delivered and sold at the waterside. It was only in times of severe glut that coal could not be sold directly out of the ship.[28] Because of the expense of breaking bulk, storage for long periods was uneconomic, and exposure to the weather reduced its quality and saleability. As Ralph Carr explained, 'I never ship any...unless the weather is dry and the coals newly wrought which very seldom happens but in summer time, for as these coals is never laid under any cover they become as heavy as lead by the rains so would less [lose] 3s p. cha. by their weighing so much.'[29] Quick disposal in the port of delivery was essential. 'As soon as the ship arrives', wrote John Blackett, acting as Rotterdam agent for his Newcastle principal, 'will go to all the Brewers houses in town and will get 'em sold if possible.'[30] Without stocks to act as a buffer, a fairly inelastic demand caused prices to react sharply in the short term, and agents in Holland continually warned of the dangers of over-supply. 'Never send coals [to Rotterdam]' warned Blackett, 'when a fleet of 80 or 100 ships are for this place, the price is always low.'[31] Conditions of scarcity were less frequent in a trade characterised by a high level of seasonal activity during the summer months, when consumers laid down stocks.

The coal trade to Holland thus represented a rare phenomenon in mercantilist terms, presenting, as it did, the appearance of a mutually advantageous commerce. It provided an outlet for the mineowner's surplus and unsaleable coal, which the Dutch processing industries obtained at relatively low prices. During the eighteenth century, Dutch reliance on English coal increased substantially as the Republic faced the exhaustion of its peat supplies, but how far did this produce a state of dependency? To what extent, in other words, did English coal enjoy a natural monopoly

---

[26] See above, pp. 223–4.
[27] ZBL192, J. Blackett to Henry Witton, Wakefield, 28 May 1709.
[28] Ibid., 20 Nov. 1708.
[29] ZCE10/16, R. Carr to Dirk van Dam, Rotterdam, 10 June 1745.
[30] ZBL192, J. Blackett to James Morton, 18 March 1709.
[31] Ibid., J. Blackett to John Kelley (?Hull), 5 May 1711; see also 12 Mar. 1709.

in Holland, and what other sources were available? In what quantities was it imported, and, since it has been regarded as a serious burden for the Dutch economy, how did the rising level of English export duties affect a trade already subject to high transport costs?

By the late seventeenth century, the formerly important Scottish export of coal to Holland had seriously declined.[32] Most suitable for household use, Scottish great coal was both expensive and wasteful,[33] and was said to be less good than English for burning.[34] By 1765, the annual Dutch import of large coals from the Firth of Forth was valued at only £5,000, most of this coming to Zeeland.[35] Richard Wolters gave an account of the continental sources of supply open to the Dutch in 1755 and included Liège, the Rhur, Lingen and Berg, 'places properly situated near the Mase & the Rhine', and, in an emergency, Mons and Charleroi.[36] Of all these sorts, he said, none but Liège coals came to Holland, 'and those in a small quantity'. The comparable costs of a hoed of English and Liège coal delivered out of the ship at Rotterdam lay within the ranges £1 4s to £1 18s and £1 12s to £2 4s respectively. This included the relatively heavy river dues to which Liège coals were subject (heavier than on the Rhine), and, twenty years earlier Thomas Lowndes had remarked: 'water carriage from Liege being only by flat-bottomed boats makes the freight of its coals so vastly expensive, that Liege cannot pretend to send coals to foreign markets'.[37] During the period of embargo, Wolters reported that the owner of a glass-house near Rotterdam had obtained his coal from the Ruhr, which had 'answered very well both in quality and price', and again in 1765, when the prohibition of English coal exports was feared, a group of Rotterdam coal traders was considering compounding with the King of Prussia and other German princes to reduce the tolls on coal brought from the lower Rhine.[38] But not until the Ruhr was made navigable in 1784 was the Dutch market fully accessible to Westphalian coal.[39]

Dutch dependence on English coal was therefore real enough until the closing decades of the eighteenth century, and increasingly so as the price of wood and turf rose. This dependence is reflected in the customs ledgers

[32] T. C. Smout, *Scottish Trade on the Eve of Union*, pp. 227–8.

[33] Nef, *British Coal Industry*, vol. I, pp. 117–20; vol. II, p. 230.

[34] I. Le Long, *Koophandel van Amsterdam* (1714), Amsterdam, 1753, p. 525.

[35] CO388/95, 'Particulars of the Trade . . . [with] Rotterdam'. This can have been equivalent to no more than 2,000 Newcastle chaldrons.

[36] Ibid. See also Nef, *British Coal Industry*, vol. I, pp. 124–30, for a short survey of continental coal-producing regions.

[37] Lowndes, *State of the Coal trade*.

[38] Wolters spoke of 'a time of long and general Imbargo in England in the year 1744 or 1745'; his chronology is here confused, for the only embargo of these years occurred from 15 June 1739 to 15 April 1740 (*CTBP*, IV (1739–41), pp. 31, 237).

[39] Nef, *British Coal Industry*, vol. I, p. 127.

which, unfortunately, have been consistently misinterpreted by historians in such a way as to underestimate greatly the volume of English coal shipped to Holland. De Zeeuw supposed that the quantities consumed during the seventeenth century 'could not have been very important', and while Unger has gone some way to modify this distorted picture, it is clear that the actual volume of the Anglo-Dutch coal trade was at least double that which he suggests for the early eighteenth century.[40] The difficulties involved in converting the baffling variety of weights and measures used in the coal trade into a standard unit of account have been described by several historians of the trade. There were innumerable local variations in the size of the chaldron alone, so that 'the same measure did not always mean the same thing in different districts, or even in the same district at different periods'. Moreover, coal was invariably measured by volume, and, even when the exact dimensions of the container can be defined, there is no way of knowing the weight of coal inside, which varied according to the size of the lumps, the type of coal, the amount of moisture and the practice of 'heaping'.[41]

The most substantial errors arise from the fact that coal exports to nearby Europe, originating mainly in the north-east, were measured by local customs officers in Newcastle and Sunderland chaldrons equivalent to about 53 cwt, while exports to Ireland, shipped mainly from Whitehaven, were measured in Winchester chaldrons of about 27 cwt.[42] The Inspectors General, however, made the formal assumption that *all* returns were made in Winchester chaldrons until the year 1765, when the entries were corrected. The official valuation of coal exported to Europe was doubled, but no retrospective adjustment was applied to the ledgers. Historians, without exception, have been misled by this serious official error ever since.[43] Additionally, there was the problem of under-recording and the widespread practice of granting 'good measure' in a

---

[40] De Zeeuw, 'Peat and the Dutch Golden Age', p. 14.

[41] Nef, *Coal Industry*, vol. II, Appendix C, pp. 367–71; Hatcher, *Coal Industry*, Appendix A, pp. 557–71. Variations in the size of the Winchester (or Winton) chaldron in the eighteenth century are given in Cust. 85/4 (Sunderland), 20 February 1755. The problem was not confined to the coal trade – it also existed to a lesser extent in the grain trade where the quarter was likewise not a uniform measure – but because of the variety of types and sizes of coal, its low value–bulk ratio, and the heavy burden of taxes on coal which encouraged the giving of 'good measure', the problem was especially serious in this branch of trade.

[42] Cullen, *Anglo-Irish Trade*, p. 79, where comparison is made between English and Irish customs figures.

[43] PRO Cust. 3/64, 65. Davis assumed the ledgers recorded Newcastle chaldrons (*Shipping Industry*, p. 185), which exaggerates the relative size of the Irish coal trade, and therefore of total coal exports. Mrs Schumpeter assumed Winchester measure until 1765, and, like the Inspectors General, recorded exports in Newcastle and Winchester chaldrons thereafter, without making any retrospective correction (*English Overseas Trade Statistics*,

Table 8.1 *Estimated English overseas coal exports, 1700–1789*

(annual averages, '000 tons)

	1 from the NE ports	2 Total exports	3 to Holland	4 percentage to Holland
1700–4	57	98.3	35.2	36
1705–9	54	102.8	44.2	43
1710–14		136.8	66.1	48
(1711–13)		*(69.7)*	*(24.7)*	*(36)*
1715–19		168.6	86.7	51
1720–4		221.5	76.4	35
1725–9		212.5	82.2	39
1730–4	111	227.9	92.4	41
(1730–4)		*(119.5)*	*(35.1)*	*(29)*
1735–9	128	258.5	95.5	37
1740–4		281.0	112.8	40
1745–9		280.7	117.9	42
1750–4		344.8	112.2	33
1755–9		280.6	97.8	35
1760–4		315.8	90.5	29
1765–9		[472.6]	106.6	[23]
1785–9		656.5	126.5	19
			(105.4)	*(16)*

Sources and notes: column 1, Flinn, *Coal Industry*, vol. II, Table 7.8, p. 226; column 2, Schumpeter, *English Overseas Trade Statistics*, Tables VIII and IX, which include exports to Ireland; column 3, PRO Cust. 3/4–89.
Italicised figures in brackets represent those suggested by Unger, 'Energy Sources', pp. 242–3. Figures in square brackets are probably inflated by the uncertain readjustment of the Irish coal export returns by the Inspector General, 1766–8.
Note that these estimates involve three sets of adjustments:
(i) exports to Ireland have been converted from Winchester to Newcastle chaldrons to provide comparability with exports to Europe; (ii) compensation for false entries involving vessels 'forced overseas' has been made on the basis of official estimates; (iii) adjusted exports have been inflated by 20% to take account of general under-recording (see text). Annual figures for declared exports only, which incorporate the first of these adjustments, are given in Appendix 8.

pp. 19–24). Her tables (VII and VIII) therefore underestimate the contribution of the European coal trade as well as total coal exports. Having worked on both Port Books and ledgers, Nef was aware of inconsistencies between the records, but did not identify their source (*British Coal Industry*, vol. II, *1700–1830*, p. 385, n. 1). M. W. Flinn also realised that the official statistics were inconsistent and made 'no attempt to adapt Schumpeter's figures for the period before 1765…because they have the appearance of being trade burdened by export duties, as well as outright duty-evasion. As we shall see, the official statistics under-recorded the real volume of overseas shipments by at least 20% during most years, and during the 1730s and '40s the practice developed of clearing overseas without making entries of any kind whatever. During the late 1730s, over 10% of vessels made 'invisible' exports of coal from Sunderland; during the early 1740s, the figure rose to 21%, while, from 1744 to 1747, it reached an astonishing 77% (Table 8.4). These shipments, and presumably those from other north-eastern ports, are entirely excluded from the Inspector General's official statistics. Finally, it is clear that the small-grade coal which comprised almost the whole of the export trade to Holland filled up the chaldron much more completely than the large coals sent to London, Dunkirk and other markets. Table 8.1 incorporates these revisions, but it is likely that the true figures could be even higher.

Since he relies on the Dutch Admiralty statistics for rough estimates of Holland's coal imports in the 1670s and the 1780s, Unger's assessment of the extent to which peat was replaced by coal may not be too wide of the mark: that coal supplied about one third as much energy as peat in the late seventeenth-century Netherlands, rising to more than half that amount a century later. The *rate* at which the shift to coal took place, however, and the extent of dependence on English rather than continental supplies, were much greater than Unger supposed.[44] After the conclusion of the Anglo-French wars, English coal exports to Holland probably exceeded 100,000 tons in the peak year of 1714, as exporters rushed to complete their shipments before the imposition of higher rates of export duty. After falling back for a few years, the steadily rising trend was resumed from the 1720s, when peat prices began to increase. Although the ledgers cannot be made to yield exact figures for bulky and taxable commodities, elimination of the most serious errors and discrepancies suggests a threefold expansion in coal exports to Holland during the first half of the eighteenth century.

incomplete'. He continues, 'the absence of any figures in Newcastle chaldrons can only suggest that, for whatever reasons, exports from the north-east ports are omitted from the table for this period. They start suddenly in 1765 at a level . . . which cannot indicate the beginning of a new trade.' Had he examined the ledgers, especially the entries relating to nearby Europe, and compared them with the authentic information from his own Table 7.8, he would have realised that the entries were included throughout, albeit in disguise (*British Coal Industry*, vol. II, pp. 226–7).

[44] For 1711–13, Unger puts exports to Holland at 25,000 tons, representing 36% of a supposed total English export of 70,000 tons; corrected figures suggest 59,000 tons, amounting to 47% of a total export of 126,000 tons. The discrepancy is higher for 1729–30, when under-recording was increasing: Unger suggests 34,000 tons went to Holland, against a corrected figure of 92,000 tons, representing 38% rather than 28% of total exports (Unger, 'Energy Sources', pp. 242–3).

Table 8.2 *Duties on overseas coal exports, 1694–1765*

Act and date passed	Duty, per chaldron when exported in:		English vessels	Foreign vessels
6 & 7 Wm. III c. 18	1694	Subsidy	3s	12s
12 Anne c. 9	1714	Impost	3s	5s
30 Geo. II c. 19	1757	Additional duty	4s	4s
5 Geo. III c. 35	1765	Additional duty	4s	4s

Taxation and the coal trade

If English coal enjoyed something of a natural monopoly in Holland during the early eighteenth century, what role did English export duties play, if any, in limiting the demand for this essential alternative energy source? Wrigley believes that 'large-scale switching' from peat to coal was hindered by English taxation, by Dutch excises and the costs of breaking bulk.[45] Unger, likewise, suggests that higher duties were more damaging to the Dutch economy than discriminatory measures against the employment of Dutch shipping in the coal trade. De Vries and van der Woude, on the other hand, play down the problem of energy shortages and costs, arguing instead that the Dutch economy decelerated because of a deficiency of demand.[46] In order to assess the impact of taxation in this area, we must examine not only the duty increases themselves but also ways in which payment was evaded, together with the significance of freight costs in determining the final selling price. In addition to export duties, English coal was also subject to an excise levied by the Dutch provincial authorities, but so too was peat. In proportion to its value, the excise bore down more heavily on the latter. A barrel of peat containing 120 turfs paid a duty equivalent to 5d sterling by the mid 1740s, or half the value of the turfs, compared with an excise equivalent to around one quarter of the selling price of coal in Holland, in the case of brewers, distillers, dyers and sugar refiners. Domestic consumers paid at a similar rate, but glass manufacturers and ironfounders paid a good deal less.[47]

Cumulative duty increases on coal exported overseas during the first two-thirds of the eighteenth century are shown in Table 8.2. After being doubled in 1714 (in the case of coal carried in English vessels), they remained at this level for over forty years, until further increases in

---

[45] Wrigley, *Continuity, Chance and Change*, p. 60; see also Nef, *British Coal Industry*, vol. I, p. 234.
[46] Unger, 'Energy Sources', pp. 247–8; J. de Vries & van der Woude, *First Modern Economy*, pp. 719–20.
[47] Lowndes, *State of the Coal trade*.

1757 and 1765.[48] With the increase of 1757, the duty on coal carried in English ships was about equal to the prime cost of the fuel in Newcastle; on that carried in foreign ships, it amounted to about twice its prime cost. In comparison Dutch import duties were trifling, amounting to the equivalent of a few pence, whereas the excise was more substantial.[49] In the province of Holland, it stood at almost exactly the same level as that of the English post-1757 export duty.

While the magnitude of export duties can be precisely known at any point in time, freight and handling charges were subject to more random variation: to seasonal fluctuation, alteration as between periods of war and peace or expectation of these, or to long-term changes in the quantity of shipping space available. Unfortunately, sufficient data of the right sort is not available to enable assessment of long-term changes in coal freight rates, although a single example might be given. In October 1727, Michael Johnson, merchant of Rotterdam, chartered the *Nathanael* of about 200 tons burthen to be laden in Rotterdam with unspecified goods; thence to Newcastle to lie for an unspecified time for unloading and reloading with coals. The vessel was to return to Rotterdam being allowed ten days for unloading. For this voyage, a freight of £103 was paid which included all port charges except those in England, which the master, John Remmortar, paid.[50] Assuming that a vessel of this size would carry at least 70 chaldrons, and that ten days would be sufficient for unloading and loading at Newcastle, the freight per chaldron would be no more than 30s. Only rarely were coal freight rates expressed in shillings (or gilders) per chaldron delivered.[51]

Without making unfounded assumptions about the fullness of loading, size of measure, and time spent loading and unloading, it is impossible to extract accurate freight costs from the Rotterdam charterparty material. It is, however, clear that freight charges bulked largest in the final supply price, and merchants were continually aware of this. 'The prime cost of the coals is small in comparison to the duty and charges', wrote Ralph Carr to Dirk van Dam in 1745.[52] In 1715, when the duty on coal exported in English ships was 6s per chaldron, William Cotesworth was quoting 8s 6d as the prime cost at Newcastle for coal which his agent in Rotterdam was selling at 40s.[53] The residue of over 20s largely represents freight charges; handling charges were relatively low and were said to be lower

[48] The duty on coal exported overseas in British vessels was abolished in 1709, but reimposed in the following year (Lipson, *Economic History of England*, vol. II, p. 117).
[49] Before 1725, 'the chaldron or half-hoed' paid 4 stivers; after 1725, the hoed paid 3 str.
[50] GAR NA2107/412, Jacobus de Bergh, 21 Oct. 1727.
[51] Ibid., 2325/265 (Jacob Bremer), 26 Oct. 1731.
[52] ZCE 10/16, R. Carr to Dirk van Dam, 7 March 1745.   [53] Table 8.3.

Table 8.3 *Coal prices, 1708–1770 (shillings per Newcastle chaldron)*

Selling price in Holland, including all duties, but excluding Dutch excise			Prime cost in Newcastle		
			1696	June	9s–10s
1708	20 Nov.	70s	1703	?	about 10s
1708	30 Nov.	72s–74s			
1708	18 Dec.	74s–76s			
1709	4 Jan.	78s			
1709	12 Mar.	88s expected			
1709	28 May	52s expected			
1709	6 Sept.	58s			
1711	5 May	56s			
1711	12 May	60s			
1711	28 June	58s			
1715	15 Aug.	40s	1715	15 Mar.	8s 6d
			1740	25 Apr.	11s, 12s
			1745	10 Jan.	9s 6d, 10s 6d, 11s 6d
			1747	8 Mar.	13s
			1752	2 Dec.	11s
1765		48s–76s			
1770	summer	48s–52s			
	winter	60s			

Sources:
Selling price in Holland
1708, 1709, 1711: Blackett Letter Book (all prices relate to the same grade of coal, sold in Rotterdam).
1715: Cotesworth Mss, CB/1, Foster & Pickfatt to W. Cotesworth (sold in Amsterdam).
1765: CO 388/95 Consular Reports, Rotterdam, 16 July 1765.
1770: Sneller, *Steenkolenhandel*, p. 122.
Prime cost in Newcastle
1696, 1703: Nef, *British Coal Industry*, vol. II, p. 397.
1715: Carr Ellison Mss, ZCE 10/2, W. Cotesworth to R. Bewicke, Amsterdam.
1740, 1745: Carr Ellison Mss, ZCE 10/12, R. Carr to Anna Brouwer, Rotterdam; ZCE 10/16, R. Carr to Dirk van Dam, Rotterdam.
1747: CLB Customs 85/4 (Sunderland), 8 March 1747.
1752: Brants 1348, Paul Jackson to J. I. de Neufville, Amsterdam.
Note: the official valuation of coal in 1701 was 48s.

in Holland than in England.[54] In proportions of this order, supply price in Holland was determined.

Table 8.3 assembles price quotations, taken mainly from merchants' correspondence, distinguishing between selling price in Holland and

[54] Lowndes, *State of the Coal trade:* 'charges of lighterage, porterage, cartage, and some other charges which might affect the consumption of coals are much less in Holland than here'.

prime cost at Newcastle. The first fluctuated widely, the second within narrower limits, suggesting that, on the supply side, it was freight costs that varied significantly on both a monthly and an annual basis. Any secular increase in the price paid by Dutch consumers for English coal seems to be less pronounced than short-term wartime price increases, particularly during the War of the Spanish Succession.[55] The Collector of Customs at Yarmouth succinctly explained the rise in coal prices at this time: '1. The great wages they [masters] give to seamen, there being great want at present of them. 2ndly., The great loss the merchants are at in having their vessels taken by privateers, wch notwithstanding their convoys are oft snapt by them. 3dly. Lying so long upon their wages wch is a vast charge to them.'[56] Although individual prices are not available, the correspondence of Ralph Carr shows that a similar situation occurred during the War of the Austrian Succession. Again, high wartime freight rates brought about a general rise in coal prices, or, in Carr's words: 'as our masters pay great wages to their men they consequently must have proportionate frat'.[57] Indeed, freights had risen to such a level in England that the difference between English and Dutch rates was said to balance the extra duty to which coal exported in foreign vessels was subject (which at this time amounted to 11s per chaldron).[58] It is for this reason that coal was occasionally exported to Holland in Dutch vessels during the '40s, a situation unknown in years of peace.[59] Clearly, the price paid by the Dutch consumer of English coal largely depended upon the scarcity of ships and seamen at any particular time, and this was obviously greatest in periods of war. In comparison, the long-term effects of English duty increases were less serious.[60]

There were in any case ways in which the burden of export duty could be evaded or alleviated. Ralph Carr for instance informed a Rotterdam customer in 1740, 'The measure you'll find very large for as the duty and other charges cut so deep, I took particular pains in that respect.'[61] Three months later, he wrote 'I wd. endeavour to get the coals reported a cha[ldron] less than jour acc. charged duty for, which is done accordingly and your acct. credited.'[62] From the customs Letter Books of Sunderland,

[55] The prices in Table 8.3 for 30 Nov. and 18 Dec. 1708, and 4 Jan. 1709 were said to be low in comparison with even higher prices in the earlier years of the war.
[56] PRO Cust. 97/2 (Yarmouth) Collector-Board, 26 June 1704.
[57] ZCE10/12, R. Carr to J. G. Liebenrood, London, 27 April 1740.
[58] Ibid., R. Carr to Anna Brouwer, Rotterdam, 18 April 1740. The embargo on British shipping had by this time been taken off (on 14 April 1740).
[59] In 1744 and 1745, 2,300 and 3,016 chaldrons respectively were shipped to Holland in foreign vessels (Cust. 3).
[60] Nef, British Coal Industry, vol. II, pp. 81–2; Davis, Shipping Industry, pp. 319–20, 329.
[61] ZCE10/12, R. Carr to Anna Brouwer, 25 April 1740.
[62] Ibid., R. Carr to Anna Brouwer, Rotterdam, 4 July 1740.

it appears that this practice was all too common during the '30s and '40s. The nature of Sunderland's harbour was such that coal ships carrying above 4 keels (32 chaldrons) were forced to load at sea, the depth of water at the bar even at high spring tide being no more than ten feet.[63] Ships engaged in the Rotterdam coal trade, it was said, carried on average 70 chaldrons,[64] so that 'the ships wch. load in the harbour for overseas are very few'.[65] Ships bound overseas might take in one third or as much as one-half of their loading in the harbour; but many of them took in their whole loading 'nigh a mile from the harbour', and it was common for over twenty vessels to be simultaneously loading for foreign parts in this way.[66] Taking coastal and overseas coal vessels together, there were sometimes 'a hundred sail' of ships loading coals simultaneously.[67] In this situation, adequate supervision of overseas shipments was well-nigh impossible, added to which was the fact that ships often loaded during the night.[68] In February 1738 for instance, Thomas Burn cleared for Amsterdam with a cargo of coal for which he had paid duty on 42 chaldrons, though it was alleged he was carrying 48.[69] This particular instance happened to elicit an enquiry from the Commissioners of Customs, to which the collector replied that the only solution was the appointment of twenty additional officers, 'a prodigious expense ... we have daily disputes betwixt the masters of ships and the officers at their clearing oversea and generally not for above one cha. of coals difference'.[70] By 1737, an inspector had been dispatched to Sunderland to investigate these abuses, which it was thought originated with the overloading of keels and lighters. Keels were normally measured to eight chaldrons and on this basis the loading of a ship was calculated; but the inspector was convinced that they could and did carry ten chaldrons.[71] In other words, one chaldron in five may have been exported duty-free. An attempt was therefore made to have the keels remeasured to ten chaldrons, but without success.[72] Six years later, it was reported that 'it is notorious that at this time, the keels receive 11 waggons

[63] PRO Cust. 85/2 (Sunderland) Collector to Board, 3 Nov. 1739.
[64] CO388/95, 'Particulars of the Trade ... [with] Rotterdam'.
[65] Cust. 85/2 (Sunderland) Collector to Board, 3 Nov. 1739.
[66] Cust. 85/1 (Sunderland) Collector to Board, 24 July 1733.
[67] Ibid., 11 Jan. 1734; Cust. 85/2 (Sunderland) Collector to Board, 14 Jan. 1737.
[68] Cust. 85/3 (Sunderland) Collector to Board: 'Ships generally take in coals as soon as they arrive in the road and sail as soon as they are loaded, whether it happen by night or day' (20 Aug. 1742).
[69] Cust. 85/2 (Sunderland) Collector to Board, 7 Feb. 1738.   [70] Ibid.
[71] Ibid., 3 Nov. 1730; 7 Sept. 1740: 'The officers do not inspect the greatest part of the keels that go to sea but inform themselves by the best ways and means they can of the no. of keels cast on board each ship, which they compute at 8 cha. each.'
[72] The incident is related at length in two reports (Cust. 85/2, 3 Nov. 1739 and 7 Sept. 1740).

at every coal staith in the river, whereas 10 waggons are esteemed equal to eight chaldrons... and the loss to the revenue on every such keel is 4s $9\frac{1}{2}$d'.[73] The extent of this practice varied according to the allegiance of the middleman fitter, who, like the exporting merchant or master, stood to gain his share of this bonus. When coal prices were abnormally high, as during the War of the Spanish Succession, the coal owners might prevail upon their fitters to withdraw any customary allowances, to the detriment of the exporting merchant. In 1704 for instance, merchants at Newcastle were complaining of such 'hard usage'.[74]

Allowances and good measure were to some extent to be expected in a bulk trade in which profits were low and in which, because of handling problems, middlemen proliferated.[75] But from the 1720s onwards, a new form of duty-evasion appeared in Sunderland's overseas coal trade which reached crisis proportions by the mid-1740s. At that time, the Collector reported that the overloading of keels was of slight importance compared to the growing practice by which masters engaged in the overseas coal trade would first clear coastwise 'and afterwards pretend to be forced oversea' by bad weather and tides.[76] The orders of the Commissioners for Customs show that the great majority of such vessels were bound for Holland.[77] Because coal carried coastwise was subject to duty only at the port of unloading and because supervision of the coastal trade was even laxer than that of the overseas trade, duty could be completely evaded with a false declaration of a coastal voyage.[78] By March 1748, it was said that, of 400 cargoes of coals annually exported overseas from Sunderland, no more than 50 were entered overseas regularly; of the duties on the remaining 350, 'none are paid till att or near the expiration of 6 months from the date of the coast bond, many not till years after the bonds are in process, some not at all, by the failure and insolvency of the bondsmen'.[79] The rapid growth of this practice is indicated in Table 8.4. The Collector of Sunderland called for 'immediate redress', and the coalfitters likewise submitted a proposal for its suppression. The fitters, of course, gained nothing from this particular fraud as they could by giving large measure; it was the exporter alone to whom the benefit of duty-evasion accrued. In the face of this evidence, the abuse was swiftly rectified by statute

[73] Cust. 85/3 (Sunderland) Collector to Board, 30 May 1746.
[74] Cust. 97/2 (Yarmouth) Collector to Board, 26 June 1704.
[75] Nef, *British Coal Industry*, vol. II, pp. 84–9.
[76] Hoon, *English Customs System*, pp. 266–7.
[77] Cust. 85/4 (Sunderland) Collector to Board, 10 Oct. 1747.
[78] Cust. 85/71B (Sunderland), Board to Collector, January 1741–May 1744, and 85/3, 24 April 1744.
[79] Cust. 85/4 (Sunderland) Collector to Board, 17 Mar. 1748. See also Nef, *British Coal Industry*, vol. II, pp. 236–7.

Table 8.4 *Coal vessels 'forced overseas' from Sunderland, 1717–46*

(Newcastle chaldrons, annual average)

	coal exported in vessels 'forced overseas'	coal regularly entered	percentage of coal exports irregularly entered
1717–19	485	13,399	3.49
1720–3	952	15,507	5.78
1724–37	na	na	na
1738–40	3,279	23,387	12.29
1741–3	5,809	18,785	23.60
1744–6	14,394	5,206	73.43

Source: Customs 85/4 (Sunderland), 23 Feb. 1748 (1717–23); 16 Feb. 1748 (1745–7); Customs 85/3, 14 Sep. 1745 (1738–44). 1724–37, figures not available.

in 1749. Henceforth, no officer was to clear any coal vessel outwards, coastwise or overseas, until the customs due for the last voyage were paid, or alternatively an authenticated certificate produced stating that this had been done. In the event of non-compliance, severe penalties were imposed.[80] Not surprisingly, the Customs Ledgers show a sharp rise in declared coal exports to Holland for the year 1749 and, although the corresponding figure for 1750 is comparatively low, a higher level appears to have been reached by the early '50s than was the case in the mid '40s.[81] The fact is, of course, that exporters were in addition making more realistic entries. The statistics of the coal trade must therefore be carefully interpreted, bearing in mind these irregularities. The growth of the '20s and '30s was probably more rapid than the table indicates and, during the '40s particularly, the true level of coal exports was considerably higher than it appears.

The extent of these abuses strengthens the impression that profits in the overseas coal trade were relatively low; under-declaration and false coastal clearances were expedients to which exporters resorted in their anxiety to widen narrow profit margins.[82] The 1749 legislation, it seems, effectively discouraged the latter procedure so that the impact of the duty increases of 1757 and 1765 may well have been quite perceptible.[83] Table 8.3 shows that a summer price of 40s for 1715 (a year when freights

---

[80] 22 Geo. II c. 37. Officers acting 'contrary to the true interests and meaning of this act' were liable to a fine of £100, while masters making false declarations were liable to payment of 5s per chaldron over and above the normal overseas duty.

[81] See annual figures in Appendix 8.

[82] See E. Hughes, *North Country Life in the Eighteenth Century*, vol. I, *The North East 1700–1750*, 1952, pp. 160–4; Cullen, *Anglo-Irish Trade*, ch. 6.

[83] Cust. 85/4 (Sunderland) Collector to Board, 11 July 1749.

had presumably returned to their normal peacetime levels) compares to summer prices of 48s to 52s for the years 1765 and 1770, by which time duties had increased by 8s.[84] It seems that, by this time, the burden of English duty increases had been fully passed on to the Dutch consumer.

Nevertheless, English observers constantly claimed that the Dutch were supplied with coal cheaper than the English themselves, and generally ignored or underestimated the impact of provincial excises on the Dutch consumer. In 1745 for instance, Lowndes vigorously argued the case for an increased overseas duty on these grounds. 'It is granted', he wrote, 'that in Holland coals generally sell for as much within eighteen pence, or two shillings p. chaldron as they do here in the pool'.[85] At this time, coals brought coastwise into London paid a total duty of 8s 4d, and to the outports, 5s, calculated on the basis of the London or Winchester chaldron. Coal exported overseas, however, paid a duty of only 6s calculated on the basis of the Newcastle or Sunderland chaldron which at 53 cwt[86] contained about twice as much coal as the London and Winchester measures.[87] This variation in measure effectively reduced the overseas duty by half for comparable quantities of coal.[88] It was for these reasons, claimed Lowndes, that the States General was able to lay an excise equivalent to 22s per Newcastle chaldron on English coal, finding 'the commodity would bear the duty, because even the manufacturers in Holland would have coals cheaper than the artificers in London and Westminster. But if the legislature here should lay a large duty upon exported coals, the prudent Dutch would instantly take off their duty.' Similar arguments were used when parliament levied the additional duty of 4s on coal exports during the early stages of the Seven Years' War, the preamble to that statute stating that, 'The duties upon coals exported to foreign parts in British vessels are less than the duties payable on coals carried coastwide to be used in this Kingdom, whereby foreigners may be supplied therewith at a less expense than the subjects of this realm,

---

[84] The increase of 1765 took effect from 1 June 1765; the 1765 prices in Table 8.3 were quoted after this date, viz. 16 July.

[85] Lowndes, State of the Coal trade.

[86] The content of the Newcastle chaldron was fixed by statute at this level in 1714 (12 Anne s. 2 c. 17). The Sunderland chaldron contained from 15 to 25% more than the Newcastle chaldron during the last years of the seventeenth century (Nef, British Coal Industry, vol. II, App. C, p. 370).

[87] There were innumerable local variations in the size of the Winchester chaldron, some of which were given by the Collector at Sunderland (Cust. 81/4, Collector to Board), 20 Feb. 1755 – number of Winchester chaldrons making 8 Sunderland chaldrons, at: Plymouth, 15.5; Rochester, 15.3; Exeter, 16; Portsmouth, 16.5; Maldon, 17; Ipswich, 17; Colchester, 17.5; Lynn, 18.5.

[88] Lowndes, State of the Coal trade; Add Ms 8133B, fo. 53.

to the great prejudice of the trade and manufactures of this Kingdom.'[89] In fact, the Dutch retained and increased the excise on coal: by 1765, it stood at 31s 6d per Newcastle chaldron, after parliament had levied a further 4s.[90] Even after the increases of 1757 and 1765, Londoners were still paying a higher duty than foreigners (although outport consumers paid 2s less), and an unsigned official memorandum noted that 'as the quantity of coals exported is nearly doubled since the year 1714 when the first 3s was imposed and has not diminished since 1765 when the last 4s duty was laid on, it is apprehended that it will bear a further increase'.[91]

It was assumed, correctly, that an expanding trade would bear increased duties without any loss of revenue. Richard Wolters, aware of the relatively untapped continental sources of supply open to the Dutch, was somewhat exceptional in warning against the dangers involved in such a proposition.[92] Contemporaries recognised the relatively inelastic nature of foreign demand for English coal, which made it an obvious source of increased revenue. As early as 1684, the Commissioners of Customs noted:

If... the cheapnesse of a commodity supporteth an increase of consumption, it will also be remembered that the supposition will utterly fail in commodities not subject to luxury. If salt were at a penny a bushel, it would not (for its cheapnesse) augment the consumption. And if all the English custom on coales were taken off, it would not amount to above $1\frac{1}{2}$d a bushel, which in the consumption of common burning would be next to nothing; but abroad, coales is only used for manufacture. And the dearer we sell a commodity abroad which the stranger cannot be without, as aforesaid, the more we bring back to enrich our own nation.[93]

The same argument was used in 1745 by Thomas Lowndes to support his case for an increase in the duty on exported coal, particularly that exported to Holland.[94]

In fact, the statistics of the overseas coal trade show that exports to Holland stagnated during the '30s and '60s, after a long period of steady expansion.[95] The depressive effects of the legislation of 1749, 1757 and 1765 together with the rise in freight rates during the Seven Years' War must in large measure be held responsible. Although the Dutch importer may still have received his coal at a price no higher than that paid by

---

[89] 30 Geo. II c. 19 (1757).
[90] CO388/95, 'Particulars of the Trade... [with] Rotterdam'.
[91] Add Ms 8133B, fo. 53, 'A plan for equalising the duties on coals by imposing renewed additional duties' (Papers of Sir Wm Musgrave, ?1780).
[92] CO388/95, 'Particulars of the Trade... [with] Rotterdam'.
[93] Add Ms 28,079, fo. 23, Mr Ettick's paper about exported coals, 20 Dec. 1684.
[94] Lowndes, State of the Coal trade.   [95] See Appendix 8.

the Londoner, the industrial and domestic consumer in Holland was in addition forced to pay a heavy excise which raised the final cost to a considerably higher level – which English observers tended to ignore.

Commercial organisation

'Business decisions in the coal trade were taken by numerous masters, whose psychology and reactions to fluctuations in price movements were more akin to those of the peasant producers in agriculture than to those of the businessman.'[96] Thus, L. M. Cullen described the organisation of the Anglo-Irish coal trade in the eighteenth century, and up to a point the same was true of the Anglo-Dutch coal trade. Masters of ships exporting coal on their own accounts controlled a high proportion of the trade,[97] a situation reflected in Wolters's remark that 'coals are sold here [Rotterdam] for ready money'.[98] Operating on a small capital margin and relying on a quick turnover to meet current expenses, ships' masters were in no position to trade otherwise. It was this state of affairs which caused the Rotterdam market to glut from time to time,[99] aggravated by the fact that coal was often used as a 'ballast cargo' to complete a loading for Holland without prior consideration of the state of the market. Servas Havart, for example, a Rotterdam merchant, chartered the 90-ton *Rebecca* in 1727 to bring 50 tons of lead and lead ore from Chester to Rotterdam; if Edward Johnson, the master, was unable to obtain a sufficient loading, he was at liberty to sail to Milford and complete his cargo with coal, presumably for his own account.[100] In the case of ships carrying lead, this was in fact usually a necessity because of that commodity's small bulk.[101] Similarly in 1740, one of Ralph Carr's Dutch customers had been unable to obtain a cargo of lead, salmon and fish oil from a northern port, so Carr deemed it 'more for your interest to order him [the master] here to load coals than that he shd. proceed to Rotterdam in his ballast'.[102] In cases such as these, satisfactory disposal of the coal so as to cover shipping costs was a more important consideration than securing sizeable profits.

---

[96] Cullen, *Anglo-Irish Trade*, p. 119.
[97] CO388/95, 'Particulars of the Trade . . . [with] Rotterdam'.
[98] Visser, *Verkeersindustrieen*, p. 23.   [99] See above, p. 251.
[100] GAR NA2106/9637 (Jacobus de Bergh), 25 Jan. 1727.
[101] Blackett spoke of the 'coals which are generally in ship that comes wth lead' (ZBL 192, letter to 'cousin' Wilkinson, 4 Jan. 1709).
[102] ZCE10/13, R. Carr to Anna Brouwer, Rotterdam, 19 Dec. 1740; ZBL192, John Blackett to John Kelley, 1 Feb. 1709: 'I would by all means have you to get a ship to load rape seed, and what is wanting to put coals or some other thing aboard.'

Unlike merchants, masters shipping coal to Holland on their own accounts did so without assistance from established correspondents, although they might make regular use of a particular factor in Holland.
As late as the 1770s, the Rotterdam coal trade was characterised by an
alarming lack of supervision of the movement of traffic, information and
people, even by contemporary standards.[103] This specific lack of business correspondence makes generalisation covering changes in the overall organisation of the coal trade questionable and possibly one-sided,
for a small amount of correspondence has survived, produced by general
merchants whose activities encompassed, amongst other things, the coal
trade. Unlike the Anglo-Irish coal trade, it seems that transactions regulated by correspondence played an important part in the export of coal to
Holland, for two reasons.[104] Firstly, coal was used to complete mixed outward cargoes consisting of other bulky commodities such as salt and glass
bottles, as well as lead, which, because of their higher value, came within
the province of the general merchant.[105] Secondly, Dutch merchant importers of coal could and did engage in the European coal trade which
offered greater opportunities for profit than the simple and somewhat
overcrowded Newcastle/Sunderland–Rotterdam trade.[106] This required
a more sophisticated organisation.

In the early years of the eighteenth century, it was common for Newcastle merchants to consign their coal to Rotterdam houses or agents for
sale on a commission basis. In 1715, William Cotesworth for instance was
consigning his to Foster and Pickfatt of Rotterdam, who charged a 2%
commission. In addition, lead, bottles and stones were sent on the same
basis in exchange for flax, madder, mull and whalefins.[107] At the same
time, however, he had persuaded Robert Bewicke, a Northumberland
merchant who was then resident in Amsterdam, to order coal on his own
(Bewicke's) account at fixed prime cost. When the usual return cargoes
of fins, madder and candle wick were not available, Bewicke shipped tiles
which Cotesworth noted 'may do well to serve a turn'.[108] An arrangement such as this was obviously preferable for the exporting Newcastle

[103] Sneller, *Steenkolenhandel*, p. 122.   [104] Cullen, *Anglo-Irish Trade*, p. 122.

[105] See, for example, Brants 1346, Paul Jackson, Newcastle, to J. I. de Neufville, Amsterdam, 2 Dec. 1752.

[106] See below, pp. 289–90, and the large volume of charterparties in the Gemeente Archief,
Rotterdam, relating to Dutch trade in English coal with Norway and France, e.g.:
NA2325 (Jacob Bremer), NA2328 (Jacob Bremer), NA2116 (Jacobus de Bergh).

[107] Gateshead Public Library, Cotesworth Mss CB, bundle 1, Foster and Pickfatt to Wm
Cotesworth, May 1716; another prominent Newcastle merchant, William Ramsay, Jr,
traded with the same house on an identical pattern: see Hughes, *North Country Life*,
p. 47.

[108] ZCE10/2, Wm Cotesworth to R. Bewicke, Amsterdam, 15 March and 14 June 1715.

merchant, as it avoided commission charges together with the possibility
of a disappointing result. It was not easy, however, to find such regular customers in Holland. During the years 1708–12, John Blackett, son
of the coalowner Sir Edward Blackett of Newby, Northumberland, had
established himself in Rotterdam as a commission agent and merchant.
He sometimes took lead which could be a highly profitable commodity in
years of war, on his own account, but, in the case of coal, he generally had
'no inclination to take a share in the loading'.[109] Instead, he kept Newcastle merchants well informed of the movement of coal and other prices
in Holland, which he often took pains to analyse. This eliminated the
more random shipments which exporting masters were inclined to make,
and the general merchant thus secured himself a place in a notoriously
unprofitable trade. In this way, Blackett disposed of the shipments of a
small group of Newcastle and Hull merchants: John Kelley, A. Shaftoe,
'Cousin' Wilkinson, Featherstone and Reay, and James Morton. In the
opposite direction, flax and tow, together with small quantities of canvas
and paper, were sent on the account of the importing English merchant.
In all these functions, Blackett was in close contact with consumers and
producers. In the case of coal, it has been noted that he dealt directly with
brewers; flax he purchased through 'a man attendant of the market' as did
'Mr Allen, Pelsant & Foster, & others . . . we allow them $\frac{1}{2}$ st a stone & pay
ready money but as you say it is much cheaper doing so than buying in the
shops'; and similarly with paper: 'here is a young man my next neighbour
who lived with a paper merchant who has promised me always to send to
the mills himself, but then must pay him ready money'.[110] This, it will be
noted, approached the classic pattern of dealing which Merchant Adventurers such as Gay and Bale followed, but with the absence of company
organisation.[111]

The only coal which Blackett took on his own account was that which
was used to ballast vessels which had been carrying lead or rapeseed, and
this was undertaken to encourage his commission trade in these other
commodities.[112] For one of his rivals in the lead trade 'always buys the
coals of Mr Wilkinson wch. are generally put in the bottom of the ship
for his own acct'.[113] It seems that this physical connection between the
shipping of coal and lead increasingly encouraged importing Dutch merchants to take coal on their own accounts, to the partial exclusion of the

[109] ZBL192, John Blackett to James Morton, 18 March 1708/9.
[110] See above, p. 00; ZBL192, J. Blackett to Featherstone and Reay, 30 Nov. 1708 and 17
May 1709.
[111] See above, chapter 4, pp. 122–3.
[112] E.g.: letter to J. Kelley, 1 Feb. 1709, 'Yr best way will be to get a ship & what she wants
besides the rapeseed to load wth coales, I will take 1/2 with you.'
[113] ZBL192, J. Blackett to M. Brommell, 5 Feb. 1709.

agent (whether English or Dutch). In the late '20s and '30s, a Rotterdam merchant such as James Spicer was regularly chartering English vessels to sail to Milford Haven, issuing the masters with instructions to 'buy and load per the first opportunity his said ships full loading of Stonecoales of Doctor Powals pits, if to be had, otherwise what is to be got'.[114] In such cases, the master's judgement and skill in selecting the coal and keeping charges down to a minimum was of some importance, but the cargo was nonetheless on the account of the importing merchant. By the late 1730s Ralph Carr, son of the coalowner Sir Ralph Carr, was exporting cargoes of coal and lead for the accounts of Dutch customers such as T. M. Liebenrood, Dirk van Dam, H. van Ijzendoorn and Anna Brouwer, all of Rotterdam.[115] (Though he was also corresponding with an agent in Dunkirk, William Norton, who disposed of coal on the joint account of Carr and Liebenrood.)[116] Similarly, Paul Jackson of Newcastle was offering in 1752 to supply J. I. de Neufville with 'smiths' coals' on the latter's account, together with salt, lead, stones and glass bottles.[117] Carr's Dutch customers supplied both Rotterdam consumers and European markets, particularly Lisbon, Bordeaux and northern France. Because of abnormally high English freight rates and the difficulties involved in trading with the enemy, Dutch ships were used for many of these voyages,[118] and profits may well have been above average. In years of peace, however, it was common for the importing Dutch merchant (or English merchant resident in Holland) to charter English vessels for a fixed freight payment.[119] From the point of view of both the English exporter and the Dutch importer, the most satisfactory arrangement was one in which the final consumer placed a fixed and regular order, as Carr explained to Norton: 'If you were to contract with the consumers in yr place for 2 loadings per month, it is an easy matter to be supplied with them at so much per keel by which you may make a much more certain calculation & if they have convenience a pat stock might be laid in during the summer when fraughts are low.'[120] Trading of this sort implied increasingly close

---

[114] GAR NA2325/197 (Jacob Bremer), 3 Aug. 1731; see also NA2325/265, 26 Oct. 1731; NA2107/412 (Jacobus de Bergh), 21 Oct. 1727; NA2108/506 (Jacobus de Bergh), 18 May 1728.

[115] ZCE10/11, 12, 13.

[116] ZCE10/11, R. Carr to Wm Norton, Dunkirk, 20 Oct. 1738.

[117] Brants 1346, Paul Jackson, Newcastle, to J. I. de Neufville, Amsterdam, 2 Dec. 1752.

[118] In December 1738, Carr declared: 'shall use my utmost endeavours to procure a large ship to take in coals tho in all my life I never see shipping worse to come by' (to Wm Norton, ZCE 10/11, 27 Dec.). The embargo of 1739–40 necessitated the use of some Dutch shipping, see ZCE 10/12, R. Carr to T. M. Liebenrood, 7 Mar. 1740; also ZCE 10/16, R. Carr to H. van Ijzendoorn, Rotterdam, 2 Oct. 1745: 'I am daily loading Dutch vessels entirely with coals for France.'

[119] See above, pp. 288–90.   [120] ZCE10/11, R. Carr to Wm Norton, 30 Jan. 1739.

contact and a high degree of trust, and if achieved it minimised those problems endemic to the coal trade: uncertain returns arising from the combination of a fairly inelastic demand with a market which tended to glut, and high freight and handling costs. It also avoided reliance upon the overseas agent who was prone to a variety of fraudulent practices: collaboration with masters in order to undersell competitors, the mixing of different grades of coal and its sale under false denominations, and wholesale combination to raise the general level of coal prices.[121] As a safeguard against such practices, it was reported that 'masters of ships in the coal trade have directions from their owners not to sell their coals at the delivering ports under a stated price at each port, and also to take turn in their delivering'.[122]

It does not follow from the above that the coal trade to Holland was undergoing fundamental reorganisation in the same way as the woollen trade.[123] The master shipping coal on his own account with a minimum amount of information remained as the backbone of the trade, and he has left behind little documentary evidence. Until at least the 1770s, the agent resident in Holland continued to operate as an important and sometimes troublesome intermediary, as Sneller showed.[124] A part of the trade, however, was undoubtedly carried on by merchants acting on the intelligence of correspondents, and, by the late 1720s, some Rotterdam merchants (and possibly consumers) were in direct contact with English merchants and coal owners, chartering ships and drawing supplies as they needed them. This tendency to trade on Dutch rather than English account is strongly paralleled by more clearly marked changes in the organisation of the English woollen export trade to Holland, which as we have seen became rather a Dutch import trade. On the import side, English merchants were at the same time refusing to take linen on their own accounts, preferring the small but steady remuneration provided by commission sales.[125] These organisational changes all represented greater claims on Dutch capital and credit.

---

[121] Sneller, *Steenkolenhandel*, pp. 122–4. One such crisis occurred in 1775. No doubt it was partly as a solution to this problem that trusted relatives of Newcastle merchants, such as Blackett and Bewicke, established themselves in Rotterdam as agents.
[122] Cust. 85/2 (Sunderland), Collector to Board, 14 April 1738.
[123] See above, pp. 134–40.   [124] Sneller, *Steenkolenhandel*, pp. 122–4.
[125] See above, pp. 174–80.

Part III

Dutch decline and English expansion

9 The shipping industry and the impact of war

The growth of Europe's trade in low-value goods, it appears, was the result not of any striking reduction of freight rates, but of a combination of factors including improved commercial organisation, better packaging, safer seas, larger markets and cheaper goods, in addition to cheaper freights in a number of trades. Low-value goods remained sensitive to shipping and handling charges throughout the early modern period, but it was modest, incremental improvements in transport and handling costs which brought about the integration of northern and southern European markets for bulk commodities. There were two prerequisites for success in the bulk trades. The first was adequate shipping capacity, or, as Child put it, '*multitudes of merchants and shipping*' which made the Dutch 'Masters of the Field in Trade'.[1] The second, which arose from the first, was the utilisation and development of the appropriate type of vessel for its cargo and trade route: in the northern European trades, unarmed, long, flat-bottomed flyboats – of which there were several variants – rather than the traditional, defensible ships used in the rich trades of southern Europe, of which Sir George Downing complained.[2] The development of the flyboat was undeniably a major factor underlying Dutch success in the bulk carrying trades, and it was the transfer of captured Dutch flyboats to English merchants which partly explains falling freight costs in the plantation trades, which utilised large numbers of these vessels.[3] Cheap to build and to operate, and needing only a small crew, the flyboat embodied no revolutionary design principles other than simplicity

---

[1] J. Child, *A New Discourse on Trade*, 1693, 1698, p. 92.
[2] The success of the rich trades to the Mediterranean, the Levant and the East Indies, as Sir George Downing noted in 1663, depended very little on improvements in ship design, and could bear the high costs of English shipping which resembled 'rather tubs than ships, made to look like a man of war', too short and lacking in hold space (quoted by V. Barbour, 'Dutch and English Merchant Shipping in the Seventeenth Century', *EcHR*, 2 (1930), repr. Carus-Wilson, *Essays*, vol. I, p. 230).
[3] Ibid., p. 237.

Illustration 9.1 W. van de Velde I, Two Dutch Merchant Ships under Sail, undated (grisaille on panel).

and commercial profitability.[4] The carrying capacity and versatility of the flyboat (or *fluytschip*), however, was by no means the only influence: operating costs, the organisation of buying and selling, and low interest rates were also crucial. Lower costs arising from superior ship design created new opportunities for commercial expansion, as Richard Unger has emphasised, but this would only materialise if other conditions were right. If they were, then 'the value of specialisation in ship design was enhanced and the design in turn generated even greater potential cost reduction', in both construction and operation.[5]

Those historians such as Menard who stress the gradualness of improvements in ship design and shipping productivity during the early modern period are, of course, presenting a European aggregate. When the aggregates are taken apart, we find a clear rise in Dutch shipping productivity during the first half of the seventeenth century, which was

---

[4] C. H. Wilson, 'Transport as a Factor in the History of Economic Development', *JEEH*, 2 (1973), p. 330.

[5] R. W. Unger, *Dutch Shipbuilding before 1800*, Assen, 1978, p. 39.

transferred to England during the decades after 1660.[6] The development of the *fluytschip* in sixteenth-century Holland was largely a response to the shortage of home-produced primary products and a growing reliance on imports. As John Evelyn put it, 'the quality and circumstances of [Holland's] situation... affords neither grain, wine, oyle, timber, mettal, stone, wool, hemp, pitch, nor, almost any other commodity of use; and yet we find there is hardly a Nation in the World which enjoys all these things in greater affluence: and all this from Commerce alone, and the effects of industry'.[7] The Dutch were dependent on the import of cheap food and raw materials from the Baltic, and shipowning had developed out of sheer necessity, when alternative investment possibilities were few: *navigare necesse*.[8] It was out of this dependency that other northern trades developed. As the 'mother trade' (*moedernegotie*), the Baltic trade fostered several other important branches of trade, especially outward cargoes brought from southern Europe for northern markets, including the salt, wine and groceries of Spain, Portugal and southern France received in exchange for re-exports of Baltic grain.[9] It was the balanced exchange of bulk cargoes between northern and southern Europe which gave the Dutch their lead in the shipping industry, accompanied by innovations in ship design and shipbuilding. Unlike those of their English counterparts, Dutch vessels bound for the Baltic were usually laden, if only with ballast cargoes such as 'delftware' tiles, bricks and roofing tiles.

Brulez has suggested that, by the late seventeenth century, Dutch freight costs had fallen so low that a further fall in the eighteenth century was impossible.[10] Contempory commentators in England were quick to point out that low interest rates helped the Dutch to maintain their position as bulk carriers. 'Where interest is high', Davenant wrote in 1699, 'the merchants care not to deal in any but rich commodities, whose freight is easy, and whose vent is certain in corrupted countries... It is the bulky goods, whose returns are not of so great profit, that breed most seamen, and that are most nationally gainful.'[11] Although Brulez may have underestimated the continuing profitability of Dutch shipowning, his critics, such as Bruijn, produce no evidence of a sustained fall in Dutch freight rates. Ralph Davis, however, showed clearly that English rates gradually

---

[6] J. R. Bruijn, 'Productivity, Profitability, and Costs of Private and Corporate Dutch Ship Ownership in the Seventeenth and Eighteenth Centuries', in Tracy (ed.), *Political Economy of Merchant Empires*, p. 177.

[7] J. Evelyn, *Navigation and Commerce, their Original and Progress*, 1674.

[8] W. Brulez, 'Shipping Profits in the Early Modern Period', *AHN*, 14 (1981), p. 83.

[9] Davis, *Shipping Industry*, p. 187, n. 3.   [10] Brulez, 'Shipping Profits', p. 84.

[11] Cited in V. Barbour, 'Dutch and English Merchant Shipping', p. 236.

Table 9.1 *The growth of English and Dutch shipping tonnage, 1567–1786*

('000 tons)

	English	Dutch
1567	–	157
1572	50	–
1582	67	–
1629	115	–
1636	–	305*
1670	–	394
1686	340	–
1702	323	–
1750	–	359*
1751	421	–
1765	543	–
1775	608	–
1780	–	394
1786	752	–

Sources: Davis, *Shipping Industry*, p. 27, and Appendix A, pp. 395–406; J. L. van Zanden, 'Economic Growth in the Golden Age', p. 19.
Dutch figures converted from metric tonnes to English equivalent (1 ton = 1.01604 tonnes).
* VOC and WIC ships excluded for 1636 and 1750.

fell from the comparatively high levels of the 1630s, and continued to do so throughout the eighteenth century, although profitability declined.[12] The Dutch comparative advantage was passed on to England, it seems, through two main channels: the capture of prize vessels during wartime and the imitation of Dutch designs and building methods. The former produced the most immediate results, and enormous gains were made during the First Anglo-Dutch War of 1652–4, when between 1,000 and 1,700 vessels were taken: the Dutch themselves estimated their losses at 1,200.[13] The Second and Third Anglo-Dutch Wars produced 1,000 more. English losses were light, not exceeding 500 vessels, and, in Davis's words, 'these were the wars which reconstituted the English merchant fleet with Dutch flyboats'.[14] This sudden growth is reflected in the statistics for English and Dutch shipping tonnage, set out in Table 9.1.

During the third quarter of the seventeenth century therefore, the proportion of foreign-built tonnage in English ownership was uniquely

[12] Davis, *Shipping Industry*, pp. 370–2.   [13] Israel, *Dutch Primacy*, p. 210.
[14] Davis, *Shipping Industry*, pp. 51, 316.

high, and while this provided English shipbuilders with few immediate incentives to compete with their Dutch rivals, English shipowners and merchants quickly came to appreciate the value of the flyboat.[15] As these old vessels wore out, English yards modified their designs and production methods along Dutch lines, encouraged by a statute of 1662 which excluded foreign-built ships, other than prize vessels, from the privileges conferred by the Navigation Acts.[16] In 1672, the Council of Trade ordered that the building of 'Pinks, flutes and other great ships, for the more convenient carryage of masts, timber and other bulky commodities, be encouraged.' By the end of the decade, Stockton builders were turning out pinks of 200–300 tons, described as 'the largest vessel[s] that ever came nigh Stockton'.[17] During the Anglo-French wars of 1689–1713, English merchants and shipowners sustained heavy net losses, but, by this time, new shipbuilding practices were well established. Davenant, in 1698, maintained that ships were now being built on the Humber and Trent as cheaply as in Holland, a judgement that was more amply confirmed by Defoe in the 1720s. The London yards, it seems, continued to concentrate on the construction of expensive defensible ships for the Royal Navy and the East India trade, and conservative work practices combined with relatively high wage levels restrained the growth of a competitive metropolitan shipbuilding industry.[18] The northern and north-eastern ports, whose merchants were committed to the coal trade and the other bulk trades of the North Sea and the Baltic, were better placed to develop the cheap bulk carrier on the Dutch pattern.

The available statistics point to a remarkable growth in the capacity of the English shipping industry during the century after 1660, and clearly reflect the predominant influences which shaped the commercial history of north-western Europe in this period: the decline of Dutch-Baltic trade and its restructuring, and the growth of the English bulk trades to nearby and northern Europe. Both can be seen as interconnected parts of a single process, which made greater demands on English shipping tonnage than the growth of long-distance trade to Asia and the Americas. But there were important differences between Dutch and English commercial expansion. The English never attempted to carry on a balanced trade in bulk goods between northern and southern Europe in the Dutch manner. Instead they developed triangular trading patterns within the North Sea / Baltic

[15] Ibid., p. 56. [16] By 14 Chas. II c. xi; Anderson, *Origin of Commerce*, vol. II, p. 473.
[17] A. McGowan, 'The Dutch Influence on British Shipbuilding', in C. Wilson and D. Proctor (eds.), *The Seaborne Alliance and the Diplomatic Revolution*, 1989, p. 95.
[18] M. Berlin, 'Shipbuilding in Early Modern London', unpublished paper circulated to the research group, 'The Growth of a Skilled Workforce in London, 1500–1750', Centre for Metropolitan History, London, 1994.

zone which relied on the distribution of their own home-produced bulk cargoes of grain, coal and rock salt, in exchange for timber and naval stores. The navigation code was applied both to exclude the Dutch from Anglo-Baltic trade and to secure a major role for English merchants in the distribution of colonial goods in northern Europe. It was in the North Sea and the Baltic that by far the greatest volume of English shipping tonnage was deployed during the period of Dutch commercial decline, and it was consequently here that Anglo-Dutch competition in the carrying trade was most intense.[19]

The decline of Dutch Baltic trade and English competition

As we have already noticed, the historiography of Dutch-Baltic trade has undergone revision in recent years.[20] Israel has questioned the centrality of the bulk trades as the underlying element in Dutch trade primacy, while emphasising the role of the 'rich trades' in supplying raw materials for the Republic's manufactured exports at the peak of Dutch prosperity. The focus on trade values rather than volumes obviously downplays the role of the shipping and the carrying trade, together with the substantial value-added elements which these generated throughout the entire commercial sector. In fact more capital was turned over on the Amsterdam Bourse in grain dealings than in any other commodity.[21] Israel's argument would carry greater weight if it were true, as Brulez speculated, that the connection between shipping and trade in the Republic was entirely fortuitous – that staplemarket traders need not have relied on their own national shipping, following the earlier pattern followed of Antwerp and Bruges merchants. In practice, however, trade and shipping *were* closely linked in Holland, especially during the first half of the seventeenth century when the productivity of Dutch European shipping was higher than that of other countries, and where specialised shipowning firms did not exist as such. Leaving aside the case of the VOC, Dutch merchants normally used their own tonnage or hired it from other traders. In the Baltic trades, shipping interests, commerce and chartering were 'united within the same group of persons and the same partnerships'.[22]

Israel's challenge to some of these established certainties, however, has served to re-focus the role of Dutch-Baltic trade and the dynamics

[19] Davis, *Shipping Industry*, p. 186.   [20] See above, pp. 209–10.
[21] See especially the debate between van Zanden, Noordegraaf and Israel on *Dutch Primacy in World Trade*, BMGN, 106 (1991), pp. 451–79; D. W. Davies, *A Primer of Dutch Seventeenth Century Overseas Trade*, 1961, p. 10.
[22] Bruijn, 'Productivity, Profitability, and Costs', pp. 179–80; A. E. Christensen, *Dutch Trade to the Baltic about 1600*, Copenhagen and the Hague, 1941, p. 153.

of its decline. Lindblad, especially, has drawn attention to the differing fortunes of its low- and high-value components (the 'bulk' and 'rich' trades existing *within* Baltic commerce), and has identified the changing balance between structural and competitive elements in the process of contraction during the seventeenth and eighteenth centuries.[23] Historians of Dutch economic decline have long debated the role of structural change in that process, commonly discussed in terms of the weakening of the central staplemarket function and associated changes in commercial organisation.[24] Qualitative changes such as these, however, are difficult to measure and describe, beyond simple generalisations about the degree to which contraction in individual branches of trade was absolute and/or relative. By focusing attention on the changing commodity composition of trade, however, it is possible to differentiate between the structural and competitive tendencies which shaped the changing course of trade of one or more countries with a given region, or with the rest of the world. Thus, we might ask, how far was the Republic's deteriorating commerce with the Baltic region the product of a falling European demand for grain, together with a failure to develop and maintain the 'rich' Baltic trades, such as timber and colonial re-exports, in an increasingly competitive world? Lindblad has applied a simple statistical technique to this problem, which has revealed a different chronology and a greater complexity than that found in the traditional literature. (A structural change in trade is identified when the Dutch share of Baltic trade in each group of commodities remains the same, but the relative importance of the groups alters; a change in competitiveness occurs when its share within the individual groups declines.)[25]

Lindblad's findings confirm earlier views of the northern trades as the mainstay of the Dutch commercial system, and place the onset of decline in Europe's trade with the Baltic as coinciding broadly with the slowing down of the Republic's overseas trade in general. A more optimistic picture, however, emerges than that provided by Faber. Although the familiar decline of Baltic grain shipments in the second half of the seventeeth

---

[23] Lindblad, 'Structuur en Mededinging', pp. 79 90; Lindblad, 'Foreign Trade', pp. 219 49.

[24] Joh. de Vries, *Economische Achteruitgang*, pp. 29 31.

[25] The method is that developed by H. Tyszynski, 'World Trade in Manufactured Commodities, 1899 1950', *Manchester School of Economic and Social Studies*, 19 (1951), p. 288. Structural change and competitiveness are isolated by computing hypothetical shares of the country in the trade of the larger region assuming that, while the structure and value of the region's trade was changing between any two years, the country maintained its initial competitive position in each group of commodities. The share of trade which it has gained or lost through changes in the structure of the region's trade is the difference between this hypothetical share in year II and its actual share in year I. The share of trade which it has gained or lost through changes in competitiveness is the difference between the hypothetical share and its actual share in year II.

century is confirmed, Lindblad shows that the Dutch share actually rose after *c.* 1650, so that annual shipments to Holland experienced only a slight fall before 1700. This is understood as a 'competitive tendency towards expansion'. The collapse of trade between 1700 and 1740 was nevertheless drastic, as Faber realised, but the Dutch at least managed to improve their share marginally during the 1720s and '30s. After the peak year of 1740, structural gain turned to loss when the share handled by Dutch grain importers declined, until the trade revived in 1756. How far, though, did expansion in the newer branches of Dutch-Baltic trade such as timber, iron, textiles and colonial re-exports counterbalance stagnation and loss?

The eastbound Baltic trades were especially hard-hit by structural contraction after *c.* 1640, especially the transport of salt, herring and wine, all dominated by the Dutch. In Lindblad's view, the fact that absolute decline was accompanied by relative decline suggests that the Republic 'suffered not only from putting high stakes in losing branches but also from intensified competition'.[26] The newer outward trades, textiles and colonial goods, made spectacular progress between 1630 and 1680 but relative Dutch decline thereafter, in the face of absolute expansion, is explained by serious English and French competition, backed by protectionist policies. In westbound commerce, structural contraction affecting grain shipments before 1700 was less damaging than some historians have supposed, and Dutch merchants responded successfully to foreign competition by shifting from rye to wheat imports. In the two principal trades which provided substantial compensation, however, timber and iron, the Dutch lost ground heavily to the English after *c.* 1650, especially in the latter. Between the 1620s and the 1690s, the Dutch share of iron transported through the Sound had fallen from one half to one quarter of all shipments. In the timber trade, contraction was less marked, falling from two-thirds to one half.[27] In general, prospects deteriorated for traditional bulk products, while competition in the newer branches of Baltic trade became intense.

In spite of their well-known defects, the Sound Toll Registers provide a reasonable indication of the long-drawn-out struggle of the European powers to maximise their share of Baltic trade.[28] The decline in

---

[26] Lindblad, 'Foreign Trade', p. 234.   [27] Ibid., pp. 237–8.

[28] *Tabeller over Skibsfart og Varetransport gennem Øresund*, vol. I, *1497–1660*, ed. N. E. Bang, Copenhagen and Leipzig, 1906; vol. II, *1661–1783*, ed. N. E. Bang & K. Korst, Copenhagen and Leipzig, 1930. Tolls were levied on the basis of documentation provided by the master, and ships were rarely inspected; weights were often understated; the ship's or master's home port was not always accurate; and Sweden was exempted from toll before 1710. Nevertheless, the registers provide a reasonably good general picture (Christensen, *Dutch Trade*, ch. 2; W. S. Unger, 'Trade through the Sound', pp. 206–21).

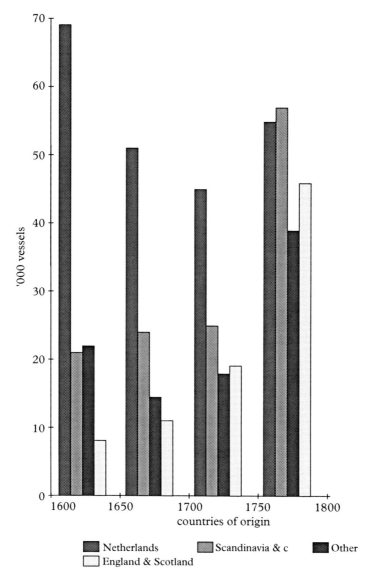

Figure 9.1 Eastward voyages through the Sound, 1600–1783

the number of Dutch vessels passing the Sound during the century after 1650 was both absolute and relative, falling from a peak share of 55% of the total during the first half of the seventeenth century, to 50% for 1650–1700, and 42% for 1700–50. Although there was a modest increase during the decades from 1750 to 1780, when European trade with the Baltic expanded very substantially, this represented a sharp relative decline for Dutch shipping of 28%. In fact the pace of structural decline during the eighteenth century was even more drastic than these figures suggest, in two respects. First, the size of Dutch vessels was reduced markedly from the late seventeenth century in response to the shift from the traditional bulk trades to high-value cargoes, and the depredations of the war. Average ship size on the Baltic–Amsterdam route fell from just over 200 tons in 1709/10 to around 150 tons in the early 1750s, to 90 tons by 1814.[29] Secondly, the proportion of vessels by-passing the staplemarket – the *voorbijlandvaart* – increased substantially as foreign competition in the carrying trade mounted. Estimates for the growth of this traffic suggest minimum levels of 40 vessels per year during the 1710s, rising to 170 by the 1750s – an increase from 9 to 16% of Dutch vessels passing the Sound – though the true level was probably much higher.[30]

The weakening of the Republic's Baltic trade opened up new opportunities for the country's rivals. Although the Scandinavian countries were extremely successful in increasing their own share of the Baltic carrying trade in the later seventeenth century, an even more striking challenge to Dutch domination came from British shipping during the eighteenth century, building up, as it did, from initially low levels.[31] In 1650, more than half the Baltic cargoes coming into England were brought in Dutch vessels, and the employment of English and Scottish vessels increased only marginally until the early 1670s, when the outbreak of war and the restructuring of the Eastland trade transformed England's position. From 1672 to 1678, the Republic was at war with France and, until 1674, with England, and in 1675 became embroiled in the Scanian war in support of Denmark. For a brief period, England was the only major European power to remain neutral, and Anglo-Baltic trade boomed as never before. The year 1675 was its *annus mirabilis*: dozens of English ships brought grain from the Baltic for re-export to Holland, France and Portugal, and returned through the Sound laden with wine and salt. For the remainder of the decade, the Dutch carrying trade to France was virtually taken over by England.[32]

---

[29] Knoppers, 'Dutch-Baltic Shipping', pp. 12, 29; J. de Vries & van der Woude, *First Modern Economy*, p. 49.

[30] J. Knoppers and F. Snapper, 'De Nederlandse Scheepvaart op de Oostzee vanaf het eind van de 17e Eeuw tot het begin van de 19e Eeuw', *ESHJ*, 41 (1978), pp. 131–3, 142–3. J. de Vries and van der Woude suggest that 200 ships per year were involved in the 1720s, rising to 'double that number in the second half of the eighteenth century' (*First Modern Economy*, p. 483).

[31] C. H. Wilson, *Profit and Power*, p. 42; Harper, *English Navigation Laws*, pp. 301–2.

[32] Hinton, *Eastland Trade*, pp. 108–9.

As the crisis in Dutch-Baltic trade deepened, English merchants benefited from the ending of the Eastland Company's monopoly, which was wound up in 1673. The company had been in difficulty since the early 1650s, when the passage of the first Navigation Act made its dwindling privileges almost unenforceable, and the closure of the Sound to English shipping during the first Anglo-Dutch War disrupted the cloth export trade and engendered a permanent balance of payments deficit with northern Europe.[33] The company unsuccessfully sought a reconfirmation of its privileges in 1649 and 1656, and on both occasions complained of interlopers and strangers meddling in its trade, of 'loose trading of unskilful persons, who... do in a manner give away our native commodity; but being shopkeers or retailers make their amends therein by their returns, which by their retail they advance far above that the merchant can make'.[34] The situation was in several respects similar to that facing the Merchant Adventurers in their trade to nearby Europe: one of stagnation of trade in the years immediately following the first Navigation Act, which, in establishing a new framework of 'national monopoly' rendered the privileges of the regulated companies redundant. There was, however, one important difference. The Eastland merchants, far from opposing the Navigation Act and striving to maintain a close working relationship with their Dutch counterparts, as the Merchant Adventurers did, strongly supported the measure as a means of undermining Dutch superiority in Baltic commerce. These aims, of course, were incompatible, and unregulated traders quickly moved into the gap vacated by the Dutch once trade revived in the 1670s. The history of the decline of the Eastland Company, according to its historian, 'is the history of the growth of the state', the 'parliamentary Colbertism' of the navigation code.[35]

How important a role, in fact, did the navigation laws play in eliminating the Dutch from handling England's trade with the Baltic? The Act of 1662 excluded Dutch shipping from the import of several, but not all, Baltic commodities into England, and covered mainly 'forest products' including timber, deals, masts, pitch, tar and potash. Iron was omitted, flax and hemp could be legally imported via Holland and Hamburg, and licences could be obtained to cover the import of most Baltic goods through continental North Sea ports in exceptional circumstances, such as war, or to meet the requirements of rebuilding activity in London

---

[33] Ibid., ch. 7.
[34] Representations by the Eastland Company desiring Restoration of Privilege, PRO SP18/205/41 [?1649] and SP18/123/16, vol. I, [1656], printed in Hinton, *Eastland Trade*, Appendix A, p. 190.
[35] Hinton, *Eastland Trade*, p. ix.

Table 9.2 *Annual average number of eastward and westward voyages through the Sound, per decade, 1661–1783*

	Dutch	%	British	%	Scandinavian	%	Total all countries
1661–70	1353	51.8	168	6.4	549	21.0	2610
1671–80	1176	45.3	558	21.5	509	19.6	2593
1681–90	1902	47.4	592	14.8	1008	25.1	4011
1691–1700	1153	31.6	336	9.2	1455	39.8	3654
1701–10	728	27.9	214	8.2	1207	46.2	2609
1711–20	880	50.1	455	25.9	161	9.2	1755
1721–30	1612	42.5	791	20.8	879	23.2	3796
1731–40	1850	42.3	867	19.8	1156	26.5	4369
1741–50	1522	36.5	734	17.6	1219	29.2	4169
1751–60	1840	34.9	1000	19.0	1593	30.2	5274
1761–70	2228	34.7	1336	20.8	1870	29.2	6414
1771–80	2216	27.6	2108	26.3	2221	27.7	8015
1781–3	174	1.9	2044	21.7	3596	38.2	9402

Source: *Tabeller over Skibsfart*, vol. II, *1661–1783*, ed. Bang & Korst, p. xviii.

after the Great Fire.[36] These circumstances help to explain the time-lag before the Acts were applied more stringently in the early 1670s, in a more favourable commercial environment.[37] Åström's examination of the Port Books for Hull, Newcastle and London, comparing the year 1635 with 1685 shows a substantial change in Anglo-Baltic trade, involving the growth of direct imports to England, yet iron imports, excluded from the Acts, also followed the same course and were obtained directly from Sweden. Scandinavian shipping soon filled the gap vacated by the Dutch and Germans, and exacerbated an already serious trading deficit with Sweden.[38] Although the navigation laws aimed a major blow against the Dutch entrepôt, Dutch capital, however, continued to play a key role in the financing of Anglo-Swedish trading ventures, and indeed it seems that Dutch owners controlled many of the ships commanded by Swedish captains, ostensibly described as Swedish.[39]

The upsurge of English Baltic trade and shipping in the 1670s and '80s is clearly reflected in the Sound Toll Registers, as the proportion

[36] PRO CO389/18, fols. 168–70, Report from the Attorney General relating to the import of Naval Stores from Holland &c, 12 January 1704.
[37] S.-E. Åström, 'The English Navigation Laws and the Baltic Trade, 1660–1700', *Scandinavian Economic History Review*, 8 (1960), pp. 3–5.
[38] Ibid., pp. 6–9; Åström, *From Cloth to Iron*, Part I, Appendix II, pp. 204–9.
[39] H. Roseveare, 'Stockholm–London–Amsterdam: the Triangle of Trade, 1660–1680', in J. M. van Winter (ed.), *The Interactions of Antwerp and Amsterdam with the Baltic Region, 1400–1800*, Leiden, 1983, pp. 93–4; Knoppers, 'Dutch-Baltic Shipping', p. 13.

of British vessels rose from insignificant numbers to equal the level of Scandinavian participation of the 1660s. The Dutch, with their large un-armed vessels, were particularly vulnerable to intermittent outbreaks of warfare in the Baltic, and during the wars of the Grand Alliance, from 1689 to 1713, both British- and Dutch-Baltic trade sank to low levels. The organisation of convoys on both sides was notoriously inadequate, as one Rotterdam merchant eloquently testified: 'It is a great pity that we who pretend to conquer kingdoms for [?one] another take no more care of our own navigation, in giving no better or more sufficient convoys.'[40] The decentralised Dutch administrative system, in which convoy monies raised by the five admiralty boards were supplemented by subsidies from the provinces, was ill fitted to provide adequate naval protection.[41] In Britain, parliamentary scrutiny – which produced inquiries in 1694 and 1708 – together with an expandable tax base and rising customs revenue laid the basis for more adequate levels of naval protection during the eighteenth century.[42] In the meantime, the Scandinavian countries, especially Sweden, took over much of the carrying trade that the British and the Dutch had involuntarily relinquished.[43] As well as the Scandinavian nations, Catalans, Portuguese and Genoese all expanded their shipbuilding industries to profit from the pressures under which the maritime powers were operating.[44] During the Great Northern War, however, the tables

---

[40] PRO C104/15 Part I, Dionysius Verburgh to David Waterhouse, London, 6 Nov. 1705; four years later, the same merchant complained 'We are very ill-served by the Admiralty as to our convoy.' See P. Crowhurst, *The Defence of British Trade, 1689–1815*, Folkestone, 1977, ch. 2.

[41] Snapper, 'Influence of British and Dutch Convoys'; see also Snapper, 'Commerce, Ships and War in the Baltic from the rise of the Hanseatic League till the French Revolution', in Heeres et al. (eds.), *Dunkirk to Danzig*, pp. 405–28.

[42] Davis, *Shipping Industry*, pp. 316–18, 327; S. R. Hornstein, *The Restoration Navy and English Foreign Trade, 1674–1688*, 1991, ch. 3.

[43] The following figures are derived from S.-E. Åström, 'The English Navigation Laws', table 4, p. 13.

Loaded vessels of different nationalities westward bound through the Sound to England, 1669–1700

	English	Swedish	others	
1669–71	51.7	35.6	12.7	Peace
1672–4	19.0	65.3	15.7	Anglo-Dutch war
1675–9	93.8	0.4	5.8	War between Sweden and Denmark
1680–8	82.9	11.4	5.7	Peace
1689–97	47.0	41.6	11.4	Nine Years' War
1698–1700	73.5	17.9	8.6	Peace

[44] Jones, *War and Economy*, p. 157.

were turned when Scandinavian shipping collapsed. The Dutch share of Baltic trade for 1711–20 rose to an eighteenth-century peak of 50%, and the British share reached a record 26%, not repeated again until the 1770s. During these years, the Dutch and British mounted combined convoy operations in the Baltic.[45]

Inevitably, the alternation between war and peace came to determine the involvement, levels of risk and profitability of the shipping industries of the maritime states in the late seventeenth and eighteenth centuries, as the scale and frequency of naval warfare increased. An element of circularity in this logic arises from the obvious fact that naval warfare itself called for increasing supplies of Baltic shipbuilding materials.[46] The rapid growth of English imports of iron, timber and naval stores, as Åström emphasised, 'was not simply a result of the termination of the entrepot trade of Amsterdam'.[47] The impact of the navigation laws in eliminating the Dutch from Anglo-Baltic trade, therefore, must be understood as operating within the broad context of warfare, the struggle for naval supremacy, and the growth of Scandinavian shipping capacity. As Davis emphasised, however, 'The Navigation Acts . . . ensured that it was Englishmen, not Dutchmen, who secured these gains.'[48]

The restructuring of Anglo-Baltic trade was completed with the demise of the Swedish empire during the Northern War of 1700–21. By 1715, Russia had gained possession of the Baltic provinces and Peter the Great's new capital and port city, St Petersburg, now provided a direct sea-route to western Europe. The balance of power in the Baltic was fundamentally changed, and England established a much firmer foothold in her trade with Russia which, by the 1730s, had become the most expansive branch of English trade in northern Europe. While imports from nearby Europe stagnated during the period 1700–80, those from the north, principally Russia, increased three-fold.[49] By the 1720s, St Petersburg had become the largest Baltic importer of English textiles, and was second only to Danzig as a consumer of English colonial goods. At the same time, Sweden began her drive to promote home industry and colonial enterprise by initiating a series of protectionist policies aimed against English textiles and imports from the Republic, together with edicts on trade modelled on the British navigation laws. Further decrees of 1734 and

---

[45] Snapper, 'Influence of British and Dutch Convoys', pp. 93–4.
[46] Between 1635 and 1700, England's direct imports of Swedish iron increased fourteen-fold in value, those of Baltic timber, linen and canvas by a factor of 3.4 (Åström, *From Cloth to Iron*, p. 32).
[47] Åström, 'The English Navigation Laws', p. 17.
[48] R. Davis, *English Merchant Shipping and Anglo-Dutch Rivalry in the Seventeenth Century*, National Maritime Museum, Greenwich, 1975, p. 33.
[49] Schumpeter, *English Overseas Trade Statistics*, Table VI, p. 18.

1735 either excluded or raised duties against British goods to prohibitive levels, and similar policies were followed by Denmark–Norway.[50] Russia thus became even more attractive to English merchants as a source of primary products and semi-manufactured goods, and the English in St Petersburg soon outnumbered the merchants of other nations.[51] The Dutch remained mainly in Archangel and the other Baltic ports of Narva, Riga and Reval, and their position in Baltic commerce was slowly eclipsed by the English, Russia's favoured trading partners.

English domination of the North Sea trades

Historians have long been accustomed to debating the significance of the decline of Dutch-Baltic trade, but have written much less about the rise of English competition in the North Sea, and still less about the interconnections between the two.[52] Several have emphasised the extent to which the former should be understood as a structural process, in which commercial rivalry and competition (taken to include efforts to impose restrictive practices) also played significant roles. Lindblad, as we have noticed, has given statistical precision to the relative contribution of these two sets of forces, and in doing so has attached an enhanced role to the competitive elements in the contraction of Dutch-Baltic trade during the seventeenth century, while emphasising major structural gains and losses during the years 1722–80, led by movements in the grain trade. However, when account is taken of changes in North Sea trade, extending the focus to the larger North Sea / Baltic zone – Braudel's 'double-sea space' – it is clear that the extent of competitive change during the eighteenth century is larger than these revisions suggest. The rise of English competition in the bulk trades of the North Sea involved not only competition with Dutch traders, but also a 'displacement effect' whereby consumers in Holland and elsewhere in Europe purchased English grain and colonial re-exports instead of alternatives previously provided by Dutch suppliers. By the early eighteenth century, Dutch merchants were also making extensive use of English shipping services for their own North Sea trading ventures, thus reversing the situation which had prevailed half a century earlier. Only in wartime did the demand for Dutch shipping revive.

---

[50] Kent, *War and Trade*, pp. 5–8.

[51] J. Newman, 'Anglo-Dutch Commercial Co-operation', pp. 95–6; J. Newman, 'Russian Foreign Trade, 1680–1780: the British Contribution', University of Edinburgh Ph.D. thesis. For a strangely negative view of these developments, see J. J. Murray, 'Baltic Commerce and Power Politics', pp. 293–312.

[52] An enormous volume of North Sea shipping, of course, never passed through the Danish Sound, but this is rarely considered alongside the information provided in the Sound Toll Registers.

As we have already noticed, English shipping tonnage grew to equal that of the Republic during the first half of the eighteenth century, perhaps by as early as the 1720s.[53] Much of this shipping was employed in the bulk trades of the North Sea, where export tonnage was much greater than that of imports: in the coal trade, steadily expanding since the late sixteenth century, and in the grain export trade which experienced a shorter burst of growth during the first half of the eighteenth century. The export of Cheshire rock salt via Liverpool also entered the North Sea trades after the close of the War of the Spanish Succession.[54] A high proportion of these bulk cargoes was disposed of in nearby European markets, especially Holland and Hamburg, but the distinction frequently made between 'nearby' and 'northern' European trades obscures the extent to which the import trades from Norway, chiefly sawn and whole timber, were drawn into the circuits of North Sea shipping, west of the Sound. The preponderance of excess import capacity, and therefore low inward freight rates, encouraged merchants and shipmasters to engage in triangular traffic, exporting grain or coal to Rotterdam, from thence in to Norway with a variety of goods, and back home with a lading of timber for London or an eastern port. Freight rates of little more than £1 per ton were charged for chartered vessels after the conclusion of the wars with France in 1713, and through the 1720s and '30s. It was during the decades from 1680 to 1720 that Dutch primacy in the European timber trade disappeared, while England's share of Norwegian exports expanded substantially. Around 1700, Norwegian timber accounted for a larger volume of English imports than any other branch of trade.[55] Triangular traffic made for intensive use of English shipping capacity, and from the numerous variants of this basic pattern there emerged, during the first half of the eighteenth century, an integrated North Sea carrying trade dominated substantially by English shipping.

Charterparties in the Rotterdam notarial archives contain numerous examples of these triangular trading patterns during the first half of the eighteenth century. Vessels were usually chartered by a single merchant and were recorded by notaries specialising in English business. The merchants involved included English and Dutch traders, amongst whom were Englishmen resident in Rotterdam for varying periods, but all voyages involved English ships and masters. In several cases, cargoes were insured with the city's own insurance company, the Maatschappij van Assurantie, Discontering en Beleening, and details, including the value of shipments,

---

[53] J. de Vries and van der Woude, *First Modern Economy*, p. 490.
[54] Earlier than Ralph Davis supposed (*Shipping Industry*, p. 204).
[55] J. de Vries and van der Woude, *First Modern Economy*, pp. 426–8; Davis, *Shipping Industry*, pp. 213–14.

can be cross-checked. The English or Anglo-Dutch merchants included Wilkinson, Whaley, Ward, Baildey, Rhodes, Cockerill and Jefferson, while Dutch firms included Konink, Rykevorsel, Ondorp, Droot and Zuylen. The involvement of Dutch merchants in the chartering of English vessels for triangular voyages across the North Sea illustrates the effectiveness of the Navigation Acts in excluding Dutch vessels from this traffic, while the continued deployment of Dutch capital in Anglo-Dutch commodity trade reflects a familiar pattern. Both developments serve to emphasise the growing separation between trade and shipping in the Republic's commerce in the early eighteenth century.

Ferand Whaley, for example, resident in Rotterdam, frequently imported cargoes of grain and lead from Bridlington, Hull, Stockton and Newcastle, at values ranging from 1,000 to 6,000 gl. Surplus English tonnage in Rotterdam was then chartered and loaded with mixed cargoes for Norwegian ports, such as Bergen and Frederickshall, from whence timber and tar were carried to the same group of English ports.[56] A fixed freight payment was usually specified for triangular routes, while tonnage charters were more common for bulk cargoes on bilateral Anglo-Dutch voyages. There were several variants of this standard pattern. Instead of sailing directly from Holland to Norway, vessels might first call at an English east coast port to complete a lading. Thus, the Rotterdam merchant William Baildey chartered the 80-ton *Mary and Elizabeth* in March 1732:

> to load with unspecified goods in Rotterdam no deeper than seven foot of water; thence to Newcastle . . . if the master runs into Yarmouth he must not stay there more than three days. At Newcastle to lie for six days and to load the ship further with grindstones, coals and glass bottles to not more than nine feet of water; thence to Bergen to lie for eighteen days to deliver cargo to John van de Velde, and to reload with stock fish and tar and other goods to be specified by J. van de Velde. To return to Rotterdam to lie for six days to unload.[57]

Other triangular North Sea voyages included Hamburg and Bremen, and ports on the west coast of England or Ireland were sometimes included as one leg of an Anglo-Dutch charter. Sneller and Ward, for example, were heavily committed to the English grain export trade to Rotterdam in the 1720s and 1730s, insuring cargoes with values ranging from 2,000 to 7,000 gl, and included the German market in a trade which also involved Dutch colonial re-exports. Their charterparty agreements describe their mixed outward cargoes from Holland in unusual detail and show how the provisions of the Navigation Acts could be neatly overcome

[56] GAR NA2082/314, 316; NA2083/260, 262, 533, 577, 757, 759, 765; NA2108/255.
[57] NA2116/234.

in traffic of this sort. In 1722, for example, the partnership chartered the 80-ton *Samuel* of Lynn to load a mixed cargo at Rotterdam consisting of:

329 wainscot boards, one basket of spa water, 33 empty hogsheads, 35 empty tar casks, four bags of pepper, two bags of nutmegs, one bag of cloves, two canasters of mace, three canasters of burnt coffy beans marked CS, ten canasters of thea marked BS, eight canasters of thea marked CS. From Rotterdam to Lynn Regis to lie there 10 working days and in that time to deliver the said wainscot boards, spawater, empty hoggsheads and tarr casks and to reload in the roome of them a cargo of corne to the full and sufficient loading of said ship, and sail with said corne, spices, coffy and thea from thence ... directly to Hamburg and lay there the time of ten working days.[58]

Although, in this case, Dutch-Asian spices were not landed in England, customs officials often turned a blind eye to the provisions of the navigation code in this area. The English, Huet explained, 'were not over severe in relation to the importation of spices from Holland, the Dutch being masters of them, and which could not be had but thro' their means'.[59]

Cheshire rock salt found growing markets in Holland, Germany and Flanders in the early eighteenth century, and provided a bulk cargo for surplus English shipping capacity lying in Dutch ports. Pieter Verbeek of Rotterdam was probably the largest single importer, with a secondary interest in tobacco. In preference to sending out ships in ballast, Verbeek gave masters the option of sailing first to Newcastle or Sunderland, laden or unladen, to take on board a cargo of coal for any port in the west of England or Ireland, before loading with rock salt at Liverpool for Holland. A preliminary voyage to Norway on the master's account was also specified in some cases. In most branches of North Sea trade, the role of ships' masters was usually circumscribed by established factors and commission agents, and orders were often sufficiently precise to leave little scope for the exercise of personal initiative. In the overseas coal trade, however, masters frequently traded on their own account and also exercised a delegated commercial role, which included purchasing. Verbeek incorporated this established practice in his contracts, but extended its scope by permitting masters to trade in other goods. A typical formula allowed the master to carry unspecified goods from Rotterdam to Liverpool 'for his own profit', before loading his vessel with as much rock salt as 'the master thinks she can conveniently carry ... the master can then load with tobacco and other light goods for himself', before returning to Rotterdam or Delft for unloading.[60] In the lead export trade too, coal shipment on the master's account was encouraged, as a ballast cargo.[61]

[58] NA2096/28; also NA2096/246.   [59] Huet, *Memoirs*, p. 67.
[60] NA2082/491 8 June 1715.   [61] NA2106/37.

The coal trade gave English shipmasters an important foothold in commercial activity, although other minor trading opportunities existed. In 1716, Sir John Elwill complained that masters in the south-west commonly bought pipe and hogshead staves for their own account and 'discourage merchants from sending the like by asking high freights', as well as buying their own sailcloth in Holland. The complaint was echoed ten years later when the Collector of Customs at Yarmouth reported that masters bought their own naval stores in Holland, 'on pretence of distress', to avoid payment of duty. Joseph Boddington, a supplier of cloth remnants, claimed that he sold to masters and mates who carried large quantities to Amsterdam and Rotterdam for their own accounts.[62] The degree to which charterparty agreements included provision for this kind of own-account trading probably reflects the concern of merchants to control a well-established practice. In eighteenth-century England, the connection between trade and shipowning was especially close, and merchants were doubly anxious to ensure that their own interests were not subordinated to those of masters, either through competition for cargoes or in the direction of a ship's operations. The Newcastle merchant William Cotesworth expressed a commonly held view when he confessed, 'I have had a long experience and always suffered by taking parts where the master had the grand bill of sale...They had rather go any voyage than that their owners recommend, because they have not a mind they should be too well acquainted with their profit.'[63] Such concern perhaps understates the mutual confidence which often existed between masters, merchants and owners, and, in the North Sea trades, a moderate degree of commercial involvement on the part of ships' masters made a major contribution to maximising the use of shipping capacity, and therefore to maintaining freight rates at a competitive level.[64]

As with Dutch-Baltic commerce, the shipping capacity required for grain cargoes played a leading role in shaping the overall pattern of bulk carrying in the English North Sea trades. Subsidised grain export, together with even larger shipments of coal, generated excess inward carrying capacity and low return freight rates, which in turn generated a competitive network of triangular trades across the North Sea and beyond. By the 1740s, it was common for English corn ships bound for

[62] Brants 924, J. Elwill, Exeter, to D. Leeuw, Amsterdam, 30 May 1716; Cust. 97/5 (Yarmouth) 10 July 1727; Brants 1344, J. Boddington, London, to J. I. de Neufville, 4 December 1749.
[63] NRO ZCE10/2, W. Cotesworth, Gateshead, to Robert Bewicke, Amsterdam, 30 April 1714.
[64] On the mutual reliance of ships' husbands and masters, see Davis, Shipping Industry, pp. 161-2.

the Mediterranean to proceed to British America after delivery, in search of return cargoes.[65] The differences, however, between the English and Dutch bulk carrying trades were greater than the similarities. The degree of balance between inward and outward cargoes which had been present during the buoyant years of Dutch-Baltic trade was absent in the English North Sea trades.[66] In 1715, the Collector of Customs at Yarmouth noted that 'our corn vessels bound for Holland mostly return light home and... bring small parcels of goods which they run to the northwards of us'.[67] In the coal export trade too, ships often returned home in ballast: the British consul in Rotterdam claimed that this was true of the great majority, 'some few of them only taking in small ventures of liquors and other trifling things'.[68] Customs officials at Newcastle, however, reported in 1708 that large numbers of coal vessels returned with ballast cargoes of pantiles, bricks and clinkers on which no duty was paid 'to the discouragement of manufacturers... and the detriment of the revenue'. Similar comments were made at other ports.[69] Clearly, the Inspector General's ledgers overstate the imbalance between export and import volumes in their omission of illegal trade and smuggling, and of the growing carrying trade which by-passed English ports, but the picture which they represent is broadly true.

How much shipping, in fact, was required for grain exports, and how did this compare with the coal trade, and with the requirements of Dutch exporters of Baltic grain? The ledgers suggest that the overseas coal trade made much larger shipping demands than the grain trade during the decades from 1700 to 1760, requiring between two and three times as much tonnage, on average. Those contemporaries, like Defoe, who argued that the corn trade employed 'more shipping than will be thought probable at first sight' tended to exaggerate, and the shipping

---

[65] Anon., *The Case of British Merchants, Owners of Ships, and others relative to the Employment and Increase of British Shipping and British Navigation*, 1750, p. 1 (Hanson 6437).

[66] On the balanced structure of Dutch-Baltic trade, see, for example, the statement presented to the French Conseil du Commerce in 1701, quoted by Macpherson, *Origin of Commerce*, vol. III, p. 8: 'That the Hollanders trade to the Baltic was so well settled, that they will ever govern the prizes of all merchandize going to, or coming from, the north. Because, carrying thither their own manufactures and merchandize, and especially their spices, of which the northern people are very fond, they can afford to take off the corn, timber, iron, copper, flax, hemp, &c. of the north, at high rates, and yet they are generally cheaper at Amsterdam than the places they are brought from, because of the great gains they make by the assortments they carry to the north.'

[67] PRO Cust. 97/3, 25 Mar. 1715.

[68] PRO CO388/95, 'Particulars of the Trade... [with] Rotterdam'; see also Add Mss 11,256, fo. 55, which explains the disparity in figures for entries and clearances at Newcastle, Sunderland and Whitehaven as arising from coal vessels returning in ballast.

[69] Cust. 84/122 (Newcastle), 5 June 1708; Cust. 64/55 (Exeter) 1717; Cust. 97/3 (Yarmouth), 25 June 1715.

Table 9.3 *Shipping tonnage employed in the English overseas coal and grain trades, 1700–1750s*

annual averages ('000 tons)

	coal	grain
1701–10	89	51
1711–20	171	66
1721–30	219	68
1731–40	257	100
1741–50	274	152
1751–60	310	105

Source: Cust. 3.

requirements of English exporters were more modest than those of Dutch-Baltic traders, in terms of an equivalent measure of grain.[70] The majority of English grain voyages, of course, were a good deal shorter than those from the Baltic. On average, between two-thirds and three-quarters of all grain voyages consisted of short hauls from London and East Anglia to nearby Europe, and small vessels, usually between 80 and 90 tons, were characteristic of the former.[71] Such vessels could complete several voyages during the course of a year. Grain was usually shipped in bulk and charterparties rarely specified more than four or six working days for loading. Nathaniel Maister of Hull, for example, observed that 180 to 200 quarters of grain per day could be shipped in good weather.[72] Dutch-Baltic voyages were longer and more expensive, involving shipment from Danzig to Amsterdam, handling and warehousing charges in the latter, and trans-shipment to final markets. Although the tendency was for Baltic carriers to decline in size during the first half of the eighteenth century, they remained substantially larger than English grain vessels, averaging over 160 tons.[73] Furthermore, English exports contained a high proportion of malt which required considerably less shipping space – perhaps as much as 40% less – than the bread grains wheat and rye of which the Baltic grain trade almost entirely consisted. This was carefully explained by the Collector of Customs at Yarmouth in 1738:[74]

[70] Defoe, *Plan*, p. 231.
[71] During the years 1699–1701, an average of 74% of English grain cargoes was destined for nearby Europe, while in 1752–4, the figure was 69%; CO388/18 Part I, fo. 22 (1710–14).
[72] Maister Letters, N. to H. Maister, London, 6 March 1738.
[73] Knoppers, 'Dutch-Baltic Shipping', Table 1, p. 29. Tonnages for Dutch shipping from the Baltic to Amsterdam ranged from 140 to 206 tons.
[74] Cust. 97/11, 18 November 1738.

A quarter of barley will fill up less room in a ship than a quarter of wheat & the reason we take to be from the form of each respective grain, barley laying lighter in a bushel than wheat: when it is poured into a ships hold, settles closer than it did in the bushel & the proportion is generally accounted as 11 to 10 & that rule has long been observed here . . . We are informed that a quarter of malt well made fine and fit for [the] London market will take up as much room in stowage as a quarter of barley, but malt for [the] Holland markets, which in making is suffered to run out to a very great length on the floors, after it is measured into a ship may be much easier compressed; besides malt being so much lighter than corn & stowed in bulk, the ships hold is generally filled quite up to the beams & for the Holland markets they force it closely into every part of the hold. For an instance hereof we humbly refer to the ship Peach . . . the ship is reported by the master at 60 tons, but we judge her at upwards of 90; in the coal trade, she make[s] about 80 chalders coals Winchester measure & carries about 400 quarters of wheat; but with malt for Rotterdam she generally clears out with 700 quarters and upwards & we are well satisfied the whole is actually on board.

It is clear, therefore, that the English grain trade made more modest demands upon shipping than those of Dutch-Baltic importers, particularly in the decades before 1730 when East Anglian malt shipments predominated. By applying the above proportions to the Inspector General's statistics, the shipping tonnage employed in the bulk export trades may be estimated as set out in Table 9.3.[75] Because overseas coal shipments were subject to heavy duties, under-declaration of exports was widespread, so that these figures doubtless underestimate the real volume of shipping tonnage in the coal trade especially in relation to that for grain exports which, if anything, would be subject to over-declaration in view of the temptation to obtain excess bounty payments. The shipping requirements of the grain trade were clearly much less substantial than those of the long-established overseas coal trade, while the combined needs of both were overshadowed by the vast tonnage employed in the domestic coal trade from the north-eastern ports to London, which averaged between 450,000 and 550,000 tons per year during the first half of the eighteenth century.[76] The English shipping industry was dominated by coal and colliers rather than grain, and the north-east remained the chief 'nursery of seamen' during these years.

In particular years, however, especially the late 1740s and early 1750s, the quantity of shipping required for grain exports could be considerable. 'Some years past', wrote the British agent in Rotterdam, in 1765, 'we have had from 800 to one thousand of these vessels [i.e. entries] here in a year', and 'from 50 to 60 corn ships have been known here at a time'.[77]

[75] See above, chapter 8, note 45.
[76] B. R. Mitchell & P. Deane, *Abstract of British Historical Statistics*, Cambridge, 1962, pp. 112–13.
[77] CO388/95, 'Particulars of the Trade . . . [with] Rotterdam'.

During peak years such as these, corn vessels would be supplemented by shipping drawn from the coal and Norway trades, since the seasonal pattern of these trades dovetailed.[78] Activity in the coal trade remained at a low level throughout the winter months. The Newcastle coal merchant Ralph Carr explained that he only shipped coal in dry weather, preferably in summer.[79]

The trade in bread grains, in contrast, was brisk from September until March.[80] By early spring, the countries of southern Europe were gathering in the harvest so that demand from that quarter, which in turn affected the demands of Dutch merchants for English grain, was slack throughout the summer months. A number of merchants therefore engaged in both these branches of bulk export, such as William Cotesworth of Newcastle, William Konink of Rotterdam, and Carr himself.[81] The seasonal rhythms of the grain and coal trades, it seems, were complementary, which helps to explain how the shipping requirements of the former were satisfied, as a virtually new bulk cargo for English merchants. The steady expansion of English grain exports thus enabled merchants to make more intensive use of shipping normally reserved for the coal trade.[82] Charterparties indicate that individual vessels operated in the coal, grain and timber trades during the course of the year, such as the 70-ton *Nancy* of Shields which in November 1734 was chartered to 'load unspecified goods at Rotterdam, thence to Bridlington Key to lie 48 hours to receive orders whether to complete [her] load with corn from thence or to proceed to Sunderland or Newcastle to load coal; thence to Christiansand to unload and reload with unspecified goods, thence back to Rotterdam to unload'.[83] During years of grain shortage in England, it was common for Sunderland vessels exporting coal to Rotterdam to return with grain cargoes to the western ports or London; and conversely it is possible to find examples of Yarmouth and Blakeney vessels, which normally carried grain cargoes, operating in the coal trade.[84] This element of flexibility obviously facilitated the expansion of England's bulk trades.

In several respects therefore, there were major differences in the structures of the English North Sea carrying trade and the deployment of

---

[78] Davis, *Shipping Industry*, pp. 191–2.
[79] ZCE10/16, R. Carr to D. van Dam, Rotterdam, 10 June 1745.
[80] Cust. 97/8, 4 January 1734, showing the seasonal pattern of grain exports from Yarmouth for 1733, heaviest at Lady Day quarter.
[81] Hughes, *North Country*, pp. 55–6; GAR NA2328/108, 116, 167, 239, 484, 567, 599.
[82] Davis, *Shipping Industry*, p. 194: 'Because there was, for one reason or another, much under-utilisation of capacity, there were important reserves available to deal with specially large crops, whether of sugar or tobacco across the ocean, or of corn in East Anglia.'
[83] NA2328/804, 10 November 1734, and NA2328/108, 116, 24 February 1734; other examples include NA2116/418; NA2325/197, 286; NA2332/70; NA2328/80.
[84] NA2198/469; NA2335/281, 487, 559, 738 (coal vessels carrying grain); NA2328/674; NA2335/265 (grain vessels carrying coal).

Dutch shipping in the Baltic: the former was characterised by a greater imbalance between outward and inward cargoes, voyages were shorter, ships were smaller, and ship's masters sometimes exercised an important commercial role, especially in the coal trade, which conferred mixed benefits. Above all, the English bulk trades were based on the export of home-produced primary products, the surpluses of a producing nation, while Dutch-Baltic trade originated in the demand for essential food imports. In the mid seventeenth century, over half of the million inhabitants of Holland, Utrecht, Friesland and Groningen depended on foreign grain, and the position changed little until the consumption of rice and potatoes became more widespread after the subsistence crisis of 1740.[85] To this exposed position was added the exceptional vulnerability of Dutch shipping in the Baltic in time of war: lightly built, unarmed *fluytships* were cheap to operate in safe waters, but in wartime required the protection of convoys.[86] As Posthlethwayt put it, 'The character of the maritime power of the Dutch is oeconomy, and that of the maritime force of the English is activity: the first, according to the republican genius, place all honour in saving; ... whatever should contribute to the strength and security of their ships they pare off to save charges as far as possible.'[87] During the War of the Spanish Succession, however, the Republic's public debt reached record levels while its navy was reduced. By the later stages of the Great Northern War, it was no longer feasible to maintain sufficient protection for Baltic shipping, and the Dutch were forced to rely on unsatisfactory combined naval operations with the English in 1715.[88]

As the Dutch position in the Baltic weakened during the decades of war from 1689 to 1720, English competition in the North Sea trades increased. Lindblad, as we have noticed, suggests that international competition played a more powerful role in the later seventeenth century than it did in the eighteenth century, when changes in its commodity composition were the key factor in the stagnation of Baltic trade (described by Lindblad as structural change). This, however, downplays the impact of English grain exports in displacing Dutch-Baltic supplies in the eighteenth century. In the 1700s and 1710s, English grain was already going a long way towards making good the shortfall of Baltic imports as trading conditions became more difficult for the Dutch during the Great Northern War. By the 1730s, the English corn surplus was making an enormous impact on European markets outside the Low Countries, reaching very

[85] J. de Vries, *Dutch Rural Economy*, p. 172; Faber, *Dure tijden*, p. 11.
[86] J. R. Bruin, 'Dutch ship owning', p. 175.
[87] Posthlethwayt, *Universal*, unpaginated, entry on 'shipping'.
[88] F. Snapper, 'Commerce, Ships and War in the Baltic from the Rise of the Hanseatic League till the French Revolution', in Heeres et al. (eds.), *Dunkirk to Danzig*, p. 425; Snapper, 'Influence of British and Dutch Convoys', pp. 93–4.

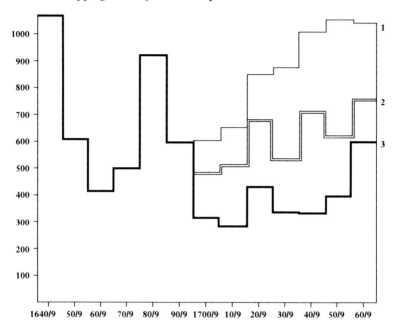

Decennial averages, 1640/9–1760/9

1 Total English grain exports + grain shipments through the Sound
2 Total grain export to Holland + grain shipments through the Sound
3 Grain shipments through the Sound

Figure 9.2 Grain shipments through the Sound, compared with English grain exports, 1640–1769 ('000 quarters)

high levels during the 1750s. As a result of wartime trading conditions, the substantial shipments of the 1740s were channelled through Holland to a much greater extent than was the case during the previous and succeeding decades, and this played a major part in the sharp decline in Dutch-Baltic grain shipments after the peak year of 1740. In the re-export of colonial goods too, English merchants provided strong competition, in the supply of groceries, tobacco and Asian textiles both to the Dutch staplemarket, and to northern Europe and the Baltic countries, especially via Hamburg.

The combined effects of competition and structural changes in trade were indeed ominous for the Republic, perhaps fatal.[89] As Europe's trade with the Baltic was becoming more diverse, particularly in textiles and colonial goods, the centre of gravity within the North Sea economy moved

---

[89] Lindblad, 'Structuur en Mededinging', p. 88.

from the Low Countries towards London, involving not so much a direct transfer of business as a dispersal or decentralisation of the staple function to existing centres, including Hamburg and even Copenhagen.[90] The restructuring of the entrepôt system indeed sprang from changes in the commodity composition of trade, yet Dutch shipping, capital and commercial enterprise continued to play a major role in the English-dominated North Sea economy in ways which facilitated the overall expansion of the larger British Atlantic trading system. Commercial rivalry and competitive behaviour were less omnipresent in the day-to-day business of merchants than some mercantilist writers suggested, and Dutch merchants were rarely constrained in their dealings by feelings of national allegiance, having long been integrated into the major commercial centres of northern Europe.[91] It was precisely this ambivalence, and the ubiquity of Dutch commercial interests, which provided some respite for the Republic's intermediary trade and her shipping industry during the difficult years of decline. As Dutch naval power collapsed during the War of the Spanish Succession, and the resources of England's merchant fleet were stretched beyond reasonable limits, a certain complementarity of interests between the maritime powers emerged in relation to the rights of neutrals and belligerents. Although English statesmen viewed the Republic's growing weakness after 1713 with concern, English merchants would derive considerable benefit from the use of neutral Dutch shipping services, as well as comfort from the notion that the Republic had passed its meridian as a commercial rival.

It was the Anglo-Dutch commercial treaty of 1674 which set out a favourable series of neutral trading rights for the Republic, but not until the struggle against Louis XIV was over was it able to exploit them fully, while drastically scaling down the level of naval and military expenditure.[92] For much of the eighteenth century, the Dutch pursued a successful policy of non-alignment, remaining neutral during the Wars of the Polish and Austrian Successions, and during the Seven Years' War.[93] The 1674 Treaty conceded the principle of 'Free Ships, free Goods', which permitted the Dutch to protect enemy cargoes from seizure, including naval stores, defining only armaments as 'contraband of war'.[94]

---

[90] K. Newman, 'Hamburg in the European Economy, 1660–1750', *JEEH*, 14 (1985); Faber, 'Structural Changes', p. 92.

[91] H. Roseveare, review of J. Israel, *Dutch Primacy in World Trade*, *EcHR*, 43 (1990), pp. 512–13.

[92] Israel, *Dutch Republic*, pp. 985–97.

[93] Not until 1747 did the Republic become an active participant in the War of the Austrian Succession (Carter, *Dutch Republic in Europe*, p. 9).

[94] Carter, *Dutch Republic in Europe*, chs. 1 and 6. See also the same author's *Neutrality or Commitment. The Evolution of Dutch Foreign Policy, 1667–1795*, 1975, chs. 6 & 7, and 'The

Although these principles caused much resentment amongst the English, and were often met by non-compliance, they were sustainable at a time when English naval power was rapidly increasing. Insofar as they represented a concession to the Dutch, this was balanced by Dutch acceptance of the Navigation Acts, which embodied the converse principle of 'Unfree ships, unfree goods' which applied to enemy vessels. As Richard Pares explained, belligerents and neutrals made a mutual concession of their rights, which encompassed Navigation Acts as well as generous neutral trading rights. The English and the Dutch were 'willing to give up the right of having their trade carried in the ships of others, if they could keep that of carrying the goods of their friends' enemies'.[95] Amongst other things, the rule enabled English producers to trade with the enemy, via third-party brokers and carriers, when appropriate and profitable. In 1747, for example, severe grain shortages in France were exacerbated by English privateering activity in the Mediterranean, which cut off French imports from the Levant. Yet it was English grain supplies transported in Dutch and Danish ships which made good the deficiency. The English consul in Rotterdam believed that most of this grain was exported on the accounts of Rotterdam residents, and reported that 'Dutch ships are daily freighted to go to England to take in a cargo part in lead and the rest in wheat or coals, which are all very welcome in France.'[96] Dutch neutral vessels also facilitated the Anglo-French wine trade and the tobacco trade of the American colonies with France, with English connivance.[97]

During the period of the Anglo-Dutch Alliance from 1689 to 1713, of course, the Dutch were unable to apply the doctrine of neutral trading rights in a formal sense, but, in practice, they engaged in large-scale 'trading with the enemy' in a wide range of staple products, including English manufactures. As we have already seen, the swollen figures for Anglo-Dutch trade during this period reflect the re-routing of what was formerly Anglo-French trade through Holland, and a variety of expedients was devised by English merchants to carry on prohibited commerce.[98] Davenant put the position in a nutshell when he explained:[99]

Dutch as Neutrals in the Seven Years' War', in Carter, *Getting, Spending and Investing in Early Modern Times*.

[95] R. Pares, *Colonial Blockade and Neutral Rights, 1739–1763*, Oxford, 1938, pp. 172–3.

[96] SP84/430, R. Wolters, Rotterdam, to Wm Chetwynd, London, 22 September and 8 December 1747.

[97] Carter, *Neutrality or Commitment*, p. 86.

[98] In the 1690s, for example, John Aylward took up residence in Saint-Malo, receiving his letters from England 'by way of Holland', making use of Messrs Hackett and Neerinex in Rotterdam as an intermediary (Aylward papers, Arundel Castle, AY51, Charles Horde, London, to J. Aylward, Saint-Malo, 26 Aug. 1692).

[99] Davenant, 'Second Report', p. 435.

The truth of the case appears to be that, especially during this last war (while our trade with France and Spain has been interrupted) large quantities of the woollen manufactures, corn, tin, tobacco, with divers other commodities, have been sent to Holland, which goods, in the former course of trade, we exported directly ourselves, and mostly in our own shipping, to the increase of our navigation, which the war having rendered difficult, and their ports being less exposed than ours to the danger of privateers, as well as in ships outward as well as homeward-bound, the Hollanders have, in a great measure, got to be the carriers of our goods.

It was thus only with considerable difficulty that the Dutch were coerced in 1703 into formally accepting the prohibition of commerce with France and Spain, but for a variety of reasons this was not renewed. By November 1705, parliament ceased to press the States General into accepting English ideas of wartime trading.[100] Dutch merchants continued their former practice of using the vessels of other nations with neutral status, as well as their own ships sailing under a variety of arrangements devised to circumvent the letter of the law. Dutch shipmasters, for example, claimed residence in neutral North Sea ports, while many Dutch vessels were temporarily transferred to neutral skippers. The French claimed that as many as 8,000 Danes and Norwegians were employed by the maritime powers in the early stages of the Nine Years' War.[101]

The revival of the staplemarket function and the substantial resort to Dutch and other foreign shipping were mutually reinforcing tendencies. In the long run, as we have seen, the Navigation Acts were successful in transferring England's import trades from the Baltic from Dutch to English shipping, but it proved necessary to modify them during the war years of the 1690s to provide for the temporary naturalisation of foreign shipping. G. N. Clark suggested that, in general, the Acts were applied less stringently at this time, but, by 1713, the Commissioners of Customs were circulating directives to ensure compliance, especially in the timber trade.[102] The enormous demand for shipbuilding materials and naval stores made this relaxation unavoidable in the northern trades: during the years 1692–7, foreign shipping accounted for almost half the nation's imports, much of which entered via London.[103] During the War of the Spanish Succession, however, the proportion was no higher than the admittedly high level of peacetime foreign tonnage of 1699–1702, at just

---

[100] Coombs, 'Debate on Franco-Dutch Trade', p. 98.
[101] J. S. Bromley, 'The North Sea in Wartime, 1688–1713', *BMGN*, 92 (1977), p. 284.
[102] During both the 1690s and the 1700s (Clark, *Dutch Alliance*, p. 135; G. N. Clark, 'War Trade and Trade War, 1701–1713', *EcHR*, 1 (1927), p. 278; Cust. 84/122 (Newcastle, Board-Collector), 8 October 1713).
[103] Clark, *Dutch Alliance*, pp. 136–7.

over 13% (Table 9.4). By the outbreak of the War of the Austrian Succession, the problem of finding sufficient shipping capacity shifted from imports to exports as the size of England's grain surplus multiplied. In 1738, not far short of a million quarters were exported. By the late 1740s, shipments were well above that figure, reaching 1.5 million quarters in 1750. The demand for foreign shipping mounted, especially that of neutral nations. In November 1738, Ralph Carr complained 'we have been obliged to give prodigious freights to all places on account of the misunderstandings with Spain', and a few weeks later was 'obliged to write to all the ports round [Newcastle] to procure small vessels for the corn trade at any rate'.[104] The Maister brothers experienced similar problems and insisted that masters signed a note binding them whilst the charterparty was being drawn up.[105]

During the early stages of the War of the Austrian Succession, English merchants realised that Dutch shipping was available at a 'much lower fraught than ours'. Carr and his agent were expecting 'sundry more foreign ships' to load for the Bay of Biscay, and five others coming to load for Holland. The lower freight charges, he calculated, 'within a trifle' balanced against the loss of bounty and higher duty consequent upon shipment of grain and coal in foreign vessels.[106] The provisions of the Corn Laws in relation to the payment of bounties restrained the use of foreign shipping, though it seems that merchants took steps to conceal the nationality of vessels when the former was unavoidable. The Inspector General's Office certainly returned suspiciously low figures for foreign vessels employed in the grain trade during wartime, which, in the light of merchants' correspondence and the remarks of pamphleteers would seem to be misleading.[107] A petition laid before the Commons early in 1750 claimed that freights between Britain and Europe had been 'engrossed by foreign ships' during the past few years, and presented detailed lists of entries of foreign shipping at English ports in 1743, 1747 and 1749. The information appears to have been extracted from the bills of entry, and included the name and tonnage of each vessel, its nationality and the number of repeated voyages. The accompanying petition concluded that 86,000 tons of foreign shipping was annually 'employ'd by England', alongside an English tonnage of 320,000 tons (including coasting and

---

[104] ZCE10/11, R. Carr to W. Norton, Dunkirk, 27 December 1738; Brants 1337, J. Coutts and Co. to J. I. de Neufville, Amsterdam, 13 February 1738, and 19 August 1749.

[105] Maister Letters, N. to H. Maister, London, 5 and 29 April 1738.

[106] ZCE10/12, R. Carr to W. Norton, Dunkirk, 24 April 1740.

[107] The customs ledgers record no foreign shipping employed in the grain export trade from 1740 to 1748 and 1756 to 1763; for the coal trade, they record a figure for foreign vessels equivalent to 4% and 5.4% of the total tonnage exported for each respective period.

Table 9.4 *Foreign vessels clearing from British ports, 1686–1751*

(as a percentage of total shipping employed)

	%	
1686	8.3	
1692–7	46.9	
1699–1702	13.4	
1710–13	13.4	(18.5)
1714–17	4.8	(6.7)
1718	3.8	
1723	6.4	
1726–8	5.2	
1740s	*21.2*	
1751	6.6	

Sources: Davis, *Shipping Industry*, p. 26; CO388/18 part I; CO390/8.
Figures in brackets show percentage of foreign shipping clearing for Dutch ports.
Figures in italics show average foreign tonnage as a percentage of estimated British-owned tonnage, plus foreign-employed tonnage, in the years 1743, 1747 and 1749 (Hanson 6437, see p. xxx, and note xx).

foreign-going vessels). A breakdown of the former is summarised in Table 9.5, although it must be borne in mind that the figures are presented in such a way as to underestimate the role of Dutch shipping in relation to that of other countries, especially Denmark.[108] It is possible that the petitioners exaggerated their case in order to attract the attention of the House, but the information which they assembled seems broadly convincing. Some years later, in 1765, the British agent in Rotterdam admitted that 'in time of war, the number of Dutch ships to the British ports was very considerable owing to the high price of assurance upon British bottoms, and dilatoriness of convoy', and went on to suggest, as the petitioners had done, that the export of bounty and debenture goods should be limited to British vessels only.

Historians have recently stressed the significance of 1740 as a decisive turning point in Dutch commercial decline, beyond which any revival

---

[108] It should be borne in mind that the distinction between Dutch, Danish and Swedish shipping may in some cases derive from the master's home-port rather than the owners' nationality, and if so, this would tend to play down the role of Dutch-owned vessels. Likewise, the figures relate to entries rather than clearances, and therefore take no account of ships which came over from Holland in ballast to collect a homeward cargo.

was impossible. Not only was the Republic faced by the rapid loss of her share of the bulk trades, she was also reduced to the role of a third-party carrier for the goods of others during the years of Anglo-French struggle for global hegemony.[109] Neutral carrying provided some compensation for loss of leverage over world markets, but in fact even this role was being undermined by the services provided by Denmark, Hamburg and other neutral states. Although English grain exporters faced a serious shortage of outward shipping from the later 1730s, the recourse to Dutch tonnage was much smaller than it had been in the 1690s. At the same time, privateering in the early 1740s presented a less serious threat than it did during the earlier conflict, as London merchants testified, while naval protection was much better organised.[110] The navies of France and Britain, indeed, were now able to perform the destructive and defensive operations which privateers had carried out by default during the War of the Spanish Succession. The establishment of the western squadron became the linchpin of British naval strategy, protecting most outward and homeward convoys, if not the Baltic trade.[111] In these circumstances, England could afford to be much less tolerant of Dutch neutral rights, and the understanding of earlier decades began to break down.

During the early stages of the War of the Austrian Succession, English privateers repeatedly intercepted the movement of Dutch ships carrying naval supplies from the Baltic to French naval bases, with the invariable support of the Admiralty Courts. The treaty provisions of 1674 were effectively disregarded, although the cargoes were not treated as contraband to be confiscated: instead, they were purchased for the Royal Navy while freight charges were duly paid.[112] Judicial opinion justified the new stance on the grounds that the transport of naval stores to an enemy would prolong the conflict.[113] The Republic gradually realised the fragility and practical limitations of the Anglo-Dutch understanding in its combination of neutrality with defensive alliance. During the Seven Years' War, the untenable basis of the relationship became even clearer. It finally broke down in 1759 when the English discovered that Dutch

[109] Israel, *Dutch Primacy*, pp. 399 400.
[110] *A Short Account of the late Application to Parliament made by the Merchants of London upon the Neglect of their Trade*, 1742 (Hanson 5624). During the War of the Spanish Succession, the value of prize goods imported amounted to £1.08 million, but more than 1,100 British merchant ships were taken (Clark, 'War Trade and Trade War', pp. 264, 266).
[111] Clark, 'War Trade and Trade War', p. 263; N. A. M. Rodger, 'Sea Power and Empire, 1699 1793', in P. J. Marshall (ed.), *The Oxford History of the British Empire*, vol. II, *The Eighteenth Century*, Oxford, 1998, pp. 174 5.
[112] Carter, *Dutch Republic*, p. 10, and *Neutrality or Commitment*, pp. 85 6.
[113] Carter, *Dutch Republic*, p. 100.

Table 9.5 *Entries of foreign vessels at British ports, 1743–1749*

	1743			1747			1749		
	repeat voyages	no. of ships	tonnage	repeat voyages	no. of ships	tonnage	repeat voyages	no. of ships	tonnage
Holland	84	45	8,941	111	66	10,542	62	45	6,282
Denmark	141	90	28,981	336	192	64,068	292	181	47,382
Sweden	8	8	928	70	62	7,963	71	56	8,400
Germany	68	37	11,370	70	42	11,415	56	44	8,739
Portugal	21	19	1,594	61	53	5,454	26	23	2,100
Others	138	105	10,061	79	62	13,005	89	74	9,367
Total	460	304	61,875	727	477	112,447	596	423	82,270

Source: Anon., *The Case of British Merchants*, p. 7 (Hanson 6437).

merchants were carrying Swedish cannon to Amsterdam, destined for trans-shipment to France via Dutch inland waterways.[114]

As neutral traders, the Dutch had been able to offer lower freight rates than English shipowners, but as the number of confiscations mounted, the need for convoy provision and consequent delay increased proportionately. The Amsterdam and Rotterdam insurance markets were, of course, well placed to cover increased risks at sea, and, by the 1740s, the additional premiums charged for sailing without convoy had fallen from 5% to 3%, compared with rates charged during the War of the Spanish Succession.[115] London's marine insurance facilities, however, had developed apace since 1720, with the founding of the Royal Exchange and its sister company, the London Assurance.[116] Two London merchants established a substantial new insurance company in Rotterdam at the same time, but, after an initial burst of enthusiasm, the number of Anglo-Dutch voyages covered declined rapidly during the first decade of its existence.[117] By 1732, even a director of the VOC had to admit that insurance of British shipping in Holland was 'not to be done for the price you can get it in London'. Some of this business returned during the mid-century wars, but the Republic had lost the clear lead in marine insurance which it had possessed fifty years earlier.[118]

Between 1713 and 1740 – most likely, during the 1720s – England's shipping tonnage came to exceed that of the Republic. Much of this new capacity was used to shift England's apparently inexhaustible supplies of coal and surplus grain across the North Sea, though some of it returned

---

[114] Ibid., pp. 91–7.

[115] In 1709, rates of 3% with convoy were offered in Rotterdam, and 8% without convoy. A copy of the convoy's sailing orders was required (NRO ZBL192, John Blackett, Rotterdam, to John Kelley, Newcastle, 28 May 1709; ZBL192, Henry Witton, Wakefield, to John Blackett, Rotterdam, 16 March 1709). In 1745, the Maatschappij van Assurantie, Discontering en Beleening in Rotterdam offered rates of 2–3% with convoy, and 5–6% without convoy (GAR MADBR, 1745 Assurantie Boek).

[116] See A. H. John, 'The London Assurance Company and the Marine Insurance Market of the Eighteenth Century', in *Economica*, n.s. 25 (1958), pp. 126–31, and B. E. Supple, *The Royal Exchange Assurance*, Cambridge, 1970, chs. 2 and 3.

[117] The company was founded by Edward Hoyle and Gerard Roeters of London, and was incorporated as Rotterdam's municipal insurance company (see P. Crowhurst, 'Marine Insurance and the Trade of Rotterdam, 1755–63', *Maritime History*, 2 (1972), pp. 140–50; Crowhurst, *Defence of British Trade*, ch. 3). The number of policies relating to Anglo-Dutch voyages declined at the following rates: 1721, 167; 1725, 90; 1730, 51 (GAR MADBR Assurantie Boeken).

[118] PRO C103/132, J. Senserf and Son, Rotterdam, to Thomas Hall, London, 4 April 1732; Violet Barbour showed that the insurance of English ships in Holland was very common during the later seventeenth century, in spite of higher premiums (Barbour, 'Marine Risks and Insurance in the Seventeenth Century', *Journal of Economic and Business History*, 1 (1928–9), p. 581). On the growth of the Amsterdam marine insurance market in the eighteenth century, see Spooner, *Risks at Sea*.

with imports of Norwegian timber, naval stores and assorted Baltic cargoes. The seasonality of trade patterns facilitated the simultaneous expansion of coal and corn exports, but merchants still found it necessary to employ Dutch and other foreign shipping during peak years and export, and during wartime. In effect, Dutch shipping used in the English North Sea trades was displacing the deployment of that same tonnage in the Republic's own, declining, Baltic trade. The neutral status of Dutch vessels may have benefited English merchants by helping to reduce the high level of wartime freight rates, but individual gains were, at least in the minds of statesmen, outweighed by the possibility that Dutch neutral services were enlarging and prolonging the Anglo-French mid-century wars. Britain's growing naval strength, improvements in naval strategy and the development of the London marine insurance market were important factors underlying the drift of British foreign policy away from reliance on Dutch neutral shipping and associated services, as well as the services of Dutch auxiliary troops promised in the defensive agreements of 1703 and 1716.[119]

By 1750, British shipowners expressed a sense of panic that as much as one-fifth of shipping employed in their overseas trade consisted of foreign tonnage at various dates during the 1740s, yet, with hindsight, it is clear that their petition to parliament came in an exceptional year – the peak year of the century for grain export.[120] The situation had changed from one of large-scale dependency, which marked the quarter-century after 1689, to one of temporary need. As the petitioners themselves noted, European nations were now purchasing ships from Britain as well as the expertise of skilled native shipbuilders. In fact their anxieties surfaced just at the moment when the shipping industry was poised on the edge of a major period of expansion, driven by the upsurge of transatlantic trade. As the tailing-off of English grain exports to Europe released surplus tonnage into the industry during the early 1750s, trade with North America and the West Indies experienced renewed growth. Its main import components were bulk cargoes of timber from Canada and the mainland colonies, and increased shipments of West Indian sugar; tobacco, rice and naval stores from the southern colonies continued their earlier growth.[121] Clearly, the English shipping industry had now acquired the competitive edge and the capacity to match its Dutch rivals, underpinned by expanding world markets. Both, however, were initially won in the trading world of the North and Baltic Seas, under the stimulus of the Navigation Acts.

[119] Carter, *Neutrality or Commitment*, pp. 72–3.
[120] Anon., *The Case of British Merchants* (Hanson 6437), p. 1.
[121] Davis, *Shipping Industry*, ch. 13.

10   Protectionism and Dutch economic decline

The connections between taxation and the decline of empires is a less unfashionable theme than it was when Charles Wilson raised the subject in the early 1960s. Wilson was primarily concerned to explore the impact of high internal taxation on the ailing economy of the eighteenth-century Dutch Republic, and arrived at conclusions which have been confirmed by more recent and detailed research: that a per capita level of taxation which stood at around 2.5 times the level of that prevailing in England in 1695 placed the Republic in an extremely vulnerable position, especially in relation to the competitiveness of its industrial sector. High wage costs impacted most seriously on the labour-intensive industries such as textiles, but also affected the carrying trade.[1] Wilson said little here about the consequences of external taxation and the protectionist policies of neighbouring states aimed against the Dutch, an issue which he had already confronted in his earlier work, and one which he felt had been seriously misinterpreted by Dutch and English historians.

The basis of Wilson's pioneering work on Anglo-Dutch commercial relations was to suggest that both contemporary and modern writers had conspired to antedate the economic decline of the Netherlands, following Sir William Temple's 'gloomy prophecy' that Dutch trade had 'past its meridian' in 1672. 'It is now safe to assume', he wrote, 'that the practical monopoly of European transport and commerce which the Dutch established in the early seventeenth century by reason of their geographical position, their superior commercial organisation and technique, and the economic backwardness of their neighbours, stood intact until about 1730.'[2] High internal taxation, rather than English and French

---

[1] C. H. Wilson, 'Taxation and the Decline of Empires', and reprinted in C. H. Wilson, *Economic History and the Historian*, pp. 114–27; J. de Vries & van der Woude, *First Modern Economy*, p. 699.

[2] C. H. Wilson, 'Economic Decline of the Netherlands', p. 254; C. H. Wilson, *Anglo-Dutch Commerce*, pp. 16–19. A revised version of the former appeared in Wilson's collected essays of 1969, which took account of the work of Johan de Vries, but still maintained that 'As late as 1730 trade was good and optimism widespread' ('Decline of the Netherlands', pp. 26–7).

protectionism, he supposed, was a more potent force in bringing about economic decline, although he recognised the strength of van Dillen's argument that the difficulties facing the Dutch sprang from an increasingly unfavourable world context, as 'the consequence of international factors, of a structural change in the economic life of Europe'.[3] Insofar as protectionism played an important role, the emphasis was placed on British industrial competition backed by high tariffs and subsidies, which gained momentum during the first half of the eighteenth century. The impact of the Navigation Acts was seen as minimal: they were 'riddled with exemptions' and frequently circumvented.[4] Not until the early decades of the eighteenth century did British merchants succeed in by-passing the Dutch staplemarket by establishing 'direct' trading links with European suppliers and purchasers, particularly in Germany. As Anglo-Dutch commodity trade languished, Dutch merchants increasingly turned towards financial activity, often via commission trade. A 'transition to finance' occurred at the expense of active trade, as Dutch investments in the English national debt expanded during the 1720s and '30s.

Wilson's analysis was consistent with the historiography of the interwar years which took an optimistic or 'delayed' view of Dutch decline, parts of which survived into the 1960s in the influential work of Johan de Vries. The latter argued that decline was only relative until *c.* 1780, since per capita incomes were maintained, and, although industrial output declined, the stability of the commercial and financial sectors provided some compensation.[5] A more pessimistic picture has emerged in the light of more recent research in demographic history, however, and although a consensus remains to be established, many would now interpret Dutch decline alongside the rhythms of the world-economy. The Republic, it seems, became 'enmeshed' in the long phase of contraction which enveloped the European economy after 1660.[6] The extent of a possible revival after 1750 remains an open question. It seems clear, however, that the Dutch golden age ended 'some time in the last third of the seventeenth century', and that Dutch overseas trade stagnated after reaching peak levels in the 1690s, in marked contrast with the sustained and rapid growth which characterised English and French commerce in

[3] 'Taxation and the Decline of Empires', p. 117.
[4] This view was revised, though not abandoned, in C. H. Wilson, *Profit and Power*, p. 99.
[5] Joh. de Vries, *Economische Achteruitgang*, pp. 167–8, 172.
[6] Joh. de Vries and van der Woude place the golden age within the period 1580–1663, the terminal date marked by the reversal of the price trend; the years after 1663 are described in terms of 'crisis and response' (*First Modern Economy*); Israel puts the 'zenith' of Dutch world-trade hegemony at 1672, but sees the period 1621–47 as one of prolonged crisis (*Dutch Primacy*, chs. 5, 6). See J. L. van Zanden, 'Dutch Economic History of the Period 1500–1940: A Review of the Present State of Affairs', in *ESHN*, 1 (1990), pp. 9–30.

the eighteenth century. Decline, as David Landes has recently remarked, is perhaps not the most meaningful term to describe the circumstances of a recurrent historical phenomenon: loss of leadership.[7]

British emancipation from the Dutch staplemarket and the impact of protectionism

The establishment of a chronology which places the onset of Dutch decline somewhere in the 1660s or 1670s and the emphasis on its character as a *relative* process, involving loss of commercial hegemony, suggests that the impact of foreign protectionism was much more complex and protracted than Wilson supposed.[8] Loss of competitiveness, of course, was rarely total and often depended on a slow, marginal deterioration of cost and price structures. It was in 1751 that Amsterdam's leading merchants concluded that one of the principal causes of the long-term decline of the Republic's trade was the adoption of protectionist policies by neighbouring states. England, France, Sweden, Norway, Russia and Prussia all deployed mercantilist measures against the United Provinces, but only the English were able to implement and (with varying degrees of success) enforce a series of protectionist measures aimed at the four main sectors of the Dutch economy: shipping, trade, industry and agriculture.[9] The financial sphere, alone, was immune from English pressure. The principal areas of legislation in each of these four sectors comprised measures designed: (1) to protect the carrying trade and English shipping – principally the navigation laws; (2) to develop the trade of the English entrepôt, in such a way as to encourage the re-export trade while protecting the home market for colonial imports – including the navigation code, and the drawback and warehousing systems; (3) to encourage and protect home industry – especially import substitution policies and import prohibitions; and, (4) to support English farming through the Corn Laws, involving duties on grain imports and subsidised export, which indirectly undermined the position of Dutch carriers of Baltic grain. Without a plentiful stock of natural resources, England's mercantilist challenge would not have been feasible, but long-term 'success' was largely the result of political advantages comprising a strong machinery of state, internal security and the use of naval power. In addition, a quasi-colonial economic policy was deployed against Ireland, which facilitated the development of the English textile industries along strategic lines.[10]

---

[7] D. Landes, *The Wealth and Poverty of Nations*, 1998, pp. 450–1.
[8] Unger, 'Energy Sources', p. 284; Lindblad, 'Foreign Trade', p. 228.
[9] Joh. de Vries, *Economische Achteruitgang*, p. 35.   [10] See chapter 5, pp. 168–9.

After the lifting of the Spanish embargoes against the Dutch in 1647, English merchants were quickly exposed to the resurgence of Dutch competition in the carrying trade, especially in the Mediterranean and the Baltic, at a time when the English economy was sliding into prolonged depression. Some years earlier, Sir Thomas Roe had pointed out that 'Our great trade depends upon the trouble of our neighbours, but if a peace happen between France, Spain and the United Provinces, all these will now share what we possess alone.'[11] The first Navigation Act of 1651 represented the government's delayed response to a major commercial crisis, by attempting to cripple the Republic's European entrepôt trade. Its failure enhanced the general 'Inclinacon to have warrs with the Dutch', to settle political as well as economic grievances.[12] Although its origins have long been disputed, it seems that the impetus behind Cromwell's Navigation Act came mainly from the Levant and Eastland merchants engaged in the European import trades, supported by the Hamburg Merchant Adventurers and prominent West Indian merchants. It was these commercial interests which the Act attempted, but failed, to satisfy. By the Restoration, however, the emphasis shifted from intra-European to transatlantic trade and shipping. Downing's new Navigation Act of 1660 tightened up the work of his predecessors by listing all those imports, European and colonial, which were to fall within the provisions of the Act, and discouraged violations of the code by designating such cargoes as prize goods. All foreign-built ships in English ownership were to be registered and, three years later, the Staple Act restricted colonial purchases of European goods to English shipping.

The revised navigation code created a national monopoly within an imperial trading system. It reflected, in a way which Cromwell's experimental Act did not, the global reach of England's developing commercial interests after the Restoration, including a range of new colonial products which fed the appetites of domestic consumers and the re-export trade. Significantly, the Second Anglo-Dutch War was fought out in the North Atlantic and the Caribbean, as well as in home waters, and its momentous result was to remove the strategic Dutch presence from the North American mainland in 1667. In the late 1640s and early '50s, Dutch merchants and shippers were conducting a vigorous transatlantic and intercolonial trade from Amsterdam to Brazil, the West Indies, Virginia and, occasionally, New England. The trade was a balanced one which combined the disposal of outward cargoes with intercolonial traffic,

---

[11] Quoted Brenner, *Merchants and Revolution*, p. 600.
[12] Harper, *English Navigation Laws*, p. 48; C. H. Wilson, *Profit and Power*, pp. 148–9; S. C. A. Pincus, *Protestantism and Patriotism. Ideologies and the Making of English Foreign Policy, 1650–1668*, Cambridge, 1996, ch. 4.

and produced returns in sugar, tobacco, indigo, cotton, ginger and beaver skins.[13] The loss of Pernambuco in 1654, however, the semi-bankrupt state of the West India Company, and Cromwell's despatch of a naval force against Virginia's pro-Dutch population in 1652 had already reduced its dimensions when the new Navigation Act was passed in 1660. The English capture of New Amsterdam in 1664, it seems, did little to alter the colonists' behaviour in the short term. Violations of the navigation laws were frequent, and private Anglo-Dutch colonial networks continued to exist for many years, not least because a strong sense of national origin was often weak amongst European settlers.[14] The Amsterdam Notarial Archives, however, show that the volume of Dutch-controlled transatlantic traffic declined substantially during the 1660s and '70s. By the late '60s in fact, Amsterdam's imports of colonial tobacco amounted to no more than one-tenth of London's, while its imports of sugar were about one third the London level.[15]

Illegal intercolonial traffic was of course easier to operate than illegal transatlantic trade which offered the prospect of larger rewards. The taking of New Amsterdam and its reinvention as New York was undertaken in the face of indifference from the majority of the English colonial population, and local English and Dutch commercial contacts persisted in the face of London's hostility. Dutch ship kits were transported to Virginia and assembled as plantation-built ships, and freighting agreements were forged to thwart the intentions of parliament.[16] Dutch traders in New York and Europe, however, were increasingly obliged to collude with and depend on their British counterparts to maintain their intercolonial and transatlantic commerce, and it is clear that the exclusion of the Dutch from the imperial trade system created new and attractive opportunities for colonial as well as British merchants.[17] An entry for September 1663 provides the first recorded instance in the Amsterdam notarial archives of a Dutch merchant relying on the services of an English master and

[13] Described in charterparties and attestations given before Amsterdam notaries: GAA, for 1650/51, NA1345/68 and 74 (H. Schaef), NA1589/387 and 390 (P. Capoen); NA2111/353 (J. Thielmans) and twelve further examples; over sixty examples exist for the 1650s.

[14] C. Schnurmann, 'Migration and Communication: Relations between Inhabitants of English and Dutch Colonies in the New World, 1648–1713', paper presented to the Conference on German Perceptions of British History, Institute of Historical Research and German Historical Institute, London, April 1997.

[15] H. Brugmans, 'Statistiek van den in- en uitvoer van Amsterdam, 1667–8', BMHG, 19 (1898), pp. 175–6; Davis, 'English Foreign Trade, 1660–1700', pp. 152–3: Steensgaard, 'Growth and Composition', pp. 131–45.

[16] Schnurmann, 'Migration and Communication', p. 11.

[17] J. J. McCusker & R. R. Menard, The Economy of British America, 1607–1789, Chapel Hill, 1985, pp. 49–50.

his vessel to tranship tobacco from Virginia to Amsterdam via a British port.[18] The notary involved, Adriaen Lock, soon began to specialise in such cases, which became increasingly common in the 1670s. The use of British shipping for Dutch-American voyages multiplied, and, by the 1680s, a standard formula was applied: that 'the ship must on the outward and return journey enter an English port and complete the necessary formalities'.[19] The position of Dutch agents in New Netherland seems to have seriously deteriorated by 1669, when a list of 53 debtors in the former Dutch colony was recorded by the Amsterdam merchants Jacob van Hummel and Jacques Outerman, most relating to tobacco and beaver skins.[20]

Although enforcement of the navigation code was initially difficult to maintain in the colonies, supervision at the European end of the chain limited the extent of illegal intercontinental trade. The network of enforcement extended from the Netherlands, Germany and Danzig to Genoa, Aleppo and Zante, with responsibility resting largely in the hands of consular officials.[21] Official supervision was supplemented by private initiative, with the encouragement of rewards on seizure, and, in practice, it seems that knowledge of the system conferred a degree of leverage and preference to British merchants over their continental counterparts.[22] In 1698, the English consul in Rotterdam reported that English and colonial ships were sailing directly from the plantations, with tobacco and other goods, to Holland, Hamburg and Bremen, without entering in English ports.[23] The concern of the Commissioners for Trade and Plantations was moderated, no doubt, by the fact that, although this was indeed an illegal trade which reduced the state's revenues, it was one which nevertheless employed British shipping and was controlled by an overseas community of British merchants. Its extent, in any case, was limited by the payments system underlying the export of colonial staples, which called for return cargoes from England. As Harper pointed out, the planters received credit, not cash, for their produce, hence they naturally made their purchases in England where their factors could debit their accounts.[24]

---

[18] GAA NA2219/434 (A. Lock), Declaration of Adriaen van Schilperoort of 12 August 1665 relating to a shipment of September 1663.

[19] NA3293/234 (H. Outgers), 25 Feb. 1688. During the Second and Third Anglo-Dutch Wars, the Navigation Acts were suspended to ease the pressure on shipping (Harper, *English Navigation Laws*, p. 68).

[20] NA1983/5–6 (Jacob van Loosdrecht), 3 Jan. 1669, List of outstanding debts in New Netherland and New York for account of Jacob van Hummel and Jacques Outerman. Of the 53 names, 51 are clearly Dutch.

[21] Harper, *English Navigation Laws*, ch. 8.   [22] See above, ch. 3, p. 74, n. 50.

[23] PRO CO388/7, fo. 68, 29 Dec. 1698. Abraham Kick's proposals for preventing frauds in HM customs.

[24] Harper, *English Navigation Laws*, pp. 268–9.

Serious efforts were made to improve colonial enforcement of the navigation code in 1673, when a system was implemented for the local delivery of bonds on enumerated goods destined for England or other plantations.[25] But it was in the wake of the revolution of 1689, as we have seen, that enforcement of the navigation code was greatly improved and tightened up. A new Navigation Act was passed in 1696, the 'Imperial Act of Frauds', coinciding with the permanent establishment of the Commission for Trade and Plantations.[26] The 1696 Act confined colonial trade in its entirety to English-built shipping, and registration of ownership was now required. Enhanced powers were given to colonial governors to prosecute offenders, and although ambiguities remained over the local jurisdiction of the vice-admiralty courts and the common law courts, efforts at imperial control were placed on a much stronger basis.[27]

In assessing the impact of the navigation code, it is important to distinguish between immediate results and long-term effects. In the short term, it is no doubt true that England's most concentrated attack on Dutch world primacy, that mounted during the years 1651–74, was less successful than its protagonists hoped. The Spanish embargoes, down to 1647, and the Anglo-French challenge arising from Colbert's 1667 tariff through to 1713, may well have produced more immediate results, as Jonathan Israel has suggested.[28] England's mercantilist project, however, resembled in today's jargon, a 'rolling programme' rather than a concerted attack underpinned by naval superiority.[29] Not only were the Navigation Acts strengthened during the 1690s, a continual series of tariff adjustments and a programme of import substitution which stimulated British manufacturing at the expense of Dutch industry were added to a broad spectrum of protectionist measures aimed against the Republic. Although the intensity of Anglo-Dutch rivalry cooled off after 1674, as French ambitions mounted, many still believed that economic progress was best achieved by imitating Dutch methods and that commercial success could only be gained at Dutch expense. Josiah Child's *New Discourse of Trade* of 1668, perhaps the most reasoned account of Dutch commercial expansion, was reprinted and enlarged in 1689, 1690, 1693 and 1694.

[25] Ibid., ch. 14.   [26] See above, chapter 2, pp. 45–6.

[27] J. M. Sosin, *English America and Imperial Inconstancy. The Rise of Provincial Autonomy, 1696–1715*, Lincoln and London, 1985, pp. 24–5. For a reasoned appraisal of the historiography of enforcement, see McCusker & Menard, *Economy of British America*, ch. 2, and p. 50, n. 20.

[28] Israel, 'England's Mercantilist Response', pp. 305–18.

[29] The value of London's plantation trade more than doubled between the 1660s and 1700, and contemporary commentators were convinced of the effectiveness of the Navigation Acts (N. Zahedieh, 'Making Mercantilism Work: London Merchants and Atlantic Trade in the Seventeenth Century', *TRHS*, 6th ser., 9 (1999)).

Diplomats and civil servants alike provided evidence to support the arguments of the political arithmeticians. In 1703, for example, the British envoy at Vienna complained to the Commissioners for Trade of the 'arts and contrivances the Dutch are using for promoting their draperies'. A few years later, Davenant reported that 'nothing was wanting to compleat the greatness of this nation', the United Provinces, 'but elbow room for their industry to work in'. Dutch competition in woollen manufacture, he emphasised, should 'give England very just fears'.[30]

Israel's view that the Dutch trading system was relatively immune to England's mercantilist challenge rests on the belief that the latter 'lacked the leverage over key markets which both Spain and France possessed'. England, he suggests, supplied the Dutch with nothing which was essential to the functioning of their entrepôt system, and was never a major market for Dutch products and re-exports.[31] Yet the Dutch processing industries, as we have seen, came to depend on British energy resources and other raw materials in the eighteenth century, including malt and barley; and although the English and Dutch textile industries developed along complementary lines during the previous century, elements of competition still remained, reflected in the English export prohibitions on wool, yarn and fuller's earth. Only when these important exceptions are made does the argument carry any weight. Unlike Anglo-French commercial competition, English rivalry with Holland did not *primarily* involve a struggle for markets for each other's native products, but rather for 'control of the carrying trade, for entrepot profits, for the gains to be made from distant, non-domestic products – spices, sugar, slaves', as Donald Coleman emphasised.[32] The essential point, indeed, is that England's challenge to Dutch commercial primacy was played out at a global as well as at a local level in the late seventeenth century, when neither Spain nor France was a serious competitor for Holland's hegemonic position at the core of the world-economy.[33] The central objective of English mercantilism, therefore, was not to exclude Dutch merchants from the English entrepôt but, on the contrary, to reduce the dependence of English merchants on the Dutch staplemarket and to detach the growing transatlantic and other long-distance trades from its orbit.

---

[30] CO388/8 Part III, fo. 488, 1 March 1703, 'Letter from Mr Stepney at Vienna'; Davenant, 'Second Report', p. 235, p. 459.
[31] Israel, 'England's Mercantilist Response', p. 315.
[32] Coleman, 'Politics and Economics', pp. 204 5.
[33] P. K. O'Brien & L. Prados de la Escosura, 'The Costs and Benefits for Europeans from their Empires Overseas', in P. K. O'Brien & L. Prados de la Escosura (eds.), *The Costs and Benefits of European Imperialism from the Conquest of Ceuta, 1415, to the Treaty of Lusaka, 1974* (Twelfth International Economic History Congress), *Revista de Historia Económica*, 16 (1998), p. 46.

Braudel followed the view established by Charles Wilson that 'it was only after 1730 that the Dutch system began to break down in Europe', as merchants succeeded in by-passing the staplemarket and undermining the intermediary trade.[34] English merchants, however, were already moving outside the orbit of the Dutch staplemarket during the early stages of the commercial revolution, especially in the linen import and woollen export trades, which formed the basis of Anglo-Dutch commercial relations. 'Direct trade' with Hamburg was already flourishing in the late seventeenth century. In absolute terms, linen imports from Germany represented about twice the value of those from Holland around 1700, and while the former increased from 1700 to 1735, at a time when the latter were stagnant, both declined together from the mid-1730s onwards, as the home and re-export markets were increasingly supplied with Scottish and Irish alternatives.[35] Exports of woollen goods to Holland and Germany followed a similar course during the first sixty years of the eighteenth century, and there is no evidence that the transit trade to the south German market, via Holland, declined – if anything, it was probably maintained, while the demands of the north German market for English woollens stagnated after 1715. The growth of new bilateral trading relations between England and Germany in the eighteenth century, then, was of negligible significance.

The changing position of Holland and Germany as sources of linen imports and as markets for woollen exports can only be properly understood in the general context of eighteenth-century English commercial growth. We have seen that English demand for most types of linen was expanding during the period 1700–60, a demand which the linen-producing areas of nearby Europe were unable to meet from the later 1730s onwards, in the face of growing Irish and Scottish competition. For much of the eighteenth century, the woollen export trade was steadily increasing, particularly from the 1740s onwards, yet, again, the traditional markets of Holland and Germany failed to keep pace. It was the markets of southern Europe and North America which absorbed increased exports.

In the case of the bulk export trades to Holland, a similar contrast can be observed between a degree of moderate expansion overshadowed by the more rapid growth of other markets. This is especially clear in the case of the coal trade. English coal exports quadrupled in volume in the period between the 1700s and 1760s, while those to Holland increased by a factor of 2.5. In the grain export trade, which grew steadily during the

---

[34] Braudel, *Perspective of the World*, pp. 260–1. Braudel also followed Wilson on the supposed ineffectiveness of the Navigation Acts.

[35] At the same time, imports of linens in the category 'Germany' via Holland were actually increasing (see above, chapter 5, p. 165).

Table 10.1 *English trade with Holland*
expressed as a percentage of total English
overseas trade, 1698–1763

	% imports	% exports
1698–1701	10.1	24.2
1702–13	13.1	33.0
1714–19	8.8	24.1
1720–9	8.3	19.5
1730–8	6.9	15.8
1739–48	6.4	20.1
1749–55	3.9	14.4
1756–63	4.6	12.1

Source: *State of the Trade of Great Britain*, ed. C.
Whitworth, 1776.

first half of the eighteenth century, the proportion destined for Holland
fell less dramatically – by around 10% between 1730 and 1750. In several
areas of export activity therefore, the decline in English trade with the
Dutch staplemarket was relative rather than absolute, a state of affairs
which has been emphasised in the context of Dutch economic decline in
general (see Table 10.1). In absolute terms, the Dutch market was fairly
stable and revived noticeably during wartime.

On the import account, however, decline was absolute, and the impact
of English protectionist policy, especially high tariffs, is reasonably clear.
The fiscal demands of war and a policy of encouraging the development
of infant industries laid the basis for a series of significant duty increases
affecting imports of paper, linen, sailcloth, cambrics and other manufactured goods imported from Europe, and Holland in particular. By the
early 1740s, a London merchant wrote to his Amsterdam correspondent
that 'our present small demand for Dutch papers prevent my ordering
anything of that kind, which is greatly occasioned by the improvements in
England made in that fabrick'.[36] It was the Irish and the Scots rather than
English producers who responded to similar encouragements in the manufacture of linen and associated products such as thread and sailcloth, but
the effects were broadly comparable. Only the higher-grade imported
fabrics could withstand heavy duty increases, and it was on the basis of
the cheaper grades that the Irish and Scottish industries developed. Few

[36] Brants 1344, Wm Holloway, London, to J. I de Neufville, Amsterdam, 4 October 1743.
D. C. Coleman, *The British Paper Industry, 1495–1860*, Oxford, 1958, ch. 5.

English merchants engaged in the linen trade quarrelled with the practice of import substitution; in common with most imported goods, duties could be 'drawn back' or reclaimed on re-export, and colonial markets were steadily expanding. The only conspicuous protest to appear in print was that of Sir Matthew Decker, himself a Dutchman by origin. The obstructive effects of high duties, according to Decker, were the main cause of the commercial recession of the early 1740s.[37]

Aside from the weight of her existing tax burden, the geographical situation of Holland ruled out any major increase in customs revenue, because of the enormous transit trade along the Maas and Rhine into the heart of Europe. Much of the Republic's internal trade was, in effect, a branch of international trade, and if combined Dutch import and export duties, together with river tolls, exceeded transport and other costs via alternative routes, the trade of the hinterland would gradually disappear.[38] In fact the transit trade increased in relative importance during the earlier decades of the eighteenth century, as Dutch-Baltic trade declined. For the most part, the Republic's merchants focused on the case for reduced customs duties. Several free-zone proposals were made during the eighteenth century, before the comprehensive proposals of 1751 were placed before the States General, but the conflict of interest between Dutch industrial interests, frequently clamouring for protection, and the intermediary trade was never resolved.[39] The general tariff reform of 1725 marginally increased the protective element, but its results were negligible.[40] The 1751 free-port scheme collapsed for several reasons: the opposition of the industrial towns and the non-seafaring provinces; the opposition of Zeeland which already provided transit facilities for the trade with the Austrian Netherlands, as well as a home for the smuggling trade; the lack of alternative revenue sources to support the navy; and the absence of strong central government.[41]

A high tariff system, moderated by drawbacks and bonding facilities, was clearly a feasible and an attractive option for British parliaments, as London rose to a position of pre-eminence within the North Sea economy and the imperial trading system. Duty increases on imports played a significant, if not a critical, role in reducing English dependence on the Dutch staplemarket, and were substantial enough to affect the course of trade in the long term. Above all, a high tariff regime enabled parliament

---

[37] M. Decker, *An Essay on the Causes of the Decline of the Foreign Trade . . . of Great Britain*, 1744, p. 1.

[38] H. R. C. Wright, *Free Trade*, pp. 73–7.

[39] Free-zone proposals were made in 1664, 1688, 1727, 1732 and 1740, before the substantial proposals of 1751.

[40] See above, chapter 4, pp. 113–16.   [41] Hovy, *Voorstel van 1751*, pp. 610–29.

to use enhanced customs revenue as an instrument of economic policy through granting concessions and inducements to different commercial and industrial interests.[42] As trade expanded and diversified from the 1670s, the range of possibilities increased enormously. The Wars of the Grand Alliance put a severe strain on England's trading performance, yet the tariff increases which those wars brought into being were achieved in spite of several daunting economic challenges, including a recoinage crisis.[43] By 1700, the state had, in effect, taken hold of the commercial revolution, and had begun to give it shape and form. Revenue policy became a vehicle for expressing economic priorities as well as the state's own strategic objectives, which included preferential duties for colonial and entrepôt trade, protective tariffs, and, in some cases, subsidies, to encourage home industry as well as grain production.

Walpole's customs reforms of 1722 simplified, consolidated and strengthened the protectionist elements, and responded to the demands of the textile and paper industries for duty exemptions on imported raw materials. This fell far short of strategic economic planning, but it contained rudimentary elements of a development programme. As we have noted, gross customs revenue was comparable in value to the yield from the excise, usually considered to be the most important branch of the revenue throughout the eighteenth century. Moreover, the decades from the 1720s to the 1750s saw a widening gap between gross and net customs revenue, accounted for by bounties, subsidies, drawbacks and management costs. This is a gap which deserves greater visibility, since commercial growth was creating additional resources for redistribution by successive British governments to promote manufacturing and processing through the granting of subsidies and bounties (Table 10.2). The bulk of these subsidies were devoted to the encouragement of grain production, via corn export bounties, although the Land Tax originally funded these. But encouragement was also given to the export of sailcloth (1713), manufactured silk (1722), spirits (1733) and gunpowder (1731), as well as shipping involved in the Greenland fishery (1731). A subsidy was granted on imports of naval stores from the colonies in 1705, subsequently extended to imports from Scotland in 1713. The amount of subsidy varied in each case: around 10% of the notional value as set out in the Book of Rates in the case of corn, 12% for gunpowder, 8% for sailcloth, and around 8% in the case of British manufactured silk. The strategic significance of several of these is obvious, including the corn bounties whose

---

[42] Davis, 'Rise of Protection', p. 307; O'Brien, Griffiths & Hunt, 'Political Components of the Industrial Revolution', pp. 395–423.
[43] Jones, *War and Economy*, ch. 2.

Table 10.2 *Allowances for bounty payments and drawback of excise,*
1689–1766

	statute	date(s) commencing	amount (£ s d)	%
Bounties on exported goods				
1 Corn (cereals and malt)	1 Wm & Mary c. 12	1689		
wheat			0.5.0 p. qr	10.4
rye			0.3.6 do.	10.9
barley			0.2.6 do.	10.4
malt			0.2.6 do.	10.4
2 British sailcloth	12 Anne c. 16	1713	0.0.1 p. ell	
	4 Geo. II c. 27	1730	0.0.2 p. ell	
3 British and Irish linen	15 Geo. II c. 29	1743		
at 6d p. yd or less			0.0.0$\frac{1}{2}$ p. yd	<8.3
at 6d–1s p. yd			0.0.1 p. yd	8.3–16.6
4 Spirits	6 Geo. II c. 17	1733	1.10.0 p. ton	
5 British manufactured silk	8 Geo. I c. 15	1722	0.3.0 p. lb	8.4
6 British-made gunpowder	4 Geo. II c. 29	1731	0.4.6 p. 100lb	12.6
7 Cordage	6 Geo. III c. 45	1766	0.2.4$\frac{3}{4}$ p. cwt	
Bounties on imported naval stores				
1 from the British plantations	3&4 Anne c. 10	1705		
hemp			6.0.0 p. ton	
masts			1.0.0 p. ton	
tar, ordinary			2.4.0 p. ton	
tar, prime			4.0.0 p. ton	
pitch			1.0.0 p. ton	
turpentine			1.10.0 p. ton	
2 from Scotland	12 Anne c. 9	1713		
hemp			6.0.0 p. ton	
masts			1.0.0 p. ton	

Drawback of excise on British-made goods, on export; payable on:
Candles; leather; leather goods; starch; soap; paper; printed or dyed silks, calicoes, linens and stuff; wrought plate; gold and silver lace, thread etc.; beer, ale, mum & cider; corn-spirits; fish and salted pork and beef; malt.

Industrial raw materials imported free of duty

1 Irish hemp and flax	7&8 Wm III c. 39	1696
2 Cochineal and dyestuffs	1 Geo. I c. 15	1714
3 Turkish silk and mohair yarn	4 Geo. I c. 7	1718
4 Dyestuffs	8 Geo. I c. 15	1722
5 Rags for paper makers	8 Geo. I c. 15	1722
3 Flax	4 Geo. II c. 27	1732
4 Irish woollen yarn	12 Geo. II c. 21	1740
5 Linen yarn	24 Geo. II c. 46	1752
	29 Geo. II c. 15	1756
6 Raw silk	6 Geo. III c. 28	1765

Sources: H. Crouch, *A Complete View of the British Customs*, 1738 and 1755 editions; *Statutes at Large*.

purpose was to maintain grain prices and preserve self-sufficiency in cereal production. The bounty on silk manufactures extended the drawbacks (or repayments of duty) already available on imported raw and thrown silk to wrought silk, together with an allowance for wastage in manufacture. The ultimate purpose, however, was to outdo the French in growing export markets, who, as Defoe pointed out, 'were our Teachers, and of whom we always bought the richest and finest broad Silks the whole World could produce,... [yet] we now sell broad Silks even into France itself'.[44]

Industrial development as such, however, did not take priority in the precepts underlying these legislative programmes, and the satisfaction of consumer preferences was frequently ignored, as Adam Smith emphasised. Production derived meaning and value from its association with commerce, and, above all, the extent to which it enlarged the nation's export surplus. Recognition of these priorities explains why governments, in pursuing policies of import substitution, levied heavy duties on goods with a high elasticity of demand, such as fine linens. The significance of import saving was equal to, if not greater than, that of enhanced revenue, and an immediate stimulus to home production was not always intended. The priority given to maintaining a favourable balance of trade also explains why the state was more willing to make concessions to manufacturing interests by allowing drawback of import duties on industrial raw materials, rather than exempting these from duty altogether. The latter policy was indeed pursued by Walpole in the early 1720s, but was extended only gradually during succeeding decades. The most favoured industrial interests were those which relied on home-produced raw materials: woollens, most obviously, but also Irish and (after 1707) Scottish linen, and, to some extent, paper. Industrial producers who relied on grain products for raw materials were only mildly damaged by the corn bounties before mid-century. But as food prices started to rise in the 1760s, brewers and distillers began to complain that the preference long enjoyed by farmers and landowners was enjoyed at their own expense, and that of the consumer.[45] Further concessions were also granted to manufacturers supplying overseas markets through the granting of drawbacks on excise payments, for exports of various domestic manufactures. The more important excise drawbacks were approved during the later years of Anne's reign, from 1710 to 1712, on goods including paper, soap, and printed silks and linens, where home production had already benefited from the imposition of protective duties.

---

[44] Defoe, *Plan*, p. 226.
[45] Combrune, *Enquiry*, pp. 108–10; Barnes, *English Corn Laws*, ch. 3.

Mercantilist practice was clear in distinguishing beneficial from damaging trades, and in discerning manufacturing interests worthy of protection from those less deserving. By granting exemptions from a high tariff regime, the state was able to exercise a moderate degree of control, and nowhere was this more evident than in entrepôt trading and colonial trade. Together with the Navigation Acts, the drawback system formed the basis of England's re-export trade to European and colonial markets. High duties on imports such as coffee, tobacco and rice, coupled with drawbacks, gave a strong stimulus to the re-export of these goods to Europe, while the prohibition on the use of printed Asian textiles on the domestic market after 1701, strengthened in 1720, redirected the legal trade to nearby Europe. In the opposite direction, drawbacks enabled colonial consumers to enjoy European re-exports traded via England at lower prices than English consumers, after making due allowance for transport costs. They also created a situation where British manufactured goods were forced to compete with European-made products in colonial markets without the benefit of protection, although some exceptions existed.[46] British linen producers, amongst others, made their opposition clear, but their trade to America and Africa surged ahead nonetheless during the 1750s, '60s and '70s, while re-exports of European linens stagnated.[47] British colonial sugar, on the other hand, entered the British home market at highly preferential rates of duty, compared with alternative supplies from foreign plantations.

From the standpoint of merchants involved in trade with nearby Europe, an increasingly high tariff structure combined with the restrictive effects of the Navigation Acts clearly exacerbated the problem of finding return cargoes. Many ships returned from the Low Countries lightly laden or in ballast, although, as we have seen, the same situation also encouraged triangular trading across the North Sea by shipmasters and owners wishing to exploit excess inward carrying capacity. The growing imbalance between export and import volumes was regarded by Charles Wilson as a sign that commercial opportunities were dwindling for Dutch merchants trading with England, and this, in turn, provided support for his argument that many were turning towards financial activity at the expense of active trade. All the evidence, however, points to the fact that these changes were well under way in the 1670s, rather than the 1720s and '30s, as Wilson supposed. As Alice Carter emphasised, 'commodity trading and finance existed side by side, supporting

---

[46] The drawback on re-exports of foreign iron and ironware to the colonies was removed in 1705 (Davis, 'Rise of Protection', p. 312).
[47] Harte, 'Rise of Protection', p. 98; J. M. Price, 'The Imperial Economy', pp. 88, 102.

each other for many decades'.[48] There was, in other words, no sudden rupture separating Dutch involvement in commodity trade from financial activity. The crisis surrounding the passage of the Navigation Acts, the establishment of a national monopoly, the collapse of regulated trading and the weakening of the English mart for woollens in the Netherlands marked the beginning of the end of English dependence on the staple-market. Declining profits for English exporters and the opening up of the Merchant Adventurers' trade, however, created new opportunities for foreign merchants and agents in London, and several began to involve themselves with the English export and re-export trades to nearby Europe after 1689. As Amsterdam's role in world trade shifted from that of an active to a passive staplemarket, Dutch traders increasingly came to London to buy on their own account, while low-risk commission trade – the handling of goods owned by others – came to characterise a larger share of business transacted in Holland.

The refinancing of the North Sea economy and the 'Atlanticisation' of British trade

Of the various sectors of the Dutch economy subject to the protectionist policies of other nations, the financial sphere was uniquely immune from attack. The substantial movement of Dutch capital into the English national debt was the subject of extensive contemporary comment, much of it adverse, and has been carefully analysed by modern writers, including Wilson, Carter, Dickson, Riley, Neal and Wright.[49] Although difficult to quantify, there was also an equally significant flow of Dutch capital into British *commodity trade*, which has passed virtually unnoticed. Both developments, of course, were the by-products of low interest rates in Holland – a fairly stable 3% in the later seventeenth century while English rates fluctuated between 4% and 6% (the legal maximum from 1651). It was

---

[48] Carter, *Dutch Republic in Europe*, p. 138.

[49] A. M. C. Carter, 'The Dutch and the English Public Debt in 1777', and 'Dutch Foreign Investment, 1738–1800', *Economica*, new ser., 20 (1953), May and November; C. H. Wilson, 'Dutch Investment in 18th-century England', together with Carter's reply, *EcHR*, 12 (1959), all reprinted in Carter, *Getting, Spending and Investing in Early Modern Times*, pp. 20–65; Dickson, *Financial Revolution*, ch. 12; J. C. Riley, *International Government Finance and the Amsterdam Capital Market, 1740–1815*, Cambridge, 1980, especially chs. 4 and 6; L. Neal, *The Rise of Financial Capitalism: International Capital Markets in the Age of Reason*, Cambridge, 1990; J. F. Wright, 'The Contribution of Overseas Savings to the Funded National Debt of Great Britain', *EcHR*, 50 (1997), pp. 657–74. See also E. S. Brezis, 'Foreign Capital Flows in the Century of Britain's Industrial Revolution: New Estimates, Controlled Conjectures', *EcHR*, 48 (1995), which extends J. C. Riley's suggestion that Dutch capital exports not only financed the commercial activity of recipients, but were 'sometimes used in the private sector to expand production in mining, industry and plantation agriculture' (Riley, *International Goverment Finance*, p. 219).

during the 1720s that the gap between Dutch and English interest rates narrowed significantly, as substantially increasing flows of Dutch investment in English securities brought about a greater degree of parity.[50] A recent examination of the market for English stocks in London and Amsterdam has shown conclusively that both markets were efficiently and closely integrated from 1723 onwards, following the South Sea crisis, with a remarkable degree of stability attained during the 'Walpole years', from the end of the decade.[51] By 1762, almost 20% of the English national debt was held in foreign (mainly Dutch) hands, particularly Bank stock, of which the Dutch owned 30% of the total.[52] The significant Dutch and Huguenot role in the financial revolution has long been recognised, but the connection between the commercial and financial revolutions deserves greater emphasis. In fact, it was precisely the period 1689–1720 which saw a significant movement of Dutch merchant capital into British commodity trade *prior* to the enormous flow of Dutch and Huguenot investment into the English funds. This in turn partly explains why the foreign share in the national debt came to be dominated by a handful of very large Dutch merchant-investors. Peter Dickson has shown that in 1723–4, 3% of Dutch proprietors owned 37% of total Dutch-held stock.[53]

These investment opportunities were related to a number of factors: the Anglo-Dutch Alliance of 1689 and the enhanced opportunities for wartime trading and the handling of remittances up to 1713; the opening-up of British overseas trade to foreign merchants; and, above all, the protracted process of Dutch economic decline. In Charles Wilson's view, Dutch foreign investment developed in parasitic fashion, at the expense of active trade, and hence acted as a major cause of the Republic's economic decline.[54] As we have noticed, this was consistent with the historiography of the inter-war years which dated the onset of decline from the 1730s rather than the 1660s or '70s. In the light of revisionist explanations of decline, however, and broad acceptance of an earlier chronology, it seems much more plausible to regard the 'transition to finance' as a delayed consequence rather than a cause of stagnation. Following the success of Colbert's drive to undermine the trade of the Dutch in the

---

[50] Dickson, *Financial Revolution*, p. 332.

[51] Neal, *Financial Capitalism*, pp. 46–55, 141–65. On the integration of Paris into the London–Amsterdam network, see E. S. Schubert, 'Innovations, Debts and Bubbles: International Integration of Financial Markets in Western Europe, 1688–1720', *JEH*, 48 (1988), pp. 299–306.

[52] C. H. Wilson, 'Dutch Investment', reprinted in Carter, *Getting, Spending and Investing in Early Modern Times*, p. 53; Dickson, *Financial Revolution*, Tables 50, 51, pp. 321, 324.

[53] Dickson, *Financial Revolution*, p. 328.

[54] C. H. Wilson, *Anglo-Dutch Commerce*, ch. 3, which broadly follows the account given by J. MacGregor, *Commercial Statistics*, 1844–50, vol. I, p. 831.

Mediterranean, and the impact of the Navigation Acts in excluding them from the trade of the British plantations, particularly in colonial sugar, Dutch merchants turned their attention to the British metropolis.[55] The years from *c.* 1689 to 1720, in fact, form a transitional stage during which highly mobile Dutch and Huguenot capital was pumped into English commodity trade with Europe, thus paving the way for the period of heavy investment in English stocks in the ensuing decades. The substantial contribution of Huguenot families to the development of English public finance after 1689 is of course well known: Alice Carter estimated that 10% of the national debt was held by Huguenot investors during this period.[56] It should be emphasised, however, that Huguenot financial involvement was also linked with commodity trade, a point which Carter was aware of, though she underrated its significance. Her analysis of the Amsterdam notarial archives for the period 1701–10 showed that the London–Amsterdam commodity trade was dominated by Huguenot and Jewish merchants: 28.5% of merchants listed as being concerned with London trade proved to be Huguenot, 21% were Jewish, 13% were Dutch, 7.5% were German, and 30% were English.[57]

It was in the financing of the English export and re-export trades to Holland, rather than the small and declining import trades, that Dutch capital and credit made its earliest and most significant impact. In 1669, the Lords' Committee on the Decay of Trade heard that several London merchants had received business loans from Holland, while others were acting as agents for Dutch lenders at 5, 6 and 7%. Josiah Child put the overall value of these loans at no more than £100,000, but evidence later emerged suggesting that much larger sums were involved.[58] By the 1690s, however, Dutch merchants in Holland were actively participating in the finance of English woollen exports to the Republic and beyond, taking consignments on their own account and paying commission to agents or clothiers in England. As we have seen, this new pattern of trade reversed the traditional method of dealing formerly practised by the Merchant Adventurers, whose monopoly was wound up in 1689, at the same time as differential duties discriminating against foreign merchants were abolished. The Adventurers had previously sent their own stock to be sold in Holland on commission by resident agents or factors, but

[55] I. K. Steele, 'The Empire and the Provincial Élites: An Interpretation of some Recent Writings on the English Atlantic, 1675–1740', in P. Marshall and G. Williams (eds.), *The British Atlantic Empire before the American Revolution*, 1980, p. 7.

[56] Neal, *Financial Capitalism*, pp. 10–13; C. H. Wilson, *Anglo-Dutch Commerce*, pp. 105–18.

[57] Carter, 'The Huguenot Contribution', pp. 76–90; A. M. C. Carter, 'Financial Activities of the Huguenots in London and Amsterdam in the Mid-eighteenth Century', *Proceedings of the Huguenot Society of London*, 19 (1952–8), p. 101.

[58] HMC 1881, part 1, item 215 (134b).

the key figure was now the large merchant–importer such as d'Orville and Leeuw of Amsterdam.[59] In a similar way, a large share of English trade with Hamburg passed into the hands of German merchants, reducing their English correspondents to the status of commission agents. In London's re-export trade to Holland, Dutch and Huguenot merchants took over a similar role from the start, as firms such as de Neufville, Loubier and Fonnereau set up London agencies to facilitate the channelling of colonial and oriental produce to Amsterdam.[60] Hamburg merchants also bought re-export goods in London for their own entrepôt trade. Foreign merchants, in fact, had always traded on the same basis as English merchants on the London re-export market, which consequently became 'cosmopolitanised' before the woollen trade.[61]

On the import side, the opportunities for Dutch merchants were severely damaged by the Navigation Acts, and, by the early years of the eighteenth century, rising import duties coupled with measures designed to promote import substitution reduced a stagnant volume of trade to low levels. Here, too, Dutch merchants were forced to invest their capital in the trade of foreigners if anything at all was to be done. By the 1690s, naturalised Dutch merchants in London, such as Cornelisen and Vandermersh, were annually importing linen to the wholesale value of over £10,000, alongside several smaller German importers. Wine imports were handled by naturalised Dutch and French merchants, and the import trade in paper was dominated by Sir Theodore Janssen, with consignments worth £22,000 in 1695.[62] By the 1730s, English merchants were refusing to take Dutch linens on their own accounts, and instead were accepting them for sale on a commission basis for Dutch houses, or, at best, on half-account with Dutch exporters. By the mid-1750s, the Amsterdam firm of de Neufville was prepared to deal on half-account in almost any commodity, up to a limit of £500 per consignment.[63]

As increasing amounts of Dutch capital became tied up in stocks of English commodities, it seems that merchants on both sides of the North Sea also responded to low profit levels by forming direct trading contacts with producers and consumers.[64] This further damaged the Dutch intermediary role. In the linen trade, drapers were importing their own Hollands linen in the 1730s and, by 1755, it was said that 'The Holland trade is now too much in the Drapers hands to be worth...engaging

[59] See above, chapter 4, pp. 136–7.   [60] See above, chapter 6, p. 201.

[61] Newman, 'Anglo-Hamburg Trade', p. 188.   [62] Jones, *War and Economy*, pp. 254–6.

[63] Brants 1344, M. and B. Harrison, London, to J. I. de Neufville, Amsterdam, 12 November 1756.

[64] In the woollen trade, 5% was regarded as a good profit by Dutch importers (Forman, *Letter to the Merchants of Great Britain*, p. xix).

in.'[65] In the 1710s, shipmasters and others were drawing their supplies of sailcloth directly from Dutch sailmakers and sailcloth producers. In the woollen export trade, Dutch merchants were corresponding directly with English manufacturers in the early 1700s, a tendency which became much more common by the 1730s; while in the coal export trade, some Rotterdam merchants (and possibly industrial consumers) were in direct contact with English coalowners, chartering vessels and drawing supplies as they needed them.[66] The influences which produced these changes were varied: in the linen and sailcloth trades, the rising level of duties and the appearance of cheaper, home-produced alternatives; in the woollen trade, heavy reliance on the Dutch staplemarket during wartime which produced poor returns and a need to reduce costs; and in the coal trade, the need for a less erratic supply. The result was to contribute towards the gradual demise of the general merchant and the accompanying growth of more specialised commercial functions which characterise eighteenth-century trade in general.[67]

The timing of these changes was strongly influenced by the emergence of new patterns of demand, as England's traditional trade to the Low Countries in woollen textiles was overtaken by colonial and Asian re-exports, and as home production was substituted for imports. The dynamism of re-exports emerges clearly from the Inspector General's statistics, summarised in Table 10.3.[68] Woollen exports, on the other hand, grew only slowly between the 1660s and 1700, as the consumption of oriental fabrics increased throughout western Europe. It was these changes in consumption patterns which underlay the emergence of new marketing structures in north-western Europe. In the early 1680s, as English clothiers and domestic producers complained increasingly of the ruin and decay of their trade, one section of the London merchant community was rapidly concentrating its traditional operations at Blackwell Hall, while others were moving into entirely new markets and exotic commodities.[69] It was during the years 1677–88 that the re-export of Asian and tropical goods to Europe became established as the fastest-growing sector of English commerce.[70] These were also the years when regulated trading weakened to the point of collapse. After the dissolution of the Merchant

[65] Brants 1344, M. and B. Harrison, London, to J. I. de Neufville, Amsterdam, 29 January 1755.
[66] See above, pp. 137–9, 267–9.
[67] Ashton, *Eighteenth Century*, pp. 131–5; Cullen, *Anglo-Irish Trade*, pp. 106–18.
[68] Davis, 'English foreign trade, 1660–1700', which incorporates Davis's estimated figure for outport woollen exports of £700,000 for 1663/9; 'English Foreign Trade, 1700–1774'; Schumpeter, *English Overseas Trade Statistics*, tables XII and XIII.
[69] Thirsk & Cooper, *Seventeenth-Century Economic Documents*, p. 304.
[70] Davis, 'English Foreign Trade, 1700–1774', p. 93.

Table 10.3 *Annual average percentage rate of growth of English exports,*
1660s–1770s

	re-exports	domestic exports	woollens (Davis)	woollens (Schumpeter)
1663 and 1669 to 1699–1701*	3.53	1.15	1.11	1.11
1699–1701 to 1722–4	1.61	0.61	−0.08	0.84
1722–4 to 1752–4	0.97	2.23	1.05	1.09
1752–4 to 1772–4	3.35	0.85	0.32	0.43

Sources: Davis, 'English Foreign Trade, 1660–1700', 'English Foreign Trade, 1700–1774',
Schumpeter, *English Overseas Trade Statistics*, Tables XII and XIII.
* London only.

Adventurers' monopoly in 1689, Dutch, Huguenot, German and other
foreign merchants moved into the export trade in English woollens. By
1695, foreign capital tied up in the nearby European trades accounted for
over £300,000, or nearly one-third of England's total domestic exports.[71]
In arriving at this estimate, D. W. Jones identified thirty-four substantial
alien merchants exporting goods worth more than £500. The majority, indeed, exported much more valuable consignments, with eight merchants
accounting for shipments worth over £10,000. The commercial life of
London thus became the province of a truly international community of
merchants, in the wake of the deregulation.

During the War of the Spanish Succession, woollen exports to Holland
experienced extraordinary boom conditions, which the aggregate figures
in Table 10.3 conceal. Exchange depreciation and the disruption of the
Leiden textile industries created exceptionally favourable export opportunities which the new 'free traders' were well placed to exploit. Unsurprisingly, this temporary state of affairs ended in 1711–12, and woollen
shipments to Holland and Germany slowly declined to a low point in the
1720s. Re-export growth, however, provided a major element of compensation. Sales of colonial and Asian goods in Europe mounted steadily
during the four decades from *c.* 1690 to 1728, when a peak value of £1.4
millions was reached for re-exports to Holland (see Appendix 6). A high
proportion of these re-export sales was financed on Dutch accounts and,
in spite of disappointing results, Dutch merchants continued to invest in
these two major branches of English overseas trade for some time.

By the early 1730s, however, the Dutch market for re-exports of groceries and Asian textiles reached a state of collapse, while sales of English

[71] Jones, *War and Economy*, p. 256 and Tables 8.3 and 8.4; Chapman, *Merchant Enterprise
in Britain*, pp. 29–35.

woollens revived.[72] If anything, the Inspector General's official values disguise the falling real value of re-exports: prices for sugar and tobacco declined sharply after 1713, while those of tea and Asian textiles stagnated during the 1720s. With the exception of Glamann, historians have barely noticed the re-export crisis of the 1730s and its serious repercussions on the Dutch staplemarket.[73] Several causes contributed to the decline of Holland as the principal market for English re-exports. To the declining quality of the VOC's textile imports was added competition from the English East India Company, especially in Chinese silks and teas, as well as the disintegrating Ostend Company, its Danish and Swedish successors, and the French Compagnie des Indes, whose combined activities generated an unsustainable boom. Prices on the Amsterdam market collapsed in 1729–30, particularly for Asian textiles, tea and other groceries. The complaints of English merchants in Amsterdam multiplied: of India goods, 'there is too much in Europe and cannot be consumed', or of tea, 'everybody is for getting out as fast as they can'. By 1735, the Rotterdam merchant Sir Jacob Senserf confessed: 'we seldom encourage our friends to engage in any commodity because we daily finde by experience how little there is to be depended upon'.[74] English merchants and their Dutch associates gradually abandoned the re-export of Asian and colonial goods to Holland, hitherto their chief market, in favour of Hamburg. More importantly, some began to move into the growing export markets of the American mainland colonies and the West Indies. From mid-century, Anglo-American trade entered a prolonged period of export-led growth, which sharply accelerated from the later 1770s.[75]

The active involvement of foreign merchants and a major influx of Dutch capital into English trade with nearby Europe had major consequences for commercial expansion. Most obviously, it released resources for deployment elsewhere, and it permitted English merchants to

---

[72] Schumpeter, *English Overseas Trade Statistics*, Tables XXXVI, XXXVIII, XLIV (bays and stuffs).

[73] Glamann, *Dutch-Asiatic Trade*, pp. 149–51, 228–30.

[74] PRO C103/131, D. Smith, Amsterdam, to Thomas Hall, London, 31 March 1730; C103/131, C. Pike, Amsterdam, to Thomas Hall, London, 8 May 1731; C103/133, J. Senserf and Son, Rotterdam, to Thomas Hall, London, 23 September 1735. See above, chapter 6, pp. 195–7.

[75] S. D. Smith, 'The Market for Manufactures', pp. 676–708; S. D. Smith, 'British Exports to Continental North America', unpublished, University of Cambridge Ph.D. thesis, 1992; B. Thomas, 'The First Atlantic Economy, 1700–60', in B. Thomas, *The Industrial Revolution*; P. K. O'Brien and S. Engerman, 'Exports and the Growth of the British Economy from the Glorious Revolution to the Peace of Amiens', in B. L. Solow, *Slavery and the Rise of the Atlantic System*, Cambridge, 1991; K. Morgan, 'Business Networks in the British Export Trade to North America, 1750–1800', in Morgan & McCusker (eds.), *The Early Modern Atlantic Economy*, 2000.

withdraw from active trade into commission business. Shortly after the ending of the Merchant Adventurers' monopoly, former company members claimed that the remaining trade was 'too small for their capitals'. By 1693, several had been 'forced to launch out into other trades'.[76] Over the next half-century, British merchants gradually abandoned their role as independent entrepreneurs in all branches of overseas trade with regions which contained strong indigenous merchant groups. Increasingly, they operated as commission agents, providing financial, shipping and commercial services for overseas producers and merchants. This new pattern extended from England's trade with Holland and Germany to Anglo-Scandinavian and Baltic trade, excluding Russia. In an important synthesis of new and older research, R. C. Nash has shown how similar processes were at work within Anglo-American commerce. In their dealings with the northern colonies in New England, New York and Pennsylvania, with the West Indies, and to a lesser extent with the Chesapeake, British merchants took on the role of commission agents handling colonial imports for the account and risk of indigenous American merchants and producers. In return, British manufactured goods were exported on colonial accounts, together with British shipping, financial and commercial services. It was indigenous Boston merchants who first emerged as independent traders in the mid seventeenth century, followed by the West Indian and richer Chesapeake planters. By *c.* 1720, New York and Philadelphia merchant groups had escaped from Boston's dominance and began to seize control of their trades from British merchants resident in London. A number of exceptions existed to this general move towards commission trade: the slave trade, the tobacco trade of the lesser Chesapeake planters, the rice exports of South Carolina, and London's shipping services were all organised on the account of British merchants, using either local or British agents.[77] But the general picture sketched out in 1759 by Joseph Massie remains true: that merchants of the mother country were now reduced to the role of servants of the colonists.[78]

---

[76] Anon., 'Reasons humbly offered', 1693, p. 3 (Goldsmiths Library, no. 2968).

[77] I am much indebted to Dr R. C. Nash for supplying a typescript copy of his 1999 conference paper on 'The Organisation of Trade and Finance in the British Atlantic Economy, 1600–1830', on which this paragraph is based, together with a reading of the same author's 1982 Cambridge Ph.D. thesis, 'English Transatlantic Trade, 1660–1730: a Quantitative Study'. See also J. M. Price, *Overseas Trade and Traders. Essays on Some Commercial, Financial and Political Challenges Facing British Atlantic Merchants, 1660–1775*, 1996; J. M. Price & P. G. E. Clemens, 'A Revolution of Scale in Overseas Trade: British Firms in the Chesapeake Trade, 1675–1775', *JEH*, 47 (1987); McCusker, *Essays in the Economic History of the Atlantic World*.

[78] For an alternative view, see D. Hancock, *Citizens of the World. London Merchants and the Integration of the British Atlantic Community, 1735–85*, Cambridge, 1995, pp. 130–1.

The restructuring and refinancing of the North Sea economy undoubtedly facilitated the expansion of British transatlantic trade during the
century after 1670. During the early stages of the commercial revolution, as Davis emphasised, the amount of capital needed for carrying on
trade grew much faster than the value of trade itself.[79] As Dutch and
other foreign merchant capital flowed into the old-established channels
of Anglo-European commerce, British merchants operating as commission agents found it easier to redirect their energies and limited capital resources towards the Atlantic periphery. After the conclusion of the
Anglo-Dutch wars, the main growth area of Anglo-European trade lay
in re-exports, and the Navigation Acts provided English merchants with
the leverage necessary to operate as the principal intermediaries between
colonial markets, the mother country and continental Europe. As we
have already noticed, England's traditional nearby European trades had
become highly specialised by the late seventeenth century. The influx
of Dutch, Huguenot and other foreign merchants into London, ready
to exploit their established international connections, increased this tendency, while the growing abundance of bills of exchange in the later
seventeenth century encouraged merchants to operate as either specialist
exporters or importers.[80] Commission trade in general, however, was a
more flexible, low-risk option than trade on one's own account, and the
handling of colonial and Asian goods for the re-export market was generally a less specialised affair than exporting or importing. Participation
in transatlantic trade on a commission basis was, therefore, an attractive
field for those merchants wishing to diversify their interests, particularly
for those with strong interests in shipowning. Several shifted the balance
of their interests from Europe to North America, particularly after the
London–Amsterdam re-export crisis of the 1730s.

A well-documented case is that of the London broker Henry Gambier,
who sent piece goods, tea and coffee to Amsterdam on his own account,
and also made purchases at the East India Company's sales on behalf of
Dutch and Huguenot firms established in London, including Mattheus
and John de Neufville, Francis and John van Hemert, and Riou and
Guinard, as well as for Amsterdam merchants. At some stage before
1720, Gambier extended his interests to include the North American re-
export market, sending consignments of tea, chinaware and Asian textiles
to South Carolina, in return for rice.[81] A proportion of these rice cargoes
was consigned and re-exported to his Dutch correspondents, excluded

[79] Davis, *A Commercial Revolution*, p. 12.   [80] Jones, *War and Economy*, pp. 260, 272.
[81] PRO C108/132, Letters to Henry Gambier. Gambier dealt mainly with Lester Clarkson
and Isaac and Willem Kops in Amsterdam, and also supplied provincial English grocers
with tea and coffee.

by the Navigation Acts from direct participation in Carolina's expanding export trade.[82] Gambier was fortunate to have at his disposal the *Carolina Galley* which he jointly owned and operated with his brother-in-law, John Smyter, who acted as master. His principal American trading contacts were with fellow Huguenots in Charleston.

Other prominent merchants active in the Dutch and North Sea trades who shifted their interests towards transatlantic ventures included Robert Hackshaw; Isaac, William and Daniel Minet; Ralph Carr; Thomas Hall; Henry Hope; and George Aufrère.[83] In the 1690s, Robert Hackshaw was a major exporter to Germany, the Low Countries, southern Europe, New England and Barbados, with total assets of £24,000 at his death. By the early 1720s, he was specialising almost wholly in commission trade for New York and New England merchants. The Minet brothers, whose banking and shipping agency business was established in London and Dover during the early 1690s, followed a similar course. In its early days, the house was heavily involved in the grain export and wine import trades with Holland and France but in 1723 turned to the colonial transit trade, which offered 'greater business and credit than ever before'. Like many others, the firm was ready to exploit the opportunities created by the Navigation Acts. The trade was described by William Minet in the 1750s as drawing 'the New York, Philadelphia, Rhode Island and Carolina ships to clear at Dover, land their goods, reship [them] for Holland and Hamboro' which was a good profit'. Fresh cargoes of tea, groceries and provisions were loaded, and the trade 'drew great numbers of ships from 25 to 41' by 1730–1.[84] At a later date, the Newcastle merchant Ralph Carr was involved in similar operations, helping to facilitate and legalise the trade of his Amsterdam correspondents with New York and New England. By completing the cargoes of westward-bound vessels with coal, glass and grindstones, Carr was able to develop a lively triangular

---

[82] C108/132, L. Clarkson, Amsterdam, to Henry Gambier, London, 5 October 1728. On rice re-exports to Holland, see R. C. Nash, 'South Carolina and the Atlantic Economy', *EcHR*, 45 (1992), p. 687.

[83] On Thomas Hall, see C. Gill, *Merchants and Mariners of the Eighteenth Century*, 1961, and his correspondence with J. Senserf and Son of Rotterdam, in PRO C103/132; for Ralph Carr, see W. L. Roberts, 'Ralph Carr: A Newcastle Merchant and the American Colonial Trade', *Business History Review*, 42 (1968), and chapter 8 above; for Robert Hackshaw, see Jones, *War and Economy*, pp. 265, 280; for Henry Hope, see Buist, *Hope & Co.*, pp. 11–12; for William and Isaac Minet, see W. Minet, *Some Account of the Huguenot Family of Minet*, privately printed, 1892, pp. 127–39; for George Aufrère, see Hancock, *Citizens of the World*, pp. 74–5, 107.

[84] Minet, *Family of Minet*, pp. 127–39; W. Minet, 'Extracts from the Letter-book of a Dover Merchant, 1737-1741', *Archaeologia Cantiana*, 32 (1917), pp. 247–81; C. Matson, 'Minet and Fector of Dover', *Archaeologia Cantiana*, 81 (1966), pp. 39–43; Brants 1335, Letters to J. I. de Neufville, Amsterdam, 1755.

trade. Although unsuccessful in promoting the export of northern textiles to New York, he exported 'large quantities' of Leeds cloths, Halifax
worsteds and Scottish Osnaburghs to Boston in exchange for Carolina tar,
whale oil, dyewoods, mahogany and barrel staves. This extensive colonial
trade compensated for declining opportunities in the grain export trade
to Holland during the 1750s, in which Carr had been deeply involved.
His American business was conducted entirely on a commission basis,
and by charging a standard rate of $2\frac{1}{2}\%$, he was able to earn sums ranging from £25 to £250 for each transaction, which could easily exceed the
profits earned in consignment trade.[85]

Aside from their role as commission traders, many of those who shifted
or extended their dealings from Holland and nearby Europe across the
Atlantic had a common interest in the provision of shipping services.
Gambier and Smyter, the Minet brothers and Ralph Carr were all
shipowners, as was Thomas Hall, one of several merchants to disengage
from the London–Amsterdam re-export trade in the 1730s when prices
collapsed. Hall moved back into shipping management and, in a series of
temporary partnerships with John Pinnell, committed himself to the West
India and Guinea trades. Jasper Waters, also a casualty of the Amsterdam
re-export crisis, followed a similar course. The Rotterdam firm inherited
by Henry Hope in the 1720s had originally concentrated on Anglo-Dutch
business, especially the grain trade to which the firm committed several
vessels. But in 1730, Henry emigrated to Boston and developed an extensive illegal triangular trade between New England, the West Indies and
Holland, in correspondence with his brothers established in Amsterdam
and Rotterdam. By the 1740s, the Rotterdam house, managed by Isaac
and Zachary Hope, specialised in the conveyance of emigrants to North
America.[86] The Amsterdam house of de Neufville also became involved
in transatlantic shipping business, with three vessels committed to the
West India trade at the time of the firm's collapse in 1763.[87]

As we have seen, British merchants and shipowners were quick to take
advantage of the opportunities provided by the Navigation Acts for facilitating Dutch trade with the American mainland colonies from the
1660s. The strengthening of the machinery of enforcement during the
1690s served merely to reinforce the intermediary position of British
merchants, shippers and commission agents, such as Gambier, Carr and
the Minet brothers.[88] The large and influential British community in
Rotterdam played a major role in obtaining British shipping for Dutch

[85] Roberts, 'Ralph Carr', pp. 271 87.   [86] Buist, *Hope & Co.*, pp. 11, 543.
[87] De Jong-Keesing, *Economische Crisis*, pp. 99 100.
[88] McCusker & Menard, *Economy of British America*, p. 49.

principals, and the Amsterdam notarial archives also suggest a similar dependence amongst Amsterdam merchants for the first four decades of the eighteenth century. Illegal direct trade between British America and the Dutch ports persisted, but the notaries more commonly recorded details of what had evidently become a formalised transit system through London or ports of convenience such as Cowes and Portsmouth. In contrast with the position before the new Navigation Act of 1696, the eighteenth-century evidence indicates that the vessels and masters involved were entirely British.[89]

It is clear, then, that the main thrust of British protectionist policy affected Dutch commercial activity at two interconnected levels. In the first place, the Navigation Acts stimulated British transatlantic trade and shipping. Although they failed to eliminate Dutch participation in the Atlantic economy in the later seventeenth century, they placed the Dutch in a subordinate role, dependent on British commercial networks. Secondly, the navigation code, combined with the rising level of import duties, greatly reduced the volume of European imports received via Holland, whether these originated in Germany or northern Europe and the Baltic. The response of the Dutch merchant was to assume a greater degree of risk by financing a higher proportion of a relatively stagnant volume of Anglo-Dutch trade – which of course still remained the most valuable branch of English foreign trade during the first half of the eighteenth century. This, in turn, facilitated the further expansion of the British Atlantic economy by freeing credit and capital resources for employment in colonial commerce, especially on a commission basis.

---

[89] GAA NA5874/374, NA6110A, NA8569 (Isle of Wight); NA6159/348 (Portsmouth); NA10232/316 (Glasgow).

11 Conclusion. Commercial growth and the divergence of England

The divergence of England during the late seventeenth and eighteenth centuries is an inescapable fact of European economic history, as striking as the meteoric rise and slow decline of the Netherlands. If England's gross national product per head was roughly similar to the rest of continental Europe in 1550, reliable estimates suggest that it was three times the continental level by 1820. The figure is even more impressive when set against England's untypically rapid rate of population growth during the same period. While the population of Europe minus England multiplied by about 80%, that of England grew by around 280%.[1]

The language of 'rise and decline', however, obscures important regional discontinuities and suggests that economic growth and change resembles a relay race. It is, of course, the world-economy which develops over time, as adjustments occur within and between its sub-units, however described. Neither the Dutch economic miracle nor England's divergence can be fully understood as 'national' exceptions to a European norm, to be explained primarily in terms of comparative resource endowments. Europe in 1700 was not yet a world of fully formed nation states, indeed the English themselves only became conscious of their identity as a trading nation during the recoinage debates of the 1690s.[2] Despite appearances, the labels invented by the Inspector General of Imports and Exports in 1696 – 'Germany', 'Italy', 'Turkey' and so on – described a commercial world of extremely diverse political structures, ranging from free imperial cities, provinces, centralised states and sprawling political empires, to crown colonies and plantations. England's commerce with the Far East, the core of Gundar Frank's 'real' world-economy, was subsumed under the label 'East Indies'. The Inspector General's purpose, of course, was to identify a taxonomy of beneficial and damaging trades, reminding us that mercantilist practice and coercion entered into the

---

[1] E. A. Wrigley, 'The Divergence of England: The Growth of the English Economy in the Seventeenth and Eighteenth Centuries', *TRHS*, 6th ser., 10 (2000), pp. 117–41.
[2] Kwarteng, 'Recoinage Crisis', ch. 4.

equation in a host of ways which modified the direction of 'Smithian' or market-led growth. Nevertheless, classical and neo-classical paradigms continue to exercise a powerful influence over economic historians. World systems theory provides a challenging alternative, but it too inclines towards a one-dimensional reading of exchange relationships, insisting on the universality of unequal exchange as the engine of growth and under-development.

Braudel's account of the rise of the European world-economy proposes an alternative frame of reference to simple neo-classical growth models, but at the same time accommodates the possibility of *interdependent* growth. The Braudellian 'divisions of space and time' are well known, the latter following alternate phases of growth and contraction within long cycles of historical time. Spatially defined phenomena, including cities, states, regions and world-economies provide its main source of explanation, and the power relations between them shape patterns of change within the world system as a whole. As well as political power and co-ercion, the 'weapons of domination' included shipping, trade, industry and credit.[3] These two dimensions, the spatial and the jurisdictional (the sphere within which power and coercion are exercised), provide a useful matrix for summarising the patterns of commercial growth and decline which we have traced in the foregoing chapters, as Europe's centre of gravity shifted from the Dutch Republic to England.

In spatial terms, Braudel emphasises the bi-polarity of the emerging European economy, and its tendency during periods of crisis to fragment into its regional components, the two great circuits of trade centring on the Mediterranean and on the North and Baltic Seas. By 1600, Europe's economic centre of gravity had shifted permanently to the north, princi-pally to Amsterdam. As the world economy began to contract during the early seventeenth century, there was no return, or partial return, of vi-tality to the Mediterranean, and, indeed, large areas of western Europe's principal markets in south Germany, France and the Southern Nether-lands suffered serious decline. The north-western European littoral was the only region able to escape from prolonged economic stagnation; and from 1650, even Amsterdam's rapidly rising population began to level off, while that of London, already nearly twice as large as Amsterdam, continued its inexorable rise. With the exception of the luxury goods industries, the dynamism had disappeared from Europe's late medieval 'poly-nuclear' urban system.[4] The core of the European world-economy was now firmly established in the North Sea zone, a complete regional

---

[3] Braudel, *Perspective of the World*, p. 35.
[4] Israel, *Dutch Primacy*, pp. 4–6; S. Ciriacono, 'The Venetian Economy and its Place in the World Economy of the Seventeenth and Eighteenth Centuries. A Comparison with

system in itself, with its own peripheral and semi-peripheral areas in the Baltic and eastern Europe.

The divergence of England, therefore, must be placed in its regional context, one of growing dominance within the North Sea economy. The steady rise in English per capita output during the seventeenth and eighteenth centuries was undoubtedly sustained by a substantial rise in agricultural productivity, which Wrigley describes as involving an 'intensification rather than an extensification of her territory'. Intensification, however, was not an undifferentiated process, spread uniformly throughout the British Isles. Wrigley leaves Ireland and Scotland out of the account, although their inclusion would bring the available estimates for Britain, France and the Netherlands into a much narrower range.[5] During the century before 1750, growth was concentrated in the southern and eastern parts of England, especially London and the home counties, all of which depended on important markets in the Low Countries and nearby Europe. The slow assimilation of waves of protestant migrants moving in both directions across the North Sea generated dense social networks amongst generations of merchants and artisans, and the Anglo-Dutch communities of Rotterdam and London handled an enormous traffic in goods, money and information.[6] Significantly, England and Holland maintained no permanent consular service in each other's ports during the seventeenth and early eighteenth centuries. The British in Rotterdam regarded consular assistance as 'altogether as unnecessary and superfluous as it would be in the City of London'. In 1697, Pollexfen described Holland as a virtual extension of the home market: 'Holland being so near us, the trade between us is like our home trade from one town to another.'[7]

Economic interdependence of this kind implies that English growth and Dutch decline cannot be discussed in isolation, and that the interactions between commercial cities formed the real basis for inter-national economic relations in the age of mercantilism.[8] As Charles Wilson showed so persuasively, England's 'apprenticeship' to the Dutch Republic in the seventeenth century produced a point of convergence between the two

the Low Countries', in H.-J. Nitz (ed.), *The Early-Modern World-System in Geographical Perspective*, Stuttgart, 1973, pp. 127–8. For an alternative view, see P. Musgrave, *The Early Modern European Economy*, 1999, ch. 5.

[5] Wrigley, 'Divergence of England', pp. 118–19, and n. 6.

[6] See above, chapter 3, pp. 89–99.

[7] J. Pollexfen, *A Discourse of Trade, Coyn, and Paper Credit*, 1697, p. 87; PRO CO388/6–A5, Copy of a Petition of English Merchants . . . in Rotterdam, 1690; V. Barbour, 'The Consular Service in the Reign of Charles II', *American Historical Review*, 33 (1928), pp. 574–5.

[8] P. K. O'Brien, 'Reflections and Meditations on Antwerp, Amsterdam and London in their Golden Ages', in O'Brien, *Urban Achievement in Early Modern Europe*, 2001, pp. 7–8.

economies around 1700.[9] Wilson and Braudel were mistaken, however, in supposing that the Dutch commercial system in Europe survived intact up to 1730. Dutch economic decline began much earlier than Wilson realised, and it is now clear that the Navigation Acts and English protectionist policies helped to secure English commercial hegemony within the North Sea and beyond by the opening of the War of the Spanish Succession. The slow decline of Amsterdam, however, was not followed in linear fashion by the rise of London, for the years from *c.* 1690 to 1730 saw a diffusion of the entrepôt system between London, Hamburg and Amsterdam. Hamburg soon became 'the continent's most English city', as the formerly predominant Dutch merchant community dwindled in size and influence, representing a reversal of the earlier pattern in which Dutch merchants settled in most of Europe's major trading centres.[10] London was the exception to this tendency in that it continued to attract Dutch merchants and brokers well into the eighteenth century. Dispersal of entrepôt trading, as Faber has explained, was a function of the diversification of northern European trade as old Baltic staples declined, especially the east–west trade in grain, supplemented by timber, iron, copper and naval stores. In the opposite direction, textiles and colonial goods moved alongside cargoes of salt, herring and wine. Population growth and rising per capita incomes helped to increase the demand for many of these commodities.[11]

It was the mercantilist state which decisively shifted the balance of power and influence towards London, through the creation of a *national* entrepôt within an imperial trading network. London's unique position in the English urban hierarchy contrasted with that of Amsterdam, which never developed into a multifunctional metropolis. London drew on the productive capacities and consumer demands of a large internal market, together with those of an enormous population within its own expanding boundaries. Braudel rightly emphasised the benefits which London drew from its hinterland, that of an integrated national economy drawing on its own surplus food and energy supplies, and exaggerated only a little when he wrote, 'the entire economy of England was ruled from London'.[12] Holland's immediate hinterland was one of provinces and principalities in the Low Countries and Germany, and its industrial base was sustained by processing rather than by primary production and manufacture. Beneath the advantages conferred on England by geography and location, however, lay the hand of a strong, centralised state, supporting and

[9] C. H. Wilson, *England's Apprenticeship*, pp. 359–77.
[10] M. North, 'Hamburg: "The Continent's most English city" ', in M. North (ed.), *From the North Sea to the Baltic*, Aldershot, 1996, p. VI–1.
[11] Faber, 'Structural Changes', pp. 92–3.   [12] Braudel, *Perspective of the World*, p. 365.

extending London's dominance within and beyond the North Sea entrepôt system. The Republic, in contrast to Britain, 'lacked the kind of clear and unambiguous political co-ordination that came from unified and uncontested territorial sovereignty'.[13]

During the earlier decades of the seventeenth century, Anglo-Dutch commercial disputes generally involved localised issues, such as restraints on the dyeing and finishing of English woollens in Holland, the privileges of the Merchant Adventurers, and the North Sea fisheries. It was not until mid-century that more challenging problems emerged, involving control of the North Sea, Baltic and colonial carrying trades, when Dutch competition revived after the conflict with Spain ended in 1647–8.[14] Cromwell's Navigation Act of 1650 marked the beginning of a drive to emancipate the nation's commerce from dependence on the Dutch staplemarket. Its successor of 1660 prohibited the indirect supply of Baltic goods and was largely effective in eliminating Amsterdam's role as a Baltic entrepôt for England, evident from the 1670s. Whereas Dutch shipping entering the Sound outnumbered English vessels by 13:1 during the first half of the seventeenth century, the ratio fell to 4:1 for the period 1661–1700.[15] The Act of 1663, however, placed an increased emphasis on colonial trade, and, by the time of the Second Dutch War which came in its wake, the theatre of naval operations had expanded to include the West Indies and New Netherland. Anglo-Dutch rivalry entered a new phase in the 1660s, which marked the beginning of the end of a significant Dutch presence in the trading world of the North Atlantic. The 1650s saw buoyant trade between Holland and its colonial territories on the North American mainland, the Caribbean and the Wild Coast, as well as a vigorous intercolonial trade. Although the latter continued after the new Navigation Acts of the 1660s and the taking of New Amsterdam, Dutch trade across the North Atlantic dwindled to low levels thereafter as Dutch merchants found themselves dependent on British commercial networks. With the loss of Brazil in 1654, Dutch Atlantic merchants turned increasingly to the West African slave trade between Guinea, Curaçao and Surinam.

The Europeanisation of America and its incorporation into the world economy marks one of the great discontinuities in global history, and it was England's role to complete what the older colonial powers had initiated. For the Dutch, the Americas were always secondary to Asia, the core of the real global economy, and, from the 1650s if not earlier, the

[13] Epstein, *Freedom and Growth*, p. 34.
[14] Israel, *Dutch Primacy*, p. 197. While the English were distracted by civil war during the 1640s, the Dutch gained a strong foothold in the tobacco and sugar trades, and the colonies showed unwelcome signs of independence from the mother country.
[15] Harper, *English Navigation Laws*, p. 316.

West India Company was unable to integrate the different regional components of its Atlantic system.[16] Compared with England, the Republic had no need for an imperial hinterland: as a continental nation, its overland European trade was already international, and religious toleration generated few pressures to emigrate. Indeed, this was a society which easily absorbed migrant labour, with little or no 'surplus population'. England's maritime imperial policy during the century after 1650 was also based on the drive to expand trade rather than to acquire territory, but she was a much less reluctant colonising nation than the Republic. Dutch merchants in America, as in Asia, preferred an intermediary role, providing shipping, financial and commercial services to other nations, and, in the long run, this made them highly vulnerable to the protectionist policies of other countries.[17]

There can be no doubt that the divergence of England during the eighteenth century was closely connected with the expansion of the Atlantic economy, a dimension largely neglected in Wrigley's model of endogenous growth, or 'intensification'. In the age of the sailing ship, transatlantic commerce was an energy-efficient means of conducting long-distance trade and one which initiated an expansive process of 'Smithian' growth. English manufactures found a growing market in the West Indies and North America, accounting for up to 40% of incremental industrial production from 1697 to 1760.[18] Expansion was even more rapid after mid-century, when population growth surged forward. To some extent, these were captive markets, dependent on home supplies. But colonial purchasing power was largely determined by Britain's capacity to absorb staple goods, and, within the closed circuit of imperial trade, by the success of British merchants in maintaining a buoyant re-export trade to Holland, Germany and northern Europe in sugar, tobacco, rice and other colonial produce. Fundamentally, the dynamism of the Atlantic economy rested on British control of the North Sea entrepôt system, together with its Baltic periphery which supplied essential shipbuilding materials. French competition intensified after the peace of 1713, particularly in the sugar and coffee trades, but American markets for French manufactures remained sluggish. The key to British success in the

[16] P. C. Emmer, 'The Economic Impact of the Dutch Expansion Overseas, 1570–1870', in P. K. O'Brien & L. Prados de la Escosura (eds.), *The Costs and Benefits of European Imperialism, Revista de Historia Económica*, 16 (1998), pp. 171–2; Emmer, 'The West India Company, 1621–1791: Dutch or Atlantic?', in Blussé & Gaastra (eds.), *Companies and Trade*, pp. 83–4.

[17] P. K. O'Brien, 'Mercantilism and Imperialism in the Rise and Decline of the Dutch and British Economies, 1585–1815', *De Economist*, 148 (2000), pp. 471–2; R. T. Griffiths, *Industrial Retardation in the Netherlands*, The Hague, 1979, p. 35.

[18] O'Brien & Engerman, 'Exports and the Growth of the British Economy', pp. 187–9.

Atlantic trades was its integrated, systemic character, and the navigation code helped to achieve this.[19]

The costs and benefits of maintaining an imperial system continue to be debated, although it must be admitted that modern critics of empire have often resorted to highly unrealistic counterfactual propositions involving perfect competition, full employment, an absence of international conflict, and virtually unlimited domestic purchasing power.[20] A simpler and more realistic counterfactual scenario might involve an Atlantic economy managed by a protestant Anglo-Dutch commercial network, without mercantilist controls, in which Dutch investors gave greater priority to colonial settlement. Statistical modelling would doubtless confirm the availability of private capital for such a project, but would underline the enormous public costs falling on the Dutch state, which in 1672 was unable to defend itself against French aggression on the European mainland. By the early eighteenth century, the Republic had reached its natural tax ceiling, and per capita tax levels were almost twice as high as Britain's.[21] In reality, the limits to growth in the premodern period were determined by geopolitics: by state power and the extent of naval protection available for merchant shipping in distant waters. In Britain's case, naval power protected commerce and also provided a front line of national defence. As a systematic policy, the 'blue-water strategy' was based on a *quid pro quo*: 'the state needed an expanding commerce as a source of customs revenue, sailors and privateers, while merchants and colonists accepted regulation and taxation as the price paid for naval protection and access to a large imperial trading zone'.[22] O'Brien reminds us that, before the publication of *The Wealth of Nations*, contemporaries failed to entertain, let alone adopt, an alternative programme.[23]

The strategy behind the Navigation Acts was in the first instance designed to undermine the Republic's European entrepôt trade in the North Sea and the Baltic, for it was here that the greatest volume of English

[19] J. de Vries, *The Economy of Europe in an Age of Crisis, 1600–1750*, Cambridge, 1976, pp. 128–46; E. J. Hobsbawm, 'The General Crisis of the Seventeenth Century', *PP*, 5 & 6 (1954), repr. in T. Aston, *Crisis in Europe, 1560–1660*, 1965, pp. 50–3; B. Thomas, *The Industrial Revolution*, pp. 34–59; S. D. Smith, 'British Exports to Colonial North America and the Mercantilist Fallacy', *Business History*, 37 (1995), pp. 45–63.

[20] P. K. O'Brien, 'Inseparable Connections: Trade, Economy, Fiscal State, and the Expansion of Empire, 1688–1815', in P. J. Marshall (ed.), *The Oxford History of the British Empire*, vol. II, *The Eighteenth Century*, Oxford, 1998, p. 75; S. Engerman, 'British Imperialism in a Mercantilist Age, 1492–1849', in O'Brien & Prados de la Escosura (eds.), *Costs and Benefits*, pp. 213–16.

[21] See above, chapter 1, pp. 22–4.

[22] D. Baugh, 'Maritime Strength and Atlantic Commerce', in L. Stone, *An Imperial State at War: Britain from 1689–1815*, 1994, pp. 185, 193; Jones, *War and Economy*, p. 51.

[23] O'Brien, 'Mercantilism and Imperialism', p. 475.

shipping was deployed during the most intense period of Anglo-Dutch competition, the 1650s and '60s.[24] Control of the colonial economy was incidental to the Acts' main purpose of securing national control of England's entrepôt trade, including the disposal of colonial re-exports in the markets of northern and north-western Europe. The changing commodity composition of Dutch-Baltic trade after 1660 made Dutch shipping much more vulnerable to these objectives. Falling European demand for Baltic grain in the 1660s and '70s was matched by a general shift towards the richer trades of the Baltic region, including timber, colonial re-exports, iron and textiles, where the Dutch lost heavily to the English. The situation deteriorated further during the first half of the eighteenth century, when the size of Dutch vessels was reduced as the proportion of bulk cargoes declined. In addition to the damaging effects of the Navigation Acts, the Dutch now faced the consequences of England's new policy of agricultural protectionism, embodied in the Corn Laws. From 1689 until the 1760s, a system of subsidised export enabled English shippers to replace the Dutch as the carriers of Europe's surplus grain – with the essential difference that their cargoes were produced at home. By 1713, England dominated the Baltic and North Sea carrying trades, to the extent that Dutch merchants were now chartering British vessels to move their own bulk cargoes.

England's mercantilist response to Dutch competition was thus born out of weakness, and the integration of its Atlantic possessions with northern European markets was initially a slow and somewhat marginal process. Dutch merchants were reluctant to accept their virtual exclusion from the North Atlantic carrying trades alongside the sustained onslaught against their formerly dominant position in the North Sea – Baltic region. The Glorious Revolution encouraged the merchants of Amsterdam to press for the repeal of the Navigation Acts and a reduction of English tariffs. William, however, was not prepared to consider this, and the States General were unwilling to endanger negotiations for an alliance by linking these with demands for a new commercial treaty.[25] English restrictions, however, applied to trade and navigation rather than finance – to the nationality of ships, crews and ports of entry. With declining investment opportunities at home and excluded from participation in the Atlantic trading system, Dutch investors turned their attention to the English commercial metropolis. During the 1690s, Dutch merchant

---

[24] See above, chapter 9, pp. 277–8.
[25] Clark, *Dutch Alliance*, pp. 24–8, 135–8. Four treaties were concluded in 1689, for the union of the fleets, the alliance, the recapture of prizes and the prohibition of commerce with France. In fact the Navigation Acts were relaxed during the 1690s in relation to the import of naval stores from the Baltic in foreign vessels, and the manning of ships.

capital poured into London, alongside increasing flows of foreign investment in the English national debt from 1694. The first branch of commodity trade to benefit was the de-regulated woollen trade. During the first half of the eighteenth century, English merchants reduced their commitment to the nearby European trades, and Dutch capital also moved into the English re-export trade to Holland and the Anglo-Dutch linen trade. In general, wholesale merchants came to occupy a much reduced role in the trade with nearby Europe, and the shift of financial responsibility to continental buyers enabled English woollen manufacturers to trade directly with their customers. In the coal export trade too, there is some evidence that direct orders from Holland came to play an increasing role.

The restructuring of the North Sea economy, however, was something more than a merely local or regional phenomenon, since the movement of Dutch commercial capital to London played a critical role in releasing resources for the expansion of England's Atlantic economy. In organisational terms, there was clearly a functional relationship between the refinancing of the North Sea trade and the 'Atlanticisation' of English trade, evident most obviously in the shift towards commission trade in both Anglo-European *and* Anglo-American commerce. As we have seen, protectionist controls and rising import duties underlay the shift to commission business in the trade with nearby Europe. In the case of Anglo-American trade, it was the build-up of indigenous American trading capital which reduced English merchants to the status of commission agents.[26] Although the underlying circumstances were different in each case, commission trade reduced risks for English merchants and facilitated the redeployment of capital and merchant enterprise from nearby Europe to long-distance trade and the New World, and from older patterns of commodity exchange into the disposal of re-exports in Europe. In its early days, the commission system did not involve the advance of substantial capital sums to colonial merchants and planters, either in the West Indies, the Chesapeake, or New England. During the 'middle years' of the colonial period, the provision of short-term credit and shipping services was more usual. From the early 1730s, however, there was a huge increase in the outflow of commercial capital from England to each of these regions.[27] In the long term, it seems that the commission system 'supplied far more capital to the colonies than independent traders had ever done'.[28]

These changes, which involved a transformation of the spatial and organisational parameters of English commerce, may be appropriately

---

[26] See above, chapter 10, p. 329.
[27] Nash, 'Organisation of Trade and Finance', pp. 23–45.   [28] Ibid., p. 23.

understood in terms of Smithian growth: of market-led growth associated with the exploitation of American markets and sources of supply, which released northern Europe from a regime of diminishing returns. Although Adam Smith denounced the machinations of the mercantilist state, there is at least one respect in which it behaved with an authentically Smithian logic. It was precisely the parliamentary attack on corporate monopolies and regulated trading from 1689 which facilitated the influx of foreign capital and merchant enterprise into England and released resources for Atlantic expansion. After several decades of instability and 'interloping', the Merchant Adventurers' monopoly in the Netherlands was wound up in 1689, and privileged access to the Republic's mart towns formally ended. 'Deregulation' – the replacement of a cluster of commercial monopolies by the overarching national monopoly of the navigation code – was the product of an opposition movement, of long-running tensions within London's merchant community and of the persistent activity of interlopers and non-merchant groups. Not until the years immediately following the revolution of 1688 was this programme brought to maturity, with the defeat of the Tory-dominated restrictive companies.[29] Only the East India Company survived the 'free-trade' movement of the 1690s, though not without major restructuring and a much greater degree of public accountability.[30]

The exercise of state power and coercion thus involved different forms of struggle, and was often mediated through the collective action of specific interest groups. Externally, the mercantilist state was driven to reduce risk by resorting to protectionism, enforcement of the national (or 'joint') monopoly of the navigation code, and naval warfare. Internally, it was prepared to apply more competitive strategies by dismantling decentralised monopolies and corporate privilege. In the language of the new institutional economics, it sought to remove the main source of premodern institutional inefficiency, the 'near-ubiquitous parcellization of sovereignty, which restricted states' ability to co-ordinate or curtail competing political and economic claims'.[31] In 1700, as S. R. Epstein argues, only the English state had achieved a sufficient degree of legitimate sovereignty, backed by a clear separation of legislative, executive and judicial powers, to enable it to mediate between competing jurisdictions and to enforce a unified fiscal and legal regime.[32] The enhanced authority of parliament after 1689, together with the establishment of the Commission for Trade and Plantations in 1696, provided the basis for a more representative and informed approach to commercial policy,

---

[29] Brenner, *Merchants and Revolution*, postscript.
[30] Neal, 'Dutch and English East India Companies', pp. 221–3; Chaudhuri, *Trading World*, p. 448.
[31] Epstein, *Freedom and Growth*, p. 36.   [32] Ibid., pp. 8, 174.

at once more professional and transparent than the traditional system of control which rested on the royal prerogative.[33]

The Dutch experience indicates that the failure of the state to provide unambiguous support for commercial enterprise and the 'excessive and debilitating hold of particular interests' were major causes of stagnation.[34] The staplemarket system was riddled with monopolistic tendencies, and inter-state and inter-city rivalries were endemic.[35] In an optimistic, Schumpeterian vein, P. W. Klein has argued that Dutch entrepreneurs reduced risks by applying 'an astonishingly wide range of monopolistic practices within the staplemarket and staple trades' which allegedly protected investment and promoted growth.[36] In fact very few goods traded on the staplemarket lent themselves to monopolisation in a thoroughgoing way.[37] Much more usual were 'monopolistically competitive' practices whereby merchants attempted to evade perfect competition in a variety of ways: through specialisation, product differentiation and the development of customer loyalty.[38] De Vries and van der Woude contend that efforts to assert monopoly power may have been a natural consequence of rapid capital accumulation in the early Republican economy, but long-term growth depended on the achievement of higher productivity in industry and commerce, agriculture and fishing.[39] Institutionalised monopoly certainly persisted. Unlike its English equivalent, the VOC preserved its privileges intact until its dissolution in 1795.[40] Monopoly powers may have been useful in the early stages of commercial expansion in the Far East, but increasing European competition weakened the Dutch position, and it seems that the companies were ill prepared to respond to changes in demand as the seventeenth century progressed.[41] The Dutch West India Company lost most of its monopoly privileges in 1638, but continued to function as a Dutch company in a larger transatlantic trading world composed overwhelmingly of private firms and informal merchant networks. The institutional framework provided by company trading proved too weak and inappropriate to handle the multilateral

---

[33] M. J. Braddick, *State Formation in Early Modern England, c. 1550–1700*, Cambridge, 2001, pp. 265–70.

[34] Epstein, *Freedom and Growth*, p. 35.

[35] J. L. Price, *Holland and the Dutch Republic*, pp. 221–34.

[36] P. W. Klein, 'Dutch Capitalism and the European World-Economy', in M. Aymard (ed.), *Dutch Capitalism and World Capitalism*, Cambridge, 1982, p. 90; Klein, *De trippen*, pp. 478–9; Klein, 'Entrepreneurial Behaviour', p. 15.

[37] Van Zanden, 'Dutch Economic History', pp. 13–14.

[38] Veluwenkamp, *Ondernemersgedrag*, pp. 129–32.

[39] J. de Vries & van der Woude, *First Modern Economy*, p. 694.

[40] Steensgaard, 'The Companies', pp. 245–6; Chaudhuri, *Trading World*, pp. 6–7.

[41] See above, chapter 6, pp. 202–6.

structures of the Atlantic economy, and the Dutch never quite succeeded in abandoning the Asian model for their American operations.

Before the English Civil Wars of the 1640s, of course, the sale of monopoly and corporate privileges had been an important revenue-raising method, and was a major impediment to the rise of competitive markets. The supremacy of parliament after 1689 ended arbitrary taxation, and the financial revolution provided the basis for a new kind of state able to mobilise its resources for warfare and imperial expansion. Although the fiscal-military state increased the burden of taxation placed on overseas trade, it liberalised the conduct of trade and applied tax concessions and penalties as instruments of control.[42] There was no detailed master plan. Through a series of discriminatory duties, drawbacks and subsidies, however, parliament was able to make marginal adjustments to relative price levels, both at home and within the imperial trading zone, so as to maximise export sales in overseas markets as a whole. Although wartime tax increases and dislocation of trade tended to produce inflationary effects in the short term, long-term price trends remained unaffected by the pattern of eighteenth-century warfare, as Brewer has emphasised.[43] In at least two respects, the mercantilist state produced a favourable climate for the growth of the British national economy, with its central aims of securing a favourable balance of trade and the increase of navigation. In the first place, as Lord Keynes argued in his 'Notes on Mercantilism', the growth of exports and import-saving helped to reduce interest rates and, in turn, to increase domestic investment. Although the state's capacity to make major public investments was limited, military and naval expenditure stimulated the metallurgical and shipbuilding industries, as well as the search for cost-reducing technical innovations. This was public spending with a self-sustaining and expansive impact, arising from its strategic character: foreign markets were 'seized, created and protected by relatively high levels of investment in naval power'.[44]

In the second place, the emphasis on self-sufficiency in English mercantilism, although not as rigorous as that promoted by Colbert, was ingrained deeply enough to encourage industrial development. High levels of military and naval expenditure created a logic which required import saving, import substitution and a degree of self-sufficiency unknown in the Republic. Mercantilist stratagems helped to enhance an already

---

[42] Davis, 'Rise of Protection', p. 307; O'Brien, Griffiths & Hunt, 'Political Components of the Industrial Revolution', pp. 395–423.
[43] Brewer, *The Sinews of Power*, pp. 191–9.
[44] A. H. John, 'War and the English Economy, 1700–1763', *EcHR*, 7 (1955), pp. 330–3; O'Brien and Engerman, 'Exports and the Growth of the British Economy', p. 189; J. M. Keynes, *The General Theory of Employment, Interest and Money*, 1936, ch. 23.

favourable endowment of natural resources, including rich mineral deposits and a broad-based but productive agricultural sector. Holland, it is true, had overcome the constraints imposed by geography by developing a highly specialised and intensive agriculture which depended on substantial imports of Baltic grain. Malthusian constraints on population growth and high living standards were lifted at an early stage, as de Vries and van der Woude argue, by 'the fruitful interaction of Holland's Baltic trade and its agricultural sector'. The consequent release of labour from rural employments helped to create a high-wage economy, with the highest capital/labour ratio in Europe; and the Republic's peat deposits, they continue, provided a uniquely large amount of available energy per worker.[45] In one sense, de Vries and van der Woude are right to stress the advanced character of the Dutch preindustrial economy, but they underestimate its vulnerability as an organic, as distinct from a mineral-based, economy, dependent on high levels of food and energy imports.[46] Dutch dependence on British coal had already reached substantial proportions by the 1720s, when imports came to exceed 100,000 tons in some years. Equally, her growing reliance on malt and cereal imports from eastern England played a major role in displacing both Dutch-Baltic grain supplies and the shipping required to carry it. Unfortunately, the accessibility of the Sound Toll Registers to historians has inhibited consideration of the larger North Sea – Baltic trading system, which this traffic helped to shape.

Insofar as the Republic's early dependence on British coal supplies has been underestimated, it follows that the exhaustion of Dutch peat supplies must have exercised an even more serious constraint on growth than writers such as Wrigley, Unger, de Vries and van der Woude have suggested. Wrigley has stressed the extent to which organic, as distinct from mineral-based, economies were subject to negative feedback: the process of growth itself produced changes which inhibited further growth because of declining marginal returns to land use.[47] During the course of the seventeenth century, the Dutch were forced to devote increasing areas of land to energy production, while substantial grain imports made up the shortfall in food production. At the same time, the destructive impact of peat cutting reduced the value of land to farmers and brought with it high reclamation costs. Against these disadvantages, peat exploitation gave rise to a series of industries based on low-intensity thermal energy, such as breweries, distilleries, tile-making, ceramics, dyeing, sugar and salt refineries, which often involved the processing of imported raw

[45] J. de Vries & van der Woude, *First Modern Economy*, pp. 688, 693–9.
[46] Wrigley, *Continuity, Chance and Change*, pp. 102–4, 113–14.   [47] Ibid., p. 29.

materials.[48] By and large, these were industries which had grown up in the shadow of the staplemarket. As an organic energy source, however, peat burned with a lower intensity than coal – which could produce more than four times as much energy as peat, for a given volume – and was subject to relatively rapid exhaustion.[49] As peat prices rose faster than general prices during the late seventeenth and early eighteenth centuries, the processing industries of Holland turned towards a commercial solution – the import of British coal.[50] This, however, was a solution which put Dutch industries at a disadvantage in relation to their British competitors, for two reasons. Firstly, rising British export duties were added to already high provincial excises. Secondly, the Dutch found themselves at the receiving end of a coal-producing, coal-exporting economy, a situation which provided few incentives towards innovation in industrial and power technology. Although they succeeded in substituting coal for peat in several of their processing industries, such as distilling, brewing, sugar refining, soap boiling and bleaching, the two major uses of fossil fuel associated with the industrial revolution eluded them: iron smelting and the conversion of thermal energy (heat) into kinetic energy (motion).[51]

Contemporaries often marvelled at Dutch success in making the most of an unpromising natural environment, including the exploitation of wind power, water and waterways. As time went on, however, the processing industries of Holland faced further serious problems arising from pollution of the surface water, especially in Rotterdam, Schiedam and Amsterdam which continued to expand throughout the seventeenth century. Sugar refining, linen bleaching, cotton printing, textile dyeing, brewing, distilling and paper making all generated noxious effluents and waste, yet also required plentiful supplies of fresh, pure water. But land reclamation, the consequent reduction of tidal action in the Zuider Zee, and river navigation schemes combined to slow down the rate at which surface water was discharged at precisely the time when these industries were expanding most rapidly. Dutch historians have stressed the deleterious environmental consequences, but have said less about the price paid by these industries in terms of the increasing struggle to

---

[48] De Zeeuw, 'Peat and the Dutch Golden Age', p. 23; J. de Vries, *Dutch Rural Economy*, pp. 31, 68; Lambert, *Dutch Landscape*, pp. 208–12.

[49] Unger, 'Energy Sources', p. 232.

[50] J. de Vries and van der Woude imply that this was an entirely satisfactory solution to the energy crisis, and that the Republic's growth 'did not decelerate because of the supply constraints of inelastic energy sources, but because of economic circumstances that limited demand' (*First Modern Economy*, pp. 719–20).

[51] Unger, 'Energy Sources', p. 234; Mokyr, *Lever of Riches*, p. 62.

maintain quality.[52] By the 1730s and '40s, as we have seen, London merchants were highly critical of the quality of Haarlem bleached linens and Dutch printed calicoes.[53]

The mercantilist ideal of self-sufficiency hardly constitutes one of the many hallmarks of modernity which have been claimed for the Republic, but it serves to remind us that the Dutch golden age was built on precarious foundations. The Republic's principal imports – food, energy supplies, and raw materials – were paid for by exports of manufactured and processed goods, colonial produce, shipping, commercial services and overseas loans. During the second half of the eighteenth century, however, prices of imported primary products rose faster than the Republic's exports of consumer goods and services, causing a substantial deterioration in the terms of trade. J. A. Faber calculates a 15% decline during the last three decades of the century, based on weighted price indexes.[54] There are, of course, obvious parallels with Britain's international trading position during the first industrial revolution, when the terms of trade deteriorated by a massive 70% from 1820 to 1860.[55] The differences, however, are more striking than the similarities. Britain's 'worsening' trading position was a consequence of a high rate of technical innovation in the cotton industry sufficient to produce an overall fall in export prices. The underlying changes were internally generated, and signalled an exceptionally high degree of industrial competitiveness and

---

[52] J. A. Faber, H. Diederiks & S. Hart, 'Urbanisering, industrialisering en milieuaantasting in Nederland in de periode van 1500 tot 1800', *AAG Bijdragen*, 18 (1973), pp. 251–71; J. de Vries & van der Woude, *First Modern Economy*, pp. 40–5.

[53] Above, pp. 166, 183.

[54] J. A. Faber, 'The Economic Decline of the Dutch Republic', pp. 107–15. Faber produced the following indexes, for the Republic's terms of trade (1721–45 = 100):

	(1)	(2)
1750–9	0.97	0.95
1760–9	0.93	1.00
1770–9	0.91	0.86
1780–9	0.91	0.84
1790–9	0.88	0.85

(1) Based on unweighted price indexes for 15 export products and 10 import products.
(2) Based on weighted price indexes for the 4 principal export products and the 5 principal import products. Insofar as the indexes exclude shipping, commercial and financial services which involved large payments for labour, the value of which was falling substantially in the later eighteenth century, they underestimate the full extent of the deterioration in the terms of trade (ibid., pp. 109–10).

[55] K. Harley, 'Foreign Trade: Comparative Advantage and Performance', in R. Floud & D. McCloskey (eds.), *The Economic History of Britain since 1700*, vol. I, *1700–1860*, Cambridge, 1981, pp. 304–7.

entrepreneurial ingenuity. The Republic's deteriorating terms of trade, on the other hand, resulted from external circumstances beyond its control, in a situation of structural dependence on foreign trade. The mercantile sector was more important to the Dutch economy than to any other in Europe, including that of Britain, yet the state lacked the revenues, an apparatus for effectively resolving conflicting commercial interests, and a sufficiently well-defined *handelspolitiek* to sustain it.[56]

The divergence of England, as Wrigley has argued, owed much to a uniquely favourable resource endowment in a world where production depended overwhelmingly on organic materials. Intensification of production, especially of food and raw materials, continued to advance beyond the stationary state envisaged by Adam Smith and evidently reached in Holland by the later eighteenth century. The breakthrough to exponential growth, according to Wrigley, was possible because of the transition to an economy based on minerals and fossil fuels, an option denied to the Dutch.[57] In fact the extent of Dutch dependence on British coal and the environmental costs of peat digging were even higher than Wrigley supposes. 'Intensification' of primary production and the exploitation of mineral-based energy sources and sectors, however, represent only half the story. Pomeranz has recently recapitulated this now familiar argument, and balances it with a powerful emphasis on the external dimension and the exploitation of the resources of the New World. Abolition of the 'land constraint' was achieved with the most dramatic results by British imperial power and coercion. If the annual energy output of the British coal industry in 1815 represented the equivalent produced by 15 million acres of forest, the land area required to produce the cotton, sugar and timber imported from North America in 1830 would have amounted to between 25 and 30 million acres. Escape from the age-old problem of diminishing returns came when the British imperial state harnessed forces outside the market, including slavery and mercantilist controls, which turned the terms and conditions of trade strongly in its favour.[58] If this was Smithian growth, it was induced and backed by substantial state support, including armed force. It was precisely the failure of the Dutch state to underwrite the costs of defending the Atlantic possessions of the WIC that hindered the development of successful plantation colonies. The disappointing results that were achieved have been explained by the absence of a protected home market.[59]

---

[56] Emmer, 'Economic Impact', p. 170; Klein, 'Entrepreneurial Behaviour', p. 14.

[57] Wrigley, 'Divergence of England', pp. 129, 136–7, and *Continuity, Chance and Change*, ch. 2.

[58] K. Pomeranz, *The Great Divergence. China, Europe and the Making of the Modern World Economy*, Princeton, 2000, p. 276.

[59] Emmer, 'Economic Impact', pp. 172–3.

In the premodern world, commercial growth, as distinct from tech-
nological or industrial growth, depended substantially on geopolitics.
The exercise of state power helped to secure access to land, essential
raw materials, 'everyday luxuries' and markets for manufactured goods.
Domestic stocks of coal and mineral ores gave Britain unique advantages over her competitors from the 1830s, but, by this time, the Dutch
economy was already in an advanced stage of stagnation, afflicted by
industrial retardation.[60] As Europe emerged from the crisis of the seventeenth century, a degree of relative decline would inevitably affect the
Dutch intermediary position in European and world trade. The extent of
'potentially avoidable decline' during the eighteenth century, as O'Brien
puts it, arose not from inefficiencies in the economic sphere, but from
the failure of the Dutch state to respond appropriately to the aggressive
mercantilist challenges of her neighbours.[61] Nowhere was this more apparent than in the trading world of the Atlantic. The logic of those who
argue that the Republic had no need for mercantilism, as a successful
'lead economy', is essentially circular, and fails to engage with the problems facing the Dutch merchant elite in the changed circumstances of
the eighteenth century. The questions presented to the States General in
August 1751, when William IV introduced his proposals for reviving the
trade of the Republic, were essentially two. Was it at this stage possible
to take concerted and purposeful action on commercial matters within
a federal state system, and, if so, was the only practicable option for a
relatively small city state like Hamburg or Genoa to offer free-zone and
transit facilities? The answer on both counts was negative, and the proposals, like numerous other attempts at reform, collapsed.[62]

We have elaborated at some length on the pre-national origins of the
staplemarket economy which evolved from the old *stapelrecht*, and its continuing dependence on imports and terms of trade which were increasingly set by others during the eighteenth century.[63] The unavoidable fact
remains that, while the Dutch system of government may or may not have
been efficient, the first moves towards establishing a unitary nation state
were not made until the later 1790s.[64] At the time of the revolt, power
had fallen into the hands of local magistrates, who explicitly rejected anything resembling a uniform system of harmonised taxes. Compared with

[60] O'Brien, 'Mercantilism and Imperialism', p. 478; Griffiths, *Industrial Retardation*,
pp. 1–37; J. Mokyr, *Industrialisation in the Low Countries, 1795–1850*, New Haven, 1976,
pp. 124–32.
[61] O'Brien, 'Mercantilism and Imperialism', p. 496; Swart, 'Holland's Bourgeoisie',
pp. 44–8.
[62] Hovy, *Voorstel van 1751*, ch. 5, and p. 654.   [63] See above, chapter 1, pp. 15–20.
[64] Schama, *Patriots and Liberators*, ch. 9; Klein, 'Entrepreneurial Behaviour', p. 18.

its absolutist neighbours in the next century, the Republic resembled an 'antistate', a condition which was in some ways beneficial for an economy which performed an extensive intermediary role for the rest of Europe. As de Vries and van der Woude emphasise, the Republic's economic interests spread far beyond the boundaries of the state, whereas the state systems of England and France were larger than their economies, in the sense that they were driven to assert territorial control over autonomous areas and colonial possessions.[65] It was precisely the transnational aspect of Dutch merchant capitalism which gave Dutch economic development its distinctive character, in terms of a minimal requirement for central state direction and the potential for rapid growth, but which in the long run turned greatly to the advantage of her neighbours.[66] After 1689, the prospect of a secure northern European entrepôt, underpinned by a stable and accountable protestant state, was sufficient to persuade large numbers of Dutch, Huguenot and other foreign merchants to base their operations permanently in London. In doing so, they helped reorganise the traditional structures of Anglo-European trade in ways which facilitated the expansion and integration of the Atlantic economy.

Economic historians habitually deal in national aggregates and the Dutch commercial empire fits uneasily into a national case study of growth, stagnation and decline. In some respects, its history is too closely interwoven with that of Britain to provide an independent benchmark of British economic progress. To repeat an earlier point: the language of 'rise and decline' of states obscures the regional dimension and suggests that economic growth resembles a relay race. It is the world-economy which develops over time, as adjustments are made within and between a diversity of regions larger than those occupied by a single nation state.

[65] J. de Vries & van der Woude, *First Modern Economy*, pp. 698, 714.
[66] Internally, the dominating role of merchant capital and the rapid growth of the staple-market led to the diminution of the Republic's agricultural sector, which increased dependence on immigrant labour and the 'disappearance of a proto-capitalist economic structure in the countryside' (J. L. van Zanden, *The Rise and Decline of Holland's Economy*, Manchester, 1993, pp. 40–1). The contrast with the dynamics of English agrarian capitalism is obvious.

Appendixes

1. English overseas trade flows, 1699–1774: annual averages, £'000 (official values).
2. English trade with the North Sea / Baltic region, 1701–1780; decennial averages, £'000 (official values).
3. English trade with Holland, 1697–1765, distinguishing exports, re-exports, and imports; annual figures, £'000 (official values).
4. English woollen exports, 1697–1765, distinguishing exports to Holland and Germany; annual figures, £'000 (official values).
5. European linens imported into England, 1697–1765, distinguishing imports from Holland and Germany; annual figures, £'000 (official values).
6. Foreign and colonial goods exported from England, 1700–1760, distinguishing re-exports to Holland and Germany; annual figures, £'000 (official values).
7. (i) English exports of wheat, rye and oatmeal, 1697–1765, showing quantities shipped to Holland; annual figures, '000 quarters.

   (ii) English exports of malt and barley, 1697–1765, showing quantities shipped to Holland; annual figures, '000 quarters.
8. Declared English coal exports, 1699–1765, showing quantities shipped to Holland; annual figures, '000 tons.

A note on the official statistics

The information contained in these appendixes is derived from the trade figures compiled annually by the Inspectors General of Imports and Exports, whose office was established in 1696 (Cust. 3). Volumes for 1705 and 1712 are missing, but information can in some cases be substituted from abstracts compiled by the Inspector General's office. (See Clark, *Guide*, 'Catalogue of Statistical Materials', pp. 151–206.) The other main sources of information are Schumpeter, *English Overseas Trade Statistics*, and *State of the Trade of Great Britain*, ed. Whitworth. The problems involved in interpreting the official statistics are discussed above, ch. 3, pp. 68–9, and at greater length in T. S. Ashton's Introduction to Schumpeter, *English Overseas Trade Statistics*, pp. 1–14. Essentially, the values entered in the Inspector General's ledgers are expressed not in current prices, but in formalised, unit values ('official values') which closely match the level of wholesale prices prevailing during the years 1696–1709, when the official list became fossilised.

In interpreting the statistics for woollen exports, a special problem should be noted arising from falling real prices in the early years of the eighteenth century. A general 'devaluation' of the official values for woollens was applied from 1709 onwards, remaining virtually unchanged thereafter. Most seriously affected were 'Spanish' cloths, reduced by 45%, and northern dozens, by 37%. All other categories were devalued by 25% or less, including perpetuanas and serges, the staple of the trade to Holland, reduced by 11%. In 1715, the Inspector General's Office produced figures for woollen exports for 1696–1714 expressed at the new post-1709 values (CO390/12), and the effect is shown in Figure 4.2 above. A second problem arises from the tendency of merchants to overstate their woollen shipments in order to impress competitors after the removal of export duties in March 1700, but this problem was probably exaggerated by contemporaries for political reasons (Ashton, Introduction, pp. 5–6).

In utilising the Inspector General's materials, I have followed contemporary usage in referring to the United Provinces as 'Holland', since virtually all Anglo-Dutch trade was carried on through the ports of that province.

In the appendixes, 'na' = 'not available', and 'n' = 'negligible'.

Appendix 1 English overseas trade flows, 1699–1774

Annual averages, £'000 (official values)

	NORTH SEA / BALTIC ECONOMY				MEDITERRANEAN and southern Europe	ATLANTIC colonies and W. Indies	ASIA	TOTAL
	nearby Europe		northern Europe	N. Sea Total				
	Holland	rest						
1699–1701								
imports	519	899	583	2,001	1,555	1,107	756	5,849
exports	1,078	781	255	2,114	1,484	539	122	4,433
re–exports	712	451	80	1,243	224	312	14	1,986
1722–24								
imports	575	784	591	1,950	1,783	1,679	966	6,758
exports	936	598	216	1,750	2,141	758	93	5,042
re–exports	970	778	46	1,794	176	487	19	2,714
1752–54								
imports	309	863	1,043	2,215	1,597	2,684	1,086	8,203
exports	938	1,214	271	2,423	2,879	1,707	667	8,417
re–exports	836	1,085	91	2,012	285	627	81	3,492
1772–4								
imports	447	795	1,599	2,841	1,829	4,769	1,929	12,735
exports	646	822	301	1,769	2,211	4,176	717	9,853
re–exports	1,240	1,766	217	3,223	453	972	63	5,818

Sources: Cust. 3; Davis, 'English Foreign Trade, 1700–1774', pp. 119–20. Ireland and British islands are omitted from the four main circuits of trade, but are included in totals.

Appendix 2 *English trade with the North Sea / Baltic region, 1701–1780*

Decennial averages, £'000 (official values)

EXPORTS AND RE-EXPORTS								
	1700s	1710s	1720s	1730s	1740s	1750s	1760s	1770s
NORTHERN EUROPE								
Denmark & Norway	44	80	72	60	76	81	150	180
East Country	115	76	120	125	152	172	193	76
Sweden	56	36	36	25	33	19	41	78
Russia	133	88	43	49	87	81	100	207
sub-total	348	280	271	259	348	353	484	541
NEARBY EUROPE								
Holland	2147	2020	1876	1867	2405	2193	1864	1553
France & Flanders	56	198	219	297	274	334	342	585
Germany	971	889	1087	1111	1482	1339	1852	1341
sub-total	3174	3107	3182	3275	4161	3866	4058	3479

IMPORTS								
	1700s	1710s	1720s	1730s	1740s	1750s	1760s	1770s
NORTHERN EUROPE								
Denmark & Norway	75	87	100	93	92	80	82	92
East Country	140	128	198	212	250	282	192	276
Sweden	189	132	168	200	184	202	211	201
Russia	124	182	192	283	342	527	861	1085
sub-total	528	529	658	788	868	1091	1346	1654
NEARBY EUROPE								
Holland	589	538	572	496	437	353	445	476
France & Flanders	15	37	70	112	68	46	102	136
Germany	605	513	681	738	704	701	639	658
sub-total	1209	1088	1323	1346	1209	1100	1186	1270

Appendix 3 *English trade with Holland, 1697–1765*

£'000 (official values)

	Domestic exports	Re-exports	Imports		Domestic exports	Re-exports	Imports
1697–8	1,028	479	649	1732	829	1,072	523
1699	922	534	510	1733	987	1,079	512
1700	1,005	764	527	1734	947	858	490
1701	1,309	837	521	1735	958	997	525
1702	1,217	470	436	1736	986	1,098	546
1703	1,700	718	522	1737	928	843	474
1704	1,555	809	757	1738	1,013	825	502
1705	1,715		572	1739	930	911	479
1706	1,716	647	623	1740	916	838	404
1707	1,730	588	595	1741	928	937	471
1708	1,774	621	700	1742	1,134	802	360
1709	1,477	603	519	1743	1,328	1,348	407
1710	1,503	568	637	1744	1,178	1,328	406
1711	1,353	998	644	1745	1,396	882	431
1712	2,153		588	1746	1,580	1,099	577
1713	1,039	1,116	500	1747	1,676	865	698
1714	1,461	1,002	487	1748	1,719	927	340
1715	1,308	638	437	1749	1,675	1,041	350
1716	1,020	644	536	1750	1,469	735	325
1717	1,056	874	545	1751	987	908	327
1718	1,073	633	634	1752	1,023	852	324
1719	954	963	527	1753	896	765	331
1720	929	987	482	1754	897	890	273
1721	964	1,081	467	1755	907	804	276
1722	920	1,211	562	1756	870	555	300
1723	889	927	570	1757	694	610	422
1724	999	774	593	1758	864	757	473
1725	957	821	564	1759	1,074	790	387
1726	914	763	557	1760	1,105	680	412
1727	886	863	540	1761	1,280	965	437
1728	764	1,442	639	1762	1,140	967	494
1729	726	1,093	654	1763	977	933	476
1730	766	1,001	568	1764	917	1,124	372
1731	764	902	500	1765	924	1,103	420

Note: combined figures for total exports (home-produced plus re-exports) shown for 1705 and 1712

Appendix 4 *English woollen exports, 1697–1765, distinguishing exports to Holland and Germany*

£'000 (official values)

	Total woollen exports	Exported to or via Holland	Exported to Germany		Total woollen exports	Exported to or via Holland	Exported to Germany
1697–8	3,168	631	201	1732	4,078	445	366
1699	2,908	475	330	1733	4,440	569	387
1700	2,909	633	261	1734	3,762	551	392
1701	3,238	774	409	1735	4,222	564	397
1702	2,617	745	458	1736	4,468	619	447
1703	3,359	1,133	329	1737	4,628	608	459
1704	3,327	1,050	369	1738	4,735	572	415
1705	na	894	507	1739	3,835	517	390
1706	3,503	1,041	525	1740	3,827	531	423
1707	3,594	1,176	503	1741	4,192	509	403
1708	3,875	1,212	548	1742	3,793	525	460
1709	3,916	1,048	592	1743	3,967	605	644
1710	4,271	1,085	478	1744	3,332	560	687
1711	3,663	987	476	1745	3,503	710	674
1712	4,181	889	583	1746	4,519	870	861
1713	3,391	689	267	1747	4,224	799	740
1714	4,361	976	511	1748	4,471	782	706
1715	4,053	893	450	1749	5,666	723	615
1716	3,765	634	487	1750	5,350	637	561
1717	4,589	664	521	1751	5,282	505	637
1718	3,262	573	420	1752	4,609	510	734
1719	3,131	505	328	1753	5,267	545	569
1720	3,493	509	271	1754	4,605	449	519
1721	3,427	531	286	1755	4,506	418	573
1722	3,919	439	268	1756	5,715	456	495
1723	3,418	312	260	1757	5,660	434	463
1724	3,570	550	276	1758	5,734	591	597
1725	4,000	531	346	1759	6,341	547	575
1726	3,284	460	367	1760	6,445	532	580
1727	3,250	497	320	1761	5,927	527	645
1728	3,521	444	345	1762	4,638	598	759
1729	3,633	420	322	1763	4,908	574	533
1730	3,840	415	369	1764	6,216	508	752
1731	3,477	403	354	1765	5,467	530	661

Appendix 5 *European linens imported into England, 1697–1765, distinguishing imports from Holland and Germany*

Annual figures, £'000 (official values)

	Total linen imports	Imported from Holland	Imported from Germany		Total linen imports	Imported from Holland	Imported from Germany
1697–8	700	153	442	1732	1,051	194	562
1699	713	171	410	1733	1,084	194	566
1700	887	188	560	1734	1,065	188	724
1701	892	166	594	1735	1,158	207	721
1702	575	141	422	1736	886	177	513
1703	810	214	560	1737	1,058	171	634
1704	929	309	566	1738	939	180	565
1705	825	226	566	1739	964	175	596
1706	582	237	303	1740	1,002	135	684
1707	954	200	704	1741	981	143	701
1708	704	206	445	1742	871	131	568
1709	731	215	484	1743	976	157	630
1710	620	220	369	1744	956	164	611
1711	554	201	298	1745	790	129	568
1712	587	170	382	1746	770	119	582
1713	812	205	552	1747	825	155	574
1714	933	221	630	1748	876	111	627
1715	835	193	553	1749	895	112	600
1716	834	249	502	1750	905	97	538
1717	873	236	566	1751	817	102	527
1718	831	229	527	1752	755	89	520
1719	863	187	590	1753	924	90	563
1720	670	180	409	1754	816	76	586
1721	703	168	459	1755	813	66	524
1722	828	213	501	1756	827	72	587
1723	743	196	409	1757	751	87	515
1724	1,089	212	707	1758	804	117	555
1725	1,031	212	617	1759	699	102	374
1726	897	216	539	1760	687	75	428
1727	877	198	545	1761	749	71	463
1728	937	224	542	1762	470	52	291
1729	897	229	561	1763	696	63	393
1730	1,017	191	697	1764	721	51	423
1731	896	194	550	1765	655	74	379

Appendix 6 *Foreign and colonial goods exported from England, 1700–1760, distinguishing re-exports to Holland and Germany*

Annual figures, £'000 (official values)

	Total re-exports	to Holland	to Germany		Total re-exports	to Holland	to Germany
1700	2,132	764	228	1731	2,782	902	521
1701	2,229	837	409	1732	3,196	1,072	584
1702	1,177	470	222	1733	3,015	1,079	596
1703	1,649	718	257	1734	2,897	858	615
1704	1,925	809	395	1735	3,402	997	692
1705	na	na	na	1736	3,585	1,098	689
1706	1,485	647	336	1737	3,414	843	623
1707	1,645	588	364	1738	3,214	825	553
1708	1,495	621	316	1739	3,272	911	598
1709	1,507	603	232	1740	3,086	838	570
1710	1,566	568	348	1741	3,575	937	645
1711	1,875	998	207	1742	3,480	802	713
1712	na	na	na	1743	4,442	1,348	982
1713	2,066	1,116	205	1744	3,780	1,328	625
1714	2,440	1,002	356	1745	3,333	882	632
1715	1,908	638	336	1746	3,566	1,099	856
1716	2,243	644	534	1747	3,031	865	524
1717	2,613	874	576	1748	3,824	927	662
1718	1,980	633	379	1749	3,598	1,041	596
1719	2,321	963	425	1750	3,225	735	522
1720	2,300	987	405	1751	3,644	908	731
1721	2,689	1,081	646	1752	3,469	853	629
1722	2,972	1,211	655	1753	3,511	765	558
1723	2,671	822	607	1754	3,470	890	554
1724	2,494	774	573	1755	3,150	804	625
1725	2,815	821	585	1756	3,089	555	599
1726	2,692	763	637	1757	3,755	610	408
1727	2,670	863	670	1758	3,855	757	673
1728	3,597	1,442	868	1759	3,869	790	603
1729	3,299	1,093	791	1760	3,714	680	773
1730	3,223	1,001	627				

Appendix 7(i) *English exports of wheat, rye and oatmeal, 1697–1765, showing quantities shipped to Holland*

Annual figures, '000 quarters

	to all markets	to Holland		to all markets	to Holland
1697–8	17.6	17.2	1732	218.9	29.9
1699	1.3	n	1733	456.8	33.0
1700	76.7	36.1	1734	512.0	13.2
1701	142.5	104.3	1735	156.6	3.3
1702	142.0	98.3	1736	120.6	2.2
1703	165.2	49.5	1737	471.4	2.5
1704	119.8	10.8	1738	618.5	64.3
1705	120.3	na	1739	310.4	35.5
1706	238.3	138.6	1740	65.9	32.3
1707	108.3	61.6	1741	54.1	20.5
1708	88.2	16.9	1742	357.9	65.4
1709	336.2	39.1	1743	461.6	200.8
1710	26.3	10.5	1744	307.8	156.5
1711	115.2	31.9	1745	418.6	134.3
1712	163.2	na	1746	196.6	72.5
1713	216.2	30.9	1747	361.7	199.6
1714	195.4	82.1	1748	651.0	240.1
1715	197.9	87.8	1749	737.9	250.1
1716	115.8	26.7	1750	1050.9	193.6
1717	46.4	28.8	1751	734.9	76.1
1718	122.1	68.1	1752	488.7	53.6
1719	173.5	51.0	1753	331.5	26.3
1720	135.8	26.9	1754	401.5	42.1
1721	151.9	41.1	1755	282.0	54.5
1722	109.3	55.3	1756	134.2	15.9
1723	171.0	24.2	1757	16.6	
1724	269.8	31.7	1758	11.1	—
1725	226.4	25.6	1759	271.0	89.5
1726	162.4	33.8	1760	443.9	117.2
1727	41.7	9.4	1761	501.1	156.8
1728	5.2	n	1762	324.3	58.8
1729	23.0	0.1	1763	441.7	50.1
1730	110.8	16.4	1764	425.3	19.8
1731	152.9	33.2	1765	181.2	11.8

Appendix 7(ii) *English exports of malt and barley, 1697–1765, showing quantities shipped to Holland*

Annual figures, '000 quarters

	to all markets	to Holland		to all markets	to Holland
1697–8	84.7	74.2	1732	174.9	170.1
1699	1.6	n	1733	240.7	205.7
1700	63.5	39.4	1734	303.3	195.1
1701	72.4	58.2	1735	277.3	187.9
1702	88.1	78.9	1736	199.5	178.6
1703	194.8	153.7	1737	127.4	101.3
1704	133.6	107.1	1738	259.3	186.6
1705	158.8	na	1739	246.3	188.0
1706	151.3	146.9	1740	169.6	150.2
1707	115.9	109.7	1741	129.9	110.3
1708	127.7	104.1	1742	201.0	161.8
1709	180.4	144.2	1743	254.2	221.8
1710	85.3	77.7	1744	239.9	200.5
1711	148.4	134.7	1745	315.2	201.6
1712	211.5	na	1746	440.7	313.6
1713	270.5	200.0	1747	464.4	352.5
1714	238.9	194.5	1748	423.2	336.6
1715	108.4	89.4	1749	408.1	316.5
1716	241.5	195.7	1750	555.3	322.5
1717	269.5	213.0	1751	289.2	203.7
1718	374.3	301.0	1752	393.9	226.9
1719	367.1	251.0	1753	341.5	172.6
1720	258.0	163.6	1754	369.8	220.3
1721	350.6	265.3	1755	374.4	237.4
1722	404.3	294.2	1756	263.9	148.7
1723	350.9	236.6	1757	63.3	11.9
1724	252.2	222.5	1758	11.4	5.4
1725	307.8	258.4	1759	188.9	134.4
1726	355.9	276.1	1760	258.8	191.0
1727	250.1	186.7	1761	376.9	295.6
1728	195.5	177.6	1762	385.3	209.9
1729	135.4	128.5	1763	203.9	126.6
1730	194.4	160.5	1764	232.4	142.9
1731	191.3	165.0	1765	227.9	134.6

Appendix 8 *Declared English coal exports, 1699–1765, showing quantities shipped to Holland*

Annual figures '000 tons

	to all markets	to Holland		to all markets	to Holland
1699	88.6	38.4	1733	180.2	67.7
1700	101.2	46.7	1734	203.1	71.8
1701	104.1	42.3	1735	209.1	75.0
1702	79.4	21.6	1736	213.0	76.1
1703	57.1	12.6	1737	198.8	68.7
1704	67.5	23.4	1738	199.5	74.5
1705	na	na	1739	227.2	74.1
1706	67.5	27.9	1740	276.6	90.1
1707	84.3	36.5	1741	214.2	81.4
1708	90.1	36.4	1742	188.1	66.1
1709	100.8	46.4	1743	224.4	82.7
1710	90.6	44.7	1744	197.8	79.5
1711	99.3	49.7	1745	198.9	64.2
1712	100.2	49.2	1746	202.7	63.1
1713	114.2	48.9	1747	174.2	66.1
1714	165.9	83.1	1748	223.0	72.0
1715	142.2	63.9	1749	261.4	116.3
1716	144.5	65.0	1750	235.5	79.2
1717	123.4	47.9	1751	329.1	106.3
1718	136.1	52.4	1752	296.7	96.9
1719	150.8	55.9	1753	300.1	96.8
1720	139.0	47.9	1754	275.1	88.4
1721	159.0	56.9	1755	261.4	88.4
1722	165.2	67.0	1756	258.7	95.4
1723	162.0	60.2	1757	217.6	70.4
1724	284.3	73.2	1758	200.9	75.5
1725	146.1	53.3	1759	210.4	77.7
1726	183.5	73.9	1760	211.2	62.3
1727	206.2	78.0	1761	261.2	84.0
1728	146.4	51.9	1762	260.6	70.8
1729	182.3	64.5	1763	285.2	73.4
1730	161.0	73.2	1764	297.6	86.7
1731	179.3	69.9	1765	315.2	82.4
1732	200.8	77.3			

Note: Column 1 ('to all markets') includes exports to Ireland, converted to provide comparability with exports to continental Europe; none of the columns include any adjustment for false entries and under-declaration (see Table 8.1 above, pp. 253–5).

Bibliography

Unless otherwise stated, place of publication is London.

MANUSCRIPT SOURCES

PUBLIC RECORD OFFICE, LONDON

Colonial Office Papers: Board of Trade, original correspondence, CO388/1–95; entry books, CO389/1–59; miscellanea, CO390/5–12.

Board of Customs and Excise: ledgers of imports and exports, Inspector General's Office, Cust. 3/1–70; Excise and Treasury papers, Cust. 48/10–16; outport records for Exeter, Newcastle, Sunderland, Hull and Yarmouth, Cust. 64, 84, 85, 92, 97.

Treasury: miscellanea, T1/106, T64/173, 232, 241, 274, 277.

Exchequer, K.R: port books, E190, Yarmouth and Sunderland.

State Paper Office, Holland: SP84/285; SP84/415–533.

Court of Chancery: Chancery Masters' exhibits, C103/131, 132, 133; C103/146; C104/15; C107/158; C107/161; C108/132; C109/19–24; C111/127.

Deposited Papers: Chatham Papers, PRO 30/8–81 and 88.

BRITISH LIBRARY

Add Mss: 4,459; 8,133; 9,293; 9,746; 10,453–4; 11,255–6; 14,027; 14,035; 15,570; 15,764–6; 17,018–19; 22,265; 28,079; 32,977; 35,125; 35,906; 36,785; 37,981.

OTHER LONDON LIBRARIES

Guildhall Library: Radcliffe Papers, Mss 6645/1–2.

British Library of Political and Economic Science: Tawney Papers, Boxes 1–5, Lectures on Economic History, 1485–1800.

PROVINCIAL RECORD OFFICES AND LIBRARIES IN ENGLAND

Northumberland Record Office: Blackett (Matfer) Mss, ZBL192, 195; Carr Ellison Mss, ZCE 10/1–16.

Gateshead Public Library: Cotesworth Mss.

Hull University Library: Maister Ledger, Ms DP/82.

Norfolk Record Office: Baret Letter Book, Ms 6360/6B8.

Hertfordshire Record Office: Delmé-Radcliffe Letters, DE4091–6.
Exeter City Archives: Jeffrey Ledger.

PRIVATE ARCHIVES

Arundel Castle (the Duke of Norfolk): Aylward Papers.
Winestead (the late Col. R. A. Alec-Smith): Maister Letters.

MUNICIPAL RECORD OFFICES IN THE NETHERLANDS

Gemeente Archief, Amsterdam
Familie-Archief Brants: business correspondence of David Leeuw, 88/923–30;
    business correspondence of J. I. de Neufville and Co., 88/1155 (from
    London), 88/1328–53 (from England, Scotland and Ireland), 88/1401–2
    (outgoing letters), 88/1472, 88/1503 (balance-book and inventory).
NA: van der Ven, 1121, 1133; Schaef, 1371; Volkaertsz, 1540; van Loosdrecht,
    1983, 3208; Lock, 2191–241; Swanenburgh, 2711; de Vos, 2973; Outgers,
    3204–93; van Breugel, 3503; van Hille, 4778–9; Boots, 5129; Hoekeback,
    5852–942; Baars, 8569–632; Schabaalje, 6097–159; de Marolles, 8021;
    Phaff, 10,232; van der Brink, 10,361–84.

Gemeente Archief, Rotterdam
Maatschappij van Assurantie, Discontering en Beleening: Assurantie Boeken,
    1721–60.
NA: van Bortel, 1509; ten Bergh, 1579; de Bergh, 2078–153; Bremer, 2325–45;
    Schadee, 2609; de Superville, 2705.

Gemeente Archief, Haarlem
Archief Merkman: business correspondence of Pieter Merkman.

THE HUNTINGTON LIBRARY, SANTA MONICA, CALIFORNIA

Ellesmere (Bridgewater) Mss, EL 9625–6, 9657, 9814, 9839–54, 9873–81.
Brydges Papers, ST57 (outgoing letters); ST 58 (incoming letters).

CONTEMPORARY PRINTED SOURCES

COLLECTIONS

Journals of the House of Commons, vols. VIII–XXXII (1660–1770).
Reports from Committees of the House of Commons, not inserted in the *Journals*, vols.
    I–IV.
Calendar of House of Lords Mss, new series, vol. X (1712–14).
Journal of the Commissioners for Trade and Plantations, 1704–1782, 14 vols., 1920.
    The *Journals* for the years 1675–1704 are included in:
Calendar of State Papers, Colonial Series. America and West Indies, IX–XXII.
Calendar of Treasury Papers, 1697–1728.
Calendar of Treasury Books, 1695–1718.
Calendar of Treasury Books and Papers, 1729–45.

ABSTRACTS AND DOCUMENTS

Tabeller over Skibsfart og Varetransport gennemØresund, vol. I, *1497–1660*, ed. N. E. Bang, Copenhagen and Leipzig, 1906; vol. II, *1661–1783*, ed. N. E. Bang & K. Korst, Copenhagen and Leipzig, 1930.

Bronnen tot de Geschiedenis van de Leidsche Textielnijverheid, vol. VI, *1703–95*, ed. N. W. Posthumus, 's-Gravenhage, 1922.

State of the Trade of Great Britain, ed. Sir Charles Whitworth, 1776.

BOOKS AND PAMPHLETS

Anderson, A. *An Historical and Chronological Deduction of the Origin of Commerce*, 2 vols., 1764; 4 vols. (1801), 1967.

Anon. 'The Dutch Design Anatomised . . . or, a Discovery of the Wickedness and Injustice of the Intended Invasion . . . written by a True Member of the Church of England, and lover of his country', 1688 (Goldsmiths Library, 2697).

Anon. 'Reasons humbly offered against the Continuation of a General Liberty for Exporting the Woollen Manufactures of this Kingdom by Foreigners, into the Privileges of the Merchants Adventurers of England', 1693 (Goldsmiths Library, 2968).

Anon. *The Beaux Merchant, a Comedy written by a Clothier*, 1714.

Anon. [T. B.] *The Holland Merchant's Companion*, Rotterdam, 1715 and 1748.

Anon. *A Short Account of the late Application to Parliament made by the Merchants of London upon the Neglect of their Trade*, 1742 (Hanson 5624).

Anon. *A Description of Holland, or the Present State of the United Provinces*, 1743.

Anon. *The Case of British Merchants, Owners of Ships, and others relative to the Employment and Increase of British Shipping and British Navigation*, 1750 (Hanson 6437).

Arbuthnot, J. 'A Short Account of the Corn Trade of Amsterdam' (1773), *Annals of Agriculture*, 27 (1796).

Beawes, W. *Lex Mercatoria Rediviva: or The Merchant's Directory*, 1st London edn, 1750; 6th Dublin edn, 1773; 4th enlarged edn, by T. Mortimer, London, 1783, reprinted 1970, Farnborough.

Burrish, O. *Batavia Illustrata*, 1728.

Carr, W. *An Accurate Description of the United Netherlands*, 1691.

Castaing, J. *The Course of the Exchange*, 1698–1761.

Child, J. 'A Treatise concerning the East India Trade', 1681.
A New Discourse of Trade, 1693, 1698.

Comber, W. T. *An Inquiry into the State of National Subsistence, as connected with the Progress of Wealth and Population*, 1808.

Combrune, M. *An Enquiry into the Prices of Wheat, Malt, and Occasionally of Other Provisions*, 1768.

Crouch, H. *Complete View of the British Customs*, 1746.

Davenant, C. *New Dialogues upon the Present Posture of Affairs . . . and the Trade now carried on between France and Holland by the Author of the 'Ways and Means'*, 1710.

'A Second Report to the Honourable Commissioners for Stating the Public Accounts', Part II, 10 December 1711, printed in Davenant's *Political and Commercial Works*, ed. C. Whitworth, 5 vols., 1771, vol. IV.

Decker, M. *An Essay on the Causes of the Decline of the Foreign Trade . . . of Great Britain*, 1744.

Defoe, D. *A Weekly Review*, 9 vols., 1704–13.

An Enquiry into the Danger and Consequences of a War with the Dutch, 1712.

A Plan of the English Commerce, 1728.

Evelyn, J. *Navigation and Commerce, their Original and Progress*, 1674.

Forbes, W. *Memoirs of a Banking House* (1803), Edinburgh, 1859.

Forman, C. *A Letter to the Merchants of Great Britain, or a Proper Reply to the London Journal, of Dec. 12, 1730, by Peregrine English*, 1732.

Gee, J. *The Trade and Navigation of Great Britain Considered* (1729), 1738.

Gervaise, I. *The System or Theory of the Trade of the World*, 1720 (Hanson 2565).

Hanway, J. *An Historical Account of the British Trade over the Caspian Sea: with a Journal of Travels from London through Russia into Persia; and back again through Russia, Germany and Holland . . . added, The Revolutions of Persia during the present century* (1752), 2 vols., 1754.

Houghton, J. *A Collection for the Improvement of Husbandry and Trade*, 3 vols., 1727.

Huet, P. D. *Memoirs of the Dutch Trade* (1698), 1718.

King, C. *The British Merchant*, 3 vols., 1721.

Le Long, I. *Koophandel van Amsterdam* (1714), Amsterdam, 1753.

Lowndes, T. *A State of the Coal trade to Foreign Parts, by way of a memorial to a supposed very great assembly*, 1744–5 (Hanson 5897).

Luzac, E. *Hollands Rijkdom*, 4 vols., Amsterdam, 1783.

MacGregor, J. *Commercial Statistics*, 5 vols., 1844–50.

Macpherson, J. *Origin of Commerce*, 4 vols., 1805.

Magens, N. *The Universal Merchant, containing the rational of commerce*, 1753.

Mandeville, B. *The Fable of the Bees, or Private Vices, Public Benefits* (1714), 6th edn, 1723.

Marshall, J. *Travels through Holland, Flanders, Germany, Denmark, Sweden, Lapland, Russia, the Ukraine and Poland; in the years 1768, 1769, and 1770* (1768), 3 vols., 1772.

McCulloch, J. R. *A Select Collection of Scarce and Valuable Tracts on Commerce*, 1859.

Mortimer, J. *Universal Director of London and Westminster and their Environs*, 1763.

Mortimer, T. *A New and Complete Dictionary of Trade & Commerce*, 1766–7.

Mun, J. *Observations on British Wool*, 1738.

Pinto, I. de. *Traité de la Circulation et du Crédit*, 1771.

Pollexfen, J. *A Discourse of Trade, Coyn, and Paper Credit*, 1697.

Postlethwayt, M. *Universal Dictionary of Trade and Commerce* (1751), 2 vols., 1774.

Serionne, J. A. de. *Le Commerce de la Hollande*, 3 vols., Amsterdam, 1765–8.

Smith, A. *Inquiry into the Nature and Causes of the Wealth of Nations*, ed. J. R. McCulloch, 1838.

Smith, C. *Three Tracts on the Corn Trade*, 1804.

Smith, J. *Chronicum Rusticum-Commerciale, or Memoirs of Wool*, 2 vols., 1747.

Temple, W. *Observations upon the United Provinces of the Netherlands* (1673), 1705.

Tucker, J. *A Brief Essay on the Advantages and Disadvantages which Respectively Attend France and Great Britain with Regard to Trade*, 1750.

Warden, A. J. *The Linen Trade, Ancient and Modern*, 1864.

MODERN WORKS

Abel, W. *Agrarkrisen und Agrarkonjunktur im Mitteleuropa vom 13. bis zum 19. Jahrhundert*, Berlin, 1966.

Anderson, P. 'Fernand Braudel and National Indentity', *London Review of Books*, 9 May 1991.

Appleby, J. *Economic Thought and Ideology in Seventeenth Century England*, Princeton, 1980.

Ashley, M. *Financial and Commercial Policy under the Cromwellian Protectorate*, Oxford, 1934.

Ashton, R. 'The Parliamentary Agitation for Free Trade in the Opening Years of the Reign of James I', *PP*, 38 (1967).

The Court and the City, 1603–1643, Cambridge, 1979.

Ashton, T. S. *An Economic History of England: The Eighteenth Century*, 1955.

Introduction to E. B. Schumpeter, *English Overseas Trade Statistics, 1687–1818*, Oxford, 1960.

Ashton, T. S. & Sykes, J. *The Coal Industry of the Eighteenth Century*, Manchester, 1929.

Åström, S.-E. 'The English Navigation Laws and the Baltic Trade, 1660–1700', *Scandinanvian Economic History Review*, 8 (1960).

From Cloth to Iron. The Anglo-Baltic Trade in the late Seventeenth Century, Helsingfors, 1963.

Atkinson, F. (ed.), *Some Aspects of the Eighteenth Century Woollen and Worsted Trade in Halifax*, Halifax, 1956.

Attman, A. *Dutch Enterprise in the World Bullion Trade*, Gothenburg, 1983.

Atton, H. & Holland, H. H. *The King's Customs. An Account of Maritime Revenue and Contraband Traffic in England, Scotland and Ireland, from the Earliest Times to the Year 1800*, 1908.

Baker, D. A. 'The Marketing of Corn in the First Half of the Eighteenth Century: North-East Kent', *Agricultural History Review*, 18 (1970).

'The Agriculture of Kent, 1660–1760' (University of Kent Ph.D. thesis, 1976).

Barbour, V. 'The Consular Service in the Reign of Charles II', *American Historical Review*, 33 (1928).

'Marine Risks and Insurance in the Seventeenth Century', *Journal of Economic and Business History*, 1 (1928–9).

'Dutch and English Merchant Shipping in the Seventeenth Century', *EcHR*, 2 (1930), repr. in Carus-Wilson, *Essays*, vol. I, 1954.

Capitalism in Amsterdam in the Seventeenth Century (1950), Ann Arbor, 1963.

Barfoot, C. C. ' "Envy, Fear and Wonder"; English Views of Holland and the Dutch, 1673–1764', in C. C. Barfoot & R. Todd (eds.), *The Great Emporium. The Low Countries as a Cultural Crossroads in the Renaissance and the Eighteenth Century*, Amsterdam, 1992.

Barnes, D. G. *A History of the English Corn Laws from 1660 to 1846*, 1930.

Baugh, D. 'Maritime Strength and Atlantic Commerce', in L. Stone (ed.), *An Imperial State at War: Britain from 1689–1815*, 1994.

Baumann, W.-R. *The Merchants Adventurers and the Continental Cloth Trade, 1560s–1620s*, Berlin, 1990.

Becht, H. E. *Statistische gegevens betreffende den handelsomzet van de Republiek der Vereenigde Nederlanden gedurende de 17e Eeuw (1579–1715)*, 's-Gravenhage, 1908.

Beier, A. L. 'Engine of Manufacture: The Trades of London', in Beier & Finlay (eds.), *London, 1500–1700*, 1986.

Beier, A. L. & Finlay, R. (eds.), *London, 1500–1700. The Making of a Metropolis*, 1986.

Bel, J. G. van. *De Linnenhandel van Amsterdam in de XVIII Eeuw*, Amsterdam, 1940.

Berg, M. 'Manufacturing the Orient. Asian Commodities and European Industry, 1500–1800', in Cavaciocchi (ed.), *Prodotti e Tecniche*, 1998.

Berrill, K. 'International Trade and the Rate of Economic Growth', *EcHR*, 12 (1960).

Bijlsma, R. *Rotterdams Welvaren, 1550–1650*, 's-Gravenhage, 1918.

Black, J. *The Rise of the European Powers, 1679–1793*, 1990.

The Grand Tour in the Eighteenth Century, 1992.

Blussé, L. & Gaastra, F. (eds.), *Companies and Trade. Essay on Overseas Trading Companies during the Ancien Régime*, Leiden, 1981.

Bosher, J. F. 'Huguenot Merchants and the Protestant International in the Seventeenth Century', *William and Mary Quarterly*, 52 (1995).

Bowen, H. V. *War and British Society, 1688–1815*, Cambridge, 1998.

Boxer, C. R. *The Dutch Seaborne Empire, 1600–1800*, 1965.

Braddick, M. J. *Parliamentary Taxation in Seventeenth-Century England*, Woodbridge, 1994.

State Formation in Early Modern England, c. 1550–1700, Cambridge, 2001.

Braudel, F. *The Mediterranean and the Mediterranean World in the Age of Philip II*, 2 vols., 1972.

Civilisation and Capitalism, 15th–18th Century, vol. III, *The Perspective of the World* (1979), 1984.

Braudel, F. & Spooner, F. C. 'Prices in Europe from 1450', in Rich & Wilson (eds.), *The Cambridge Economic History of Europe*, vol. IV, 1967.

Brenner, R. 'The Social Basis of English Commercial Expansion, 1550–1650', *JEH*, 32 (1972).

Merchants and Revolution. Commercial Change, Political Conflict, and London's Overseas Traders, 1550–1653, Cambridge, 1993.

Brewer, J. *The Sinews of Power. War, Money and the English State, 1688–1783*, New York, 1988.

Brezis, E. S. 'Foreign Capital Flows in the Century of Britain's Industrial Revolution: New Estimates, Controlled Conjectures', *EcHR*, 48 (1995).

Bromley, J. S. 'The North Sea in Wartime, 1688–1713', *BMGN*, 92 (1977).

Bromley, J. S. & Kossman, E. H. (eds.), *Britain and the Netherlands. Papers delivered to the Anglo-Dutch Historical Congress*, vol. I (London, 1960), vol. II (Groningen, 1964), vol. III (London, 1968), vol. IV (The Hague, 1971), vol. V (The Hague, 1975).

Brugmans, H. 'Statistiek van den in- en uitvoer van Amsterdam, 1667–8', *BMHG*, 19 (1898).

Bruijn, J. R. 'Productivity, Profitability, and Costs of Private and Corporate Dutch Ship Ownership in the Seventeenth and Eighteenth Centuries', in Tracy (ed.), *Political Economy of Merchant Empires*, 1991.

Bruijn, J. R., Gaastra, F. S. & Schoffer, I. *Dutch-Asiatic Shipping in the Seventeenth and Eighteenth Centuries*, vol. I, The Hague, 1987.

Brulez, W. 'Shipping Projects in the Early Modern Period', *AHN*, 14 (1981).

Buist, M. G. *At Spes Non Fracta: Hope & Co. 1770–1815*, The Hague, 1974.

Butler, J. *The Huguenots in America. A Refugee People in New World Society*, Cambridge, Mass., 1983.

Cain, P. J. & Hopkins, A. G. *British Imperialism, Innovation and Expansion, 1688–1914*, 1993.

Campbell, R. H. (ed.), *States of the Annual Progress of the Linen Manufacture, 1727–54*, Edinburgh, 1964.

Carter, A. M. C. 'The Dutch and the English Public Debt in 1777', *Economica*, 20 (1953); repr. in Carter, *Getting, Spending and Investing in Early Modern Times*, 1975.

'Dutch Foreign Investment, 1738–1800', *Economica*, 20 (1953); repr. in Carter, *Getting, Spending and Investing in Early Modern Times*, 1975.

'The Huguenot Contribution to the Early Years of the Funded Debt, 1694–1714', *Proceedings of the Huguenot Society of London*, 19 (1952–8); repr. in Carter, *Getting, Spending and Investing in Early Modern Times*, 1975.

'Financial Activities of the Huguenots in London and Amsterdam in the Mid-eighteenth Century', *Proceedings of the Huguenot Society of London*, 19 (1952–8).

'The Ministry to the English Churches in the Netherlands in the Seventeenth Century', *BIHR*, 33 (1960).

'The Dutch as Neutrals in the Seven Years' War', *International and Comparative Law Quarterly*, 12 (1963); repr. in Carter, *Getting, Spending and Investing in Early Modern Times*, 1975.

The English Reformed Church in Amsterdam in the Seventeenth Century, Amsterdam, 1964.

'Britain as a European Power, from her Glorious Revolution to the French Revolutionary War', in Bromley & Kossman (eds.), *Britain and the Netherlands*, vol. III, 1968.

The Dutch Republic in Europe in the Seven Years' War, 1971.

Neutrality or Commitment. The Evolution of Dutch Foreign Policy, 1667–1795, 1975.

Getting, Spending and Investing in Early Modern Times, Assen, 1975.

Carus-Wilson, E. M. *Essays in Economic History*, vol. I, 1954, vol. II, 1962.

Cavaciocchi, S. (ed.), *Prodotti e Tecniche d'Oltremare nelle Economie Europee Secc. XIII–XVIII* (Istituto Internazionale di Storia Economica 'F. Datini'), Atti delle XXXI settimana di studi, Prato, 1998.

Chandaman, *The English Public Revenue, 1660–1688*, Oxford, 1975.

Chapman, S. D. *Merchant Enterprise in Britain, from the Industrial Revolution to World War I*, Cambridge, 1992.

Chartres, J. 'The Marketing of Agricultural Produce', in Thirsk (ed.), *The Agrarian History of England and Wales*, 1985.
    'Food Consumption and Internal Trade', in Beier & Finlay (eds.), *London, 1500–1700*, 1986.
    'City and Towns, Farmers and Economic Change in the Eighteenth Century', *Historical Research*, 64 (1991).
Chaudhuri, K. N. *The Trading World of Asia and the English East India Company, 1660–1760*, Cambridge, 1978.
Chaudhuri, S. & Morineau, M. (eds.), *Merchants, Companies and Trade. Europe and Asia in the Early Modern Era*, Cambridge, 1999.
Cherry, G. L. 'The Development of the English Free Trade Movement in Parliament, 1689–1702', *JMH*, 25 (1953).
Christensen, A. E. *Dutch Trade to the Baltic about 1600*, Copenhagen and The Hague, 1941.
Cipolla, C. 'The Economic Decline of Italy', in B. Pullan (ed.), *Crisis and Change in the Venetian Economy in the Sixteenth and Seventeenth Centuries*, 1968.
Ciriacono, S. 'The Venetian Economy and its Place in the World Economy of the Seventeenth and Eighteenth Centuries. A Comparison with the Low Countries', in H.-J. Nitz (ed.), *The Early-Modern World-System in Geographical Perspective*, Stuttgart, 1973.
Clapham, J. H. 'The Transference of the Worsted Industry from Norfolk to the West Riding', *Economic Journal*, 20 (1910).
Clark, G. N. *The Dutch Alliance and the War Against French Trade, 1688–1697*, Manchester, 1923.
    'War Trade and Trade War, 1701–1713', *EcHR*, 1 (1927).
    The Later Stuarts, 1660–1714, Oxford, 1934.
    Guide to English Commercial Statistics, 1696–1782, Royal Historical Society, 1938.
Cole, W. A. 'Trends in Eighteenth Century Smuggling', *EcHR*, 10 (1958).
    'The Arithmetic of Eighteenth Century Smuggling; A Rejoinder', *EcHR*, 28 (1975).
Cole, W. A. & Deane, P. *British Economic Growth, 1688–1959*, Cambridge, 1964.
Coleman, D. C. 'The Economy of Kent under the Later Stuarts', University of London Ph.D. thesis, 1951.
    The British Paper Industry, 1495–1860, Oxford, 1958.
    'Textile Growth', in Harte & Ponting (eds.), *Textile History and Economic History*, 1973.
    'Politics and Economics in the Age of Anne: The Case of the Anglo-French Trade Treaty of 1713', in Coleman & John (eds.), *Trade, Government, and Economy*, 1976.
    The Economy of England, 1450–1750, Oxford, 1977.
Coleman, D. C. & John, A. H. (eds.), *Trade, Government, and Economy in Pre-Industrial England. Essays presented to F. J. Fisher*, 1976.
Coleman, D. C. & Mathias, P. (eds.), *Enterprise and History. Essays in Honour of Charles Wilson*, Cambridge, 1984.
Colley, L. *Britons. Forging the Nation, 1707–1837*, 1992.

Coombs, D. 'Dr Davenant and the Debate on Franco-Dutch Trade', *EcHR*, 10 (1957).

Crafts, N. 'The Industrial Revolution', in R. Floud & D. McCloskey (eds.), *The Economic History of Britain since 1700*, vol. I, *1700–1860*, 1981.

Crouzet, F. 'England and France in the Eighteenth Century: A Comparative Analysis of two Economic Growths', in F. Crouzet, *Britain Ascendant: Comparative Studies in Franco-British Economic History*, Cambridge, 1990 (first published in *Annales*, 21 (1966)).

Crowhurst, P. 'Marine Insurance and the Trade of Rotterdam, 1755–63', *Maritime History*, 2 (1972).

The Defence of British Trade, 1689–1815, Folkestone, 1977.

Cullen, L. M. *Anglo-Irish Trade, 1660–1800*, Manchester, 1968.

Cunningham, W. *The Growth of English Industry and Commerce in Modern Times*, vol. I, *The Mercantile System* (1882), Cambridge, 1912.

Curtin, P. D. *Cross-Cultural Trade in World History*, Cambridge, 1984.

Daudin, G. 'French International Trade 1716–1792: What Do we Know, and Why Do we Care?', *Papers presented to the Annual Conference of the Economic History Society*, Oxford, 1999.

Davids, C. A. 'Beginning Entrepreneurs and Municipal Governments in Holland at the Time of the Dutch Republic', in Lesger & Noordegraaf (eds.), *Entrepreneurs and Entrepreneurship in Early Modern Times*, 1985.

Davids, K. & Lucassen, J. *A Miracle Mirrored. The Dutch Republic in European Perspective*, Cambridge, 1995.

Davids, K. & Noordegraaf, L. (eds.), *The Dutch Economy in the Golden Age. Nine Studies*, Amsterdam (NEHA), 1993.

Davies, D. W. *A Primer of Dutch Seventeenth Century Overseas Trade*, 1961.

Davies, G. 'The Seamy Side of Marlborough's Wars', *Huntington Library Quarterly*, 15 (1951).

Davis, R. 'English Foreign Trade, 1660–1700', *EcHR*, 6 (1954); repr. with Davis, 'England and the Mediterranean', in Minchinton (ed.), *The Growth of English Overseas Trade in the Seventeenth and Eighteenth Centuries*, 1969.

'England and the Mediterranean, 1570–1670', in F. J. Fisher (ed.), *Essays in the Economic and Social History of Tudor and Stuart England*, Cambridge, 1961.

'English Foreign Trade, 1700–1774', *EcHR*, 15 (1962).

The Rise of the English Shipping Industry in the Seventeenth and Eighteenth Centuries, 1962.

'The Rise of Protection in England, 1689–1786', *EcHR*, 19 (1966).

Aleppo and Devonshire Square. English Traders in the Levant in the Eighteenth Century, 1967.

A Commercial Revolution: English Overseas Trade in the 17th and 18th Centuries, 1967.

English Overseas Trade, 1500–1700, 1973.

The Rise of the Atlantic Economies, 1973.

English Merchant Shipping and Anglo-Dutch Rivalry in the Seventeenth Century, National Maritime Museum, Greenwich, 1975.

The Industrial Revolution and British Overseas Trade, Leicester, 1979.

Deane, P. 'The Output of the British Woollen Industry in the Eighteenth Century', *JEH*, 17 (1957).

Dickson, P. G. M. *The Financial Revolution in England. A Study in the Development of the Public Credit, 1688–1756*, 1967.

Finance and Government under Maria Theresa, 2 vols., Oxford, 1987.

Diederiks, H. 'The Netherlands, the Case of a Decentralised Metropolis', in E. Aerts & P. Clark (eds.), *Metropolitan Cities and their Hinterlands in Early Modern Europe*, Leuven, 1990.

Dillen, J. G. van. 'Stukken betreffende den Amsterdamschen graanhandel omstreeks het jaar 1681', *EHJ*, 3 (1917).

'Amsterdam's Role in Seventeenth-Century Dutch Politics and its Economic Background', in Bromley & Kossman (eds.), *Britain and the Netherlands*, vol. II, 1964.

'Dreigende hongersnood in de Republiek in de laatste jaren der zeventiende eeuw', in J. G. van Dillen, *Mensen en achtergronden, studies, uitgegeven ter gelegenheid van de tachtigste verjaardag van de schrijver*, Groningen, 1964.

Van Rijkdom en Regenten: Handboek tot de economische en sociale geschiedenis van Nederland tijdens de Republiek, 's-Gravenhage, 1970.

'Economic Fluctuations and Trade in the Netherlands, 1650–1750', in P. Earle (ed.), *Essays in European Economic History, 1500–1800*, Oxford, 1974.

Dunthorne, H. *The Maritime Powers, 1721–1740. A Study of Anglo-Dutch Relations in the Age of Walpole*, New York and London, 1986.

Durie, A. J. *The Scottish Linen Industry in the Eighteenth Century*, Edinburgh, 1979.

Earle, P. *The World of Defoe*, 1976.

Eatwell, J. 'Import Substitution and Export-led Growth', in J. Eatwell, M. Milgate & P. Newman (eds.), *The New Palgrave. The World of Economics*, 1987.

Eeghen, I. H. van. *Inventaris van het Familie-Archief Brants*, Amsterdam, 1959.

Einzig, P. *The History of Foreign Exchange*, 1962.

Emmer, P. C. 'The West India Company, 1621–1791: Dutch or Atlantic?', in Blussé & Gaastra (eds.), *Companies and Trade*, 1981.

'The Economic Impact of the Dutch Expansion Overseas, 1570–1870', in P. K. O'Brien & L. Prados de la Escosura (eds.), *The Costs and Benefits of European Imperialism, Revista de Historia Económica*, 16 (1998).

Engelhard, J. L. F. *Het generaal-plakkaat van 31 juli 1725 op de convooien en licenten en het lastgeld op de schepen*, Assen, 1970.

Engerman, S. 'British Imperialism in a Mercantilist Age, 1492–1849', in O'Brien & Prados de la Escosura (eds.), *Costs and Benefits of European Imperialism*, 1998.

Epstein, S. R. *Freedom and Growth. The Rise of States and Markets in Europe, 1300–1750*, 2000.

Evans, N. *The East Anglian Linen Industry. Rural Industry and Local Economy, 1500–1850*, Aldershot, 1985.

Faber, J. A. *Dure tijden en hongersnoden in preindustrieel Nederland*, Amsterdam, 1959.

'The Decline of the Baltic Grain Trade in the Second Half of the Seventeenth Century', *AHN*, 1 (1966); revised version in Heeres *et al.* (eds.), *Dunkirk to Danzig*, 1988 (first published in *AAG Bijdragen*, 9 (1963)).

'Structural Changes in the European Economy during the Eighteenth Century as Reflected in the Baltic Trade', in Heeres *et al.* (eds.), *Dunkirk to Danzig*, 1988 (first published in *Tijdschrift voor Zeegeschiedenis*, 1 (1982)).

'The Economic Decline of the Dutch Republic in the Second Half of the Eighteenth Century and the International Terms of Trade', in Heeres *et al.* (eds.), *Dunkirk to Danzig*, 1988.

Faber, J. A., Diederiks, H. & Hart, S. 'Urbanisering, industrialisering en milieuaantasting in Nederland in de periode van 1500 tot 1800', *AAG Bijdragen*, 18 (1973).

Faber, J. A., Roessingh, H. K. *et al.*, 'Population Changes and Economic Developments in the Netherlands: An Historical Survey', in *AAG Bijdragen*, 12 (1965).

Farnell, J. E. 'The Navigation Act of 1651, the First Dutch War and the London Merchant Community', *EcHR*, 16 (1964).

Firth, C. H. (ed.), *The History of England, from the Accession of James II*, by Lord Macaulay, 6 vols., 1914.

Fisher, F. J. 'London as an "Engine of Economic Growth"', in Bromley & Kossman (eds.), *Britain and the Netherlands*, vol. IV, 1971.

Fisher, H. E. S. *The Portugal Trade*, 1971.

Flinn, M. W. *The History of the British Coal Industry*, vol. II, Oxford, 1984.

Floud, R. & McCloskey, D. *The Economic History of Britain*, vol. I, *1700–1860*, Cambridge, 1981.

Forbes, W. *Memoirs of a Banking-House* [1803], Edinburgh, 1859.

Frank, A. G. *World Accumulation, 1492–1789*, 1978.

Re-Orient: Global Economy in the Asian Age, Berkeley, Los Angeles, London, 1998.

Friis, A. *Alderman Cockayne's Project and the Cloth Trade*, Copenhagen and London, 1927.

Fritschy, W. 'Taxation in Britain, France and the Netherlands in the Eighteenth Century', *ESHN*, 2 (1990–1).

Furber, H. *Rival Empires of Trade in the Orient, 1600–1800*, vol. II, Minnesota, 1976.

Gaastra, F. S. *De Geschiedenis van de VOC*, Haarlem and Antwerp, 1982.

Gauci, P. *The Politics of Trade. The Overseas Merchant in State and Society, 1660–1720*, Oxford, 2001.

Gibbs, G. C. 'The Reception of the Huguenots in England and the Dutch Republic, 1680–1690', in O. Grell, J. Israel & N. Tyacke (eds.), *From Persecution to Toleration. The Glorious Revolution and Religion in England*, Oxford, 1991.

Gierowski, J. & Kaminski, A. 'The Eclipse of Poland', in J. S. Bromley (ed.), *New Cambridge Modern History*, vol. VI, Cambridge, 1970.

Gill, C. *The Rise of the Irish Linen Industry*, Oxford, 1925.

Merchants and Mariners of the Eighteenth Century, 1961.

Glamann, K. *Dutch-Asiatic Trade, 1620–1740*, Copenhagen and The Hague, 1958.

'European Trade, 1500–1750', in C. M. Cipolla (ed.), *The Fontana Economic History of Europe*, vol. II, 1974.

'The Changing Patterns of Trade', in Rich & Wilson (eds.), *The Cambridge Economic History of Europe*, vol. V, 1977.

Glennie, P. 'The Social Shape of the Market for Domestic Linens in Early Modern England', unpublished working paper presented to the Conference on 'Clothing and Consumption in England and America, 1600–1800', Victoria and Albert Museum, London, June 1992.

Gomes, L. *Foreign Trade and the National Economy. Mercantilist and Classical Perspectives*, 1987.

Grassby, R. *The English Gentleman in Trade. The Life and Works of Sir Dudley North, 1641–1691*, Oxford, 1994.

The Business Community of Seventeenth Century England, Cambridge, 1995.

Grell, O. P. *Dutch Calvinists in Early Stuart London. The Dutch Church in Austin Friars, 1603–42*, Leiden, 1989.

'From Persecution to Integration: The Decline of the Anglo-Dutch Communities in England, 1648–1702', in O. P. Grell, J. Israel & N. Tyacke (eds.), *From Persecution to Toleration. The Glorious Revolution and Religion in England*, Oxford, 1991.

'Merchants and Ministers: The Foundations of International Calvinism', in A. Pettegree, A. Duke & G. Lewis (eds.), *Calvinism in Europe, 1540–1620*, Cambridge, 1994.

Griffiths, R. T. *Industrial Retardation in the Netherlands*, The Hague, 1979.

Groenveld, S. & Wintle, M. (eds.), *State and Trade: Government and Economy in Britain and the Netherlands since the Middle Ages*, Zutphen, 1992.

Gunn, J. A. W. *Politics and the Public Interest in the Seventeenth Century*, 1969.

Gwynn, R. D. *Huguenot Heritage. The History and Contribution of the Huguenots in Britain*, 1985.

Haley, K. H. D. *The British and the Dutch*, 1988.

Hamilton, H. *An Economic History of Scotland in the Eighteenth Century*, Oxford, 1963.

Hancock, D. *Citizens of the World. London Merchants and the Integration of the British Atlantic Community, 1735–85*, Cambridge, 1995.

Harley, K. 'Foreign Trade: Comparative Advantage and Performance', in R. Floud & D. McCloskey (eds.), *The Economic History of Britain since 1700*, vol. I, *1700–1860*, Cambridge, 1981.

Harper, L. *The English Navigation Laws*, New York, 1939.

Hart, M. 't 'Freedom and Restrictions. State and Economy in the Dutch Republic, 1570–1670', in Davids & Noordegraaf, *Dutch Economy in the Golden Age*, 1993.

The Making of a Bourgeois State. War, Politics and Finance during the Dutch Revolt, Manchester, 1993.

Harte, N. B. 'The Rise of Protection and the English Linen Trade', in Harte & Ponting (eds.), *Textile History and Economic History*, 1973.

(ed.), *The New Draperies in the Low Countries and England*, Oxford, 1997.

Harte, N. B. & Ponting, K. G. (eds.). *Textile History and Economic History. Essays in Honour of Miss Julia de Lacy Mann*, Manchester, 1973.

Hatcher, J. *The History of the British Coal Industry*, vol. I, Oxford, 1993.

Hatton, R. M. 'John Drummond in the War of the Spanish Succession', in R. Hatton & M. S. Anderson (eds.), *Studies in Diplomatic History*, London, 1970.

Hazewinkel, H. C. *Geschiedenis van Rotterdam*, 3 vols., Amsterdam, 1940.

Heaton, H. *The Yorkshire Woollen and Worsted Industries from the Earliest Times up to the Industrial Revolution*, Oxford, 1920.

Heckscher, E. F. 'Multilateralism, Baltic Trade, and the Mercantilists', *EcHR*, 3 (1950).

Mercantilism (1931), revised edn, ed. E. F. Soderlund, 1955.

'Mercantilism', in D. C. Coleman, *Revisions in Mercantilism*, 1969.

Heeres, W. G., *et al.* (eds.), *From Dunkirk to Danzig. Shipping and Trade in the North Sea and the Baltic, 1350–1850*, Hilversum, 1988.

Helleiner, K. F. 'The Population of Europe', in Rich & Wilson (eds.), *The Cambridge Economic History of Europe*, vol. IV, 1967.

Henderson, W. O. *The State and the Industrial Revolution in Prussia, 1740–1870*, Liverpool, 1958.

Studies in the Economic Policy of Frederick the Great, 1963.

Hinton, R. W. K. *The Eastland Trade and the Common Weal in the Seventeenth Century*, Cambridge, 1959.

Hobsbawm, E. J. 'The General Crisis of the Seventeenth Century', *PP*, 5 and 6 (1954), repr. in T. Aston (ed.), *Crisis in Europe, 1560–1660*, 1965.

Hohenberg, P. M. & Lees, L. H. *The Making of Urban Europe, 1000–1950*, Cambridge, Mass., and London, 1985.

Hoon, E. E. *The Organisation of the English Customs System, 1696–1786* (1938), repr. Newton Abbott, 1968.

Horner, J. *The Linen Trade of Europe during the Spinning-Wheel Period*, Belfast, 1920.

Hornstein, S. R. *The Restoration Navy and English Foreign Trade, 1674–1688*, 1991.

Horwitz, H. *Parliament, Policy and Politics in the Reign of William III*, Manchester, 1977.

Houtte, J. A. van. *An Economic History of the Low Countries, 800–1800*, 1977.

Hovy, H. J. *Het voorstel van 1751 tot instelling van een beperkt vrijhavenstelsel in de republiek*, Groningen, 1966.

Hughes, E. *North Country Life in the Eighteenth Century*, vol. I, *The North East 1700–1750*, Durham, 1952.

Huvelin, M. *Essai historique sur le droit des marchés et des foires*, Paris, 1897.

Israel, J. I. *Dutch Primacy in World Trade, 1585–1740*, Oxford, 1989.

'The Phases of the Dutch *Straatvaart*, 1590–1713: A Chapter in the Economic History of the Mediterranean', in Israel, *Empires and Entrepots. The Dutch, the Spanish Monarchy and the Jews, 1585–1713*, 1990.

The Anglo-Dutch Moment. Essays on the Glorious Revolution and its World Impact, Cambridge, 1991.

The Dutch Republic. Its Rise, Greatness, and Fall, 1477–1806, Oxford, 1995.

'England's Mercantilist Response to Dutch World Trade Primacy, 1647–74', in Israel, *Conflicts of Empires. Spain, the Low Countries and the Struggle for World Supremacy, 1585–1713*, 1997.

Jackson, G. *Hull in the Eighteenth Century*, 1972.

Jansen, P. 'Het ritme van de dood: sociale conjunctuur in Amsterdam, 1750–1800', *Ons Amsterdam*, March 1973.

'Armoede in Amsterdam aan het eind van de achttiende eeuw', *TvG*, 88 (1975).

Janzen, O. U. (ed.), *Merchant Organization and Maritime Trade in the North Atlantic, 1660–1815*, St. John's, 1998.

Jenkins, D. T. & Ponting, K. G. (eds.), *The British Wool Textile Industry, 1770–1914*, Aldershot, 1982.

Johansen, H. C. 'How to Pay for Baltic Products?', in W. Fischer, R. McInnis & J. Schneider (eds.), *The Emergence of a World Economy, 1500–1914*, Part I, *1500–1850*, Wiesbaden, 1986.

John, A. H. 'War and the English Economy, 1700–1763', *EcHR*, 7 (1955).

'The London Assurance Company and the Marine Insurance Market of the Eighteenth Century', in *Economica*, n.s. 25 (1958).

'Aspects of Economic Growth in the First Half of the Eighteenth Century', *Economica*, 28 (1961), and repr. in Carus-Wilson, *Essays*, vol. II, 1962.

'English Agricultural Improvement and Grain Exports, 1660–1765', in Coleman & John (eds.), *Trade, Government and Economy*, 1976.

Jones, D. W. 'London Merchants and the Crisis of the 1690s', in P. Clark & P. Slack (eds.), *Crisis and Order in English Towns, 1500–1700*, 1972.

War and Economy in the Age of William and Marlborough, Oxford, 1988.

'Sequel to Revolution: The Economics of England's Emergence as a Great Power, 1688–1712', in Israel, *The Anglo-Dutch Moment*, 1991.

Jong-Keesing, E. E. de. *De Economische Crisis van 1763 te Amsterdam*, Amsterdam, 1939.

Joutard, P. 'The Revocation of the Edict of Nantes: End or Renewal of French Calvinism?', in M. Prestwich (ed.), *International Calvinism, 1541–1715*, Oxford, 1985.

Kearney, H. F. 'The Political Background to English Mercantilism, 1695–1700', *EcHR*, 11 (1959).

Keith, G. S. 'A General View of the Corn Trade and Corn Laws of Great Britain', *Farmers' Magazine*, 11 (1802).

Kent, H. S. *War and Trade in Northern Seas*, Cambridge, 1973.

Kerridge, E. *Textile Manufactures in Early Modern England*, Manchester, 1985.

Keynes, J. M. *The General Theory of Employment, Interest and Money*, 1936.

Kindleberger, C. P. *World Economic Primacy, 1500–1990*, Oxford, 1996.

Kinross, Lord. *The Kindred Spirit. A History of Gin and the House of Booth*, 1959.

Klein, P. W. *De trippen in de 17e eeuw. Een studie over het ondernemersgedrag op de Hollandse stapelmarkt*, Assen, 1965.

'Entrepreneurial Behaviour and the Economic Rise and Decline of the Netherlands in the Seventeenth and Eighteenth Centuries', *Annales Cisalpines d'Histoire Sociale*, 1 (1970).

'De zeventiende eeuw, 1585–1700', in J. H. van Stuijvenberg (ed.), *De economische geschiedenis van Nederland*, Groningen, 1977.

'Handel, geld- en bankwezen', in *Algemene Geschiedenis der Nederlanden*, vol. VIII, Haarlem, 1979.

'The Origins of Trading Companies', in Blussé & Gaastra (eds.), *Companies and Trade*, 1981.

'Dutch Capitalism and the European World-Economy', in M. Aymard (ed.), *Dutch Capitalism and World Capitalism*, Cambridge, 1982.

' "Little London": British Merchants in Rotterdam during the Seventeenth and Eighteenth Centuries', in Coleman & Mathias (eds.), *Enterprise and History*, 1984.

'A New Look at an Old Subject: Dutch Trade Policies in the Age of Mercantilism', in Groenveld & Wintle (eds.), *State and Trade*, 1992.

Klein, P. W. & Veluwenkamp, J. W. 'The Role of the Entrepreneur in the Economic Expansion of the Dutch Republic', in Davids & Noordegraaf (eds.), *Dutch Economy in the Golden Age*, 1993.

Knoppers, J. 'Dutch-Baltic Shipping from the late Seventeenth to the early Nineteenth Century' (Papers presented to the Fifth Conference on Baltic Studies, Columbia University, May 1976).

Knoppers, J. & Snapper, F. 'De Nederlandse Scheepvaart op de Oostzee vanaf het eind van de 17e Eeuw tot het begin van de 19e Eeuw', *ESHJ*, 41 (1978).

Kooy, T. P. van der. *Hollands Stapelmarket en haar Verval*, Amsterdam, 1931.

Korte, J. P. de. *De Jaarlijkse Financiele Verantwoording in de VOC*, Leiden, 1984.

Kossman, E. H. 'The Development of Dutch Political Theory in the Seventeenth Century', in J. S. Bromley & E. H. Kossman (eds.), *Britain and the Netherlands*, vol. I, 1960.

Krantz, F. & Hohenberg, P. (eds.), *Failed Transitions to Modern Industrial Society: Renaissance Italy and Seventeenth Century Holland*, (Interuniversity Centre for European Studies) Montreal, 1975.

Krey, G. S. de. *A Fractured Society. The Politics of London in the First Age of Party, 1688–1715*, Oxford, 1985.

Kwarteng, K. A. A. 'The Political Thought of the Recoinage Crisis, 1695–7', unpublished Cambridge Ph.D. thesis, 2000.

Lambert, A. M. *The Making of the Dutch Landscape*, 1971.

Landes, D. *The Wealth and Poverty of Nations*, 1998.

Laslett, P. 'John Locke, the Great Recoinage, and the Origins of the Board of Trade: 1695–1698', *William and Mary Quarterly*, 14 (1957).

Lemire, B. *Fashion's Favourite. The Cotton Trade and the Consumer in Britain, 1660–1800*, Oxford, 1991.

'East Indian Textiles and the Flowering of European Popular Fashions, 1600–1800', in Cavaciocchi (ed.), *Prodotti e Techniche*, 1998.

Lesger, C. 'Intraregional Trade and the Port system in Holland, 1400–1700', in Davids & Noordegraaf (eds.), *Dutch Economy in the Golden Age* 1995.

'Clusters of Achievement. The Economy of Amsterdam in its Golden Age', in O'Brien *et al.* (eds.), *Urban Achievement in Early Modern Europe*, 2001.

Lesger, C. & Noordegraaf, L. (eds.), *Entrepreneurs and Entrepreneurship in Early Modern Times. Merchants and Industrialists within the Orbit of the Dutch Staple Market* (Hollandse Historische Reeks, 24), The Hague, 1995.

Levasseur, E. *Histoire du commerce de la France*, 2 vols., Paris, 1911.

Lindblad, J. T. 'Structuur en Mededinging in de Handel van de Republiek op de Oostzee in de Achttiende Eeuw', *ESHJ*, 47 (1984).

'The Foreign Trade of the Dutch Republic in the Seventeenth Century', in Davids & Noordegraaf (eds.), *Dutch Economy in the Golden Age*, 1993.

Lindeboom, J. *Austin Friars. History of the Dutch Reformed Church in London, 1550–1950*, The Hague, 1950.

Lingelbach, W. E. 'The Internal Organisation of the Merchant Adventurers of England', *TRHS*, n.s., 16 (1902).

Lintum, C. Te. *De Merchant Adventurers in de Nederlanden*, 's-Gravenhage, 1905.

Lipson, E. *The History of the English Woollen and Worsted Industries*, 1921.

The Economic History of England (1931), vols. II and III, 1948.

Loosjes, J. *History of Christ Church, Amsterdam 1698–1932*, Amsterdam, 1932.

Mann, J. de L. 'A Wiltshire Family of Clothiers: George and Hester Wansey, 1683–1714', *EcHR*, 9 (1957–8).

'Clothiers and Weavers in Wiltshire during the Eighteenth Century', in L. S. Pressnell (ed.), *Studies in the Industrial Revolution Presented to T. S. Ashton*, 1960.

The Cloth Industry in the West of England, from 1640 to 1880, Oxford, 1971.

Marshall, J. D. (ed.), *The Autobiography of William Stout of Lancaster, 1665–1752*, Manchester, 1967.

Mathias, P. *The Brewing Industry in England, 1700–1830*, Cambridge, 1959.

Mathias, P. & O'Brien, P. K. 'Taxation in England and France, 1715–1810: A Comparison of the Social and Economic Incidence of Taxes Collected for the Central Governments', *JEEH*, 5 (1976).

Matson, C. 'Minet and Fector of Dover', *Archaeologia Cantiana*, 81, 1966.

McCusker, J. J. 'The Current Value of English Exports, 1697–1800', *William & Mary Quarterly*, 28 (1971); repr. in McCusker, *Essays*, 1997.

Money and Exchange in Europe and America, 1600–1775, 1978.

Essays in the Economic History of the Atlantic World, 1997.

McCusker, J. J. & Menard, R. R. *The Economy of British America, 1607–1789*, Chapel Hill, 1985.

McGowan, A. 'The Dutch Influence on British Shipbuilding', in C. Wilson & D. Proctor (eds.), *The Seaborne Alliance and the Diplomatic Revolution*, 1989.

Menard, R. R. 'Transport Costs and Long-Range Trade, 1300–1800. Was there a European "Transport Revolution" in the Early Modern Era?', in Tracy (ed.), *Political Economy of Merchant Empires*, 1991.

Meuvret, J. 'Les oscillations des prix des céréales aux XVIIe et XVIIIe siècles en Angleterre et dans les Pays du Bassin Parisien', *Revue d'Histoire Moderne et Contemporaine*, 16 (1969), and repr. in Meuvret (ed.), *Études d'Histoire Économique* (Cahiers des Annales, 32), 1971.

Minchinton, W. E. (ed.), *The Growth of English Overseas Trade in the Seventeenth and Eighteenth Centuries*, 1969.

Minet, W. *Some Account of the Huguenot Family of Minet*, privately printed, 1892.

'Extracts from the Letter-book of a Dover Merchant, 1737–1741', *Archaeologia Cantiana*, 32 (1917).

Mitchell, B. R. & Deane, P. *Abstract of British Historical Statistics*, Cambridge, 1962.

Mitchell, D. M. ' "It will be easy to make money." Merchant Strangers in London, 1580–1689', in Lesger & Noordegraaf (eds.), *Entrepreneurs and Entrepreneurship in Early Modern Times*, 1995.

'The Linen Damask Trade in Haarlem. Its Products and its Markets', in Teylers Museum, *Textiel aan het Spaarne. Haarlem: van linnen damast tot zijden linten*, 1995.

Mokyr, J. *Industrialisation in the Low Countries, 1795–1850*, New Haven, 1976.

Lever of Riches, Oxford, 1990.

Morgan, K. *Bristol and the Atlantic Trade in the Eighteenth Century*, Cambridge, 1993.

'Business Networks in the British Export Trade to North America, 1750–1800', in Morgan & McCusker (eds.), *The Early Modern Atlantic Economy*, 2000.

Morgan, K. & McCusker, J. J. (eds.), *The Early Modern Atlantic Economy*, Cambridge, 2000.

Morineau, M. 'La balance du commerce franco-néerlandais et le resserrement économique des Provinces-Unies au XVIIIème siècle', *EHJ*, 30 (1965).

Mui, H.-C. & L. H. 'Trends in Eighteenth Century Smuggling Reconsidered', *EcHR*, 28 (1975).

Murray, J. J. 'Baltic Commerce and Power Politics in the Early Eighteenth Century', *Huntington Library Quarterly*, 6 (1942–3).

George I, The Baltic and the Whig Split, 1969.

Musgrave, P. 'The Economics of Uncertainty: The Structural Revolution in the Spice Trade, 1480–1640', in P. L. Cottrell & D. H. Aldcroft (eds.), *Shipping, Trade and Commerce; Essays in Memory of Ralph Davis*, Leicester, 1981.

The Early Modern European Economy, 1999.

Nash, R. C. 'English Transatlantic Trade, 1660–1730: A Quantitative Study', University of Cambridge Ph.D. thesis, 1982.

'South Carolina and the Atlantic Economy', *EcHR*, 45 (1992).

'The Balance of Payments and Foreign Capital Flows in Eighteenth-Century England: A Comment', *EcHR*, 40 (1997).

'The Huguenot Diaspora and the Development of the Atlantic Economy: Huguenots and the Growth of the South Carolina Economy, 1680–1775', in Janzen, *Merchant Organization*, 1998.

'The Organisation of Trade and Finance in the British Atlantic Economy, 1600–1830', unpublished conference paper, 1999.

Neal, L. 'The Dutch and English East India Companies Compared; Evidence from the Stock and Foreign Exchange Markets', in Tracy, *The Rise of Merchant Empires. Long Distance Trade in the Early Modern World, 1350–1750*, 1990.

The Rise of Financial Capitalism: International Capital Markets in the Age of Reason, Cambridge, 1990.

Nef, J. U. *The Rise of the British Coal Industry*, 2 vols., 1932.

Newman, J. 'Russian Foreign Trade, 1680–1780: the British Contribution', University of Edinburgh Ph.D. thesis.

'Anglo-Dutch Commercial Co-operation and the Russia Trade in the Eighteenth Century', in J. M. van Winter (ed.), *The Interactions of Amsterdam and Antwerp with the Baltic Region, 1400–1800*, Leiden, 1983.

Newman, K. 'Anglo-Hamburg Trade in the late Seventeenth and early Eighteenth
   Centuries', University of London Ph.D. thesis, 1979.
   'Hamburg in the European Economy, 1660–1750', *JEEH*, 14 (1985).
Niermeyer, F. *De Wording van onze Volkshuishouding*, 's-Gravenhage, 1946.
Noordegraaf, L. 'Domestic Trade and Domestic Trade Conflicts in the Low
   Countries; Autonomy, Centralisation and State-formation in the Pre-
   industrial Era', in Groenveld & Wintle (eds.), *State and Trade*, 1992.
   'Dutch Industry in the Golden Age', in Davids & Noordegraaf (eds.), *Dutch
   Economy in the Golden Age*, 1993.
   'The New Draperies in the Northern Netherlands, 1500–1800', in Harte (ed.),
   The New Draperies, 1997.
North, D. C. & Weingast, B. R. 'Constitutions and Commitment: The Evolution
   of Institutions Governing Public Choice in Seventeenth-Century England',
   JEH, 49 (1989).
North, M. 'Hamburg: "The Continent's most English city"', in M. North (ed.),
   From the North Sea to the Baltic, Aldershot, 1996.
O'Brien, P. K. 'European Economic Development: The Contribution of the
   Periphery', *EcHR*, 2nd ser., 35 (1982).
   'The Political Economy of British Taxation, 1660–1815', *EcHR*, 2nd ser., 41
   (1988).
   'Political Preconditions for the Industrial Revolution', in P. K. O'Brien &
   R. Quinault (eds.), *The Industrial Revolution and British Society*, 1993.
   'Inseparable Connections: Trade, Economy, Fiscal State, and the Expansion of
   Empire, 1688–1815', in P. J. Marshall (ed.), *The Oxford History of the British
   Empire*, vol. II, *The Eighteenth Century*, Oxford, 1998.
   'Mercantilism and Imperialism in the Rise and Decline of the Dutch and British
   Economies, 1585–1815', *De Economist*, 148 (2000).
   'Reflections and Meditations on Antwerp, Amsterdam and London in their
   Golden Ages', in O'Brien (ed.), *Urban Achievement in Early Modern Europe*,
   2001.
O'Brien, P. K. & Engerman, S. 'Exports and the Growth of the British Economy
   from the Glorious Revolution to the Peace of Amiens', in B. L. Solow, *Slavery
   and the Rise of the Atlantic System*, Cambridge, 1991.
O'Brien, P. K. & Hunt, P. H. 'The Rise of a Fiscal State in England, 1485–1815',
   Historical Research, 66:160 (1993).
O'Brien, P. K. & Prados de la Escosura, L. 'The Costs and Benefits for Europeans
   from their Empires Overseas', in O'Brien & Prados de la Escosura (eds.),
   *The Costs and Benefits of European Imperialism from the Conquest of Ceuta,
   1415, to the Treaty of Lusaka, 1974* (Twelfth International Economic History
   Congress), *Revista de Historia Económica*, 16 (1998).
O'Brien, P. K., Griffiths, T. & Hunt, P. 'Political Components of the In-
   dustrial Revolution: Parliament and the English Cotton Textile Industry,
   1660–1774', *EcHR*, 44:3 (1991).
O'Brien, P. K., Keene, D., 't Hart, M. & van der Wee, H. (eds.), *Urban Achieve-
   ment in Early Modern Europe. Golden Ages in Antwerp, Amsterdam and London*,
   Cambridge, 2001.
Ogg, D. *William III*, 1956.

Ormrod, D. J. 'English Re-exports and the Dutch Staplemarket in the Eighteenth Century', in Coleman and Mathias (eds.), *Enterprise and History*, 1984.

'R. H. Tawney and the Origins of Capitalism', *History Workshop*, 18 (1984).

'The Demise of Regulated Trading in England. The Case of the Merchant Adventurers, 1650–1730', in Lesger & Noordegraaf, *Entrepreneurs and Entrepreneurship in Early Modern Times*, 1985.

English Grain Exports and the Structure of Agrarian Capitalism, 1700–1760, Hull, 1985.

'Industry: 1640–1800', in W. A. Armstrong (ed.), *The Economy of Kent, 1640–1914*, Aldershot, 1995.

Overton, M. *Agricultural Revolution in England. The Transformation of the Agrarian Economy, 1500–1850*, Cambridge, 1996.

Page, W. (ed.), *The Victoria History of the Counties of England*, vol. III, *Kent*, 1932.

Palgrave, R. H. I. *Dictionary of Political Economy*, vol. I, 1894.

Pares, R. *Colonial Blockade and Neutral Rights, 1739–1763*, Oxford, 1938.

Merchants and Planters, EcHR, Supplement 4, 1960.

Pettegree, A. *Foreign Protestant Communities in Sixteenth Century London*, Oxford, 1986.

Phillips, H. *The Thames about 1750*, 1951.

Pincus, S. C. A. *Protestantism and Patriotism. Ideologies and the Making of English Foreign Policy, 1650–1668*, Cambridge, 1996.

Plumb, J. H. *The Growth of Political Stability in England, 1675–1725*, 1967.

Plummer, A. *The London Weavers' Company, 1600–1970*, 1972.

Pomeranz, K. *The Great Divergence. China, Europe and the Making of the Modern World Economy*, Princeton, 2000.

Portal, R. 'Manufactures et classes sociales en Russie – 18e siècle', *Revue Historique*, 201 (July and Sept. 1948).

Posthumus, N. W. *De Nationale Organisatie der Lakenkoopers tijdens de Republiek*, Utrecht, 1927.

De Geschiedenis van de Leidsche Lakenindustrie, vols. II and III, 's-Gravenhage, 1939.

Nederlandsche Prijsgeschiedenis, vol. I, Leiden, 1943.

Inquiry into the History of Prices in Holland, vol. II, Leiden, 1964.

Pottle, F. A. (ed.), *Boswell in Holland, 1763–4*, 1952.

Price, J. L. *Holland and the Dutch Republic in the Seventeenth Century. The Politics of Particularism*, Oxford, 1994.

Price, J. M. 'Multilateralism and/or Bilateralism: The Settlement of British Trade Balances with "the North", ca. 1700', *EcHR*, 14 (1961).

'The Economic Growth of the Chesapeake and the European Market, 1697–1775', *JEH*, 24 (1964).

'Economic Activity', in J. S. Bromley (ed.), *The New Cambridge Modern History*, vol. VI, 1970.

Overseas Trade and Traders. Essays on Some Commercial, Financial and Political Challenges Facing British Atlantic Merchants, 1660–1775, 1996.

'The Imperial Economy, 1700–1776', in P. J. Marshall (ed.), *The Oxford History of the British Empire*, vol. II, *The Eighteenth Century*, Oxford, 1998.

Price, J. M. & Clemens, P. G. E. 'A Revolution of Scale in Overseas Trade: British Firms in the Chesapeake Trade, 1675–1775', *JEH*, 47 (1987).

Quinn, S. 'Gold, Silver and the Glorious Revolution: Arbitrage between Bills of Exchange and Bullion', *EcHR*, 49 (1996).

Ramsay, G. D. *The Wiltshire Woollen Industry in the Sixteenth and Seventeenth Centuries*, Oxford, 1943.

The Queen's Merchants and the Revolt of the Netherlands, Manchester, 1986.

Regin, D. *Traders, Artists and Burghers. A Cultural History of Amsterdam in the 17th Century*, Assen, 1976.

Regtdoorzee Greup-Roldanus, S. C. *Geschiedenis der Haarlemmer Bleekerijen*, 's-Gravenhage, 1936.

Rich, E. E. & Wilson, C. H. (eds.), *The Cambridge Economic History of Europe*, vol. IV, *The Economy of Expanding Europe in the Sixteenth and Seventeenth Centuries*, Cambridge, 1967.

The Cambridge Economic History of Europe, vol. V, *The Economic Organization of Early Modern Europe*, Cambridge, 1977.

Rijswick, R. B. van. *Geschiedenis van het Dordtsche Stapelrecht*, 's-Gravenhage, 1900.

Riley, J. C. *International Government Finance and the Amsterdam Capital Market, 1740–1815*, Cambridge, 1980.

'The Dutch Economy after 1650: Decline or Growth?', *JEEH*, 13 (1984).

Rimmer, W. G. *Marshall's of Leeds, Flax Spinners, 1788–1886*, Cambridge, 1960.

Roberts, W. L. 'Ralph Carr: A Newcastle Merchant and the American Colonial Trade', *Business History Review*, 42 (1968).

Rodger, N. A. M. 'Sea Power and Empire, 1699–1793', in P. J. Marshall (ed.), *The Oxford History of the British Empire*, vol. II, *The Eighteenth Century*, Oxford, 1998.

Roessingh, H. K. *Inlandse Tabak* (*AAG Bijdragen*, 20), 1976.

Roseveare, H. *The Treasury. The Evolution of a British Institution*, 1969.

'Stockholm–London–Amsterdam: The Triangle of Trade, 1660–1680', in J. M. van Winter (ed.), *The Interactions of Antwerp and Amsterdam with the Baltic Region, 1400–1800*, Leiden, 1983.

Markets and Merchants of the Late Seventeenth Century. The Marescoe–David Letters, 1668–1680 (British Academy, Records of Social and Economic History, n.s., 12), 1987.

Rothermund, D. 'The Changing Pattern of British Trade in Indian Textiles, 1701–1757', in S. Chaudhuri & Morineau (eds.), *Merchants, Companies and Trade*, 1999.

Schama, S. *Patriots and Liberators: Revolution in the Netherlands, 1780–1831*, 1977.

Schilling, H. 'Innovation through Migration: The Settlements of Calvinistic Netherlanders in Sixteenth- and Seventeenth-Century Central and Western Europe', *Social History*, 16 (1983).

Schmitthoff, C. M. 'International Business Law: A New Law Merchant', in C.-J. Cheng (ed.), *Clive M. Schmitthoff's Select Essays on International Trade Law*, Dordrecht, Boston and London, 1988.

Schnurmann, C. 'Migration and Communication: Relations between Inhabitants of English and Dutch Colonies in the New World, 1648–1713', paper presented to the Conference on German Perceptions of British History,

Institute of Historical Research and German Historical Institute, London, April 1997.

Schöffer, I. 'Did Holland's Golden Age Coincide with a Period of Crisis?', *AHN*, 1 (1966).

Schubert, E. S. 'Innovations, Debts and Bubbles: International Integration of Financial Markets in Western Europe, 1688–1720', *JEH*, 48 (1988).

Schumpeter, E. B. *English Overseas Trade Statistics, 1697–1808*, Oxford, 1960.

Scott, W. R. *The Constitution and Finance of English, Scottish and Irish Joint-Stock Companies to 1720*, vol. I, Cambridge, 1912.

Scouloudi, I. 'Alien Immigration into and Communities in London, 1558–1640', University of London M.Sc. thesis, 1936.

Shammas, C. *The Preindustrial Consumer in England and America*, Oxford, 1990.

'The Revolutionary Impact of European Demand for Tropical Goods', in Morgan & McCusker (eds.), *The Early Modern Atlantic Economy*, 2000.

Smail, J. *Merchants, Markets and Manufacture. The English Wool Textile Industry in the Eighteenth Century*, 1999.

Smith, S. D. 'British Exports to Continental North America', unpublished University of Cambridge Ph.D. thesis, 1992.

'British Exports to Colonial North America and the Mercantilist Fallacy', *Business History*, 37 (1995).

'Prices and the Value of English Exports in the Eighteenth Century: Evidence from the North American Colonial Trade', *EcHR*, 48 (1995).

'The Market for Manufactures in the Thirteen Continental Colonies, 1698–1776', *EcHR*, 51 (1998).

Smith, W. D. 'The Function of Commercial Centers in the Modernization of European Capitalism: Amsterdam as an Information Exchange in the Seventeenth Century', *JEH*, 44 (1984).

Smout, T. C. *Scottish Trade on the Eve of Union, 1660–1707*, Edinburgh, 1963.

Snapper, F. *Oorlogsinvloeden op de Overzeese Handel van Holland, 1551–1719*, Amsterdam, 1959.

'Commerce, Ships and War in the Baltic from the Rise of the Hanseatic League till the French Revolution', in Heeres *et al.* (eds.), *Dunkirk to Danzig*, 1988.

'The Influence of British and Dutch Convoys on the Development of British Baltic Trade', in W. E. Minchinton (ed.), *Britain and the Northern Seas*, Pontefract, 1988.

Sneller, Z. W. *Rotterdams bedrijfsleven in het verleden*, Amsterdam, 1940.

Geschiedenis van den Steenkolenhandel van Rotterdam, Groningen, 1946.

Sosin, J. M. *English America and Imperial Inconstancy. The Rise of Provincial Autonomy, 1696–1715*, Lincoln and London, 1985.

Sperling, J. G. 'Godolphin and the Organisation of Public Credit, 1702–1710', unpublished University of Cambridge Ph.D. thesis, 1955.

'The International Payments Mechanism in the Seventeenth and Eighteenth Centuries', *EcHR*, 14 (1962).

Spooner, F. C. *Risks at Sea. Amsterdam Insurance and Maritime Europe, 1766–1780*, Cambridge, 1983.

Sprunger, K. L. *Dutch Puritanism. A History of English and Scottish Churches of the Netherlands in the Sixteenth and Seventeenth Centuries*, Leiden, 1982.

Steele, I. K. *Politics of Colonial Policy. The Board of Trade in Colonial Administration,*
1696–1720, Oxford, 1968.

'The Empire and the Provincial Élites: An Interpretation of some Recent Writings on the English Atlantic, 1675–1740', in P. Marshall & G. Williams
(eds.), *The British Atlantic Empire before the American Revolution,* 1980.

Steensgaard, N. 'The Companies as a Specific Institution in the History of
European Expansion', in Blussé & Gaastra (eds.), *Companies and Trade,*
1981.

'The Growth and Composition of the Long-distance Trade of England and the
Dutch Republic before 1750', in Tracy (ed.), *The Rise of Merchant Empires,*
1990.

Stuijvenberg, J. H. van. *De Economische Geschiedenis van Nederland,* Groningen,
1977.

Supple, B. E. *Commercial Crisis and Change in England, 1600–1642,* Cambridge,
1959.

The Royal Exchange Assurance, Cambridge, 1970.

'The Nature of Enterprise', in Rich & Wilson (eds.), *Cambridge Economic*
History of Europe, vol. V, 1977.

Swart, K. W. *The Miracle of the Dutch Republic as seen in the Seventeenth Century,*
Inaugural Lecture, University College, London, 1969.

'Holland's Bourgeoisie and the Retarded Industrialization of the Netherlands',
in Krantz & Hohenberg (eds.), *Failed Transitions,* 1975.

Tawney, R. H. *Business and Politics under James I. Lionel Cranfield as Merchant and*
Minister, Cambridge, 1958.

Thirsk, J. 'The Fantastical Folly of Fashion; The English Stocking Knitting Industry, 1500–1700', in Harte & Ponting (eds.), *Textile History and Economic*
History, 1973.

Economic Policy and Projects. The Development of a Consumer Society in Early
Modern England, Oxford, 1978.

(ed.), *The Agrarian History of England and Wales, 1640–1750,* vol. V (II),
Agrarian Change, Cambridge, 1985.

Thirsk, J. & Cooper, J. P. *Seventeenth-Century Economic Documents,* Oxford, 1972.

Thomas, B. 'Britain's Energy Crisis in the Seventeenth Century', repr. in
B. Thomas, *The Industrial Revolution,* 1993.

The Industrial Revolution and the Atlantic Economy, 1993.

Thomas, P. J. *Mercantilism and the East India Trade. An Early Phase of the Protection*
v. Free Trade Controversy, 1926.

Tilly, C. 'Entanglements of European Cities and States', in C. Tilly & W. P.
Blockmans (eds.), *Cities and the Rise of States in Europe, AD 1000–1800,*
Boulder, 1994.

Tracy, J. D. (ed.), *The Rise of Merchant Empires. Long-Distance Trade in the Early*
Modern World, 1350–1750, Cambridge, 1990.

The Political Economy of Merchant Empires. State Power and World Trade,
1350–1750, Cambridge, 1991.

Tyszynski, H. 'World Trade in Manufactured Commodities, 1899–1950', *Man-*
chester School of Economic and Social Studies, 19 (1951).

Unger, R. W. *Dutch Shipbuilding before 1800,* Assen, 1978.

'Energy sources for the Dutch Golden Age', *Research in Economic History*, 9 (1984).

Unger, W. S. 'Trade through the Sound in the Seventeenth and Eighteenth Centuries', *EcHR*, 12 (1959).

Unwin, G. 'De Leidsche Textielnijverheid', in R. H. Tawney (ed.), *Studies in Economic History. The Collected Papers of George Unwin*, 1927.

'The Merchant Adventurers' Company in the Reign of Elizabeth', in R. H. Tawney (ed.), *Studies in Economic History. The Collected Papers of George Unwin*, 1927.

Veluwenkamp, J. W. *Ondernemersgedrag op de Hollandse Stapelmarkt in de tijd van de Republiek. De Amsterdamse handelsfirma Jan Isaac de Neufville & Comp., 1730–1764*, Leiden, 1981.

Viner, J. 'Power versus Plenty as Objectives of Foreign Policy in the Seventeenth and Eighteenth Centuries', *World Politics*, 1 (1948), repr. in D. C. Coleman (ed.), *Revisions in Mercantilism*, 1969.

Visser, C. *Verkeersindustrien te Rotterdam in de tweede helft der achttiende eeuw*, Rotterdam, 1927.

Voort, J. P. van der. *De Westindische Plantages van 1720 tot 1795, Financien en Handel*, Eindhoven, 1973.

Voorthuijsen, W. D. *De Republiek der Verenigde Nederlanden en het Mercantilisme*, 's-Gravenhage, 1965.

Vries, Joh. de. 'De ontduiking der convooien en licenten in de Republiek tijdens de achttiende eeuw', *TvG*, 71 (1958).

De Economische Achteruitgang de Republiek in de Achttiende Eeuw, Amsterdam, 1959.

Amsterdam–Rotterdam. Rivaliteit in economisch-historisch perspectief, Bussum, 1965.

Vries, J. de. *The Dutch Rural Economy in the Golden Age, 1500–1700*, New Haven, 1974.

The Economy of Europe in an Age of Crisis, 1600–1750, Cambridge, 1976.

'Barges and Capitalism. Passenger Transportation in the Dutch Economy, 1632–1839', *AAG Bijdragen*, 21, 1978.

'The Decline and Rise of the Dutch Economy, 1675–1900', in G. Saxonhouse & G. Wright (eds.), *Technique, Spirit and Form in the Making of Modern Economies: Essays in Honour of William N. Parker*, Greenwich, 1984.

European Urbanization, 1500–1800, 1984.

'Problems in the Measurement, Description, and Analysis of Historical Urbanisation', in A. M van der Woude, J. de Vries & A. Hayami (eds.), *Urbanisation in History. A Process of Dynamic Interactions*, Oxford, 1990.

Vries, J. de & Woude, A. M. van der. *The First Modern Economy. Success, Failure, and Perseverance of the Dutch Economy, 1500–1815*, Cambridge, 1997.

Waddell, D. 'Charles Davenant (1656–1714): A Biographical Sketch', *EcHR*, 11 (1958).

Wadsworth, A. P. & Mann, J. de L. *The Cotton Trade and Industrial Lancashire. 1600–1780*, Manchester, 1931.

Walker, J. 'The English Exiles in Holland during the Reigns of Charles II and James II', *TRHS*, 4th ser., 30 (1948).

Wallerstein, I. 'Failed Transitions or Inevitable Decline of the Leader?', in Krantz & Hohenberg (eds.), *Failed Transitions to Modern Industrial Society*, 1974.

The Modern World-System, vol. I, *Capitalist Agriculture and the Origins of the European World-Economy in the Sixteenth Century*, 1974.

The Modern World-System, vol. II, *Mercantilism and the Consolidation of the European World-Economy, 1600–1750*, 1980.

Weatherill, L. *Consumer Behaviour and Material Culture in Britain, 1660–1760*, 1988.

'Consumer Behaviour, Textiles and Dress in the Late Seventeenth and Early Eighteenth Centuries', *Textile History*, 22 (1991).

Westerfield, R. B. *Middlemen in English Business, particularly between 1660 and 1769*, New Haven, 1915.

Westerman, J. C. 'Statistische gegevens over den handel van Amsterdam in de zeventiende eeuw', *TvG*, 61 (1948).

Willan, T. S. *The English Coasting Trade, 1600–1750*, Manchester, 1938.

Wilson, C. H. *Anglo-Dutch Commerce and Finance in the Eighteenth Century*, Cambridge, 1941.

'Treasure and Trade Balances: The Mercantilist Problem', *EcHR*, 2 (1949).

'Treasure and Trade Balances: Further Evidence', *EcHR*, 4 (1951).

'The Economic Decline of the Netherlands', *EcHR*, 9 (1939), and repr. in Carus-Wilson (ed.), *Essays*, vol. I, 1954.

Profit and Power. A Study of England and the Dutch Wars, 1957.

'Dutch Investment in 18th-century England', *EcHR*, 12 (1959).

'The Other Face of Mercantilism', *TRHS*, 5th ser., 9 (1959).

'Cloth Production and International Competition in the Seventeenth Century', *EcHR*, 13 (1960).

'Dutch Investment in Eighteenth Century England: A Note on Yardsticks', *EcHR*, 12 (1960).

'Taxation and the Decline of Empires, an Unfashionable Theme', *BMHG*, 77 (1963).

England's Apprenticeship, 1603–1763, 1965.

The Dutch Republic and the Civilisation of the Seventeenth Century, 1968.

Economic History and the Historian: Collected Essays, 1969.

'Transport as a Factor in the History of Economic Development', *JEEH*, 2 (1973).

'The Anglo-Dutch Establishment in Eighteenth Century England', in A. G. Dickens (ed.), *The Anglo-Dutch Contribution to the Civilization of Early Modern Society*, British Academy, 1976.

Wilson, C. H. and Parker, G. (eds.), *An Introduction to the Sources of European Economic History, 1500–1800*, 1977.

Wilson, R. G. *Gentlemen Merchants, The Merchant Community in Leeds, 1700–1830*, Manchester, 1971.

Woude, A. M. van der. *Het Noorderkwartier. Een regionaal historisch onderzoek in de demografische en economische geschiedenis van westelijk Nederland van de late middeleeuwen tot het begin van de negentiende eeuw*, 3 vols. (*AAG Bijdragen*, 16), 1972.

Wright, H. R. C. *Free Trade and Protection in the Netherlands, 1816–1830*, Cambridge, 1955.

Wright, J. F. 'The Contribution of Overseas Savings to the Funded National Debt of Great Britain, 1750–1815', *EcHR*, 50 (1997).

Wrigley, E. A. 'The Growth of Population in Eighteenth-century England: A Conundrum Resolved', *PP*, 98 (1983).

'Urban Growth and Agricultural Change: England and the Continent in the Early Modern Period', *Journal of Interdisciplinary History*, 15 (1985).

People, Cities and Wealth. The Transformation of a Traditional Society, Oxford, 1987 (where the above two articles are reprinted).

Continuity, Chance and Change. The Character of the Industrial Revolution in England, Cambridge, 1988.

'The Divergence of England: The Growth of the English Economy in the Seventeenth and Eighteenth Centuries', *TRHS*, 6th ser., 10 (2000).

Wyczanski, A. 'Le niveau de la récolte des céréales en Pologne du XVIe au XVIIIe siècle', in *Contributions and Communications, First International Economic History Conference, Stockholm*, Paris, 1960.

Zahedieh, N. 'Credit, Risk and Reputation in Late Seventeenth-Century Colonial Trade', in Janzen (ed.), *Merchant Organization and Maritime Trade*, 1998.

'Overseas Expansion and Trade in the Seventeenth Century', in N. Canny (ed.), *The Oxford History of the British Empire*, vol. I, *The Origins of Empire. British Overseas Enterprise to the Close of the Seventeenth Century*, Oxford, 1998.

'Making Mercantilism Work: London Merchants and Atlantic Trade in the Seventeenth Century', *TRHS*, 6th ser., 9 (1999).

Zanden J. L. van. 'Dutch Economic History of the Period 1500–1940: A Review of the Present State of Affairs', *ESHN*, 1 (1990).

'Economic Growth in the Golden Age: The Economy of Holland, 1500–1650', in Davids & Noordegraaf (eds.), *Dutch Economy in the Golden Age*, 1993.

The Rise and Decline of Holland's Economy, Manchester, 1993.

Zanden J. L. van, Noordegraaf, L. & Israel, J. J. 'Discussie over J. I. Israel, *Dutch Primacy in World Trade*', *BMGN*, 106 (1991).

Zeeuw, J. W. de. 'Peat and the Dutch Golden Age. The Historical Meaning of Energy Attainability', *AAG Bijdragen*, 21 (1978).

Index

Abel, W., 214
'acrospiring', 225
Act of Union with Scotland, 170
Adams, Nathaniel, 38
Admiralty Colleges, Dutch, 20, 229
Admiralty Courts, in England, 303
African trade, 196
agricultural improvement in England, 213, 217
agricultural protectionism, 207
Alkmaar, 146
Allan & Roycroft, 200
Allenson, Robert, 117, 138
Allix, Gilbert, 176
American mainland colonies
  as market for English manufactures, 328–30
  linen imports, 152
  population growth, 64
American War of Independence, 7
Amsterdam, 5, 9
  aversion to luxury, 3
  Bourse, turnover, 278
  colonial trade, compared with London, 311
  English church, 90–1
  government, 93
  granaries, 229
  linen production, 146
  merchants, 115, 309
  rise of, 13
  trans-shipment of grain, 216
Anderson, Adam, 1, 110
Andrews, Benjamin, 118, 139
Andrews, John, 117
Anglo-Baltic trade
  and demise of Swedish power, 286
  dependence on Baltic linen products, 171
  scale of deficit, 73
  strategic character, 72
  use of Dutch shipping, 282

Anglo-Dutch alliance, 1689–1713
  'trading with the enemy', 299
Anglo-Dutch mercantile co-operation, 74, 298
Anglo-Dutch rivalry, 6, 8, 33, 35, 61, 103, 106, 313, 314, 338
Anglo-Dutch trade
  as percentage of total English trade, 316
  chronology of decline, 308
  commercial treaty of 1674, 298
  composition, 76–7
  imbalance, 321
  main trends, 315
  transfer of risk
  use of Dutch shipping, 282
Anglo-Dutch wars, 1, 33
  Dutch ship losses, 276
  impact on Anglo-Dutch trade, 37
Anglo-French trade
  diverted through Holland, 79, 142
Anglo-French wars, 1689–1713, 79, 142
Anglo-German trade, 75, 315
  'direct trade', 132, 315
Anglo-Irish trade, 142, 173
Anglo-Portuguese trade, 82, 134
Anglo-Russian trade
  growth, 74
  value, 286
Anglo-Swedish trade
  and Dutch capital, 284
Antwerp, 5, 62
Archangel, 287
arms trade, 185
ash trade, 178
Asian textiles
  valuation, 187
Åström, S.-E., 284
Atlantic economy, 298
  Dutch role, 339
  expansion of, 63, 71, 306, 333
Attwood, William, 121–5
  comparison with Cranfield's trade, 124

Cambridge Studies in Modern Economic History

Edited by CHARLES FEINSTEIN, PATRICK O'BRIEN, BARRY
SUPPLE, PETER TEMIN and GIANNI TONIOLO

1 *Central and Eastern Europe 1944–1993:*
Detour from the periphery to the periphery
Ivan Berend
ISBN 0 521 55066 1

2 *Spanish agriculture*
The long siesta 1765–1965
James Simpson
ISBN 0 521 49630 6

3 *Democratic socialism and economic policy*
The Attlee years 1945–51
Jim Tomlinson
ISBN 0 521 55095 5

4 *Productivity and performance in the paper industry*
Labour, capital and technology, 1860–1914
Gary Bryan Magee
ISBN 0 521 58197 4

5 *An economic history of the silk industry, 1830–1930*
Giovanni Federico
ISBN 0 521 58198 2

6 *The Balkan economies c.1800–1914*
Michael Palairet
ISBN 0 521 58051 X

7 *Grain markets in Europe, 1500–1800*
Integration and deregulation
Karl Gunnar Persson
ISBN 0 521 65096 8

8 *Firms, networks and business values*
The British and American cotton industries since 1750
Mary B. Rose
ISBN 0 521 78255 4

9 *Statistics and the German state, 1900–1945*
The making of modern economic knowledge
J. Adam Tooze
ISBN 0 521 80318 7

10 *The rise of commercial empires*
England and the Netherlands in the age of mercantilism, 1650–1770
David Ormrod
ISBN 0 521 81926 1